A GUIDE TO TEA(...)
PRACTICE
Revised fifth edition

A Guide to Teaching Practice is the most comprehensive text available for students on initial teacher training courses across all phases in the UK. The book's focus on the quality of teaching and learning and consideration of the latest regulations and guidelines ensures that it fits comfortably within current statutory frameworks.

Revised and updated, this authoritative yet accessible textbook covers all the important basic skills and issues that students need to consider during their practice, such as planning, classroom organisation, behaviour management and assessment, as well as chapters on:

- the Early Years Foundation Stage (EYFS)
- legal issues
- learning and teaching and using ICT in the classroom
- teaching and learning numeracy
- teaching and learning literacy
- children's rights, and
- gifted and talented children.

This respected and widely used textbook will be an essential resource for any student teacher. Additional learning resources for students are provided on a companion website, which contains further research, important links and downloadable materials. The website also contain information to make this book more relevant to international audiences.

Louis Cohen is Emeritus Professor of Education at Loughborough University, UK. **Lawrence Manion** was formerly Principal Lecturer in Music at Manchester Metropolitan University, UK. **Keith Morrison** is Professor and Registrar at the Macau University of Science and Technology, China. **Dominic Wyse** is Senior Lecturer in Early Years and Primary Education at the University of Cambridge, UK.

WITHDRAWN
2 3 FEB 2023

A Guide to Teaching Practice – Companion Website

This fully updated fifth edition of *A Guide to Teaching Practice* is accompanied by a companion website which features downloadable* supplementary material for students and lecturers, and also a wealth of signposts and weblinks to useful material.

Organised thematically, reflecting the chapter structure of this textbook, the website will be a valuable tool for any teacher or student teacher wanting to improve their practice.

Featured material includes:

- a variety of adaptable lesson plan templates
- additional original material on subjects including the use of ICT in the classroom, assessment and legal issues and copyright
- signposts to further reading
- a wealth of weblinks to sites containing material relevant to students, and also practical sites offering classroom resources for teachers and pupils
- presentation outlines for course lecturers.

It is intended that the companion website will provide real added value to this already comprehensive textbook – we hope you find it of use.

Visit the website at www.routledge.com/textbooks/9780415485586.

Also, please feel free to browse the Routledge site at www.routledge.com for information about a wide range of books and resources for teachers and student teachers.

* Please note that material downloaded is copyright, for personal use only and is not to be distributed or resold.

A GUIDE TO TEACHING PRACTICE

Revised fifth edition

Louis Cohen,
Lawrence Manion,
Keith Morrison and
Dominic Wyse

Routledge
Taylor & Francis Group

LONDON AND NEW YORK

First published 1977
by Routledge

Second edition published 1983

Third edition published 1989

Fourth edition published 1996
by RoutledgeFalmer

Fifth edition published 2004

Revised fifth edition published 2010
by Routledge
2 Park Square, Milton Park, Abingdon, Oxon, OX14 4RN

Simultaneously published in the USA and Canada
by Routledge
711 Third Avenue, New York, NY 10017

Routledge is an imprint of the Taylor & Francis Group, an informa business

© 2010 Louis Cohen, Lawrence Manion, Keith Morrison and Dominic Wyse

Typeset in Times New Roman and Helvetica by FiSH Books, Enfield
Printed and bound in Great Britain by TJ International, Padstow, Cornwall

The publishers have made every effort to contact authors/copyright holders
of works reprinted in *A Guide to Teaching Practice* (rev. 5th edn). This has not
been possible in every case, however, and we would welcome correspondence
from those individuals/companies whom we have been unable to trace.

British Library Cataloguing in Publication Data
A catalogue record for this book is available from the British Library

Library of Congress Cataloging-in-Publication Data
A guide to teaching practice : revised edition / Louis Cohen ... [et al.]. — 5th ed.
    p. cm.
  Prev. edition cataloged under Cohen, Louis
  Includes bibliographical references and index.
  1. Student teaching—Great Britain. 2. Teachers—Training of—Great Britain. I. Cohen, Louis, II. Cohen, Louis,
Guide to teaching practice.
LB2157.G7G85 2010
370.71'141—dc22

2009052934

ISBN 10: 0-415-48558-4 (pbk)
ISBN 10: 0-203-84862-4 (ebk)

ISBN 13: 978-0-415-48558-6 (pbk)
ISBN 13: 978-0-203-84862-3 (ebk)

Contents

● introduction ● a plethora of innovations: standards and targets ● democracy and control in question ● stress in teaching ● indiscipline and bullying ● school diversity ● changing the nature of teaching

● introduction ● standards for the award of qualified teacher status ● skills tests in numeracy, literacy and ICT ● mentoring ● conclusion

● introduction ● the Early Years Foundation Stage ● the National Curriculum ● statutory tests ● the National Strategies ● conclusion

● introduction ● what is ICT? ● claimed advantages of ICT ● concerns about ICT ● constructivism and ICT ● higher-order thinking and ICT ● differentiation ● administration ● social learning ● pedagogy ● assessment ● evaluating websites ● finding out about the school's ICT for teaching practice ● evaluating your own use of ICT on teaching practice

Boxes

Foreword to the Revised Fifth Edition

It is six years since the fifth edition of *A Guide to Teaching Practice* was published and we are indebted to Routledge for the opportunity of updating and extending the text with a revised edition. The book has been comprehensively updated, with inclusion of new material addressing:

- the Early Years Foundation Stage (EYFS)
- advances in neuroscience and the implications for teaching and learning
- the Primary Curriculum
- *Every Child Matters* and *The Children's Plan*
- children's rights.

The revised fifth edition also includes outlines and/or discussion of:

- educational reforms and developments in England and Wales
- school diversity
- reviews of the national curriculum
- important changes to the professional standards made by the Training and Development Agency for Schools (TDA), and information about the tests of numeracy, literacy and ICT
- stress in teaching
- the use of ICT for planning and teaching
- useful websites for teachers
- brain-based approaches to teaching and learning
- developing higher order thinking
- direct instruction and whole-class interactive teaching
- characteristics of effective teaching and learning
- motivation and learning
- inclusion and equal opportunities
- the role of special needs co-ordinators
- Attention Deficit/Hyperactivity Disorder
- raising the achievements of boys in school
- gifted and talented students
- bullying in schools, and how this is addressed
- homework and marking work
- assessment for learning
- authentic, portfolio and performance assessment

- test construction
- record keeping.

The book is comprehensively referenced to websites, to government documents, and to the latest research and scholarship in its fields. We should like to think that the updating and additions of this revised fifth edition will ensure that *A Guide to Teaching Practice* continues to be a major, standard text on preparing student teachers to work in contemporary classrooms.

Acknowledgements

The publishers would like to thank the following for permission to reprint their material:

Assessment Reform Group, for *Assessment for Learning: Ten Principles* © Assessment Reform Group, www.assessment-reform.group.org.uk; BECTA, for *Technology Works! Stimulate to Educate* by the National Council for Educational Technology; Basil Blackwell, for *School Discipline: A Whole-School Approach* by C. Watkins and P. Wagner and *Teaching Infants* by T. Kerry and J. Tollitt; Booth, I. for permission to reprint material from Booth, I. G. (1998) *The Law and the Teacher*. University of Durham Whole School Issues PGCE Secondary Course Document, 1997–8. School of Education, University of Durham. Reprinted with permission of Ian Booth; Cengage Learning, for From GRABE, *Integrating Technology for Meaningful Learning*, 5E. © 2007 Wadsworth, a part of Cengage Learning, Inc. Reproduced by permission. www.cengage.com/permissions; Continuum, for *Reflective Teaching in the Primary School* by A. Pollard and S. Tann; reprinted by kind permission of Continuum International Publishing Group. Reprinted by permission of the Continuum Book and *Changing English Primary Schools? The Impact of the Education Reform Act at Key Stage One* by A. Pollard, P. Broadfoot, P. Croll, M. Osborn and D. Abbott; Crown Copyright material is reproduced with the permission of the Controller of HMSO and the Queen's Printer for Scotland, for *Records of Achievement: A Statement of Policy* by the Department of Education and Science (1984), *The National Curriculum from 5–16: A Consultation Document* by the Department of Education and Science (1987), *Education Observed 5: Good Behaviour and Discipline in Schools* (1989 edition) by the Department of Education and Science (1989), *National Record of Achievement letter* to accompany the publication of the National Record of Achievement by the Department of Education and Science and the Employment Department (1991), *National Record of Achievement: A Business Guide* (ref. PP3/2267/891/55) by the Employment Department, *Circular 9/93* by the Department for Education (1992), Curriculum Organisation and Classroom Practice in Primary Schools: A Discussion Paper by the Department for Education, written by R. Alexander, J. Rose and C. Woodhead (1992), *Circular 14/93* by the Department for Education (1993), *Mathematics in the National Curriculum* by the Department for Education (1995), *Guidance on the Inspection of Schools* by the Office for Standards in Education (1995), *Circular 02/98: Reducing the Bureaucratic Burden on Teachers* (1998), *Health and Safety of Pupils on Educational Visits* (1998), *School Standards and Framework Act 1998. Circular 11/98: Supporting the Target Setting Process* (1998), *The National Literacy Strategy: Framework for Teaching* (1998), *Circular 10/99: Social Inclusion: Pupil Support* (1999), *The National Curriculum* (1999), *The National Curriculum: Handbook for Primary Teachers* (1999), *The National Numeracy Strategy: Framework for Teaching Mathematics* (1999), *The Structure of the Literacy Hour* (1999), *Circular 15/2000: Curriculum Guidance for the*

Foundation Stage (2000), *National Standards for Headteachers* (2000), *Schools: Building on Success* (2001), Education Bill 2001. *Inclusive Schooling* (2001). *Schools Achieving Success* (2001), *Special Educational Needs Code of Practice* (2001). *Supporting the Target Setting Process* (2001), *Gender and Achievement: The Tool Kit* (2001). *14–19: Extending Opportunities, Raising Standards* (2002), *Autumn Performance Report 2002*. Cmnd. 5689, *Bullying: Don't Suffer in Silence* (2002), *Cutting Burdens* (2002), Education Act 2002. *Education and Skills: Delivering Results: A Strategy to 2006* (2002). *Gender and Achievement* (2002), *Guide to the National Record of Achievement* (2002), *Key Stage 3 National Strategy: Designing the Key Stage 3 Curriculum* (2002), *Progress File Achievement Planner, Supplement 2* (2002). *Progress File Achievement Planner, Supplement 3* (2002). *Safe Schools* (2002). *Statistics of Education: Permanent Exclusions from Maintained Schools in England* (2002). *Target Setting at Key Stage 2* (2002). *Transforming the Way We Learn: A Vision for the Future of ICT in Schools* (2002), *About the School Curriculum* (2003). *Choosing Strategies for Reducing Bullying, Definition of SEN* (2003), *Inclusion: Providing Effective Learning Opportunities for All Pupils* (2003). *Planning Guidance* (2003), *Statement of Values* (2003), *Research into Teacher Effectiveness: A Model for Teacher Effectiveness*. Report to Department for Education and Skills. London: Hay McBer. Office for Standards in Education (1999), *Principles into Practice: Effective Education for Pupils with Emotional and Behavioural Difficulties*, para 104. 2001 Special Educational Needs & Disability Act, part II, para 11–13. Ofsted Statistics of Education (2002), Permanent Exclusions from Maintained Schools in England; The Development Education Centre (Birmingham) for *A Sense of School* by C. McFarlane and S. Sinclair; *Educational Research*, for the article 'Curriculum planning in multicultural education' by R. Jeffcoate in vol. 18 (3), 192–200; Education World, for *Technology in Schools: It Does Make a Difference*, by G. Chaika, *Education World* [online]. Retrieved 21.6.2003 from: http://www.education.world.com. Estate of E. C. Wragg, for *Class Management and Control: A Teaching Skills Workbook* by E. C. Wragg (DES Teacher Education Project with Focus Books). Reprinted with permission of Mrs J. Wragg, the Estate of Professor E. C. Wragg. George Allen and Unwin, for *Classroom Control: A Sociological Perspective* by M. Denscombe; Learning Matters Ltd, for *Primary ICT: Knowledge, Understanding and Practice* by J. Sharp, J. Potter, J. Allen and A. Loveless (2000); Longman, for *A Practical Guide to Improving Your Teaching* by E. Perrot; McGraw-Hill, (Boston, MA) for *Learning to Teach* (1998) by Arends, R. I.; National Council for Educational Technology for *Technology Works! Stimulate to Educate* (1994). Coventry, NCET. Nelson Thornes, for *Essential Teaching Skills* (2nd edn) by C. Kyriacou (1998); NFER-Nelson, for *Educating Pupils with Special Needs in Ordinary Schools* by S. Hegarty, K. Pocklington and D. Lucas; Paul Chapman Publishing Ltd, for *Relationships in the Primary Classroom* by P. J. Kutnick; Pearson Education, Inc., for *Authentic Assessment in the Classroom: Applications and Practice* by Tombari/Borich, © reprinted by permission of Pearson Educational Inc., Upper Saddle River, NJ; Pearson Education Ltd, for *The Language of Teaching* by A. D. Edwards and V. J. Furlong (1978), London: Heinemann, now owned by Pearson Education Ltd.; Qualifications and Curriculum Authority for kind permission to reprint the following: QCA (1999) *Early Learning Goals*, London: QCA, pp. 4–5, 27; QCA (1999) *Keeping Track; Effective Ways of Recording Pupil Achievement to Help Raise Standards*, London: QCA; QCA (2000) *Feedback: 'Not very good work' doesn't help me know how to do it better – The LEARN Project, Guidance for Schools on Assessment for Learning* (2000). University of Bristol – CLIO Centre for Assessment Studies; QCA (2000) *Curriculum Guidance for the Foundation Stage*, London: QCA, pp 8–9, 11–12; QCA (2001) *Planning for Learning at the Foundation Stage*, London: QCA, pp. 4, 9, 10, 15, 20; QCA (2002) *Designing and Timetabling the Primary Curriculum*, London: QCA, pp. 25, 29; QCA (2002) *Designing the Key Stage 3 Curriculum*, London: QCA, p. 4; QCA (2002) *Including All Learners*, London: QCA, www.qca.org.uk/ca/inclusion/key_principles.asp; QCA (2002) *Guidance on Teaching the Gifted and Talented: Characteristics to Look for*, London: QCA, www.nc.uk.net/gt/general/01_characteristics.htm; QCA (2002) *Guidance on Teaching the Gifted and Talented: Good Practice*, London: QCA. www.nc.uk/gt/general/01_identifying.htm; QCA (2002) *Guidance on Teaching the Gifted and Talented: Developing an Effective Learning Environment*, www.nc.uk.net/gt/general/05_environment.htm; Sage Publications Ltd, for 'Effective use of homework', in *Effective Teaching: Evidence and Practice* by D. Muijs and D. Reynolds, reprinted by permission of Sage Publications Ltd, © Sage Publications Ltd, 2001; Sage Publications Inc. Books, for *How the Brain Learns: A Classroom Teacher's Guide*, 2nd Edn (Paper) by De Souza. Copyright 2001 by Sage Publications Inc. Books. Reproduced with permission of Sage Publications Inc. Books in the format. Other book via Copyright Clearance Center; School Curriculum and Assessment Authority, for *Planning the Curriculum at Key Stages 1 and 2* (1995), *A Curriculum for All*, NCC (1992); Solution Tree, for *Assertive Discipline: Positive Behavior Management for Today's Classroom* by Canter, L. and Canter, M. (1992). Canter & Associates, Inc., now published by Solution Tree. Stanley Thornes, for 'Essential Teaching Skills' by Chris Kyriacou, reproduced with the permission of Nelson Thornes Ltd, isbn 978-0-7487-8161-4, first published in 1991; Taylor & Francis Books/Routledge, for *Learning to Teach in the Primary School* by A. Proctor, M. Entwistle, B. Judge and S. McKenzie-Murdoch, *Explaining* by E. C. Wragg and G. Brown, *Questioning* by G. Brown and E. C. Wragg, *Bullying: Effective Strategies for Long-term Improvement* by D. Thompson, T. Arota and S. Sharp, *Assessment, What's In It for Schools?* by P. Wedeen, J. Winter and P. Broadfoot, *Learning to Teaching in the Secondary School* by S. Capel, M. Leask and T. Turner (eds) (paper by T. Turner: 'Moral development and values'), *Testing: Friend or Foe?* by P. Black, *Understanding Assessment* by D. Lambert and D. Lines, *ICT, Pedagogy and the Curriculum* by A. Loveless, G. L. DeVoogd and R. M. Bohlin, *Special Education Re-formed: Beyond Rhetoric?* by H. Daniels (ed.) (paper by B. Norwich: 'Inclusion in education: from concepts, values and critique to practice'), *Developing Topic Work in the Primary School* by S. Tann (1988), 'Situated cognition. Vygotskian thought and learning from the communities of practice perspective: implications for the design of web-based e-learning', in *Education Media International*, 38 (1), 3–12 by D. W. L. Hung and D. T. Cheng (2001); Taylor & Francis Journals/The National Communication Association for D. W. L. Hung and D. T. Cheng (2001) 'Situated cognition. Vygotskian thought and learning from the communities of practice perspective: implications for the design of web-based e-learning', in *Education Media International*, 38 (1), 3–12. Copyright © National Communication Association, reprinted by permission of (Taylor & Francis Ltd, http://www.tandf.co.uk/journals) on behalf of The National Communication Association; Teachers College Press for *Teaching with Technology: Creating Student-Centered Classrooms* from Sandholtz, J. H. Ringstaff, C. and D. C. Dwyer, New York © 1997 by Teachers College Press, Columbia University. All rights reserved. Reprint by permission of the publisher; Training and Development Agency for Schools (TDA), for *Qualifying to Teach: Professional Standards for Qualified Teacher Status and Requirements for Initial Teacher Training* (2002), *Guidance on the Requirements for Initial Teacher Training* (2002); Trentham Books Ltd and the Runnymede Trust, for *Equality Assurance in Schools*; Ward Lock Educational, for *The Integrated Day – Theory and Practice* by J. Walton (ed.); WestEd, for *Summary of Current Research and Evaluation Findings on Technology in Education* by John Cradler, copyright © 1994 WestEd (Far West Laboratory). See: http://www.wested.org/techpolicy/refind.html. Reprinted by permission of WestEd, San Francisco.

The authors would like to thank the following people for their advice: Paul Warwick, Jane Warwick, Helen Bradford and Roland Chaplain (all University of Cambridge); David Spendlove (University of Manchester); Steven Ford QC.

Disclaimer

The publishers have made every effort to contact authors/copyright holders of works reprinted in *A Guide to Teaching Practice* (rev. 5th edn). This has not been possible in every case, however, and we would welcome correspondence from those individuals/companies whom we have been unable to trace.

PART I

SOME PERSPECTIVES ON TEACHING AND LEARNING

Education is context-specific and context-dependent. Context refers to the settings or surroundings in which education takes place. A student teacher is faced with the exciting but challenging task of assimilating a variety of contexts very rapidly when embarking upon teaching practice, whether during a course of initial teacher pre-service education or as a newly qualified teacher entering a first appointment in a school. These contexts vary from the very broad and general macro-contexts at a societal level to the very specific micro-contexts of a particular individual in a particular school, class and lesson. The prospect can be daunting. The thrust of this book is to support students in their initial teaching experiences – the micro-contexts of everyday life in classrooms. However, localised education is set in broader contexts of society. This part of the book sets the contemporary scene for daily teaching and learning in these broader contexts. It also describes some of the major themes of education in the last decade. Significantly, these include several developments and reforms from the government, changes to the requirements for student teachers and revisions to the National Curriculum. Important amongst these are the statutory requirements for the Early Years Foundation Stage (EYFS), an area addressed by new sections in this book. Further, with the exponential rise of information and communication technology, a new, large chapter is devoted to this. In an increasingly litigious age there is a need for student teachers to know key legal matters, and a chapter discusses these. The convention used in discussions throughout the book will be to refer to students in initial teacher education as 'student teachers' and to children and young adults attending school as 'students' (or 'pupils' if there is possible ambiguity). Similarly, the terms 'he' and 'she', 'him' and 'her', are used alternately in order to avoid the more cumbersome 'he/she', 'him/her'.

1 A Background to Current Developments in Education

INTRODUCTION

It is the first day of your school visit for teaching practice. You may have a mixture of anticipation, anxiety, excitement, eagerness, trepidation and more than a few butterflies in your stomach. That is entirely natural and to be expected. Maybe you have made a positive decision to be a teacher and this is the first time you are going into school not as a pupil. All change! You are one of life's successes; you have gained a range of qualifications that have enabled you to reach this point. But here you are, a comparative novice whose only experience of education so far has been on the 'receiving end'.

You want to teach; your experience of being taught may have been enjoyable (perhaps with a few negative aspects); you like the company of young learners and you have enjoyed the environment of a school; you like learning; you like knowledge; you like people and you like children. Maybe one of your relations has been a teacher and this has inspired you to want to teach; maybe you have been impressed by a particular teacher who taught you and you want to model yourself on him or her. There are many and varied reasons for wanting to teach.

So, here you are at the school gate. What will you want to find out? What will you need to learn? What will you have to teach? What will the class(es) be like? Where will you teach? What resources will you have? What will be appropriate for the pupils to learn? How will you teach? How will you keep order? How will you handle pupils with different abilities, motivations and interests? What will be your timetable? Will you like your class teacher or mentor? Will you meet the head teacher? Will the children like you? How will you gain respect? How will you plan your teaching? The stomach churns a little more!

These are all legitimate questions and concerns, and it is right that student teachers will have an expectation of answers; indeed, we hope that this book will help you to address them all. The point here is that, as a novice teacher, you need to find out a range of matters, and quickly. You need to look at the specific circumstances of the school, teachers, children, resources, curricula, assessment, discipline and so on; in short you need to conduct a rapid situational analysis and learn from this very quickly. You need information, guidance and support, and we hope to indicate how you can gain these.

How can you do this? We intend to set some of the terms of this situational analysis in this book and in this chapter. For example, with regard to the 'what' of teaching, we will draw attention to, amongst other matters, the National Curriculum and the detailed and helpful guidance that the government has provided for its implementation with children at all ages so that there is no uncertainty about what should be taught, to whom, when and in what sequence. With regard to the 'how' of teaching, we will cover a range of issues in, amongst other matters, pedagogy, planning, discipline, motivation, learning and assessment, and the government's requirements for, and guidance in, these matters. With regard to the support for teaching, we will draw attention to the government's guidance documents, to the roles of significant teachers at school (for example mentors, subject leaders and class teachers). With regard to what may be uppermost in student teachers' minds – how to keep order and maintain discipline in order to promote learning – we will draw attention to the current situation in schools, how discipline and order can be approached, what are the government's guidelines on discipline, and what to expect from the school.

The situation in schools is one of permanent change, with many innovations and developments designed to boost learning, raise standards and achievement, energise learning and meet the diverse needs and conditions of learners. This chapter outlines several of these, as they provide the necessary backdrop for understanding schools and the tasks of teachers. We hope that this eases student teachers' initial anxieties by providing information and by providing details on how to find more information and support. We paint a picture of extensive government involvement in education with the expressed intentions to raise standards, to improve social inclusion, to provide guidance and documentary support – in short, to help teachers in their daily work. We hope that by providing such an outline, we both inspire student teachers to teach and also inject a note of realism into what their expectations of teaching might be.

There will be many days when student teachers will experience a sense of achievement in school, just as there will be some days where they experience a sense of frustration, disappointment and downright dislike. That is the world of work. We hope that this book will help to increase the sense of achievement in accomplishing effective teaching and learning, and promote a sense of enjoyment of teaching. Effective teaching is pleasurable and richly repays the investment of time and energy that it requires.

If you do a web search with the words 'I had always wanted to be a teacher' you will find some 374 websites which include these exact words. If you key in 'I have always wanted to be a teacher' there will be over 4,670 websites returned to you. If you key in 'I want to be a teacher' you will find close to 182,000 sites returned. If you key in 'I love teaching' you will have over 293,000 sites returned. If you key in 'I want to teach' you will have nearly 311,000 sites returned. One might suppose that the popularity of teaching is not in jeopardy. The rewards from teaching have traditionally included the opportunity to work with young and developing minds, to be a member of a human service, to share the excitement of learning and knowledge, to work with personalities and people, young and old, to be with the next generation and to be with young people, shaping their personal development. These are their own rewards and they are very powerful.

How is it, then, that the government's statistics[1] showed that in the year 1997–98, 15,700 teachers left the profession (not including those moving to part-time service or retiring) but in 2005–06, 20,300 teachers left, or that the figures for premature retirement have shown year on year increases from 2,380 in 1998–99 increasing to 7,460 in 2006–07? In England about 40 per cent of people who start a training course (on all routes) never become teachers, and of those who do become teachers, about 40 per cent are not teaching five years later.[2]

A survey in 2001[3] found several reasons for teachers leaving. The reasons given by secondary teachers were: workload (57.8 per cent); pupil behaviour (45.1 per cent); government initiatives (37.2 per cent); salary (24.5 per cent); stress (21.6 per cent); and resources and facilities (14.7 per cent). For primary teachers the most commonly cited reasons were: workload (73.9 per cent); government initiatives (42.1 per cent); stress (26.3 per cent); and pupil behaviour (15.8 per cent). We address these items in this chapter.

One cannot presume perversity in government circles in trying to render teaching as unattractive as possible, yet many people seem to be turned off teaching. In 1997 the New Labour government soundbite 'education, education, education' became a slogan for reform of UK schools. There was, and continues to be, no shortage of government documentation for teachers; indeed a litany of government prescriptions and interventions continues to flow thick and fast. This chapter charts some of these and sets a context for the remainder of the book.

A PLETHORA OF INNOVATIONS: STANDARDS AND TARGETS

Since the last edition of *A Guide to Teaching Practice* numerous developments, trends and initiatives have taken place in education. In 1984, perhaps portending the gloom of Orwell's book with the same date for its title, a small publication appeared entitled *The Tightening Grip: Growth of Central Control of the School Curriculum*.[4] In it, the author suggested that 'in a democracy, dispersion of control, rather than concentration at one level, is what is needed'.[5] Some two decades later, the situation does not appear to have been ameliorated. Rather, the opposite is the case. In the earlier 1990s, in a compelling analysis, Hargreaves[6] suggested an 'intensification' thesis: teachers' workload and responsibilities were increasing at an exponential rate, evidenced by lack of time for personal and professional development and preparation, limited professional control and personal discretion over workplace activities and decision making, 'chronic and persistent overload', lack of time for relaxation, indeed for even a proper lunch break. The effects of this, he argued, were the creation of cultures of dependency on externally produced materials and reliance on others' decisions, and because there was inadequate time, to reduction in the quality of services provided in education. His analysis was remarkably prescient.

One response to this situation, he suggested, was for governments and national agencies to treat teachers as 'recovering alcoholics'[7] who depend on step-by-step guidance on instruction, and monitoring by inspection, imposed tests and curricula. Indeed, if we remain with his analysis, we can identify specific government interventions to address the issues.

In connection with teachers' workload and responsibilities the government issued a circular on reducing the bureaucratic burden on teachers,[8] with advice on well-run meetings, written communications, preparing documents, receiving documents, pupils' reports, schemes of work and lesson plans, and use of school resources, most of which requirements were generated by the government itself. What spectacular naivety! If only the solution were that easy. The problem did not go away.

The requirement for personal and professional development, and lack of time for decision making, was addressed by relieving teachers of the responsibility to think for themselves: witness the production of copious documents covering every aspect of education and planning, cascading into schools in abundance, with thousands of pages of print. Exactly as Hargreaves had predicted, the rush of documents, prescriptions and requirements has not been stemmed, constituting a litany of consultations and responses from the centre to the periphery of education providers.

We are witness to the rise and fall of departments, agencies, individuals, governments and decision makers. Out go the Teacher Training Agency (TTA) and the Department for Education and Skills (DfES); in come the Training and Development Agency for Schools (TDA) and the Department for Children, Schools and Families (DCSF) (mischievously called the Department for Curtains and Soft Furnishing by some!). David Blunkett has long departed in spite of not resigning as promised when the national target for statutory tests at age 11 was not met. Since then there have been many Secretaries of State for Education, all united under the banner of 'standards'. Old wine, new bottles?

Perhaps one should not be uncharitable. There are many bold initiatives under way to improve education, and the government has been active in pushing through multiple agendas for reform and improvement. Under the flags of raising standards, excellence and social inclusion there have been several initiatives; these are summarised in Box 1.

Box 1: Interventions for school improvement

- Continued attention to standards and target setting.
- Moves to reduce violence and bullying in schools.
- The imposition of synthetic phonics teaching following the report by Sir Jim Rose.
- Government establishes statutory control of the whole education system from birth to 18 by adding the Early Years Foundation Stage requirements.
- Introduction of the concept of 'school diversity' to include 'specialist' schools (those offering a particular specialism, e.g. technology, languages, arts, humanities), 'academies', training schools and 'Leading Edge Partnerships'.
- The advocacy of personalised learning.
- The legislation of the Children Act 2004 followed by the guidance *Every Child Matters*.
- The introduction of the new National Curriculum at Key Stages 3 and 4.
- The rewriting of standards for the award of qualified teacher status and requirements for initial teacher education.
- The provision of copious amounts of support materials and guidance for schools implementing the National Curriculum.
- A range of new Education Acts and White Papers designed to improve standards and effectiveness.
- A package to encourage disadvantaged 'gifted and talented' pupils to apply for top universities.
- The establishment of learning mentors.
- The provision of guidance for raising the achievement of boys.
- Test statistics and analysis available for schools from the RAISEonline (Reporting and Analysis for Improvement through School Self-Evaluation) service coupled with even more detailed analyses from local authorities.
- New diplomas for the 14–19 age range.
- The development of e-learning.
- The review of the primary curriculum which was preceded by review of the teaching of reading and mathematics.

If one were to judge the effectiveness of a government by the quantity of initiatives then surely the government would be close to 'top of the class'. Yet, the very same innovations that have been designed to bring improvements, to render teaching a more attractive option, to reduce the pressure and workload on teachers, in many ways have had the opposite effect to that sought. One could not fault the valuable documentation support provided by the government, and the need for support for overworked teachers seeking guidance on a range of educational matters; yet it is rather like hitting the jackpot on the 'one-armed bandit' in Las Vegas, only to find that one cannot possibly catch or contain all the coins that are spewed out from the machine. The sheer weight of government documents is staggering. But even this pales into insignificance compared with the extraordinary growth of government guidance on the internet.

In 2003 the government published the Green Paper *Every Child Matters (ECM)* prompted by the tragic death of Victoria Climbié. Although such events are rare, sadly every year children continue to die at the hands of those who are supposed to care for them. The response to such events has repeatedly been calls for better communication between the services who work with children including teachers, doctors, social workers and the police. Following consultations the government published *Every Child Matters: The Next Steps* and passed the Children Act 2004. In 2005 the government published *The Children and Young People's Plan (England) Regulations 2005*. This provided the statutory basis for the *Children's Plan: Building Brighter Futures*, which was presented to Parliament in December 2007. The Children's Plan is a comprehensive ten-year strategy with the aim 'to make England the best place in the world for children and young people to grow up'.[9] The desire for a world-class system, which has motivated governments since 1997, is still present in this aim.

Goals and targets to drive up standards remain the government's main mechanism for measuring the success of the Children's Plan:

Goals for 2020

35. The Children's Plan also sets out goals for what we can and should achieve for our children by 2020. These should be aspirational for both children and young people's educational attainment and for their wider wellbeing. We will consult widely over the next year on whether these goals represent the right national ambitions:

- enhance children and young people's wellbeing, particularly at key transition points in their lives
- every child ready for success in school, with at least 90 per cent developing well across all areas of the Early Years Foundation Stage Profile by age 5
- every child ready for secondary school, with at least 90 per cent achieving at or above the expected level in both English and mathematics by age 11
- every young person with the skills for adult life and further study, with at least 90 per cent achieving the equivalent of five higher-level GCSEs by age 19; and at least 70 per cent achieving the equivalent of two A levels by age 19
- parents satisfied with the information and support they receive
- all young people participating in positive activities to develop personal and social skills, promote wellbeing and reduce behaviour that puts them at risk
- employers satisfied with young people's readiness for work
- child health improved, with the proportion of obese and overweight children reduced to 2000 levels
- child poverty halved by 2010 and eradicated by 2020
- significantly reduce by 2020 the number of young offenders receiving a conviction, reprimand or final warning for a recordable offence for the first time, with a goal to be set in the Youth Crime Action Plan.

(p. 14)

To a certain extent, the Children's Plan has become the focus of attention more than *ECM*. This and the increasingly complex web of goals and targets can be seen in the revised outcomes framework for *ECM* published in 2008 (http://www.everychildmatters.gov.uk/aims/outcomes/).

Since 1997, the government has expressed a laudable commitment to raising standards. The White Paper *Excellence in Schools 1997*[10] outlined the government's commitment to assessment and accountability for raising quality. It placed social inclusion, partnerships and modernisation at the heart of its agenda for education, and suggested requiring local education authorities to prepare education development plans for raising quality. It included target setting by schools. Indeed the Department for Education and Skills set requirements for specific statutory target setting. Since 1997, we now have the benefit of research evidence to show the extent to which government target setting has really resulted in improved education. The majority of evidence has been collected in relation to primary education, and it is not particularly good news for government. For example, although there was evidence of improvement in statutory test scores for maths and English up to 2000, these plateaued from 2000 onwards. Even the gains up to 2000 can be explained by teachers getting better at teaching to the tests.[11]

Whether the setting of such targets is unrealistically optimistic (particularly when there is limited indication of resources to accompany such targets beyond advocacy of partnerships and associations that might be involved),[12] an important motivating feature or simply an irrelevance for many schools and teachers battling with daily problems of indiscipline, staff shortages, curriculum overload and a whole host of pressures is an open question. It is easy to set targets but difficult to achieve them. Indeed one wonders what the penalties could possibly be for schools that fail to achieve them. Does simply raising the bar alone improve performance? Surely not.

DEMOCRACY AND CONTROL IN QUESTION

The government's approach to improving education is increased prescription and centralisation; nothing in education is left untouched by the government and the overall picture appears water-tight. The response to lack of time for personal and professional development is increased centralisation and prescription, simply removing from teachers their need to make many professional judgements. The response to putatively falling standards is increased centralisation and prescription, with an arguably unholy alliance with standards, targets and testing. It is a leap of faith to rely so heavily on these as the engine of improved performance, or to employ testing to destruction as a way of ratcheting up quality. Weighing the pig does not necessarily cause the pig to grow. Underlining all of these agendas is a response to the perceived ills of education by increasing control, direction and prescription. Whether nailing down required performances in documents and statutory requirements ensures that performance flourishes is an open question; a bird whose wings are clipped cannot fly. Owners clip birds' wings so that they will remain with their mate rather than fly away; birds become used to, even enjoy, their captivity. As Orwell indicated, we come to love Big Brother!

There are more substantive issues at stake here than the simple transmission of government prescriptions.[13] It is over fifty years since Karl Popper published the two volumes of *The Open Society and Its Enemies*,[14] which presents an analysis of democracy and the challenges that he saw to it. In the open society individuals enjoy freedom, are aware of the dangers of power and illegitimate authority, and have regard for a plurality of values and opinions. For Popper, dissent is not only to be tolerated but also actively encouraged, not least because it fits with his view of knowledge and learning as essentially conjectural (incomplete, tentative, provisional, open) and subject to constant refutation.[15] Dissent and challenge are essential ingredients if freedom, democracy and human development are to thrive. By contrast, for Popper, a closed society is characterised by the domination of a given and uncontested set of values, to which members have to assent, either by force or by consent – hegemony.

Social and political institutions, including schools, Popper argued, need to put their practices to the test of critical scrutiny and debate, and to be judged by the extent to which they promote democracy. The open society, for Popper, is democratic, and practises tolerance, dignity, justice, respect for individual freedoms and differences of view, free speech and, at its foundation, the freedom to judge one's rulers. *Respect* for difference, rather than merely tolerance of it, is central, as we learn from difference and dissent. Humans are fallible, society is fallible, knowledge is fallible, so they must constantly be open to critique, and the development of critique is essential for democracy.

Teachers, Popper suggests, have the task of educating developing minds to think critically and democratically, so that the open society can flourish. Democracy *requires* education, and free speech in a democracy must require its free speakers to have something useful to say. The open society is both an educated and an educative society. Such education bears several hallmarks; it:

- concerns itself with the furtherance of democracy
- fosters critical judgement in students and teachers
- requires students and teachers to question and justify what they are doing, saying, believing and valuing
- respects evidence and argument, even if it refutes currently held positions, i.e. views are open to challenge and change
- recognises individual fallibility and the tentative, conjectural and refutable nature of knowledge
- respects others as having equal value in society
- values and respects diversity and independence of ideas, views and values
- gives all participants a voice
- places the greater social good over self-interest.

Education, in this scenario, is not simply schooling in obedience or passivity – 'specialised training in the art of keeping down its human sheep or its human cattle'[16] – nor is it instrumental as a service activity, e.g. schooling for jobs or for entrance to higher education, but it is to provoke learning, critique, the pursuit of the just, open society and a search for truth. Rather than being indoctrinatory, education is a potentially subversive activity since it develops the ability in students to question, challenge and demand rational justifications for educational practices. For Popper, critique and the opportunity for critique are fundamentals of the open society.

The consequences of Popper's views for education are several. For example, the transmission/ delivery of a received curriculum is criticised for being, at heart, authoritarian, and hence illiberal, however benevolent. In this vein the use of texts and prescriptions (as in the National Curriculum and its associated assessment) as if they hold unassailable truths, and the practices of teachers who do not, or may not be enabled to, expose themselves to challenge or critique are untenable. Transmission teaching, reinforced by tests which simply check the learner's abilities to reproduce given knowledge, is a one-way process, from the expert to the ignorant empty vessel. Moreover, it is not only an impoverished characterisation of sentient humans but a misrepresentation of the uncertainty of knowledge. Education and its associated testing is more than simply checking a student's failure or success in reproducing given material against given criteria. The criteria themselves have to be open to critical scrutiny, and, where knowledge is tentative and conjectural, assessment leads to learning from errors (refutations from conjectures) rather than public recognition of failure, as in league tables of performance and the 'naming and shaming' of schools in difficulty.

Popperian education is more than telling people what to think; indeed, given the fallibility of knowledge, it concerns raising doubts and uncertainties – 'conjectures and refutations'.[17] Of course, that pushes education out of the comfort zone of teachers, students, societies, politicians and the state.

It is an open question whether the government's prescriptions, reinforced through statute, assessment, inspection and all the instruments of constant surveillance (not least the terminology of its key proponent, the Qualifications and Curriculum *Authority*), further Popper's vision of democracy or his nightmare of a totalitarian state policed by mind control and the 'nanny state', emanating from a *dirigiste* government. We have great concern that the government's prescriptions, for all their benevolent intentions, may be contributing to a closed, monitored and undemocratic citizenry. The issue of centralisation and prescription has a clearly antinomial character: on the one hand it can promote learning, entitlement and the range of benefits that it ascribes to itself. But let us not be naïve; there is a powerful sub-text of control, compliance, conformity and instrumentalism within it. Does the degree of centralisation, direction and prescription from the government's interventions in education promote or inhibit freedom, or both? The jury is out.

We have argued that the student teacher entering the world of school will encounter a situation in which there is little latitude for personal autonomy. In the name of improving quality – surely an endeavour with which one could not disagree – the government has taken an aggressively interventionist stance in telling people what they should do in education. We have been critical of this on three counts: first, because it is not the task of government to do this, but in the interests of democracy to adopt a much more 'hands off' approach, albeit, as Popper would argue, with a safety net to prevent poor quality; second, because the fall-out from such actions is causing more problems than it solves, e.g. the narrowing of the curriculum as a result of statutory testing; and third, because the reliance on standards, testing, quality and their accompanying bureaucracy are a misplaced response to the problems that education faces.

On the other hand, one could speculate whether teachers and schools, if left alone to exercise their own autonomy, would arrive at a set of practices that differed widely from some of the prescriptions of, say, the National Curriculum. Perhaps not. It is not an either/or situation – *either* one supports the government's actions *or* one is against them; that is simplistic. There is no doubt that some of the government's interventions have brought improvements, and its expressed concern for social inclusion, be it out of desire or necessity in the face of the breakdown of social order, is laudable. Further, we have painted a picture of teaching in which there seems to be little room for autonomy; that could be contested and an overstatement – the day-to-day world of classrooms necessarily relies on considerable teacher autonomy and routine on-the-job judgement to be exercised; that is the professional duty and judgement of teachers interacting with learners in order to promote learning.

Issues of control are clearly reflected in two distinct areas that have received attention from government: creativity and the teaching of reading. The publication of the influential report by the National Advisory Committee on Creative and Cultural Education (NACCE)[18] coincided with a growing feeling in education that pupils' experiences were too constrained by centralised prescription. In particular there were fears that creativity was not being engendered in children and young people in England. The importance of creativity was supported by the view in wider society that the modern workplace puts a premium on those workers who can think creatively in order to innovate and solve problems. In education, some government documents began to pay more attention to creativity. The development of the National Strategies and the new National Curriculum at Key Stages 3 and 4 were cases in point. Frequently, though, tensions were evident in such documents because of the government's approach to standards through the testing system, on the one hand, but on the other the recognition that creativity was important. One of the most promising government initiatives to emerge was *Creative Partnerships* (which is now part of the national agency Creativity, Culture and Education). Considerable government money was invested in Creative Partnerships with the aim of fostering creativity for children, young people and teachers.[19] However, in spite of this positive development, creativity remains an endangered element of children's education.

In 2006 Sir Jim Rose's report on the teaching of early reading was published. One of the report's conclusions was: 'Having considered a wide range of evidence, the review has concluded that the case for systematic phonic work is overwhelming, and much strengthened by a *synthetic approach*' (p. 20, italics added). The report was enthusiastically accepted in full by government who moved quickly to develop a synthetic phonics programme called *Letters and Sounds*, which schools can adopt or, if they prefer, use another government approved commercial synthetic phonics programme (see http://www.standards.dfes.gov.uk/phonics/rosereview/). The Rose report was criticised for the weakness of its evidence base.[20] However, one of the other controversial features was that for the first time government moved from only prescribing curriculum content to prescribing teaching method. This continued a pattern of increasing control of teachers' work. Pre-1988 teachers had a relatively high level of teacher autonomy but the passing of the Education Reform Act

1988 and the implementation of the first National Curriculum and testing system changed that because secretaries of state for education were given powers to determine the curriculum. In 2006 there was another significant shift because government took control of teaching methods for the first time (see Chapter 3 for more comment on this in relation to the curriculum).

STRESS IN TEACHING

We cannot escape the fact that teachers are under very great pressure, and, despite the pleasures of working with developing minds and young people, their morale is low and they are leaving the profession in droves. As the start of this chapter indicated, teachers hold the government responsible for this in terms of workload and prescribing initiatives – more means less.

That teachers are under stress is well documented.[21] Teachers were highlighted by medical insurers in 1997 as being at high risk of stress-related illnesses, reinforced in 1998, 1999, 2000 and 2001 by further studies that indicated that:[22]

- 41.5 per cent of teachers reported themselves to be 'highly stressed'
- 36 per cent of teachers felt the effects of stress all or most of the time
- calls to the Teacher Support Line (http:// www.teacherline.org.uk/) show that the most common concern is stress (25 per cent of calls) (http://www.teachersupport.info/index.cfm?a=63)
- long working hours and workload were significant causes of stress, coupled with pressure of inspections and pupil misbehaviour.

In 2001 the Department for Education and Skills commissioned PricewaterhouseCoopers to review teachers' workload[23] and found that:

- teachers work more intensive weeks than other comparable managers and professionals, routinely working more than a 50-hour week
- teachers perceive a major problem to be lack of control and ownership over their work
- rising expectations coupled with pupils' misbehaviours and lack of parental support were significant problems
- more guaranteed non-contact time was needed for teachers to plan and prepare.

Teaching has consistently been ranked as a high-stress occupation. When compared with 26 other professions teaching was found to be one of the six most stressful occupations. As a result of this, specific websites for contact by teachers have been set up to cope with burgeoning teacher stress:

- The Teacher Stress website (http://www.teacherstress.co.uk)
- The Teacher Support Network (http://www.teachersupport.info/index.cfm?a=63)
- The Stress and Work website (htttp://channel4.com/health/microsites/H/health/magazine/stress/work_teachers/html)
- The Teacherline Organization (http://www.teacherline.org.uk)
- The National Healthy School Standard at the Wired for Health website (http://www.wiredforhealth.gov.uk)

The Department of Health[24] published a significant document on teacher stress, its causes, treatment and legal framework, indicating, for example, that 31 per cent of calls to a teacher support line concerned workplace stress in state schools, in comparison with 8 per cent of calls from private organisations.

Too much stress leads to 'learned helplessness', a situation in which, because one is unable to alleviate the situation because impossible tasks are set, one simply capitulates, surrendering one's autonomy to others; or it can lead to burnout and breakdown. Or one gets out.

Troman[25] reported that the main causes of teacher stress were: chronic strains in personal life; the 'intensification of work' (cf. Hargreaves's 'intensification thesis' mentioned earlier); teacher/pupil relationships; staff relationships, and accountability. Kyriacou[26] reported that the main sources of stress facing teachers were:

- teaching pupils who lack motivation
- maintaining discipline
- time pressures and workload
- coping with change
- being evaluated by others
- dealing with colleagues
- self-esteem and status
- administration and management
- role conflict and ambiguity
- poor working conditions.

Whilst he makes it clear that an individual's stress is a unique and personal matter, nevertheless there are social facts that indicate common patterns, and one can see that government interventions in education bear some of the responsibility for this.

INDISCIPLINE AND BULLYING

A major source of teacher stress is the amount and handling of indiscipline in schools. There is scarcely a day passes without the media reporting cases of bullying and violence between students and towards teachers. The matter gained huge coverage with the murder of the head-teacher Philip Lawrence in London, and the earlier murder of Nikki Conroy, a teenager in a Teesside school, by an intruder, but these were only two incidents out of thousands.

In a study of over 2,000 schools,[27] some of the school violence was found to be crime- and drug-related, over a third of the schools (38.7 per cent) had been burgled (43.9 per cent of these with more than one burglary), with theft (38.3 per cent), robbery with threat and actual violence (1.9 per cent), malicious damage (56.6 per cent) and arson (7.2 per cent) reported. Staff had been verbally abused by parents in 50.3 per cent of the schools, in the majority of cases more than once, with other outsiders verbally abusing teachers in 26.9 per cent of cases. The severity of assaults was graded on a three-point scale: Level 1 comprising spitting, pushing and unwanted touching; Level 2 comprising hitting with a fist, being punched or kicked; Level 3 comprising being hit with a weapon or other object. 16.1 per cent of respondents reported physical abuse on teachers by pupils at Level 1 and 18.7 per cent at Level 2, in the majority of cases more than once, with 2.9 per cent at Level 3. 12 per cent of the schools had found pupils carrying weapons on the school premises. 27.1 per cent reported outsiders causing disturbance on school premises, and 26.7 per cent of parents causing disturbance on school premises. More schools reported assaults by pupils on pupils at Level 2 than Level 1 (50.7 per cent and 47.4 per cent respectively), and around one in 14 schools reported Level 3 assaults on pupils by pupils.

The responses to this state of affairs have been several. For example, most schools have restricted entry and increased security systems, including the identification and registration of visitors and the locking of entrances to schools; most schools have policies to deal with bullying, intruders, and violence; staff and pupils have been trained in personal safety and restraint; links to the local police have been strengthened. Dealing with discipline problems and maintaining discipline were reported to be major causes of stress in teachers.[28] The government's policy of inclusion has had the effect of having classes each with a significant number of disruptive students, the problem being worse in secondary schools than primary schools.[29] Indeed, after workload, pupils' behaviour was the most frequent reason that teachers gave for leaving the profession. In one study reported in 2001, 61 per cent of 700 teachers reported that they had either witnessed or been involved in physical or verbal abuse, and in another report of the same year one in ten teachers had been physically assaulted by a pupil in the previous year. The problem is not confined to physical assault; rather it is the daily dose of verbal abuse and misbehaviour that wears down teachers, with pupils lighting textbooks, throwing furniture, slamming doors, swearing and screaming, threatening teachers sexually, refusing to work, and general physical restlessness. Such behaviour is not the preserve of teenagers; it happens in the infant school.[30]

One government response to this has been the issuing of guidelines on procedures for dealing with intruders, violence, safety and bullying, with specific indication of legal redress.[31] Teachers and student teachers should not have to put up with violence or abuse, racial or sexual harassment; these are not part of the job. Student teachers will need to find out the school's procedures for handling violence, bullying, assault and discipline matters.

With regard to bullying, it was reported in 2001 that over half of all British school children had been bullied. One in ten of those reported severe bullying which included physical violence; one third of all girls and one quarter of all boys reported that, at some time, they had been frightened of going to school, and at least 16 pupils' suicides each year were attributable to bullying.[32] 4.1 per cent of all children reported being bullied several times a week, and 32.3 per cent of children reported being bullied once or twice a week. 18.7 per cent of 10-year-olds, 13.1 per cent of 11-year-olds, 12.1 per cent of 12-year-olds, 10.5 per cent of 13-year-olds and 7.5 per cent of 14-year-olds reported being bullied. Perhaps equally alarming were the reports on children as bullies in the same document: 5.3 per cent of 10-year-olds; 1.4 per cent of 11-year-olds; 2.8 per cent of 12-year-olds, 3.6 per cent of 13-year-olds, and 3.3 per cent of 14-year-olds.[33] For 10- and 11-year-olds this extrapolates to around 35 bullies in the 10–11 age range in a school of 500 students, and 97 bullies in the 12–14 age range in a secondary school of 1,000 pupils. The statistics are more than alarming. Indeed the same report indicated that, in a survey of 300 secondary schools in England and Wales, 82 per cent of teachers were aware of verbal incidents and 26 per cent were aware of physical incidents (p. 15).

Three categories of bullying have been identified:[34]

1 *physical* (e.g. kicking, hitting, theft, being pushed about, attack, having one's possessions thrown around, being forced to hand over money or property (extortion), pinching, use of a weapon, hiding property (e.g. a school bag, clothes, shoes), spoiling things such as clothes, writing on books or homework, destroying a game, and sexual harassment)
2 *verbal* (e.g. name calling, taunts and gestures, threats, racist remarks, teasing, comments about looks, or religion, sarcasm, ridicule)
3 *indirect* (e.g. spreading rumours, being ignored, excluding someone from a social group).

In 2007, the government introduced new overarching guidance for schools within their *Safe to Learn* documents.[35] *Safe to Learn* defines bullying as: 'Behaviour by an individual or group, usually repeated over time, that intentionally hurts another individual or group either physically or emotionally' (p. 6).

Government has repeatedly made suggestions for action, including policies, monitoring, intervention, implementation of interventions, reporting, investigating bullying, whole-school approaches, tackling the issue through the school curriculum (e.g. in Personal, Social and Health Education) from age 5, assertiveness training for pupils, liaison with other services (the police, social services, libraries, leisure services), punishments, procedures for identifying bullies and victims, support groups for victims, how pupils should react to bullies, handling specific forms of bullying (racist, sexual, special needs, homophobic), reducing the risk of bullying (e.g. playground action), working with parents, and advice for pupils, parents and families.

One of the newer forms of bullying is *cyberbullying* which is the use of ICT, particularly mobile phones and the internet, deliberately to upset someone. Cyberbullying has to be taken just as seriously as other forms of bullying. One aspect of it is that bystanders can easily become perpetrators if they are not careful. For example, taking part in online polls or discussion groups can mean that they become *accessories* to the bullying. Schools have to have sanctions for this kind of behaviour just as they do for other forms of bullying. The government documents also cover racist bullying and homophobic bullying (for a powerful example of a secondary teacher who's teaching for citizenship involves challenging pupils' use of sexist, racist and homophobic language see Keddie's article in the *Cambridge Journal of Education.*[36]

The Directgov website (http://www.dfes.gov.uk/bullying) has useful information for teachers, pupils and parents on bullying, as it does for many other topics.

The prescriptions appear sensitive, sensible and helpful. How far they improve the situation is another open question. Simply writing documents could be seen as cosmetic. The problem of indiscipline and bullying seems less than tractable; if there were simple solutions we would have found them. How far the government has contributed to the very problems that teachers face through its unwavering and uniform prescription, with a massively disaffected set of pupils (one estimate puts a figure of 50,000 pupils truanting each day),[37] being forced to learn, and teachers being forced to teach contents in which pupils have little interest, is debatable. Real ground-level developments are needed, and they cost money.

SCHOOL DIVERSITY

In the past, *beacon* schools (phased out in 2005) were an example of what is now part of *school diversity.* Government describes school diversity as a structural element of the education system which enables schools to develop an individual ethos, special character and areas of specialism. The information on the *Standards Site* claims that the government actively promotes diversity in education and that this is part of Britain's educational history. However, the kind of government-controlled diversity is rather different from the diversity that is part of, for example, A.S. Neill's famous Summerhill School, or early years settings inspired by Reggio Emilia which recognise the need for children to exercise control over their learning, or even the diversity that is part of schools in the private sector. The two ideas that underpin school diversity are specialisation and collaboration, which can be seen in the ways that diversity is promoted.

Leading Edge Partnership programme

High-performing specialist schools are encouraged to play a central reform role to help schools in their locality, that are struggling to raise standards by sharing their expertise and resources.

Academies

Academies are all-ability, state-funded schools established and managed by sponsors from a wide range of backgrounds, including high-performing schools and colleges, universities, individual philanthropists, businesses, the voluntary sector and the faith communities. According to government, the sponsors of academies 'challenge traditional thinking on how schools are run and what they should be like for students. They seek to make a complete break with cultures of low aspiration which afflict too many communities and their schools.' At the time of writing there were 85 academies open.

Specialist schools

Specialists schools have a particular focus on certain subjects in the curriculum while at the same time continuing to offer a broad and balanced education. The specialisms are: arts, business and enterprise, engineering, humanities, languages, mathematics and computing, music, science, sports, and technology. The schools are in partnership with private sector sponsors and supported by additional government funding.

Training schools

Training schools are centres of excellence for training. As well-managed and successful institutions they are expected to add to this by supporting the training of teachers including those in other schools and those who are new to the profession. They are expected to work with teacher training providers and they are encouraged to evaluate their impact through research.

There is always the danger that with a multitude of initiatives there can be a loss in policy coherence. In recognition of this, government emphasised the wider idea of planning school diversity. This is where local authorities and schools in an area work towards a shared strategic pattern of specialist provision. Diversity Pathfinder Projects were set up in six areas in England in order to plan for school diversity. However, these were only expected to run until 2005, so it is not clear how coherence will be maintained.

The most controversial aspect of school diversity that has been a feature of academies has been the idea of partnership between private and public institutions in order to raise finance. Many people are concerned about the particular influence that private companies might have on children's education. One of the ways that academies are being evaluated is the extent to which test and examination scores compare to other kinds of schools in similarly deprived areas. This is likely to be a highly contested area that has many parallels with the *Charter Schools* debates in the USA. Although the commitment to improving standards is welcome, the main solution seems to be through relatively short-term initiatives that are, in terms of time, related to the political cycle. However, research would suggest that improving schools in challenging circumstances requires much more sustained work.[38]

CHANGING THE NATURE OF TEACHING

The effect of many interventions is to change the nature of teaching very considerably. From being a key macro-decision maker, the scope of a teacher's decision making has been attenuated considerably; teachers are largely the agents of, the implementers of, major decisions taken elsewhere. The sphere of their decision making concerns how to implement others' agendas, and their own classroom role in this. Many teachers may feel comfortable with this, as it reduces the burden of their decision making and because it is seen as a move toward the creation of 'high-reliability schools'.

High-reliability schools possess several characteristics, many of which are characterised by standardised procedures:[39] schools where reliability through policies, procedures and consistency of practice and behaviour is a powerful device for raising achievement (bureaucracies lift the trailing edge of organisations to an acceptable minimum).[40] This might be the case for 'failing schools', where the absence of procedures or consistency contributes to their weakness. High-reliability might be a useful concept, in that it involves:[41]

- massive investment in training
- detailed identification and rectification of weaknesses
- a limited number of explicit goals
- standard operations which are applied consistently
- adequate resources for the school's operations
- the alignment of management, administrative, curricular, pedagogic and cultural subsystems towards achievement of the school's goals
- a blend of centralisation and controlled delegation
- efficient and extensive communication
- extensive back-up facilities and knowledge about the operations
- close monitoring of activities and people.

Documenting everything, having procedures for everything, in short bureaucratising teaching, is one approach to raising standards. For other schools the procedures-driven mentality undermines their excellence (and bureaucracies can suppress excellence),[42] identity and uniqueness. Indeed it misrepresents the nature of education, as *in essence* it is non-standardised (because individuals are individual!), and because the impersonality and dehumanisation of a procedures-driven view misses the heart of the educative process.

We ought not to be too dismissive of this approach. For example the benefits of consistency have been well documented in school effectiveness research, not least in reducing bad behaviour in schools. That this is an important matter is well attested to by the reported incidence of bullying and violence in schools, on pupils and on teachers, reported earlier.

Teaching risks becoming a delivery system, a given rather than a negotiated activity. Somewhere buried in the whole picture there are people, not robots. Many teachers, having come into the profession with high ideals, find that these soon evaporate; teaching becomes simply a job, an occupation not a vocation. Education becomes a commodity like any other. This is a terrible loss.

The context of teaching practice, then, is mixed. Student teachers should be under no illusions: teaching is tough. It is not a profession for the faint-hearted. There are multiple issues to be faced in entering classrooms. On the one hand there is a range of statutory requirements and initiatives whose effect has been seen to be the creation of stress, a flight from teaching, innovation fatigue and a very heavy workload, and a surfeit of documentation for teachers to absorb.

On the other hand, lest we be accused of being merely negative, we have to keep in mind that at the heart of education lie people, sentient, creative, full of potential, interacting with humour, imagination and personalities. That separates teaching from many other walks of life. We perhaps have to remind ourselves frequently about this, to restore the sense of vocation that may have brought us into teaching.

Further, though it is easy to carp about governments, nevertheless it would be difficult to criticise the beneficent intent of government in tackling deep and problematic issues in the education service. Whether we think they are going to the heart of the problem, whether we think their interventions are desirable, whether we think that the resources that they are putting into education are well targeted or misguided, whether we believe that the government is straying into areas of control and prescription into which it ought not be straying, or whether we think the government has 'got it right', nevertheless it would be a hard-hearted commentator who would not wish to applaud its commitment to improvement of the education service for all.

The government's provision of guidance documents on all aspects of teaching is a worthy accomplishment. Student teachers will find much to praise in them, and will be able to draw valuable guidance from them together with practical advice and concrete suggestions. For some they reduce teacher autonomy, thinking and decision making; for others they provide welcome support and give a clear picture of expectations and actions.

We have tried to paint a realistic picture of the context of teaching and for teaching practice. Our palette has frequently been a little unattractive; it has also been replete with references to government actions. Nonetheless we have a duty to be faithful to the real situation in many schools, and considerable government involvement in education is quite simply the order of the day. We pick up the issues that this raises throughout the book. However, most schools are not negative places, and they are not all bear gardens; most schools are delightful and many children never let us down in their positive desire to learn, to work, to have good relationships with each other and with their teachers. It is good to be with them. We must be optimists.

Teacher Training Requirements

INTRODUCTION

The Training and Development Agency for Schools (TDA) has responsibility for providing guidance, frameworks and enactment of government policy for important aspects of initial teacher education (also called Initial Teacher Training (ITT)). The TDA's published remit is as follows:[1]

The TDA will work with the DCSF to ensure:

- High-quality teaching and learning in every classroom, by securing a sufficient supply of new teachers and effective continuing professional development.
- Ongoing workforce reform in schools to secure effective staff deployment that addresses local needs so teachers, schools and children realise the benefits.
- Closer co-operation between, and integration of, schools and other children's services to meet the needs of children and families.
- Support for the development and roll out of extended schools.

We are also responsible for:

- Increasing the number and quality of science, technology, engineering and maths teachers.
- Leading on the development of a new qualification for teachers: the Masters in teaching and learning.
- Supporting special educational needs and disability training for the workforce.
- Providing training and development opportunities to support staff.
- Supporting the implementation of the national agreement.

Government control of ITT has been extended in order to cover teachers' professional development throughout their career. There are standards not only for ITT but also for the various career stages:[2]

Q – qualified teacher status
C – core standards for main scale teachers who have successfully completed their induction
P – post-threshold teachers on the upper pay scale
E – excellent teachers
A – advanced skills teachers (ASTs)

Each set of standards builds on the previous set. So, for example, an advanced skills teacher has to satisfy the A standards as well as those for C, P and E.

Much of ITT takes place in schools, on variants of an internship model. This has been both welcomed and criticised. It has been welcomed as an opportunity to break the perceived stranglehold of initial teacher education by institutions of higher education and to ensure a highly professionally, relevant ITT programme. It has been criticised for trying to offload onto schools responsibilities which they neither have time to undertake, nor should be undertaking (schools exist to promote learning in pupils, not to train teachers, or to use pupils as 'guinea pigs' for novice teachers). Indeed Maguire et al.[3] comment on an anomaly, wherein schools are being blamed for poor performance yet are being used to train the very teachers who might work in such schools following the completion of the ITT courses. All trainee teachers must be prepared to teach across at least two or more consecutive age ranges:

- Foundation Stage, age 3–5
- School years 1–2, age 5–7
- School years 3–4, age 7–9
- School years 5–6, age 9–11
- School years 7–9, age 11–14
- School years 10–11, age 14–16
- School years 12–13, age 16–19

and they must also be familiar with the expectations, curricula, strategies and teaching arrangements in the age phases immediately before and after the ones they are trained to teach. The TDA has tied ITT very closely into the preparation of teachers to teach the National Curriculum alone, or largely alone. The desirability of this is a moot point.

The requirement to have much of the ITT taking place in schools means significant periods of school placement, as follows:[4]

- a four-year undergraduate QTS programme – 160 days (32 weeks)
- a two- or three-year QTS undergraduate programme – 120 days (24 weeks)
- a secondary graduate QTS programme – 120 days (24 weeks)
- a primary graduate QTS programme – 90 days (18 weeks)
- employment-based schemes – determined by the training programme.

Each student teacher must have experience in at least two schools or other settings (provided that these enable the student to achieve the standards required for qualified teacher status (QTS)).

There is a differential proportion in the amount of school-based work in ITT programmes. For all secondary and Key Stage 2/3 postgraduate programmes the proportion of school-based work is very high; for primary postgraduate programmes the proportion is smaller. How this is justified is opaque. In its effects it means that, for students preparing to teach in primary postgraduate programmes, the pressure on non-school-based work taking place in higher education institutions and work in school is immense, in order to cover all the aspects of ITT to meet the standards required for QTS, indeed to be fit to teach a spectrum of subjects and to take on the extended role of teachers. For intending postgraduate secondary school and KS2/3 teachers the pressure is similarly huge, as the amount of time out of school is minimal.

For ITT to happen effectively requires the development of active partnerships between schools and institutions that provide initial teacher education in respect of:[5]

Partnership requirements

R3.1 That partners establish a partnership agreement setting out the roles and responsibilities of each partner.

R3.2 That partners work together to contribute to the selection, training and assessment of trainees against the QTS standards.

Moderation of assessments of trainees is required to ensure reliability, accuracy, parity and standardisation across schools and providers.

STANDARDS FOR THE AWARD OF QUALIFIED TEACHER STATUS

Those who are awarded QTS are required to meet the following standards, set into three interrelated sections of:

1   professional attributes
2   professional knowledge and understanding
3   professional skills.

These standards apply to teachers of all the age ranges and are not differentiated according to age phases. These are set out below.[6]

Those recommended for the award of QTS (Q) should meet the following criteria:

Professional attributes

Relationships with children and young people

Q1   Have high expectations of children and young people including a commitment to ensuring that they can achieve their full educational potential and to establishing fair, respectful, trusting, supportive and constructive relationships with them.

Q2   Demonstrate the positive values, attitudes and behaviour they expect from children and young people.

Frameworks

Q3 (a)   Be aware of the professional duties of teachers and the statutory framework within which they work.

Q3 (b)   Be aware of the policies and practices of the workplace and share in collective responsibility for their implementation.

Communicating and working with others

Q4   Communicate effectively with children, young people, colleagues, parents and carers.

Q5   Recognise and respect the contribution that colleagues, parents and carers can make to the development and wellbeing of children and young people and to raising their levels of attainment.

Q6   Have a commitment to collaboration and co-operative working.

Personal professional development

Q7 (a)   Reflect on and improve their practice, and take responsibility for identifying and meeting their developing professional needs.

Q7 (b)   Identify priorities for their early professional development in the context of induction.

Q8   Have a creative and constructively critical approach towards innovation, being prepared to adapt their practice where benefits and improvements are identified.

Q9   Act upon advice and feedback and be open to coaching and mentoring.

Professional knowledge and understanding

Teaching and learning

Q10   Have a knowledge and understanding of a range of teaching, learning and behaviour management strategies and know how to use and adapt them, including how to personalise learning and provide opportunities for all learners to achieve their potential.

Assessment and monitoring

Q11   Know the assessment requirements and arrangements for the subjects/curriculum areas they are trained to teach, including those relating to public examinations and qualifications.

Q12   Know a range of approaches to assessment, including the importance of formative assessment.

Q13   Know how to use local and national statistical information to evaluate the effectiveness of their teaching, to monitor the progress of those they teach and to raise levels of attainment.

Subject and curriculum

Q14   Have a secure knowledge and understanding of their subjects/curriculum areas and related pedagogy to enable them to teach effectively across the age and ability range for which they are trained.

Q15   Know and understand the relevant statutory and non-statutory curricula and frameworks, including those provided through the National Strategies, for their subjects/curriculum areas, and other relevant initiatives applicable to the age and ability range for which they are trained.

Literacy, numeracy and ICT

Q16   Have passed the professional skills tests in numeracy, literacy and information and communications technology (ICT).

Q17   Know how to use skills in literacy, numeracy and ICT to support their teaching and wider professional activities.

Achievement and diversity

Q18   Understand how children and young people develop and that the progress and well-being of learners are affected by a range of developmental, social, religious, ethnic, cultural and linguistic influences.

Q19   Know how to make effective personalised provision for those they teach, including those for whom English is an additional language or who have special educational needs or disabilities, and how to take practical account of diversity and promote equality and inclusion in their teaching.

Q20   Know and understand the roles of colleagues with specific responsibilities, including those with responsibility for learners with special educational needs and disabilities and other individual learning needs.

Health and wellbeing

Q21 (a) Be aware of the current legal requirements, national policies and guidance on the safeguarding and promotion of the wellbeing of children and young people.

Q21 (b) Know how to identify and support children and young people whose progress, development or wellbeing is affected by changes or difficulties in their personal circumstances, and when to refer them to colleagues for specialist support.

Professional skills

Planning

Q22 Plan for progression across the age and ability range for which they are trained, designing effective learning sequences within lessons and across series of lessons and demonstrating secure subject/curriculum knowledge.

Q23 Design opportunities for learners to develop their literacy, numeracy and ICT skills.

Q24 Plan homework or other out-of-class work to sustain learners' progress and to extend and consolidate their learning.

Teaching

Q25 (a) Use a range of teaching strategies and resources, including e-learning, taking practical account of diversity and promoting equality and inclusion.

Q25 (b) Build on prior knowledge, develop concepts and processes, enable learners to apply new knowledge, understanding and skills, and meet learning objectives.

Q25 (c) Adapt their language to suit the learners they teach, introducing new ideas and concepts clearly, and using explanations, questions, discussions and plenaries effectively.

Q25 (d) Demonstrate the ability to manage the learning of individuals, groups and whole classes, modifying their teaching to suit the stage of the lesson.

Assessing, monitoring and giving feedback

Q26 (a) Make effective use of a range of assessment, monitoring and recording strategies.

Q26 (b) Assess the learning needs of those they teach in order to set challenging learning objectives.

Q27 Provide timely, accurate and constructive feedback on learners' attainment, progress and areas for development.

Q28 Support and guide learners to reflect on their learning, identify the progress they have made and identify their emerging learning needs.

Reviewing teaching and learning

Q29 Evaluate the impact of their teaching on the progress of all learners and modify their planning and classroom practice where necessary.

Learning environment

Q30 Establish a purposeful and safe learning environment conducive to learning and identify opportunities for learners to learn in out-of-school contexts.

Q31 Establish a clear framework for classroom discipline to manage learners' behaviour constructively and promote their self-control and independence.

Teamworking and collaboration

Q32   Work as a team member and identify opportunities for working with colleagues, sharing the development of effective practice with them.

Q33   Ensure that colleagues working with them are appropriately involved in supporting learning and understand the roles they are expected to fulfil.

The TDA website provides guidance 'to help providers exercise their professional judgement' when using the standards and ITT requirements. *QTS Standards Guidance*,[7] includes details of the *scope* of each of the statements and the *expectations*. Each standard has separate guidance broken down to the following sections: rationale; scope; questions; cross-references; sources of evidence; resources. For example, standard Q1 has the following rationale:

> Education is part of the process through which people acquire values and learn to apply those values in the attitudes they adopt and the ways they behave. Teachers recognise the role they play in this process and demonstrate appropriate values, including a professional commitment to raising the educational achievement of all learners.
>
> Children and young people are more likely to thrive if they feel that they are valued and are confident that their teachers and their peers will support them. They are more likely to behave in a positive and constructive manner, and adopt appropriate values and attitudes, when they encounter such behaviours, values and attitudes in their teachers.

The suggested sources of evidence to demonstrate this standard:

> Evidence about trainee teachers' commitment, attitudes, behaviour and expectations of learners' achievement are likely to emerge from most aspects of their professional practice including the ways they conduct themselves throughout the school and in the wider learning environment. Trainees' planning will demonstrate how they aim to develop specific values, attitudes and behaviour in children and young people.

The idea that this level of prescription will help those working in ITT to 'exercise their professional judgement' (and, by implication, help trainee teachers more effectively) is highly questionable. This is spoon-feeding at an extraordinary level given that most ITT tutors and mentors have many years of teaching and management experience themselves, often coupled with Masters or doctoral-level study, as well as, for some, considerable academic track records.

It is a good idea for students to acquaint themselves with this guidance because it will show them the way that their training, and increasingly their careers, will be structured. If the situation smacks of Foucault's[8] constant surveillance and 'interrogation without end', then we consider this to be a fair assessment of actuality. The requirements for evidence suggest that student teachers themselves may have to ensure that they have had the opportunity to experience and demonstrate the contents that are assessed during their teaching practice.

Since the inception of the competence-based movement in initial teacher education (and though the terminology of 'competence' has been dropped, the concept is still alive and well in practice in the 'standards'), the achievement of standards/competencies is usually recorded in a developing profile or portfolio called a record of professional development (or RPD). The standards for QTS feature significantly in action planning. An action plan is the outcome of a review of present achievements of the standards and a process wherein the student teacher is guided into electing which standards need to receive attention and when they are to be addressed – in schools and during a student teacher's course. If a student teacher is to meet the standards during the course then an initial appraisal of 'threshold' performance is necessary and becomes the springboard into future action planning. Though the nature of the development of student teachers in principle is student teacher-driven, the reality of the situation is that usually student teachers often do not have the appropriate background or expertise to assess their own performance or to plan for its development. Indeed that is why they come onto the course in the first place!

It is possible to meet this problem by having experienced and significant others – often tutors and mentors – *prescribing* a route or sequence through the lists of the standards and advising on areas for development and action planning. We address just such a sequence throughout the book, for example Box 2.

Box 2: A sequence of elements to meet the standards for the award of QTS

Professional values and practice

E.g. how to have high yet realistic expectations; taking account of pupils' backgrounds; treating learners with respect and consistency; being a model of good learning; effective communication with all stakeholders; contributing to the corporate life of schools; learning from a range of parties; self-evaluation.

Knowledge and understanding

E.g. knowledge of the subject they are to teach; understanding of the National Curriculum that they are to teach: its aims and values, contents and programmes of study, general teaching requirements, teaching arrangements in their key stages, understanding of how learning takes place and the factors that affect it, use of ICT in teaching and learning, understanding the Special Educational Needs Code of Practice; understanding of a range of strategies for promoting positive behaviour.

Teaching and class management (discipline and relationships)

E.g. being proactive, vigilance, transitions, routines and rules, controlling movement, setting realistic and manageable tasks, acting reasonably and fairly, use of praise and encouragement, being clear in demands and expectations, promoting a positive environment, communicating, timing, developing motivation in children, maintaining tolerance and a sense of humour.

Teaching and class management (teaching techniques)

E.g. introducing, explaining, questioning, summarising, use of voice, dividing attention, listening, eliciting, demonstration, giving feedback, class, group and individual teaching, timing, beginning, continuing, finishing, transitions.

Teaching and class management (teaching and learning styles)

E.g. use of whole-class, group, individual work, formal, informal, didactic, experiential, gain insights into how children are learning and what affects this.

Planning, expectations and targets

E.g. subjects, topics, cross-curricular skills, matching, differentiation, breadth, balance, continuity, progression, sequence, timing, subject knowledge, objectives, coverage of Attainment Targets and programmes of study, analysis of task demands and task, drawing up schemes of work and lesson plans, communicating purposes to children, providing for children with special educational needs, creativity and imagination.

Monitoring and assessment

E.g. providing valid diagnoses, diagnostic teaching, judging, recording, observing, reporting, use of Level Descriptions, covering core and foundation subjects and other aspects of children's development, selecting appropriate assessment criteria, providing feedback, providing for children with special educational needs, recording and reporting, carrying out a range of types of assessment for a range of purposes and audiences.

The sequence in Box 2 draws on the experience of tutoring many student teachers before the first whisper of 'standards' was heard. This box addresses from very early on the questions that are usually uppermost in many student teachers' minds: 'Can I keep order?' 'Can I avoid a riot?'

Moreover this sequence recognises that very little teaching, attention to teaching and learning styles, and curriculum planning can be considered unless discipline has been established. This box also reflects the sequence in which student teachers learn to teach during their teaching practice, whereby initially they work alongside a teacher, taking the initiative from the teacher and, typically, begin by working with small groups, trying out teaching techniques and teaching and learning styles (discussed in Parts II and III). Gradually the responsibility for curriculum planning (initially perhaps for a small group, increasing by stages as confidence grows until working with the whole class) passes from the class or subject teacher to the student teacher. As confidence and accomplishment grow in these areas so the student teacher can begin to take stock of individual differences in the students and plan appropriately for differentiation and progression, both of which are contingent on formal and informal assessment (discussed in Part IV).

The standards for QTS are addressed not only during teaching practice but also through those elements of courses that typically take place in institutions of higher education. Typically, the understanding required to demonstrate the standards begins in the early input at the institution. However, full understanding for the standards can only be demonstrated through the active process of teaching in schools. One part of the assessment of standards comes from students' writing assignments. These assignments are often structured so that students can reflect on school experience in the context of the wider picture of theory and research. In recent years, many PGCE courses have moved towards offering Masters level accreditation for some written assignments. The need to engage critically with theory, research and practice is an essential part of this work. This kind of critical reflection is also an essential part of the most effective ITT partnerships and of the most effective teaching.

Each of the statements of standards for the award of QTS is an amalgam of different types, numbers and orders of sub-components; some are task-related, some person-related, some generic, some discrete, some low-level and others of a higher-order.[9] The operationalisation of each standard risks the same problems as behavioural objectives, namely that it becomes impossible to avoid devising and endeavouring to complete lengthy lists of sub-components for each standard – an unworkable system.[10] Hence a degree of professional judgement must be exercised by those involved in assessing and planning for the achievement of these standards.

SKILLS TESTS IN NUMERACY, LITERACY AND ICT

In addition to the evidential bases for the standards for the award of QTS, student teachers are required to take skills tests in numeracy, literacy and ICT. There is no limit to the number of times the skills tests can be taken, but the award of QTS is contingent on passing them. Support and sample/practice interactive test materials are available from the TDA, as are details of how and where to register for the tests (http://www.tda.gov.uk/skillstests.aspx).

The QTS skills test in numeracy is intended to ensure that everyone qualifying to teach has a good grounding in the use of numeracy in the wider context of their professional role as a teacher.

The numeracy QTS skills test requires you to show that you can:

- carry out mental calculations using time, fractions, percentages, measurements and conversions
- interpret and use statistical information accurately, and
- use and apply general arithmetic correctly.

The numeracy test involves mental arithmetic, using and interpreting statistical information, and using and applying general arithmetic. The test is in two parts and covers:[11]

Mental calculations of:

● time
● amounts of money
● proportions, fractions and/or decimals
● percentages
● measurements (e.g. distance, area)
● conversions (e.g. from one currency to another, from fractions to decimals or percentages), and
● combinations of one or more of the following processes: addition, subtraction, multiplication, division.

On-screen work on:

● Interpreting and using statistical information. Candidates will be expected to:
  – identify trends correctly
  – make comparisons in order to draw conclusions, and
  – interpret information accurately.
● Using and applying general arithmetic. Candidates will be expected to use and apply general arithmetic correctly using:
  – time
  – money
  – proportion and ratio
  – percentages, fractions and decimals
  – measurements (e.g. distance, area)
  – conversions (e.g. from one currency to another, from fractions to decimals or percentages)
  – averages (including mean, median, mode and range where relevant), and
  – simple given formulae.

On-screen questions may draw on graphs, charts and tables, using information that teachers are likely to meet in school (e.g. test results, absences, reading ages, student numbers).

The literacy test begins with an audio spelling section, then moves to questions on punctuation, grammar and comprehension. It requires student teachers to be able to:[12]

● spell correctly, including words which appear in a teacher's professional written vocabulary
● punctuate texts with a professional content, in a helpful and consistent way
● understand and analyse the kind of texts teachers encounter in their professional reading
● recognise where writing does not conform to standard English, where it fails to make sense and where the style is inappropriate.

The ICT test contains tasks which require use of word-processing, presentation packages, databases, spreadsheets, e-mail and web-browsers. The test covers:[13]

● general skills
● researching and categorising information

- developing and modelling information
- interrogating and manipulating information
- presenting and communicating information.

MENTORING

The success of the use of standards for developing and assessing student teachers' achievements relies on the sensitive support given to the student teacher in the school by the mentor and in the institution of higher education by the appropriate tutor. The development of a realistic action plan by, with and for student teachers is often the outcome of a review with a mentor. A mentor is a named teacher in the school (often in a middle or senior management position) who has responsibility for:

- advising student teachers how to teach their particular subjects
- developing student teachers' understandings and appreciation of how students learn and how learning can be planned
- advising student teachers on class management and the planning of curricula and assessment.

In short the mentor has a significant role to play in the student teacher's development as a reflective practitioner.[14] The role of the mentor is multifaceted and complex, for in addition to providing content and skills-focused advice and support there is a large interpersonal and psychological dimension. The role includes some aspects of apprenticeship,[15] but moves beyond these to co-mentoring, mutual learning, co-operative learning (mentor and mentee) in ways in which the mentor acts as a support for the student teacher, motivating, empowering, raising awareness, providing feedback and advice, reviewing sessions and guiding future planning, acting as a 'critical friend' – an unthreatening source of student teacher improvement and, in some cases, simply being on hand to discuss matters with the student teacher as they arise in school, acting as a link person between the school and the college or university tutor.[16] Being a mentor requires the ability to employ several sensitive and sophisticated skills,[17] for example:

- being a model of good teaching practice
- listening, responding and advising
- understanding situations through the eyes of the student teacher – empathy
- developing observation skills in order to recognise and crystallise specific issues for discussion and the development of sound practice
- the ability to conduct reviews and appraisals of lessons seen in a supportive manner.

(See www.routledge.com/textbooks/9780415485586, Chapter 2 Teacher training requirements, Some tasks of the mentor.)

A mentor needs to be an experienced and effective practitioner, committed to the task, to be an effective and sensitive counsellor, and to have excellent interpersonal and communication skills. The mentor will need several qualities in communicating, for example: showing empathy, having positive active listening skills: listening, clarifying, responding, summarising, eliciting, questioning, challenging, reflecting, confronting, probing, taking the lead, acting as a sounding board, encouraging, advising and supporting, providing feedback, sharing ideas, reassuring, drawing on his/her own experience. The mentor will have an important role in inducting the student teacher into the rules and norms of the school.

A student teacher has a reasonable expectation of guided support from the mentor.

Reciprocally, a mentor has a reasonable expectation of co-operation in meeting negotiated targets by the student teacher. Typically a mentor will discuss the teaching file and lesson plans with the student teacher, negotiating what the mentor will be observing. The mentor then observes her/him teaching one or more of these lessons each week. Following the observation the mentor conducts a review meeting with the student teacher during which feedback is given and debriefing occurs. This meeting is timetabled and is designed to provoke reflection on the part of the student teacher – both through the setting of a predetermined agenda and the opportunity for an open discussion to be held about other matters. At the meeting an action plan for further development will be negotiated.

Not only does the mentor have an important substantive role to play in the professional development of the student teacher but s/he has an important facilitatory role to play. For example the mentor is the link not only to the college or university tutor but to teacher colleagues in the school. Thus, the mentor might arrange for a student teacher to be attached for some time to another member of staff, to meet other departmental staff (in secondary schools) or teachers of other age phases (in primary schools); the mentor may put the student teacher in touch with a colleague with a particular expertise, e.g. information technology, multimedia resources, a music specialist, contacts with outside organisations and agencies, etc. The mentor will apprise the student teacher of protocols, rules and routines in the school, in short, the 'hidden curriculum' of the school.

Mentoring in schools accords significance to the part that experienced teachers can play in the initial preparation of teachers. Some schools do not wish to follow the mentoring road, arguing that it is too time-consuming, expensive (in supply teacher cover) and onerous for teachers whose prime responsibility is to teach children not student teachers. Indeed these sentiments often accord not only with those of parents but of governing bodies concerned that standards do not fall because students are taught by novice student teachers.

Clearly it may be the case that schools have to nominate identified teachers to undertake the mentoring role. ITT providers may require mentors to be accredited or registered, and, indeed, to undergo mentor training programmes. It may be the case that the most effective teachers could become the mentors; schools may be reluctant to undertake this, as it could represent a 'loss' in teaching terms of their most experienced and effective teachers and, indeed, their replacement with novices. The issue at stake here is that mentoring is not an additional, bolt-on task that is undertaken at spare moments during the school week; rather it is integral to the school week, and requires dedicated time specifically set aside for its operation. It *replaces* rather than *adds onto* teaching time.

It can be seen from this that the processes of target setting and action planning which are being advocated for pupils in school are also being applied to student teachers.

(See Career entry and development profile, available on www.tda.gov.uk/teachers/induction/cedp.aspx)

CONCLUSION

We close this chapter with some observations about the standards for the award of QTS. This chapter has laid out the several areas for focus and development of student teachers; in some respects they constitute a job description for teaching. There is no doubt that there is plentiful detail and supporting material for student teachers wishing to learn about the several aspects of their progression to be teachers. The standards for the award of QTS seek transparency through the publication and free availability to all of the requirements of the several parties involved in ITT. There is no stone left unturned in the prescriptions from the government and the TDA. The documents emanating from these two parties offer an almost seamless web of specification, and their coverage is very useful. It would be difficult to disagree with many of the proposals and identified qualities of effective teachers, or even with the notion that an elected government that administers the disbursement of public taxation to bring the best return for that income has a duty to ensure high-quality teacher education.

However, we offer two lines of critique of the standards: (a) that in practice they leave much to be desired; and (b) that the model of education that the standards represent is deficient. The standards have to be used by trainee teachers, teachers, mentors, tutors, examiners and inspectors. For some, at times, their use is on a daily basis. For this reason it is important, leaving aside momentarily the idea that we should have the system at all, that the standards are coherently organised and clear. The basic idea behind the standards is a straightforward one: they are a tool for assessing trainee teachers. Assessment tools are used in a variety of contexts, not least in teaching itself, so there is no reason that a valid tool could not have been devised. This is particularly true in view of the many revisions that have been made to the standards since an early version represented by government Circular 4/98. The problems are as follows:

- There are far too many standards for an efficient assessment tool. If you count the additional lettered standards there are 40 in total.
- The subheadings that structure the standards were unnecessary and have resulted in a lack of clarity. The distinction between attributes, knowledge and understanding, and skills is arbitrary and incoherent. For example, how is 'Be aware of the professional duties of teachers and the statutory framework within which they work' (Q3 (a)) an attribute? This is knowledge, not an attribute.
- The addition of sub-subheadings adds nothing to the coherence of the standards.
- The standards feature repetition and overlap largely because of the unnecessary use of subheadings, but also because of a lack of attention to detail. For example, Q12 requires trainees to 'Know a range of approaches to assessment, including the importance of formative assessment', and Q26 (a) requires trainees to 'Make effective use of a range of assessment, monitoring and recording strategies.' If we ignore the grammar of this standard, which clumsily links 'a range' with 'including the importance of', the underlying requirement is that teachers are able to assess their pupils effectively, something which could be covered in one standard. But because of the subheadings, the writers saw the need for two standards: one covering the knowledge required and the other covering the practice. Of course, it is not possible to use assessment strategies effectively in practice if you don't have the necessary knowledge about assessment!
- Some of the standards try to address too many concepts, which makes them unnecessarily diverse and therefore difficult to assess appropriately:

  > Q10 Have a knowledge and understanding of a range of teaching, learning and behaviour management strategies and know how to use and adapt them, including how to personalise learning and provide opportunities for all learners to achieve their potential.

Knowledge and understanding are two different things. For example, I might know that transmission teaching is commonly known as 'chalk and talk' but it takes a lifetime to understand the implications of the place of transmission teaching, its deficiencies and its possibilities. Knowledge and understanding are different things, the assessment of which necessitates some separation. Table 2.1 shows just some of the many concepts that Q10 addresses and how onerous the assessment process would have to be to genuinely assess the standard. The framework in Table 2.1 would also need to be applied to the remaining concepts that are part of standard Q10: a range of learning strategies (e.g. using a more hands-on approach); and a range of behaviour-management strategies (which also overlaps with standard Q25 (d)).

Table 2.1 Breakdown of the concepts and their assessment for standard Q10

Standard requirement	Concept	Examples	Assessment of standard
Have knowledge of	a range of teaching strategies	transmission teaching; interactive teaching; collaborative group work	Discussion with trainee or evidence in written assignment
Have understanding of	a range of teaching strategies	transmission teaching; interactive teaching; collaborative group work	Observe trainee teaching over several lessons where different teaching strategies are used and discuss teaching in order to assess level of understanding
Know how to use	a range of teaching strategies	transmission teaching; interactive teaching; collaborative group work	Observe trainee teaching over several lessons where different teaching strategies are used
Know how to adapt	a range of teaching strategies	transmission teaching; interactive teaching; collaborative group work	Observe trainee for a further set of several lessons to see how they adapt strategies for different groups of children
Have knowledge of	personalise[d] learning	read definition of the term	Discussion with trainee or read evidence in written assignment
Have understanding of	personalise[d] learning	interacting with pupils to elicit their understanding during a lesson. Change teaching to accommodate the pupils' views	Observe trainee in such a position that interaction with pupil can be clearly heard

If some of the responses to the consultation about the standards had been acted on then a much simpler framework of standards could have been developed, such as the example that we have drawn up:

Teachers with QTS:

1   help learners enjoy learning
2   promote learners' independence
3   have high expectations of learners
4   form positive relationships with learners and other members of the school community
5   are aware of learners' needs and rights and support these
6   have appropriate knowledge of the curriculum they teach
7   plan the curriculum appropriately
8   establish a purposeful and well-managed learning environment
9   use a range of teaching strategies effectively
10 have the necessary skills to teach effectively

11 assess learners effectively and use the information to enhance teaching and learning
12 provide appropriate feedback to learners
13 understand the contribution that extra-curricular activities make to children's learning
14 evaluate and critically reflect on practice in order to improve teaching
15 understand school policies and have a critically evaluative response to changes in practice
16 be aware of school organisation and management
17 collaborate and work effectively with people in the school community
18 communicate effectively with people in the school community and wider professional community
19 keep up to date with approaches to teaching in learning, particularly those supported by rigorous research and evidence
20 take responsibility for CPD with the support of school and local authority.

The main reason for the practical deficiencies of the standards is the model that underpinned their development. A seamless web has the whole scene 'sewn up'. We suggest that the picture is all too neat and complete. It offers a totalising picture and a 'grand narrative' that leaves little room for people, for values, for the very relationships that it purports to affirm between all stakeholders in education. Student teachers are told what to think, when to think it, how to think, and how well they have thought about it. The agenda is given and received, not constructed. There is little room for negotiation, disagreement, modification or question. That seems to be a striking contradiction: the aims of education, indeed of the very National Curriculum from the government, are to promote flexibility and decision making, and to produce resourceful and adaptable citizens. Yet the degree of prescription, uniformity, centralisation, conformity, standardisation and rigidity in the contents and degree of specification runs counter to these aims.

Let us be very clear: the prescriptions demonstrate an overwhelming control mentality in which the government seeks to exert control over the contents and framing of education and teacher education, a process of the homogenisation of initial teacher education. This control shows no signs of diminishing in view of the extension of the standards throughout teachers' careers. Though this might be intended benevolently – to help teachers and students teachers to become more effective – nevertheless, in its effects, teachers are reduced to technicians; an instrumental rationality is at work here, with little or no room for disagreement or debate. The frequent use of the term 'initial teacher training' by the government reveals, perhaps, a view of initial teacher preparation as train-ing rather than as education. The effect of the plethora of government documents prescribing what student teachers need to do and think, and how they will be assessed, leaves little space for disagree-ment. Taking a conspiratorial line, one could argue that this is precisely what the government requires – teachers as technicians who will not question, think, debate and set agendas, but simply carry out orders; teachers who will not disagree but who roll over and acquiesce. However, teach-ers do not do this; they leave.

It strikes us as ridiculous that the most straightforward and widely understood principle of workplace motivation – people having some control over their work – is either not recognised or not valued by a government struggling to fill thousands of vacant teacher positions in schools. It is a classic management ploy – overwhelm teachers with paperwork and documentation so that they have no time to disagree or even to think for themselves. Maybe this is what the government desires; whether it is or not, that is its effect. Do we really want the sort of teachers that these docu-ments and prescriptions will produce: clones of government-speak? Do paperwork, prescriptions and documents really improve practice and quality? We have serious reservations about this. Given the flight out of teaching and the problems of retention and recruitment, it seems that we are not alone.

This is a factory model of teacher education and education (and it is interesting to note the use of the term 'corporate life' in clause 1.5 of the section on Professional Values and Practice in the requirements for QTS); factory models have for long been discredited in industries, yet the government appears reluctant to abandon such command-and-control models in education.

Do we really want education to echo Seneca, where human excellence aims to be 'like the stars: pitiless, passionless, perfect', or do we wish to invoke Pindar's response: 'but human excellence grows like a vine tree fed by the green dew, raised up, among wise men [*sic*] and just, to the liquid sky. We have all kinds of needs for those we love'. The fluidity, uncertainty, open-endedness and humanity of education have little place in a government apparently obsessed with statutory control of what people should do and think, reinforced through inspections and constant surveillance in the name of quality assurance such that, true to Foucault's analysis cited earlier in this chapter, institutions become self-surveilling. As management-speak reminds us: quality is built-in, not bolt-on: given enough imposition and total control, workers become self-surveilling and self-controlling. This is paternalism and control run rife. Little wonder that there are so many dispirited teachers and teacher educators. Student teachers have little option but to follow the required elements of ITT. However we would hope that they would adopt a healthy scepticism about the degree to which these requirements adequately define the task of teaching, or the legitimacy of governments to be so prescriptive.

It is perhaps invidious to constantly 'second guess' the next policy initiative that emanates from government and which will go out of fashion, and so, whilst this book provides the latest material from the government at the time of writing, nevertheless to forestall too early an outdating of the book, we focus on many key constants in teaching: effective relationships, humanistic teaching, effective planning, management, teaching, learning and assessment. The particular political hue given to these varies as the wind, but their underlying importance and relevance remain.

3 The Curriculum

INTRODUCTION

The tasks of a teacher, during teaching practice or otherwise, are multi-dimensional. The teacher is not only the person who teaches a particular subject or subjects, but he or she has responsibility for the curriculum, widely interpreted. There are several interpretations of the curriculum which have evolved over decades.[1] For example, the former Schools Council[2] defined the curriculum as:

- subjects
- processes (e.g. skills of observation, communication, problem-solving, physical and practical, creative and imaginative, numerical, personal and social)
- the study of problems (e.g. ecology, poverty)
- areas of knowledge or experience
- that which the child defines as the curriculum.

This final statement can be a salutary lesson for teachers: the curriculum is that which the pupil takes from the learning situation in school, not necessarily that which was intended.

In 1985 Her Majesty's Inspectorate (HMI) defined the curriculum as comprising five main strands:[3]

1   areas of experience (aesthetic and creative, human and social, linguistic and literary, mathematical, moral, physical, scientific, spiritual, technological)
2   essential issues (e.g. environmental education, health education, information technology, political education, education in economic understanding, preparation for work, careers education, equal opportunities, meeting the needs of students from ethnic minorities)
3   elements of learning: knowledge, concepts, attitudes and skills (communication, observation, study, problem-solving, physical and practical, creative and imaginative, numerical, personal and social)
4   informal, extra-curricular activities
5   characteristics (breadth, balance, relevance, differentiation, progression and continuity).

One can clearly see the influence of this important document reaching into England's National Curriculum. Since 1997, countries in the UK have become increasingly independent. The national curricula of the different countries reflect this:

●   Northern Ireland (http://www.nicurriculum.org.uk/)
●   Scotland (http://www.ltscotland.org.uk/curriculumforexcellence/index.asp)
●   Wales (http://new.wales.gov.uk/topics/educationandskills/curriculumassessment/?lang=en).

HMI provided a very broad interpretation of the curriculum to include the formal and informal programme of content, pedagogy, organisation, assessment, and the extra-curricular elements which contribute to the school's ethos. The issue here is that the curriculum is not simply the syllabus, but all the experiences that the student has at school. This includes the significant area of the hidden curriculum, masterly defined by Jackson[4] as comprising everything that is learnt without being specifically or deliberately taught, for example:

●   the experience of crowds, praise, power, delay and denial
●   the recognition that the teacher has considerably more power than the students
●   rules, routines and rituals
●   public evaluation
●   individual interests being subordinated to group interests (e.g. the whole class) and management strategies.

For Jackson, pupils' success in school depends as much on their learning, and working with, the hidden curriculum as with the formal curriculum. The hidden curriculum also concerns the values, attitudes, ethos, norms, relationships, discipline and organisational aspects of the school. This is an extremely important area, for it presses teachers to ask what their pupils are learning without specifically being taught, and it has found voice in discussions of the experience of prejudice, cultural clashes between school and society, equal opportunities, and student 'voice'.[5]

Emerging from, and clearly informed by the seminal document from HMI, several formulations for the school curriculum were devised. For example Wragg[6] discusses a 'cubic curriculum' in which the three dimensions of the cube comprise:

1   subjects
2   cross-curricular themes
3   teaching and learning strategies.

Dowson[7] identifies the subject curriculum, the cross-curricular elements, the pastoral curriculum (including equal opportunities, personal and social education, form and year groupings), the hidden curriculum, and the extra-curricular curriculum. Indeed the Qualifications and Curriculum Authority used the term 'curriculum' to 'describe everything children do, see, hear or feel in their setting, both planned and unplanned'.[8] Wyse locates the pupils' 'self' at the heart of his curriculum, which addresses text, images, numbers and environment.[9]

It had been argued for many years that the most satisfactory account of the curriculum has its expression in Tyler's[10] famous and influential rationale for the curriculum in terms of four questions (see below). Underlying this rationale is a view that the curriculum is controlled (and controllable), ordered, predetermined, uniform, predictable and largely behaviourist in outcome. However, this view has been criticised. It is important to recognise the behaviourist sympathies in this approach, for it embodies the debate on both the attraction and the problems with the behaviourist approach that are rehearsed in several pages of this book. For some the great attraction is that such curricula lead to behavioural and measurable outcomes; for others this is their greatest weakness, narrowing down education to that which is measurable, and missing the less tangible but no less significant aspects of education.[11]

We regard it as curious that, as Chapter 9 remarks, the significance of the use of constructivist approaches over instructivist and behaviourist approaches, together with the employment of the Tylerian rationale as the clear model for the National Curriculum, represent an adherence to a style of curriculum planning which has been widely discredited not only for its undesirability but for its failure to meet the demands of a changing world. Doll[12] argues that it represents a closed system of planning and practice that sits uncomfortably with the notion of education as an opening process and with the view of society as open and diverse, multi-dimensional, fluid and with power less monolithic and more problematical.

This is not the place to rehearse such debates in detail. However, it is important to note that the National Curriculum and the National Strategies use a largely Tylerian rationale, albeit wrapped up in different terminology. The Tylerian rationale is perhaps irresistible for politicians (and it was initially devised as a managerial response to large-scale curriculum planning and decision making), as it suggests that curriculum outcomes can be prespecified, practical and demonstrable; that they are measurable. It offers the security of putative certainty in curriculum planning. Once such a model has been accepted (even though the Tylerian rationale has been highly contested since its inception), it is a short step to holding teachers and schools accountable for the students' achievements. It is an even shorter step, perhaps, to specifying: the contents in detail, the time allowances and the standards of achievement expected of students at different ages. Indeed, the Early Years Foundation Stage and the National Curriculum have addressed all of these matters.

1	What educational purposes should the school seek to attain?	AIMS/OBJECTIVES
2	What educational experiences can be provided that are likely to attain these purposes?	CONTENT
3	How can these educational experiences be effectively organised?	PEDAGOGY
4	How can we determine whether these purposes are being attained?	EVALUATION

THE EARLY YEARS FOUNDATION STAGE

Principles and aims

Humans are characterised by the longevity of their learning and the time it takes for them to reach adulthood. Education is 'either about learning, or it is about nothing',[13] and early years education is the *foundation* for that learning, as the title of the curriculum at this stage suggests. The quality of the young learner's education has far-reaching effects that persist into later life,[14] a feature which has resulted in early intervention programmes such as *Sure Start* (for research on the effectiveness of *Sure Start* see Rutter (2006).[15]

Early childhood education is more than simply the starting line for school education; it is cognitively, socially, affectively, morally, physically, personally and behaviourally the foundation of lifelong learning. The Early Years Foundation Stage in England runs from birth to age 5. The range of settings in which children experience their education and care is much more varied than in the later years of schooling. Here are some examples: crèches, toddler groups, childminders, nannies, playgroups, nursery class as part of a primary school, nursery school, private day nursery, children's centres. Children's centres are a more recent kind of setting. One of the important early years principles that they are founded on is the idea of multi-professional care and education. They provide early education and full day care for children younger than 5, as well as a range of other services such as family support and health services.

The government's most determined effort to bring services together to support children and families is represented by *Every Child Matters*:

> The government's aim is for every child, whatever their background or their circumstances, to have the support they need to:
>
> - Be healthy
> - Stay safe
> - Enjoy and achieve
> - Make a positive contribution
> - Achieve economic wellbeing.
>
> This means that the organisations involved with providing services to children – from hospitals and schools, to police and voluntary groups – will be teaming up in new ways, sharing information and working together, to protect children and young people from harm and help them achieve what they want in life. Children and young people will have far more say about issues that affect them as individuals and collectively.[16]

The changes in children during these years can be dramatic. Three-year-old children have usually developed many of the features of oral language necessary for standard speech but still have some way to go in terms of discourse development.[17] Adults in early years settings can too easily underestimate the positive experiences and learning young children bring to the setting. Having said that, young children do have particular needs. They come to nursery still learning how to feed themselves, egocentric, unused to sharing with larger groups of children, with very limited self-control and used to being the centre of their family's attention. It may be their first main break with home, which is sometimes equally as traumatic for the parents as for the children. They quickly learn the hidden curriculum of schooling[18] – rules, routines, delay, denial, praise, power, control, authority, self-reliance, being only one out of many children vying for the teacher's attention – and they leave the early years as sophisticated, if embryonic, learners. What has happened during this time? This chapter indicates some significant factors of early years education.

An early years classroom can be a bewildering place for the new student teacher and child alike. Tables and centres of activity are set up, both inside and outside, and children move around them, talking, playing and concentrating. The teacher adopts a combination of roles – from nurse to judge, from social worker to expert catalyst for learning. The task is as subtle as it is complex. Knowing when to intervene and when to stand back is a critical matter for the teacher. Teaching becomes an art, not simply an amalgam of competencies; an emerging, self-choreographed dance rather than a programmed, mechanistic routine.

Underpinning these experiences are fundamental and significant principles of learning, for example:

- Learning is a social as well as an individual activity (and Vygotsky[19] reminds us that all higher-order cognition is socially learned and transmitted).
- Sensory learning is closely linked to cognitive learning and young children need sensory stimuli.[20]
- Feelings, motivation and effective learning are closely linked.[21]
- Learning begins with the learner and 'where the learner is', and where the learners are considerably in control of their learning.[22]

- Motivation, interest, engagement and enjoyment are key elements of learning.
- Language and communication are fundamental to learning and should be accorded high priority.[23]
- Even complex ideas and concepts can be learned in an intellectually honest way by young children.[24]
- Activity (physical and mental), experience, concrete learning and operations – learning by doing and applying – are fundamental to effective learning rather than passive, programmed behaviourism.[25]
- Ideas and knowledge are interconnected and networked in the learner's mind, hence there is a need to integrate and link knowledge in the learner.
- Children communicate in a variety of ways: 'a hundred languages'.[26]
- Teachers and learners are involved in the co-construction of meaning, rather than simple transmission and reception, respectively, and collaboration, language, verbalisation, discussion and dialogue are critical elements here.[27]
- Learning concerns investigation, exploration and the formulation and solution of problems; it is problem-solving.[28]
- Trial and error are significant aspects of learning; children must be able to make choices and mistakes, and to learn from these.
- Multiple intelligences are addressed through integrated learning and knowledge.
- Social and emotional factors feature centrally in learning – to separate cognitive/academic learning from social and emotional learning (typically, in many schools, to reduce the significance of social and emotional factors), and from all-round personality development, misrepresents the nature of learning.
- Active learning is important for young children; children are active learners.[29]
- A secure (emotionally, cognitively, socially), caring environment and the promotion of children's self-esteem, sense of accomplishment, experience of achievement and positive feedback (not least praise) are essential ingredients for young children's learning.[30]
- Learning must be meaningful if it is to be effective.[31]
- Exploration and divergent thinking are often essential precursors of learning and convergent thinking.
- Learning must be unhurried and unpressured, with time to explore, develop and reflect on ideas and feelings.[32]
- A competitive atmosphere must be reduced.[33]
- Early reading, writing and numeracy must be embedded in young children's preferred experiences and interests, rather than being too formal or disconnected from other areas of learning.[34]
- Pressurising young children is frequently counter-productive.[35]
- Punitive environments hamper growth, and enjoyment promotes learning.[36]
- Early years learning must build on prior and ongoing rich experiences on which children reflect.[37]
- Children must be encouraged to take risks and make mistakes in order to develop independence.[38]
- People, cultures and the community all have a significant influence on children's learning.[39]
- Adults can expedite learning through careful diagnosis, monitoring, assessment, talk and intervention.[40]
- Too early a formalisation of learning into planned 'lessons' can inhibit effective learning.[41]

These principles have to accommodate several constraints, be they physical (space and layout), material (resources), human (the number of children in the class, the number of adults in the class – teachers, parents, classroom assistants, nursery nurses, learning support teachers – the developmental stages of children), curricular (for example, the prescriptive approach to reading pedagogy adopted by government, and, in some settings, pressure from Key Stage 1 teachers to start preparation for statutory tests) or assessment and its uses (the formal testing at the end-of-Key Stage 1 that contributes to 'league tables' of schools).[42] Underpinning these principles are two views of constructivism.

Curriculum matters

In September 2008 the requirements of the Early Years Foundation Stage (EYFS) became statutory (see Chapter 5 for the legal basis for this). The requirements that much of the following information is based on can be found at the early years section of the National Strategies website (http://nationalstrategies.standards.dcsf.gov.uk/earlyyears).

The EYFS unified previous frameworks that had been developed for education and care, although as far as education is concerned, the previously non-statutory guidance became statutory. The idea that all children and families have an equal right to be included is an essential part of this stage of learning, just as it is at all stages. It is recognised that children develop individually, but that there are also common developmental patterns shared by most children.

Learning and development in the EYFS is organised into four key aspects: Play and Exploration; Active Learning; Creativity and Critical Thinking; and Areas of Learning and Development.

The Areas of Learning and Development are:

- personal, social and emotional development
- communication, language and literacy
- problem-solving, reasoning and numeracy
- knowledge and understanding of the world
- physical development, and
- creative development.

One of the recurrent tensions in government's curriculum planning has been the disagreements about whether curricula should be organised as subjects or not. Although the areas of learning development are broader than National Curriculum subjects, it is not hard to see that they reflect a similar philosophy of curriculum organisation, particularly as one looks closer at the guidance (see Chapter 8 on planning). The tension is evident from the statements that suggest that children's learning is not compartmentalised, but which is contradicted to a certain extent by the 'requirements' for the separate areas. So on the one hand the EYFS is structured as The EYFS Themes and Principles/Commitments (A Unique Child; Positive Relationships; Enabling Environments; Learning and Development), which are inter-disciplinary and cross-curricular, but on the other hand the areas of learning and development are divided up into curricular areas. It is also somewhat confusing to have Learning and Development as both a theme and a sub-section of its own theme (Areas of Learning and Development).

Each area of learning and development is accompanied by extensive guidance material, so we will not detail all of them; instead we will explain a little of the detail from one of the areas. The Communication, Language and Literacy area requires children to be supported in their communication and in their reading and writing. The aspects are: Language for Communication; Language for Thinking; Linking Sounds and Letters; Reading; Writing and Handwriting. It is at this point that some of the lack of conceptual clarity begins to creep in. In particular, the isolation of 'Linking Sounds and Letters' from 'Reading'. This is a direct consequence of Sir Jim Rose's report on reading, which is referred to in the 'research' section of the site (for a commentary on the evidence base for this report see Wyse and Goswami (2009).[43]

In addition to links to government resources, which are included alongside each area of learning and development, there are also some video clips available to download, which usefully show practitioners at work in the area concerned.

Making the EYFS statutory caused a great deal of controversy. One of the reasons for this is that it meant that alternative approaches to the early years curriculum and pedagogy would not be able to operate unless they were seen to be addressing the EYFS. The English government's decision to make the EYFS statutory was part of their increasing control of the curriculum, which began in 1988 with the National Curriculum.

THE NATIONAL CURRICULUM

Since the National Curriculum of England and Wales was given statutory weight, it has been subject to intense debate. One of the recurrent concerns about the National Curriculum has been the amount of content to be taught and whether state prescription of schools' curricula (and pedagogy) is appropriate. As a result of the professional opposition to the framing, contents, forms of assessment, elements of assessment, methods of assessment, levels of prescription, unworkability and teacher overload, and the hostility to the deprofessionalisation of teachers caused by having too many decisions taken for them, attempts have been made, through government-initiated enquiries, to reduce the amount of content in the National Curriculum.

The National Curriculum has gone through several versions and mutations since its inception, including:

- the reduction of a ten-level sequence to an eight-level sequence
- the considerable trimming down of its prescription of content
- the inclusion of a new subject (Citizenship) for certain Key Stages
- the inclusion of a new stage (the Foundation Stage)
- the reduction in the number of attainment targets for certain subjects
- the closer focus on a few subjects for national assessment rather than coverage of every subject
- the reduction of the standard assessment tests and tasks, typically (though not entirely) to written tests
- a regularisation of what, in earlier versions, had been differences in terms of the framing of subjects, e.g. some had not included level descriptions, preferring to indicate end-of-Key Stage statements
- greater clarification of Key Stage 4 curricula with their associated qualifications
- the provision of a far greater amount of teacher support materials from the government, with guidance on schemes of work, sample assessments and tests, and planning guidelines.

Another new National Curriculum for Key Stages 3 and 4 was published in 2007 and implemented in 2008. The phasing for this is as follows: Year 7 from 2008, Year 8 from 2009, and Year 9 from 2010, and the new attainment targets to be used for assessment from 2011. This change to the curriculum resulted in some key differences between the curriculum at Key Stages 1 and 2, and the curriculum at Key Stages 3 and 4 (see Box 5 for differences between the main elements). One of the main ideas behind the new curriculum at Key Stages 3 and 4 was to give schools greater flexibility and coherence by having less prescribed subject content. However, the greater emphasis on key concepts and processes, arguably, did not result in much greater opportunity for schools to genuinely control their curriculum.

The year 2009 was historically another key moment for primary education. Sir Jim Rose published another report that had been commissioned by government, this time on the primary curriculum. The select committee for Children, Families and Schools completed its bi-partisan review of the primary curriculum, and the independent Cambridge Primary Review based at the University of Cambridge (http://www.primaryreview.org.uk/) published its findings. Rose's interim report[44] had some welcome features, the most important being the idea that 'an important aim of primary education is to instil a love of learning for its own sake'.[45] 'Love of learning' is an emotive phrase but an appropriate one which we think should be used as the basis for the systematic evaluation of the success or otherwise of changes to the curriculum. *A rewarding curriculum that results in a love of learning* depends on children being encouraged to make meaningful choices in their curriculum, which requires that teachers are empowered to enable such choices. The empowerment of teachers requires encouragement for each individual teacher in the primary school to develop interests and knowledge unique to them that may colour their teaching in ways that make the school experience more varied for pupils. This was recognised implicitly in the report: 'many believe that the government, the QCA, Ofsted, and the National Strategies, or a combination of all four, effectively restrict their [teachers'] freedom' (p. 19). Steps need to be taken to mitigate this restriction on professional decision-making.

There were other areas of the interim report that were less positive (an extended version of the following points, and the points made in the previous paragraph, can be found in Wyse *et al.*, 2009):

- The idea of child-centred education was addressed somewhat sceptically in the report yet such education has a sound cultural, philosophical and increasing empirical basis for it.
- The voices of children themselves were absent from the report.
- The suggestion to organise the curriculum in six areas of learning was promising but the rationale for this and the specific wording and conception of these areas lacked rigour. The pragmatics of accepting that 'the aims and values for primary education must be seen in the light of the Children's Plan' (p. 15) were not a sufficient rationale for the development of an outstanding curriculum for the country.
- One could sympathise with Sir Jim Rose's comments on the Review website, which suggested that the distinction between cross-curricular work and subject-based work had been polarised by some in the media; yet the report also appeared to emphasise 'cross-curricular studies' merely as a vehicle for applying understanding learned in the context of subject teaching. Effective 'topic work' or theme-based work is, in fact, valuable in its own right as a coherent and intellectually defensible way to organise teaching in the primary classroom.
- The idea that teaching pre-1988 was a 'do as you please' (p. 17) curriculum was an unfortunate caricature that cannot seriously be defended. It also neglects the fact that serious problems occurred post-1988 because of the introduction of the National Curriculum and the associated high-stakes testing system[46] (testing was something which the report would not address, claiming that the remit prevented this).
- The Review recognised that the curriculum is more than just subjects and linked areas of learning; for example it embraced links from schools to sites outside schools and relationships with external partners to support learning. So it was unfortunate that matters of place, space, time and the design of schools, classrooms and other spaces for play, socializing and learning were given such minor consideration in the Review. The first new schools built as a result of the Primary Capital Programme (a massive investment programme to renew at least half of all primary school buildings by 2022/23 in order to create twenty-first-century schools that are at the heart of their communities) will be opening at a time when the new primary curriculum is in effect. It is vital that these two policy initiatives be connected imaginatively and systematically if an education fit for the twenty-first century is to be achieved.

The 'New Primary Curriculum' published in 2010 by the Qualifcations and Curriculum Development Agency (QCDA) was replete with support material, either available as hard copy in schools or to be downloaded from the website (http://curriculum.qca.org.uk/index.aspx). Indeed, so great is the degree of support material, arguably to reduce the bureaucratic burden on teachers and the time they have to spend on planning, that the de facto homogenisation of the curriculum is almost inevitable. It is a curious anomaly that, at a time when greater flexibility is being called for in the workforce, the response to this has been through greater degrees of prescription and nonstatutory guidance from the government, leading to a degree of uniformity redolent of the Victorian era. Perhaps we are only one step away from the 'payment by results' of that era. Though the intention might be honourable – to reduce the burden on teachers – the outcome is a climate in which teachers are increasingly becoming technicians, serving given agendas with little say in the construction of those agendas. The mentality of government control, reinforced through the constant surveillance of testing and inspection, is all-pervasive. The situation is not confined to the UK; governments across the world are imposing forms of national or prescribed curricula, and, indeed, some have emulated that of England. The drive for greater and greater control of teachers' and students' lives seems difficult to stop.

Perhaps that is being uncharitable. If we have faith in the government's 'league tables' of students' results, the increase in examination successes, then the National Curriculum may have driven up certain academic standards in schools. But at what cost is an important question. The industrialist Peter Senge wrote in 1990 that yesterday's solutions are today's problems;[47] the National Curriculum may come to be viewed as both a force for lifting the trailing edge of poor schools' performance and creating 'high-reliability schools', or as a suppressant of excellence and creativity, or, indeed both (and bureaucracies, as Lieberman[48] suggests, lift weak performance but reduce excellent performance). The bureaucratic burden which accompanies the National Curriculum is intolerable; teachers are becoming first and foremost form fillers rather than teachers, and, as mentioned in Chapter 1, the flight out of teaching, coupled with stress-related absence, appears insuperable.[49] We should not be blind to both the advantages and disadvantages of the National Curriculum; whether it is a force for good or a poisoned chalice is a moot point.

The National Curriculum and the EYFS covers children's early years education and state schooling from birth to age 16. The National Curriculum does not apply to independent schools, though such schools may choose to follow it. Originally the government was clear that it did not constitute a school's complete curriculum. However, reviews of the curriculum have led to changes. At Key Stages 3 and 4: 'A school's curriculum consists of everything that promotes learners' intellectual, personal, social and physical development. As well as lessons and extra-curricular activities, it includes approaches to teaching, learning and assessment, the quality of relationships within school, and the values embodied in the way the school operates.'[50]

The National Curriculum is organised into Key Stages that are age-related. It comprises statutory elements and non-statutory elements (see Box 4 below, which shows the Statutory requirements for Key Stage 3; Key Stages 1 and 2 were to be clarified following the outcome of the general election in 2010). The key components of the National Curriculum, in terms of coverage, are: subjects, programmes of study, attainment targets and level descriptions.

The main elements and the cross-curricular elements of national curricula from birth to age 16 are set out in Box 5.

STATUTORY TESTS

One of the most controversial features of the Education Reform Act 1988 was the proposal to establish a national system of testing. These statutory tests are known in everyday language as SATs (this dates back to the time when they were called Standard Assessment Tasks, but due to a copyright

Box 3: The stages of education

Age	Stage	Year	Statutory assessments
3–4	Early Years Foundation Stage		Early Years Foundation Stage Profile
4–5		Reception	
5–6	Key Stage 1	Year 1	
6–7		Year 2	National tests and tasks (SATs) in English and maths
7–8	Key Stage 2	Year 3	
8–9		Year 4	
9–10		Year 5	
10–11		Year 6	National tests (SATs) in English and maths. Teacher assessment of National Curriculum subjects
11–12	Key Stage 3	Year 7	
12–13		Year 8	
13–14		Year 9	Teacher assessment of National Curriculum subjects
14–15	Key Stage 4	Year 10	Some young people take GCSEs
15–16		Year 11	Most young people take GCSEs or other national qualifications
16–17	Sixth form (can be school or college)	Year 12	Many young people take AS (Advanced Subsidiary) level assessments, which are stand-alone qualifications valued as half a full A level qualification
17–18		Year 13 Upper Sixth/ Second Year College	Many young people complete A level courses by taking the final year A2 assessments

Box 4: Statutory requirements for Key Stage 3

What is statutory?

The National Curriculum applies to pupils of compulsory school age in community and foundation schools, including community special schools and foundation special schools, and voluntary controlled schools.

The statutory subjects that all pupils must study are art and design, citizenship, design and technology, English, geography, history, information and communication technology, mathematics, modern foreign languages, music, physical education, and science. The teaching of careers education, sex education and religious education is also statutory.

What is non-statutory?

The curriculum also includes non-statutory programmes of study for:

● religious education, based on the Framework for Religious Education
● personal well-being, which includes the requirements for sex and relationship education and drugs education
● economic well-being and financial capability, which includes the requirements for careers education.

Box 5: The main elements and the cross-curricular elements of statutory curricula from birth to age 16

Main elements

The Early Years Foundation Stage:
Four themes and principles: a unique child; positive relationships; enabling environments; learning and development

National Curriculum Key Stages 1 and 2:
Values, aims and purposes, subjects, general teaching requirements, inclusion, assessment, learning across the curriculum

National Curriculum Key Stages 3 and 4:
Aims, subjects, personal development, skills, cross-curriculum dimensions, organising your curriculum, developing your curriculum, evaluating your curriculum, curriculum in action, assessment

Cross-curricular elements

Foundation Stage learning and development requirements (cross-curricular delivery through play):
Personal, social and emotional development; communication, language and literacy; problem-solving, reasoning and numeracy; knowledge and understanding of the world; physical development; creative development.

KS 1 and 2: Learning across the curriculum:
Creativity
ICT in subject teaching
Spiritual, moral, social and cultural development
Skills across the National Curriculum (key skills and thinking skills)
Financial capability and enterprise education
Education for sustainable development

KS 3 and 4: Cross-curriculum dimensions:
Cultural diversity and identity
Healthy lifestyles
Community participation
Enterprise
Global dimension and sustainable development
Technology and media
Creativity and critical thinking

problem in relation to an American private company, the correct term is now statutory tests). In the period from 2007 onwards, opposition to the tests intensified. Initially, the only sign shown by government that change to the system might be possible was the trialing of 'single-level tests' in December 2007 and June 2008. Single-level tests are designed to confirm that a pupil is working securely at a particular National Curriculum level, from level 3 to level 8. The idea behind single level tests was that teachers would not have to wait until the end of a Key Stage for pupils to be assessed. This has the advantage of minimising some of the stress caused by all pupils sitting in an exam room together but fails to address the underlying problem with high-stakes testing systems such as the one in England. The rather conservative proposal for single-level tests was trumped in dramatic fashion by the sudden abolishment, by government, in 2008 of the statutory tests at Key

Stage 3. This decision was prompted by at least three factors: 1. the serious problems caused as a result of the marking of statutory tests being contracted to an external company in 2008; 2. the tireless work by educational researchers, teachers, head teachers and parents in resisting the imposition of statutory tests; 3. a series of reports by the Cambridge Primary Review critiquing government policy on assessment and the curriculum including Wyse, McCreery and Torrance[51] which was front page news in a number of newspapers including *The Independent* and which was featured on the BBC's Radio 4 *Today* programme.

The assessment arrangements for the end of each Key Stage comprise:

- Key Stage 1: Statutory Key Stage 1 tests and tasks, combining teacher assessment judgements with national tests in mathematics and English
- Key Stage 2: Statutory Key Stage 2 tests and tasks, combining teacher assessment judgements with national tests in mathematics and English. Additionally, the government provided optional tests in English and mathematics for students at the end of each of Years 3, 4 and 5.

In 2008 a major reform of 14–19 education was being rolled out. The changes included those made to the assessment system. One of the key features of the reforms was the introduction of new diplomas to complement existing qualifications such as GCSEs and A levels (see Box 6). The diplomas combine theoretical study with practical experience. All diplomas require students to achieve minimum standards in English, maths and ICT, complete a project and do a minimum of ten days work experience. The diplomas were designed by partnerships led by employers and higher education to ensure that progression to employment or university was catered for. The diplomas are available at three levels, with level 3 being equivalent to A level. The government's aim was to ensure that those who prefer practical learning were not disadvantaged by an academic curriculum and to try to ensure that at least 90 per cent of young people continued in education and training to the age of at least 17.

Box 6: Diploma options and first teaching dates

Diploma area	First teaching
IT Society, Health and Development Engineering Creative and Media Construction and the Built Environment	September 2008
Environmental and Land-based Studies Manufacturing and Product Design Hair and Beauty Studies Business Administration and Finance Hospitality	September 2009
Public Services Sport and Active Leisure Retail Business Travel and Tourism	September 2010
Humanities Languages Science[52]	September 2011

Qualifications at the 14–19 stage are diverse and subject to much review. Options include: apprenticeships, diplomas, functional skills, applied learning programmes, GCSEs, A levels, the Baccalaureate, to name but a few. A large amount of information is available at the DCFS and DirectGov websites. Having identified some of the options available in the school that you are working in it is a good idea to then check these websites for detailed guidance.

Each year the government updates and produces a handbook of guidance for the assessment and reporting arrangements at the end of each Key Stage, and these are sent directly to schools. They provide guidance on changes to assessments, the nature and operation of tasks and tests, teacher assessment, reporting and timetables. It is advisable to check these annually in order to meet the requirements. Assessment is a sizeable topic, and it is discussed in considerably more detail in Part IV.

In terms of pedagogy, though the government indicated that the National Curriculum would leave room for schools and teachers to decide how to deliver the contents,[53] in fact contained in the National Curriculum document are specific principles for pedagogy, e.g. a requirement for using group work, collaborative work, whole-class interactive teaching, ICT-based teaching and learning, active learning and independent work. Indeed, the National Strategies (discussed below) were very specific in prescribing pedagogic issues. In terms of the whole curriculum the National Curriculum is designed to address certain features that were signalled in 1985 by the then HMI:[54] breadth; balance; relevance; continuity; progression; and differentiation. To these can be added coherence. These issues will be discussed later in this book. Suffice it here to say that, even though they are problematic,[55] the level of prescription in the National Curriculum attempts to ensure: breadth, balance and relevance by prescribing the contents of the curriculum; continuity by prescribing the curriculum from ages 5 to 16 largely in subject terms; progression by describing eight levels within subjects. The overall elements of the curriculum – the National Curriculum, the whole curriculum and the school planning – are presented in Box 7.

The intention in presenting this introduction to the National Curriculum is to indicate that when student teachers go into schools and discuss what and how they will be teaching, to whom and with whom, they will encounter very many changes from the days when student teachers were able to have a 'free hand' in deciding what to teach. Many people involved in teacher education feel that even if trainee teachers or young/relatively inexperienced teachers *were* faced with the possibility of devising their own curriculum the changes to education since 1988 have resulted in teachers being *deskilled*. The ever-increasing control of the curriculum by government is a concern to many people[56] and is an issue that you should think about as part of your professional development both during teacher training and beyond.

Schools are required to have a yearly plan that indicates the main contents and organisation of the curriculum. Student teachers going into schools can expect to be told what they will be teaching and to have explained to them the context of their teaching in terms of the plans that have been drawn up by the school, the department and faculty, the age phase leaders, curriculum leaders and co-ordinators, subject and age phase teams as well as individual teachers with whom they will have contact. Though there may be latitude in planning specific activities and in pedagogical matters, student teachers will have to slot into the school curriculum planning that has already preceded their arrival in school. They will have to work within the frameworks of a received curriculum, the parameters and contents of which teachers, in turn, have received from external sources.

In many respects the need to operate within a received curriculum can be very helpful to student teachers as it provides a considerable amount of support and guidance on what to teach and what will be matched to particular students, groups and whole classes. By placing some parameters on student teachers they are freed to consider other aspects of planning and pedagogy in more detail;

Box 7: Elements of the whole curriculum

Element	National	Local	Whole school	Faculty	Department/ subject	Individual teacher
1 Context: situational analysis						
2 Rationale						
3 Aims						
4 Objectives						
5 Learning objectives						
6 Intended learning outcomes						
7 Desirable learning outcomes						

8 Relationship to overall prescribed curricular frameworks:
  ● core and foundation subjects
  ● cross-curricular themes, issues, dimensions, skills
  ● non-statutory subjects						

9 Relationships to National Curriculum Attainment Targets, programmes of study, Level Descriptions, assessments						

10 Components of the curriculum:
  ● Knowledge and understanding
  ● Concepts/key concepts
  ● Skills
  ● Attitudes and values
  ● References to hidden curricula
  ● Sequence
  ● Prioritisation						

11 Characteristics of the curriculum:
  ● Breadth
  ● Balance
  ● Relevance
  ● Progression
  ● Continuity
  ● Differentiation
  ● Coherence						

12 Pedagogy and implementation:
  ● Structure and organisation
  ● Time and timetabling
  ● Teaching and learning styles
  ● Resources and their organisation: time, people, finances, administration, materials, space						

13 Specific activities and experiences						
14 Planning documents: long-term, medium-term, short-term						
15 Student assessment and measuring 'value-added'						
16 Course evaluation						
17 Recording						
18 Reporting (to several audiences)						
19 Curriculum policy documents and links to other school and curricular policy documents						
20 Identifying/auditing/monitoring existing practices						
21 Planning change and innovation						
22 Quality assurance, quality control, quality development						
23 Management issues						
24 Development of whole department/institution plan						
25 Contribution to institutional development plan						
26 Links to school inspection						

it reduces stress. The issue of planning is taken up in considerably more detail later; at this point the intention has been to indicate that part of an initial or subsequent visit to the school will be to find out where and how student teachers will fit into existing curriculum plans and organisation in the school.

The point here is that during teaching practice the student teacher can expect to be involved in a range of activities, not simply teaching a single subject. The curricular responsibilities of teachers, within the range of the National Curriculum and more widely, are immense. Clearly it is unrealistic to expect student teachers to immerse themselves in all of these, but it does raise important issues for the planning of curricula and the activities that student teachers undertake in schools during their teaching practice. These are issues that we discuss in the remainder of this book.

The fact that the National Curriculum is framed in terms of subjects has caused some consternation to those teaching in the primary and foundation years.[57] For many years primary teaching had been cast in terms of integrated, cross-curricular topics (e.g. 'Myself', 'Communication', 'Trees'), and, indeed in early years education, an almost seamless web of activities which touched on several aspects of the curriculum simultaneously had been the order of the day. Indeed Blenkin and Kelly[58] suggest the National Curriculum sits very uncomfortably with early years education in this respect. Further, Coltman and Whitebread[59] argue that it exerts a downward pressure on the early years curriculum which is of questionable value, risking using early years education as a preparation for the National Curriculum diet of subjects and tests, putting pressure on children to press through curricula without ensuring a firm foundation of understanding or, indeed, enjoyment of learning, and reducing meaningful learning for young children, all reinforced by a vocabulary of teaching which places emphasis on 'delivering' a pre-packaged curriculum.

On the other hand, it is clear from the government's own guidelines that framing the primary and early years curriculum in subject terms does not necessarily mean that it is to be taught as discrete subjects (though quite how realistic this is, when the curriculum is reinforced by subject-specific assessment, is questionable). Further, within subjects, care has been taken by the Qualifications and Curriculum Authority to identify links that can be made to other subjects and areas of the curriculum, and in many subjects specific topics have been indicated (e.g. 'How do we know about the great fire of London?' for history; 'Going to the seaside' in geography).

THE NATIONAL STRATEGIES

In addition to the National Curriculum, in 1998 and 1999 the government launched two important initiatives: the National Literacy Strategy (NLS) and the National Numeracy Strategy (NNS), conceived as part of the government's commitment to raising standards through target setting. Though these did not have statutory status, many schools put them into practice, not least because they had to defend the decision not to enact them. Originally conceived for primary schools, the strategies were extended to secondary schools as part of the Key Stage 3 National Strategy.

The Literacy Strategy included one hour daily on literacy (the literacy hour),[60] including word-level, sentence-level and text-level work, organised thus: the first 15 minutes devoted to whole-class shared-text work, followed by 15 minutes of focused word and sentence work, followed by 20 minutes of group and independent work, e.g. independent reading, writing or word work, while the teacher works with one or two ability groups each day (two for Key Stage 1 and one for Key Stage 2) on guided text work (reading or writing), followed by ten minutes of whole-class work, reviewing, reflecting, consolidating teaching points and work covered in the session.

The National Numeracy Strategy,[61] with a recommended daily coverage of 45 minutes at Key Stage 1 and 50–60 minutes at Key Stage 2, was based on four basic principles:

1   dedicated mathematics lessons each day
2   direct teaching and interactive oral work with the whole class and groups
3   an emphasis on mental calculations
4   controlled differentiation, with all children engaged in mathematics relating to a common theme.

In practice this meant increased focus on direct teaching, with a balance between several strategies: directing, instructing, demonstrating, explaining and illustrating, questioning and discussing, consolidating, evaluating responses, and summarising. A typical lesson might involve: oral work and mental calculation (5–10 minutes) with whole-class work, to hone mental and oral skills, followed by the main teaching activity (30–40 minutes) combining teaching input and children's activities in whole-class, group, paired or individual work, followed by a plenary session (10–15 minutes) to resolve, with the whole class, any misconceptions, to identify progress, to summarise key facts and ideas, to link to other work, for forward planning and to set homework.

The strategies were subject to strong criticism from very early on. For example, with regard to literacy, the prescriptive nature of the pedagogy and the inappropriateness of many of its features were questioned.[62] In spite of many well-made criticisms, modest concessions to the ruthless pressure from government to conform to their prescriptions were only made in relation to the necessity for allocation of timings to lessons, the problems with one-off lessons and the lack of attention paid to pupils' responses to the teaching if they deviated from the objectives set for the lesson.[63] On a more positive note the government maintained an explicit commitment to ensuring that teachers support children with particular needs.

Excellence and Enjoyment, England's Primary National Strategy (PNS) (DfES 2003), published in 2003, offered hope to many in education of a more flexible and creative approach to the curriculum. However Ofsted's report on the primary curriculum, the National Literacy Strategy (NLS), and the National Numeracy Strategy (NNS), based on visits between 2002 and 2004 (Office for Standards in Education (Ofsted), 2005) noted that few schools had made significant progress in adopting more flexible and creative ways of managing the curriculum. They also found that, 'In English, teachers' planning focuses too much on covering the many objectives in the NLS framework for teaching, instead of meeting pupils' specific needs. This inflexibility hinders improvements in the quality of English teaching' (p. 2). The claimed lack of progress by schools with regard to flexibility and creativity is perhaps indicative of the contradictions that are part of *Excellence and Enjoyment*. Although the PNS exhorted schools to be more flexible and creative, at the same time the emphasis on the literacy and numeracy strategies remained, and was intensified.

One of the key features of the strategies has been the organisation of learning as a sequence of teaching objectives. In the report on the first four years of the NLS based on inspection visits carried out during 1998–2002 (Office for Standards in Education (Ofsted, 2002) it was noted in relation to the teaching of literacy that, 'There is more direct teaching, the lessons have a clearer structure and learning objectives are more precise' (p. 2). The encouragement by Ofsted in this and other publications, including school and teacher-training institution inspection reports, to focus on teaching objectives resulted in the practice of teachers' lessons being strongly objective-led, to the extent that objectives were written onto classroom boards and pupils were encouraged to write the objective of the lesson in their exercise books. Ofsted's change of emphasis from positive findings on precise objectives in 2002 to the criticism that teachers were focusing on them too much in 2005 could be seen as a reflection of government policy, represented in the change of guidance from the

NLS to the PNS, rather than a rigorous and objective analysis of the evidence from inspection observations. A persistent problem with Ofsted national reports on the English and literacy curriculum has been the lack of consistent attention to particular main findings from one report to the next.

In October 2006 the National Strategies new frameworks for literacy and mathematics were released with an expectation that 'the majority of schools and settings are likely to be making extensive use of the renewed framework at some stage during this academic year.'[64]

We have commented about the ever-increasing documentation provided by government. One of the most striking images of the original National Curriculum documents was of a school that had piled all the documents on top of each other creating a tower the height of a single-storey building. Since then, in spite of regular complaints about overload, if anything this process has intensified. One of the key changes to the strategies in 2007 was the move to web-based documentation. The ease of publishing web pages and making changes to them has resulted in even greater amounts of government documents, requirements, guidance etc. On the positive side, they are all easily accessible! At the time of writing, the web pages for the strategies had been reorganised again to bring them all together: early years, primary, secondary, inclusion, leadership, CPD. The Primary section includes the following main elements:

- primary framework
- improving schools programme
- mathematics subject area
- publications
- assessment
- literacy subject area
- behaviour, attendance and Social and Emotional Aspects of Learning (SEAL).

The introduction to the framework explains that the principles of both *Every Child Matters* and *Excellence and Enjoyment* (see above) are embedded in the practice for children aged 3–11 that is outlined in the frameworks. Even at this introductory page of the guidance the Rose report on phonics teaching is explicitly referred to, which is an indication of its influence. Another section of the introductory material provides 'Overviews of learning' for each year of pupils' lives in the primary school. These overviews seem to be more about the government's agenda than a genuine attempt to characterise learning. For example, there is no comment on children's motivations or the real choices over learning that they might make. The opening paragraph of 'Year 6 – the learner' is indicative of the familiar emphasis on testing and assessment dressed in slightly new web-based clothes:

> Year 6 children are coming to the end of the primary phase of their education. The end of Year 5 assessment provides a clear benchmark of their attainment in literacy and mathematics, enabling teachers and children to identify how much progress they have made and what they still need to do to meet end-of-Key Stage expectations. These assessments will identify both the achievements children have made and those areas or aspects where gaps in understanding remain and need to be addressed in order to secure the necessary progression in learning. Use of the assessment profile, together with ongoing teacher assessment, informs planning and teaching across the broader curriculum. Helping children to recognise their progress maintains their motivation and desire to improve.[65]

The National Strategy for secondary addressed both Key Stage 3 and Key Stage 4 and included the following main elements: Introduction; English; Mathematics; Science; and ICT. The introductory material identified some of the key issues that were part of the redevelopment of the strategy. It was claimed that the changes were linked to the previous strategies as they were 'Building on success'; the evidence of this success is debateable. The ideas of *personalised learning* and the need for flexibility and locally determined curricula were explicitly mentioned but contradicted by the prescriptive nature of all the guidance. In 2010 the status and development of the national strategies was called in to question because of the government's decision not to continue the funding after 2011.

With regard to Key Stage 4, it can be seen in this chapter that the curriculum for Key Stage 4 and beyond has been covered more skeletally than for the other Key Stages. This reflects the considerable state of flux that characterises the education of 14- to 19-year-olds, not only in terms of qualifications and examinations (discussed earlier) but also in terms of curriculum coverage, specialisation and commonality, and degree of student choice. Attention is focused on this age phase by the government,[66] not least because of the low performance of many such students in the UK compared to France and Germany, and the low uptake of university by lower socio-economic groups. The government's proposals for this age group include:

- higher attainment
- reform of qualifications and curriculum
- the importance of local delivery
- the new secondary curriculum
- introduction of the new diplomas
- renewed emphasis on personal learning and thinking skills
- increased attainment by age 19
- increasing the number of young people completing apprenticeships
- increasing the number of young people participating in education at age 17
- the 14–16 re-engagement programme
- learning visits and twinning networks to share good practice
- race equality impact assessments
- disability and gender assessments.

These initiatives are part of a new vision for 14–19 education, which it is hoped will prepare students for the constant changes that are a feature of the world they live in. The creation of the diplomas does seem to be a promising development that could motivate many more students and will offer greater choice over qualifications. Part of the plan for ensuring that students do have this greater choice is the idea to encourage institutions in local areas to work together more, in order to provide the wide range of learning opportunities that are being promised by government.

CONCLUSION

This chapter commenced with an indication that the roles and tasks of the student teacher on teaching practice will be diverse and plentiful. If the scope of the task appears daunting, then, perhaps with little solace, this is because it is. Clearly a teacher, at whatever level or age group, has a wide range of responsibilities, having to be more than simply a subject teacher. Whilst the size of these responsibilities is very considerable, some of them will have a greater priority than others, depending on local circumstances. This is a matter to be discussed on preliminary school visits, with the mentor and the class or subject teachers. It is entirely unrealistic to expect a student teacher to move from a zero starting point to taking on the range of these responsibilities overnight, and, indeed, some of them may not have to be addressed on a teaching practice at all, e.g. aspects of items 20 to 26 from Box 7. Further, the student teacher should expect to receive information from the school on its practices in respect of the National Curriculum, not to have to go fishing for it.

The range of responsibilities is formidable, by any standard, and the rate at which these responsibilities can be addressed and assumed by student teachers is a matter of individual discussion and development.

Information and Communications Technology

INTRODUCTION

The rise of information and communication technology (ICT) in schools is apparently unstoppable and developments in ICT seem to many to encapsulate broader trends in education. ICT touches most aspects of education, leading to the formation of new networks of teachers, promoting the development of new approaches to teaching and learning and, through the use of such technological advances as video-conferencing, online forums, blogging tools etc. puts teachers and students in contact with each other on a global scale.[1] For most young people the use of technology is a part of their daily lives, and with greater access to a wider range of digital technology than ever before, these young people are using technology to access, communicate, share and support their learning in many different ways. Schools, too, are using their own websites, technology systems and intranets (or virtual learning environments/learning platforms) to make learning resources available online at any time of day. The harnessing of technology in this way remains an important aspect of government and local agendas with the intention of having a strategic impact on the education system.[2]

In this environment, where the use of technological tools is increasingly embedded in school and everyday life, some broad trends in education can be seen. For example:

- There is less certainty about what counts as important knowledge.
- Knowledge generation and construction have replaced knowledge replication and repetition as important.
- Views of effective learning and how learners learn have moved away from an emphasis on drill and practice, rote learning, memorisation and repetition.
- A premium is placed on higher-order thinking for creativity, imagination, evaluation and flexibility in order to keep pace with the information age and for learners to be able to judge what is needed and worth learning.
- Students have to take responsibility for their own learning and thinking, with assessment for learning practices in school emphasising the need for learners to understand not just what but also how they learn.
- Higher-order thinking is socially learned and developed, not with students sitting and working in isolation but collaboratively and in co-operation through dialogue.
- Motivation and engagement are seen as central requirements for effective learning.
- Teachers' roles are changing from transmitters to facilitators and supporters of learning.
- The emphasis in education is moving away from teacher-centred teaching to learner-centred learning.

- Learning is not simply a result of instructional teaching but of networking – the linear view of teaching and learning is replaced with a networked view of learning.
- Changing practice requires changing the culture of teachers, teaching, and getting into the minds and hearts of teachers and schools.
- Learning takes place outside classrooms and the walls of the school.

The role of Information and Communication Technology (ICT) in schools is increasingly being viewed as connected to the development of both teaching and learning. ICT on its own is not sufficient to influence education in the direction of the trends noted above. The key, critical component in this process is teachers and their pedagogy. If a new culture of teaching is to be developed, ICT may be one feature that can help to support this.

WHAT IS ICT?

ICT is a means of accessing, storing, sharing, processing, editing, selecting, presenting and communicating information through a variety of media.[3] It involves finding, sharing and restructuring information in its diverse forms.[4] A range of technological devices are now used as tools (both technical and cognitive), as media, as resources, and even as tutee (where the computer is being programmed by students).[5]

Different kinds of ICT have evolved over the past decades, e.g. programming, drill and practice, LOGO, software, CD ROMS, simulations, databases and word processing, multimedia, internet usage and interactive technologies.[6] Castro[7] indicates that the early use of computers tended to mimic teachers and used 'drill and practice' programs to practise what teachers do in conventional classrooms, e.g. spelling and multiplication tables. From here computer usage became more imaginative, moving to simulations and explorations. The turtle, which moved around on the screen, was seen as a means to teach programming algorithms, with LOGO as a landmark in this. The turtle, and associated programmable toys, use computers to develop higher-order cognitive skills. Further, simulations and animations enable students to grasp theoretical principles, e.g. from models of the solar system to inferential statistics, and they have the advantages of concreteness, control, cost-effectiveness, and safety.[8] Computers can do what is impossible or impracticable in real life. The introduction of multimedia, interactivity and the internet for communication have the potential for transforming teaching and learning.

The types of ICT usage are diverse (see Box 8), in terms of both hardware and software, and include a range of devices (e.g.speech-sensitive devices, touch-screens, interactive boards) to enable students with a variety of learning difficulties to participate in learning. Examples of the diversity of teachers' and students' usage include: writing and publishing through the web using blogs, wikis and collaborative forums; accessing resources through virtual libraries; experiencing exploratory situations through adventure games, simulations and virtual learning; using real-time and asynchronous conversations; and sharing resources.[9] It is worth noting at this point that ICT encompasses many aspects of technological devices and is not simply to do with computers.[10] In their research with computers and pre-school children, Plowman and Stephen (2005) included within their definition of ICT a variety of audio-visual devices, photocopiers, telephones, fax machines, televisions and computers. They also included toys that simulated appliances such as mobile phones, laptops, cash registers and microwave ovens.[11]

There are several major forms of ICT set out in the following pages, each of which addresses the implications for practice. Allen et al.[12] and Woolard[13] suggest that teachers need to know several features of word-processing software in order to teach effectively with and about word processing (Box 9). These authors also suggest several issues that teachers need to know about spreadsheet software in order to teach effectively with and about spreadsheets (Box 10).

Box 8: Different uses of ICT in education

Find things out

Understanding and using electronic information to handle data and undertake research using:

- database entry programs and spreadsheets
- database packages
- internet and the World Wide Web.

Developing ideas and making things happen

Knowing that a simulation can represent real or imaginary situations. Identifying patterns, sequences, and cause and effect using:

- adventure and problem-solving-type games
- simulations
- ideas processors/mind mapping tools
- LOGO programming
- measurement and control equipment and software
- modelling programs.

Exchanging and sharing information

Being able to communicate effectively with others through the sharing of information and in the presentation of their ideas in electronic format using:

- word processing
- desktop publishing
- digital cameras and digital scanners
- online bulletin boards and forums
- web conferencing
- web authoring
- e-mail and chatrooms
- talking books
- presentation packages
- animation and film-making techniques
- graphics packages
- multimedia
- software CD-ROMs and virtual libraries
- virtual learning communities and study centres.

And there will be many other simultaneous uses of ICT relating to the Management and Information System (MIS):

- personal data collection
- assessment programs
- the tracking storage and retrieval of personal data
- transferring data/files
- recording and reporting.

Databases are structured stores of information such that retrieval and presentation are very straightforward, enabling graphical representation of information, even by young children. Allen *et al.* and Woollard suggest that it is advisable that teachers need to know several factors about databases and that students start by adding data to existing databases in order to be able to learn how to interrogate them effectively (Box 11).

Box 9: Teachers' knowledge of word processing

- Creating, opening, saving, closing, deleting and printing documents.
- Selecting font, font size, colour, style (italic, bold), line spacing and justification.
- Altering default font, font size, colour, background colour, margins, page size and orientations.
- Inserting, deleting, selecting, cutting, copying, pasting and undoing.
- Utilising the 'help' function.
- Inserting bullet points, tables, clip art, borders, shading and columns.
- Altering page orientation (landscape, portrait) and margins.
- Forcing page breaks.
- Utilising tabs and indents.
- Utilising spelling and grammar checkers (including how to switch on and off), thesaurus, print preview, high-lighter and talking facilities (including how to switch on and off) and find and replace.
- Connecting alternative input devices (overlay keyboards, touch-screens).
- Inserting page numbers.
- Inserting text, graphics, tables and documents from other applications.

Box 10: Teachers' knowledge of spreadsheets

- Creating, opening, saving, closing, deleting and printing documents.
- How to set up spreadsheets so that children can enter data.
- Selecting worksheet and cell size.
- Inserting, modifying and deleting row and column labels.
- Inserting, modifying, moving and deleting textual and numerical data.
- Inserting, modifying and deleting formulae and functions.
- Inserting and deleting cells, rows and columns.
- Formatting data.
- Searching and sorting data.
- Adding, modifying and deleting borders and shading.
- Selecting, modifying and displaying graph types.
- Formatting graphs to include axes labels, key and text.
- Exporting graphs and spreadsheets to other applications.
- Importing information from other applications.
- Selecting font and font size.
- Navigating through records.
- Searching and retrieving information.
- Plotting and replotting graphs/reports etc.
- Entering data.
- Designing a new data file.
- Inserting titles.
- Importing and exporting information.
- Utilising help.
- Copying and pasting.
- Altering defaults.
- Customising the spreadsheet program.
- Protecting cells and documents.

Box 11: Teachers' knowledge of databases

- Creating, opening, saving, closing, deleting and printing documents.
- Adding, modifying and deleting data and questions.
- Navigating through records.
- Searching and retrieving information.
- Plotting and replotting graphs/reports etc.
- Entering data.
- Designing a new data file.
- Inserting titles.
- Importing and exporting information.
- Selecting font and font size.
- Utilising help.
- Inserting text, images, borders, arrows.
- Copying and pasting.
- Altering defaults.
- Protecting documents.

Box 12: Teachers' knowledge of graphing programs

- Choice of variables (categorical, discrete, continuous).
- Types of data.
- Grouping data.
- Collecting and recording data.
- Presenting data.
- Creating, opening, saving, closing, deleting and printing documents.
- Adding, modifying and deleting data.
- Plotting and replotting graphs.
- Selecting and displaying graph types.
- Selecting and modifying constituent elements of graphs.
- Selecting, resizing, cutting, copying and pasting graphs.
- Selecting and modifying graph scales and autoscaling.
- Selecting two-dimensional or three-dimensional representations.
- Inserting graph titles, axes labels, key and text.
- Selecting font and font size for graph and axes headings.
- Exporting graphs into other applications.
- Importing information from other applications.
- Utilising help.
- Altering defaults.
- Customising the graphing program.
- Utilising alternative input devices.
- Selecting appropriate colours and/or patterns depending on printer availability.
- Protecting documents.

Graphing

Graphing software can be used for preparing resources, interrogating and presenting information. Graphs enable students to focus on the content of the information, not solely the problems of presenting data and constructing graphs. They can be produced directly from stored data (e.g. from databases and spreadsheets) and from data collected through sensing and measurement (e.g. temperature from data loggers).[14] Further, ranges of different types of graph are available, and the scale of graphs is usually selected automatically on software packages. Teachers need to know several factors about graphing in order to be able to teach with them effectively (Box 12).

Graphics packages, clip art and sound packages

Graphics software allows images to be created, entered, stored, retrieved and manipulated. In using graphics, it is important that students should be aware of the difference between paint and draw packages, that they should have opportunities to develop their abilities to scan, edit, enhance and customise images, whilst avoiding plagiarism of work (see Chapter 5) and the overuse of irrelevant images. Allen *et al.* and Woollard suggest that teachers need to know several factors about graphics packages, clip art and sound packages in order to be able to teach with them effectively (Box 13).

Box 13: Teachers' knowledge of graphic, clip art and sound packages

- Creating, opening, closing, deleting and printing documents
- Altering default page size, margins and page orientation
- Inserting, modifying and deleting background colours
- Selecting, modifying and utilising tools from the toolbar
- Utilising fill
- Utilising undo/redo
- Grouping and ungrouping elements
- Selecting, cutting, copying, pasting, cropping, resizing, reshaping, reordering and rotating elements and drawings
- Switching grid on and off
- Utilising zoom/magnifier
- Exporting images to other applications
- Utilising help
- Altering defaults
- Customising set-up
- Connecting alternative input devices
- Protecting documents
- Using sound software for manipulating sounds
- Avoiding using the computer simply as an expensive form of cassette recorder

---

Desktop publishing

Desktop publishing is a way of producing high-quality textual and graphics presentations. In using desktop programs teachers need to be able to know several key points (Box 14).

Box 14: Teachers' knowledge of desktopping

- Laying out a page with text blocks, borders, shading, illustrations and photographs.
- Using word-processing skills and saving processed word data.
- Using draw or paint packages and saving such data as a file.
- Using template page designs in the software.

Multimedia

The claims for multimedia usage are considerable. Whilst it might be suggested that multimedia presentation of information could lead to more effective learning and increased interaction in the classroom, there is a danger of over-emphasis on image over content, presentation over substance and entertainment over learning. If multimedia is to be used then users need to be media-literate, aware of the impact and effect of still and moving images and sound (Box 15).[15]

Box 15: Teachers' knowledge of multimedia

- Students must be clear about the purposes of using multimedia.
- Teachers and students must know how to gather and present multimedia information.
- Assessment criteria must be made clear for multimedia projects (particularly if they are group projects).
- Teachers and students must be clear on the kinds of information that are best handled with multimedia, and the forms of visual display.
- The limits and disadvantages of multimedia usage must be understood, together with the added cognitive and pedagogical benefits brought about by visual or auditory inputs over textual material.
- Teachers and students must be clear how the main messages of the multimedia are being conveyed (through text, through visual channels and through auditory channels).
- Teachers and students must know how the pictures, text and sound interact to make meaning.
- Students must be actively involved in multimedia creations, preferably as a group activity, with appropriate levels of challenge.
- Appropriate higher-order skills must be assured in students.
- Students must understand the difference between linear and branching programs.
- Teachers will need to accept that multimedia writing by students is time-consuming but that the results are usually worth it.
- Judicious use of multimedia is required, in order to avoid converting every project to a multimedia project.

Internet

Related to multimedia presentation is the use of the internet. We are already seeing that the internet is becoming the major driving force for new developments in teaching and learning, such that a paradigm shift in conceptualising teaching and learning, teachers and learners, may occur. To maximise the value of the internet, Allen *et al.* and Woollard suggest that teachers will need to consider several issues (Box 16).

Box 16: Teachers' knowledge of the internet

- How to access the internet and how to access and use browsers.
- How to access, search, and navigate the World Wide Web.
- How to design, create, save, modify and publish on the World Wide Web.
- Use of e-mail, discussion forums, texting, podcasting and video-conferencing for teaching and learning.
- Awareness of E-safety issues
- Detailed knowledge of the school's policy and protocols for internet usage. Bookmarking favourite websites.
- Copying and pasting text, images and materials from web pages into other applications.
- Downloading and saving websites and files.
- Checking for, and preventing damage from viruses.
- Altering default browser settings.
- Utilising cache facilities.

Synchronous and asynchronous communication

Electronic mail has been for some time now a powerful way of supporting teaching and learning. Discussion forums, blogging, texting, podcasting and video-conferencing are now being used frequently to support both teaching and learning across a variety of contexts. Teachers need to acknowledge that a wider range of communicative forms is part of acceptable practice within and beyond the school environment. These popular, communicative forms are supported by mobile technology and have the potential to enable teachers and learners to work flexibly, anytime and anywhere. In discussing mobile technologies Naismith et al.[16] suggest that learning is improved through synchronous (real-time) and asynchronous communication, that it makes for increased equality in group dynamics and greater collaboration, and can ensure rapid dissemination and sharing of information to all parties.

Games and simulations

Games and simulations have considerable attractions as pedagogical tools.[17] Computer games and simulations can:

- improve the speed and quality of learning and performance
- stimulate and develop motivation and curiosity
- enhance learning and memorisation through visualisation, experimentation, prediction, manipulation and logical thinking
- enable students to experience success and a sense of achievement.

Whilst the range of attractions is very considerable, several voices have cautioned against over-use of games and simulations, suggesting, for example, that they can:

- reduce dialogue and interaction
- tend towards rote learning
- only lead to predictable rather than open-ended or novel outcomes
- are too removed from everyday life and over-simplify complex matters and everyday realities.

These are telling concerns that require teachers to ensure 'fitness for purpose'. This entails careful preparation and follow-up when using games and simulations to ensure that they do not replace deep learning with superficial entertainment.

CLAIMED ADVANTAGES OF ICT

There are many benefits claimed for using ICT in classrooms. Principal amongst these are that it can:

- raise student achievement in all subjects and for all students
- promote higher-order thinking in order to evaluate knowledge
- promote learning for capability and problem-solving
- foster collaborative learning
- raise students' motivation and engagement significantly.

Some time ago, Lajoie[18] showed how ICT could support cognitive processes such as memory and sharing cognitive load, particularly by engaging the learner in 'out of reach' cognitive activities. Hennessy[19] shows clearly that this may only be possible if teachers have a clear grasp of how pedagogy and the use of ICT in classrooms are linked.

The Department for Children, Schools and Families[20] suggests that:

The evidence from the literature shows a positive effect of specific uses of information and communication technology (ICT) on pupils' attainment in almost all the National Curriculum subjects, the most substantial being in mathematics, science and English at all Key Stages. There is a strong relationship between the ways in which ICT has been used and pupil attainment. This suggests that the crucial component in the use of ICT within education is the teacher and his or her pedagogical approaches. Specific uses of ICT have a positive effect on pupils' learning where the use is closely related to learning objectives and where the choice of ICT use is relevant to the teaching and learning purposes. The positive effect on attainment is greatest for those ICT resources which have been embedded in some teachers' practices for a long time.

Indeed, ICT, it is claimed, enables students to take greater control of their learning and enhances learning on a variety of fronts.[21] It seems that there may be improvements on several fronts:

Student outcomes

- Performance increases, particularly when there is interactivity and multiple technologies (video, computer, telecommunications).
- Attitudes improve and confidence increases particularly in 'at risk' students.
- Instructional opportunities are provided that otherwise might not have been possible.

Educator outcomes

Teaching with technology brings several benefits:

- moving from a traditional, directive approach to a student-centred approach
- increased emphasis on individualised programmes of learning
- greater revision of, and reflection on, curricula and instructional strategies.

CONCERNS ABOUT ICT

However, the situation is not one of unbridled advantage. Higgins,[22] for example, found few indications that ICT could bring about improvements in understanding, and considered that the benefits reported by studies of Computer Assisted Learning (CAL) and Computer Aided Instruction (CAI) were both relatively low and not as effective as other approaches such as homework and peer learning. Hokanson and Hooper[23] question the initial claims for ICT as being both over-optimistic and unrealistic in predicting gains in student learning, achievement and test scores.

In considering the use of interactive whiteboards (IWBs) in primary classrooms, Smith *et al.*[24] have suggested that IWBs may reinforce established styles of whole-class teaching unproductively, rather than promoting new, innovative teaching approaches. As has been the experience with other uses of technology in classrooms, IWBs are often made to fit pre-existing instructional practices (Nordkvelle and Olsen).[25]

It appears that the promise of ICT, and the very many claimed benefits of ICT sometimes remain unfulfilled or unrealised. More significantly, many studies report that it is only under the right conditions that the claimed benefits can be realised. Central to these conditions is the teacher and the way in which she/he promotes learning through ICT – the teacher is still at the heart of the process of learning.[26] The teacher is still critical in newer forms of teaching; computers are no substitute but a powerful tool for teachers and learners to use. They help people, not vice versa. Schools are communities of people, not computer banks. Teachers are infinitely more responsive and sensitive to students' learning and development than computers. Indeed the teacher, in very many cases, will be making decisions on the most effective ways of using computer technology to enhance learning.[27] The provision of ICT is therefore a necessary but not sufficient condition for effective development, and that teachers are the critical factor, rather than hardware or software.[28]

CONSTRUCTIVISM AND ICT

The argument that is developed in this book is that teaching and learning have moved from instructivism to constructivism, and also that constructivism underpins the more effective use of ICT. A corollary of constructivism is the development of:

- situated learning
- metacognition
- higher-order thinking
- the social basis of learning
- a move away from didactic approaches to teaching
- an emphasis on the process of learning, not simply on the product
- the breaking of subject boundaries and the development of project-based, real world ('authentic') learning and authentic assessment
- student-centred learning, and
- the significance of intrinsic motivation.

Many of these issues derive from, or are related to, the work of Vygotsky, whose work inspired many of the ideas about teachers helping learners by 'scaffolding', and ensuring that teaching and learning take place within a 'zone of proximal development'.[29]

There has been a change in education from using ICT to deliver and control instruction to using ICT to support learners' creation of knowledge, and their investigation and thinking. A change from representation, using ICT to transmit information, to generation (for knowledge construction), from linear logic to non-linear, networked logic.[30] The use of computers, it is argued, is best conceived in terms of metaphors from biology rather than instruction, being a medium for growth – intellectually and cognitively – rather than simply a tool. Schools have moved some way from an emphasis simply on linear logic and programmed instruction and learning, towards non-linear, networked, branching, hypertext views of learning, in which connections between knowledge are made and developed. ICT has considerable potential to catch the tentative nature of knowledge in constructivism, as the use of ICT involves drafting and redrafting, editing and selecting, making connections and reflecting.

In a context where neither the teacher nor the textbook is the repository of all knowledge, the internet is an embodiment of, and medium for, the practice of constructivism. This is because it is an expanding store of accessible information and requires students to evaluate and select that information[31] and to select their own pathways for learning. The internet calls into question conventional notions of authority, validity, the nature and ownership of knowledge. Knowledge is non-hierarchical in the internet. Student-centred learning is a natural consequence of internet usage; indeed learner control of learning is a significant feature of ICT usage.[32]

The implications of adopting constructivist principles are to suggest that learning is situated; it is context- and individual-specific and it must place emphasis on social interaction and active learning,[33] with the locus of control of learning moving from the teacher to the learner. The significance of the social basis of learning and 'situated cognition' owes much to Vygotsky. Hung and Cheng[34] categorise this into four headings – situatedness, commonality, interdependency and infrastructure – and draw out their implications for e-learning (Box 17).

Further, with regard to ICT, the internet has been claimed to have considerable potential to develop metacognition,[35] as the non-linear nature of the internet and its use promote reflection and networked learning, both of which are essential ingredients of metacognition. Indeed it may be that the development of metacognitive strategies must be built into the design of ICT use, and that this, using Vygotsky's notion of 'scaffolding' (discussed in a later chapter) can be facilitated through ICT. Scaffolding can be provided by the teacher but Wegerif and Dawes[36] suggest that collaborative work on ICT with small groups of children can also enable them to provide scaffolding for each other. During internet use Grabe and Grabe[37] have suggested that the teacher can provide scaffolding by helping students to locate and evaluate material (e.g. from a web search), presenting students with challenging but achievable tasks, helping students to develop enquiry skills, identify problems and tasks, together with strategies for addressing them. This requires the teacher to locate learning within Vygotsky's 'zone of proximal development'. The zone of proximal development is defined as 'the distance between the actual development of the child and the level of potential development as determined by adult guidance or in collaboration with more capable peers'.[38]

If the teacher is to provide appropriate scaffolding to fit the learner's zone of proximal development, then this requires both the development of higher-order thinking and attention to the social basis of learning. For Vygotsky, one cannot have the former without the latter; for him all higher-order functions and cognition are socially learnt and transmitted.

HIGHER-ORDER THINKING AND ICT

Wegerif[39] suggests that using ICT in classrooms, particularly in a constructivist approach, has great potential to develop students' higher-order cognitive skills. A section of the report summary reveals how the relationship between ICT, thinking skills and pedagogy is a complex one:

> There are three main ways of thinking about the role of information and communications technology (ICT) in teaching thinking skills: as tutor or teaching machine, as providing

Box 17: Four features of learning from Vygotsky

Principles of situated cognition and Vygotskian thought	Design considerations for e-learning
Situatedness Learning is embedded in rich cultural and social contexts. Learning is reflective and metacognitive, internalising from the social to the individual.	E-learning environments should be internet- or web-based. E-learning environments should be as portable as possible. E-learning environments can focus on tasks and projects, enabling learning through doing and reflection. E-learning environments can focus on depth over breadth.
Commonality Learning is an identity formation or act of membership. Learning is a social act/construction mediated between social beings through language, signs, genres and tools.	E-learning environments should create a situation where there is continual interest and interaction through the tools embedded in the environment. E-learning environments should capitalise the social communicative and collaborative dimensions allowing mediated discourse. E-learning environments should have scaffolding structures.
Interdependency Learning is socially distributed between persons and tools. Learning is demand driven – dependent on engagement in practice.	E-learning environments should create interdependence between individuals where novices need more capable peers capitalising on the zone of proximal development (ZPD). E-learning environments should be designed to capitalise on the diverse expertise in the community. E-learning environments should be personalised to the learner with tasks and projects embedded in the meaningful activity context. E-learning environments can track the learner's history, profile, and progress and tailor personalised strategies and content.
Infrastructure Learning is facilitated by an activity – driven by appropriate mechanisms and accountability structures.	E-learning environments should have structures and mechanisms to facilitate the activity (project) processes in which the learners are engaged. E-learning environments have the potential to radically alter traditional rules and processes that were constrained by locality and time.

'mindtools' and as a support for learning conversations. A review of the evidence suggests that using technology does not, by itself, lead to transferable thinking skills. The success of the activity, crucially, depends on how the technology is used. Much depends on the role of the teacher. Learners need to know what the thinking skills are that they are learning and these need to be explicitly modelled, drawn out and re-applied in different contexts.

The evidence also suggests that collaborative learning improves the effectiveness of most activities... The positive effect of collaborative learning is amplified if learners are taught to reason about alternatives and to articulate their thoughts and strategies as they work together. Technology is therefore best thought of as a support and resource for dialogues in which thinking skills are taught, applied and learnt.

Some of this echoes the much earlier findings of Wishart,[40] who reported that computer programs can act as cognitive tools which facilitate the construction of higher-order schemata and use of cognitive skills such as formal, abstract reasoning, which were previously considered to be unattainable by younger children. But the key message is that the teacher is the crucial mediator. A well-constructed multimedia programme of study, with co-operative and situated learning, with an exploratory approach being adopted and with students working at their own pace and in their own sequences, can fulfil the potential of multimedia learning. Self-paced learning, they aver, can provide space for reflection and the integration of experience, understanding and conceptual development

One impact of ICT and new technologies is to shift the emphasis from teaching to learning, and from the product to the process of learning. Students need to focus on how and where to acquire, store and utilise knowledge rather than to remember it all.[41] Effective teachers will be those who can scaffold learning for students, and support them in the navigation of their own learning.

Faced with massive potential information overload as a consequence of ICT, the notion of a 'lesson' or a 'subject' might have to change dramatically, moving toward a variety of types and contents of learning taking place simultaneously and towards project-based work, often using primary sources, in a variety of settings.[42] Further, teachers are faced with a situation in which their students may know more about ICT than they do, and the notion of increased student choice is opened. Indeed, the content of curricula becomes debatable beyond fundamental literacy and numeracy. Project-based learning[43] should also encourage students to make decisions, encourage exploratory 'what-if' questions, actually require discussion and communication, and enable a final product or solution to be prepared. In particular, the content of curricula has increased potential to provide authentic, real-world learning and materials.[44]

What is being suggested here is the need for engaged and meaningful learning, with real-life tasks, which will be multidisciplinary, project-based, participative ('minds-on' as well as 'hands-on') and collaborative.[45] Collaborative work will require fluid and ad hoc grouping of students, with active pedagogies.

DIFFERENTIATION

One of the great claims for ICT is its ability to provide differentiated learning and differentiated activities: by task, process, materials (inside and outside schools), routes through learning, outcomes, pacing, timing, learning styles, abilities, kinds of knowledge, difficulty of material, personal involvement of the learner, enabling student choice, assessment and individual learning.[46] Another attraction of ICT and computer-mediated learning is its ability to engage learners affectively – their emotions, motivation and personality development.[47] For some students their enjoyment lies in being able to work with computers in private and at their own pace. For others it is the control of the learning which they value – they control their own learning[48] and the computer can be tailored to individual learning needs. For others it is the ability of the computer to set appropriately challenging and achievable tasks at their own levels.

The power of ICT to make learning possible for a diversity of students is well documented. Underwood[49] reports that students with special educational needs are viewed, and often view themselves, as failures, and that they have difficulty in completing work. With different technologies Bruntlett[50] suggests that several of these needs can be addressed; for example, learners who are dyslexic can use voice-activated computers; learners with visual impairments can use screen magnifier and talk-back facilities; learners with cerebral palsy can use lightweight laptops. There are concept keyboards for a range of learning needs. Further, the Department for Education and Skills[51] indicates the use of ICT can make learning available to students who have been excluded from school (NotSchool.net), reinforcing the principle of inclusive education and social inclusion.

In examining issues of equity, Grabe and Grabe[52] point out that females predominated in learning clerical skills with ICT and that fewer females than males took computer sciences at higher education level. Indeed, they report that females rated themselves as lower than males in computing abilities. They found that recreational software and competitive games were more geared to males and that, in school, there was more computer use as a tool for mathematics and science, both typically male-dominated subjects. If there was limited access to computers then males were more aggressive in gaining access to computers. It was important, therefore, for teachers to ensure equity of access, content and outcome in computer usage. Lachs[53] found that, generally, boys were more confident than girls in using computers and tended to take control (e.g. of the keyboard) more than girls. Clearly the teacher must be vigilant here to ensure equality of access and use. Further, Underwood[54] found that girls-only groups collaborated and co-operated better than the boys-only groups or mixed groups. This notwithstanding, boys-only groups performed well when given explicit instructions to co-operate. The teacher, then, will need to decide on the most judicious grouping – boys only, girls only or mixed-sex groups.

ADMINISTRATION

Schools use ICT in a variety of administrative ways. Bialo and Sivin-Kachala[55] found that teachers used ICT to streamline record keeping and administrative tasks, to decrease isolation through e-mail, and to increase their own professional development through distance education. Telem[56] noted that, with ICT, reports became more reliable, updated, timely and easy to retrieve and read, that there was a reduction in the need to sort through piles of documents and that statistical and comparative analyses were available immediately. Further, through ICT, teachers and head teachers became more accountable (p. 354), e.g. in terms of student achievements, complaints about teachers, and deviation from curriculum planning and timetables. Transparency was increased. School management information systems impacted on accountability, the evaluation of teaching and learning, supervision, record keeping (e.g. of attendance, writing reports, assessment marking, writing of lesson plans, resources), feedback, meetings (and their frequency) and shared decision making, shared values and continuous development of leadership, with increased efficiency in all areas.[57] However, Kwok et al.[58] found limited gains in terms of administrative time or personnel, though the Teacher Workload Study in 2001 found savings of up to 3.75, 3.25 and 4.55 hours each week in primary, secondary and special schools, respectively, in the UK.[59]

Student teachers are advised to find out the school's practices on using ICT for lesson planning, preparation and recording, communication, timetabling, recording (e.g. student progress, attendance, personal details, electronic mark-books) and administrative work. They are advised to find out about the school's intranet and e-mail practices.

SOCIAL LEARNING

A major claim for ICT in schools is its ability to foster social learning,[60] which, as was suggested earlier, is a major factor in the development of higher-order cognition. ICT is also valuable in supporting co-operative learning.

In planning for social learning the teacher must consider the number of users at each work station, the duration of the use, the nature of the access to the computer, and turn taking. For example, if one user alone has access this gives highly individual and possibly closely matched work, but it is very expensive in terms of time at the computer, and other students may suffer from not having access. If a small group of students is at the computer, positive peer interaction may take place but there may be arguments about turn taking in the group. If a large group or class is working with the computer then teachers may need to be much stricter about access. Further, if the teacher is using the computer for a presentation then the traditional issues arise as for other audio-visual media – the ability of every student to see and hear the presentation on screen.

The social basis of ICT cannot be underestimated. It promotes higher-order cognition, collaborative learning, authentic tasks and rich feedback. However, it has to be learnt, practised and developed.[61] Vygotsky[62] encapsulates the significance of the social basis of learning when he writes that 'social relations or relations among people genetically underlie all higher functions and their relationships'. Indeed he regards this position 'as a law'. In the age of Web 2.0 technology, social learning has perhaps taken on a new meaning. It would seem that anybody who is anybody wants to be part of an online social networking scene. Sites like Bebo, Friendster and MySpace have fuelled the social networking trend and statistics are starting to show that young people today spend many hours online communicating, learning and socialising in a way that only a few years ago would have been difficult to imagine.

PEDAGOGY

Work in the area of ICT and learning has involved considerable thought about pedagogy. This work features a number of links with constructivist theories. Research suggests that individual teachers' educational beliefs are associated with specific uses of computers in the classroom (Ertmer, 2005).[63] Low-level computer use tends to be associated with teacher-centred practices, whereas high-level use tends to be associated with pupil-centred or constructivist practices. Tondeur *et al.* (2008)[64] investigated individual teacher characteristics and their influence on the adoption of three specific types of computer use in the primary school classroom: 'basic computer skills', 'the use of computers as an information tool' and 'the use of computers as a learning tool'. Teachers with constructivist teaching beliefs were a significant predictor for all three types, especially with regard to 'the use of computers as an information tool'.

Schools exist to promote learning; that is their primary purpose. ICT will need to extend and improve student learning, and pedagogy concerns enhancing learning.[65] We have made several allusions so far to the view that ICT will bring about changes to pedagogy. Further, we cited earlier instances where brain-based research suggested a vital role for motivation and for networked learning (joined-up thinking). Under the umbrella of changes to pedagogy brought about by ICT are several areas, for example: approaches to teaching and learning, teaching and learning styles and behaviour, and contexts in which teaching and learning take place. The move is away from teacher-centred instruction and towards the facilitation of learning with ICT, particularly through group work and student-centred learning. Teachers and learners are partners in the co-construction of knowledge. With ICT the roles and tasks of teachers are still vital and add value to learning, but they change.

What is being argued here is that the computer is not a proxy for the teacher, there to reinforce traditional teaching styles or to help to soften the blow by employing 'edutainment', but is there to bring about new teaching and learning styles. Indeed if it is used only to buttress existing teaching styles then its novelty value will soon tarnish and wither, and student achievements will fall. Many teachers may feel uncomfortable in moving to new roles and tasks, not least because they might see it as a threat to their control and authority and also because many students know more about ICT than their teachers. Futurelab, based in Bristol, provide a fascinating insight into contemporary projects that explore the relationship between ICT and learning (http://www.futurelab.org.uk/).

The moves towards greater collaboration and interaction in students' learning is not something which will happen quickly. Many students will need to be taught, and to practise interaction and collaboration.[66]

It seems that students will need regular exposure to different roles and learning situations in order to maximise their benefit, for example having activities which:

- require regular participation and response (e.g. dialogue)
- set up 'conflicting opinions'
- place students in different roles (e.g. the *agent provocateur*, the visiting expert)
- require role playing
- involve formal debate
- develop writing groups
- develop group/team projects
- require groups to work autonomously and independently of the teacher.

Effective use of ICT requires teachers to be able to operate in different learning situations,[67] for example: the student and teacher engaged in individual one-to-one learning activity; students, teacher and other pupils engaged in whole-class teaching and learning; the student working with other students in a group activity; and the student working alone and independently.

Similarly teachers will need to develop their expertise in promoting interaction,[68] for example:

- when to intervene and when to stand back
- how to help students to search for information
- how to help students to define the task, use information-seeking strategies, locate and access information, evaluate and synthesise information
- how to help students to search, edit, draft, format, collate, connect, model, summarise and present information for a particular purpose and audience.

One claim of ICT is that it is able to accommodate different learning styles (a much-abused and misused term). Here it is taken to mean the characteristic or preferred ways in which particular learners learn and interact with the learning environment.[69] On average, both trainees and teachers in primary schools prefer learners who adopt the style of 'abstract conceptualisation' and 'active experimentation'. For ICT to be able to accommodate different learning styles teachers will need to be actually aware of how their students learn and like to learn, and build this into their planning for learning. It seems that the younger the children are, the more they prefer direct contact with the teacher, as this maintains a necessary sense of security in the young learner's mind.

What is being suggested here is that ICT has very considerable potential to change teaching and learning styles and behaviour, but that this is conditional upon a range of factors, at the heart of which lie people – learners and teachers. This suggests that we must still hold to models of effective teaching,[70] which emphasise:

- motivation
- explicit sharing with students the desired outcomes
- modelling, demonstration and supporting students towards the outcomes
- active approaches to learning in which students spend more time doing than listening
- formative assessment aimed at providing plenty of opportunity to practise new skills, to learn and create new knowledge and gain feedback
- opportunities for students to engage collaboratively with new learning
- authentic real-world contexts for the learning
- learning which leads to production of some kind for real audiences

- summative assessment which is closely tied to the desired learning outcomes
- assessment and reporting which clearly signal the next stage of learning.

The authors suggest that these are fundamental principles of teaching and learning, irrespective of ICT, and that technology makes them easier and more fun to achieve.

Similarly, the National Council for Educational Technology[71] provides practical advice for teaching and learning with ICT, in the form of seven 'don'ts' (Box 18).

Box 18: Seven 'don'ts' with ICT

- Don't devise a task which has no relevance to anything else in school or at home.
- Don't assign pupils to computers before preparing them for the task they will be doing.
- Don't let the pupils sit at computers while you are talking to them at the start of the lesson.
- Don't leave the pupils for the whole lesson just working on their task with no intervention to remind them of the educational purpose.
- Don't expect the pupils to print out their work at the end of every lesson.
- Don't end the lesson without drawing them together to discuss what they have achieved.
- Don't rely on the technology to run the lesson.

ASSESSMENT

Much traditional assessment has taken the form of testing of recall, memorisation and factual knowledge, leavened with some informed personal opinions. Students sometimes have to wait for several days or, in the case of public examinations, months for feedback in the form of a simple indication of the grade reached. Whilst we examine issues of assessment in later chapters, it is opportune here to suggest that ICT has the potential to develop and use alternative and maybe more fruitful assessment methods.

Assessment with ICT has several claimed advantages (Box 19). Research suggests that rapid feedback improves learning, the provision of rich feedback improves motivation.[72] Assessment and motivation are profoundly linked. ICT can indicate the number of attempts a student has made, the number of clues that needed to be supplied, the percentage of correct responses and the success of completion of the task.

Assessment for Learning practices attempt to strengthen the links between assessment and learning. Whereas traditional assessment frequently took the form of summative – end-of-course – testing, the provision of diagnostic assessments of strengths, weaknesses, difficulties, achievements and ways of learning and thinking is enriched and facilitated by ICT, not least in terms of speed, but also in terms of the quality of feedback. Assessment becomes the springboard into learning, having a strong formative potential[73] Authentic assessment (see Chapter 15) embodies constructivist learning principles, for example through real-world simulations which enable students to demonstrate the extent to which they can transfer knowledge from classrooms to typical real-life situations. It has been suggested that much learning with ICT is collaborative and requires different thinking strategies. To be able to reflect and embrace these new forms of learning and to present evidence of learning, a suitable form of assessment is portfolio assessment, in which students compile their own portfolios of work, selecting what to include and how to present the material. It seems that such portfolio assessment is motivating for learners[74] because it makes them agents of their own

Box 19: Advantages of assessment with ICT

- Feedback can be very rapid, if not immediate.
- Feedback can be private, avoiding public humiliation.
- As students are working with ICT in groups, this frees time for the teacher to give feedback to individuals.
- Feedback is richer because the computer can analyse the learner's performance in more detail and with more closely targeted feedback than the busy teacher can.
- The computer can assess higher-order thinking and learning.
- Longitudinal assessment is possible through stored databases of each student, enabling progress to be tracked and presented easily.
- Authentic assessment is developed, and linked to real-world learning. Multidisciplinary tasks are able to be assessed.
- Assessment is based on performance of real tasks.
- The links between learning, diagnosis and assessment are strengthened; assessment is linked to learning.
- Student self-assessment is facilitated.
- Computer-adaptive testing enables assessment to be tailored to individual levels.
- Examination anxiety is reduced, and less emphasis is placed on a single 'right' answer recalled at high speed.
- Non-academic achievement and skills can be accredited and recognised.
- The gap between learners and assessors is bridged; teachers, peers and individual students become both learners and assessors.

assessment, building in involvement and engagement. Portfolios require students to collect, select, present and reflect on their work and their learning.

Traditional assessment has usually been the task of teachers, and, indeed, Dykes[75] suggests that this task will not be relinquished with the arrival of ICT. Rather, it will mutate, so that teachers set up learning activities and opportunities for rich assessment and students themselves become involved in assessment. For example, the 'PbyP' system (www.camb-ed.net/pbyp/) allows children to upload their work for comment by their peers across the world; students may provide feedback comments on the work on which the submitter(s) can reflect and from which learning may occur and improvements can be made before making the submission of the final piece of work for assessment. Feedback might include comments on projects, for example: coverage of content, data collection and presentation, argument and its clarity, screen layout, graphics, team and individual involvement, team support. Collis *et al.*[76] make several claims for the potential benefits of providing feedback through the internet. For example:

- It can provide personal feedback to a group of students who have all carried out the same assignment.
- It can provide public feedback when the teacher wishes students to learn from each other's answers or maybe incorporate each other's ideas into a new assignment.
- It can provide group feedback to groups whose size is too great to enable individualised feedback to be given.
- It can indicate common errors made by many students and provide common remedies.
- It can enable peer feedback.
- The teacher can enable students to learn how to give and receive feedback and how to act on it, i.e. to learn responsibility.

It is clear that ICT has the potential to make for greater provision of opportunity for portfolio assessment, self-assessment, peer assessment and authentic assessment. One should not be too sanguine, perhaps, that these changes will be rapid, as there is still a long way to go to address the incorporation of higher-order learning into assessment with ICT, to clarify what should be assessed and what may or may not be assessed with ICT, and to ensure that ICT will enable the realisation of newer forms of assessment for learning. Further, if ICT is to be used for large-scale and newer forms of assessment, then there is a need to guarantee that all students and schools have access to equivalent ICT facilities. The problem is that technologies change and are outdated very rapidly, rendering standardisation difficult. Moreover, it may become harder to find out whether the work is the student's own and that it is not always easy to find out if the student understands what she or he has written. Indeed, a surfeit of computer-assisted assessment might lead to student boredom, rote learning and cheating.

A recent trend in testing is towards computerised adaptive testing. Here a test is flexible and it can be adaptive to the testees. For example, if a testee found an item too hard the next item could adapt to this and be easier, and, conversely, if a testee was successful on an item the next item could be harder. In an adaptive test the first item is pitched in the middle of the assumed ability range; if the testee answers it correctly then it is followed by a more difficult item, and if the testee answers it incorrectly then it is followed by an easier item. Computers here provide an ideal opportunity to address the flexibility, item discriminability and efficiency of testing. Testees can work at their own pace, they need not be discouraged but can be challenged; the test is scored instantly to provide feedback to the testee, a greater range of items can be included in the test, a greater degree of precision and reliability of measurement can be achieved, indeed test security can be increased and the problem of understanding answer sheets is obviated.

The use of computer adaptive testing has several attractions but it requires different skills from traditional tests, and these might compromise the reliability of the test, for example:

●   The mental processes required to work with a computer screen and computer program differ from those required for a pen and paper test.
●   Motivation and anxiety levels increase or decrease when testees work with computers.
●   The physical environment might exert a significant difference, e.g. lighting, glare from the screen, noise from machines, loading and running the software.
●   Having so many test items increases the chance of inclusion of poor items.

EVALUATING WEBSITES

The use of ICT in education requires a developed ability in teachers and students to evaluate websites. The internet is a vast and growing store of disorganised and largely unvetted material, and teachers and students alike will need to be able to ascertain quite quickly how far the web-based material is appropriate. Murphy (2006)[77] considers a set of generic pedagogical issues which developers, in consultation with subject matter experts, should address in all courseware, including web pages for interactive use in the classroom. These issues suggest that teachers need to be clear on the following:

●   the purpose of the site, as this will enable users to establish its relevance and appropriateness
●   the authority of the material, which should both be authoritative and declare its sources
●   the content of the material – its up-to-dateness and relevance
●   the design of the material, which should be appropriate to its purposes, intended audiences and content

◉ the readability of the material for the target audience and purposes (including words, sounds, pictures and other graphics)

◉ the implementation of the site, which should be easy to use by the target audience.

Some sites might provide assistance here, by including details of standards, courses, units, projects, lessons and lesson plans, student activities, information resources, interactive resources, assessments. Others give no guidance at all, and teachers and trainees will need to be able to evaluate them for themselves.

In evaluating educational materials on the web teachers can ask themselves several questions:

◉ Is the author identified?
◉ Does the author establish her/his expertise in the area, and institutional affiliation?
◉ Is the organisation reputable?
◉ Is the material referenced; does the author indicate how the material was gathered?
◉ Does the website work well or badly?
◉ What is the role that this website is designed to play (e.g. informational, as a supplement) in the class?
◉ Is the material up to date?
◉ Is the material free from biases, personal opinions and offence?
◉ What is the teaching philosophy on which this website is based?
◉ What assumptions are made about the students' learning styles who are using this website?
◉ How do we know that the author is authoritative on this website?
◉ Is this website useful for all kinds of learners (e.g. those with visual impairments)?

Boklaschuk and Caisse[78] suggest that a website should be evaluated in terms of its audience, credibility, accuracy, objectivity, coverage, currency, aesthetic and visual appeal, navigation, accessibility. Software and websites can be evaluated on several criteria (Box 20).

It is important for the teacher to keep records of the name of the program, website, author, level intended, curriculum areas covered, some details of the contents, and an overall evaluation (maybe a mark) of is general quality and utility, for future reference.

FINDING OUT ABOUT THE SCHOOL'S ICT FOR TEACHING PRACTICE

Student teachers have a limited time to find out about ICT in the school before they are faced with the task of having to use it. It will be useful, then, for students to ascertain the following:

◉ What hardware and software is available?
◉ Is there a reference list/resource list of software and resources? Where is it held?
◉ Are there records of the kind and level of programs available, and details of their suitability/ usage? Where are these held?
◉ What CD-ROM or preloaded software is there, where is it stored and how is it accessed?
◉ Which ICT resources can students access with and without supervision, and which are for teacher use only?
◉ What hardware can be used by students with and without supervision and what are the protocols for logging onto the system?
◉ What hardware can be used by teachers for their own preparation and for classroom use?
◉ What hardware has to be booked (e.g. digital cameras)? How is this done?

Box 20: Evaluating software and websites

- Clarity of information
- Authenticity and up-to-dateness of content
- Speed of downloading and permission to access through school/county system access (e.g. too many graphics can slow down the process)
- Cost of items (if any)
- Spelling (UK/US), language levels, vocabulary and jargon
- Usefulness of pictures and photographs
- Use of sound and animation
- Appropriateness for the project/work in hand
- Information overload or underload
- Clarity of focus
- Ease of navigation around the material
- Ease of capability to select, cut and paste material
- Copyrighted or with copyright clearance
- Safety and ability to select out items (e.g. games, undesirable material)
- Guidance on how to use the material in teaching
- Comparative advantage over books
- Compatibility and ease of use with the intended curriculum
- An indication of the level/age of the intended students and suggestions for how the materials can be used and followed-up
- Accuracy and efficient presentation of the content
- Motivating presentation and ease of navigation and structure
- Potential to stimulate active thinking
- Cost benefit (in terms of time and money)
- Suitability of pacing and sequence through the materials
- Degree to which users can control the pace, sequence and activities included
- Ability to save ongoing work
- Provision of suitable and useful feedback to users
- Quality of the materials, including supplementary materials, handbooks and manuals
- Provision of virus-free downloads
- The extent and coverage of the material
- Capability for being used in different curriculum areas
- Compatibility with existing and preferred learning styles
- Indication of whether it is mainly a teacher or student resource
- Quality of the presentation, graphics, audio and video materials
- Degree and kind of interactivity
- Additional facilities (e.g. bookmarking, recording progress)
- Indication of how it has been used with learners

- Does the school have an intranet, or access to a Learning Platform and how is it used? Who has access to it? How? Are passwords/login required?
- How many computers are there available in the classroom(s) and what are the rules, routines and practices for using them?
- How do teachers usually organise the computer use in the class/suite?
- Is there a rota for student use of the computers?
- Are there dedicated computer rooms, or banks of laptops and how are they timetabled for use?
- How is e-mail used in the school?

● Can students use e-mail?
● Do students and staff have individual passwords and identifiers?
● What are the requirements for teachers in terms of computer use for administrative purposes (e.g. for recording marks, attendance, lesson notes, feedback to students, report writing, working out statistics)?
● What levels of clearance are required for stored information (e.g. personal details of students)? Who has access to which information and which databases?
● Who are the ICT specialists in the school? How can they be reached?
● What back-up facilities and support are there (e.g. who are the computer technicians and how can support be found if there are problems)?
● Can teachers take home school laptops? If so, what insurance protections are there?
● Are students and staff permitted to use their own diskettes and CDs on school ICT equipment?
● How is ICT currently used for teaching, learning, assessment and recording keeping?
● Are there 'open access areas' for ICT use by students? If so, what are the procedures for students using them?
● What services does the school have in terms of purchased licences and membership of ICT groups? How are these accessed?
● What are the policies, practices, procedures and packages in the school for: word processing, spreadsheets, databases, graphing, graphics, sound packages, desktop publishing, multimedia, sensing and measurement, control, framework programs, internet, games, intranet, e-mail?
● Where is the E-safety policy? How does the school ensure that pupils are kept safe?

EVALUATING YOUR OWN USE OF ICT ON TEACHING PRACTICE

In planning and evaluating teaching and learning with ICT, the following questions are designed to draw together the several issues on ICT which have been raised in this chapter for student teachers using ICT on teaching practice.

For you

● How have you used ICT in lesson planning, evaluating, recording and record keeping?
● How have you used ICT for assessing students?
● What records have you kept of information about: CD-ROMS, websites, databases, software, multimedia, games and simulations?
● What have you learned about teaching and learning with ICT from your teaching practice, for planning, implementing and evaluating your teaching?
● How have you used ICT to differentiate work and learning?
● What ICT did you use, and how effective was it, with regard to:
    - word processing
    - spreadsheets
    - databases
    - graphing software
    - graphics and sound packages
    - desktop publishing
    - multimedia (use and authoring)
    - internet (use and publishing)
    - distant communication
    - games and simulations?

- How effective have you been in your teaching roles in ICT-driven teaching and learning?
- How effective have you been in providing scaffolding for students in their ICT use?
- How have you helped students to search, retrieve, select, evaluate, store, edit, communicate, share, present information from ICT?
- How well balanced was the use of ICT with individuals, groups, the whole class?
- How successfully did you monitor and intervene in learning with your and students' use of ICT?
- What theories of learning and motivation have you employed in your and students' use of ICT?
- What value-added benefits did ICT bring to your teaching and students' learning?
- What were your strengths and weaknesses in using ICT in your teaching?
- What areas of ICT and teaching do you need to improve?

For the learners

- How have you used ICT to develop creativity?
- How have you used ICT to develop higher-order thinking in students?
- How have you used ICT to promote collaborative learning, group work and team work?
- How have you used ICT to develop student-centred learning and learner control of learning (e.g. contents, sequencing, timing, pacing)?
- How have you used ICT to improve student motivation and curiosity?
- How have you used ICT to develop inter-disciplinary and within-discipline/subject project and topic work?
- How have you used ICT to develop students' enquiry skills and exploratory work?
- How have you used ICT to make learning enjoyable?
- How have you used ICT to develop real-world learning and real-world, authentic assessment?
- How have you used ICT to share information?
- How have you used ICT to vary teaching and learning styles, strategies and practices?
- How have you used ICT to accommodate students' different and preferred learning styles?
- How have you used ICT to improve your own and students' presentations?
- How have you used ICT to raise students' self-esteem, confidence and experience of achievement and success?
- How have you used ICT to address and develop equal opportunities (equal access, use, uptake and outcome of the ICT curriculum and the other areas of the curriculum through ICT)?
- How have you used ICT to increase student concentration?
- How have you used ICT to improve the quality, rate and quantity of learning?
- How have you used ICT to develop students' autonomy and responsibility for learning?
- How have you used ICT to develop students' social and interpersonal behaviour?
- How have you used ICT to develop students' abilities to apply knowledge?
- How have you used ICT to promote active learning?
- How have you used ICT to develop students' metacognition?
- How have you used ICT to develop portfolios for assessment?
- How have you used ICT to provide rich feedback to students?
- What ICT did the students use, and how effective was it, with regard to:
  - word processing
  - spreadsheets
  - databases
  - graphing software
  - graphics and sound packages

- – desktop publishing
- – multimedia (use and authoring)
- – internet (use and publishing)
- – e-mail
- – games and simulations?
- What evidence is there of raised student achievement as a result of ICT use?

The use of ICT in education has tremendous potential to improve learning. As can be seen here, that is critically dependent on the effectiveness of the teacher.

5 Legal Issues

INTRODUCTION

A teacher's legal responsibilities and obligations are legion. Legal matters touch every aspect of a teacher's work, for example: equal opportunities, school visits, photocopying, use of computer software, use of equipment, hours worked, discipline and punishment, physical restraint, health and safety, responsibilities to students, school uniform, reporting and assessment, confiscation of property, supervision and duties of care. Some legal obligations are written specifically for teachers (see below); others are for all employees and employers, which include teachers, e.g. the Health and Safety Act 1974 and the Management of Health and Safety at Work Regulations 1999. Though student teachers will need to know all the legal requirements when they are qualified, there are many immediate concerns on teaching practice which this chapter discusses. In particular this chapter discusses issues which might be most in student teachers' minds when considering teaching practice:

- duty of care, supervision and the avoidance of negligence
- discipline and its related fields of detention, confiscation and uniform
- safety
- educational visits
- child protection
- data protection
- copyright.

The discussion here is introductory only, and student teachers are advised to pursue the matters with their teaching practice schools.

DUTY OF CARE, SUPERVISION AND THE AVOIDANCE OF NEGLIGENCE

Teachers bear a significant responsibility for the students in their care; indeed they have a legal responsibility or 'duty of care' for the students under their charge. There are aspects of both civil law and criminal law that apply to teachers. In civil law, for example, teachers have a 'duty of care' and, if negligence is proven, then compensation can be secured, 'commensurate with any loss or damage suffered from the negligent action of the offender'.[1]

The 'duty of care' depends on several factors,[2] for example:

- whether it is possible to anticipate harm
- the 'neighbourhood principle', wherein acts must be avoided which are likely to cause harm or injury to a neighbour, defined as 'persons who are so closely and directly affected by my act that I ought reasonably to have them in contemplation as being so affected when I am directing my mind to the acts or omissions which are so called into question' (*Donoguhe* v. *Stevenson* [1932]), and
- whether the court considers it 'just and reasonable to hold that there is a duty'.[3]

Teachers are in loco parentis, that is, they act in the place of parents. They must act as a reasonably prudent would act, bearing in mind that the teacher usually has many more children in the class than the parent has at home. This is enshrined in the phrase that a school's duty is to take care such as a 'careful father could take of his boys' (*Williams* v. *Eady* [1893]), though quite what this means in practice can be confusing.[4] Clearly circumstances differ between parents and teachers, home and school, and so more recently courts have tended to abide by principles of negligence rather than by the in loco parentis principle.[5] So, for example, schools have to ensure that their premises are reasonably safe and that all reasonable steps have been taken to prevent damage and injury by other students (this obligation arises under the Occupiers Liability Act 1957). The issue of the degree of risk in educational activities has to balance safety and protection from injury with the need for children to take risks in order to learn independence (and to engage in educationally worthwhile experiences).[6] As Palfreyman reports, in the case of *Jeffrey* v. *London County Council* [1954], it would be 'better that a boy [*sic*] break his neck than allow other people to break his spirit'.[7] The duty of care, demonstrated by close supervision of students, is tempered by the need to enable students to have enough space to learn to take responsibility for their actions, to learn independence and autonomy, to demonstrate creativity and exploration. A balance must be struck, and this depends on the age, maturity and ability of students to anticipate the consequences of their actions. For example, some young children are fearless to the point of recklessness in PE lessons, and they must be prevented from hurting themselves. As a result of the Compensation Act 2006 courts are now required to consider the balance between risk and the benefit inherent in the activity in order to decide whether a teacher has acted negligently.

Section 1: Deterrent effect of potential liability

A court considering a claim in negligence or breach of statutory duty may, in determining whether the defendant should have taken particular steps to meet a standard of care (whether by taking precautions against a risk or otherwise), have regard to whether a requirement to take those steps might:

(a) prevent a desirable activity from being undertaken at all, to a particular extent or in a particular way, or
(b) discourage persons from undertaking functions in connection with a desirable activity.

During school hours teachers, as part of their contractual terms of employment, do not have to supervise children during the lunch break, though the school is under an obligation to provide adequate supervision during this time. Generally schools are not responsible for children arriving at school before the start of the school day, though, if they are allowed into school premises (including outside premises) then health and safety requirements must be in place, and schools may be both responsible and liable if they have not provided adequate supervision. Indeed many schools do not let students into the school until supervising adults have arrived. At the end of the day the school has a duty to hand over children to parents or carers. This is particularly in the case of younger children. So, a school has a responsibility to hand over a child to a parent or responsible adult who is known to the child, or, indeed, to keep the child in the school until he or she is collected, or to arrange for social services or police to be involved, so that the child does not simply wander off. Children should never be let out of school early unless parents have plenty of notice of this; in the event of an accident the school or local authority could be liable (*Barnes* v. *Hampshire CC* [1969]).

If the school has taken all reasonable precautions to ensure safety, then it is unlikely that negligence will be established. So, for example, if a child runs away and is injured, and the school has taken all reasonable precautions, then it is unlikely that the duty of care will have been breached. Of course, it is incumbent on student teachers to take steps not only to prevent this but to alert the senior staff of the school immediately if a pupil runs out of the school premises.

In other cases the notion of reasonable prevention may depend on the age and characteristics of the children. So, for example, in *Black* v. *Kent CC* [1983], negligence was established, and an award made, in the case of a 7-year-old child who stabbed himself in the eye with a pair of sharp-nosed scissors, as it was deemed to have been inappropriate for such a young child to have been using the equipment in question and the injury could have been avoided had blunt-ended scissors been used. Teachers have a duty to address and communicate health and safety issues with the students themselves, giving warnings as appropriate. Not to give such warning could be deemed to be negligent.

The issue of breach of duty is influenced by the age, developmental stage and abilities of the students, the numbers of children in the class, the activity in question and the resources being used, and the school should have clear policies and established practices on these matters, which the student teacher should ask to see. Negligence must be proved before an individual can be held legally responsible for injury or loss, and so it is incumbent on student teachers to find out the precautions, policies and practices that the school has in order to prevent problems from arising. If the duty of care has been shown to have been breached, for legal redress to be established it is still necessary to prove that injury or damage has resulted from the breach. It is highly likely that the school will have insurance policies, but prudent student teachers would be advised to check this matter, to ascertain whether, and in what ways, they are covered. If in doubt then do not put children or yourself at risk. The school and the teacher education institution have a duty to prepare teacher training students adequately for the matters of discipline, supervision, welfare and safety, so that a safe working environment is provided for student teachers.

Negligence is guided by the 'prudent and reasonable man' (*sic*) principle, which is the 'omission to do something which a reasonable man [*sic*] . . . would do, or something which a prudent and reasonable man would not do' (*Alderson* v. *Birmingham Waterworks* [1856]). In addition to this Booth, citing *Wilsher* v. *Essex Area Health Authority* [1998], indicates that the law expects additional responsibilities of a professional person, viz., that the person must demonstrate an average amount of professional competence and that 'no allowance may be made for age or inexperience',[8] i.e. a novice teacher must have the same level of competence, e.g. for a duty of care, as a more experienced teacher.

For negligence to be proven several factors must be addressed:[9]

● *duty:* the defendant must be shown to have a 'duty of care'
● *breach:* the defendant must be shown to have failed in that duty, either 'by an act of commission or omission'
● *damage:* the plaintiff must have been shown to have suffered damage as a result of the failure.

In addressing the legal aspects of supervision and negligence courts will take into consideration:[10]

- the adequacy of supervision for the students and activity in question
- the extent to which teachers have followed guidance and statutory requirements of safety and supervision
- the extent to which teachers have followed school policies and procedures in their teaching, supervisory and health and safety arrangements
- whether the students have been told the health, safety, supervisory and procedural arrangements
- whether the teacher has 'given clear and specific warnings to children not following rules'.

It must be noted here that a student teacher is not a qualified teacher. Therefore the student teacher cannot be used for supply cover for absent teachers; schools should not put pressure on student teachers to act in this way. If there is any question about this, the student teacher must politely refuse.

Another aspect of teachers' and schools' duty of care is in relation to bullying. Schools must take reasonable steps to prevent children being injured by bullying. This is related to the main principles of negligence that we outlined above. Generally, to avoid liability, schools need to show that they have a reasonable policy to prevent bullying and that they put it into effect.

DISCIPLINE

Related to the issue of supervision is the complex issue of discipline. Teachers have a contractual responsibility to maintain good order and discipline, under the School Teachers' Pay and Conditions Act, 1991. Discharging this role is one of the most difficult tasks of the teacher, and we devote several chapters of this book to it. There are several kinds of incident for which a legal consideration might be useful.

Corporal punishment is illegal. Period. Under section 131(4) of the Schools Standards and Framework Act 1998, corporal punishment is defined as the 'doing of anything for the purpose of punishing the child... which, apart from the justification, would constitute battery'. The same document makes it clear that corporal punishment excludes anything done to prevent personal injury to the person or property of any person, including the child. Hitting a student, or a student hitting a teacher, is a criminal assault.

Restraint is permissible, and staff may use reasonable force to prevent a pupil from committing or continuing to commit an offence, causing personal injury or damage to property (including their own) or from engaging in any behaviour prejudicial to the maintenance of good order and discipline at the school or among any of its pupils, whether that behaviour occurs during a teaching session or otherwise (e.g. off-site activities, but this must not contravene corporal punishment laws).[11] According to the DfES, schools should have a policy on the use of force; if the school is aware of the potential need to use force with a child it is advisable that the parents be involved in the planning of this. Too much force may result in a police or social services child protection investigation and procedures.

Restraint may be necessary in the interests of the safety of the child and others. It should be the minimum necessary. Desirably more than one adult should be present,[12] though this is not always possible. Physical restraint is permissible only in circumstances of the child causing harm to himself/herself or others, damaging property, or committing a criminal act which risks harm to people or property, and 'where verbal commands will not control the behaviour'. Schools have a duty to prevent assault and battery on one student by another (e.g. bullying) and on staff by students. 'The purpose of the intervention is to restore safety, and restraint should not continue for longer than is necessary. Physical contact and restraint should never be used in anger, and teachers should avoid injury to the child.' In practice charges of battery are seldom brought, though teachers should be guided by the use of the term 'reasonable force'. Parents should be told how restraint may be used (particularly in the case of children with emotional and behavioural difficulties); there should be a written policy for handling a specific child if necessary. Staff should be trained in proper and safe restraint.

In a litigious age school students are often only too keen to cause trouble to their teachers, and unfortunately some will not hesitate to cause extreme difficulty to teachers by wrongful accusations of assault, abuse and suchlike. Student teachers, and indeed experienced teachers, feel that talking to students in private may be useful. The advice we give is to be extremely cautious about this to the point of not doing it without another experienced teacher present, and not to be alone in a class-room with a student, even if it means leading a student out of the classroom into a public place. Many schools provide guidelines on physical contact with students. Clearly this may vary with the age of the child; it would be ridiculous not to have physical contact with very young children. However, teachers have to be extremely cautious about any physical contact, and should expect the school to have guidelines on this, and then to adhere to them. Our advice is to avoid physical contact if at all possible; this is perhaps an unfortunate sign of the times, but such is the position nowadays.

It is advisable to be very wary of accepting a child's account of an incident (particularly if it is the child's hearsay) until it has been tested against other evidence. If it is deemed that the child is of 'sufficient age and understanding' then it may be wise not to take instructions from, or in the presence of, the parent, not least because some parents may be quick to condemn their own child and other parents may not wish to condemn their own child or accept that their child could do any wrong. It is unrealistic to expect parents to have kept school correspondence (e.g. on disciplinary matters). If a parent complains about a teacher it is important to investigate it professionally rather than to leave it or dismiss it.

If a criminal act is suspected then the head-teacher can invite the police in to investigate. Here good practice suggests that parents or someone with parental responsibility should be present, even social workers. Police have the power to enter schools without invitation to search for offensive weapons. There is no requirement to caution a pupil before questioning him or her while investigating crimes, since the head teacher is not a person who is 'charged with the duty of investigating offences or charging offenders' *DPP* v. *G* [1997].

On the other hand, as we saw in Chapter 1, the incidence is rising of students themselves committing acts of violence against teachers, as well as against other students. Not only this, but teachers are also subject to acts of violence, both physical and verbal, from outsiders who may be parents, carers or even intruders. In the case of such assaults or acts of violence teachers have protection from the law as follows:

- the Crime and Disorder Act 1998 (applicable in the case of pupils aged 10 or over who commit an assault)
- the Criminal Justice Act 1988, for common assault, carrying an offensive weapon
- the Offences Against the Persons Act 1861, for assault on staff by parents, carers or children
- the Public Order Act 1986, where a parent or carer causes a disturbance inside or outside the school

Increasingly, teachers are taking court action. In our view, this is entirely correct as they should not have to suffer assault in the workplace. Violence against teachers, where proven, is usually grounds for exclusion or prosecution. Student teachers are strongly advised to find out the school's policies and procedures for such eventualities.

Detention

Teachers use detentions for discipline. Detentions must be reasonable and moderate.[13] To hold someone in detention for an excessive time for a small offence may be classed as false imprisonment. In *Terrington* v. *Lancashire County Council* [1986], the judge found that it was unlawful to detain the whole class when only one unidentified pupil had actually done something wrong.

The Education Act 1996, Section 550B, permits a student to be kept in detention after school without specific parental consent if:

- the head teacher has notified both parents and pupils in advance in general terms that detention is a punishment that may be imposed on pupils
- the head teacher, or someone else authorised by the head, has imposed the detention as a punishment
- it is reasonable in all the circumstances
- the parent has been given at least 24 hours' notice in writing that the detention will take place.

The detention must:

- be in proportion to the circumstances of the case
- be with due consideration to the special factors about the pupil – age, special needs, religious requirements, travel arrangements for the child to return home.

The detention must be supervised and a record kept of it (including the reasons for imposing it); care must be taken with travel arrangements for the child to return home.[14]

The letter to parents may be sent by hand or by post or left at the parents' address. Avoid sending it via the pupil. Seek confirmation, particularly if a fax is used. E-mail is not generally advised.

If a student fails to attend the detention then the head teacher must be notified and she/he should decide the course of action to be taken.

Confiscation

Teachers frequently use confiscation in the promotion of discipline. Some items must be taken from pupils, e.g. unlawful materials (drugs, pornography) must be taken and handed to the police. Others should be taken (e.g. offensive weapons). Taking someone's property may be construed as theft, though it may be hard to prove, as it implies dishonest appropriation of property and intention never to return; both parts must be fulfilled for it to count as theft. So, even if a teacher were to take away a toy, with the intention never to return it, this would probably not be construed in law as dishonest behaviour. Destruction of a student's property could be considered unlawful unless it was deemed to be necessary in the interests of safety. Confiscation could be deemed unlawful if it were taken for the confiscator's personal use. Confiscation rarely results in a legal case. In civil law there is 'trespass to goods', described as wrongful physical interference, when someone else's belongings are taken and the person refuses to give them back.

It is not a good idea to take property away and keep it for too long, particularly if it is valuable, and it is perhaps best to return it at the end of the school day. Return of goods and property may involve the pupil's parents, rather than giving it back to the child. It is important that parents and pupils know what may and may not be brought to school. It is also important to have a safe place where confiscated items (e.g. mobile phones) can be stored.

It is an arrestable offence to carry a knife or other offensive weapon on school premises without reasonable excuse (Offensive Weapons Act, 1996, sections 1 and 4), and police have powers to search; the law is unclear whether teachers have the right to search pupils or their property (e.g. locker, bag, pockets). If pupils do not consent to their property being searched then it is inadvisable to force the issue of a personal search of their bags or pockets without the involvement of parents, unless there is a suspicion of danger, in which case the police should be involved. Not to abide by these cautions is to risk the charge of assault. It is extremely inadvisable to resort to force, as it may constitute a breach of the Human Rights Act. It is less troublesome in searching a locker or a storage place, as it could be argued that it is a condition of use that consent has been given to reasonable searches provided that no damage is done to pupils' property.

Uniform

Schools are entitled to have rules on uniform, and this is often a matter of school discipline. Rules which forbid Sikhs wearing turbans, or insist that girls wear skirts may offend the race relations and sex discrimination legislation. Consideration of health and safety may apply in the school's duty of care (e.g. the wearing of certain jewellery and bracelets, footwear, toys, sweets, food and hair fashions). Schools should have a clear policy on these and on the enforcement of school uniform rules, and parents should know of these.

Exclusions (see Table 5.1)

School exclusions, though reducing, continue to be a significant problem in UK schools, with numbers of permanent exclusions moving from 12,668 in 1996/97 to 8,680 in 2006/07, which represents 0.12 per cent of the number of pupils in schools (or 12 pupils in every 10,000). Pupils of age 13, 14 and 15 are much more likely to be excluded than any others, with three times more boys being permanently excluded than girls.[15] Nearly twice as many special school pupils were excluded than secondary pupils (as a proportion of the respective total school populations).

Previous data showed 'a far higher proportion of Black Caribbean, Black African and Black Other groups [being] excluded than of other ethnic groups', but the data for 2006/07 did not include a breakdown of ethnic origin in relation to exclusions.[16] Although any permanent exclusion is serious, these figures provide a useful counterbalance to the suggestion that school pupils are running amok. However, these figures obviously do not shed light on the day-to-day problems that are not serious enough to result in permanent exclusion.

In an attempt to reduce the number of exclusions the government issued guidance on non-excludable offences in 1999.[17] Exclusion was not to be used for minor incidents (e.g. failure to do homework or bring dinner money; lateness; poor academic performance; truancy; pregnancy; breaches of the school's uniform policy, including hairstyle and jewellery).

Exclusion represents the 'end of the road' for students and schools alike; it is a last resort, and is not usually invoked until all other avenues for discipline (including asking parents to remove their child voluntarily) have been exhausted. Exclusions may be for a fixed period of time (not more than 45 days of a school year) or permanently, and the head teacher alone has the power to exclude. If a student is to be excluded, parents must be informed about the commencement and duration, the reasons for the exclusion, and appeals procedures, arrangements for the student to continue his/her education, the parents' rights to see their child's school record, and whom the parents can contact in connection with the exclusion. If a student is to be temporarily excluded for more than five days in a single term, or will miss an examination as a result of the exclusion, the head teacher must inform the governing body of the school and the local education authority. The governing body must

Table 5.1 Primary, secondary and special schools[1][2][3]: number and percentage of fixed-period exclusions by reason for exclusion, England, 2006/07

	Primary schools		State funded secondary schools[2]		Special schools[3]		Total	
	Number of fixed period exclusions	Percentage of all fixed period exclusions[4]	Number of fixed period exclusions	Percentage of all fixed period exclusions[4]	Number of fixed period exclusions	Percentage of all fixed period exclusions[4]	Number of fixed period exclusions	Percentage of all fixed period exclusions[4]
Physical assault against a pupil	11,210	24.5	65,390	18.0	2,580	15.6	79,180	18.6
Physical assault against an adult	6,710	14.7	8,560	2.4	3,320	20.0	18,590	4.4
Verbal abuse/ threatening behaviour against a pupil	2,520	5.5	12,910	3.6	660	4.0	16,090	3.8
Verbal abuse/ threatening behaviour against an adult	5,590	12.2	81,770	22.5	2,530	15.2	89,880	21.1
Bullying	560	1.2	5,710	1.6	530	3.2	6,800	1.6
Racist abuse	350	0.8	3,790	1.0	230	1.4	4,370	1.0
Sexual misconduct	260	0.6	3,080	0.8	160	1.0	3,500	0.8
Drug and alcohol related	60	0.1	7,840	2.2	280	1.7	8,180	1.9
Damage	950	2.1	10,070	2.8	800	4.8	11,820	2.8
Theft	340	0.7	8,980	2.5	120	0.7	9,440	2.2
Persistent disruptive behaviour	14,020	30.7	79,270	21.8	3,470	20.9	96,760	22.7
Other	3,180	6.9	75,910	20.9	1,922	11.6	81,000	19.0
Total[5]	45,730	100	363,270	100	16,600	100	425,600	100

Source: School Census

(1) Includes middle schools as deemed.

(2) Includes both CTCs and Academies. Information is as reported by schools. See Notes to Editors 2.

(3) Includes both maintained and non-maintained special schools.

(4) The number of exclusions by reason expressed as a percentage of the total number of exclusions.

(5) There was one fixed-period exclusion for which circumstance were not known – this is included in the 'total' column only.

Totals may not appear to equal the sum of component parts because numbers have been rounded to the nearest 10.

take part in a review of the decision to exclude, at the parents' request, and may uphold the exclusion or reinstate the student at a named date. There is an appeals panel which is specially constituted by the local education authority.[18]

The nature of the offence for which exclusion is the penalty is indeterminate, but it may include:

- possession of an offensive weapon (for example a knife, gun, bicycle chain, matches) (e.g. *R v. Solihull BC ex parte H* [1997])
- possession of a controlled substance (drugs)
- physical assault (e.g. *R v. Cardinal Newman's School, Birmingham and another, ex parte* [1997])
- indecent assault (e.g. *R v. Newham LBC and another, ex parte X* [1995])
- swearing at a teacher (e.g. *R v. Governors of St Gregory's Roman Catholic Aided High School, ex parte Roberts* [1995])
- bullying and intimidatory behaviour (e.g. *R v. Headmaster of Fernhill Manor School, ex parte Brown* [1992])
- spitting on the public
- theft.

Permanent exclusions are often the culmination of a series of fixed term exclusions.[19]

The practical effect of exclusion (apart from the stigma) is that the student receives less education. Indeed Circular 10/99 indicates that, if an exclusion is to be for a block of more than 15 days, plans must be made for the student's ongoing 'full-time and appropriate education', reintegration, and intervention to address the student's problems.[20] The government indicated that, in September 2002, almost half of the permanently excluded students were receiving fewer than 12 hours education per week, whilst 40 per cent of students at Key Stage 4 were receiving over 20 hours per week.[21] The government has taken several steps to address the issue of provision of education for excluded pupils, as part of its programme for social inclusion. For example, the Education Act of 1996[22] established Pupil Referral Units, to cater for students who, for a variety of reasons, including exclusion from school, need exceptional arrangements to receive education. Home tuition is another option for excluded students (often for younger rather than older students), as is placement in the voluntary sector, FE college, work-related placements, or 'mixed provision' (a combination of provision). That said, the government's own figures indicate that 10.4 per cent of permanently excluded students still have no provision,[23] with the problem being particularly acute for those in Key Stage 3.

SAFETY

Teachers are required to ensure their children's health and safety, under the Health and Safety at Work Act 1974 and the Management of Health and Safety at Work Regulations 1999. These Acts seek to prevent accidents and to ensure that the workplace is as free from risk as possible. If the Health and Safety Acts are violated then criminal prosecution can follow, even if no accident has occurred. The employer is vicariously liable for civil wrongs of an employee,[24] e.g. some aspects of negligence (*Gower v. London Borough of Bromley* [1999]), though not for criminal wrongs, i.e. there may be cases where, if the Health and Safety Act 1974, is breached, then it is the teacher alone who is liable. The student teacher should find out, indeed be told, who is responsible for Health and Safety matters in the school, and what the procedures are in respect of health and safety, e.g. dangerous substances or equipment, school visits, reporting accidents, first aid treatment.

Certain activities carry a higher risk to children than others. For example, in sports, physical education and various science activities there may be a greater degree of risk than in mathematics or language activities. Here greater exertion of the duty of care must be applied, and, indeed, Health and Safety regulations must be observed in schools. In any activity that carries risks teachers must ensure that it is undertaken in a safe manner and with regard to foreseeable risks. So, for example, if dangerous chemicals are to be used then appropriate safety measures must be observed. If children are cooking with hot ovens then safety measures must be in place. In physical education and sporting activities, demands placed on children must not exceed their reasonable capabilities (and great care must be observed for children with special needs), in order to avoid the charge of negligence (e.g. *Moore* v. *Hampshire CC* [1981]).

Some two-thirds of accidents to students take place in PE lessons. The British Association of Advisers and Lecturers in Physical Education has produced several materials on safe practice in physical education, and, indeed, many other associations have produced similar guidance. The issue remains that supervision and reasonable demand on students head the list of concerns about safety in PE, particularly in respect of dangerous equipment, lack of proper safety equipment (*Povey* v. *Rydal School* [1969]), broken limbs (*Moore* v. *Hampshire CC* [1981]), and teachers joining in with dangerous tackles in rugby (*Affutu-Nartoy* v. *Clarke and ILEA* [1984]).

In science and technology lessons, in addition to government guidance on safety, several other associations[25] have produced guidelines for schools. Some of these include statutory requirements (e.g. safety glasses and safety screens, the Control of Substances Hazardous to Health, and requirements on the use of low-level radioactive materials). Care must be taken to point out the dangers of chemicals (e.g. phosphorus in *Shepherd* v. *Essex CC and Linch* [1913] and caustic soda in *Crouch* v. *Essex CC* [1966]), not only in terms of saying that they are dangerous, or 'don't touch', but in pointing out what the exact dangers are (*Noon* v. *ILEA* [1974]). Equipment must be in good order (*Barnes* v. *Bromley LBC* [1983] in respect of a riveting tool), and care must be taken to instruct children in its safe use. In *Hoar* v. *Board of Trustees* [1984] the school was found to be 50 per cent negligent in the use of a woodworking machine because it had not taken care to instruct a child in its safe use, as the child had been absent on the day when the explanation had taken place. In *Fryer* v. *Salford Corporation* [1937], negligence was established, as insufficient care had been taken to protect children and their clothing from a gas flame.

The student teacher must seek advice from qualified teachers about any proposals which might present a risk, and, if there is any doubt or the advice has not been able to be found, then that lesson cannot go ahead, and an alternative lesson must take place. In lessons where there is a risk, the regular class teacher must be available, either in the classroom itself or close at hand. In some lessons (e.g. PE, some science lessons) the class teacher must be present or else the planned activity should cease and an alternative take place.

In many situations the school may not be found negligent if it has taken due care to prevent danger (e.g. *Suckling* v. *Essex CC* [1955], where a pupil stole a handicraft knife and attacked another boy with it; *Smith* v. *Hale* [1956], where a pupil attacked another with a home-made arrow; *Ellesmere* v. *Middlesex CC* [1956], where a pupil attacked another with scissors in a handicraft lesson).

It must be made very clear that staff, unless they are specifically employed for the purpose, are under no obligation to, indeed should not, administer medicine. The Medicines Act of 1968 indicates that only a qualified practitioner should administer medication, including injections except in life or death emergencies, though, as part of the prudent parent principle, medication may be administered with parental permission. The government has issued *Supporting Pupils with Medical Needs: A Good Practice Guide*, which makes clear what schools should and should not do in the administration of medication. Student teachers are very strongly advised not to administer medication without having gained clearance from the appropriate party in the school, and to find out what is the school rule on administering medication. Clearly, if a school suspects that a child needs medical attention then it has a duty to ensure that it is provided, but from suitably qualified people. Teachers are not medics, and are not trained to deal with such cases. So student teachers are strongly advised not to administer first aid unless the emergency is extreme.

If there is an accident then the student teacher must send for help if it is necessary. In the case of an accident there are school procedures which must be adhered to in terms of notification, reporting, recording, and informing parents. Student teachers are advised not to admit liability for any accident in their lessons, but to take advice. Indeed if a case comes to court under civil law then vicarious liability often applies in cases of negligence,[26] i.e. 'the employer is held responsible for the actions of the employee whilst fulfilling any duties within the scope of employment' (p. 24), though the employer may seek a contribution to the award from an employee. The student teacher is strongly advised to find out the legal cover that the school provides for him/her (e.g. whether the student teacher is classed as an employee); indeed the school should feel an obligation to make this clear to the student teacher.

Student teachers are strongly advised to find out the school's policies on health and safety, equipment and usage, and to find out whether they are covered by the school's insurance policies. In particular, student teachers are strongly advised to have a qualified teacher present with them in risky situations. So, for example, in PE lessons the student teacher may have to stop the lesson if he or she is left alone without the class teacher or suitably qualified adult present and if adequate supervision and insurance are not provided. For some subjects it is important to find out the school's policies and rules on children entering or not entering classrooms, laboratories, workshops, swimming pools and gymnasia before the teacher arrives.

Educational visits

On school and educational visits, legislation was brought in after a series of tragic events in which children were injured or killed for want of proper supervision or protection, and an important document from the government is *Health and Safety of Pupils on Educational Visits.*[27] In recent years concerns have been expressed by teachers that in view of the possibility of being sued for negligence if there is an accident during a school trip, there is a question about whether it is too risky to take children on trips at all. The phrase 'risk averse' society has been used to characterise these and similar concerns. However, the Compensation Act 2006 that we referred to earlier was introduced so that proper consideration could be made of whether taking certain precautions might have prevented a desirable activity being undertaken at all.

It is folly to take students on educational visits if they are unprepared and if the safety and supervisory arrangements are not already assured and in place. Schools should have policy documents and rules/procedure for educational visits, and student teachers need to consult these. Before undertaking any educational visit or school trip there is a legal requirement that a written risk assessment is prepared and given to all the teachers and adults concerned, not least to show explicitly that 'all reasonable precautions' have been taken. A risk assessment will include addressing the following considerations:[28]

● What are the hazards?
● Who might be affected by them?
● What safety measures need to be in place to reduce risks to an acceptable level?
● Can the group leader put the safety measures in place?
● What steps will be taken in an emergency?

Supervisory, health and safety considerations in planning an educational visit will vary according to several factors, for example:[29]

- the type and suitability of the activity in question and its associated risk (e.g. sporting, water activities, walking and climbing may require not only proper equipment but proper preparatory training for the children and may need to be led by a qualified instructor/leader)
- the location of the visit (e.g. a visit to a local library may be easier to plan and supervise than a visit to a more distant farm, and a visit abroad will need meticulous preparation)
- the competence, experience and qualifications of the supervisory staff
- the ratio of pupils to teachers and supervisory staff
- the duration of the visit (e.g. an afternoon, a day, a week)
- the quality and suitability of the available equipment
- seasonal and weather conditions
- the age, developmental stage, nature and temperament of the children (including those with particular emotional, behavioural, physical and medical needs)
- the statutory requirements for health and safety (e.g. in visiting a power station)
- the provision of supervision on site by the staff at that site (e.g. at outdoor centres or in other schools if students are going to visit other schools, or if students are visiting a museum)
- the time of day of the visit (e.g. out-of-school hours (evening or weekend) visits to a theatre may need additional insurance cover and preparation)
- the safety provisions existing on the site (e.g. in sports stadia for local sporting competitions)
- the availability of first aid, emergency and medical services
- procedures for handling situations when students are either unable or unwilling to continue (including how to send children home early, if appropriate)
- procedures for ongoing risk assessment and risk management during the activity (e.g. in the event of worsening weather conditions during a mountain activity)
- communication arrangements and contingency measures.

Student teachers are strongly advised to visit the site themselves before taking the students, to check out the educational potential, the Health and Safety matters, the supervisory arrangements and all aspects of reasonable prevention of accidents and injury. During the educational visit teachers are responsible for all the students in their care; if non-teachers accompany the trip then they are bound by the same common law principle of acting as a 'reasonable parent', though they are not held as accountable as the teachers themselves. The message is simple: regardless of which other non-qualified adults are present, it is the teachers who share the supervisory Health and Safety responsibility. Non-teacher adults (including student teachers) should not be left in sole charge of children unless this has been cleared as part of the risk assessment (student teachers are cautioned not to put themselves in a position of being in sole charge).

In planning the number of adults required to accompany an educational visit, the DfEE 1998 and RoSPA make it clear that there is no absolute formula on ratios, but that there must be a high enough ratio of adults to students for the visit to be safe. The advice is very clear: err on the side of extreme caution, particularly with students with special needs. The schools and local education authorities should provide guidelines on staff/student ratios. Some local education authorities insist on a minimum number of teachers and/or adults for any trip out of school, and student teachers are advised to find out what they are for the school in question. The teacher unions also provide guidelines for school trips, indicating, for example, a minimum of two teachers per visit, a minimum ratio of 2:20, reducing to 1:5 or 1:4 for particularly hazardous activities. The advice to student teachers is unequivocal: do not take out a group of students on your own, however small the group; you must have a qualified teacher present with you. In mixed groups, have a male and a female adult/teacher. For very young children the ratio could be as low as 1:2, i.e. one adult to hold the hands of two children. early years classes often use the guideline of 1:4, but for some classes of very young children this is simply inadequate. Parents will need to be informed in advance of the educational visit and to have given their consent in writing; they have the decision on whether their child should go on the visit. Parents must not pay a compulsory charge, though they may be asked for a contribution.

If insurance is not provided then the trip cannot take place. The insurance should cover:

- personal injury
- public liability
- medical and related expenses
- extra expenses (e.g. travel if the intended travel arrangements do not happen, e.g. a rail strike, a flight cancellation)
- personal effects
- hired equipment
- special activities (e.g. special arrangements and clauses may need to be inserted into policies to cover particularly risky activities)
- cancellations.

The provider of the transport has the legal responsibility for the children's safety whilst in transit (e.g. seatbelts and wearing of seatbelts), together with adequate insurance, and there must be adequate supervision whilst in transit (e.g. it may not be enough to devolve supervision to the driver). During the visit very judicious vigilance must be observed with students. Although there have been cases where negligence has not been established when children break into small groups on their own (e.g. *Murphy* v. *Zoological Society* [1962], in respect of a group of boys who entered the lion's cage at Whipsnade Zoo) it would be very foolish to court danger in this respect.

(See www.routledge.com/textbooks/9780415485586, Chapter 6 Legal issues, Educational visits, staff:student ratios.)

Child protection

Under the Children Act, 1989 and following a series of high-profile legal cases, the issue of child protection has become a matter for schools and teachers. Schools and teachers must be vigilant to observe signs of abuse and harm, defined as physical injury, neglect, sexual abuse, emotional abuse and mental abuse. Schools are obliged to have protocols and procedures for action in the event of abuse being suspected, and teachers should only act in accordance with these, and not take the law into their own hands here. If a teacher suspects that abuse and non-accidental injury have taken, or is taking place, then he or she must report it to the head-teacher or the designated person in the school, as there are legal procedures to be observed. Sometimes this may be as a result of something that a child has said, or that the student teacher has observed.

The Safeguarding Vulnerable Groups Act 2006 introduced a new vetting scheme for all people working with children and young people to be implemented from 2008. Previous guidance was consolidated in the document *Safeguarding Children and Safer Recruitment in Education.*[30] The main objective of the guidance is to ensure that children and young people are safe by providing a safe environment for learning, and identifying children and young people who are suffering or likely to suffer significant harm, and taking appropriate action to support them. The emphasis on preventing unsuitable people working with children and young people was strengthened following the tragic case of two children murdered by a school caretaker. The guidance also emphasises: the promotion of safe practice and the need to challenge unsafe practice in educational settings; the identification of instances where there are grounds for concern and the need to initiate appropriate action; and the requirement to contribute to effective partnership between people who work with children.

In 2006 it became mandatory for schools to obtain enhanced Criminal Records Bureau (CRB) disclosures for anyone employed by a school including those employed to deliver extended services; this includes trainee teachers and unsupervised volunteers. Trainees on teacher training courses are required to undergo a CRB check but they cannot initiate this themselves. The law requires the employer to initiate the process. In practice, this means that trainees are given a form to complete by their training institution, which results in the CRB check being made so that they are allowed to work in schools (detailed guidance about the form can be found at http://www.crb.gov.uk/Default.aspx?page=0).

DATA PROTECTION

Information about an identifiable living person held on a computer is subject to the Data Protection Act 1984, and the individual about whom the data are kept has a legal right to see that information and to ask for it to be amended if it is incorrect.[31] This right extends to the parents of children under the age of 18. The Data Protection Act 1984 and the Data Protection Act 1998 require schools to be registered with the Data Protection Registrar as data users.[32] The 1984 Act applies to electronic records, including references stored for more than two months, though the 1998 Act extends this to manual records which are held in a filing system.

With regard to the disclosure of information the Education (School Information) (England) Regulations 1996, indicate that some information should either not or never be disclosed save to other educational establishments; such information might concern, for example:

- child abuse, be it suspected or proven
- material which might cause serious physical, emotional or mental harm to the individual
- material prepared for a juvenile court
- statements of students' special educational needs
- data on a student's ethnic origin.

Student teachers will have to abide by these regulations; we advise caution, therefore, in committing thoughts to record – be it in paper or electronic form.

Copyright

Teachers need to use printed and electronic resources for the purposes of teaching. For example, they may want to discuss a page from a children's picture book or use a film as the basis for a series of lessons. This brings teachers into the realm of the law on copyright. The Copyright, Designs and Patents Act 1988, as amended, is part of the wider body of intellectual property rights laws (the Act and some important amendments can be found at http://www.patent.gov.uk/copy/legislation/index.htm). Copyright in the UK is automatic, provided the work is in writing or some other material form, has some originality and has been produced by a British subject. It is useful to mark work with the copyright symbol ©, the author's name and the date of first publication, but this is not a requirement for protection under copyright law in the UK, unlike some other parts of the world. (The information in this section on copyright is informed by guidance from the University of Cambridge Centre for Applied Research in Educational Technologies (http://www.caret.cam.ac.uk/copyright/).

In view of the fact that copyright law applies to work in writing or other material form, most works that teachers might use are covered; for example:

● literary works including books, poems, journal articles, tables, etc.
● films
● artistic works including all pictures
● musical works;

in other words, work that has been created by someone and that has been recorded in any form, including electronically on the internet. To sum up, teachers cannot copy work (e.g. by using a photocopier for printed materials, or a scanner) that is still within copyright (normally within 70 years of its creation) without applying for written permission (even if this is granted, fees are sometimes payable). Although some of the specific details of electronic rights are still being worked out, copyright law is applied in much the same way to printed and electronic materials. The detail of copyright law is complex; hence it is not possible to cover everything in this section, so we briefly address teachers' use of images and use of texts as two examples to illustrate some key aspects of the law.

The good news is that trainees and teachers can show images to their classes by using the internet live through an electronic whiteboard. They are also permitted to write sections of copyright material on the more traditional blackboard or flip chart for the purposes of teaching. However, scanning images into a computer, or photocopying images, is not allowed. According to the letter of the law, teachers are not allowed to make an OHT, a slide or a photograph of an image for classroom use because this would infringe copyright. However, there are many sources of free-to-use images, for example:

Freely available images

There are some sources of images that may be used free of charge for educational purposes[33]:

● AICT (Art Images for College Teaching): this is a royalty-free image resource for the educational community
● DHD photo gallery: over 13,000 very varied images, clip art, sounds and video clips (from carbon resister strips to Victoria Falls) that may be used subject to very reasonable terms and conditions
● FreeFoto.com: over 67,000 images in 117 sections, available for non-commercial use subject to FreeFoto terms and conditions
● Flickr hosts a huge and growing library of photographs submitted by individuals. It is possible to search for images with Creative Commons licences allowing educational use.
● FreeImages.co.uk: over 2,500 photographs that may be freely used or adapted for use on websites or in publications, under FreeImages terms and conditions, which include that a credit/link is given to the site
● Pics4Learning: copyright-friendly images for education. The site is aimed at primary- and secondary-education teachers but the images available are broad in range and applicability.
● Visual Arts Data Service: access to collections of images that may be used for research or teaching purposes but, if used for teaching, must be restricted so that access is only available to students who have signed an appropriate undertaking – see VADS conditions for use
● Philip's House of Stock Photography (www.photo.net/stock/). This site provides many free images and also provides links to other free-image sites.

- NASA (http://spaceflight.nasa.gov/home/index.html). As with most US government agency websites, NASA allows the use of NASA imagery, video and audio material (except the NASA insignia logo) for educational or informational purposes provided proper credit is included. The terms of use are set out at http://www.jsc.nasa.gov/ policies.html. For a full list of US government graphics and photographs available, see http://www.firstgov.gov/Topics/Graphics.shtml
- Botanical Society of America Online Image Collection: education images on botany for instructional use
- Earth Science World Imagebank (http://www.earthscienceworld.org/) is a service provided by the American Geological Institute designed to provide quality geoscience images to the public, educators and the geoscience community. Most of the images are available free of charge for educational purposes, provided the straightforward terms of use are followed (http://www.earthscienceworld.org/imagebank/imageuse.html).
- The Centre for Bioscience ImageBank: thousands of images are available free of charge with copyright cleared for educational use, with due acknowledgement.
- Geology by lightplane – 335 colour aerial images of landforms and geological features (in USA) taken from a small aircraft, free for non-commercial educational use
- Graphic Maps (www.graphicmaps.com) – free images of maps, flags and globes. (The site also contains many maps and images available for a fee, but the free ones are easy to find.)
- Health Education Assets Library: a digital library providing freely accessible digital teaching materials aimed to meet the needs of today's health sciences educators and learners.
- Microsoft ClipArt Gallery – copyright-free images if you have Microsoft Office software legally installed on your computer. This is a searchable gallery of thousands of images. N.B. Do not forget to read the licence information on each site. A web page that promotes a department, as opposed to being part of teaching materials, may or may not be considered 'educational purposes'.

With regard to texts, one way that teachers *are* allowed to make a copy of a literary, dramatic, musical (printed not sound recording) or artistic work is if they wish to use it for research for a non-commercial purpose and private study, which can be regarded as fair dealing. The key test that the courts have used in relation to fair dealing is whether the economic impact on the owner of copyright is likely to be significant. If not then it would generally be regarded as fair dealing. With regard to a literary work, fair dealing usually means making only one copy. Full acknowledgement such as thorough bibliographic information is necessary, not least to avoid plagiarism.

Plagiarism

You may think that the subject of accurate citation and referencing of sources has more relevance to university students than school teachers and their pupils. However, even at GCSE level, students are given guidance on how to show the sources they have used to complete coursework and to avoid plagiarism. It is not an infringement of copyright to quote directly from a source provided it is not a *substantial part* and provided the source is acknowledged. Unfortunately what constitutes a substantial part rather depends on the kind of source being used. In some cases it could be a headline or a list of concluding points if they are particularly significant. For larger texts an informal rule of thumb is that you should quote no more than 800 words in total extracts, with no single extract from the work exceeding 300 words. For poems, 40 lines is regarded as a good rule of thumb, provided that does not constitute more than 25 per cent of the poem (University of Cambridge Centre for Applied Research in Educational Technologies, online).

Plagiarism is most serious in the context of examinations because it can reflect the intention of a candidate to deceive the examiners in order to get unfair advantage. It is also a way of taking credit for work that someone else has done. The University of Cambridge defines plagiarism as follows:

> Candidates are advised that plagiarism can be defined as: the unacknowledged use of the work of others as if this were your own original work.
>
> In the context of an examination, this amounts to a candidate passing off the work of others as his/her own to gain unfair advantage.
>
> Examiners must be left in no doubt as to which parts of the work are the candidate's own and which are the rightful property of someone else.

The guidance goes on to say[34]:

Plagiarism may be due to:

- *Copying* (using another person's language and/or ideas as if they are your own)
- *Collusion* (where collaboration is concealed or has been expressly forbidden, in order to gain unfair advantage).

Methods include:

- *quoting directly* another person's language, data or illustrations without clear indication that the authorship is not your own and due acknowledgement of the source
- *paraphrasing* the critical work of others without due acknowledgement – even if you change some words or the order of the words, this is still plagiarism if you are using someone else's original ideas and are not properly acknowledging it
- *using ideas* taken from someone else without reference to the originator
- *cutting and pasting* from the internet to make a 'pastiche' of online sources
- *colluding* with another person, including another candidate (other than as might be permitted for joint project work)
- submitting as part of your own report or dissertation *someone else's work* without identifying clearly who did the work (for example, where research has been contributed by others to a joint project) or submitting work that has been undertaken in whole or in part by someone else on your behalf (such as employing a 'ghost writing service')
- submitting work you have submitted for a qualification *at another institution* without declaring it and clearly indicating the extent of overlap
- *deliberately reproducing someone else's work in a written examination.*

Plagiarism can occur in respect to *all types of sources and all media*:

- not just text, but also illustrations, musical quotations, computer code etc.
- not just text published in books and journals, but also downloaded from websites or drawn from other media
- not just published material but also unpublished works, including lecture handouts and the work of other students.

The most difficult point in the list above is the idea that even if you change someone else's words this would still be regarded as plagiarism if you did not accurately *cite* their work and provide an appropriate entry in a reference list.[35]

THE EDUCATION AND INSPECTIONS ACT 2006

The Education and Inspections Act 2006 was a significant addition to educational law. The act addresses eight key areas: trust schools; local authorities; fair access; behaviour; 14–19-year-olds; school food; Young people; and inspectorate reform. From the point of view of the trainee teacher the reforms on behaviour, 14–19-year-olds and school food are the most immediately relevant and are the ones we discuss here (the government has produced a helpful guide to the law available from teachernet.gov.uk which informs this section).

There had been a growing feeling by many in education that it was difficult for teachers to discipline students for poor behaviour, epitomised in the 'you can't tell me what to do' attitude by some pupils (although the power that teachers and schools have over pupils is often interpreted rather differently by those who advocate children's rights). Sections 90 and 91 of the Act provided new powers for teachers (and others in lawful charge of pupils) to discipline pupils for inappropriate behaviour. The Act also extends contracts for parents to encourage them to take more responsibility for their children's behaviour.

The Act also paved the way for further reforms of the curriculum and qualifications, for example the changes to the National Curriculum at Key Stage 3 (see Chapter 3). One of the key changes was the introduction of the 14 new specialised diplomas which will be available to every 14–19-year old in the country. Given the range of these diplomas it is not expected that every school delivers all of them. In many cases this will require schools and colleges to collaborate in order to ensure a range of provision. The Act requires local authorities to ensure that the schools and colleges in the area offer the full range of diplomas.

The issue of school food was brought to high-profile media attention by the celebrity chef Jamie Oliver. Memorable images from the time included Jamie dissecting turkey twisslers to reveal a grey gloop, and some parents passing burgers and chips to their children through the railings of schools who had changed their menus to more healthy ones. The Act allows for nutritional standards to be applied to all food and drink supplied on school premises. This may not seem to be quite as important as some of the other areas addressed in the Act but society has become increasingly concerned about obesity and children's health. For the first time the statistics for life expectancy have been decreasing for some groups as a result of poor diet. This is why this aspect of the Act, and the associated moves to ensure that pupils learn about cooking, are so important.

TEACHERS' PROFESSIONAL RESPONSIBILITIES

The Education Act 2002 provides a legal basis for important aspects of teachers' work. The Act implemented proposals from a government white paper and five related consultation papers published in 2001. One interesting part of the Act is the power it gives to the Secretary of State for Education to suspend legal requirements over the curriculum through the 'power to facilitate innovation' if, in the opinion of the Secretary of State, the innovation will contribute to the raising of educational standards. But perhaps the most important part of the Act is its role in determining teachers' pay and conditions. The Act requires that, each year, an Education (School Teachers Pay and Conditions) Order is made. This requires the School Teachers Review Body to meet and prepare a report (which informs the School Teachers Pay and Conditions Document and guidance for the year in question).

In 2008 the detail of teachers' professional responsibilities was a subject of considerable debate by the School Teachers Review Body. They proposed a draft 'new statement of responsibilities', which was succinct and meaningful:

TEACHERS' PROFESSIONAL RESPONSIBILITIES

Teachers are responsible and accountable for helping children and young people to achieve their full potential, by providing education of a world class, continually-improving standard and contributing to the delivery of excellent services for children and young people.

As professionals, teachers act in accordance with the values, code of practice and standards of their profession; and fulfil the requirements of their employer and the law.

This is achieved through teachers' excellence in:

- teaching, learning and assessment
- leadership
- management
- support for the achievement and well-being of children and young people as diverse individuals
- relationships with children and young people, families and local communities
- team-working and collaboration with colleagues in the school or service and wider services for children and young people
- continuing professional development, and
- support for colleagues' development.

The roles and responsibilities of individual teachers and the outcomes for which they are accountable are agreed locally and reflected in job descriptions and performance objectives.[36]

One area in this statement that we might wish to challenge is the rationale and place of 'world class' in such a document, the mantra that has purveyed the government's approach since 1997. However, the review body did outline some important principles underpinning the statement. Most important of these was that:

The statement is short and high-level. It reflects teachers' important role in improving the all-round achievement and well-being of children and young people. It does not prescribe: as professionals, teachers themselves are best able to determine what they need to do to achieve good outcomes and they will also be guided by a shared professional commitment to their pupils, their institutions and the wider community.[37]

The Review Body went even further than this, confirming what many have been saying about government reforms for a long time:

The current fragmented plethora of regulation is confusing for teachers and governors, makes it difficult to get a full picture of the legal framework, creates risks of duplication, and presents barriers to distributed leadership. Regulations in the education field affecting schools and services should be clear, mutually consistent and non-duplicatory.

This plethora of regulation includes the curriculum, standards and discipline. Let us hope that government clearly heeds these messages.

The complexity of the legal requirements for education is further seen in one final example of an addition to the legislation: the Childcare Act 2006. In general, this Act was designed to enhance the well-being of children. With regard to education specifically, it is the legal basis for the change to early years education that made the Early Years Foundation Stage statutory for the first time in England's history. This means that education from birth to 18 is now controlled by government. The move to consider education less as a discrete part of children's lives and more as part of a holistic picture of children and the services that they receive has been a slow one but, increasingly, one that is being reflected in policy. *Every Child Matters* and the Children's Plan initiatives are two examples of outcomes of such legislation.

IMPLICATIONS FOR STUDENT TEACHERS

In preparing for teaching practice students will need to discuss the following questions with their host schools:

●   What are the school policies, procedures, requirements and practices in terms of:
- planning and preparing courses and lessons
- special needs and equal opportunities
- setting and marking work (including homework)
- assessing, recording and reporting on the attainment, development and progress of pupils
- providing guidance and advice to pupils on social, educational and career-related matters (where relevant)
- communicating and consulting with parents and outside bodies
- reviewing their own teaching
- maintaining good order and discipline, and what sanctions rewards are in place to reinforce discipline
- policies on detention, confiscation, uniform and parental notification
- safeguarding health and safety (on and off school premises, the latter if an educational activity is taking place)
- attending staff meetings
- preparing students for public examinations
- being involved in management activities and required administration; registration and supervision of pupils
- attending assemblies?

●   Who is the Health and Safety officer in the school?
●   What Health and Safety documents does the student teacher need to have?
●   What information does the Health and Safety officer need to have from the student teacher?
●   What are the school policies, procedures, requirements and practices in terms of:
- Health and Safety matters, school visits, risk assessment and formal reporting
- accidents, emergencies, administering first aid and medication
- supervision at the start and end of the lesson, session, day
- discipline, bullying and assault
- child protection
- suspected child abuse
- data protection
- copyright?

- What are the school policies, procedures, requirements and practices in terms of educational visits, and their related issues of adult/student ratios?
- What insurance cover does the school have for student teachers? (It is highly likely that the school will have such insurance.)

Many schools will have an 'induction pack' for new teachers and student teachers, in which such details are contained. If this is not available then student teachers are very strongly advised to ask specifically about these matters.

PART II

PREPARATION AND PLANNING

Within the contexts of education identified in Part I, student teachers are faced with a battery of tasks upon their immediate arrival in schools for their teaching practices. They quickly have to assimilate a range of issues in their planning for teaching and learning, and to ensure that their planning accords with the existing practices in the school. They will have demands placed upon them by the school, by their tutor, by their mentor and by the students. Careful attention to planning is informed by the rapid gathering of information about the school and the students.

The first visits to a school and the first meetings with classes can be nerve-wracking; this part is designed to reduce some of that anxiety by providing detailed support on planning for teaching, gathering information from and about the school and the students, and how to develop teaching and learning plans that work. It suggests what kind of information is useful to collect on initial visits to school.

Much has been made of objectives in educational literature and the prescriptions for the National Curriculum, planning for teaching and learning, and school inspections are couched in variants of objectives models. These include, for example: attainment targets, target setting, intended learning outcomes and desirable learning outcomes. The objectives model is a useful starting point for student teachers' curriculum planning as it provides a sense of direction to the planning for teaching and learning. We utilise the objectives model in this part and indicate how it can be used to promote effective teaching and learning. Student teachers are usually required to prepare detailed teaching and learning plans, yet they are unfamiliar with how to do this. Part II provides a careful, staged guide to this process, from the most general and long-term to the most specific and short-term levels, and for all age groups. It provides copious examples of planning documents.

Further, student teachers are typically required to evaluate the planning and implementation of their teaching and the students' learning, and Part II provides extensive examples of how this can be approached.

6 The Preliminary Visit

INTRODUCTION

Student teachers are normally given the opportunity to visit their schools before the period of teaching practice formally begins. This may take the form of an observation week or a system of school attachments in the period leading up to the block practice.

The preliminary visit enables the student teacher to meet the head teacher, the mentor or teacher in charge of students (where such an office exists), and the rest of the staff; to become acquainted with her class or subject teacher; to see the students she will be teaching; to get to know the nature, layout and resources of the school; and to gather specific information relevant to the work she will undertake during the practice. The following points will be of interest to student teachers offered such facilities.

BEFORE THE VISIT

It is ridiculous to expect to go into a school and simply absorb everything that you need to know reactively. Student teachers must be proactive in their planning for the preliminary visits, so that they go into the school with an agenda for information. This entails considerations of exactly what they need to know about the school, what they need to gather and collect from the school, whom they need to meet (e.g. the head teacher, the mentor, the class teacher(s), the subject teachers, the curriculum co-ordinators, the students), what they need to find out about the students, curriculum, assessment, special needs and so on – the list is exhaustive, and it is the intention of this chapter to set that agenda.

An initial familiarisation exercise might be to have sight of the school prospectus before you go into the school (maybe your HE institution has a copy, or you can approach the school in question about this). Further, many schools have their own websites, and these are very valuable introductions to the school, as, typically, they present a considerable amount of both general and detailed information about many aspects of the school. Student teachers are strongly advised to find out if the school has a website and to conduct a search of that website before the first visit.

Schools are subject to inspection, and it would be useful, again as a familiarisation exercise, to have looked at the school inspection report. These are freely available on the internet (http://www.ofsted.gov.uk/reports) and they provide an initial introduction to the school's performance. Further, you may find it helpful to look at the school's position in the national league tables of school performance (www.dfes.gov.uk/statistics). Although this latter is, at best, only an indicator of one aspect of the school, and arguably does not present a fair picture of the school, nevertheless, as an initial sensitiser to the school it may be useful.

The issue here is that you do not go into the school 'cold'; rather, you go in with an initial briefing about the school and an initial agenda. You must show that you have 'done your homework' about the school. That makes your visit(s) more efficient, as well as presenting a positive initial image of yourself in the school.

WHAT TO LOOK FOR AND WHAT INFORMATION TO COLLECT

It follows from what we said in the preceding paragraph that to make the most of the preliminary visit, the student teacher must systematically take note of and, where she feels it helpful, record those aspects of the school's organisation, policy and methods in so far as they will relate to her own work in the school.[1] To help her in these respects, we offer the following guidelines which arise from: the physical features, the school in general, its philosophy, grouping of students, schools' expectations of student teachers, policies and other relevant documentation (e.g. the school prospectus), significant people and organisational matters, the classroom, control and discipline, rules, routines and protocols (e.g. for involving others), resources, record keeping, timetabling, curriculum organisation and planning, teaching and learning styles used, other adults involved (e.g. support assistants) and particular information to record (e.g. resources, schemes of work, details of students, timetable, curriculum planning, use of the photocopier, accessing resources – including computers, television and video). We stress that some of the points raised, e.g. in the physical features, may be more pertinent to the work of the primary teacher than the secondary specialist.

The physical features

We suggest you begin by investigating features and resources of the neighbourhood in which the school is situated. Some of these may prove to be relevant to the lessons you will be teaching and organising, e.g. the social nature of the area – is it urban, suburban or rural, for instance? You could then build up a basic topography of the locality to include the pattern of the main roads; churches and other buildings of significance; places of historical, geographical or social interest; recent developments; means of transport; details of houses, shops, businesses and industries; parks and beauty spots; museums; canals, rivers and bridges; docks; reservoirs; and markets. If there is a library nearby, the librarian may be able to supply information on local history, or even arrange a special display for your class.

The layout of the school should next engage your attention. Observe the general architectural style. Is the school's design conventional or open plan, for example? Approximately how old is the building? When might it have been built – in the late Victorian period or between the wars, for instance? Has the school an annex or other buildings on another site? The latter is quite common where previously separate schools have merged as a result of reorganisation. Find out where the head teacher's room, the staffroom, the general office and assembly hall are to be found (if these are not immediately apparent). Are any rooms used for specialisation? Where are these located? How is their use timetabled? Is there an audio-visual centre? Or a resources centre? How are the rooms numbered? If the school is a single-storey construction and extensive in its layout, you may find it useful initially to draw a rough plan of the building.

The school in general

Find out how many pupils there are in the school, the size of its annual intake and the approximate location of its catchment area or areas. The school's recent history may prove interesting, especially if it includes reorganisation or inspection.

The school's ethos has an important bearing on the work of both teachers and students. Check nerve points in the school's life to ascertain what the prevailing atmosphere is like in this respect, e.g. the staffroom, or morning assembly, for instance. Make provisional assessments of the quality of the relationships between the head and the staff, between staff and students, and among the staff themselves. If the school has a healthy atmosphere, you should have little difficulty fitting in and helping to maintain it. Where the atmosphere is less than wholesome, however, then you must decide what personal and professional qualities you can display that will improve it.

The prevailing system of control and discipline operating in the school is of very great importance and you should find out how it works. What are the school rules, for example? Are there dos or don'ts? Who decides the rules? How explicit are they? Do all members of staff enforce them? What rewards and punishments are used? Who determines them? How effective are they? Which rules are broken? And how often? How are the more extreme forms of misbehaviour like classroom violence handled? Alternatively, how do individual teachers cope where there is no such clearly defined framework of rules? Or where an ineffectual one exists? Or where chaos reigns? Which teachers appear to be most effective in such circumstances? And why? How will you relate to one or other of these situations when you have to work in the school?

It can also be of value to find out what the school's philosophy of education is. It may be voiced explicitly in the school's prospectus, mission statement and website, or it may not be voiced explicitly, and there may even be a clash of philosophies in some schools. However, one can get some idea of the way in which teachers think in these respects by studying the organisation of the school and the lessons. Some schools, for example, foster and encourage competition; others, co-operative behaviour. Some enforce a school uniform, others do not. Some are restrictive and authoritarian; others, by contrast, encourage autonomy and freedom of expression. Teaching methods are another obvious indication of a school's philosophy or philosophies. An important question arises for the student teacher in this connection: given an established system of teaching in the school, how does he or she fit in? The answer is that whereas the student teacher will generally adopt whatever method or methods are already in use, especially if they are well tried and effective, there is no reason why he or she should not introduce alternative ones. One could, for instance, employ group methods with a class that had only experienced the traditional or teacher-centred approach. As a matter of courtesy, however, the class teacher should be consulted before introducing such a change, not the least reason being that rearrangements of the room may be required.

It is particularly important to discover what forms of grouping are employed in the school, e.g. setting (and, if so, for what subjects), age groupings, ability groupings, team-teaching and so on. Likewise, where integrated days and integrated curricula operate, how are they organised? A student teacher placed in a school where one or more of these approaches are used should make a special effort to find out how work and routines are organised.

It can also be helpful to get to know something of the school's expectations of him and her with respect to time of arrival, attendance at morning assembly, involvement with extracurricular activities, free periods, leaving the school premises, dress, general appearance, preparation of lessons and behaviour *vis-à-vis* the rest of the staff. Box 21 provides a list of basic points one should try to keep in mind on teaching practice.

Box 21: Professional courtesy on teaching practice

- If you are absent, let the school know promptly.
- On return from an absence, let the head teacher know you're back. Do not let him/her find out from hearsay.
- Lateness calls at least for an apology and possibly an explanation.
- Be respectful to senior colleagues, e.g. concerning chairs in the staffroom.
- Be prompt, tidy and accurate in whatever administrative work you have to do, e.g. registers.
- Maintain adequate standards of dress and appearance.
- Leave a classroom tidy and the whiteboard clean at the end of a lesson.

There will be a number of significant people in the school whom you should at least meet and, better still, become acquainted with. These will include the head teacher and deputy head-teacher(s), the teacher in charge of the pastoral and counselling aspects of the students, subject co-ordinators, heads of year, your school mentor and the class teacher(s) with whom you will be working. If you are in a secondary school where students will be involved in vocational preparation and work experience, it will be important to meet the co-ordinator for this. It can also be useful to introduce yourself to the school secretary, technicians or laboratory assistants (where relevant), and the caretaker.

Finally, if the school has its own librarian or resources organiser, find out what the procedures are for borrowing books for yourself, and for utilising the library's resources with the children you will be teaching, for example in topic or project work. You can save yourself a lot of time and trouble by preliminary enquiries of this kind before your block practice begins.

The classroom

We have already stressed the importance of finding out what systems of control and discipline operate in the school. It is even more important to ascertain what management and control systems are used in the class(es) you yourself will be teaching. Where the class is taught chiefly by one teacher, make a note of established rules and routines, especially those relating to day-to-day matters such as speaking to the teacher, moving about the room, asking and answering questions, talking, finishing early and so on. (To help you make a start in these respects, we have listed guidelines in Box 22).[2]

UNDERSTANDING RULES, PROTOCOLS, PROCEDURES AND ROUTINES

We cannot overstate the importance of the student teacher understanding the 'hidden curriculum'. The hidden curriculum 'oils the wheels' for the smooth running of the school and of the classes of students within it. In coining this term Jackson[3] suggested that a key factor of students' success in school was their ability not only to learn, but to work within, the hidden curriculum of the school.[4] Indeed he argued that survival and success in school was a function of students' achievements in the hidden rather than the formal curriculum. Exactly the same is true for the student teacher. Jackson argues that students in school have to learn very quickly to live with rules, routines, crowds, praise, power, denial and delay. So, too, do student teachers. The student teacher's success depends in part on her ability to understand and work within the hidden curriculum of the school.

THE PRELIMINARY VISIT

Box 22: Classroom routines

The following checklist was designed by Haysom and Sutton for use in science lessons. Selecting whatever items you feel relevant, use them in one of your observation lessons to discover the rules and routines governing the classroom behaviour of the pupils.

Is it the standard practice for pupils to:

- stand up at the beginning of a lesson?
- choose where they sit?
- go to allotted spaces?
- work in self-selected groups?
- help each other in their work?
- expect not to consult each other?
- put hands up before speaking to the teacher?
- speak directly to the teacher, butting in at any time?
- be silent when the teacher begins to speak?
- carry on with what they're doing when the teacher speaks?
- leave the room on own initiative?
- move about freely during lessons?
- compose their own notes?
- copy notes from the board?
- be expected to have with them pencils, rulers, rubbers etc.?
- be allowed to borrow these items?
- be allowed, if they finish early, to get on with homework?

You may feel it necessary to extend this list to accommodate rules and routines making up the standard practice in the particular situation you find yourself in.

Some of the elements of the hidden curriculum are enshrined in the formal administrative and managerial aspects of the school at a whole-school level. Schools have formal, sometimes statutory protocols, e.g. for registering authorised and unauthorised absence, for reporting and handling suspected cases of child abuse, for handling aggressive parents, for security within the school, for arranging educational visits. Schools will also have protocols for handling students who arrive late for lessons, students who seek permission to be out of school, movement around the school, arrangements for break times and lunch times, use of the school library, access to computers, incidence of illness during school time, disciplinary matters, wearing uniform and jewellery, completing homework, failure to bring the correct equipment for lessons, matters of confidentiality, pastoral and tutorial responsibilities, meeting parents, handling complaints, ordering and collecting stock from central resource areas, use of the telephones, dealing with and reporting accidents (i.e. Health and Safety matters). The student teacher will need to find out about the formal arrangements that the school has for all of these matters so that she knows exactly what to do and whom to contact in particular circumstances. Some of these matters are contained in school prospectuses; others are contained in 'information for staff' booklets; others might be found out in conversation with the mentor and other teachers.

Not only are there rules and routines at a whole-school level; at a classroom level the student teacher will need to ascertain very quickly – from observation and discussion with relevant parties (e.g. the teachers with whom she will be working) – the rules and routines that individual teachers adopt with different classes. Knowledge and practice of these provides security for students and for student teachers alike. Within each class there will be several strategies that teachers routinely use to ensure that learning is productive, efficient and effective and that behaviour is acceptable. These routines and rules operate at every stage of the lesson. Examples of the practical matters that the student teacher will need to find out about are set out as follows.[5]

RULES AND ROUTINES AT DIFFERENT POINTS DURING THE LESSON

At the beginning of the lesson

- how the students enter the classroom and where they sit
- whether the teacher enters the classroom before the students or vice versa
- where the teacher is as the start of the lesson
- whether any initial registration is taken
- whether the students enter the room in silence or whether they are permitted to speak
- whether the students are permitted to bring in bags, outdoor wear and where they are supposed to place them
- how the teacher gains and maintains the students' attention and interest
- how long the lesson takes to start
- what the teacher does when students arrive without appropriate materials (e.g. books, pens, paper, sports equipment)
- how homework is collected/returned/commented upon/followed up
- how the objectives/intended learning outcomes and contents of the lesson are introduced
- how the teacher settles the class
- how a clear start to the lesson is signalled
- how reference is made to the previous work/ lesson and how the present lesson will build on this
- how initial resources are distributed.

The transition from the introduction to the lesson

- how the teacher prepares the students for the transition
- how the teacher manages the transition from the introduction to the subsequent activities of the students
- what the teacher does, says, where she stands, where she goes, how she uses her voice and non-verbal behaviour immediately prior to the transition, during the transition, immediately after the transition
- how the teacher monitors the transition and settles the students after the transition
- how the teacher introduces individual, collaborative and group work
- how the teacher explains the purpose of post-transition activity/work
- how clearly the teacher explains what is expected to happen straight after the transition
- what the teacher says and does to make sure that all the students know what they have to do and what they must not do during and immediately after the transition
- how the teacher manages the use of resources immediately after the transition (e.g. access, uptake, organisation)
- how long the transition is expected to take and how the students are made aware of this (e.g. 'you have three minutes to . . .').

During the lesson

- how, whether, and in what numbers the students are able to move around the classroom
- where the teacher is at different points of the lesson
- how the teacher ensures that she can see all the students all the time
- how the teacher and students access, use and replace resources
- how students may ask for the teacher's attention
- in what kinds of activity collaborative work is used
- how ICT is accessed and used in the classroom
- when, where and how much talk is acceptable to the teacher
- how the teacher gains and maintains silence and 'on-task' behaviour
- how the teacher divides her attention amongst the class
- how the teacher sustains the students' interest, motivation and self-esteem
- what verbal and non-verbal means the teacher uses to gain and maintain the smooth running of the lesson
- how the teacher handles difficult situations and students
- how the teacher gives praise/rewards/sanctions/ punishments – and for what
- how the teacher uses her/his own questioning (e.g. low to higher-order, closed to open, handling incorrect or incomplete responses, giving 'thinking time' for students to reply, prompting and probing students)
- how the teacher handles difficult questions or questions that she cannot answer
- how the teacher deals with unacceptable behaviour (to her and to other students)
- what happens if equipment is deliberately or accidentally damaged
- what happens if a student feels unwell
- how the teacher copes with students who work more slowly/more quickly than others (i.e. what the teacher does with students who do not complete work in the lesson and with students who complete work before the lesson time has elapsed)
- how the work is differentiated for individual needs
- what teaching and learning styles are being used
- what happens if a lesson is not going well
- how the teacher works with students with special needs and learning difficulties
- how the teacher works with other adults in the classroom
- how the teacher balances her instructional, procedural and managerial talk
- how the teacher circulates round the class and monitors everything that is happening
- how the teacher keeps up with marking during the lesson
- how the teacher responds to different requests and to different students (verbally and non-verbally)
- how the teacher assesses students.

Towards the end of the lesson

- how the teacher draws the lesson to a conclusion in practical management terms – what she does, what she says
- how students are made aware of how much time they have left to complete the work of the lesson
- what happens with students who finish the work before the end of the lesson or who do not finish the required work by the end of the lesson
- how plenary and feedback sessions are managed

● how students clear away and return apparatus and materials
● how the work is gathered together for the teacher – who does it, where it is put
● how students are to be seated at the end of the lesson
● how the teacher draws together – summarises – the cognitive aspects of the lesson
● how homework is set
● how the teacher dismisses the class.

More specifically the student teacher may find it useful to focus on a specific feature during a lesson that she observes. In this instance she will need to plan in advance what she will be looking for – maybe by posing a series of questions. For example, let us imagine that she wishes to see what strategies the class teacher uses to motivate students during a lesson. The questions that the student teacher might wish to ask are contained in Box 23.

A focused observation of one or more aspects of a lesson enables the student teacher to find out how the smooth running of the lesson and working with the class is managed. This requires the student teacher to attend to the rules and routines in the lesson. It is often the case that student teachers are not in the school or with a group of students for a long enough period of time to enable them to stamp their own way of working on the students. Student teachers inherit from, and hand back to the teacher a set of rules, routines, ways of working. Indeed a student teacher would be ill-advised to try to overturn an established way of working with a class for the comparatively short duration of a teaching practice. Hence in most cases the student teacher will have to find out about, understand, and operate within a given set of procedures – cognitive, behavioural, interpersonal – rather than attempting to replace an inherited system. This is not to deny the need for student teachers to try new ways of teaching and to experiment to some extent; it is to suggest that if the student teacher wishes to try something different she discusses it first with the class teacher.

Box 23: Motivation questions for use in an observation lesson

● What techniques and approaches, if any, did the teacher use at the outset of the lesson to engage the class's interest?
● How did he sustain the interest, once aroused?
● How did she deal with the problem of flagging motivation?
● In what ways did the teacher capitalise on the children's own interests?
● Could any parts of the lesson be explained in terms of the concepts of intrinsic and extrinsic motivation? Did the teacher, for example, arouse the students' curiosity, challenge them or offer them some form of reward?
● What part did feedback play in the lesson? How was it conveyed? And what was its effect on the class?
● Could you establish any relationship between motivation and (a) social class; (b) ability; (c) age; (d) sex; or (e) aspects of the subject being taught or investigated?
● What effect did the personality of the teacher appear to have on the overall success (or failure) of the lesson?
● Were threats used as a means of motivating the students?
● Examine the relationship between motivation and the instructional approach or approaches used by the teacher, e.g. formal class teaching; discussion; group work; guided instruction etc.
● How would you describe (a) the teacher's attitudes towards his class, and (b) his expectations of their performance? Could either of these be seen to affect his class's motivation?
● Which forms of motivation did the class appear to respond to best?

Observe what sanctions the teacher employs with her class in order to enforce the rules. Are individuals kept in after school, for instance, or are they asked to stay behind at the end of a lesson, or reprimanded in front of the other children? Does isolation of disruptive students figure in a teacher's tactics? What happens if a student swears at a teacher? What happens if students refuse to work? What happens if a student bullies another, or bullies the teacher? For what actions are immediate removal from the classroom a rule of the school? For what kinds of offences are detentions used? Are there established rules for handling very difficult children (e.g. calling for assistance from a colleague)?

On a more positive note, find out what kinds of motivators and rewards the teacher uses. If the class is taught by other teachers, you can subsequently compare the different methods of control used and check how the class responds to them. The advantages of ascertaining prior knowledge on these matters is that you will then be able to relate your own control systems to the existing framework where this proves to be effective.

The reality of classroom life, unfortunately, is often very different from what one would like to see. Control systems may be either ineffective or non-existent. Where such is the case, you will have to decide what you can do to achieve some measure of control over the class when you eventually take over. In this connection, we recommend you read Chapter 15.

Successful class teachers' methods of organisation will have evolved in the light of their experience and knowledge of the particular students they teach. The student teacher does not have this experience or knowledge, nor obviously the time to acquire them, so it is advisable that he perpetuates effective routines established by the class teacher throughout the period of his practice (e.g. what is the established procedure for tidying up at the end of an art lesson? Or what is a child expected to do when he finishes his allotted task five minutes before the rest of the class?) Studying the classroom routines of an experienced and successful teacher requires close observation because the most effective methods are often the least obvious.

What should student teachers do, however, when they find themselves working with a disorganised teacher who has no routines? Having made a quick assessment of the position, they must then decide what they can do to improve the situation even though the extent of their influence is limited (they are, after all, in a position of dependence in a host school, and perhaps only teaching two or three lessons each day). Between the preliminary visit and the block practice, they should decide on a few basic classroom rules and routines that would impose some structure on the situation so that when they meet the class they can spend some time discussing them with the students to find out where they stand with them. They can thus improve the original situation at worst marginally and at best significantly.

PARTICULAR INFORMATION TO RECORD

You will need to bring back a certain amount of information from your preliminary visit, chiefly for your own use. Thus it is important to find out details of the resources and equipment available in the school – the size and range of the library, the ICT hardware, software, intranet and internet facilities, the audio-visual equipment you may use, apparatus you may require, facilities for word processing and duplicating, resources for individual and group work (topics and projects, for example). Check that the school has the resources, equipment and materials that you will require. Teachers of practical subjects like PE or specialist subjects like art or music need to be particularly alert in this respect. A PE teacher, for instance, may want to know how many badminton rackets are available; an art specialist, whether there's a sink in the room she will be using; and a music teacher, the extent of facilities for creative music making. Teachers of science subjects, too, will need to anticipate equipment they will need for practical work, particularly whether there is sufficient equipment for class practicals. Find out about Health and Safety matters and procedures.

You will need to gather details of the schemes of work you will be required to teach, together with any explanatory or ancillary information your class teacher may provide. You will need to find out what pro-formas you will be required to use and complete for planning and other aspects of the school's life, and how ICT is used in planning. You will need to find out when planning takes place, with which teams and groups, and what are the long-term, medium-term and short-term planning formats and contents in the school, so that you can fit into the school's requirements here. These aspects are examined in more detail in Chapter 8.

Coupled with details of schemes of work is the need for information on the students you will be working with, together with some indication of their previous experience and learning in the subject areas you will be teaching. This kind of information is crucial, as you need to know where to begin your work. The obvious source of information of this nature is the class teacher or subject teacher. If he or she keeps records on each student, ask if you may have a look at them.

You may find that you are involved in teaching courses leading to state or external examinations such as GCSE, GCE Advanced Level, the Scottish Certificate of Education, or additional arrangements. If you are, and are unfamiliar with the nature of these systems, find an introductory guidebook relevant to your needs. This may particularly be the case with the GCSE. One important factor in examinations and courses leading to these examinations is the inclusion of compulsory coursework for examination and this you may very well be involved with if you are a secondary specialist.

Though student teachers may not be involved in public examinations, nevertheless most likely they will be involved in formal and informal assessment requirements, for the National Curriculum and for the ongoing, formal and informal reporting of students' progress to parents and documentation of progress within the school. Student teachers will need to become conversant with the procedures required here, and they should expect to have to work within them.

The preliminary visit also gives you the opportunity to ascertain details of text books, worksheets, ICT usage and other materials used by the class. Where you feel it necessary, borrow copies or examples of the ones you will be using as they will help you when planning your lessons.

Details of topic work and related approaches, where relevant, should also be noted. These could include organisational procedures: individual or group work, for example; topics recently covered; the stage of development of the class or individuals in this kind of learning; and ways in which topics have been presented and evaluated in the past.

Specific information on the class(es) you will be teaching should include:

- the name of the class and, if relevant, the significance of the name
- the size of the class (the number of students makes a difference to the organisation and presentation of the various subject areas and curricular activities)
- the average age of the class, or its range if it is inter-age
- the band/set of the class, or range of ability
- the names of the students and a seating plan (the latter can be particularly useful in the early stages of the practice as an aid to getting to know a class)
- details of the classroom(s) in which you will be working; an annotated layout plan may be useful here
- details of groups (if appropriate) – their organisational basis
- details of students with special needs (again where relevant) – ones with emotional problems, communication difficulties, physical disabilities or home background problems, for instance
- details of particular problematic students, in terms of control and discipline, together with suggestions from the class teacher as to possible ways of handling them.

It is also important to find out as much as you can about curriculum planning in the school, routines, rules, specific students, discipline policies and strategies, classroom organisation, resources, teaching styles, topic work and subject-based work, schemes (e.g. for language, mathematics and other curriculum areas, matching and differentiated work, assessment), school policies, ICT and technology usage.

Additionally the student teacher may find it useful to ask questions to find out about:

- access to reprographic equipment
- use of ICT for planning and personal, as well as student, use
- timetabling of fixed times (e.g. use of the hall)
- what to do with latecomers
- rules for moving around the classroom/school
- arrangements for break times and lunch times (e.g. are the students allowed inside buildings, where are they allowed to go, where are they forbidden to go?)
- use of the school library
- what to do if someone is taken ill during school time
- the school's uniform policy
- what to do if students do not bring equipment (e.g. PE kit)
- arrangements for meeting parents
- ordering and collecting stock from centrally held resources
- use of the telephone
- reporting accidents
- insurance cover for personal accident, injury, damage or theft
- handling money (e.g. for school lunches, students' personal money for safe-keeping)
- use of support assistants and teaching assistants
- when parent helpers come in and what they do
- which teachers have responsibilities and what they are responsible for
- arrangements for planning times with other teachers (i.e. team meetings)
- whether students can take school property home (e.g. reading books)
- if the students go to another teacher, and if so, when, where, what for
- if students join other classes, if so, when, where, what for
- which work is done in books, jotters, loose-leaf sheets, saved in software or the intranet
- permission for going to the toilet
- how the day starts
- how the children change their reading books (for primary schools)
- the school's handwriting style(s)
- which children print and which children do 'joined up' writing (largely for primary schools)
- details of the students – names, ages, abilities, students with statements of special educational needs
- which students it is advisable to keep apart
- seating arrangements and layout of the classroom.

The timetable operating in the school should be noted. Finally, details of your own timetable should be recorded. These will include:

- lesson details – their times and duration
- class(es) and subjects or activities to be taught or organised
- indications of rooms and locations to be used (Room 3, Main Building; Room 23, Lower School; Room 7, Annex, for instance)

- details of other teachers' lessons you will be observing (where appropriate)
- non-contact periods
- extra-curricular activities (if relevant: Science Society after school Mondays; choir practice Thursday lunchtimes, for example)
- indications of when the school will be closed in the course of the practice period (local elections, half-term, special holidays)
- indications of when you will be prevented from teaching your normal timetable (because of school examinations, for example, or rehearsals for a school play)
- the name of the school, its address and its telephone number; the names of the head teacher, the teacher in charge of student teachers (if appropriate), your mentor and the class teacher(s), and appropriate contact details for these (e.g. telephone, e-mail).

The range of suggestions given above on what information to collect includes little reference to the kinds of problems and pitfalls you may encounter in seeking this information. We conclude this section, therefore, by highlighting some of them and indicating possible ways of dealing with them.

First, there is the problem of time. Some students spend as much as a whole week on their preliminary visit, but others are not so fortunate. If you are only in for one day, and time does therefore present a problem, decide on an order of priorities and begin by noting the most immediately important information that you need. The remainder can then be collected visit by visit, or during the first week of the practice itself. Even in the most favourable circumstances, it is going to take time to build up a total picture of the school, so do not expect to do it in half a day.

A second kind of problem may arise when you are confined to one or two rooms during your initial visit (if this only lasts one day) and cannot therefore move about the building. What you must do if you are in this position is to ask politely and tactfully if you may see other features of the school.

One final point: what do you do when essential information you need is just not forthcoming? Or when the source of it is unreliable? Or when it is misleading? You cannot complain to the head, or ask the students! The best course is to ask the teacher in charge of students or school mentor to help you, or possibly the tutor from the HE institution who will be supervising you during the practice.

It must be remembered that schools will have experienced inspection visits, and, as part of the inspection process, as part of statutory requirements, and as part of their best professional practice, they should have to hand a battery of policies, prospectuses, records of attendance, examination and assessment results, documents, planning schedules, protocols, schemes and review pro-formas covering all aspects of the school's life. It would be useful for student teachers to enquire about these, to have copies of significant and relevant documents and to ensure that they act within the requirements of these documents.

7 Aims, Objectives and Intended Learning Outcomes

INTRODUCTION

Aims, objectives and intended learning outcomes refer to expressions of educational intention and purpose, which may be expressed with varying degrees of generality and specificity. An aim is a general expression of intent, and the degree of generality contained in the statement may vary from the very general in the case of long-term aims to the much less general in the case of short-term aims. An objective or intended learning outcome, by contrast, is characterised by greater precision and specificity. Again, at one extreme will be objectives that are fairly specific, and at the other, objectives that are extremely so. An aim is, in principle, infinite (e.g. to become educated, a process which never stops), whereas an objective tends to be more finite (e.g. to understand why heat melts ice).

An objective is more like an achievable target than an unachievable goal. One can see the attraction of both aims and objectives to educationalists.

For the former, targets link into action planning for, and by, students in their own learning. For the latter it links into target setting at a systems level, to which we alluded in Part I, where explicit targets were set for school achievement, e.g. for secondary schools: in June 2008 the target was described as the National Challenge. This was a programme to secure higher standards in secondary schools so that by 2011, at least 30 per cent of pupils in every school will gain five or more GCSEs at A* to C grade including both English and mathematics.[1]

It is argued that setting targets is a useful strategy for accountability. For example, the Autumn Performance Report 2007, which evaluates government's achievement against public service agreement targets found the following:

Objective II: Raise standards and tackle the attainment gap in schools

6　Raise standards in English and mathematics so that:
- by 2006, 85 per cent of 11-year-olds achieve level 4 or above, with this level of performance sustained to 2008 (Element 1); and
- by 2008, the proportion of schools in which fewer than 65 per cent of pupils achieve level 4 or above is reduced by 40 per cent (Element 2).

Element 1: Not met
Element 2: Ahead[2]

The very existence of this kind of national target *per se* is the reason that target setting is such a dominant and distorting feature of the work of teachers and pupils in England.

Targets, like many objectives, are specific, finite, frequently measurable, often time-bound, and strive for realism. In short, targets, objectives and intended learning outcomes are SMART: Specific, Measurable, Achievable, Realistic and Time-bound. This can apply to governments, schools, individual teachers and learners, curricula and curriculum planning.

Long-term aims form the basis of a school's raison d'être, defining the nature and character of its overall educational programme in relation to societal and individual needs. Short-term aims will constitute the logical starting point for curricula construction and the devising of schemes of work. Objectives and intended learning outcomes expressing varying degrees of specificity will be derived from such aims, especially the short-term ones, and will represent their translation into specific and tangible terms necessary for planning a course of lessons, individual lessons or units of learning on which the ultimate realisation of the aims depends.

Aims constitute the basic elements in educational planning. Although existing at different levels of generality, collectively they make up the building blocks of the total programme. The most general aims, being broad and often abstract in their expression, will simply offer guidance as to the general direction of educational intention and will in no way indicate particular achievements within specified time limits (e.g. 'To prepare children to meet the challenges of a technological age'). Aims of this nature, frequently social in character, express basic concepts of the purpose of the school and its overall intended outcomes. In this sense aims are perhaps synonymous with values. For example the New Labour vision for education was one of inclusion:

> One nation, in which each citizen is valued and has a stake; in which no one is excluded from opportunity and the chance to develop their potential; in which we make it, once more, our national purpose to tackle social division and inequality.[3]

The following examples of aims and objectives will help the reader to see the distinction between them more clearly.

Aims

1   To enable pupils to develop an appreciation of art in the twentieth century.
2   To introduce the class to the concept of heat.
3   To educate the whole child.

Objectives

1   To introduce the class to the principal characteristics of the violin.
2   A review of the events leading up to the First World War.
3   To further the students' appreciation of Hardy's 'The Darkling Thrush'.

Designers of educational programmes cannot always be too legislative on the question of what constitutes an aim and what constitutes an objective. What a teacher plans to do with a given statement of intent is the ultimate determinant of its nature. Aim 2 above, for instance, 'To introduce the class to the concept of heat', could conceivably form the basis of a lesson of one hour, in which case it would be seen as an objective. Alternatively, objective 1 listed above, 'To introduce the class to the principal characteristics of the violin', could equally form the basis of four weekly lessons, in which case it would be more appropriately labelled an aim.

The National Curriculum sets out two main aims:[4]

1   The school curriculum should aim to provide opportunities for all pupils to learn and to achieve.
2   The school curriculum should aim to promote pupils' spiritual, moral, social and cultural development and to prepare all pupils for the opportunities, responsibilities and experiences of life.

It also sets out four main purposes:[5]

1   to establish entitlement
2   to establish standards
3   to promote continuity and coherence
4   to promote public understanding.

When the National Curriculum was first written, people rightly questioned what the values were that underpinned it. This resulted in a separate statement of values being added following an extensive consultation by the National Forum for Values in Education and the Community in May 1997. These values remained unchanged until the publication of the new secondary curriculum. The four areas of: the self; relationships; the diversity in our society; and the environment were simplified:

- **the self**, recognising that we are unique human beings capable of spiritual, moral, intellectual and physical growth and development
- **relationships** as fundamental to the development and fulfilment of ourselves and others, and to the good of the community. We value others for themselves, not only for what they have or what they can do for us
- **the diversity in our society**, where truth, freedom, justice, human rights, the rule of law and collective effort are valued for the common good. We value families, including families of different kinds, as sources of love and support for all their members, and as the basis of a society in which people care for others. We also value the contributions made to our society by a diverse range of people, cultures and heritages
- **the environment**, both natural and shaped by humanity, as the basis of life and a source of wonder and inspiration which needs to be protected.

However, in addition to the simplification, the following paragraphs were added (the first paragraph as a preamble to the values and the second paragraph as a conclusion):

Education should reflect the enduring values that contribute to personal development and equality of opportunity for all, a healthy and just democracy, a productive economy, and sustainable development. These include values relating to: ...

At the same time, education must enable us to respond positively to the opportunities and challenges of the rapidly changing world in which we live and work. In particular, we need to be prepared to engage as individuals, parents, workers and citizens with economic, social and cultural change, including the continued globalisation of the economy and society, with new work and leisure patterns and with the rapid expansion of communications technologies.

It is a moot point whether 'a productive economy' is appropriate, or can even be regarded as a value at all. Also we question whether 'we should be prepared to engage [with] the continued globalisation of the economy'. This should surely be a matter of personal choice and conviction; it is certainly not something that necessarily would command the support of the majority of people in society. What is particularly troubling about these kinds of additions is that they do not appear to have been through the same process of consultation that the original values had. They are also another indication of the way that government has tried to strengthen its control of the school curriculum.

The aims of the National Curriculum should of course be reflected at all levels of the curriculum including the programmes of study, which are the vehicle for delivering the aims. White[6] found that, broadly speaking, the best match between subjects and the National Curriculum aims was with newly introduced subjects such as design and technology, ICT, citizenship and PSHE. Longer-established subjects matched much less well with the aims of the National Curriculum.

The Foundation Stage doesn't have an explicit statement of values, although the Themes and Principles are similar:

The EYFS is based around four Themes:

- A Unique Child
- Positive Relationships
- Enabling Environments
- Learning and Development.

Each Theme is linked to an important Principle:

A Unique Child
- Every child is a competent learner from birth who can be resilient, capable, confident and self-assured.

Positive Relationships
- Children learn to be strong and independent from a base of loving and secure relationships with parents and/or a key person.

Enabling Environments
- The environment plays a key role in supporting and extending children's development and learning.

Learning and Development
- Children develop and learn in different ways and at different rates, and all areas of Learning and Development are equally important and interconnected.

The value that is missing from this list, when compared with the National Curriculum, is Society. This is particularly surprising in view of the explicit inclusion of points about families as part of this value statement.

At other levels, aims will express less generality. Such will form the basis of curricula (e.g. 'To achieve certain specified standards in the skills of reading and writing'). Unlike the more general aims noted above, they will suggest tangible achievements and imply rather more specified time limits. They are often statements of what can be expected to have been achieved at given stages over the formal educational period. There is a relationship between the degree of generality expressed in an aim and the time limit within which it can be expected to have been achieved. It may be expressed thus: the more general the aim, the more difficult to specify when it will be achieved, or, conversely, the less general the aim, the greater the likelihood of its being achieved within definable and predictable time limits. Thus, 'To prepare children to meet the challenges of a technological age' could only be achieved at some time in the relatively distant future; one could not be any more specific than that. The aim 'To be able to decode the words and comprehend the meaning of age appropriate texts', however, could, conceivably, be achieved by, at the latest, the age of 6.

This relationship has very real and practical implications for the student teacher on teaching practice. Since she is only in school for a comparatively short time (four, six, eight or ten weeks, depending on the college or university and the particular school placement), the aims that will form the basis of her schemes of work may be even less general than some of the aims referred to above.

The relevance of aims for the student teacher is that they make up one of the major sources from which lesson objectives are derived; and it is essential to understand the relationship between aims and objectives, and between schemes of work and the individual lessons to be taught.

In conclusion, you may find the following checklist useful when formulating aims for schemes of work:

- Does the aim express the appropriate level of generality?
- Is it expressed simply, clearly and economically?
- Does its content relate to the ability and previous experience of the class?
- Can appropriate lesson objectives and intended learning outcomes be derived naturally from it?
- Is it attainable in relation to the facilities and time available?

TWO KINDS OF OBJECTIVES AND INTENDED LEARNING OUTCOMES: (1) BEHAVIOURAL AND (2) NON-BEHAVIOURAL

Objectives and intended learning outcomes are formulations of educational intent that are much more specific and precise than aims. While the latter serve to indicate the overall direction and purpose of educational activities they are, by comparison with objectives and intended learning outcomes, general, imprecise and lacking in specificity. They are thus of little immediate value to the teacher in planning a particular lesson or unit of learning in that they cannot inform his decisions on precise content, teaching strategy and evaluation. To meet these needs, the teacher must utilise objectives and intended learning outcomes for individual lessons. Desirable learning outcomes are differentiated from intended learning outcomes by their degree of requirement. Intended learning outcomes are seen as a minimum necessary requirement; desirable learning outcomes are seen, perhaps, as a maximum possible, or a bonus to the minimum requirement, and they do not have such a degree of obligation as intended learning outcomes; indeed intended learning outcomes may be statutory whilst desirable learning outcomes are not. Intended learning outcomes, like objectives, must be developmental and sequential to ensure continuity and progression as topics/themes are revisited throughout the Key Stages.

An example of an intended learning outcome might be, for example in a Key Stage 3 geography unit of work: 'Students should learn to use maps to identify climatic patterns in western Europe', or 'Students should learn to interpret weather maps and compare their information with that shown on satellite images.' The schemes of work from the Department for Education and Skills (www.standards.dfes.gov.uk/schemes2) include the intended learning outcomes for all of the elements of the National Curriculum.

A desirable learning outcome may be: 'Students should learn to take turns in a class discussion.' The intended learning outcome of the lesson may be that students are learning some of the causes of the outbreak of civil war in Ireland in the early part of the twentieth century. As a by-product of this they are also learning to share ideas and take turns, as the lesson is discussion-based. The by-product is the desirable learning outcome.

Box 24: An example of a non-behavioural and a behavioural lesson objective in poetry

Non-behavioural
To further the class's understanding of Hardy's 'The Darkling Thrush'.

Behavioural
At the end of a 45-minute lesson on Hardy's 'The Darkling Thrush' the class will be able to:

● detail the images which conjure up a landscape of winter and death
● compare the rhythms of the winter mood with those associated with the thrush
● explain the meanings in the context of, or give synonyms for: coppice, spectre, bine-stems, crypt, canopy, germ, fervourless, illimited, gaunt, carollings, terrestrial, air
● account briefly for the poem's date (December 1900)
● assess whether the poem is mainly pessimistic or optimistic in meaning
● describe their own emotional responses to the poem.

An example of objectives and intended learning outcomes is given in Box 24, together with their referent – Hardy's poem (Box 25).

Some objectives refer to overt, visible, potentially quantifiable student behaviours. These may be termed behavioural objectives, and they identify the learner's overt achievements. Other objectives refer to more intangible qualities, are more open-ended, and do not explicitly state the

Box 25: 'The Darkling Thrush'

The Darkling Thrush
by *Thomas Hardy*

I leant upon a coppice gate
    When frost was spectre-gray,
And Winter's dregs made desolate
    The weakening eye of day.
The tangled bine-stems scored the sky
    Like strings of broken lyres,
And all mankind that haunted nigh
    Has sought their household fires.

The land's sharp features seemed to be
    The Century's corpse outleant,
His crypt the cloudy canopy,
    The wind his death-lament.
The ancient pulse of germ and birth
    Was shrunken hard and dry,
And every spirit upon earth
    Seemed fervourless as I.

At once a voice arose among
    The bleak twigs overhead
In a full-hearted evensong
    Of joy illimited
An aged thrush, frail, gaunt, and small,
    In blast-beruffled plume,
Had chosen thus to fling his soul
    Upon the growing gloom.

So little cause for carollings
    Of such ecstatic sound
Was written on terrestrial things
    Afar or nigh around,
That I could think there trembled through
    His happy good-night air
Some blessed Hope, whereof he knew
    And I was unaware.

December 1900

behavioural outcomes. These may be referred to as non-behavioural objectives since they do not specify the precise terminal behaviour by means of which a teacher can assess whether his objectives have been achieved. They may indicate what the teacher plans to do ('To introduce the class to...'), or list the elements of content in some way or other ('A review of...'), or invoke patterns of behaviour in abstract terms ('Appreciation of...'). None of these manifestations can be perceived directly or measured, however.

Behavioural objectives, if used competently, are tools which can do much to improve teaching and learning. It is important to remember, however, that they are not in and of themselves better than non-behavioural ones. Each type has its place and contributes in its own way to the enhancement of learning. It would therefore be naïve and doctrinaire to claim that all objectives could be specified in precise behavioural terms. Some subject areas and certain kinds of learning – especially in the realms of attitudes, feelings and values – are not amenable to such specification and quantification; and 'open-endedness' is the *sine qua non* of teaching methods emphasising creativity and discovery. We recommend therefore that you give careful thought to which of your lessons should lead towards behavioural objectives/intended learning outcomes and which to non-behavioural objectives/intended learning outcomes. In order to help you with such decisions, a little more will now be said about behavioural and then non-behavioural objectives.

SOME CHARACTERISTICS OF BEHAVIOURAL OBJECTIVES

A behavioural objective indicates a desired state in the learner; what a student will be able to do after a prescribed lesson; a behaviour that can be perceived by the teacher's unaided senses. When the learner can demonstrate that she has arrived at this state, she will then be deemed to have achieved the objective (e.g. the student teacher will select five behavioural objectives from a list of 15 miscellaneous aims and objectives). Thus the behavioural objective describes the desired outcome of a lesson in such a way that most people can agree that the lesson has been a success or a failure.

Other terms used to describe behavioural objectives include measurable objectives, learner objectives, instructional objectives, performance goals, intended learning outcomes and terminal objectives. All these terms emphasise the importance of, first, writing objectives that describe what a student should be able to do after he completes a learning experience; and second, describing the behaviour in such a way that it can be observed and measured.

So far, so good. But what are the characteristics of meaningful behavioural objectives? And how does one write them so as to maximise the probability of achieving them?

The most important characteristic concerns the need to identify the terminal behaviour of the learner that the teacher desires. Thus a behavioural objective is useful to the extent that it indicates what the learner must be able to do, or say, or perform when he is demonstrating his mastery of the objective. It must describe observable behaviour from which the teacher can infer particular mental skills. This observable behaviour or performance may be verbal or nonverbal. Thus the learner may be asked to respond to questions orally or in writing, to demonstrate his ability to perform a certain skill or to solve a practical problem.

A second characteristic follows from the first and arises from the need for specificity and precision in phrasing the behavioural objective. There are many words which we use in everyday life that meet our need to communicate with others well enough. But for behavioural objectives they are often too general and vague. Consider the following two columns of words:

to know	to write
to understand	to explain
to be aware of	to demonstrate
to appreciate	to evaluate
to be familiar with	to list
to grasp	to construct

The words and phrases in the left-hand column are too vague and imprecise to be of use in the formulation of behavioural objectives. They are ambiguous and open to various interpretations (they are, of course, perfectly legitimate as aims and non-behavioural objectives, where their very ambiguity can be an advantage). The terms in the right-hand column, however, are more precise, open to fewer interpretations and indicate what the learner will be doing when demonstrating that he has acquired information or skills that will contribute to, or lead to, knowing, understanding, appreciating or grasping. Objectives using such words, then, will have been given behavioural specification. Thus if a student can list events in Europe leading up to the First World War and can evaluate their significance, his teacher can infer that he has some understanding of the subject.

A note of caution needs to be sounded here. It must not be assumed that understand and list are one and the same simply because one substitutes for the other. As Hirst[7] has pointed out, states of mind should never be confused with the evidence for them. That a child can list events in Europe leading up to the First World War merely indicates minimal student mastery of the facts which, together with the achievements of related objectives on other occasions, may lead to fuller understanding subsequently. The same caution applies to similar pairings.

As suggested in parenthesis above, the kinds of words listed in the left-hand column are perfectly acceptable in the wording of aims and non-behavioural objectives. The problem for the student teacher is one of knowing how to translate words and phrases of this kind into observable behaviours. Perhaps the best way is to take a simple example. It begins by stating an aim of moderate generality. From this is derived a non-behavioural objective in which the crucial phrase is to develop...awareness of. This is then translated into a behavioural objective, the phrase now being replaced by the word list (see diagram below).

The problem is thus one of replacing open-ended infinitives such as to appreciate, to understand, to develop an awareness of and so on, with appropriate 'hard and clear' action verbs such as to state, to write, to demonstrate, to identify, to distinguish, to construct, to select, to order, to make and to describe. Rowntree's[8] example illustrates the point: a student would be able to design an

---

Aim
To further the class's
understanding of the
significance of propaganda
in the twentieth century
↓

Non-behavioural objective		*Behavioural objective*
To develop the child's awareness of an author's bias in selected extracts	→	The child will list six sentences from a passage of propaganda that reveal bias and indicate which viewpoint the author holds

---

experiment, list the precautions to be taken, describe his results, evaluate conflicting interpretations, participate in out-of-class discussions, etc. Gerlach and Ely[9] consider that all 'action' infinitives of this kind have their roots in five basic types of behaviour, namely, identifying, naming, describing, ordering and constructing.

Two further characteristics of behavioural objectives may be mentioned; these sharpen the focus even further. The first concerns the conditions under which the mastery will be tested. These could include such factors as time limitations, evaluative procedures or situational factors (see below for examples). The second characteristic relates to the standards by which the objective is to be judged. These may include such conditions as the percentage of problems a child must answer correctly; the number of correct answers she must obtain; or the tolerance within which she must learn.

In summary, behavioural objectives should ideally contain the following four elements:

1   An indication of who is to perform the desired behaviour (the student, the learner, the class).
2   A precise and succinct statement of the specific terminal behaviour that the learner is to perform. This will indicate what he will actually do and will comprise an 'action' verb and its object (list the events, identify the causes, write an essay).
3   Specifications of the relevant conditions under which the behaviour is to be performed. These will indicate the givens, the limitations, the restrictions imposed on the student when demonstrating the terminal behaviour (time factors, details of materials, equipment, information, sources to be used or not used).
4   Reference to the standard that will be used to evaluate the success of the product or performance (80 per cent correct; 7 out of 10 correct; will give six reasons for).

Wiles and Bondi[10] indicate that behavioural objectives are helpful because they address the ABCD rule, specifying the audience of the objective (who will be displaying the behaviour), the intended behaviour to be demonstrated, the context of the behaviour – the tasks, activities and resources, and the degree of completion – the criteria for assessing successful demonstration of the behaviour.

Example: given one hour and no reference materials, the pupil will write an essay synthesising the causes and consequences of the Second World War. The essay must contain at least three of the causes and three of the consequences that were discussed in the lesson.

THE STUDENT TEACHER AND BEHAVIOURAL OBJECTIVES

The example of a behavioural objective given in the preceding section, 'the child will list six sentences from a passage of propaganda that reveals bias and indicate which viewpoint the author holds', is a relatively simple one and merely illustrates the principle. It is capable of extension and may even take the form of a number of itemised sub-objectives (see Boxes 24, 26, 27 and 28 for examples). The extent of its further elaboration in this way would depend on a number of situational factors – the ability of the class or group; its previous experience in the subject area; the direction of the lesson; the teacher's knowledge of the class; her skill as a teacher; the methods she uses and so on. Simply to frame a behavioural objective *in vacuo* without reference to the kinds of factors just noted and expect it to result in favourable outcomes is seriously to violate the principle of behavioural objectives.

The practical implications of this point for the student teacher are considerable. The use of behavioural objectives in contrast to non-behavioural ones places a much greater responsibility on the user. A behavioural objective has to be tailor-made to be effective; it will therefore require more thought and preparation in relation to the situational factors than would be the case with a non-behavioural objective. The latter, being open-ended, covert and less specific, places the onus on the

Box 26: An example of a non-behavioural and behavioural lesson objective in the visual arts

Non-behavioural

To increase the class's appreciation of Roy Lichtenstein's painting 'WHAAM!'.[11]

Behavioural

At the end of a 45-minute lesson on Roy Lichtenstein's painting 'WHAAM!' the class will be able to:

- identify the essential visual qualities of the composition
- compare the imagery with the comic strip sources and recognise the changes it has undergone
- analyse the unity of the structure within the composition
- explain the significance of the composition as part of the imagery of the 1960s
- separate the idea of 'depiction' in the comic strip from the idea of 'unification' in the painting
- describe their personal responses to the painting.

Box 27: An example of a non-behavioural and a behavioural lesson objective in music

Non-behavioural

To develop the class's appreciation of Mendelssohn's *Hebrides* overture.

Behavioural

At the end of a 45-minute appreciation lesson on Mendelssohn's *Hebrides* overture, the class will be able to:

- summarise in one paragraph the circumstances surrounding its composition
- compare the two main themes with respect to mood, shape and instruments used
- describe how Mendelssohn deals with the middle section
- account for the overture's description as programme music
- say whether the work is 'realistic' or 'impressionistic'
- comment briefly on the performance.

learner to make of it what he will, to match it up in so far as he is able with his own cognitive structures.

It follows from this that the student teacher who is only prepared to pay lip-service to behavioural objectives and go through the motions by using superficially conceived, off-the-peg ones would be better advised to eschew them altogether. For those prepared to take them seriously, the following checklist will serve as a framework, at least initially, for setting them up:

1   Decide whether a behavioural objective is appropriate to the particular learning situation you are preparing. If it is, then proceed as in points 2–7.
2   Consider the relevant situational factors the objective must relate to. These may include: the ability of the class, group or individual; the duration of the lesson; the class's previous experience of the subject; your knowledge of the class; your skill as a teacher; and the teaching methods you intend to employ.

Box 28: An example of a non-behavioural and a behavioural lesson objective in the visual appreciation of architecture

Non-behavioural

To increase the class's appreciation of F. L. Wright's building Kaufmann House, 'Falling Water', Connellsville, Pennsylvania, USA.[12]

Behavioural

At the end of a 45-minute lesson on F. L. Wright's building Kaufmann House, 'Falling Water', Connellsville, Pennsylvania, USA, the class will be able to:

- recognise the essential visual and spatial qualities of the building
- recognise Wright's belief in architecture's relationship to landscape and the unique suitability of a building to a site
- explain what Wright meant by 'organic' architecture and 'spatial continuity' and how these relate to Kaufmann House
- analyse the spatial structure of the house and recognise the unity between its parts
- list the materials Wright uses and explain their integral relationship with structure, void and solid
- give a brief account of their own responses to the building.

3   Specify who is to perform the behaviour (e.g. the student, the individual, the learner, the class, the group).

4   Specify the actual behaviour in terms of 'action' infinitives (e.g. to write, to list, to enumerate, to name, to specify, to demonstrate, to distinguish, to order, to identify, to construct, to describe, to state, to mark, to compute, to supply).

5   State the result or outcomes (the product or performance) of the behaviour which will be evaluated to determine whether the objective has been achieved (an essay, six sentences..., the first four problems on page 5, or whatever). This is invariably the object or object-clause of the infinitive stated in 4.

6   Specify the relevant conditions under which the behaviour is to be performed (the information, equipment, source material etc. that the student or class can or cannot use. Time limitations).

7   Indicate the standard that will be used to assess the success of the product or performance. This will often take the form of an expression of the minimal level of performance (the percentage to be correct; so many out of ten correct;...must list all the reasons;...must distinguish at least four characteristics, etc.).

NON-BEHAVIOURAL OBJECTIVES

A desirable common characteristic of non-behavioural objectives, whatever their source and whatever form they take, is that they should be expressed simply and clearly so that appropriate learning experiences may follow naturally. Tyler[13] considers that such objectives can be conveniently placed in one or other of three groups.

First, they are sometimes expressed in a manner which indicates what the teacher does, e.g.:

- to outline the theory of relativity

- to explain the principles of operant conditioning
- to introduce the work of the war poets.

This is a common way of phrasing non-behavioural objectives though, as Tyler notes, because such statements tend to indicate what the teacher plans to do they are not, strictly speaking, statements of educational ends. The particular weakness of this kind of objective from the teacher's point of view is that they do not provide a satisfactory guide 'to the further steps of selecting materials and devising teaching procedures for the curriculum'.[14]

The second form often taken by non-behavioural objectives is in stating topics, concepts, generalisations or other elements of content to be covered in a lesson or course, e.g.:

- transport problems in urban areas
- the concept of space
- the air we breathe.

Here, the emphasis is on the content to be dealt with by the teacher and, like the preceding form, they are unsatisfactory in that they do not specify what the students are expected to do with the elements of content.

The third form of non-behavioural objectives identified by Tyler are those expressed in the form of generalised patterns of behaviour which usually relate to particular content areas, e.g.:

- to develop a fuller understanding of Picasso's paintings
- to develop an appreciation of the variety of architectural styles within a five-mile radius of the school
- to increase the students' sensitivity to manifestations of beauty in art and nature.

Behaviour patterns in this context are often expressed through infinitives like to know, to appreciate, to be aware of, to understand, etc. Objectives of this kind can sometimes be so generalised as to be of questionable educational value. Providing, however, they possess a behavioural aspect and a content aspect, then they are the most useful of the three forms from the student teacher's point of view. As they achieve a suitable balance between the two they will find that this will assist the structuring of their lessons and aid their decisions about teaching method, e.g. to further the student's knowledge of the local social services.

Curriculum planners opposed to the use of behavioural objectives advocate the more general, flexible and open-ended approach of non-behavioural objectives. Class teachers, too, tend to prefer this broader interpretation and no doubt it is the one that student teachers are most familiar with. Arguments which have been advanced in favour of non-behavioural objectives include the following:

- They permit the 'opening-up' process by means of which a student is able to match her own cognitive structures with the perceived content of the objectives. She must negotiate this match-making between her internal structures and the external world for herself.[15]
- Human behaviour is broader in scope and purpose than the sum of specific bits of behaviour learned in isolation. Behavioural objectives fail to take account of the higher or more complex levels of functioning whereas non-behavioural objectives do not.[16]
- Non-behavioural objectives also take account of the broad, interrelated categories of human activity and are often more in line with the long-term aims of the school.

THE DEBATE SURROUNDING THE USE OF BEHAVIOURAL OBJECTIVES

We shall be adopting the objectives model as a basis for our discussions on preparation and planning. Briefly, this involves specifying the desired outcomes of the learning situation in advance so that the means to achieving them can be ordered in a logical and systematic way. The objectives model itself is associated with the rational approach to curriculum planning and as such has its critics. Those holding progressive views on education, for example, would argue that such an approach, in which the teacher pre-specifies the learning outcomes, ignores objectives the children may have and tends to discount the value of unintended outcomes. As one writer[17] puts it:

> The teacher's task is not to prespecify outcomes, rather to place children in learning situations which stimulate them in a host of ways but whose outcomes will emerge gradually from the constant interaction and negotiation between teacher and pupil.

Other critics point to the mismatch between the cold rationality of the objectives model and the constantly changing realities of school life. Shipman,[18] for instance, writes:

> Curriculum development does not proceed through a clear cycle from a statement of objectives to an evaluation of the learning strategies used. It consists of interaction, accommodation and compromise. Horse trading and horse sense are the concrete curriculum scene, not the clinical alignment of means with ends; that is the official version.

While conceding that such criticisms are perfectly valid, we for our part share the belief of the objectives school that the purpose of formal education is to bring about desired changes in children. Indeed it is a salutary exercise to ask oneself what students are able to do at the end of the lesson that they were unable to do at the beginning of the lesson.

Kelly[19] identifies a number of theoretical problems with the objective model. Firstly, it is a direct threat to the individual freedoms of pupils and teachers to make decisions about their curricula. He also argues that the model is particularly damaging to subjects such as those in the arts where good teaching encourages personal interpretation, which should not be determined in advance by teaching objectives. As far as the teaching of English is concerned, Kelly says:

> In literature too the whole purpose of introducing pupils to great literary works is lost if it is done from the perspective of intended learning outcomes ... Again that purpose is to invite the pupil to respond in his or her own way to what he or she is introduced to. To approach a reading of *Hamlet*, for example, in any other way is either to reduce it to an instrumental role, designed to promote an understanding of words, poetic forms, even philosophy, or to attempt to impose one's own moral and aesthetic values, one's own subjective interpretation of the play and response to it on one's pupils. If appreciation of literature or any of the arts means anything at all and has any place in education, it cannot be approached by way of prespecified objectives. (p.61)

Another way to address the issue of objective-led learning is to ask whether there is research evidence to back up the claim that it is the most effective kind of teaching. The recent manifestation of the objective model was supported by claims that school effectiveness research provided evidence that objective-led lessons were the most effective. One influential publication was an Ofsted review.[20] In a list of factors of effective schools, Sammons, *et al.* (1995: 16) cite three studies they say show that 'effective learning occurs where teachers clearly explain the objectives of the lesson at the outset and refer to these throughout the lesson to maintain focus'. Wyse (2003)[21] examined each of these three studies, and other publications that were cited, to support the point about objective-led teaching. The evidence was not as strong as suggested.

One of the stronger publications cited in the Ofsted review pointed out that the links between appropriate instructional behaviour and the teacher's objectives had rarely been studied directly; an 'assumption' is made about objectives based on opportunity to learn data. Brophy and Good (1986)[22] also observe that objectives vary in their nature and that this necessitates a range of teaching approaches such as: problem-solving; decision-making; essay composition; preparation of research reports; or construction of some product. In other words some effective lessons may well be tightly focused around a short-term and clearly formulated lesson objective. Other lessons will be more effective if there is an overall goal, such as the publication of a class book, presentation or drama performance, which guides the teaching and learning. The teacher knows that this process will lead to a range of valuable learning outcomes that do not need to be pre-specified because they will depend on the pupils' response to the task and to the teacher's interaction with them.

It is interesting to think about teaching and learning in the context of learning skills outside school. Learning to play a musical instrument, for example, involves the teaching of a skill. The teacher sets homework in the form of pieces of music to be practised and then responds to the students' playing during the lesson. The setting of pre-specified objectives would be completely counter-productive because it would not allow the teacher to respond to the specific needs of the students demonstrated by their playing of the music. Given that learning to play a musical instrument involves the learning of a complex set of skills, it is easy to see the parallels with learning to read and write. If pre-determined, short-term objectives are normally inappropriate for the learning of a musical instrument, then perhaps they are not always appropriate in the context of other lessons in school. The contexts of whole-class teaching, small-group teaching or individual teaching may well also change what is the most appropriate way to plan and structure learning.

Given that there is a weak theoretical and empirical justification for the objective model, which is so forcefully employed currently, it is difficult not to see this as a means of control over pupils, teachers and educationists exercised by politicians and policy-makers. In reviewing the changes to education over the period of the five editions of his influential book on the curriculum, Kelly shows that this level of political control has undoubtedly increased, has stifled democratic debate about the curriculum and is even beginning to look somewhat sinister.

The strengths and weaknesses of behavioural objectives are summarised in Box 29.[23] It can be seen that several strengths also appear as claimed weaknesses. This indicates the ideological nature of aspects of the debate, reflecting the personal preferences of their advocates or critics. If we want students to acquire certain kinds of knowledge and skills and to develop particular attitudes, we must identify these propensities at the outset and formulate them in terms of aims and objectives. At the same time, we do not necessarily see them as fixed and unchanging; all kinds of chance factors are operating in the classroom which will affect our planning. There is, moreover, room for accommodation and modification. Indeed, Jeffcoate[24] suggests that:

> Prespecified objectives should not acquire the status of sacrosanct unalterable absolutes. Instead they should be open to constant review, adaptation and revision...Hilda Taba[25] best conveys this notion of flexibility in the definition and use of objectives when she suggests they should be seen as 'developmental', representing 'roads to travel rather than terminal points'.

The great attraction of objectives and intended learning outcomes is that, carefully constructed, they provide criteria for evaluation and assessment. This is in direct keeping with the notion of action planning. Moreover, the National Curriculum is cast in an objectives model. It will be argued later that by stating objectives and intended learning outcomes, student teachers will have a set of criteria to use to judge the effectiveness of the lesson, i.e. the extent to which the objectives and intended learning outcomes were reached or achieved (see the discussion earlier in this chapter about target setting). The teaching–learning process is improved by, first, informing the children of the outcomes

Box 29: Strengths and weaknesses of behavioural objectives

Strengths
- They are performance-based, measurable and observable.
- They are easily communicated to teachers and students.
- They facilitate organisation by specifying goals and outcomes.
- They clarify thinking and planning and resolve ambiguities.
- They are 'teacher-proof' and clear to anxious teachers.
- They are highly prescriptive.
- They make clear assessment and evaluation criteria.
- They specify behaviours.
- They render planning logical, sequential and linear.
- They expose trivialities and emphases.

Weaknesses
- They are highly instrumental, regarding education as instrumentally rather than intrinsically worthwhile.
- They render students and teachers passive recipients of curricula rather than participants in a process of negotiation.
- They only cover the trivial, concrete and observable aspects of education, thereby neglecting longer term, unobservable, unmeasurable, deeper seated aims and elements of education.
- Education becomes technicist, tending towards low-level training rather than high-level thinking.
- Because they are 'teacher-proof' they build out teachers' autonomy.
- They lead to predictability rather than open-endedness, discovery, serendipity, creativity and spontaneity.
- The process of education is overtaken by outcome dependence.
- They replace the significance of understanding with an emphasis on behaviour.
- Epistemologically they mistake the nature of knowledge, seeing it as products and facts, supporting a rationalist rather than an empirical view of knowledge.
- They mistakenly 'parcel up' and atomise knowledge.

of their efforts; and second, checking these same outcomes against the original aims and objectives to assess the extent to which they have been achieved. However, there are considerable dangers if the process of communicating objectives to pupils becomes monotonously applied by every teacher in the same way.

It must be emphasised that the separation of the teaching–learning process into stages is necessary for the purposes of analysis and subsequent discussion. In practice, however, some stages may interact with others and occur at the same time. Objectives and intended learning outcomes, for example, cannot really be separated from the means of achieving them, nor the content of a lesson from the methods of teaching and learning being used.

An objectives model can apply at several levels and to several areas. For example, one can have whole-school curriculum objectives, objectives for a year group or a curriculum subject, for schemes of work, for individual lessons, for groups of students, for individual students. One can have objectives and intended learning outcomes for curricula, for physical, emotional and social environments, for behaviour and discipline, for teaching and learning styles, for addressing special needs, for equal opportunities, for school improvement.

You will have deduced from what you have just read that the issue of behavioural objectives has incurred a degree of odium scholasticum in some quarters. The reasons why some are inimical to their use are numerous. Principally, they arise from a rooted hostility to behaviourism, a view of psychology which in its radical form rejects concepts like 'mind' and 'consciousness' and emphasises the importance of the environment in influencing behaviour at the expense of hereditary potential.

Accordingly, learning theorists adopting this extreme position, and who perceive education with similar orientations, see behavioural objectives as tools for achieving their ends. It is thus the fear that the organism will be subjected to the 'shaping' processes of this particular instructional approach without taking mental experiences into account or acknowledging the complexity of human beings that provokes reaction from its opponents. Peters,[26] for example, writes:

> If the inner life of man [sic] is banned from investigation, actions which necessarily involve intentions, emotions which necessarily involve appraisals of a situation, together with imagination, memory, perception, dreaming and pain must all be ruled out as scientifically proper objects of investigation; for none of these phenomena can be described or identified without reference to consciousness. There is precious little left of human behaviour to investigate. So the sterility of this approach to human learning is not surprising.

Advocates of behavioural objectives, on the other hand, view them from the context of a systematic approach to education. For them, behavioural objectives have been a central concept in programming and planning learning. While readily conceding the weaknesses of such objectives, those promoting their cause have cogently argued a case for their limited use in some contexts. MacDonald-Ross,[27] for instance, says:

> For the present, behavioural objectives provide a well-worked-out tool for rational planning in education. They have made possible certain improvements in the technique of curriculum design and should not be discarded in disgust just because they fail to meet more exacting standards. But the application of these objectives should be tempered by a deep understanding of their limitations.

There will be occasions when behavioural objectives and intended learning outcomes will be useful, when student teachers have acquired the skills to formulate them and have had some practice in using them. Equally, there will be frequent opportunities to utilise the more familiar non-behavioural objectives and non-behavioural intended learning outcomes.

OBJECTIVES AND INTENDED LEARNING OUTCOMES IN INDIVIDUALISED LEARNING

So far, we have chiefly considered aims, objectives and intended learning outcomes in relation to communities, groups, and classes. But they can also be used to guide and structure the learning intentions of the individual student, often in an independent learning situation. In addition to the intellectual, emotional and personal achievements possible with individualised objectives, there are longer term gains to be had. The student, for example, can take greater responsibility for his own learning, and his ability to learn other things is enhanced. We look briefly at three possible areas where individualised objectives are relevant: students with learning difficulties, mixed-ability teaching, and projects and special studies.

When a teacher is dealing with children with learning difficulties (in particular, reading), short-term individualised objectives and intended learning outcomes can be specified, preferably in performance terms, which greatly aid the teacher (and/or the parent, if he or she is involved) to keep a check on systematic and cumulative improvement. For success here, objectives and intended learning outcomes need to be considered in relation to frequency of instruction, the amount of practice and the kinds of rewards used. In addition, there needs to be a carefully thought out system of recording to keep a check on progress over time. Or course, as students become older, they may also be involved in the specifying of objectives.

Where individualised objectives are used in mixed-ability teaching, possibly in conjunction with worksheets, a thorough understanding of individual differences is required on the part of the teacher. As we say later in the book, it will require not only knowledge of intellectual skills but awareness of those who require more time, who lack self-confidence, or who are impulsive. Student involvement in formulating objectives is a possibility at this stage.

Individual objectives and intended learning outcomes play a central role in projects and special studies. This will be particularly the case where these make up the coursework for examination, for example in the GCSE.

CONCLUSION: SOME SUGGESTIONS

We have been concerned here with the problems surrounding the expression of educational intentions. Aims were seen as general goals formulated in clear and simple language which define the nature and direction of a school's programme or an area of work within that programme. Objectives and intended learning outcomes, by contrast, were seen as more precise expressions of purpose and of particular value in planning lessons and other units of learning. We then attempted to trace a path between the behavioural view, advocates of which recommend the use of behavioural objectives as their principal tool of learning, and the more traditional practices in English education which employ non-behavioural objectives.

We conclude with suggestions that will guide the reader in deciding whether to use behavioural or non-behavioural objectives or intended learning outcomes. A behavioural objective may be used when the desired outcome is a skill that can be performed, or when the results of instruction can be expressed or demonstrated overtly in writing or speech (language learning would apply here). The acquisition of factual knowledge may likewise be formulated in behavioural terms. Where students are experiencing some difficulty in learning, the particular problem might be broken down into simpler steps or stages, each of which could then be expressed behaviourally. Individualised learning is another area where behavioural objectives would seem appropriate; and if one is producing material for programmed learning, behavioural objectives will be required.

However, when the intended or desired outcomes of learning are more general, developmental or complex in nature and need not, or cannot, be demonstrated by acts of fragmented behaviour, then behavioural objectives or behavioural intended learning outcomes are inappropriate. For example, the aesthetic and appreciative aspects of subjects like literature, art and music are better expressed in less prescriptive ways, since they involve the building up of complex, interrelated and subjective responses and the establishing of favourable attitudes. Broad, open-ended statements of intent serve teacher and student alike better in such contexts, though it must be remembered that some of the adjuncts to appreciation (historical, biographical or social, for instance; or technical, linguistic or stylistic) are often capable of being expressed behaviourally.

8 Beginning Curriculum Planning

INTRODUCTION

The days when students could elect what to teach have long gone. Student teachers can expect to go into school and, with different degrees of specificity, be told what they will be expected to teach. There are three main areas of curriculum planning that we wish to address: (a) the context and levels of planning; (b) elements of planning; (c) evaluation and review.

THE CONTEXT AND LEVELS OF PLANNING

The content and style of planning is heavily influenced by the publications from the government, most notably the Qualifications and Curriculum Authority and The National Strategies reinforced by the Office for Standards in Education, which set out some useful points for curriculum planning (see Box 30).[1]

These several elements from Ofsted provide student teachers (and teachers) with important criteria for evaluating their planning, implementation and assessment of curricula and students, viz. the extent to which their plans demonstrate the potential to meet the Ofsted criteria. The Ofsted framework recognises that for curriculum planning to be effective it needs to take account of external and internal factors to the school, in short it rehearses the 'situational analysis' that is an important feature of curriculum planning.

Another important context for planning draws on the literature of school effectiveness. This movement gathered impetus through research throughout the 1980s and 1990s and was concerned to identify and document the factors that made for effective schools. Several pieces of research found common factors that made for success:[2]

- effective leadership by the head teacher and senior staff, including their interest and involvement in the quality of the teaching and learning in the school and a sense of 'mission'
- a balance of collegiality and clear decision making by senior managers
- the establishment of clear academic goals and a widely understood set of principles for teaching – a clear thrust toward achievement and academic excellence
- consistency of practices with regard to discipline and instruction, together with increased instructional talk
- developed relations with parents
- the involvement of students (in academic planning and extra-curricular activities), the development of the social basis of learning

Box 30: Ofsted's aspects of the curriculum

1 *Standards of Achievement* compared to national norms; application to new situations; to be as high as possible.

2 *Quality of Learning* pace; motivation; ability to use skills and understandings; progress; learning skills; attitudes to learning; variety of learning contexts; acquisition of new knowledge and skills; development of understanding; showing engagement, application and concentration; productive outcomes; use of assessment for subsequent planning.

3 *Quality of Teaching* rigour; teacher expectation; strategies; development of skills and understandings; clarity of objectives (of which children are fully aware); subject knowledge; suitable content of lessons; activities chosen to promote learning of content; engaging, interesting, motivating and challenging activities; pace; range and fitness for purpose of teaching techniques; positive relationships with children; effectiveness of lesson planning, classroom organisation and use of resources; clarity of explanations; quality of questioning; imaginativeness; links between ATs; progression, continuity, relevance, matching, differentiation, balance, richness of provision; regular and positive feedback to students; encouragement of students; good behaviour and classroom climate; effective use of homework.

4 *Assessment, Recording and Reporting* accurate and comprehensive records; suitability of arrangements for assessment; outcomes of assessment useful to pupils, teachers, parents, employers; formative assessments; frequency and regularity of reports; consistency of reporting practice; frequency of reports to parents and for transfer; regularity of review of assessment procedures; staff-discussion of records received.

5 *The Curriculum* quality and range; equality of opportunity to an entitlement curriculum.

6 *Management and Administration* ethos and sense of purpose; effective leadership which is positive, which provides direction, which enables staff to understand their roles in the development of the school and which makes the best of people and resources available and which promotes positive attitudes to teaching and learning; planning (including school development plans and their usefulness as an instrument for improvement); audit of existing work and planning beyond the next school or financial year; implementation and monitoring of plans; working relationships; communication – with and among staff, parents, pupils, community; school self-evaluation and analysis of its own performance.

7 *Resources and their Management* teaching and non-teaching staff – expertise, deployment of specialist and non-specialist teachers, development (INSET and updating which are built into the school development plan), fairness of teaching loads; resources for learning – availability, accessibility and equality of access, quantity and quality, efficiency of use; in-school and out-of-school; relationship of resource provision to school development plan; accommodation – availability, condition, efficiency of use, specialist facilities, accessibility, quantity, quality, conduciveness to learning.

8 *Pupils' Welfare and Guidance* identification and meeting of pupils' academic, personal and career needs.

9 *Links with Parents and Other Institutions* informing parents and using their contributions; links to commerce and industry; quality of liaison; using others to promote learning; use of community resources; transfer documents.

- an orderly atmosphere throughout the school where the promotion of positive discipline pervades all aspects of the life of the school
- the application of careful grouping criteria within classes
- raised teacher expectations of students together with intellectually challenging teaching and carefully matched work
- greater use of whole-class teaching in the primary school
- flexible use of staff in primary schools
- having a limited focus within lessons together with limited organisational complexity.

It can be seen from this that effective learning has to be planned, that curriculum planning for effective learning entails attention to overall (long-term) planning, medium- and short-term planning, and planning very specifically for the contents, organisation, pedagogy and feedback of every aspect of every lesson. Hence the literature from the school effectiveness movement provides us with several important principles for planning.

In primary schools the Office for Standards in Education[3] found that the most effective schools held a firm belief that each student could achieve the highest standards possible, and that the curriculum was tailored to individual needs, that it was broad and challenging, that it should involve first-hand experience. Further, the curriculum was taught in a way which developed students' self-esteem and confidence. Indeed, emphasis was placed on the arts, physical education and humanities, as these were found to motivate students generally. Such a curriculum, it is reported, was largely planned and organised in separate subjects, with links drawn between subjects where relevant so that students could apply their knowledge and skills. The curriculum in school was enriched by the use of visits, residential work and the use of subject experts from within and outside the school.[4]

In primary schools student teachers will probably be involved in teaching the literacy and numeracy hours, and so student teachers will need to gather information on how these are addressed in the class.

In addition to the contexts of planning, the Department for Education and Skills[5] identifies three levels of planning: long-term planning, medium-term planning and short-term planning. Recommended planning examples such as schemes of work are provided at the National Curriculum site,[6] and the National Strategies site.[7]

Long-term planning resonates with the notion of aims, discussed in the previous section. Medium-term planning sets objectives and goals, maybe of a non-behavioural nature. Short-term planning – focused on intended learning outcomes – may be performance-based, possibly including behavioural objectives.

Long-term planning is that in which the whole school, departments, subjects and faculties set out the overall curriculum framework that fits with the school's declared aims and policies, the programmes of study for the National Curriculum, the time available for teaching, resources (both within and outside the schools), reference to individual students' needs, abilities and interests, the balance of subjects on the overall curriculum diet for students, the need to establish continuity and progression within and across units of work. Long-term planning will have taken place before the student teacher enters the school.

It is envisaged that schools have a degree of flexibility in their long-term planning.[8] The long-term planning will embody:

- the school's ethos, values and aims
- the curriculum priorities and emphases
- curriculum enrichment
- the packaging and labelling of the curriculum (which subjects will be taught separately and which will be combined with other subjects)
- the distribution of the curriculum across the Key Stage
- curriculum inclusion and differentiation
- continuity and progression.

That the notion of 'packaging and labelling' renders the curriculum like a commodity may be distasteful for those who regard as retrogressive any movement to make education like any other market commodity.

Medium-term planning is that in which the programmes of work for each group (however defined, e.g. class, year group) are set out, together with an outline of how the programmes will enable assessment to be undertaken. Medium-term planning is that which identifies units of work over a half term or full term (discussed later: schemes of work). The student teacher can reasonably be expected to be part of this planning when involved in a long block practice (e.g. a term or most of a term). Medium-term planning is often written either in outline form only, with the detail being reserved for the short-term planning, or the opposite, with medium-term planning being written in detail and the short-term planning being written in outline form. Student teachers will need to find out how the school undertakes its planning, so that they can follow the required school practice here. Indeed, many schools use ICT to facilitate their planning, and student teachers may need to access this.

Short-term planning is that in which individual teachers set out what they will be teaching on a week-by-week, day-by-day, and lesson-by-lesson basis. Clearly this is the stuff of teaching practice. Short-term planning is usually drawn up on a week-by-week basis, or a day-by-day basis, and depends, for its construction, on the actual events and learning that have taken place. Hence it is almost impossible to have a whole teaching practice's short-term planning worked out in advance of the commencement of the teaching practice, as that would be to take no account of observations and assessment of learning that have taken place during the teaching time. Short-term planning is unavoidably evolutionary; that is its purpose. A short-term plan will indicate the specific experiences, activities, learning, tasks, knowledge and skills that the students are expected to acquire, undertake, learn, practise, consolidate and apply.

Successful planning must demonstrate a strong logical coherence between the medium-term and short-term planning,[9] both of which are nested within the school's aims and values. This is also made explicit to the students themselves, so that everybody is 'in the picture' and knows what is being expected. The Office for Standards in Education found that it was the co-ordinators for each subject who often had led the planning of the subjects and units of work for each year group in primary schools, and that, even with such leadership, in fact the planning was frequently a collaborative affair.[10] Primary schools were found to draw together their overall plans into a cohesive curriculum, apart from mathematics and English, which tended to be planned separately. Long-term planning is usually with whole groups, classes and forms of students in mind, rather than being differentiated for individuals or sub-groups.

The student teacher can expect to have sight of the long-term planning that has preceded her teaching practice as she will have to fit her proposals into that framework. The student teacher will probably be concerned only with medium-term and short-term planning. With regard to medium-term planning it could well be the case that she becomes part of a team that plans the content and 'delivery' of the curriculum for, say, a half term or full term. This planning would probably take place during the initial visits to the school, from which the student has sufficient guidelines to be able to go ahead with short-term planning – the specific lessons that she will teach for each week and each day.

Curriculum coherence 'can be strengthened by linking together, where appropriate, units of work from different subjects or aspects of the curriculum'.[11] This can take place when:

- they contain common or complementary knowledge, understanding and skills
- the skills acquired in one subject or aspects of the curriculum can be consolidated in the context of another (e.g. the notion of generic and 'transferable skills')
- the work in one subject or aspect of the curriculum provides a useful stimulus for work in another.[12]

It is very clear that, for the sake of curriculum coherence, a team approach is required. Gone are the days when an individual teacher could plan what she would do with her class(es); teams can be within and across subjects, departments, faculties and age phases. The student teacher will need to find out what the teams are in a school, how they operate together and of which teams she is to be a member or which she is to consult.

THE ELEMENTS OF PLANNING

Morrison[13] suggests that a full curriculum strategy addresses several features:

● a situational analysis (the contexts of curriculum planning, with reference to the wider society, the local community, and 'within-school' factors – e.g. students, teachers, resources)
● a rationale for the curriculum that is being planned for the teaching practice – its purposes, priorities and principles
● a statement of how breadth, balance, coherence, continuity, progression, differentiation and relevance are addressed. All students should have a broad and balanced curriculum that is relevant to their particular needs
● an indication of how the cross-curricular dimensions, themes and skills will be addressed
● a plan of how the curriculum content will be addressed – its sequence (logically and chronologically), organisation (e.g. by topics and/or subjects) and resourcing (time, space, materials, staff, administrative support, money)
● an indication of teaching and learning styles to be employed
● an indication of how assessment, evaluation and record keeping operate.

CHARACTERISTICS OF THE CURRICULUM

It is necessary to comment upon the 'characteristics of the curriculum'[14] that have been alluded to above: breadth, balance, relevance, coherence, continuity, progression and differentiation within curricula defined in terms of 'areas of experience', which comprise:

● aesthetic and creative
● human and social
● linguistic and literary
● mathematical
● moral
● physical
● scientific
● spiritual
● technological.

They represent an augmented version of a liberal curriculum. Many found the notion of 'areas of experience' attractive as it emphasised experiential learning and permeable subject boundaries (HMI themselves indicated that children could gain mathematical experiences from art and vice versa).[15] However these were overtaken by the subject framed version of the National Curriculum in 1988. Morrison and Ridley[16] argue that breadth should extend beyond curriculum content to include a student's entitlement to breadth of pedagogic styles, learning processes and experience of types of classroom organisation. In the United Kingdom a prescriptive notion of breadth has now prevailed, interpreted as the National Curriculum in its several elements.

The same happened to the HMI notion of 'balance'. The open-endedness of the term was reflected in the looseness of the phraseology that HMI[17] used in defining this as being addressed through 'appropriate attention' being given to the areas of experience and the 'elements of learning' – knowledge, concepts, skills and attitudes. Balance was able to be exerted not simply over the course of a week's work but in a longer time frame, so, for example, scant attention to science in term one could be rectified by greater attention to science in term two. For secondary schools the notion of balance was accompanied in the HMI report by a castigation of too narrow an emphasis on examination syllabuses in the years immediately preceding public examinations.[18]

To some extent the National Curriculum has silenced the debate on exactly what is meant by balance. For example, Morrison and Ridley,[19] using the analogy of a balanced diet, comment that one person's balanced diet is another's unbalanced diet because people have individual dietary needs and preferences. The analogy holds in relation to the world of the curriculum; it misrepresents the individualistic notion of balance to prescribe a common curriculum diet. We know from our experience that some students need more social education than others simply to prepare them for adult life; others need more reading practice in order to be able to access the entitlement curriculum; others have a particular enthusiasm for, say, mathematics, such that to deny them an increase in this area is to demotivate them. The implications of the argument here is to suggest that the simplistic prescriptions of the National Curriculum misrepresent the complexity of the issue. One could argue that an attenuation of the simplistic view of the balance in the National Curriculum can be seen in the notion of 'differentiation', wherein individual needs and differences are intended to be addressed. However, as will be discussed below, this turns out not to be the case.

In addition to curriculum breadth and balance, the notion of 'relevance' implied for HMI[20] students' entitlement to a curriculum that would serve their present and future needs as adults and workers. HMI bracketed together relevance and practicality; for students HMI advocated experiential, practical learning and problem-solving, the need to relate experiences in school to the wider society. As with the notion of breadth, so HMI's suggestion for relevance was pre-empted by the National Curriculum programmes of study and cross-curricular issues, salted with reference to periods of work experience in secondary schools. It was the National Curriculum that was to be relevant.

Though HMI did not specifically address curriculum 'coherence' in its 1985 report, nevertheless one can detect this in the National Curriculum, where, for example, planners are exhorted to try to ensure that different subjects in the overall curriculum relate to each other where possible and that different areas within each subject relate to each other. So, for example, a student studying weather and climate in geography might use statistics and data about weather in mathematics, or study some important historical or religious events that turned on the weather, or undertake some poetry writing about the weather, or study (or compose) stormy and calm music. Clearly this is a matter that requires the careful co-ordination of subject teams in secondary schools and phase teams in primary schools so that the programmes of study of the National Curriculum are accessed without duplication or repetition.

It is, perhaps, an irony that the calls for coherence, wherein logical connections are to be made across subjects, are made in the face of the framing of the National Curriculum in subject terms. The notion of coherence argues very powerfully for integrated topic work; that seems to fly in the face of the arguments against topic work that have been voiced by government representatives (discussed later in this part).

However there is another different but no less compelling view of coherence that interprets it as intelligibility. In this sense we move away from a prescriptive view of coherence, viz. the coherence that curriculum planners plan, to a constructivist view of coherence. In this latter interpretation it is the student who causes subject matter and knowledge to cohere in the sense of being able to assimilate it and accommodate it to existing conceptual structures in her own mind, a view that resonates with Gestalt psychology. Though we can plan for coherence to our heart's content it might not in fact occur for the student if we do not endeavour to communicate and facilitate it in the student's conceptual framework – their 'zone of proximal development'.[21] This argues for a view of learning through the student's eyes rather than the curriculum developer's, and echoes the salutary definition from the former Schools Council[22] that the curriculum is what each child takes away. It is perhaps utopian, then, to think that student teachers can plan for coherence in a teaching practice, for coherence-as-intelligibility requires an intimate knowledge of how each individual student learns. Though the teachers in school may have some of this knowledge it is perhaps unreasonable to expect a student teacher to be able to find out very much about this in the short period of a teaching practice. The safer, if less relevant, way is to plan for curriculum coherence rather than coherence-as-intelligibility!

The notion of 'continuity' is an important educational principle, arguing that the curriculum that is planned for a teaching practice must build on prior curricular experiences that the students have had. There can be continuity of:

● experiences
● skills
● concepts
● knowledge
● attitudes
● in-school and out-of-school experiences
● pedagogy
● organisation
● aims and objectives
● management styles
● social experiences
● record keeping.

Continuity applies vertically as students progress through school, and laterally across different teachers and subjects.[23] The latter has increased significance in primary schools with the rise in subject and subject specialist teaching. The student teacher can plan for continuity, first, by discussing with relevant teachers what the students have done before and what they are doing in other curriculum areas, and second, by looking at records of work undertaken.

The list above refers not only to curriculum matters but also to management matters, interpreting continuity as consistency. Much attention has been given to generating whole-school policies on every aspect of a school's work in an attempt to bring about greater consistency of practice. For example, many policies on behaviour in school lay great stress on consistency of rewards, sanctions, referral systems, handling difficult students, being fair, and promoting positive behaviour. Moreover, the literatures both on behaviour management and on school effectiveness combine to indicate that consistency in behaviour policies has positive spin-offs in curriculum matters in terms of improved standards of student performance.[24] What we are arguing here is that a curriculum plan will make reference (if tacitly) to other aspects of school life – discipline, pedagogy, organisational arrangements.

As with the notion of coherence, the notion of continuity has two very different interpretations whose impact on practice is significant. We saw that an alternative to a prescriptive view of coherence was a view that saw coherence residing in the student's mind – a constructivist interpretation. The same applies to continuity. It is the student ultimately who establishes the continuity between existing knowledge, concepts, skills, ways of working, teaching and learning styles in her own mind, even though we might be able to facilitate that process of building links.

This draws on the work of Vygotsky[25] who argues that teachers ought to be able to identify the 'zone of proximal development' in students – the distance between the actual and potential intellectual, social, cognitive, emotional development in the student. This argues for careful assessment of where the student is in intellectual development etc. in order that her subsequent learning can be planned without it being so close to her existing knowledge and abilities as to render learning boring or so distant from her existing knowledge and abilities as to render learning impossible – to stretch rather than to dislocate. As with the student-centred version of coherence above, it is perhaps unrealistic to imagine that a student teacher can go very far in seeing a situation through a student's cognitive lenses in the short period of a teaching practice. That is not to argue that it should not be attempted; it argues for realistic expectations to be held about what is possible.

The partner to continuity is 'progression'. The National Curriculum is overtly and massively prescriptive in its interpretation of progression. Whether one agrees or disagrees with the interpretation offered, nevertheless at least there is a clear view of what the National Curriculum considers progression to be. It is this: progression is seen as the cumulative, systematic and incremental acquisition of the knowledge, understandings and matters of the National Curriculum through its ten-level sequence for planning and assessment purposes and its programmes of study.

It is possible, in some cases, to detect a logical sequence through the levels and programmes of study (addressing the notion of logical connections that was raised in the discussion of curriculum coherence). However, a logical sequence, even if it were total, which, in the National Curriculum, it is not, does not necessarily imply a psychological sequence of learning.[26] Students' learning is eclectic, lateral and recursive rather than following the clean lines of the National Curriculum. For example, what one student finds difficult another will find straightforward; what one student finds easy another finds difficult. There are no unequivocally objective criteria for ascribing levels of difficulty to tasks; indeed there are several ways in which progression[27] can be defined that may stand as polar opposites to each other:

- simple to complex/complex to simple
- general to specific/specific to general
- singular factors to multiple factors/multiple factors to singular factors
- low order to high order/high order to low order
- unique instance to overarching principle/ overarching principle to unique instance
- concrete to abstract/abstract to concrete
- familiar to unfamiliar/unfamiliar to familiar
- present to past/past to present
- present to future/future to present
- near to distant/distant to near.

In fact when one turns to the documentation of the National Curriculum one can see a range of different views of what constitutes progression:

- the development of an enquiring attitude
- increasing attention, concentration and ability to sustain study
- greater range of purposes, applications, activities, audiences, resources, equipment, demands and contexts
- greater quantity of knowledge, skills, understandings, breadth and depth of study
- greater complexity of ideas, concepts, sequences, stages and applications.

In planning for progression, therefore, the student teacher has to temper the view of progression that is sometimes implicit in the National Curriculum with student-centred and alternative views of progression. As with the notions of coherence and continuity mentioned above, the expectation that student teachers will be able to understand the learner in sufficient detail to be able to plan for a learner-centred view of progression in the period of a teaching practice is almost certainly unrealistic.

With regard to the final characteristic of the curriculum – 'differentiation' – a major study in 1984[28] reported not only that work was poorly matched but that teachers were blind to their under-estimation of children's abilities and hence held unnecessarily low expectations of their students. In mathematics only 43 per cent of work was well matched, with 28 per cent being too difficult and 26 per cent being too easy. In language only 40 per cent of the work was well matched, with 29 per cent being too difficult and 26 per cent being too easy. Low attainers were overestimated on 44 per cent of tasks and high attainers were underestimated on 41 per cent of tasks. These figures cast serious doubt on the extent to which students were working 'at their own rate'. These are crude statistics; the full data set is more sophisticated than this. The research analysed matching in terms of five types of task:

1 *incremental tasks*, involving the learning of new knowledge
2 *restructuring tasks*, where students use familiar materials but are required to discover, invent or construct new ways of looking at a problem for themselves
3 *enrichment tasks*, where students use familiar materials in unfamiliar contexts, i.e. applying knowledge
4 *practice tasks*, where familiar knowledge is rehearsed to speed up thinking processes
5 *revision tasks*, where students restore to their working consciousness knowledge that had been learnt some time previously.

The study found that underestimation included teachers setting what they thought would be incremental tasks but which, in fact, turned out to be practice tasks. Others overestimated students by setting what they thought would be practice tasks but which were, it turned out, incremental tasks.

The implications of this research are clear for student teachers; that they should conduct an analysis of the demands of the task for each individual, or, more realistically, for each group of students and adjust the demands accordingly to avoid boredom, demotivation, upset or frustration. That is not an easy task for several reasons. In practice students, particularly perhaps inarticulate students, do not always want to reveal their weaknesses, whilst more able students do not wish to reveal their strengths as this will only attract more work! In theory, as was mentioned in Part I, the notion that one can diagnose a student's abilities with a sufficient degree of precision to be able to make more than a crude estimate of how well the work can be matched, is flawed. Nevertheless the implications are clear for planning: as careful a diagnostic assessment as possible is needed of the students' abilities in order to be able to approach anything close to a good match of work.

The discussion of differentiation so far has been at a cognitive level, matching the child's abilities to the demands of different types of task – the 'zone of proximal development' mentioned earlier. However, Morrison and Ridley[29] argue for a more extended and complex view of matching. They argue not only for the need to analyse task requisites but to take account of characteristics of the learners in question: their preferred modes and ways of working and learning (e.g. on their own, in small groups, in large groups, with the teacher, without the teacher, with a lot of apparatus, with little apparatus, writing, reading, drawing, listening, talking, doing, problem-solving). The characteristics of children go beyond simply their preferences for learning and include, for example, their interests, self-concept, motivation, degree of autonomy. Indeed Withers and Eke[30] argue for a social constructivist view of matching that embraces social context and teachers' and students' discourses, i.e. 'matching' embraces more than a narrowly intellectual field. Differentiating learning, thus, will need to take account of personality characteristics, social interaction, emotional development, interest, involvement, potential for and willingness to study.

Nor does the discussion of differentiation end there, for just as there are factors that reside in students so there are important factors that reside in student teachers: their personalities, abilities, interests, preferred teaching styles, levels of subject knowledge, preferred organisational arrangements (of students, curricula, classrooms, resources), previous experiences, willingness to take risks, uses of resources, interaction with students, values, potentials. These exert an influence on matching and differentiation.

What we are arguing for is a notion of differentiation that moves beyond the simplistic and facile views of differentiation by outcome (where the same relatively open-ended task is set with the expectation that children of differing abilities will produce differentially successful outcomes) and differentiation of input (where different tasks are set to different children, depending on their abilities). What we are suggesting is that the student teacher will need to consider, for example, differentiation of:[31]

- time allowances and pacing
- the amount, type and quality of teacher attention, prompting, support, demand and challenge
- the type of language that the teacher uses and the level and order of questioning
- the style of teaching
- the social arrangements, groupings and working arrangements in the class
- the activity, task type (e.g. extension, application, practice), demands, cognitive challenge and expected outcomes, covering, for example, similar content but at different levels
- responsiveness to students' optimum and preferred styles of learning.

This is merely an introductory list,[32] the intention of which is to suggest that differentiation is not simply a matter of the speed and order in which individuals progress through the National Curriculum, but that the concept of differentiation is itself differentiated and refracted through a host of different lenses – intrapersonal, interpersonal, cognitive, affective, behavioural, cultural, and so on.

SUBJECT-BASED AND TOPIC-BASED APPROACHES TO THE PRIMARY CURRICULUM

A key feature in the planning of primary school curricula is their framing. In particular the debate about topics and subjects refuses to go away. The Plowden Report[33] gave legitimacy to a child-centred approach to primary curricula in which topic work featured large. This was taken up by others[34] who suggested that:

- primary children naturally view the world holistically and therefore integrated curricula would be more meaningful to them
- children unify rather than atomise and fragment knowledge in their minds by assimilating new knowledge to existing knowledge
- a child's 'whole personality' was best served by a holistic approach to the curriculum
- to bind learning into subject compartments would prevent important links between subjects from being explored and would close up channels of investigation
- a rhythm of learning would be better served by not requiring young children to switch from

subject to subject, and this should lead to the planning of topics that integrated subjects and areas of knowledge

● parcelling up knowledge into discrete subject areas misrepresented the nature of knowledge or knowing

● many key concepts straddle subject boundaries

● new knowledge is not always subject-bound

● subject-based curricula reflect traditional academic and 'preparatory school' values that are out of place in a complex, information-rich world

● subject-based curricula, marked by strong classification and framing, i.e. with clear boundaries put round them which neither students nor teachers have the power to control or remove, are indicative of a conservative and elitist curriculum that reproduces inequality in society

● transferable skills will become increasingly necessary in a changing world and these are best served by integrated approaches.[35]

Many of these arguments in favour of a topic-based approach operated at the level of ideology and values. Hence it is not surprising to see in the literature a range of counter-arguments that also operate at the level of ideology and values. Alexander,[36] for example, suggests that the world is only integrated if we wish to view it that way, a view that echoes Walkerdine's[37] powerful argument that what is perceived to be a 'natural and given' ability to view the world in an integrated way is, in fact, no more than a social construction, a production rather than an uncovering of those characteristics that are deemed to be natural in children. Entwistle[38] suggests that integrated studies provide a poor basis for acquiring knowledge in a manageable or disciplined form; Eggleston and Kerry[39] argue that to talk in terms of integration is, contrafactually, to suggest that the basic building blocks of the curriculum are in fact the disciplines of knowledge and that it is unhelpful to students to neglect the disciplines of knowledge and their methods of enquiry. A strongly worded attack on topic work is mounted by Alexander et al.,[40] who argue that to deny children access to subjects is to deny them access to some powerful ways of regarding the world. They advocate stripping out the ideological argument in favour of or against subject teaching and recognising the empirical limitations of topic work and the empirical possibilities in the promotion of subject teaching for effective learning.

Their views echo Morrison[41] who argues that subject knowledge in teachers and subject specialist teaching could help to raise standards because teachers with expert subject knowledge could better diagnose a student's needs and plan more carefully and knowledgeably for a differentiated and well-matched curriculum that would build in progression. He argues that a subject specialist teacher might thereby, in fact, be more child-centred than the progressivist teacher. Indeed a teacher's subject knowledge is a critical factor in successful teaching and, for children in the upper end of the primary school, subject and subject specialist teaching might bring a depth and richness to their studies that they had previously been denied. Further, much of what had passed for topic work in primary schools had been unchallenging, superficial, undemanding copying out from texts and that progression was marked by its absence over the years of a primary school child's exposure to topics.

STAGING CURRICULUM PLANNING

There is a saying that the best way to eat an elephant is by eating little pieces at a time![42] The same applies here; though the list of factors above that require planning seems perhaps to be overwhelming it can be made manageable by careful staging. The following pages provide an indication of how this can be done. Essentially the process of planning involves the funnelling of issues and contents from the general to the specific, from outline areas of study to particular lessons. In essence this can follow a staged sequence, set out in Box 31.

Box 31: A planning sequence

	General
1 Select the area of study (e.g. a topic or curriculum subject) with reference to the programmes of study, non-statutory guidelines and attainment targets of the National Curriculum. 2 Brainstorm – read around the area, collect relevant resources, investigate the possibilities in the area for study. 3 Organise the topic by curriculum areas (for primary schools) – the core and foundation subjects and the cross-curricular areas. 4 Note the knowledge, concepts, skills and attitudes that are to be developed overall and in specific lessons. 5 Identify the specific attainment targets and levels that the programme addresses. 6 Plan the sequence (logical and chronological) through the work. 7 Indicate how continuity and progression will be addressed. 8 Indicate how work will be differentiated in terms of tasks, knowledge, skills, abilities, needs and interests. Plan for differentiation of input, process and outcome. 9 Plan for good matching – looking at the type of task and the level of demand. 10 Plan appropriate resources – first-hand, second-hand, materials, time, space, display, people, e.g. whole-class, group, individual work, problem-solving, investigational work, didactic and instructional, informal, experiential, practical. 11 Decide resources – first-hand, second-hand, materials, time, space, display, people – anticipating problems and how they might be addressed. 12 Plan how to introduce, develop and conclude activities and sessions. 13 Plan your evaluations and assessments.	
	Specific

Box 31 moves from the medium term to the short term. It provides a conceptual planning map that can be operationalised straightforwardly. The figure addresses a divergent, all-accepting phase of planning (stages 1 and 2) and a convergent, organisational phase (stages 3–13). It addresses the features of a situational analysis and, from such an analysis, identifies priorities and practices. This addresses the third major area of planning mentioned above – the focus of planning. We identify four stages in addressing the several focuses of planning:

- Stage 1: a situational analysis
- Stage 2: the construction of schemes of work
- Stage 3: weekly and daily plans
- Stage 4: individual lesson plans.

These stages are addressed in order below.

Stage 1: situational analysis

This draws together the material that you have gained during the preliminary visit(s), identifying:

- the physical features of the school
- the school in general
- the classroom
- particular information to record.

Out of this spring priorities to be addressed in the planning of curricula, teaching and learning. In terms of keeping a school experience file the contents might be presented thus:

- *title page:* this could provide the following information:
    - date of the practice
    - name of the student teacher
    - name of the school, its address and telephone number
    - name of the head teacher
    - name of the class teacher (if appropriate)
    - name of the supervising tutor and mentor

- *page 2* and following: details of the class(es) to be taught:
    - number in the class
    - its composition (i.e. boys, girls, mixed)
    - age range and abilities
    - names of the students
    - seating plan(s)

- a plan of the school
- the timetable, indicating fixed slots, e.g. use of the hall, television rooms, computer suites, swimming (in primary schools), assemblies, lessons taken by other teachers (for primary schools), work experience (for secondary schools)
- further information (e.g. notes and information on the students; details of specialist and other resources, the predominant catchment area of the students)
- overall aims and purposes of the school, teaching practice, curriculum content (with reference to how some 'characteristics' of the curriculum will be addressed – breadth, balance, coherence) and students' learning
- schemes of work
- charts, diagrams and words which indicate the sequence of the work, i.e. so that it is possible to see at a glance the development within each subject and activity and the relationship (where applicable) between the subject and other curriculum areas
- weekly plans
- daily plans
- lesson plans (with evaluations)
- records
- additional materials.

The focus here is on medium-term planning and short-term planning; indeed, as mentioned earlier, long-term planning will have probably been undertaken before the student teacher arrives at the school. The student teacher inherits the long-term plan and works within it.

Stage 2: the construction of schemes of work (i.e. planned possibilities)

Having reviewed aims and objectives in the preceding part, we now consider two important tools in the preparation for teaching practice where they play a vital part – schemes of work and lesson notes. The broader aims will provide a focus for a student's schemes of work and the more specific objectives, the starting point for individual lesson notes, enabling the reader to see how each of these tools 'fits in' to the objectives model presented there.

A scheme of work in the context of school practice may be defined as that part of a school/class syllabus that the student teacher will be required to teach during her/his teaching practice. In addition to its primary function in providing an outline of the subject matter and content, it may also include information on the children (age, sex, ability, number, class, groups, etc.) as well as on organisational matters, evaluative procedures and ancillary aids. As already indicated, it is also advisable for the student teacher to find out what has gone before in the particular area he will be responsible for and include some reference to this in the scheme.

The scheme will therefore indicate the amount of ground a student is likely to cover in her stay with the host school. It will be a survey of the work she will undertake and will enable her to clarify her own thinking and to plan and develop those particular curriculum experiences which she may feel will require more time and attention in preparation. Although part of a school or class syllabus, a scheme should not be seen as fixed and rigid; modifications may be made to it subsequently in the light of new ideas or further experience of the children. One knows what the broad aim is, and there is nothing to stop one taking a detour along the route – like devoting a lesson to a topic that has arisen incidentally from the students' own interests.

Planning schemes should be done in consultation with the class teacher. The criteria to bear in mind when planning one's schemes in this context are continuity in learning and progression of experience. Let us be very clear: most schools plan by subjects and most make extensive and heavy use of the planning examples from the National Strategies and the National Curriculum. Each subject or area of learning is divided into schemes, units and sections; a scheme comprises several units, and each unit is divided into several sections.

A scheme usually provides guidance on:

- teaching the subject
- aims and objectives
- principles of constructing a scheme
- links to other subjects and aspects of the curriculum, including the literacy and numeracy frameworks, where relevant
- an overview of the units
- progression and inclusion
- sequencing the units
- time allocations
- useful organisations and websites.

Units, which are intended to be medium-term plans, indicate:

- how they address the programmes of study and non-statutory framework for each Key Stage
- links to other subjects and aspects of the curriculum
- how the work relates to previous work and what can follow from the work in question
- vocabulary to be used and learned by students
- resources needed for the unit
- intended outcomes in terms of knowledge, skills and understanding.

Within each unit, the sections provide a series of lessons, as short-term plans, which indicate:

- learning objectives and the small steps to be taken to reach them
- teaching and learning activities
- intended learning outcomes and how they provide indications of student progress
- examples of usage
- short-term lesson plans
- points to note, e.g. about teaching and learning, class management, Health and Safety, home-work and links to other subjects.

Examples of planning at the different Key Stages is given later in the chapter.

The comments that follow are informed by the very extensive guidance on planning at different Key Stages that is provided by the government.

Of particular use in the planning of schemes of work for primary and secondary pupils are the programmes of study for the National Curriculum as they indicate what students should be taught at each Key Stage; the 'matters, skills and processes'[43] that should be taught to students of a range of abilities during the Key Stage. Student teachers will also need to plan within the context of the skills and cross-curricular dimensions.

What to include in a scheme of work

The following information should generally be included in a scheme of work:

- Particulars of the children in the class or group; these will cover number, age, sex, ability and stream (if appropriate).
- Previous knowledge and experience of the class in respect of the subject matter.
- Reference to the National Curriculum programmes of study, attainment targets and level descriptions.
- Reference to the government's schemes, units and sections, where appropriate.
- The number and duration of the lessons, i.e. the amount of time available overall and for each lesson.
- The aim of the scheme: an outline of the subject matter and content, possibly with the teaching and learning objectives for each lesson or unit of learning.
- The main content to be covered, in terms of knowledge, concepts, skills, understandings and attitudes.
- An indication of how the scheme will demonstrate relevance, differentiation, continuity and progression.
- An indication of how the scheme demonstrates coherence (including relatedness to other curriculum areas).
- Some indication of organisational factors, such as: how are the pupils to learn? What kind of work units are planned – class, group or individual? Methods of teaching and learning to be employed – formal class teaching, self-direction under guidance, etc.
- Sources of information – books, worksheets, pictures, software, videos, speakers, visits, etc. The manner in which the children's work will be presented, for example oral, written, dramatic, folders, booklets, murals, display, exhibition, etc.
- Means of evaluation: how are the pupils' achievements to be assessed against the lesson objectives? What criteria will be used?

- Equipment available to be used: books, materials, apparatus, computers, whiteboard, chalk-board, LCD equipment and PowerPoint projectors, learning aids, audio-visual equipment, etc.
- What the work will lead on to after the student teacher has completed the practice (i.e. when the class is returned to the class teacher).

It is usually recommended that schemes of work should be acquired or prepared before teaching practice begins. One such arrangement is as follows:

SUBJECT .... CLASS ....

PARTICULARS OF CHILDREN: age, sex, ability, number, groups, etc.

1 Lessons – number and duration (where appropriate).
2 Aims, objectives and priorities for each scheme (general and very specific).
3 Previous knowledge and experience of the area(s).
4 Outline of content and key concepts to be covered (possibly with lesson objectives):
   Week 1 Lesson 1, 2, etc.
   Week 2 Lesson 4, 5, etc.
5 Organisational factors, teaching styles, learning styles to be adopted.
6 Evaluative procedures and assessment evidence.
7 Equipment.

Schemes of work must demonstrate sequencing. A sequential scheme is one in which the components are logically related to one another and in which the achievements of the later components will depend in large measure on having mastered the earlier ones, i.e. the notion of progression. Much successful learning in 'linear' subjects (like mathematics) depends on such organisation and continuity.

An exception to the sequential scheme is a plan for topic work, an example of which we give in Box 32.

Stage 3: making weekly and daily plans

Stages 3 and 4 of the four-stage model concern short-term planning – the tactical level of planning rather than the strategic levels of medium-term planning, clarifying specific learning objectives and intended outcomes. It was stated earlier that schemes of work are to be considered as planned possibilities, i.e. there is some potential for lessons not to go as originally planned; classroom processes are non-linear. Hence whilst the devising of schemes of work is a necessary feature of planning, it is also necessary to review what takes place over a day or week, and from that review springs refinement of the scheme or lesson. This repeats the significance of action planning that takes place as a result of a careful review of what has taken place. There is a danger of student teachers being so over-prepared in their planning that the plans are cast in tablets of stone, unable to be altered as a result of what happens in the day-to-day activities in class. For example, it is inadvisable to draw up specific lesson plans for more than two or three days in advance in primary schools or for more than two or three lessons in a subject in secondary schools.

At the end of each lesson, day and week, careful stock has to be taken of what happened in the classroom. For example, was too much or too little planned? Did the students grasp the teaching points clearly or do they need further work in the area? Did some children fail to grasp the points whilst others found them very simple, i.e. is there a need for better matching and differentiation? Had the students covered some of the work prior to your teaching, and if so, what are the

Box 32: A topic plan for a Year 6 group

Topic: Food **Duration:** January and February	**Year Group:** 6

English	**Mathematics**
Debating the location of a supermarket; should we use pesticides? drama on angry customers returning purchases; writing advertisements; should we all be vegetarians? Evaluating evidence – the Kava story; language modelling – making a fish and potato pie; topic books on food; reading work sheets and information sheets; reading indexes to fruit and vegetables (non-fiction); Writing recipes, letters of support/opposition to supermarket proposal; narratives, diaries; devising a questionnaire to gather local opinion on supermarket; narrative/poetry – when I was left to make the dinner; writing a report on the survey made.	Comparing prices for different amounts of food; giving change; calculating averages; percentages and fractions (link to pie charts); comparing prices. Pictograms, histograms, line graphs of likes and dislikes in food; actual food eaten (by type); Venn diagrams of food types in bought products; estimation of seed density in fruits; handling data – gathering, processing and presenting data about supermarket; considering national trends in growth of fast-food outlets; problem-solving – the milk bottle and crates problem; timelines of when food is eaten.

Science	**Design and Technology**	**Information and Communication Technology capability**
Purposes of different food types – growth, repair, protection, energy, digestion, chemical balance; ways of preserving food; healthy and unhealthy foods; nutritional and energy values; dissecting and labelling fruits. Heating and cooking food – changes (sugar, eggs, margarine, custard, milk, potatoes) – permanent and impermanent changes; making butter; decaying food; yeast and bread making.	Making and calibrating a weighing machine; design and test machine to test the 'crispiness 'of crisps; making model shops and market stalls; making a 'good food' board game; making a food dominoes game.	Software – balance your diet; the fishing game; what do you eat? Generate and interrogate databases on food eaten; simple statistical packages; preferences and dislikes; word processing of recipes, questionnaires; letters; accounts of how the survey was done.

Geography	**History**	**Music**
Locating original sources of imported food; locating fishing grounds; primary and secondary food-related industries; siting a supermarket; effects of climate on vegetation and crops; a survey of types of shops in the locality and why out-of-town shopping is growing.	Voyages to the Spice Islands and food on board ship; typical foods in Tudor times (using facsimile first-hand documentary resources); preserving food in history.	Food songs with accompaniments – ostinati and pitched percussion.

Art and Design	**RE**	**PE**
Posters to indicate healthy and unhealthy foods; vegetable and fruit prints; observational drawing of still life fruits; market scenes.	Foods and festivals – Chinese new year, Divali, Easter and Christmas, Hannukah, wedding ceremonies.	Emphasis on keeping healthy through exercise and diet (ref. the Happy Hearts project).

Personal, Social and Health Education	**Citizenship**
Uses and abuses of alcohol; healthy and unhealthy diets; the need for exercise; nutritional value of foods; obesity and diet; safety in handling foods; dangerous effects of some foods – e.g. additives, sugar. Arranging a tea party for a group of elderly residents – who to invite; source of finance for project; expenses and costing; supermarket packing problem.	Legal protections for products bought; how to complain; protecting shop workers' rights and work routines; should shops open on Sundays? Types of jobs done by women and men in shops – managers, supervisors, senior executives, cleaners, shop assistants, checkout operators; pay differentials; employment and unemployment for ethnic minorities in the food trade; making shops accessible to those unable to walk.

implications for motivation, curriculum content, teaching and learning styles, extension activities, progression and continuity? What needs to be reinforced and with whom? Did it turn out that what was planned to be straightforward turned out to be very complex and confusing? How did relationships and groupings facilitate or impede learning?

What we are arguing, of course, is for evaluation to take place at the end of each lesson, day and week, and for the implications of the outcomes of the evaluations to be fed into subsequent modifications and coverage of the scheme of work. This is not to relegate the importance of a scheme of work. On the contrary, it is to reaffirm its central role in planning. Without it teaching and learning are literally aimless. What is being advocated here is that the students themselves have a part to play in the teaching and learning; they can cause student teachers to modify their original plans. Whilst that is to be desired it means that a scheme of work is mutable, as are its timing, its sequence, its contents, its planned processes. It provides a framework rather than a blueprint. This echoes the early work of Stenhouse[44] when he describes the curriculum as a proposal and a basis for planning that is refined by, and grounded in, practice and the everyday realities of classrooms.

The implications of this view of a scheme of work render it essential that shorter-term action planning for teaching takes place as a result of reviewing events and learning in schools and lessons. This is the stuff of weekly, daily and lesson-by-lesson planning. For primary student teachers a weekly plan will be useful because of the extended contacts that they have with a single class of students. For some secondary student teachers a weekly plan may be useful provided that they see the students for more than one or two occasions per week (as is the case for core subjects – mathematics, English and science). For other secondary student teachers a weekly plan may not be so useful because of the limited contact that they have with students. For example, many secondary school students will only have one lesson of each of the foundation subjects per week – geography, history, art, music, technology, PE, a modern foreign language and RE.

Having introduced stages one, two and three of the planning process let us look at some examples of teachers' planning before we move on to stage four: individual lesson plans.

EXAMPLES OF PLANNING: FOUNDATION STAGE

Scheme of work

The Early Years Foundation Stage became statutorily controlled for the first time in September 2008. Prior to 2008 the early years curriculum was controlled by teachers and, to varying degrees, the children they taught. An important feature of early years planning has been the idea of topics or themes. Children's knowledge and understanding is not naturally compartmentalised into school subjects, hence the importance that many teachers put on planning work in topics, in order to help children to understand more fully. This principle has been upheld most strongly by early years educators, and it is in part why the guidance for the Foundation Stage has slightly broader areas of learning and development than the school subjects of the National Curriculum (although in 2010 the Qualifications and Curriculum Development Authority (QCDA) published a new national curriculum organised into areas of learning). The government advice says that the areas of learning and development cannot be delivered in isolation.[45] However, it is interesting to note that as the new guidance was being developed in 2008, it was the areas of communication; language and literacy; and problem-solving, reasoning and numeracy (in other words English and maths) that had additional guidance on planning published before the other areas of learning and development (see Box 33).

Planning for the Foundation Stage is considerably different from planning at primary and secondary levels, and these differences are reflected in the way that schemes of work are developed.

Box 33: Overview of learning[46]

Example of literacy planning and resourcing[46]
What we want children to learn (development matters)
- Extend their vocabulary, exploring the meanings and sounds of new words

Related Early Learning Goals
- Recognise and explore how sounds can be changed, sing simple songs from memory, recognise repeated sounds and sound patterns and match movements to music (CD)
- Find out about their environment, and talk about those features they like and dislike (KUW)

Possible contexts
- Take children on visits and walks, discovering new things and places.
- Use stories, poems, rhymes and songs. Investigate the meanings of particular words and share the pleasure of their sounds.
- Use word banks and labels for shared interests; involve the children in making their own and discussing meanings.
- Provide opportunities for children to share a variety of languages including sign language.
- Introduce and extend vocabulary in play.

Example of adult-led activities
Context: sharing stories and rhymes, for example 'Rumble in the Jungle' by Giles Andreae and David Wojtowycz
- Read 'Rumble in the Jungle' by Giles Andreae and David Wojtowycz.
- Play at being some of the different animals. Ask the children to listen carefully to the words to see how the animal is described. Use highlighting pens on a scanned or photocopied page, or scan into the interactive whiteboard and enlarge or colour the adjectives. Ask the children what some of the words mean; when they are not sure use dictionaries (can be web-based) to find out.
- Make a collection of other things that that word could describe, for example what else could shine?
- Act out the chosen animals, again with strong intonation on the adjectives.
- With the children's help, make a display that shows the animal, uses the text for the animal and labels the animal with the adjectives.
- Children could make their own animals, using a variety of media. Encourage the children to have a go at writing words that describe their animal using models, the labels in the display or books as above, and word banks with picture support.
- Read and share their descriptions of their animals with each other.

Adult role
- Share and enjoy a wide range of rhymes, music, songs, poetry, stories and non-fiction books.
- Give opportunities for linking vocabulary with physical movement in action songs and rhymes.
- Provide time and opportunities to develop spoken language through conversations between children and adults, both one-to-one and in small groups, with particular awareness of, and sensitivity to, the needs of children learning English as an additional language, using their home language when appropriate.
- Provide opportunities for children who use alternative communication systems to develop vocabulary.
- Scaffold children's spoken and written language, recasting sentences and providing new vocabulary.
- Participate alongside children's role play activities to develop use of language, for example talking with customers and answering the phones.
- Connect children's vocabulary development with their growing phonological awareness.
- Use visits and walks as a base for vocabulary development.
- Introduce specific and accurate vocabulary across all areas of learning, for example the vocabulary of mathematics.

Opportunities for children to explore and apply

● Create word banks and labels for shared interests, involving the children in making their own and discussing meanings.
● Provide opportunities for the children to become familiar with stories, poems, rhymes and songs. Investigate the meanings of particular words and share the pleasure of their sounds with the children.
● Encourage the children to share their languages and bring in others by naming and, where appropriate, labelling or listing familiar items such as food.
● Introduce and extend vocabulary in play, for example positional vocabulary in 'small world' play and the language of quantity and measures in cooking.
● Recast children's sentences positively to increase use of vocabulary. For example: 'I did it' can become 'Oh, well done, you took the register back to the office; thank you.'
● Use visits and walks to see new objects and gather new vocabulary.

Adult role

● Make a language-and-literacy rich environment. For an audit see Early Reading Audit.
● Share and enjoy a wide range of rhymes, music, songs, poetry, stories and non-fiction books.
● Give opportunities for linking vocabulary with physical movement in action songs and rhymes, role play and practical experiences such as cookery and gardening.
● Provide opportunities for sharing languages and using vocabulary from a variety of languages in the environment, for example in signs, notices and labels.
● Provide time and opportunities to develop spoken language through conversations between children and adults, both one-to-one and in small groups, with particular awareness of, and sensitivity to, the needs of children learning English as an additional language, using their home language when appropriate.
● Provide opportunities for children who use alternative communication systems to develop vocabulary.
● Scaffold children's spoken and written language, recasting sentences and providing new vocabulary.
● Participate alongside children's role play activities to develop use of language, for example talking with customers and answering the phones.
● Connect children's vocabulary development with their growing phonological awareness.
● Use visits and walks as a base for vocabulary development.
● Introduce specific and accurate vocabulary across all areas of learning, for example the vocabulary of mathematics.

Look, listen and note

● Do children display an increased use of vocabulary?
● Do they make up their own rhymes or alternative versions of favourites using their phonic knowledge?
● Do they take pleasure in using language and trying out new words?
● Are they curious about words and their uses?

Assessment opportunities

● Are children developing confidence in speaking to adults?
● Are children developing confidence in speaking in a group?
● Observe how children use specific vocabulary, for example in cooking.
● Do children show an interest in words and language through comments or questions, for example in listening to songs, stories and rhymes?
● Observe how children use new words, for example in play.

Related profile scale points

● LCT 2, 4, 5, 6, 8, 9 LSL 2

Note: The 'scale points' show the progression that is assessed by using the EYFS profile.
LCT = Language for communication and thinking; LSL = Linking sounds and letters

Children's learning in the early years consists of child-initiated learning through play and adult-initiated learning which teachers and other adults plan. A scheme of work will identify the topics which will be covered throughout the year. The topics are often planned to last for half a term; typical examples include Ourselves; Food; and Toys. The scheme of work needs to show how the areas of learning and development of the Early Years Foundation Stage will be covered through the activities and experiences that are planned for the children. However, it must be remembered that planning in the early years begins with observations of children and reflection on their learning in order to plan the most appropriate experiences (arguably this should be more a priority for other Key Stages as well). For that reason, the longer-term planning that is a feature of schemes of work is likely to be less complete than the schemes at primary and secondary level. Records of learning and development, which parents are encouraged to contribute to, also provide evidence from which planning can draw. The records of observations of children feed directly into weekly and daily plans.

Weekly/daily plans

Box 34[47] and Box 35[48] are examples of weekly planning at the Foundation Stage. Box 36 shows how one of the areas of learning and development, communication language and literacy, is planned in much greater detail.

Box 34: A weekly plan for the Foundation Stage

Theme: Fruit	**Date:** 3–7 July
Personal, social and emotional development Encourage children to listen to others ' questions and take turns. Choose own utensils. Safety reminders: prickly branches, use of knives, hygiene.	**Knowledge and understanding of the world** How gooseberries grow, conditions of growth, sun, rain, soil. Use magnifying glass to look at the inside and outside of gooseberries. Allow to see, feel, smell, taste.
Communication, language and literacy Listen to explanations. Make list of fruit growing in the garden. Vocabulary: parts of plants: root, branch, stem, leaf, flower, fruit, seed.	**Physical development** Keep to the narrow path around the garden/climb steps. Fine motor skills: use of knives/magnifying glass.
Mathematical development Compare size of gooseberries and count them. Order sizes. Vocabulary: bigger than, more than, less than, how many (take turns).	**Creative development** Colours of leaves and ripening berries. Textures: smooth, rough, prickly. Paint pictures of the garden.

Notes:
Only allow children to feel, smell and taste gooseberries under supervision.
Katy explained to Jess that we have to be careful with knives because they can cut you.
Dan brought a book on fruit and vegetables from home that had a picture of gooseberries in it – could also be useful for learning about vegetables/seasons.
Next time we go shopping, look at the different fruits in the shop and discuss where they come from.
Use photos to introduce ideas and encourage discussion.

Box 35: A plan for one week in the Foundation Stage

Week commencing 26 April 2010	Monday	Tuesday	Wednesday	Thursday	Friday
Activities/resources					
Themed activity	Walk to local church using maps made by the children KUW5, CLL1, PSED4	Making pancakes for Shrove Tuesday KUW6, PSED5, CLL1,	Walk to local shops using maps made by the children KUW5, CLL1, PSED4	Investigate remote-control cars with large-sized maps PD4, CLL1, KUW1	Mini treasure hunt in the sand tray CLL2, CD4, MD3
PSED activity	Introducing our own objects of interest PSED, CLL, KUW, CD	Circle time – sharing news PSED, CLL, CD	Sharing items collected on our walk PSED, KUW, CD, CLL	Creating an interest table showing maps and treasure PSED, CLL, KUW, CD	Exploring our treasure box and talking about our own treasure PSED, CLL, CD, KUW
Reading/writing	Looking at a selection of maps CLL, KUW	Creating our own maps CLL, KUW	↑	↑	↑
Maths	Completing colour and shape puzzles MD, PSED, PD	Completing number puzzles MD, PSED, PD	Sorting shapes MD, PD, PSED	Matching shape and colour game MD, PD, PSED	Matching and grid game MD, CLL, PSED
Science	Looking through a microscope at slides KUW, PSED, PD	Exploring slopes using tractors, lorries and cars KUW, PD, PSED	Looking through magnifying glass at items found on our walk KUW, CLL, PSED	Exploring magnets and things they stick to PD, KUW, PSED	Looking through magnifying glasses at our treasure KUW, CLL, PSED
ICT and computers	Playing mouse control games PD, CD, CLL	↑	Exploring our touch game (mapping) PD, PSED, KUW	↑	Listening to guess the sound game KUW, CLL, CD
Sand tray	Exploring the texture of wet and dry sand PD, CD, CLL	Using sand and blocks to create models PD, CLL, PSED	Building sand castles using buckets and spades MD, PD, PSED	Using lorries, diggers and tractors on the building site KUW, PSED, PD	Pouring and measuring with sieves, funnels and scales MD, PSED, PD

Box 35: A plan for one week in the Foundation Stage (continued)

Week commencing 26 April 2010	Monday	Tuesday	Wednesday	Thursday	Friday
Activities/resources					
Water tray	Using whisks in different-sized containers PD, CLL, MD	Imaginary cooking with a tea set, pots and pans PD, CLL, PSED	Looking at coloured water using tubes and funnels MD, KUW, CLL	Measuring using jugs and pouring equipment MD, KUW, CLL	Exploring items that float and sink KUW, MD, CLL
Physical activity (indoors/outdoors)	Blowing and chasing bubbles PD, KUW, CD	Balancing using small equipment – beanbags, balls and hoops PD, PSED	Navigating an obstacle course PSED, PD	Dancing to fast and slow music PD, PSED, CD	Music and movement – vehicles we have seen PD, CD, PSED
Creative areas	Constructing junk model buildings PD, KUS, CD	→	→	Creating junk model town PD, PSED, CD	Creating junk model town PD, PSED, CD
Sensory area	Manipulating Play-doh with cutters and rollers PD, CLL, CD	Handling wet and dry pasta PD, CD, KUW	Using the conveyor belt with moulded Play-doh objects PD, CD, CLL	Discovering properties of cornflour PD, CD, PLL	Mixing and blending paint PD, CD, PSED
Imaginative play	Navigating cars around a road map CD, KUW, PD	Connecting a train track for magnetic trains PD, CD, KUW	Building a garage for cars on a road map CD, KUW, PD	Aeroplanes and helicopters landing at the airport PD, CD, PSED	Dolls from the doll's house going to the zoo CD, KUW, CLL
Role play	Going on a bus/train journey CD, CLL, KUW	Opening our own ticket office CD, PSED, CLL	Having a picnic CD, CLL, PSED	Shopping in the supermarket CD, KUW, CLL	Booking a holiday at the travel agents CD, PSED, CLL

PSED = personal, social and emotional development; KUW = knowledge and understanding of the world; CLL = Communication, language and literacy; MD = mathematical development; PD = physical development; CD = creative development

Box 36: A flow chart for planning

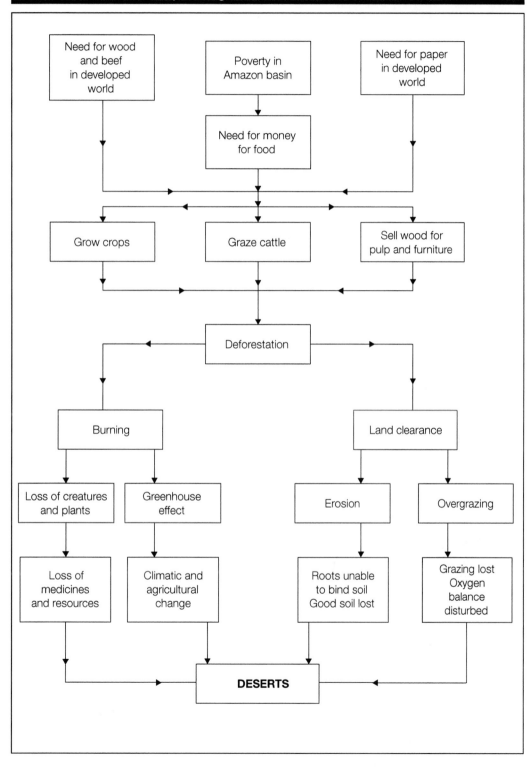

PRIMARY SCHOOL KEY STAGE 2

Scheme of work

In the case of the primary school Year 6 class, Box 32 represented the results of an initial 'brain-storming' of ideas about an integrated topic that had been refined into a subject-based plan. The student teacher has made certain that her proposals for the curriculum content fit with the other programmes of study, schemes, units and sections of the National Curriculum for each of the subjects indicated. The student teacher has gone one stage further, which is to check that the scheme of work is correctly matched in terms of the attainment targets for each subject where applicable.

The next task, where applicable, is to address the level descriptions of the National Curriculum for each attainment target so that the work is appropriately matched in difficulty to the abilities of the students (though, as mentioned earlier, in fact the level descriptions are to be used more as guides for assessment rather than as guides for planning). At this stage the student teacher will have to clarify how the scheme of work builds on previous knowledge, concepts, skills and attitudes and how it addresses progression and differentiation. What the student teacher has done so far is to create the framework for a scheme of work in each of the curriculum areas.

The final task is for her to go through each curriculum area in turn and for each devise a programme of work that has a clear sequence and structure. This means that she has moved from outlining an overall statement of content to subject-specific, detailed descriptions of the curriculum content to be covered. The schemes of work, then, will probably be subject specific, with each subject setting its aims and objectives, priorities, content, key concepts to be taught, teaching and learning styles to be employed, resources, and a delineation of what the expected learning outcomes will be and what the assessment evidence will be during and at the end of the programme. Once the schemes of work for each subject have been planned they can be transferred rapidly (particularly if the process is computer-assisted) onto a matrix, with subjects listed on the vertical axis, and Weeks 1–4 along the horizontal axis.

Using the matrix the student teacher will be able to see how each subject will develop over the four weeks by looking across the rows. Looking vertically down the columns enables her to see how each subject area relates to the others in any given week. Further, looking along the rows indicates how progression will be addressed in each subject, whilst looking down the columns indicates how continuity will be addressed by identifying the relationships between activities and subject areas in a single week. This is particularly valuable if topic work is to be introduced that integrates several curriculum areas.

Weekly/daily plans

Weekly/daily plans based on curriculum subjects are shown in Box 37[49] and Box 38.[50] The weekly planning sheets provide a useful summary of what will be attempted. They enable student teachers to see at a glance what is happening, when it is happening, with whom, what precedes it and what proceeds from it. Because of the limited space in a weekly matrix plan, student teachers, in a sense, are compelled to identify priorities. A daily plan can adopt the same format as a weekly plan, identifying priorities and the sequence of events, be it for specific students, groups or classes, depending on whether it is referring to a primary school or a secondary school. It must be noted here that, increasingly in primary schools, teachers teach classes other than their 'own'; the daily plan should indicate the class that the student teacher will be teaching, i.e. it is a plan of the student teacher's programme rather than a single class's programme. A small planning matrix can act as an *aide-mémoire*, reminding the student teacher of specific points, for example in connection with preparing resources, meeting others, major teaching or organisational points.

Box 37: A weekly timetable for a primary school

	Monday	Tuesday	Wednesday	Thursday	Friday
8.55	REGISTRATION				
9.00	Understanding English, communication and languages (60 minutes)	Mathematical understanding (60 minutes)	Assembly (20 minutes)	Mathematical understanding (60 minutes)	Assembly (20 minutes)
	Assembly (20 minutes)	Assembly (20 minutes)	Mathematical understanding (60 minutes)	Assembly (20 minutes)	Scientific and technological understanding (60 minutes)
10.30	BREAK				
10.35	Understanding physical development, health and well being (45 minutes)	Scientific and technological understanding (45 minutes)	Understanding the Arts (30 minutes)	Understanding the Arts (45 minutes)	Understanding physical development, health and well being (45 minutes)
			Sustained reading/'catch up 'groups (15 minutes)		
	Mathematical understanding (60 minutes)	Sustained reading/'catch up' groups (30 minutes)	Understanding English, communication and languages (60 minutes)	Understanding English, communication and languages (60 minutes)	Mathematical understanding (60 minutes)
		ICT (30 minutes)			
12.30	LUNCH AND REGISTRATION				
13.15	Sustained reading/'catch up' groups (30 minutes)	Literacy – sustained writing (75 minutes)	Understanding the Arts (75 minutes)	Scientific and technological understanding (75 minutes)	Sustained reading/'catch up' groups (15 minutes)
	ICT (45 minutes)				Understanding English, communication and languages (60 minutes)
14.30	BREAK				
14.45	Historical, geographical and social understanding (45 minutes)	Understanding physical development, health and well being (45 minutes)	Historical, geographical and social understanding (45 minutes)	Sustained reading/'catch up' groups (15 minutes)	Religious education (45 minutes)
				PSHE (30 minutes)	
15.30	FINISH				

Box 38: An alternative weekly timetable for a primary school

		Monday	Tuesday	Wednesday	Thursday	Friday
	8.50	REGISTRATION				
60 mins	9.00	Science	English	Mathematics	PE	English
50 mins	10.00	Mathematics	Mathematics	English	Mathematics	Mathematics
	10.50	BREAK				
70 mins	11.05	English	RE	Science	English	Drama
	12.15	LUNCH				
	13.15	REGISTRATION (conferences on Mon, Wed and Thurs – 5 mins) and quiet hours when support available. Mathematics or reading – pupil target-setting				
50 mins	13.25	History/ICT	Music	English	Geography	Art and Design/ICT
50 mins	14.15	History/ICT	PE	English	Geography	Art and Design/ICT
	15.05	Junior assembly	Junior assembly	Class assembly	Year group assembly	Whole-school assembly
	15.20	FINISH				

One possibility is to divide the daily planner into four teaching sessions with morning, lunchtime and afternoon break. Many schools do not adhere to this plan, reducing the time of lunch breaks (often in an attempt to avert troublesome behaviour) and not having an afternoon break. In some regions of the UK this decision is also based on finances, as it means that school heating costs can be reduced in the colder months of the year if school finishes in the mid-afternoon each day. It may be also that in any single 'session' there is more than one lesson, or there is a school assembly followed by one or more lessons before the first break. Clearly, this might mean that the format of the daily planner might have to be altered to accommodate these.

SECONDARY SCHOOL KEY STAGE 3

Scheme of work

Another example of a planning matrix is of a scheme of work for Geography for Year 8 students, again over a four-week period, and places a strong emphasis on planning by key concepts, e.g. the concepts of (a) desertification, (b) the economic imperatives of the developed world that lead to the economic exploitation of the third world, and (c) the concept of deforestation. In conceptual terms the plan is represented in Box 36 and, in essence, falls into a four-week teaching practice thus:

● Week 1: The poverty of the rainforest dwellers, coupled with the need for the developed countries to have wood for pulp and furniture and beef for food, create a situation where income for the rainforest dwellers can be gained by deforesting the rainforests in order to sell the wood and to clear land for grazing cattle and growing crops.

- Week 2: As deforestation increases (because of the need for new grazing and for more wood) the 'slash and burn' principle for clearing the forest is difficult to halt because of the income that it generates.
- Week 3: The burning of the forest permanently upsets the climate and contributes to the green-house effect whilst the soil, now lacking any tree roots to hold it together, is eroded by the rain. This problem is compounded by overgrazing.
- Week 4: A dust-bowl effect is caused, resulting in loss of medicines from plants, the diminu-tion of bio-diversity, permanent climatic change, yet it still continues because of the exploitation of the underdeveloped world by the developed world. Considerations of how to remedy this complete the four-week practice.

As it stands this scheme of work is incomplete, being conceptual only. It requires amplification by detailing aims and objectives; how it builds on previous work (i.e. progression); how it relates to the relevant areas of the programmes of study and the levels within the National Curriculum; resources; specific content that will be approached to address the concepts listed here; teaching and learning styles; intended learning outcomes; progression and differentiation; and assessment crite-ria and methods. Though the scheme sets outs its priorities at present – the key concepts to be addressed – it needs much greater detail.

This second example is of one scheme of work for one secondary class. Typically the student teacher will be teaching several classes, hence several schemes of work will be required, one for each class/set/group (falling in with the organisation of students in the school). Again a matrix approach to planning can be useful for the student teacher, to chart the commitments and prepara-tions that will be needed over the teaching practice.

Weekly/daily planning

Box 39 shows some planning done by a secondary English teacher, which is one of the examples made available to teachers through the National Strategies secondary site.[51]

Stage 4: individual lesson plans

The lesson plan is the clearest example of short-term planning. There is no single format for a lesson plan. The format of a lesson plan is contingent upon a number of factors, for example: the school's pro-formas for lesson planning, the students, the curriculum area, the type of lesson, the individual preferences of each student teacher, the level of detail required, the level of detail that is useful. Some lessons are introductory, some continue work from a previous lesson, some build on and develop the work from a previous lesson, some practise skills learnt in previous lessons, some are designed to enrich and extend – laterally – points made and concepts studied in previous lessons, some complete a blocked unit or module of work, some lessons are overtly diagnostic (see the discussion of assessment in Part IV), some are directly concerned with 'input'. Some student teachers keep slight lesson plans, releasing them to think creatively; others find that having to include much detail in a lesson plan helps them to think creatively, clearing their mind.

Box 39: An example of secondary English planning

Medium-term plan – sheet 1			
Title of unit: Parallel worlds	**Year 7**	**Term 3**	**Duration: 6 weeks**

Overview

Stage 1 (week 1): Pupils will explore a range of texts, images and related ideas about how writers (and some artists) have drawn on the idea of 'parallel worlds' in their work, both in literary heritage texts such as *Gulliver's Travels*, through non-fiction work – accounts of the so-called 'Cottingley fairies' fake photos in 1917, to the initial study of the novel *Elsewhere* by Gabrielle Zevin.

Stage 2 (weeks 2–4): Detailed study and exploration of *Elsewhere* with associated exploration of the 'parallel worlds' genre and publishing for it in children's and adult commercial literature.

Stage 3 (weeks 5–7): Development of own 'parallel worlds' concept for publication – with both spoken presentation and written work as a core outcome.

Link to key concepts

- Pupils will make 'fresh connections between ideas, experiences and texts' (Creativity) when exploring the 'parallel worlds' focus, and use 'inventive approaches ... taking risks' when 'playing with language' in their own writing.
- They will need to demonstrate being adaptable 'when they present their ideas for their short story in an unfamiliar context', as well as a 'secure understanding' of language and grammar conventions (Competence).
- They demonstrate 'Cultural understanding' in their exploration of important texts in the literary heritage, but also gain a sense of how 'ideas and values are portrayed differently' in other cultures and traditions when they explore how other cultures have written about 'parallel worlds' (e.g. via creation myths).
- Throughout, 'critical understanding' will be important in getting a real sense of how writers marshal and shape ideas to create meaning, but also then drawing on this to develop their own and others' ideas.

Key learning focus

Speaking and listening:

3.1 developing and adapting discussion skills and strategies in formal and informal contexts

Reading

5.2 understanding and responding to ideas, viewpoints, themes and purposes in texts

6.1 relating texts to the social, historical and cultural contexts in which they were written

6.2 analysing how writers' use of linguistic and literary features shapes and influences meaning

Writing

7.2 using and adapting the conventions and forms of texts on paper and on screen

8.44 developing varied linguistic and literary techniques

Language

10.2 commenting on language use.

Assessment opportunities*

Speaking and listening (AF1, AF2, AF6)

Contribution to group and class discussion.

Group oral presentation on 'parallel worlds' in fiction.

Individual 'pitch' to a publisher about own idea for a story.

Reading (AF2, AF3, AF5, AF6)

Contribution to group and class discussion.

Written analysis of how Zevin presents her 'world'.

Writing (AF1, AF2, AF6)

Own 'parallel worlds' story or novella.

Commentary on process and plans (link to reading assessment).

* AF = Assessment Focus

Core texts and resources

Elsewhere by Gabrielle Zevin; *Gulliver's Travels* by Jonathan Swift; OHTs/slides of extracts and illustrations related to 'parallel worlds'; 'The Witch' by Mary Coleridge.

'Miller's End' by Charles Causley; Article from *Boston Journal*, 1904 on Fox sisters case (see Wikipedia for link); access to internet, or downloaded web-screens of teenage publisher websites, blurbs, promos and so on.

Medium-term plan – sheet 2

Week 1	Week 2	Week 3	Week 4	Week 5	Week 6	Week 7
Lesson 1: discussion and exploration of fragments of poems, articles and texts linked by parallel worlds focus. Causley and Coleridge poems.	**Lesson 1:** Chapters 1/2 of *Elsewhere* – tracking story development – prediction, anticipation, retrospecting – what will the world of *Elsewhere* be like?	**Lesson 1:** parallel stories – how characters in *Elsewhere* have their own stories.	**Lesson 1:** endings and beginnings – how is the structure of the novel both circular and linear? Initial ideas for own texts/stories.	**Lesson 1:** pitching an idea for a novella/story – what are publishers looking for? How do you know?	**Lesson 1:** one-minute pitch to 'publisher' (teacher) on ideas; notes on changes and so on needed.	**Lesson 1:** continued workshop/ interventions and modelling where needed.
Lesson 2: focus on *Gulliver's Travels* – text analysis and biographical information on Swift.	**Lesson 2:** making links to other reading: exploration of setting/ world created in novel.	**Lesson 2:** further reading and focus on structure of novel: key moments, the 'arc' of the narrative.	**Lesson 2:** reviewing the novel, writing about it, its issues and themes – personal response and links to other texts.	Linking content to an oral presentation and key strategies needed. **Lesson 2:** planning/generating ideas for own 'parallel worlds' story. Publisher brief/requirements.	**Lesson 2:** continued drafting of novella/ short story – sharing of fragments, peer evaluation, editing, proofing and so on.	**Lesson 2:** blurbs, covers and promo; getting the target audience right (if time, digital design, font, layout and so on). Link to Business Studies – team teaching.
Lesson 3: focus on contemporary news article on the Cottingley fairies – how influenced Conan Doyle; brief synopsis of what has been read, explored. Read first page of *Elsewhere*.	**Lesson 3:** focus on character of Liz and her 'journey'. What is target audience of text, why and so on? Short role play drama in pairs.	**Lesson 3:** comparison and contrast of Thandi and Liz, how their stories start, divide, links to social backgrounds.	**Lesson 3:** Gabrielle Zevin's work – presentation of her text/s; promos, blurbs and so on; 'parallel worlds' story genre – research and analysis.	**Lesson 3:** drafting openings – trying out ideas; writing a synopsis and preparing short pitch.	**Lesson 3:** focused workshops/ intervention with teacher on key aspects, especially how meaning shaped by specific literary effects.	**Lesson 3:** presentation of manuscript to 'publisher'. Evaluation of format and so on as required by initial brief.

Medium-term plan – sheet 3

Teaching strategies

Range of explorations via pair and group discussions.

Shared and guided reading – focused analysis, predicting, empathising, anticipating and retrospecting.

Eliciting links between texts and ideas via range of closed and open questions.

Detailed focus on short elements of text composition; using modelling, redrafting, and peer evaluation to improve.

Teacher-in-role as publisher, using rigour of the role to stress high quality of writing needed, and value invention and originality.

Personalising this unit for your pupils

Gifted and talented to look at Conan Doyle's view of the Cottingley fairies case and how it influenced his writing; also perhaps to read all of *Gulliver's Travels* and write a more extended analysis of how parallel worlds are presented in a range of texts.

For group and guided reading sessions, group pupils based on APP reading levels and targets. Sessions differentiated by tasks, questioning/prompts, and so on.

Teaching assistant (TA) to give additional support to level 3 writers with planning and writing of own narrative (see Progression map) – working with 'Group 1' below.

Notion of choice also provided via three-group model for work which follows initial set-up of work:

Group 1: directed learning, supporting group with guided work; working closely with teacher/TA prompts, structures, eliciting learning before move to greater independence.

Group 2: periodic intervention through teacher/TA support, but extended independent work with strategic plenaries.

Group 3: independent work with intervention as required by group themselves, deciding focuses, direction for exploration and development of ideas.

Despite these variations there are some constants that student teachers are advised to include in their lesson plans. These include:

- a statement of objectives (a statement of aims may not be appropriate here because, as the earlier discussion indicated, aims are long-term, generalised and infinite, whereas objectives are short-term, specific, concrete and finite); objectives might refer to the knowledge, concepts, skills and attitudes that will feature in the lesson
- an indication of the subject/curriculum area (in the terms of the National Curriculum, or a topic that straddles the National Curriculum subjects or works within one National Curriculum subject)
- an indication of the attainment targets, programmes of study and level descriptions (where appropriate, defined as where they are mentioned in the National Curriculum itself and whether the lesson seeks to address the National Curriculum subject matter or whether it moves outside it)
- an indication of resources to be used (which need to be assembled and tried out by student teachers before the lesson)
- an indication of the time available and timing of the different stages of the lesson, e.g. introduction, development, conclusion (to address the items from the Ofsted criteria (Box 30) mentioned earlier, in particular the items included in the quality of learning, the quality of teaching and resources and their management)
- an indication of the intended learning outcomes (for the students and the student teachers – student teachers experience a teaching practice in order to learn how to teach)
- an indication of the organisation of the lesson – its sequence, use of resources, pedagogical intentions, groupings of students (where relevant)
- an indication of the specific teaching points in the lesson; these might be framed in terms of key concepts, knowledge, skills and attitudes
- an indication of the precise activities that will be taking place in the lesson and the times at which they will be taking place
- an indication of how continuity/progression/differentiation are addressed;
- an indication of what the student teacher will be doing at the various stages of the lesson, with particular groups and individuals, and what her priorities are for the lesson
- an indication (if not already covered in the preceding points) of criteria for evaluation of the lesson and self-evaluation of the student teacher
- anticipated difficulties (e.g. in behaviour, cognitive content, teaching points) and how they will be addressed
- an indication of assessment evidence that the lesson will provide (so that the student teacher can complete formal assessment requirements and informal – often diagnostic – assessments).

We are suggesting here that if student teachers provide clear details of intentions for the lesson, for learning, organisation and outcomes, this facilitates evaluation and self-evaluation because the criteria for evaluation and self-evaluation have been clarified. The student teacher can then evaluate the extent to which the objectives for all aspects of the lesson have been achieved and why that was or was not the case. This brings us back to the notion of action planning in order to facilitate review and subsequent action planning.

In most cases student teachers are well advised to include more detail than experienced teachers keep in their planning. Experienced teachers have a tacit understanding of planning, organisational and pedagogical issues that do not necessarily need to be committed to paper. Inexperienced student teachers do not have that tacit knowledge or it is embryonic, hence it is a useful principle to over-plan rather than to under-plan.

For example, many student teachers put on a lesson plan the words to the effect that 'the class will discuss such-and-such'; when they come to take the lesson they find that it goes awry quite badly, that the students are not motivated or engaged on the task, that it seems to go nowhere and that nothing useful seems to have come out of it. It could well be that this is because that section of the lesson plan that mentioned the discussion was not clear on its objectives; on what was required to come out of the discussion; on what the main features of the discussion were to be; on how the student teacher could prompt and lead the discussion; on the specific questions that the student teacher was going to ask, and why these questions were chosen. The lack of purpose in the plan was conveyed in the implementation – anything could become relevant, any direction become acceptable. The lack of focus in fact meant that very little became relevant and very little became acceptable. The free-floating nature of the discussion meant that it was at the whim of the students; it encouraged caprice rather than logic.

At its simplest, because many student teachers come to teaching practices as comparative novices in working with large numbers of students, they are unused to phrasing questions (see the discussion of questioning in Part III). There is a powerful case for student teachers writing down the actual words that they will use to ask questions, to prompt discussions, to clarify exactly what is required to come out of the discussion, to lead the discussion to a conclusion, to link the discussion to the contents of the lesson which precede it and the activities that follow after it. What we are advocating here is that the lesson plans are absolutely specific in their objectives and that these objectives are made clear to the school students. This rehearses the argument that we have made throughout the book that an objectives model of planning can be a very positive organising principle.

We are not necessarily advocating that student teachers spend hour upon hour writing down every fine detail of the lesson, often as a cosmetic exercise to please a tutor or class teacher. On the contrary, we are suggesting that the student teacher will need to be explicitly clear on every aspect of the lesson and that this should be committed to paper at a level of detail and prioritisation that is useful for the professional preparation of the student teacher and useful to colleagues – for example, class teachers, mentors, tutors from the institution of higher education, visiting examiners – so that they can trace back through the teaching practice file to find out how the lesson relates to previous work and understand at speed what is supposed to be taking place in the lesson. Further, the delineation of detail enables self-evaluation and review to have some clear foci (see the discussions of evaluations, self-evaluations, self-assessments and review later).

We have argued that there are several constants that should appear in a lesson plan if it is to be useful. How these are set out in a lesson format is a matter of judgement. Some formats will provide much space for organisational matters and for details of how each group in a class will be working; other formats might emphasise the curriculum contents; others will emphasise particular teaching points and roles of the student teacher and so on. The formats that we provide here are examples only; clearly individual formats will depend on their appropriateness to the task in hand and the student teacher.

A lesson plan particularly designed for groups within a single class or set of students is presented in Box 40.

When planning for group work it is essential to make certain that the student teacher will be able to 'be in the right place at the right time'; she cannot see to all groups at once and she needs to be able to set a group off working in the knowledge that they will not need her attention for, say, ten minutes, so that she can be freed to see to other groups. After that ten minutes has passed the student teacher needs to have planned to be free to return to the first group. Further, the tasks set must be such that the student teacher can be reasonably certain that despite unpredicted events occurring in the normal course of the day:

●   the students will finish together (if that is desired); or

Box 40: A lesson plan for group work

Date:	Group 1	Group 2	Group 3	Group 4
09.00–9.20	Registration, news, assembly	Registration, news, assembly	Registration, news, assembly	Registration, news, assembly
09.25	*Mathematics* Children's activities Teacher's tasks/teaching points	*Reading and writing* Children's activities Teacher's tasks/teaching points	*Painting, shop, Play-doh* Children's activities Teacher's tasks/teaching points	*Sand/water tray, home corner* Children's activities Teacher's tasks/teaching points
09.45	→	→	*Mathematics* Children's activities Teacher's tasks/teaching points	*Reading and writing* Children's activities Teacher's tasks/teaching points
10.00–10.30	*Painting, shop, Play-doh* Children's activities Teacher's tasks/teaching points	*Sand/water tray, home corner* Children's activities Teacher's tasks/teaching points	→	→
10.45	*Measuring and recording* Children's activities Teacher's tasks/teaching points	*Mathematics* Children's activities Teacher's tasks/teaching points	*Reading and writing* Children's activities Teacher's tasks/teaching points	*Painting, shop, Play-doh* Children's activities Teacher's tasks/teaching points
11.15–11.55	*Sand tray, water tray, home corner* Children's activities Teacher's tasks/teaching points	*Painting, shop, Play-doh* Children's activities Teacher's tasks/teaching points	*Model making* Children's activities Teacher's tasks/teaching points	*Mathematics* Children's activities Teacher's tasks/teaching points
13.00	*Music corner/cassette work* Children's activities Teacher's tasks/teaching points	*Library corner* Children's activities Teacher's tasks/teaching points	*Model making* (from morning) Children's activities Teacher's tasks/teaching points	*Measuring and recording* Children's activities Teacher's tasks/teaching points
13.50–14.30			Physical Education	
14.45	Complete audio cassette work Children's activities Teacher's tasks/teaching points	Complete Lego models from previous day, jigsaws Children's activities Teacher's tasks/teaching points	Continue model making, tidy up Children's activities Teacher's tasks/teaching points	Finishing the measuring and recording, tidying up Children's activities Teacher's tasks/teaching points
15.05–15.30			Story	

● that students who have completed the task before the end of the lesson are able to be gainfully employed in another activity – maybe an extension activity, or completing a previous piece of work from another occasion, or undertaking a 'holding' activity that does not require the student teacher's attention but is educationally worthwhile; or

● that the stage of completion of an incomplete task is such that it is able to be picked up easily (with cognitive as well as practical ease) at a future occasion, i.e. that the main features of the task have been completed.

Indeed, so careful must be the planning that it may be necessary to have a more detailed activity plan for each activity, and we provide an example in Box 41.[52]

The significance of these points is marked. They direct attention to the need to consider carefully in planning for group work: (a) the type and size of the tasks; (b) the timing and time scales of the tasks; (c) the sequence of the lesson so that the student teacher can use her own time most efficiently and effectively. That is a tall order that requires considerable planning. It was Bernstein[53] and Sharp and Green[54] in the 1970s who alluded to the fact that the most apparently 'free' classrooms were, in fact the most planned and carefully structured; it was simply that the pedagogy was 'invisible'. That is a salutary message that teachers of very young school children know – sometimes to their cost! For lesson planning, then, a device in the format must be used that will give special attention to task type, timing and sequence. An example of this is given in Box 40 – a format that is used by many teachers of young children.

Box 41: An activity sheet for the Foundation Stage

Activity
Learning to manipulate a remote control car to follow a route to the shops
Show the children how to use the controls, take turns to practise moving the car along different routes to the shops

Grouping of children
3–4 children

Main learning intentions	**Key vocabulary**
Know how to operate simple equipment (KUW).	Forwards/backwards
Show an interest in why things happen and how they work (KUW).	Further away/nearer to
	Left/right
Share and take turns (PSED).	Next/to
Work as part of a group (PSED).	– Can you make the car stop?
	– Can you make the car move forward?

Resources	**Adapting the activity for individual children**
Remote control car.	Children sequence two or three moves together.
Materials/boxes to customise the car.	Children teach other children how to use the remote
Large sheet of paper with route on.	control car.
Large sheet of paper for children to draw new	Children draw out new routes on large sheets of paper.
routes on.	Children manipulate the remote control car to a set of
	verbal instructions.

Children for whom this activity is particularly appropriate
Full time Ruth, Nadid, Sam, Katy
Part time Alex C (am) Luke (am) David (pm) Callum B (pm)

PSED = personal, social and emotional development; KUW = knowledge and understanding of the world

In this example the time line in the left-hand column provides the student teacher with a very clear outline of what should be taking place and when; it indicates group work and whole-class work; it indicates the sequence of activities for each group and shows that each group is receiving a spread of activities over a single day. One can see, for example, that Group 1, for whatever reason – is being given longer than Group 2 for mathematics; Group 2, in turn, is being given longer for reading and writing than Group 3; it has been recognised that model making for Group 3 requires a considerable amount of time – longer than the completion of the Lego models for Group 2; Group 4 is experiencing two types of mathematics activity – one in the morning and another in the afternoon. Group two completes a Lego model from the previous day, ensuring that a comparatively large task is completed over a two-day span, so that children do not become bored with it by making it last too long.

By looking across the rows the student teacher is able to see what activities should be taking place at any one time, so that he can make the most use of himself. For example at 11.15 he may wish to concentrate on setting away the work of Group 4 because the work of the other three groups does not necessarily require his immediate presence – as the model makers (Group 3) will be getting their resources ready and their protective clothing whilst Groups 1 and 2 have been able to observe the activities in the sand, water, home corner, painting, shop and Play-doh in the four groups in the first session of the morning. Then, when Group 4 has been started the teacher can then go to Groups 3, 2 and 1, probably in that order. Once he has completed the round of these three groups, Group 4 will be ready for his attention. At a pedagogical level this plan has to be set in the context of the debate on school and teacher effectiveness that questions the efficiency of learning when multiple groups of children are working on multiple curriculum areas simultaneously; that message strikes at the very heart of learning in the early years.

Though the matrix, for the sake of clarity here, has indicated that there will be children's activities and teachers' tasks, it has not indicated what these will be. A full plan for the day will probably spread over two or more sides of paper so that space is provided for a delineation of the student teacher's and children's tasks. One can speculate in this plan that the mathematics, reading and writing are continuing activities whilst the model making is more of a blocked activity.

This type of planning could well be 'front loaded', that is, it will take a considerable amount of time to prepare for four groups but it could well last the student teacher more than one day, as children will rotate round the activities over the course of two or more days. This is an important feature of lesson planning, for it indicates that:

- each lesson draws on and relates to one or more schemes of work
- a single lesson plan might last the student teacher for more than one session.

The folly of 'cosmetic' lesson planning is where a student teacher virtually duplicates a lesson plan from a previous day simply because the students did not complete the previous day's work. That is a sheer waste of time. Sense tells us that if a coherent lesson is planned to take two or more sessions then it is unnecessary to duplicate the lesson plan for each session. In our experience this is particularly true for mathematics lessons, as (a) the same concepts, objectives and content may take several lessons to achieve, and (b) the objectives for the mathematics may be contained in the scheme of work or the teacher's manuals for published schemes of work. This is not to invite student teachers to be lazy; it simply recognises that duplication may be needless.

EVALUATION AND REVIEW

So far this part has been concerned with aims and objectives, the planning of curriculum content and organisation and an indication of the need to plan the teaching and learning styles that will be used (discussed in more detail in Part III), together with the planning of resource use and the sequencing of the lesson and schemes of work. The point was made earlier that action planning – at whatever level (overall curriculum strategy, schemes of work, lesson plans) – requires, at some point, a review of the extent to which the plan has been realised in practice, so that the next cycle of action planning can be undertaken.

Moreover, the levels of planning discussed earlier indicated that action planning could apply to: (a) an overall curriculum policy (long-term planning); (b) schemes of work (medium-term planning), (c) weekly and daily plans (short-term planning); (d) lesson planning (short-term planning). It was argued that a major component of planning at these levels was the need to set appropriate aims and objectives – objectives for the whole teaching practice, for individual schemes, for a week's work, for a day's work, and for individual lessons. Further, it was suggested that the statements of objectives should apply not only to the children and students but to the student teachers themselves because student teachers undertook teaching practice in order to learn how to teach.

The outcome of these issues is to suggest that evaluation must take place with regard to (a)–(d) above. The form of evaluation is largely an objectives model[55] that takes its lead from the work of Stake.[56] Stake argues that teaching and curriculum planning begin with a statement of intentions (or objectives) with regard to:

1   antecedents (the putative initial conditions or state of the class, the student teacher, the students, the curriculum, the resources)
2   transactions (the proposed processes that will be experienced in achieving the objectives, with regard to, for example, the teaching and learning styles, the structuring, sequencing and organisation of the content, the organisation of classroom groups, the nature of the use of resources)
3   outcomes (the proposed outcomes with respect to the achievements of the objectives, the students' and student teacher's learning and behaviour, the curriculum knowledge, skills and attitudes that have been learnt).

The task of this objectives-based form of evaluation is to chart the extent to which the intentions (objectives and expectations) have been realised in practice, the match between intentions and actuality in respect of 1–3.

With reference to antecedents the student teacher, for example, might expect the students to have understood simple addition of fractions. She commences work to build on that which she has planned to find as an initial condition, only to discover that in reality several students have no understanding of the addition of fractions. The intended antecedents of another student teacher might have included, for instance, an expectation that resources for teaching the history of the Victorian age would be plentiful, only to find that the resources are very meagre. Another student teacher might expect to be teaching in a room with enough chairs and tables for every student to be able to sit and see the student teacher, only to find that the room is L-shaped and that, because of the small working areas, there are only enough chairs and tables for three-quarters of the class with the regular class teacher always planning for one group to be out of the L-shaped room and in a 'wet' area that is shared with another class. These messages suggest the pressing need for a full situational analysis of the school and the class before the teaching practice begins, including gathering information on children's abilities and prior knowledge.

With reference to transactions the student teacher might have planned collaborative group work, only to find that the students cannot handle the apparent freedom and opportunity to talk (often about matters unrelated to the lesson!). Another student teacher might have planned for multi-media resource-based learning, only to find that on the days on which she had planned for this to occur some of the computers were booked out for another class, some children were unsure how to operate equipment, others saw the change of student teacher's role from an instructor to a facilitator as a licence to misbehave. Clearly the intentions for how the sessions would run would have to be rethought.

With reference to outcomes, these fall into a variety of fields. The student teacher may wish to know the extent to which the students have learnt the knowledge, concepts, skills and attitudes that had been intended that they should learn. This is the model of evaluation-as-assessment that underpins the formal assessment of student achievement at the end of each Key Stage of the National Curriculum. The student teacher might have set targets for her own learning – the achievement of specified TTA competencies that were introduced in Part I – and wishes to reflect on and evaluate her achievement of these. The student teacher may want to evaluate the extent to which her planning for flexible learning arrangements to improve students' ability to work autonomously (mentioned in Part I) and to speed up their learning progress have been successful.

With regard to the evaluation of outcomes a student teacher might have intended the students to have come to an understanding of the water cycle, only to find at the end of the teaching practice when a summative – terminal – assessment is undertaken (see Part IV on assessment) that, though they can identify different elements of the water cycle, say evaporation and precipitation, they have been unable to grasp the cyclical nature of the water cycle, i.e. they have failed to understand the key concept in question.

In all of these examples the purpose of an objectives model is to evaluate the degree of match between that which was proposed and that which occurred. This is a very powerful form of evaluation for it is ruthless. It asks what student teachers and students can do at the end of the teaching practice, week, day and lesson that they could not do at the beginning. Having made explicit what the objectives are for each level and element of planning, this model (we suggested earlier that objectives were to be very specific and concrete) assesses, maybe measures, a level of success or failure in achieving them. The objectives become the criteria for evaluation. As a result of the evaluation a new plan of campaign can be drawn up – the commencement of the next round of action planning.

This model does not look for reasons why the objectives were or were not achieved; instead it confines itself to what was achieved – the cold, hard edge of success or failure. That is both its strength and weakness. For example, its strength may be to reveal that a clear 30 per cent of the class had understood the multi-faceted notion of social class in a sociology programme; its weakness here is to consign 70 per cent of the class to failure, with the concomitant problems of negative labelling and the lowering of self-esteem.

The argument so far points to three major difficulties in using an objectives model. First, Morrison[57] argues that:

> [w]hilst the objectives model is very useful in detailing which objectives have been achieved and their level of achievement, it does not address those types of evaluation which seek to explain why the objectives may or may not have been achieved. Hence its simplicity is bought at the price of explanatory potential. It is the model which is useful for describing rather than explaining.

The model is weak on suggesting ways forward for improvement; it has little formative potential. Lawton[58] said of this model that it is akin to undertaking intelligence after the war is over.

Second, in evaluating the achievement of the objectives the model takes little or no account of matters that were not stated in the objectives. For example, a host of unanticipated but worth-while matters might have arisen during the course of the teaching practice that the objectives fail to catch. Further, some educationally beneficial activities (for student teachers and students) are not susceptible to formulation in neat objectives; longer term and deeper qualities that education can develop over time are not easily captured in objectives.

Third, there is a risk in an objectives model that the objectives themselves are not evaluated, their worthwhileness is not considered. This misrepresents the semantic root of evaluation, the notion of value. To overcome this problem the student teacher should have considered overall aims of the teaching practice and should have prefaced each scheme of work with a statement of aims. As was mentioned in the earlier discussion of aims, these indicate the main purposes, rationales, principles and values that the school sees itself as serving – the stuff of 'mission statements' that appear in school prospectuses.

The implications of this discussion are to suggest that the student teacher, in undertaking evaluations and reviews for the purpose of action planning, will find it useful:

●   to use an objectives model at all levels (relating to schemes of work, weekly, daily and lesson-by-lesson plans)
●   to amplify an objectives-based evaluation with an analytical aspect, a diagnosis of why the objectives were or were not achieved
●   to amplify an objectives-based evaluation with comments on the development of qualities and longer term, underlying matters that are not measurable
●   to recognise that achievement of objectives may be partial in terms of which aspects of objectives were achieved, the levels of success in achieving of objectives
●   to evaluate matters that arose in the teaching practice that were not anticipated
●   to relate the evaluation of objectives to the development of the TTA competencies
●   to include in evaluation the question of value, the worthwhileness of activities and plans, particularly of overall aims of the teaching practice and schemes of work
●   to use evaluations formatively, as springboards into further action, rather than summatively.

We can use these points and the preceding discussion to arrive at a definition of evaluation as 'the provision of information about specified issues upon which judgements are based and from which decisions for action are taken'.[59] Using these principles the evaluations that student teachers conduct will address their success in achieving their overall aims for the teaching practice; their schemes of work; their weekly and daily plans, and their lesson plans. These evaluations will differ in their focus, form, methods, evidence – types and sources, and outcomes. This is not the place to look at the whole range of issues in evaluation as some of these go wider than the needs of a student on teaching practice (though some of these are addressed throughout the book by way of suggesting success criteria in terms of content and pedagogy and others feature in Part IV on assessment). This section concerns a student teacher's self-evaluation.

An evaluation of successes or achievements will need to make clear what the success criteria are (a feature which, as Part I indicated, is a requisite for effective school development plans). If a lesson note contains clear, specific, concrete (often behavioural) objectives then these can be used as success criteria, for example learning the use of the full stop, understanding that ice has a greater volume than its equivalent weight in water. However, as indicated above, it is not always possible, or indeed desirable, to cast objectives or their outcomes in behavioural terms, or be able to conduct this tightly focused form of evaluation, because events and outcomes are not always precise and tight. This is less true of lesson plans but more true of daily and weekly plans, schemes of work and overall aims of the teaching practice. We address these in turn below.

EVALUATION OF ACHIEVEMENT OF OVERALL AIMS FOR THE TEACHING PRACTICE

The statement of aims and priorities that student teachers write as the outcome of their situational analysis and overall planning are couched in general, non-operational terms (see the earlier discussion of aims and objectives). In this sense, also, it is both invidious and impossible to discuss 'achievement' of the aims; because they are infinite (e.g. it is impossible to say that a person has achieved a finite state of creativity, imaginativeness, being educated) they will never be achieved finally and completely. The overall aims are qualitative; they describe qualities rather than outcomes. It is advisable, then, to address an evaluation of how, how fully and how successfully the aims have been addressed, in qualitative terms – words, informed opinions, judgements based on the professional insights of connoisseurs,[60] in this case experienced teachers, mentors, tutors from institutions of higher education who are examples of reflective practitioners (see the discussion in Part I of reflective practice).

This evaluation will be summative, that is, a retrospective, summary review of that which has taken place during the practice that is conducted at the end of the teaching practice in terms of the match of intentions and actuality (see the discussion of Stake's 'countenance' model of evaluation above). This evaluation will address points 2–7 from the list of considerations outlined above. It will also focus on the student teachers' own development of reflective practice, e.g. the move beyond a technical, recipe-driven view of teaching to a flexible style of teaching that is underpinned by relevant theory (see the discussion of reflective practice in Part I). The evaluation will both describe the ways in which the aims have been addressed and explain (and justify) why they were addressed in that way.

EVALUATION OF ACHIEVEMENTS OF THE SCHEME OF WORK

The discussion of issues in evaluating the achievement of the aims of schemes of work rehearses that of the overall aims of the teaching practice and so will not be repeated here. In judging the success of the achievement of objectives an evaluation can focus on objectives that were set out for:

- the student teacher, what she has learned about: students; preparation; curriculum planning, topic work and subject planning; organisation, sequencing and structure; assessment; behaviour, relationships, discipline and control; resource preparation and management (e.g. time, space, materials, staff, children, audiovisual, books, charts, displays, ICT); relationships with colleagues
- the students/children, e.g. interests, motivations; behaviours; abilities, progress; achievements, independence and autonomy; self-esteem; interactions; equal opportunities
- the organisation of the classroom(s), layout, seating arrangements, resource access
- the curriculum, framing (e.g. knowledge, concepts, skills, attitudes), content, coverage, breadth, balance, relevance, differentiation, progression, continuity, coherence, prioritisation, variety, organisation, structure, sequencing, resourcing
- the pedagogy, e.g. structuring activities; use of first- and second-hand experiences; drawing on students' contributions; stimulating and motivating students; teaching and learning styles and strategies; the resource access and use; the use of different types of display; timing and pacing; matching and differentiation; class, group and individual work
- assessment and monitoring, opportunities for diagnostic teaching.

The breadth of the review of the achievement of the plans that were contained in the schemes of work is a function of the breadth of the schemes. Part of the summative review might consider the appropriateness of the breadth of the schemes that was addressed. As with the overall aims discussed above, the review of the success of the schemes of work will also consider their worth-whileness. Again, as with the evaluation of the overall aims and priorities, the evaluation of the success of the schemes of work will be summative and retrospective and qualitative (using evidence from people and student outcomes that have been recorded in the students' ongoing records, weekly, daily and lesson-by-lesson comments and students' work and results on formal and informal assess-ments). Additionally there may be 'marks', grades or other forms of 'hard data' that might be used in judging the success of the schemes of work. The evaluation of the scheme of work, like the eval-uation of the overall aims, will describe the main features that have come out of a review of the schemes with significant adults; though this may include an analytical or explanatory element it will be slight here, being reserved largely for the shorter term weekly, daily and lesson evaluations.

WEEKLY AND DAILY EVALUATIONS

These evaluations will identify key points that the student has learnt over the previous week or day respectively. They identify priorities for the student teacher in terms of (a) what she has learnt about teaching, and (b) what the implications of this are for subsequent weekly and daily planning. They are not concerned with description; rather they are concerned with analysis of and explanations for the incidence or importance of the major features selected. For example, they might focus on significant points that the student teacher has learned about behaviour and discipline, e.g. promo-tion of positive behaviour patterns, encouraging self-esteem, a range of strategies to avert or minimise bad behaviour, managing the whole class, transitions, use of voice, praise, maintaining high expectations; students; classrooms; curriculum planning and implementation; pedagogy, e.g. successful and unsuccessful strategies, collaborative and group work and seating arrangements; problem-solving and investigational work; resource access, use, organisation and storage; particu-lar types of activity; particular successes and failures and reasons for these.

These evaluations are formative, that is, they suggest implications for the immediate future during the teaching practice. They concern day-to-day matters and tactics for subsequent planning. Weekly evaluations might draw on the student teacher's discussions with her mentor, other teach-ers and involved adults, and they might include personal, subjective comments and self-review. The purpose of these evaluations is to shape what happens next; analyses and reviews of this nature lead into action planning. It is also the case that a weekly review is an appropriate time for the student to refer to her developing abilities in the Teacher Training Agency competencies.

EVALUATIONS OF SPECIFIC LESSONS

Though these evaluations will be very specific and focused, a student teacher who is developing as a reflective practitioner will need to be selective, to avoid reportage and low-level description and to be able to extract from the minutiae of classroom processes the significant issues for subsequent practice. The evaluation is at the level of issues rather than low-level accounts of what took place (except where they provide important detail to accompany the analytical commentary). A lesson evaluation will ask (and hopefully answer) why a specific lesson and elements of that lesson were more or less successful or unsuccessful and what the implications of this analysis are for the imme-diate future. This will focus on the achievement of the concrete objectives that were set out in the lesson plan and the level of success in achieving the elements of the lesson that were included in the lesson plan (see above for the contents of a lesson plan), for example:

●   the motivational, managerial and organisational factors at the introductory stages

- the clarity of communication – questioning, responding, explaining – at the introductory, development and concluding stages of the lesson
- the success of different stages of the lesson – introduction, development, conclusion
- the smoothness of the transition from one stage of a lesson to another or from one activity to the next in the lesson
- the quality of the student teacher's feedback that was given to individuals, groups and the whole class; the timing and pacing of different stages of the lesson
- the organisation, location, access and uses of resources for the lesson
- the success in addressing the key teaching points and key questions in the lesson
- the degree of success of the planned matching and differentiation
- the development of positive relationships between the student teacher and the students and between the students themselves
- the degree of success in achieving the intended learning outcomes for the student teacher
- the degree of success in achieving the intended learning outcomes for the students/children
- the degree of success in gaining data for assessment purposes – formal and informal
- the extent to which the activities drew on subjects and cross-curricular elements of the National Curriculum.

These are outline areas only. From our experience of teaching and supervision we would suggest that student teachers will find it useful to consider the following questions in evaluating lessons.

The curriculum

- *Aims and objectives:*
  - Are they clear, worthwhile, useful, appropriate?
- *Curriculum content:*
  - Is it appropriate for the objectives?
  - Is it appropriate for the skills to be learned or practised?
  - Is it appropriate for the teaching and learning styles used?
  - How far does the content address new knowledge?
  - How far does the content provide enrichment and application of existing knowledge?
  - How far does the content introduce new skills?
  - How far do the new skills reflect the students' experience and development?
  - How far does the content develop students' attitudes – what are they?
  - How interesting is the content?
  - How far does the content provide for breadth, balance, depth, relevance, coherence, continuity and progression?
  - What criteria are being used to address matching?

The teaching and learning

- *Task:*
  - Is the work sequenced at the optimal level?
  - Is the work well structured?
  - Is there an appropriate balance between choice and direction?
- *Time:*
  - Is the time used most effectively?
  - Is the time scale effective and appropriate?

  – Is time used flexibly to respond to students' learning styles?
● *Space:*
  – Is space used effectively – to reflect the range and nature of the activities?
  – Can students move round the room easily where necessary?
  – Can students understand the classroom organisation?
● *The student teacher:*
  – Are praise and blame used appropriately and effectively?
  – Is discipline effective?
  – Are students well motivated?
  – Is there a good rapport between the student teacher and the students?
  – Is the student teacher's approach well thought-out?
  – Is the student teacher's approach varied and stimulating?
  – Does the student teacher's approach respond to the complexity of the content?
  – Is the voice used effectively?
  – Are the student teacher's gestures and movements used effectively?
  – Are instructions clear?
  – Is the pacing of the lesson clear, brisk and appropriate?
  – Is questioning appropriate, varied and effective?
  – Are the exposition, explanation, discussion, summary effective?
  – Is the student teacher clear at the beginning, continuation and close of the lesson in the time allotted?
● *The students:*
  – Can they see and hear as necessary?
  – Is allowance made for students' different preferred learning styles?
  – Is there a suitable use of group, class and individual activities?
  – Are the students developing socially and emotionally as a consequence of the lesson?
● *Resources:*
  – Do the resources reflect the range of the curriculum?
  – Do the resources reflect the focus of the curriculum (e.g. first-hand and second-hand experience)?
  – Do the resources reflect the level of the curriculum for each student?
  – Are they stimulating?
  – Are they used?
  – Are they well maintained?
  – Are they accessible?
  – Are they appropriate to the task?
  – Are they of good quality?
  – Are there sufficient?
  – Are displays attractive?
  – Are displays used for learning?
  – Are displays changed as appropriate?
● *Record keeping:*
  – Are records appropriate, thorough, comprehensive, useful, used?
  – What is recorded?
  – How is the progress of each student recorded and monitored?[61]

Many schools and teacher education institutions devise their own evaluation pro-formas, raising questions as follows (Box 42).

Box 42: An evaluation pro-forma

Learning objectives
- Were there clear targets, consistently set?
- Did the targets show progression?
- Were the learning objectives made clear to the students?
- Were the learning objectives suitable?
- Did the learning objectives link to prior learning?

Curriculum content
- Was the planning clear?
- Was the content suitable, well matched and differentiated for the students?
- Were there targets and time limits set?
- Were the appropriate resources to hand and well used?
- Were there high yet realistic expectations of the students, in terms of work and behaviour?
- Were key skills addressed?
- Did the learning build on previous learning?
- Did the tasks address and involve new learning (incremental), consolidation, practice, enrichment, application tasks?

Teaching methods and strategies, activities, timing and sequence
- Did the student teacher have adequate subject knowledge and vocabulary?
- Were the exposition, activities and follow-up clear, well-timed, interesting, well-paced, focused?
- Was the time well spent?
- Were the links between the lessons clear?
- Were the beginning, middle and end of the session clear?
- Was the questioning effective?
- Was there an appropriate range of teaching and learning strategies?
- Was there formative evaluation?
- Was any assessment made clear?
- Was there differentiation?
- Was provision made for SEN/gifted and talented students?
- Did the student teacher respond appropriately to students' emergent needs?
- Was the learning active and engaging?
- Did the students apply their knowledge and learning?
- Were the methods chosen such that all students could learn effectively?

Learning
- What did the students learn?
- Did the students learn what was intended?
- Did the students respond positively to the challenges set?
- Did the students understand what they learnt?
- Did the students know what was expected of them for successful performance?
- Did the students support each other?
- Did the students participate well?
- Did the students take responsibility for their learning?
- Did the students take pride in their work and present it well?
- Did the students try hard?
- Was there progress in knowledge, understanding and skills?
- Was there progress in students developing their own learning skills?
- Did the student teacher develop students' confidence, motivation and self-esteem?
- Were students encouraged and praised?
- Were the students responsive and positive/enthusiastic?
- Did the students learn independently?
- Did the students sustain their concentration?

Management
- Was the class management effective?
- Was the start of the lesson clear and orderly?
- Was the class management appropriate?
- Were support staff used effectively?
- Was the student behaviour acceptable?
- Were praise, rewards, sanctions, negative comments used appropriately?
- Did the student teacher intervene effectively to deal with unacceptable behaviour?
- Were all students involved in their learning?
- Was the classroom environment conducive to learning?
- Was there an understanding of classroom rules and routines?
- Did the students listen, contribute and question?
- Did the student teacher insist on high standards of behaviour?
- Were the relationships good?
- Was the end of the lesson orderly, e.g. collection of resources?

Homework
- Was homework set?
- Was homework used in the class?
- Was time given for reflection on the results of the homework?
- Was homework useful?
- Was homework relevant?
- Was homework adequately prepared for in the session?
- Did the homework link well into the session?

Attainment
- Was there evidence of progressive improvement in attainment?
- Are different groups achieving as they should be for their age/ability?

Marking
- Do the marking and feedback enable students to know how to improve?
- Is marking up-to-date and regular?
- Is assessment thorough and consistent?
- Is feedback used constructively?
- Is the feedback motivating and encouraging?

Assessment
- Was the assessment formative?
- Was the assessment effective, and for what?
- Was there a review of learning achieved?
- Did students evaluate themselves?
- Did the students know how to improve?
- Were students aware of their own strengths and weaknesses?
- Did the students make the progress expected?
- Was it made clear what the criteria for success were?

Evaluation
- What session evaluation has there been?
- How have the evaluations contributed to improvement in the lessons, teaching, learning, levels of achievement and attainment?
- How have the evaluations led into subsequent planning?

Another way for student teachers to evaluate their own teaching, or, indeed for them to be evaluated, is to refer to the work of the Office for Standards in Education. By going through its frameworks and handbooks for inspection it is possible to distil a series of questions for evaluating teaching and learning, based on several different sources of evidence. We present such a distillation in Boxes 43 and 44.

Below is an example of a student's self-evaluation of a lesson and a tutor's evaluation of the same lesson with a class of 28 Year 3 children. Neither evaluation is perfect! For example, the student's evaluation is descriptive, lacking in analysis, rather unselective, and unsuggestive of how it will affect future practice, even though it is clearly touched by authenticity. The tutor's evaluation, by contrast, is very long, rather pointed and maybe rather negative.

Box 43: Evaluation of the quality of learning

The effectiveness with which children:

• are paced through the lesson	1	2	3	4	5
• use skills and understanding	1	2	3	4	5
• progress appropriately in knowledge, understandings and skills	1	2	3	4	5
• experience a variety of learning contexts	1	2	3	4	5
• develop learning skills, including observation and information seeking, looking for patterns and deeper understanding, communicating information and ideas in various ways	1	2	3	4	5
• are willing to ask questions, to try to find answers, to solve problems	1	2	3	4	5
• apply what has been learned to unfamiliar situations	1	2	3	4	5
• evaluate the work that they have done	1	2	3	4	5
• foster and utilise enquiry skills	1	2	3	4	5
• offer comments and explanations	1	2	3	4	5
• demonstrate motivation, interest and the ability to concentrate, co-operate and work productively	1	2	3	4	5
• persevere and complete tasks when difficulties arise	1	2	3	4	5
• undertake practical activity which is purposeful and which encourages them to think about what they are doing	1	2	3	4	5
• respond to challenge of the tasks set	1	2	3	4	5
• are willing to concentrate	1	2	3	4	5
• can adjust to working in different contexts	1	2	3	4	5
• appear to be committed to and enjoying learning	1	2	3	4	5
• experience achievement that matches their abilities	1	2	3	4	5
• remain on task	1	2	3	4	5
• listen attentively to the teacher	1	2	3	4	5
• participate in the lesson	1	2	3	4	5
• can work independently	1	2	3	4	5
• can work co-operatively	1	2	3	4	5
• take responsibility for their own learning	1	2	3	4	5
• select appropriate resources	1	2	3	4	5
• demonstrate their learning both orally and practically	1	2	3	4	5
• understand the purposes of learning	1	2	3	4	5
• learn from their mistakes	1	2	3	4	5
• behave well in lessons	1	2	3	4	5

1 = very little; 2 = a little; 3 = quite a lot; 4 = a lot; 5 = a very great deal.

Box 44: Evaluation of the quality of teaching

The effectiveness with which:

teachers promote effective learning	1	2	3	4	5
teachers' expectations of children are high and appropriate	1	2	3	4	5
teachers develop skills and understanding in children	1	2	3	4	5
lessons are planned, their imaginativeness and links to attainment targets	1	2	3	4	5
progression and continuity are planned and appropriate	1	2	3	4	5
matching, differentiation of individual needs are addressed	1	2	3	4	5
the objectives of the lesson are appropriate	1	2	3	4	5
the objectives are clear	1	2	3	4	5
children are made aware of and understand the lesson objectives	1	2	3	4	5
expectations of the outcomes are appropriate	1	2	3	4	5
the approach, methods and materials match the lesson objectives	1	2	3	4	5
teachers have a secure command of their subject knowledge	1	2	3	4	5
the lesson content is appropriate and suitable	1	2	3	4	5
the activities are chosen to promote the learning of that content	1	2	3	4	5
the activities are engaging, interesting and challenging	1	2	3	4	5
teachers motivate children	1	2	3	4	5
teachers communicate their high expectations of the children	1	2	3	4	5
focus on high attainment and good progress is maintained	1	2	3	4	5
teachers support and encourage children	1	2	3	4	5
resources are used: their availability, accessibility, quality	1	2	3	4	5
teachers assess children's progress and provide constructive feedback to them	1	2	3	4	5
the lesson is conducted at an appropriate pace	1	2	3	4	5
the range of teaching techniques (e.g. individual, pairs, small group, large group, whole class) demonstrates fitness for purpose	1	2	3	4	5
teaching methods are varied, appropriate and promote learning	1	2	3	4	5
all children are encouraged to participate	1	2	3	4	5
positive relationships are developed with children	1	2	3	4	5
classroom organisation and resources (time, space, people, materials) promote learning	1	2	3	4	5
strategies for consolidating and accelerating learning are used	1	2	3	4	5
regular and positive feedback is given to children to enable them to become aware of their achievements and progress	1	2	3	4	5
teachers explain matters clearly	1	2	3	4	5
teachers use questions	1	2	3	4	5
teachers use instructional talk	1	2	3	4	5
teachers conduct discussions	1	2	3	4	5
teachers engage in procedural talk – the extent to which children know what they have to do	1	2	3	4	5

1 = very little; 2 = a little; 3 = quite a lot; 4 = a lot; 5 = a very great deal.

The student teacher's evaluation of an art and technology lesson

'I felt fairly confident about this lesson even though I had not done this sort of thing with children before. I thought the children would like to use all different sorts of materials and beads and to stick them onto paper. James and Donna made a mess of theirs and then went round spoiling others' work; I got cross with them and made them sit in the reading corner out of the way. James, as usual, didn't stay there but got up and carried on wandering round the room. I had to get very cross with him. The children enjoyed looking at the beads and holding them up to the light. I felt very harassed in this lesson as the red group kept arguing about nothing and the group in the corner (Joanne, Billy etc.) kept shouting for me to go and look at what they were doing. I could have killed Julie when she spilled the box of small beads and everyone came to tell me. At one point I had to stop everyone as too many children were being silly. I think I should have told them about their behaviour and the way to behave in this sort of lesson rather than say how nice some of their pictures were.

This lesson seemed endless. It took them ages to get everything and then they were on the go all the time. I seemed to spend my time stopping things from being spilled and stopping the children from being noisy. I had to get cross with Sharon as she used up three bits of paper. I think I must have told them what to do about a hundred times!

Some of the children made some good pictures and were pleased with them. I let the finished pictures go home.

Points for the future: get everything ready beforehand; show them more clearly what to do; cut down the numbers of children out of their seats; put out fewer materials and spread them round the room rather than having them all in one place with children crowding round each other; stop them much sooner if the lesson is getting noisy.

I enjoyed this lesson (I think) and wouldn't mind doing it again but I need to think about my organisation of the children, materials and classroom.'

The tutor's evaluation of an art and technology lesson

'Whilst your weekly evaluations are fairly analytical I think your daily and lesson descriptions need a lot more detail and analysis otherwise they simply describe and comment in a way which is not very useful for yourself and future planning. Further, in lesson plans more detail is needed to expose knowledge/concepts/skills/intended learning outcomes more extensively and then to see how these are translated into practice. We need to see evidence in the file of anticipation of organisational problems and how you will deal with these. If you are moving to differentiated work then you will sometimes need to have differentiated objectives.

This is a very ambitious lesson – all doing potentially chaotic activities. Therefore ask yourself: is this the best way to get through the task or would it be better just to have one or two groups on the "sticky" work? You have set up a situation which requires a lot of movement – are you happy with this? If you are happy with this you will need to talk the children through the getting of equipment far more closely, e.g. "You have two minutes to get what you need; don't start, just get what you need and then sit still." Then stop them all, talk about the task, then set them away on it. Or just have one table at a time getting the equipment. There was a time when only five children were actually sitting down, and only three of them were really doing anything.

The lesson note peters out after the introduction – what will you be doing/teaching during the lesson? We need to know!

You will have to question the wisdom of putting all the resources together, e.g. there was a constant (i.e. for ten minutes) throng round the beads – could this have been rearranged, or are you making a rule that if there are two or three children there then no one else is to go there? After five or six minutes stop them all, sit them down, calm them, talk (maybe about teaching points), then set the children away again. This sort of lesson puts you in a high-stress situation – where you are working ten times as much as the children – are you happy with this? When you stopped all the children (after 12 minutes) the effect was positive – you were able to make teaching points – do insist on their attention – tell them to put down scissors, brushes, glue, materials. The dangers of this mass activity is that you end up by having to devote your time to instructions and behavioural points rather than to teaching points – are you happy with this? How else could the lesson have been organised? Was there a fair payoff in children's work for all your effort? Could you have got a better pay-off by only having one or two groups at a time doing this?

Some of the children are using the materials for patterns, pictures and bas-relief 3D work (using beads for snowmen) – are you happy with this (you grew aware of this as the lesson went on – it should have been anticipated – proactive rather than reactive teaching)? There are different degrees of accuracy and precision at work here. How will you know how well each child is performing, or are there some children giving less than their best? How can you ensure that the glue keeps off the desk tops? Three desks have sizeable spillages. Are you happy that the children make up their pictures as they go along, rather than trying things out before they start gluing – arranging and rearranging and then gluing – i.e. are they planning and developing aesthetic criticism or just plonking things on uncritically? Many children were becoming increasingly frustrated because they were 'going wrong'; placing before gluing would have averted this.

How can you use this lesson and yourself to develop aesthetic awareness, criticism, awareness of media, materials, form, skills of fine motor control? This is all the stuff of a lesson plan.

It seems on rereading this that I have been rather negative about this lesson. In fact the children are getting on quite well (after 35 minutes) and the results are interesting. You have provided a good variety of materials, the children are quite absorbed in the topic; they are clearly learning about the mechanics of the activity. I am concerned that more could have come out of the activity and that your classroom organisation, organisation of the lesson, questioning of the efficacy of a whole-class activity of this sort, would have maximised the high potential of this lesson to really develop the aesthetic aspects of children's development. Do allow a good amount of time to clear up and round off the lesson with comments.'

Comment

Though the style and degree of detail are different in the two evaluations, nevertheless the two parties focus on the same issues: organisation of time, resources, children, layout of the classroom, discipline, degrees of involvement and engagement, rules and routines, anticipating problems and being proactive. The tutor was concerned not only with the 'management' aspects of the lesson but the lesson content itself and the ways in which the activity could address the curriculum objectives of the lesson. The tutor suggested that more detailed attention to the 'nuts and bolts' of the lesson would have been useful, both in the planning and implementation stages. In this former respect the tutor suggested that a more detailed lesson plan might have assisted the student in anticipating problems, rather than waiting for them to happen in the lesson. Clearly the tutor is more analytical than the student teacher and the tutor suggests ways of improving matters rather than merely describing the difficulties in the lesson. On the other hand the student's evaluation is honest and formative, suggesting 'points for the future'.

The evaluation of a lesson should be formative; it should shape very concretely and specifically the subsequent lessons that the student prepares – maybe to avoid certain types of activity, maybe to emphasise other types of activity, maybe to focus on organisational matters more in the lesson note and the running of the lesson in situ. A lesson evaluation should feed directly into the action plan for the next lesson or series of lessons. If it does not do this then its utility is limited. A summary of issues in evaluation and self-evaluation is presented in Box 45.

(See www.routledge.com/textbooks/9780415485586, Chapter 9 Beginning curriculum planning – further examples of weekly/daily lesson plans varying by age of students and degree of structure.)

Box 45: A summary of issues in evaluation and self-evaluation

ASPECTS OF EVALUATION AND SELF-EVALUATION

Level	Purposes	Type	Nature	Data sources	Types of data	Focuses	Reliability
Achievement of overall aims	Review	Summative	Generalised	Significant adults and self	Qualitative, words, informed opinion	Aims	Reference to other adults
Achievement of schemes of work	Review	Summative	General and key points	Significant adults	Qualitative, words, informed opinion	Aims, objectives, student teacher, students, classroom organisation, curriculum, pedagogy, assessment	Reference to other adults and student outcomes
Achievements of weekly and daily plans	Review, analysis of main priorities	Formative	Priorities and key points	Significant adults, self, students' work	Qualitative and quantitative from informed opinion and students' work	Aims, objectives, student teacher, students, classroom organisation, curriculum, pedagogy, assessment	Reference to other adults and student outcomes
Achievements of lesson plans	Review, analyse, explain, shape future practice	Formative	Specific, detailed, concrete	Significant adults, self, students' work	Qualitative and quantitative from informed opinion and students' work	Objectives, student teacher, students, classroom organisation, curriculum, pedagogy, assessment	Reference to other adults and student outcomes

PART III
PRACTISING TEACHING

Successful teaching is a composite of skills, competencies, artistry and much more besides. Some is learned by experience; some by preparation and reflection. Part III addresses a range of significant matters in practical day-to-day teaching and learning. There is a generic core of issues in considering teaching and learning, regardless of the age group with whom one is working and regardless of their learning potential and abilities. Part III commences with a new chapter on key issues in the practice of effective learning and teaching, and these inform subsequent chapters on primary and secondary teaching. We strongly advocate that student teachers take these three chapters together, rather than only reading the chapter that might apply to the age group for which they are currently preparing to teach. Effective teaching relies on effective communication, and the chapter on language in classrooms has been updated and extended to incorporate recent developments on direct instruction and whole-class interactive teaching. Further, with recent emphasis being placed on the identification of, and planning for, gifted and talented students and those with a range of special educational needs, themselves part of the inclusion policy of recent governments, we indicate the issues to be faced in the teaching and learning of students with a range of needs and interests. This includes the topical matter of raising the achievements of boys in schools.

Uppermost in the minds of many student teachers on teaching practice is the concern to maintain effective discipline and positive working relationships in classrooms. This concern is not confined to novice teachers, of course, but routinely exercises the mind of the most seasoned teachers. More recently the attention given to the reduction of bullying has come to the fore. All of these issues are addressed in the chapter on managing behaviour in classrooms, expanded from the 4th edition to reflect the growing significance of this aspect of teaching. The chapter is concerned to provide sound, practicable and tested advice on managing behaviour and effective relationships in classrooms.

9   Learning and Teaching

INTRODUCTION

Schools exist to promote learning. Teachers are facilitators of learning. In promoting learning there is no single blueprint for effectiveness, though there are very many characteristics of what constitutes effective teaching and effective learning. This chapter sets out some of the key principles for effective teaching and learning. At heart there is a move away from direct instructing (instructivism) towards constructivism. Many of the pedagogical issues that we raise in this book are premised on constructivism. We begin this chapter by looking at several principles of constructivism and then move to looking at other characteristics of effective teaching and learning. We organise our discussion of effective learning and teaching in two main areas.

First, we look at aspects of the moves to constructivism and their implications for considering learning and teaching. These include: higher-order thinking; brain-based learning; metacognition, learning styles, motivation and co-operative learning. Essentially we argue that effective learning uses higher-order thinking, and metacognition, which in large part are learned socially and co-operatively. We argue that effective learning must be intrinsically motivated and draw on learners' emotions as well the purely cognitive aspects of their make-up; developing intrinsic motivation and the affective side of learning can be facilitated through higher-order thinking and co-operative learning. In addition, effective teaching for learning entails looking at individual learners' styles and strategies for learning, and accommodating these in planning for learning. In short, we argue that these aspects are interrelated and mutually potentiating.

Second, we examine some issues in effective learning. This is deliberate, as it signals a significant move from attention on teaching to attention on learning; classrooms are places in which pupils learn rather than being mainly places in which teachers teach. In this section we examine teaching skills, professional characteristics and classroom climate. These entail a discussion of teaching styles and strategies, non-verbal teacher behaviour, modelling, student teachers' attitudes and expectations and the influence they exert on classroom behaviour, and the organisation of learning.

CONSTRUCTIVIST THEORY

Constructivist theory regards learning as an active process in which learners construct and internalise new concepts, ideas and knowledge based on their own present and past knowledge and experiences. Knowledge is constructed rather than received.[1] There are two types of constructivism which we address here: cognitive constructivism and social constructivism, though they both share common characteristics such as the view that knowledge is constructed through the learner's cognitive structures and processing, through active and participative learning (rather than passively

Box 46: Characteristics of cognitive constructivism

- Pupils construct their own knowledge of the world.
- Knowledge and understanding are constructed internally by the learner rather than transmitted from an external source such as the teacher.
- What someone knows is not passively received but actively assembled by the learner.
- Learners continuously organise, reorganise, structure and restructure new experiences to fit them to existing schemata, knowledge and conceptual structures through an adaptation process of assimilation (taking in knowledge and incorporating it into existing knowledge structures) and accommodation (changing ways of thinking as a result of learning and new knowledge) to accord with new views of reality, in striving for homeostasis (equilibrium) – the balance between assimilation and accommodation.
- Learning is a search for meaning, looking for wholes as well as parts.
- Learning is self-directed and active.
- Learning derives from experiences.
- Learning takes time.
- Learning involves language.
- Learning involves higher-order thinking.
- Learning is an individual and a social activity.
- Learning is self-regulated.
- Learning is, in part, an organisational process to make sense of the world.
- Learning is marked by the learner's capacities to explore and experiment.
- Motivation is critical to effective learning.
- Knowledge is uncertain, evolutionary, pragmatic and tentative.
- Knowledge is socially and culturally mediated and located.
- People generate their own mental models to make sense of their experience.
- Knowledge is creative, individual and personal.
- Intelligent thought involves metacognition.
- To teach well, we have to understand what pupils are thinking.
- Standardised curricula are antithetical to constructivism.

accepting meaning) and through a recognition that learning is not fixed and inert, but is continually developing. Learning moves away from the stimulus-response/behaviourist paradigm to the ongoing development of conceptual structures in generative, creative and often unique ways.[2]

Cognitive constructivism owes its genesis largely to Piaget[3] and is concerned with thinking and learning. Some key characteristics of cognitive constructivism are set out above (Box 46).[4] Social constructivism owes much of its pedigree to Vygotsky.[5] Whilst there are considerable overlaps between Piaget and Vygotsky, the latter is differentiated by reference to the social basis of much learning, particularly higher-order cognition.

One of Vygotsky's most well-known ideas was the 'zone of proximal development'. He recognised that most psychological experiments assessed the level of mental development of children by asking them to solve problems in standardised tests. He showed that a problem with this was that this testing only measured a summative aspect of development. In the course of his experiments Vygotsky discovered that a child who had a mental age of 8 as measured on a standardised test was able to solve a test for a 12-year-old child if they were given 'the first step in a solution, a leading question or some other form of help'.[6] He suggested that the difference between the child's level working alone and the child's level with some assistance should be called the zone of proximal development (ZPD). He found that those children who had the greater ZPD did better at school.

There are a number of practical consequences to ZPD. Vygotsky's ideas point to the importance of appropriate interaction, collaboration and co-operation. He suggested that, given minimal support, the children scored much higher on the tests. All teachers must make decisions about the kind of interventions that they make. Although the tests showed the influence of appropriate support they also remind us that collaboration is an important way of learning and that in the right context there is much that children can do *without* direct instruction.

If we accept the idea of ZPD, it leaves a number of questions about how teacher interaction can best support pupils' learning within the ZPD. The term 'scaffolding' has become commonplace in discussions about teaching; for example, the idea that teachers should 'model' and scaffold aspects of the writing process. Unfortunately, the didactic context for these recommendations is not the same as the original concept of scaffolding. David Wood coined the term 'scaffolding' in his research on the teaching techniques that mothers used with their 3–4-year-old children. Mothers were asked to become parent tutors, helping their children complete a task that could normally only be completed by children older than 7. The mothers who were able to help their children complete the task successfully scaffolded their children's learning in specific ways:

- They simplified problems that the child encountered.
- They removed potential distractions from the central task.
- They pointed things out that the child had missed.

Less successful parent tutors showed their child how to do the task without letting them have a go themselves, or using direct verbal instructions too much.

Overall, Wood identified two particularly important aspects of the successful parent tutors' scaffolding process. When a child was struggling, immediate help was offered. Then, when help had been given, support was gradually removed, encouraging the child's independence. 'We termed this aspect of tutoring "contingent" instruction. Such contingent support helps to ensure that the child is never left alone when he is in difficulty, nor is he "held back" by teaching that is too directive and intrusive.'[7] The vital point here is that scaffolding happens in the context of meaningful, one-on-one, interaction that is not inappropriately didactic. This idea of scaffolding is not what is happening when a teacher is demonstrating to the whole class some aspect of the process of learning. Although demonstration has a useful purpose it should not be called scaffolding and given dubious theoretical authenticity by inaccurate reference to Vygotsky.

Those who advocate constructivism suggest that, in practice, it emphasises:

- situated learning
- metacognition
- higher-order thinking
- the social basis of learning
- a move away from didactic (instructivist) approaches to teaching
- an emphasis on the process of learning, not simply on the product
- the breaking of subject boundaries and the development of project-based, real world ('authentic') learning and authentic assessment
- pupil-centred learning, and
- the significance of intrinsic motivation.

Behind the move from instruction and representation to knowledge generation and growth lie different theories of learning (Hung).[8] For example, there is a move from behaviourist, stimulus–response theories, through cognitivism, with its emphasis on information processing and transmission, to constructivism. Hung represents these as shown in Box 47.[9]

Box 47: Learning theories

	Behaviourist	Cognitivist	Constructivist	Social Constructivist
Learning	Stimulus and response	Transmitting and processing of knowledge and strategies	Personal discovery and experimentations	Mediation of different perspectives through language
Type of learning	Memorising and responding	Memorising and application of rules	Problem-solving in realistic and investigative situations	Collaborative learning and problem-solving
Instructional strategies	Present material for practice and feedback	Plan for cognitive learning strategies	Provide for active and self-regulated learner	Provide for scaffolds in the learning process
Key concepts	Reinforcement	Reproduction and elaboration	Personal discovery generally from first principles	Discovering different perspectives and shared meanings

The implications of these matters are significant, for they point to the need for teachers to ensure that learning is about problem-solving, communication, and the ability to evaluate and apply information, far beyond the recitation paradigm of traditional learning and an emphasis on 'correct' responses. Schools have to move away from the over-emphasis on linear logic and programmed instruction and learning, towards non-linear, networked, branching, hypertext views of learning, in which connections between knowledge are made and developed.

In this situation, argue Hokanson and Hooper,[10] new conceptions of intelligence emerge: facts give way to capabilities, the ability to find and handle emerging knowledge overtakes the ability to reproduce knowledge, and memorisation of facts takes second place to knowledge of where information is stored, how it can be utilised and an understanding of what it means. Whereas traditional pedagogy emphasises remembering as much as possible, the newer forms of education emphasise knowing what to know and how to use it.[11] Knowledge is evolutionary, not fixed and static. Sandholtz et al.[12] set out the differences between instruction and construction very clearly (Box 48).

Doherty[13] suggests that teachers have an important role to play in structuring learning in which learners take control of the process, and indeed of the cognitive processes. Teachers help to design the environment for learning and ensure that it engages the learner, collaborating with other learners, resources and experts to construct knowledge. Doherty argues (p. 2) that learner control over his or her own experiences and the depth and range of studies, content and delivery media, enable him/her to tailor the learning experience to meet his or her specific needs and interests. These are essential features of effective learning, not least in the self-efficacy which they promote in pupils and its effect on motivation and achievement (p. 4).

In terms of implications for teaching and learning, constructivism suggests radically different forms of teaching from those which take place in conventional, traditional classrooms. There are several principles which have been identified, for example:

Box 48: Differences between instruction and construction

Function	Instruction	Construction
Classroom activity	Teacher-controlled;didactic	Learner-centred,interactive
Teacher's role	Fact teller; expert	Collaborator, learner
Student role	Listener, always the learner	Collaborator, sometimes the expert
Instructional emphasis	Facts, memorisation	Relationships, inquiry and invention
Concept of knowledge	Accumulation of facts	Transformation of facts
Demonstration of success	Quantity	Quality of understanding
Assessment	Norm-referenced, multiple-choice items	Criterion-referenced, portfolios and performances
Technology use	Drill and practice	Communication, collaboration, information access and retrieval, expression

- encouraging and accepting pupil initiative and autonomy
- following pupils' responses to learning – be prepared to change to meeting pupils' needs
- checking pupils' understanding of concepts
- entering into dialogue with pupils about their learning
- asking thought-provoking, open-ended and higher-order questions
- asking pupils to elaborate on their initial responses
- challenging pupils' thinking, ideas and assumptions
- promoting pupils' curiosity and enquiry.
- engaging pupils in meaningful and relevant problem-solving
- seeking out pupils' values and concepts
- using diagnostic and formative assessment to guide learning
- reducing grading and standardised testing.

Discovery, guided discovery and meaningful learning replace rote, receptive and transmissive teaching,[14] and meaningful learning places relevance to real life at its heart. Education becomes 'education for capability' rather than 'education for repetition'.

It is impossible to introduce learning and its constructivist base without mentioning cognition – thinking, learning, understanding, how we perceive, learn and know something. Grabe and Grabe[15] suggest that learning which is informed by constructivist principles, and which is 'situated', bears several hallmarks. They suggest that meaning must be constructed from experience and information and that the goals of learning are to create meaningful and coherent representations of knowledge, linking new knowledge to the learner's existing knowledge. Further, the task of the teacher is to develop in learners a range of thinking skills and strategies.

Underpinning such strategies is the development of metacognition – thinking about one's own thinking, knowledge of one's own cognitive strategies and how one learns, and the ability to control or regulate this,[16] the development of which improves pupils' learning and accomplishments.[17] Indeed Scardamalia and Bereiter[18] found improved pupil reflection and progressive thought to be increased when attention was placed on metacognition, with pupils taking multiple perspectives and demonstrating independent thinking.

Grabe and Grabe[19] suggest that metacognition is the individual's ability to evaluate, plan for and regulate and adjust his or her own learning and its characteristics. Clearly it is the partner to self-directed and pupil-centred learning, in which, in part, pupils decide on requirements, set their own goals and decide the best strategies to reach them. The development of metacognition, the authors aver, can turn passive learning into active and more efficient learning. In terms of planning for the development of metacognition the teacher has the task of ensuring that learning involves both exploration and reflection.[20]

(See www.routledge.com/textbooks/9780415485586, Chapter 10 Learning and teaching, Implications of constructivism for teaching and learning.)

	Box 49: Conventional and restructured learning settings	
	Conventional settings	**Restructured settings**
Pupil role	Learn facts and skills by absorbing the content presented by teachers and media resources.	Create personal knowledge by acting on content provided by teachers, media resources and personal experiences.
Curriculum characteristics	Fragmented knowledge and disciplinary separation. Basic literacy established before higher level inquiry is encouraged. Focus on breadth of knowledge.	Multidisciplinary themes, knowledge integration and application. Emphasis on thinking skills and application. Emphasis on depth of understanding.
Social characteristics	Teacher-controlled setting with pupils working independently. Some competition.	Teacher functions as facilitator and learner. Pupils work collaboratively and make some decisions.
Assessment	Measurement of fact knowledge and discrete skills. Traditional tests.	Assessment of knowledge application. Performance of tasks to demonstrate understanding.
Teacher role	Present information and manage the classroom.	Guide pupil inquiry and model active learning.
Possible use of internet	Source of information for absorption.	Source of information for interpretation and knowledge creation. Outlet for original work.

HIGHER-ORDER THINKING

A key feature of effective learning is the development of higher-order thinking. Higher-order thinking is not a new concept (see Bloom's Taxonomy of Educational Objectives in 1956[21]). Higher-order thinking is complex; it concerns synthesis, evaluation, interpretation, hypothesising, prediction, conjecture, critical thinking and judgement. It further involves reflection, self-regulation, testing of ideas, and problem-solving.[22]

The highest form of 'cognitive engagement' is where learners plan and manage their own learning and exercise considerable autonomy,[23] together with reflection on the learning experience and the incorporation of new knowledge into existing knowledge. Hence planning, living with uncertainty, prediction, making meaning, and adopting multiple perspectives on an issue are all characteristics of higher-order thinking. Critical thinking involves finding information suitable for a specified purpose, analysing and evaluating arguments, information and sources, separating fact from opinion, exposing unstated assumptions, weighing evidence, evaluating the logic of the argument and reaching conclusions.[24]

This stands in stark contrast to many conventional models of learning, in which a lock-step approach is adopted (everyone proceeding uniformly at the same rate and in the same sequence), often with lower-order skills preceding higher-order skills. Such an approach overlooks the significant point that not only can higher-order skills be taught and learned concomitantly with lower-order skills, but that this actually benefits the learning of lower-order skills. Learning, application, evaluation and problem-solving are simultaneous.

Higher-order thinking is appropriate for all ages, abilities and levels of pupil; it is not something that is addressed after the lower-order skills have been learned, but is simultaneous with them. Learning lower-order skills and knowledge is achieved most effectively when it is in the context of learning and using higher-order skills. Effective teachers use powerful teaching strategies,[25] e.g. those which are suitably flexible to be tailored to the needs of learners, which encourage pupil talk and dialogue, and which encourage divergent thinking in which there is no single right answer or solution, i.e. higher-order thinking (Box 49).

(See www.routledge.com/textbooks/9780415485586, Chapter 10 Learning and teaching, Higher-order thinking – constituent elements and Higher-order thinking – how it is learnt.)

THE BRAIN AND LEARNING

In recent years there has been a resurgence of interest in neuroscience and the possible implications that this might have for teaching and learning. A very useful review of the contribution of brain science to teaching and learning was published in 2005[26] followed by a Teaching and Learning Research Programme commentary in 2007, addressing issues and opportunities for education.[27] Some of the key findings from both documents were:

- The brain has an evolved modular structure in which elementary functions are widely distributed.
- It is a parallel processor, with high connectivity, and high redundancy, and operates in a probabilistic manner.[28]

Although it is true that some areas of the brain have specialist functions, for complex functions (i.e. most learning in classrooms including seemingly basic things like number recognition), there are a range of areas of the brain that contribute.

- Contrary to popular belief, there is no convincing neuroscientific case for starting formal education as early as possible.
- There may be sensitive periods for the development of key learning, which last into teenage years and possibly further.

The idea that nearly all brain development happens at a critical phase (a specific period of time when a child can learn a particular skill) in the early years has little evidence to support it. There is therefore no neuroscientific case for starting formal education as early as possible.[29] Although the changes are less radical than during childhood, the brain does continue to change and develop through adolescence and adulthood. What is now proven is that structural changes that take place during puberty and adolescence do have direct implications for education [ibid, p.9].

- Neuroscience is confirming earlier psychological theories about the importance of emotional engagement in learning.

Hall (2005) argues that further research to increase our understanding of the link between emotion and learning is needed.[30] It is known, for example, that the amygdala and the hippocampus (the 'emotional brain') are linked to the frontal cortex (the reasoning part of the brain). The links between the two are only just beginning to be understood; however psychologists have known for some time that excess stress and fear can inhibit cognitive performance. This has clear implications for education. By default, learners are more likely to remember things better when they are emotionally engaged with their learning.

- Education has invested a vast amount of time and money in 'brain-based' ideas that have not been substantiated by any recognisable scientific understanding of the brain.

There is no robust neuroscience research to support the following, in spite of hints and claims to the contrary: Brain Gym (with the possible exception of the importance of the link between exercise and alertness generally); Accelerated learning; Labelling children as visual, auditory or kinaesthetic (VAK) learners; left- and right-brained children; enforced water drinking when children are not thirsty; etc. (ibid).

The 2007 TLRP commentary further summarises existing research in the area of specific aspects of brain care; for example, good regular dietary habits as being probably the most important nutritional issues influencing educational performance and achievement. Sleep is also cited as an important part of learning. Neuroscience is beginning to reveal the processes by which sleep helps us to 'lay down' and consolidate our memories so that they remain more robust when we come to access them later (p.11).

NEUROSCIENCE AND WORKING MEMORY

Neuroscience has enabled us to think further about the potential role of working memory in relation to education and learning. Working memory refers to the capacity of the brain to remember what is a limited set of information in order to carry out processing. Neuroimaging (studying the brain at work *in vivo*) has deepened our understanding of complex processes underpinning speech and language, thinking and reasoning, and reading and mathematics.[31]

In relation to our understanding of language processing, it has been proposed that working memory consists of three parts: a phonological loop for storing verbal information; a visuo-spatial sketchpad for visual information and a central executive, which regulates the other two parts[32] There is disagreement as to whether some parts of working memory are not involved in the basic decisions of writing processing such as planning, reading and editing, or whether all three parts of working memory are involved at all times (ibid). Bradford and Wyse (2008)[33] hypothesise that all three elements of working memory are used at all times during the writing process but that different aspects of the writing process will demand different balances of emphasis on use of the phonological loop and the visuo-spatial sketchpad. Empirical work has examined the extent to which the effort required by transcription can compromise other aspects of writing.[34] Evidence suggests that for beginner writers in particular, the heavy demands on working memory lead to limitations of writing output. For example, when trying to compose sentences, handwriting may not be fluent enough for children to record everything they want to say before they start to forget some of their original thoughts.[35]

One of the practical outcomes of the TLRP research was the development of evidence-informed pedagogic principles.[36]

1   *Effective pedagogy equips learners for life in its broadest sense.* Learning should aim to help individuals and groups to develop the intellectual, personal and social resources that will enable them to participate as active citizens, contribute to economic development and flourish as individuals in a diverse and changing society. This means adopting a broad conception of worthwhile learning outcomes and taking seriously issues of equity and social justice for all.

2   *Effective pedagogy engages with valued forms of knowledge.* Pedagogy should engage learners with the big ideas, key skills and processes, modes of discourse, ways of thinking and practising, attitudes and relationships, which are the most valued learning processes and outcomes in particular contexts. They need to understand what constitutes quality, standards and expertise in different settings.

3   *Effective pedagogy recognises the importance of prior experience and learning.* Pedagogy should take account of what the learner knows already in order for them, and those who support their learning, to plan their next steps. This includes building on prior learning but also taking account of the personal and cultural experiences of different groups of learners.

4   *Effective pedagogy requires learning to be scaffolded.* Teachers, trainers and all those, including peers, who support the learning of others, should provide activities, cultures and structures of intellectual, social and emotional support to help learners to move forward in their learning. When these supports are removed the learning needs to be secure.

5   *Effective pedagogy needs assessment to be congruent with learning.* Assessment should be designed and implemented with the goal of achieving maximum validity both in terms of learning outcomes and learning processes. It should help to advance learning as well as determine whether learning has occurred.

6   *Effective pedagogy promotes the active engagement of the learner.* A chief goal of learning should be the promotion of learners' independence and autonomy. This involves acquiring a repertoire of learning strategies and practices, developing positive learning dispositions and having the will and confidence to become agents in their own learning.

7   *Effective pedagogy fosters both individual and social processes and outcomes.* Learners should be encouraged and helped to build relationships and communication with others for learning purposes, in order to assist the mutual construction of knowledge and enhance the achievements of individuals and groups. Consulting learners about their learning and giving them a voice is both an expectation and a right.

8   *Effective pedagogy recognises the significance of informal learning.* Informal learning, such as learning out of school or away from the workplace, should be recognised as at least as significant as formal learning and should therefore be valued and utilised appropriately in formal processes.

9   *Effective pedagogy depends on the learning of all those who support the learning of others.* The need for lecturers, teachers, trainers and co-workers to learn continuously in order to develop their knowledge and skill, and adapt and develop their roles, especially through practice-based inquiry, should be recognised and supported.

10   *Effective pedagogy demands consistent policy frameworks with support for learning as their primary focus.* Organisational and system-level policies need to recognise the fundamental importance of continual learning – for individual, team, organisational and system success – and be designed to create effective learning environments for all learners.

These are the kind of research-informed ideas that should receive teachers' attention more than so-called brain-based learning, however, we recognise that the way ideas are presented, in addition to the merit of the ideas themselves, is a crucial factor in their popularity. As a student teacher it is important that you develop a critically evaluative mind set when presented with any new teaching methods.

(See www.routledge.com/textbooks/9780415485586, Chapter 10 Learning and teaching, Deep and superficial learning and Improving deep learning.)

METACOGNITION

Metacognition has come to the fore in identifying how to improve pupils' learning. Metacognition means that pupils understand their own learning, how they learn, how they learn best, how they learn less effectively, i.e. a process of self-evaluation of their learning strategies and successes. Metacognition can be deliberately developed through a variety of means (see Box 50).

Box 50: Developing metacognition

- Requires pupils to reflect on their own learning.
- Involves working through problems visually/graphically.
- Involves conducting debriefings.
- Uses co-operative learning and feedback from, and to, pupils.
- Introduces, and builds on, cognitive conflict (a puzzling experience which contradicts others) and constructive disagreement.
- Promotes the use of a considerable amount of pupil talk and interaction.
- Encourages pupils to consider:
  - examining aims, goals and objectives
  - examining all sides of an issue/argument
  - the plus, minus and interesting points in a situation
  - the consequences of, and sequels to, a situation.

LEARNING STYLES

There are several ways in which learning styles and strategies have been discussed. A well-known example derives from the work of Kolb:[37]

- *Divergers:* learners who need to be personally involved in the task, who perceive information in concrete terms and who reflect on it.
- *Convergers:* learners who prefer detailed steps in learning, who perceive information abstractly and who reflect on it.
- *Assimilators:* learners who thrive on problem-solving activities, and who perceive and process information abstractly and actively respectively.
- *Accommodators:* learners who enjoy taking risks, who thrive on flexibility in learning activities, and who process information actively.

Kolb argues that learning follows a cyclical process of concrete experience (doing it), leading to reflective observation (reflecting on the experience), leading to abstract conceptualisation (making sense of the experience) and active experimentation (planning what to do) and then moving back to repeat the cycle. The learner can enter the cycle at any point. Within this cyclical process there are four styles of learner:

1   The *reflector*, who seeks alternatives to create options, who is prepared to wait and watch others until the time is ripe for action, and who tries to retain a sense of perspective.

2   The *theorist*, who tries to gather all the facts and who is well organised, reviewing alternatives and calculating probabilities, working well independently and learning from his or her own past experiences.

3   The *pragmatist*, who is keen to try out new ideas, techniques and theories, who evaluates options and is good at finding out information, who sets goals and takes positive action to meet them, working well independently.

4   The *activist*, who is prepared to take risks, to become involved with others and to gain new ideas and insights from them, who is active and relies on personal 'gut feeling' to drive his or her actions.

Pachler[38] identifies ten 'types' of learner. Focusers 'concentrate on one aspect of a problem at a time and proceed in a step-by-step manner' through the problem, as opposed to scanners, who 'tackle several aspects of a problem at the same time and allow ideas to crystallise slowly'. Serialists (pupils who 'operate with single-proposition hypotheses' are contrasted to holists, who operate with multiple-proposition hypotheses). Further, there are 'impulsive versus reflective thinkers', 'divergent versus convergent thinkers', field-dependent learners (where 'perception [is] strongly dominated by the overall organisation of the surrounding field') versus field independent learners (where 'parts of the field are experienced as discrete from organised ground'). Ellis[39] and Hartley *et al.*[40] suggest visual learners, auditory learners, kinaesthetic learners, tactile learners, those with a concrete learning style, analytical learning style, communicative learning style, and authority-oriented learning style.

At issue here is not so much the description that one places upon a learning style, but what one does when faced with a class of pupils whose learning styles and preferences are varied within a single class. As suggested earlier in this chapter, it is important that teachers resist the temptation to label children as particular kinds of learners and instead try to vary their teaching so that children have the opportunity to learn in different ways.

MOTIVATION

There are several different views of motivation. They do not necessarily conflict with each other but rather complement each other because very often they focus on different things.

Behaviourism

Behaviourism, sometimes known as the stimulus–response theory, has several characteristics:

- A particular stimulus provokes a particular response.
- Behaviour that is positively reinforced is learned.
- Repetition and rote lead to learning.
- Learning is largely for extrinsic purposes.
- Negative reinforcement leads to forgetting.
- Lack of repetition leads to extinction.
- Learning is conditioned behaviour.
- Learning is evidenced in observable behaviour.
- Learning can be programmed.

Behaviourism lays emphasis on external rewards, e.g. grades and test scores, working to avoid being told off and working to please the teacher/parents. Motivation is extrinsic and instrumental – for an end beyond personal satisfaction and gain. The theory is one of external reward for the learning and demonstration of particular desired behaviours. It can become very mechanistic learning, dehumanised and reward-oriented – we only learn in order to pass the test, to gain the marks. It leads to rote, repetition and mechanical jumping-through-hoops, and superficial rather than deep learning.

Expectancy theory

Expectancy theory suggests that the learner is motivated by the anticipated gain/benefit, the likelihood of achieving the gain/benefit and the importance of the gain to the learner. In this sense it involves some intrinsic motivation as well as some extrinsic motivation. If we are using expectancy theory to motivate pupils then we have to work on their expectancies and the values that they attribute to the learning – to make the learning clearly worthwhile in the learner's eyes.

In expectancy theory, motivation for learning (M) is a function of the expectancies and likelihood of success by the learner (E) and the value that the learner attributes to the goals and outcomes of the learning (V). The amount of effort people expend on an activity is a function of the degree of expectancy that they have that a particular activity will lead to better performance, rewards and meeting their own desired objectives.

Needs theories

Needs theories regard motivation for learning as rooted in a humanistic, whole-person view of learning. Learning motivation is intrinsic, and cognitive, affective and physical needs are all interlinked in this theory.

Learning is a humanistic activity, engaging all aspects of the person's make-up, and learners have needs which must be met hierarchically. Lower-order needs must be satisfied before higher-order needs can be met (we cannot expect people to learn well if they are hungry or cold!). Self-esteem and self-actualisation are high in the hierarchy, and physical, security and emotional needs precede cognitive needs. In Maslow's hierarchy of needs, understanding and knowledge are at the top of the hierarchy, and require self-esteem and a sense of autonomy (self-actualisation) if they are to be attained. This is important if we reconsider activities, where many of the pedagogical practices damaged self-esteem. We progress through the hierarchy, from lower to higher-order fulfilments.

(See www.routledge.com/textbooks/9780415485586, Chapter 10 Learning and teaching, Enhancing pupils' self-esteem.)

Self-perception and self-worth

If motivation is to be successful then it must draw on the whole person and develop his/her self-esteem and self-worth. It is important to note that self-esteem is related to control over learning. In many schools the teachers tell the pupils what to think, when to think it, and, through testing, how well they have thought; this is a very impoverished view of learning that damages self-esteem. Rather, needs theories, through Maslow and issues of self-worth and self-esteem, emphasise the importance of pupils experiencing control over their learning, success and a sense of achievement, and being given rich and positive feedback. Learning motivation must be intrinsic, not just extrinsic. Theories of motivation which emphasise self-perception and self-worth suggest that learning is effective if self-esteem and self-worth are high and deserved and that, conversely, low self-esteem and self-worth are major barriers to effective motivation and learning. The theory suggests that learners must be given rich and positive feedback and must be shown respect if self-esteem is to stay high.

Self-esteem is a critical factor in educational and scholastic achievement. It has been defined[41] as the individual's evaluation of the discrepancy between his/her self-image and his/her ideal self. It is a measure of the extent to which the individual cares about the discrepancy. Since high self-esteem is going to improve the emotional ambience of a classroom, it is in the student teacher's best interests to enhance and develop this factor in individual students, mainly through fostering suitable interpersonal relationships and providing opportunities for success.

Learned helplessness

Many pedagogical practices in schools promote learned helplessness and can be attributed, in part, to teachers. It is a significant problem, which, if we want powerful learning to occur, must be solved. Many pupils are taught to be obedient, compliant, docile and passive, often through negative behaviourist motivational strategies. They are taught not to challenge or object. Learned helplessness is related to loss of control over one's learning; it occurs when we feel there is no response that we can make to a situation to change the course of events, even if we exert maximum effort. Often learned helplessness is a consequence of taught dependency, obedience, passive learning, compliance and docility, didactic and irrelevant teaching, with an over-emphasis on rewards and punishments (behaviourism). Learned helplessness, as a motivational problem, can result from pupils and teachers being trained to be locked into a prescribed system viewed as beyond their control.

There are several symptoms of learned helplessness. For example, there may be lowered initiation of voluntary responses by pupils; they may have a negative cognitive set (self-reproach and guilt and a tendency to underestimate their effectiveness). They may demonstrate passivity, a lack of self-confidence and a feeling of hopelessness. Such pupils may be poor at problem-solving; they may have wandering attention and poor social skills. Learned helplessness children are extrinsically motivated and not so much intrinsically motivated because of their failures. Children suffering from learned helplessness eventually give up. Indeed the only way in which they feel that they may gain attention or be noticed is if they fail.

Social theories

Social theories of learning emphasise the social learning environment. The social learning environment is highly significant for promoting learning. People are powerful teachers of each other and learners from each other, and, recalling the discussion of brain-based education, learning collaboratively is one of the most powerful ways of guaranteeing effective learning. Higher-order cognition is motivating, and is socially learned and transmitted, and indeed Vygotsky suggested that it is only in social groups that higher-order thinking is learned and transmitted.[42] Group and collaborative work, for example, is not an arbitrary learning strategy, perhaps used for the sake of variety; rather it is a necessary learning strategy. So the message is simple: use collaborative and interactive learning if you want to develop learning and higher-order thinking. Cognitive, behavioural and environmental factors constantly interact to promote motivation and learning in social theories of learning, not least because pupils model their learning on their observation of other learners.

CO-OPERATIVE LEARNING

Another important factor in helping to establish good relationships and one which lies in part within the teacher's control is that of teaching and learning styles. In this respect, the importance of co-operative learning must be stressed, with pupils working together in small groups to accomplish shared goals. Cullen *et al.*[43] suggest that constructivism spawns interactive methods and conversational methods. As Kutnick[44] explains, putting pupils into groups enables them to learn very effectively with collective reinforcement – more effectively than in individualistic and competitive reward situations. It is a win– win situation for all participants. He considers that co-operative learning should become a dominant learning style because of the social and emotional developments that ensue. Some of the benefits of co-operative learning gleaned from research are listed in Box 51.[45]

Box 51: Some benefits of co-operative learning

- Interracial school friendships have been shown to develop in heterogeneously structured groups. These friendships were generally reciprocated, and minority-group academic performance correspondingly improved.
- Co-operative learning has been shown to help to overcome interactional barriers in groups including mixed-ability and physically handicapped children.
- Children's self-esteem has been shown to be enhanced in a majority of studies.
- Children generally increase their within-classroom friendships, with corresponding increases in their feelings of altruism and social perspective taking.

In addition, pupils come to learn that they can only achieve if they become interdependent.[46] This, as Schmuck and Schmuck[47] aver, is an increasingly important lesson in a networked and shrinking world. Co-operative learning requires the structuring of positive interdependence, such that the successful outcome is only achievable through such interdependence and requires face-to-face interaction with individual and group accountability. Clearly many pupils will need to be taught to work co-operatively, as it may not come naturally to some of them; hence interpersonal skills and behaviour may have to be deliberately taught.

Collaborative learning can take many forms,[48] for example: team work; 'jigsaw' work, where the whole work (the jigsaw) is apportioned (the jigsaw pieces allotted to groups through a division of labour); team games; peer-group learning (e.g. dyadic learning); individual learning which in turn contributes to group learning which contributes to the whole-class project; complex instruction using discovery methods. Slavin[49] suggests that, regardless of the form that it takes, co-operative learning requires: group goals, individual accountability, equal opportunities for success, team competition, task specialisation, and adaptation to individual needs. One may wish to question the desirability of team competition here, as it appears to run counter to the purposes of co-operation. Summarising 99 studies of co-operative learning, Slavin[50] reports that group rewards based on individual learning of all members of the group are important in producing positive achievement outcomes. Further, he suggests that pupils need some kind of group goal based on group members' learning if they are going to be prepared to spend large periods of time helping each other. Hence group rewards and explicit instruction in group strategy are important for co-operative learning to be effective.

Slavin writes that one of the greatest benefits from co-operative learning is the raising of self-esteem.[51] Put simply, pupils learn that they are valued, valuable and important. Self-esteem rises because members feel valued by their peers and because they feel that they are achieving in academic terms. Indeed Slavin reports that pupils achieve more highly in co-operative classrooms than in traditional classrooms.[52] As we know from brain-based research, cognitive and non-cognitive outcomes are very closely linked. Co-operative learning produces positive results in terms of self-esteem, peer support and being liked by peers, internal locus of control, liking of the class, time on task, and, indeed, co-operativeness itself.[53]

Of course, co-operative learning faces its difficulties, such as:[54]

- failure to work together successfully or to 'get along'
- pupil misbehaviour
- classroom noise
- pupil absence
- ineffective use of time
- too great a range of performance levels within the group.

These may be important, but not insuperable, given preparation and thought. For further material on collaborative learning we refer readers to our discussions of group work.

(See www.routledge.com/textbooks/9780415485586, Chapter 10 Learning and teaching, Fundamentals of effective learning.)

KEY CHARACTERISTICS OF EFFECTIVE TEACHING

What do we expect effective teachers to be like? School effectiveness (including effective teaching) and school improvement are large research areas, so it is with some caution that we focus on the following study. It was funded by government and received considerable attention in the media in the year 2000.[55] The study suggested three main factors associated within teachers' control that exert a significant influence on pupils' learning, making up to a 30 per cent difference in their progress:

- teaching skills
- professional characteristics
- classroom climate.

Teaching skills were divided into seven major areas, contributing to the time on task and lesson flow, set out in Box 52.

For each of these areas the researchers provided a series of questions which could be used to evaluate the effectiveness of the teacher.

KEY QUESTIONS FOR TEACHING SKILLS

High expectations[56]

- Does the teacher encourage high standards of:
  - effort
  - accuracy
  - presentation?
- Does the teacher use differentiation appropriately to challenge all pupils in the class?
- Does the teacher vary motivational strategies for different individuals?
- Does the teacher provide opportunities for pupils to take responsibility for their own learning?
- Does the teacher draw on pupil experiences or ideas relevant to the lesson?

Box 52: Time on task and lesson flow

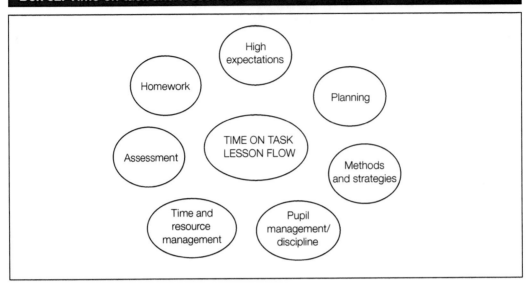

Planning

● Does the teacher communicate a clear plan and objectives for the lesson at the start of the lesson?

● Does the teacher have the necessary materials and resources ready for the class?

● Does the teacher link lesson objectives to the prescribed curriculum?

● Does the teacher review what pupils have learned at the end of the lesson?

Methods and strategies

● Does the teacher involve all pupils in the lesson?

● Does the teacher use a variety of activities/learning methods?

● Does the teacher apply teaching methods appropriate to the prescribed curriculum?

● Does the teacher use a variety of questioning techniques to probe pupils' knowledge and understanding?

● Does the teacher encourage pupils to use a variety of problem-solving techniques?

● Does the teacher give clear instructions and explanations?

● Does practical activity have a clear purpose in improving pupils' understanding or achievement?

● Does the teacher listen and respond to pupils?

Pupil management/discipline

● Does the teacher keep the pupils on task throughout the lesson?

● Does the teacher correct unwanted behaviour immediately?

● Does the teacher praise good achievement and effort?

● Does the teacher treat all children fairly?

Time and resource management

● Does the teacher structure the lesson to use the time available well?
● Does the lesson last for the planned time?
● Are appropriate learning resources used to enhance pupils' opportunities?
● Does the teacher use an appropriate pace?
● Does the teacher allocate his/her time fairly amongst pupils?
● Does the teacher manage other adults in the classroom (e.g. parent helpers, teaching assistants) well?

Assessment

● Does the teacher focus on:
  – understanding and meaning
  – factual memory
  – skills mastery
  – applications in real-life settings?
● Does the teacher use tests, competitions, etc. to assess understanding?
● Does the teacher recognise misconceptions and clear them up?
● Is there evidence of pupils' written work having been marked or otherwise assessed?
● Does the teacher encourage pupils to do better next time?

Homework

● Is homework set either to consolidate or extend the coverage of the lesson?
● Is homework which has been previously set followed up in the lesson?
● Does the teacher explain what pupils will gain from homework?
● Is the homework being set purposeful?

Time on task and lesson flow

● Does the teacher use the following effectively:
  – whole-class interactive teaching
  – whole-class lecture
  – individual work
  – collaborative group work
  – classroom management
  – testing or assessment?

The classroom climate was divided into nine main areas; see Box 53.
   The professional characteristics comprised:

● planning and setting expectations (with a drive for improvement and information-seeking initiatives)
● professionalism (challenge and support, confidence and creating trust, respect for others)
● thinking (analytical and conceptual thinking)
● relating to others (impact and influence, teamwork, and understanding others)
● leading (flexibility, holding people accountable, managing pupils, a passion for learning).

Box 53: Classroom climate

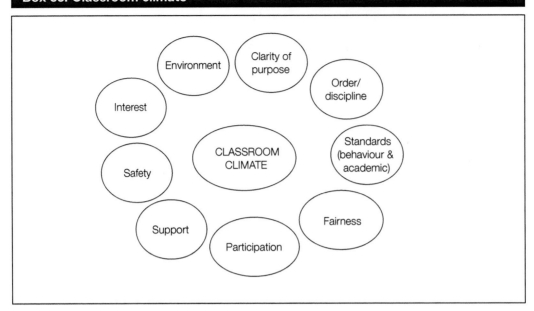

Effective teachers, then, have a battery of competencies. They:

● demonstrate professional competence
● plan effectively
● have secure subject knowledge
● promote a positive climate
● monitor and assess thoroughly
● use effective teaching strategies
● manage discipline
● manage time
● set useful homework appropriate to the age group they teach.

In their oral communication they utilise a range of language skills, for example: questioning, listening, explaining, demonstrating (modelling), challenging, instructing, managing, praising and assessing.

In their planning, effective teachers address several issues; see Box 54.

Effective teachers demonstrate (model) positive attitudes and behaviour; they:

● work safely, carefully and considerately
● demonstrate involvement, application and enjoyment
● have pride in their achievements
● respect the views of others
● work independently and collectively
● can solve problems
● take responsibility for their own learning
● sustain concentration on their task
● are reflective.

Box 54: An effective lesson plan

- Uses prior evaluations to inform planning.
- Shows evidence of continuity and progression.
- Sets high expectations of effort, attainment, achievement, progress and behaviour.
- Has clear learning objectives linked to national curricula and written in child-friendly language.
- Details what pupils have to do to achieve the learning objectives (success criteria).
- Details how pupils are going to learn: whole class work, group-work, independent activities.
- Has activities related to learning objectives.
- Has activities that are timed.
- Uses subject-specific language.
- Includes key vocabulary and key questions.
- Matches provision to pupils' needs (is appropriately differentiated).
- Addresses classroom organisation and says how resources will be used.
- Includes assessment opportunities, e.g. observation or pupil self-evaluation.
- Uses homework, when and if appropriate, to consolidate, extend, and apply learning.

Teaching styles and strategies

Effective teachers employ a range of teaching strategies and styles. Barnes[57] reports three significantly different teaching styles, thus:

1 *closed* (a formal, didactic style with little or no negotiation between teachers and pupils)
2 *framed* (where an overall structure for a lesson was given by the teacher but within that there was room for pupils' own contributions)
3 *negotiated* (where teachers and pupils largely negotiated the content and activities between themselves).

Galton *et al.*[58] promoted an alternative tripartite classification of teaching styles. These are:

- *class enquirers* (characterised by whole-class teaching together with individuals working on their own, a high level of teacher questioning and a high degree of control exercised by the teacher)
- *individual monitors* (characterised by teachers tending to work with individuals rather than with groups or the class as a whole, and making very stressful demands on the teacher)
- *group instructors* (characterised, as its title suggests, by teachers organising pupils into groups and working with them in the group situation).

This third style was seen by the researchers as an organisation that minimised the potentially disruptive effect of 'attention seekers' in the class. They would disrupt a group rather than the whole class, whereas the first style – the whole-class approach that is heavily under the control of the teacher – provided a theatre for the attention seeker, with an audience of the remainder of the class.

The student teacher will draw on a range of teaching styles using the criterion of fitness for purpose. Some activities will require the student teacher to be very formal and didactic, with little negotiation with the pupils. In other activities a group- or pupil-driven approach might be more suitable, particularly if there is a wide spread of ability in the class; group work can be seen as a manageable means of organising mixed-ability classes that steers a course between under-differentiated, poorly matched work and work that is so differentiated that it is impossible for the teacher to keep up with each individual's demands. That said, the rise in information technology heralds new possibilities for planning and managing individualised programmes of study for some of the teaching time.

We suggest that the student teacher takes the opportunity on teaching practice to try several different styles so that she can begin to match up appropriate teaching styles with appropriate learning styles, different curricular areas, different types of activity, different pupils and different resources.

Flanders,[59] found that teachers who were not successful in the classroom tended surprisingly to use many of the same instructional procedures and methods as those who were, except that they used them in more or less rigid fashion. They displayed little variation from one classroom situation to the next and seemed to lack the ability to expand or restrict the freedom of action of the children through verbal control.

The successful teachers, by contrast, reflected four elements in their teaching:

1   spontaneously varying their classroom roles from dominative to supportive ones, securing both pupil co-operation and initiative as the situation demanded
2   switching at will from one role to another and not blindly following a single approach to the exclusion of others
3   moving easily from their diagnosis of a classroom problem to a follow-up course of action, and
4   being both critical of their classroom pupils and sensitive (i.e. being fair) to their needs as human beings.

Briefly, the study suggests that successful teachers are flexible in their teaching styles and can shift easily and naturally from the direct to the indirect, from being critical observers to sympathetic counsellors, depending on the need.

Flanders subsequently reported that when pupils' ideas are incorporated into the learning activities, they seem to learn more and to develop more positive attitudes to the teacher and the learning situation; and that teachers who are over-critical in class appear consistently to achieve less in most subject areas.

Hamacheck,[60] reports that effective teachers seem to be superior in the following ways:

- their willingness to be flexible
- their capacity to perceive the world from the pupil's point of view
- their ability to 'personalise' their teaching
- their willingness to experiment
- their skill in asking questions
- their knowledge of subject matter
- their skill in establishing definite examination procedures
- their willingness to provide study helps
- their capacity to reflect an appreciative attitude, and
- their conversational manner in teaching.

The perceptual differences between good and poor teachers investigated by Combs[61] suggest that good teachers can be distinguished from poor ones with respect to the following perceptions about other people. The good teacher:

- is more likely to have an internal rather than an external frame of reference. That is, she seeks to understand how things seem to others and then uses this as a guide for her own behaviour
- is more concerned with people and their reactions than with things and events
- is more concerned with the subjective– perceptual experience of people than with objective events. She is, again, more concerned with how things seem to people than just the so-called or alleged facts
- seeks to understand the causes of people's behaviour in terms of their current thinking, feeling, beliefs, and understandings rather than in terms of forces exerted on them now or in the past
- generally trusts other people and perceives them as having the capacity to solve their own problems
- sees others as being friendly and enhancing rather than hostile or threatening
- tends to see other people as being worthy rather than unworthy. That is, she sees all people as possessing a certain dignity and integrity
- sees people and their behaviour as essentially developing from within rather than as a product of external events to be moulded or directed. In other words, she sees people as creative and dynamic rather than passive or inert.

Another indispensable feature contributing to a favourable classroom atmosphere is humour. In the well-structured, purposeful organisation of an effective classroom, there will be many opportunities for humour. Its manifold functions are more or less self-evident; it relaxes tension, helps establish natural relationships, facilitates learning and is of great value as a means of restoring sanity to a classroom after a disciplinary incident. Pupils relish humour, and its use can defuse challenging situations more effectively than many harsh words. Marland's[62] advice on humour bears the stamp of experience:

> A joke goes a long way. Try to be light-hearted whenever you feel up to it. Try to chivvy recalcitrant pupils jokingly rather than by being indignant . . . Be willing to make jokes at your own expense, and to laugh at your own foibles. Teachers' jokes don't have to be very good to be nevertheless highly acceptable.

He goes on to warn young teachers with high ideals and considerable theoretical understanding from taking themselves, their responsibilities and their pupils too seriously. Their 'humourless indignation' and 'sad intensity' may alienate their charges.

NON-VERBAL TEACHER COMMUNCIATION

Many factors that contribute to effective teacher–pupil relationships, e.g. the personality of the pupils, are clearly beyond the control of the teacher and have therefore to be taken as 'given' when interactions occur. Nonetheless, effective relationships do not just 'happen'; teachers must plan for particular relationships and not leave their occurrence to the 'hidden curriculum of everyday life in the classroom'.

Non-verbal language such as facial expression, effective eye contact, posture, gesture and interpersonal distance or space is usually interpreted by others as a reliable reflection of how we are feeling.[63,64] Mehrabian devised a series of experiments dealing with the communication of feelings and attitudes, such as like-dislike. The experiments were designed to compare the influence of verbal and non verbal cues in face-to-face interactions, leading Mehrabian to conclude that there are three elements in any face-to-face communication; visual clues, tone of voice, and actual words. Through Mehrabian's experiments it was found that 55 per cent of the emotional meaning of a message is expressed through visual clues, 38 per cent through tone of voice and only 7 per cent from actual words. For communication to be effective and meaningful, these three parts of the message must support each other in meaning; ambiguity occurs when the words spoken are inconsistent with say the tone of voice or body language of the speaker.

The student teacher needs to be aware of the messages they are sending out to a child via their use of non-verbal language. It is important to remember that whenever we are around others we are communicating non-verbally, whether intentionally or not, and children need to feel comfortable in the presence of the adults around them. According to Chaplain (2003, p. 69), 'children are able to interpret the meaningfulness of posture from an early age.'[65] Even locations and positions when talking can be important. For example, it is beneficial when speaking with a young child to converse at their physical level, sitting, kneeling or dropping down on one's haunches alongside them. This creates a respectful and friendly demeanour and communicates genuine interest in the child and what they are doing.

The way practitioners communicate with children is therefore a very important part of their role. Some key points include:

- talking with pupils so that they feel that you respect them, are interested in them and value their ideas
- giving pupils your full attention as you talk with them; using direct eye contact to show that you are really listening
- finding ways of encouraging pupils to talk in a range of contexts
- using specific positive praise such as 'I really liked the way that you waited patiently for your turn on the computer'
- smiling!

The work of Andersen and Andersen is helpful in expanding and extending the above points. They used the term 'non-verbal immediacy behaviours' when describing student teachers' non-verbal communication.[66] Non-verbal immediacy behaviours signal that the initiator, namely the student teacher, is approachable and available for communication. In that they can thus communicate interpersonal closeness and warmth, they can contribute positively to relationships. Indeed, research on immediacy constructs suggests that they can be a positive force in the classroom, particularly in bringing about better teacher–pupil relationships. Andersen and Andersen review a range of non-verbal immediacy behaviours in the context of the classroom. They include the following:

Proxemics, or the use of interpersonal space and distance. There are two aspects here – physical distance and bodily orientation. In the case of physical distance, many student teachers fail to establish interpersonal closeness with a class because they remain physically remote in the sense that they stand at the front of the classroom or sit at a desk. Confident, effective student teachers use the entire room and move among pupils. As regards orientation of the speaker, more 'immediacy' is communicated when the student teacher faces the class. As the authors say:

> Many teachers do not fully face their class when teaching. They hide behind desks, podiums and tables, and often continuously write on the blackboard, with their backs to the class. Not only does this reduce the immediacy between teachers and their classes, it also removes any visual communication between them.

Kinetics, or communication by body movement. Four aspects are relevant here – smiling, head nods, bodily relaxation and gestural behaviour, though a very full analysis of this is provided by Neill and Caswell:[67]

1   One of the most effective immediacy cues is smiling. Smiling produces substantial positive therapeutic effects in relationships, including an increase in interpersonal acceptance. As Andersen and Andersen[68] say, 'Teachers who frequently smile are communicating immediacy in one of the easiest and most powerful ways. Pupils at all levels are sensitive to smiles as a sign of positive affect and warmth.'

2   Head nods are another effective means of indicating immediacy, especially when used by a listener in response to a speaker. When used by a teacher to his class they provide reinforcement and indicate that the teacher is listening to and understanding what they say.

3   Bodily relaxation communicates immediacy by indicating freedom from stress and anxiety. It has been found that more 'immediate' teachers are more relaxed, whereas tense and anxious teachers communicate negative attitudes to their pupils who perceive them as cold and inaccessible.

4   Gestures, particularly hand and arm movements, communicate interest, warmth and involvement. In these respects they contribute positively to both interpersonal transactions and teaching.

Oculesics, or the study of messages sent by the eyes. Eye contact is an invitation to communicate and a powerful immediacy cue.[69] Student teachers who use eye contact can more easily monitor the behaviour of their classes. They can also communicate more warmth and involvement to their pupils. The authors advise that student teachers should position themselves so that they can and do establish eye contact with every pupil in the class, warning that immediacy cannot be successfully established by a student teacher in the absence of eye contact.

(See www.routledge.com/textbooks/9780415485586, Chapter 10 Learning and teaching, Teacher–pupil relationships.)

MODELLING

Good and Brophy[70] have noted that many things may be learned in classrooms without deliberate instruction by the teacher or deliberate practice by the learner; and that such observations are supported by a growing body of experimental evidence. The learner only needs to see a particular behaviour demonstrated by another person before imitating it himself, sometimes consciously, sometimes not. The person who demonstrates the behaviour is called the model and the form of learning, modelling.

Modelling can be a most useful device for the student teacher. Many skills, for example, can be learned more easily through observation and imitation than by trying to understand and respond to only verbal explanation and instruction. This is especially true for younger children whose abilities to follow detailed verbal instructions are limited.

Modelling effects can occur at any time. In this connection, if pupils detect discrepancies between what the student teacher says and what she actually does, they will ignore what she says and be affected much more by what she does. Further, if they see discrepancies between what she says she expects and what she allows, they will tend to be influenced by what she allows. This aspect of modelling has important consequences for discipline, and especially so for the student teacher who, having once established a particular standard of behaviour, should insist that it is maintained.

Factors affecting what is learned from observing a model

The amount and kind of learning that results from observing others depends on a number of factors, one of the more important of which is the situation. Modelling effects are far more likely to occur in new situations where the expected behaviour of both the student teacher and learner is unclear. When such ambiguous situations occur in the classroom, the potential for modelling will be considerable, especially at the beginning of a new academic year or, in the case of the student teacher, at the start of a teaching practice spell. As a result of such early contacts with a student teacher, then, pupils will make inferences about her and will decide whether they like her, what kind of person she is and how they ought to respond to her. Further, the student teacher's early behaviour will contribute to establishing the emotional and intellectual climate of the classroom.

It is thus vital for student teachers to model appropriate behaviour from their first day in the school. Opportunities to teach through modelling will be greater at this time because many things will still be fluid and ambiguous. Later, when both student teacher and class settle into predictable routines, it will be more difficult to bring about changes.

A second factor affecting what is learned from modelling is the personality of the teacher. A warm and enthusiastic teacher whom the pupils like will be imitated by them. There is the possibility that some of the pupils will adopt, or be influenced by, his attitudes and beliefs; and they may imitate his behaviour. However, pupils will be less likely to imitate a student teacher whom they dislike or do not respect, particularly in the sense of adopting or conforming to his ideals.

STUDENT TEACHERS' ATTITUDES AND EXPECTATIONS AND THE INFLUENCE THEY EXERT ON CLASSROOM BEHAVIOUR

The attitudes and expectations a student teacher holds with respect to the pupils she teaches considerably affect her behaviour towards them; and this, in turn, influences their responses in a variety of ways. Studies conducted in the United States, for instance, indicate that pupils of differing achievement levels were treated differently by their teachers and that there were important differences in both the frequency and quality of the contacts between them.[71] Some of the consequences were that high achievers received more opportunity to respond than low achievers. They also tended to ask more questions. Further, teachers waited significantly longer for the more capable pupils to respond before giving an answer or calling on another pupil.

The findings disclosed, too, that teachers praised high achievers more than low achievers, the latter being more likely to be criticised for a wrong answer. Teachers also tended to 'give up' more readily with pupils who did not know, or who answered incorrectly, and this suggests that they expect and demand higher performance from high achievers.

Attitudes and expectations may be a teacher's allies if properly maintained and used. However, as Lawrence[72] has pointed out, although a teacher may influence a pupil to behave in ways which the teacher expects, this will only occur when the relationship between them is a close one. The expectation factor therefore does not operate in all circumstances. Nevertheless, teachers need to be aware of what is possible in this respect and act accordingly.

One further point of interest may be added which again stresses the reciprocity of the relationship in this connection and it is this: a pupil will tend to fulfil the positive expectations of a teacher whom he or she respects. It is therefore incumbent upon the student teacher to strive to earn such respect from the outset.

THE ORGANISATION OF LEARNING

There are many ways of organising pupils, e.g. teaching them as a complete class or dividing the class into a number of groups. There are a number of forms of interaction between teacher and pupils and among pupils themselves which may be found in school learning situations. The particular one operating at any given moment will depend upon the objective of the lesson, the nature of the task in hand and the implied educational philosophy. We now consider six characteristic learning situations which account for the principal patterns of interaction, both formal and informal, which may be found in the context of the school. Our analysis is based upon the work of Oeser.[73]

Situation 1: the teacher-centred lesson

The principle of interaction underlying the teacher-centred situation may be illustrated as in Example 1. Although only five pupils are represented in the diagram, this figure may vary, with perhaps a notional 30–35 pupils being a more representative number in this kind of situation.

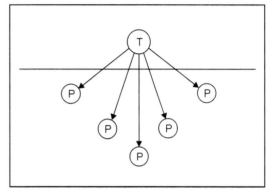

The interaction pattern here is one in which the teacher speaks and the pupils listen. Their relationship to the teacher is confined to listening, perceiving and assimilating; and there is no interaction among the pupils themselves.

A social structure of this kind is found in the talk or lecture where there is a sharp distinction between the teacher and the class (depicted in the diagram by a continuous horizontal line), and in which the teacher's role is authoritarian, exhortatory and directive. This kind of interaction style may also form part of a class lesson as, for instance, at the outset when the teacher introduces new learning, or in the course of a lesson when he demonstrates a skill, or towards the end of a lesson when he sums up what has gone before. Preparation for a formal examination would present occasions when the teacher-centred approach would be an efficient means of teaching and learning. This model corresponds closely to the method of direct instruction and whole-class interactive teaching.

Situation 2: the lecture-discussion

The second situation may be seen as a variant of the first, being one in which the pattern of interaction is not wholly dominated by the teacher. It is represented diagrammatically in Example 2. Again, the number of pupils may vary, depending upon the circumstances.

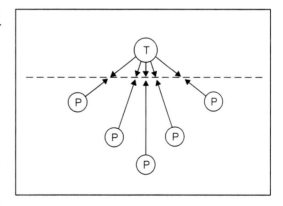

This model corresponds closely to the method of whole-class interactive teaching.

Three of the most important aims of the educator are: to turn the latent leadership of a group in the direction of the educational process; to encourage the individual development of leadership; and to encourage co-operative striving towards common goals while discouraging the exercise of authoritarian leadership. The social structures evolving through Situations 2, 3, 4 and 5 provide a framework for the achievement of these aims.

The arrowheads in the diagram indicate more or less continuous verbal interaction between teacher and pupils. Although, as leader, the teacher asks questions, and receives and gives answers, the initiative need not always be hers or his; and competition may develop among the pupils. The sharp distinction between teacher and taught which was an important feature of the first situation and which was represented in Example 1 by means of a continuous horizontal line is now less obvious – hence the broken horizontal line in Example 2.

This kind of learning situation, the pattern of interaction depicted in Example 1, could develop into the pattern illustrated in Example 2.

Situation 3: active learning

Example 3 depicts a social situation in which the teacher encourages discussion and mutual help between pupils. Practical work in a science lesson would be an occasion for this kind of situation. The letters TE in the diagram indicate that the teacher now begins to assume the additional role of expert. As Oeser notes: 'He, of course, retains his other roles as well; but the emphasis in the teaching process now fluctuates between the needs established by the task and the needs of the individual pupils.'[74] For this reason, the situation may be described as task-and pupil-centred and as one beginning to have a co-operative structure.

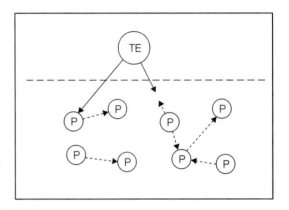

Situation 4: active learning; independent planning

Scrutiny of Example 4 shows how this fourth situation evolves logically from the preceding one. The pupils are now active in small groups, and the teacher acts more or less exclusively as an expert-consultant (indicated in the diagram by a wavy line).

As Oeser says: 'Groups map out their work, adapt to each other's pace, discuss their difficulties and agree on solutions. There is independent exploration, active learning and a maximal development of a task-directed leadership in each group.'[75] The social climate is co-operative and the situation may be described as pupil- and task-centred.

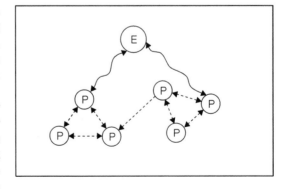

Situation 5: group task-centred

A characteristic situation in which a smallish group of individuals is concerned with a particular topic, project or problem, is illustrated in Example 5.

A pattern of this kind may thus be found in a seminar or discussion session. The arrowheads indicate that the group as a whole is concerned with the task – its elucidation, clarification and solution.

The situation is clearly a task-centred one in which there is an absence of hierarchical structure. Ideally, the role of the teacher here is simply that of a wise and experienced member of the group (depicted as 'expert' in the diagram). The more coercive roles traditionally associated with the teacher are out of place in this kind of social structure. The attitudes of members of the group to each other will tend to be co-operative and consultative.

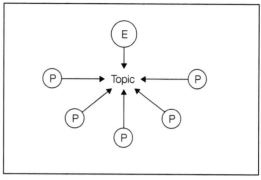

Situation 6: independent working; no interaction

This final situation, illustrated in Example 6, arises when pupils are working quite independently and there is no interaction.

This situation will occur when pupils are working at exercises 'on their own'.

In planning for reduced teacher direction and greater individual and group work, i.e. with the move from Example 1 to Example 6, many teachers develop worksheets. The worksheet is best seen as one of a number of teaching resources, though an unrelieved diet of worksheets is a certain recipe for boredom and indiscipline in any classroom. We indicate some considerations in planning and using worksheets in Box 55.

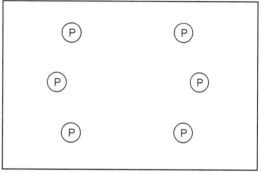

In summary, Oeser observes that from Situation 1 to 4 there is a progressive change from teacher-centred through task-centred to pupil-centred activities, from passive to active learning and from minimal to maximal participation, with a progressive diminution of the coerciveness of the teacher's roles. In Situation 5, the situation is again task-centred, but the teacher's status as such has disappeared.

The six situations outlined above will help the reader not only to understand classroom-based social and learning situations, but also patterns of interaction occurring outside the classroom.

Box 55: Considerations in planning worksheets

- What exactly is the purpose of the worksheet? Is it to provide information, ask questions, set tasks, record information, promote new learning, revise or apply knowledge, keep pupils busy, or a combination of these (and others)?
- Do you actually need a worksheet (e.g. if everyone is to have the worksheet could its contents simply be written on a whiteboard slide)?
- The worksheet must make clear exactly what the pupils are to do and how they are to record.
- The language level must be appropriate for the pupils in terms of vocabulary and readability. Will the children understand the language?
- How will different worksheets for different pupils in a single lesson be organised and introduced?
- Will the worksheet become progressively harder in the knowledge that only the brighter or faster workers will reach the end of the sheet?
- The worksheet must be attractive and motivating.
- Will the worksheet be handwritten or word-processed/desktopped? If it is handwritten will it be written in print/'joined up' writing/capitalised/lower case/in the school's adopted handwriting style? If they are word-processed the letters may be able to be printed in an interesting font or style or in an interesting manner (e.g. a worksheet on eggs could have the words written around the perimeter of an egg, a worksheet on houses could be shaped like a house). How will the student teacher be sure that her spelling is correct?
- Will the pupils know how to answer the questions on the sheet? If they do not, what will be the student teacher's role? How will the pupils find the answers to the questions?
- What resources and equipment are required for the tasks on the sheets?
- What prior knowledge is assumed on the sheets? Whereabouts in the programme of work will the worksheets come, e.g. to lead off a programme, to follow it up, to extend and apply knowledge? How will the worksheets be introduced? What preliminary activities are necessary?
- How will pupils access textbooks for answers – is it necessary to specify to which books etc. the pupil is to refer?
- How many activities are there on the sheet? Are there too many/too few?
- Will there be many activities of the same type on the sheet or activities of a differing type on a single sheet?
- How attractive is the sheet? Are there too many or too few words?
- Do some tasks require the student teacher to be on hand for safety reasons, e.g. cutting, heating, handling dangerous equipment?
- How will the sheets prompt and promote discussion as a whole class or group?
- Are the questions an appropriate mixture of low and high order, open and closed (see Chapter 13: Questions and questioning)?
- Have time scales been specified or anticipated for the completion of the worksheets (i.e. so that the student teacher can plan the most efficient use of herself)?
- How will the worksheets be linked to displayed material for accessing information?

10 Early Years and Primary Teaching

INTRODUCTION

Having looked in the last chapter at some of the principles, concepts and theories that underpin teaching in general, we now refine our focus to look more specifically at the different phases of education. A good teacher has many skills that are transferable to different age groups. However, there are also some specific areas of knowledge and experience that need to be acquired in order to be most effective with children of different ages.

EARLY YEARS TEACHING

The Reggio Emilia pre-schools in northern Italy have been celebrated around the world because of the philosophies that underpin and guide their practice. Gardner[1] reports a much-celebrated example of 'good practice' from Reggio. This approach has several key principles that are a very good starting point for our thinking about early years teaching:[2]

- the image of the child as a possessor of potential, creativity, curiosity, wanting to interact and establish relationships, constructing her/his own learning, negotiating
- the importance of children's relationships to peers, family, teachers, the school, the community and the wider society – an ever-widening circle of relationships in which all participants are partners in learning
- children, parents and teachers together, with rights to the highest quality education, to be involved in education, and to grow as professionals, respectively
- parents' roles as essential participants in their children's education (e.g. sitting on school committees, working in the school, taking part in special events, being consulted)
- the layout of the school, in which physical space is open, with close attention to detail and a rich, pleasing environment, a combination of natural and made objects and personal space (each child has her/his own box/pigeon-hole) and a profusion of children's work, exquisitely presented
- multiple interactions between teachers, students and parents, in groups of flexible size and arrangements, and the opportunity to be alone
- continuity of learning: time follows the sequence of learning, activity, concentration span and task in hand, not the clock, with time provided for interaction
- collaboration, co-operation and collegiality as cornerstones of learning (e.g. non-hierarchical staff relationships amongst teachers, *atelieristi* (artists in residence), *pedagogisti* (pedagogical

co-ordinators of all adults)), and in which everyone learns from each other – adults and children alike

● copious documentation and presentation in multiple media by teachers and others, serving several functions – to inform planning, to communicate with parents, to understand and diagnose children, to facilitate internal school communication, to create a school archive, for teachers' self-evaluation

● the dynamic, emergent curriculum, which is not pre-ordained but which emerges with the children (often as a consequence of discussion with them, together with documentation and review)

● project-based learning, which is integrated rather than subject-specific, with active, first-hand and experiential learning, and which emerges in discussions between children and teachers. These can last from a few days to weeks and months, as deemed appropriate by the participants, and can originate in a chance remark or observation that catches the students' interest.

At the Reggio schools, parents and the community have an active and central role in education as equal partners (an 'extended family') with shared responsibilities. For Gardner, the Reggio Emilia schools embody his multiple intelligences and encourage exploration of the child's world in the child's terms, for example socially, emotionally, cognitively and physically. Respectful relationships and community public-spiritedness are key watchwords of the approach. Empowerment of the children is part of the empowerment of the community. As Siraj-Blatchford[3] suggests, in the Reggio Emilia approach children are co-constructors of knowledge, identity and curricula.

PLAY

Far from being the non-serious, escapist, indolent, insignificant activity that the label often carries, Drummond[4] indicates that play is a central, highly significant activity in children's lives and learning.[5] It evokes the most intense personal and interpersonal feelings in children,[6] and they take it very seriously indeed; they become completely absorbed in it; it is very real for them. Play is a magnificent means of addressing and integrating several aspects of young children's development and of stimulating profound growth.[7] Play catches and develops children's intrinsic motivation, addresses their self-posed questions, offers the possibility for children to engage in divergent thought in which there is no single right answer, promotes socialisation and creativity, and prompts the development of both the left and right hemispheres of the brain.[8]

Edgington[9] argues that 'play is a powerful motivator of young children' and that it has a long-term impact on adult life, enabling children to:

● handle setbacks and anxieties
● experience fulfilment and a sense of well-being
● develop social awareness and interaction
● foster creativity and imagination
● explore ideas and feelings
● take risks and experiment[10]
● try out, combine and recombine ideas,[11] and
● make decisions and take responsibility for them.[12]

Play enables them to create alternative worlds and stories[13] and, as Bruner[14] reminds us, we make meaning of our lives through narrative and creating stories of our experiences.

Play improves learning in young children and long-term achievement has been seen to be present in children who have been exposed to such child-centred methods.[15] Indeed, Sylva[16] cites US-based research that shows that young children who have been exposed to sharing experiences with carers and who bring mathematical experiences into their everyday worlds outperform children who experience more formal 'lessons' in mathematics.

Play, be it epistemic (knowledge-based: what does this thing do?)[17] or ludic (game-based: what can I do with this?), is a central element of young children's learning, as is the role of the practitioner in maximising learning from play.[18]

It is sometimes noisy, sometimes quiet, sometimes gentle, sometimes boisterous, sometimes planned, sometimes spontaneous, sometimes rule-governed, sometimes rule-free. Siraj-Blatchford[19] suggests that play is central to young children's learning in that it can motivate them and enhance their learning, and provide a context in which they can explore and experiment; it is under the child's control; it is the child's 'work'. As with many species, she argues, childhood is a separate stage of development and is qualitatively different from adulthood.[20] Childhood is a state in itself, not a training ground or apprenticeship for the promised land and distant shores of adulthood.[21]

Siraj-Blatchford[22] argues that play is 'developmentally appropriate', as, in it, children make meaningful choices and explore their worlds through active, experiential, first-hand learning. Developmentally appropriate programmes are informed by what is known about: child development; learning; children's interests, motivations, needs and abilities; and local and situational factors. Such programmes have several key features, for example: positive relationships between all adults and children; teaching to enhance learning and children's development; assessment that is linked to planning for learning; mutual relations between home and school, and all the adults participating; developing a wide, all-round curriculum; and authentic, diagnostic and formative assessment. The symbolic significance of developmentally appropriate programmes is that they start with the learner, not the teacher, not the curriculum and not knowledge. They resist the pressure to force young learners to jump through the hoops of national curricula.

In developmentally appropriate programmes teachers provide support, scaffolding (e.g. helping the child to understand, explore, extend and handle activities) and interventions to promote learning, and in them each child has the opportunities to work in solitary mode, flexible and collaborative group arrangements (with mixed ages and abilities) and as a member of the whole-class group. In these, the location and use of human and material resources is critical. Whole-class activities might be in singing, story work, dancing and music, though in terms of the proportion of the day, whole-class activity is usually slight. In small-group and individual activities, the teacher adopts a range of different roles – guiding, suggesting, reflecting, expanding, demonstrating, directly teaching, probing, prompting, modelling, leading, answering questions and giving feedback. Underpinning the teacher's role is the need for the child to be engaged and involved in her/his own learning and to be initiating much of it. The adult–child relationship here is crucial and, avers Siraj-Blatchfold,[23] symbiotic. Adults must know how to plan for children's play.[24]

Providing scaffolding enables the teacher to extend what Vygotsky terms the child's 'zone of proximal development'. Vygotsky,[25] perhaps more than Piaget's more solipsistic turn, is clear that social interaction and collaboration are critical in developing the young child and that certain developmental processes are only able to operate when the child is interacting with people. Solitary and independent learning is simply less effective than social and interactive learning. Indeed, argues Vygotsky, children actively seek out others with whom to interact.

Consider the young child playing in a water area with another child. What are they learning? Socially they may be learning to share and take turns with equipment and they may be learning that co-operative play can be enjoyable and valuable – the early stages of teamwork that employers will value maybe 20 years later! Emotionally, they may be learning frustration tolerance and they may experience the pleasure of exploration. Morally, they are learning that it is not acceptable to hit other children if they have what you want, and they are learning how to solve conflicts and disagreements.

Cognitively, their senses are being sharpened through touch, sight, speech, maybe even taste (as babies, our first reaction to something new is to put it in our mouth!); they are:

●   learning about the properties of water, capacity and conservation
●   laying the foundation for early scientific methodology in terms of the 'what if ...?' questions (early experimentation and hypothesis formation)
●   learning about problem-solving:
    –   how can I put this amount of water into x number of containers?
    –   how can I prevent the water from escaping through my fingers?
    –   why do heavy boats float?
    –   why do some objects float and others sink?
    –   why does the water seem to push my hand up to the surface?
    –   why does the empty sealed bottle feel as though it is being pushed to the surface and yet the half-full bottle doesn't feel like this so much?
    –   why are there bubbles coming out of that bottle?
    –   how can I make a bubble?
    –   where does a bubble go when it reaches the top of the water?
    –   how can I make this object sink?

Mathematically, they may be learning simple counting ('how many objects float?'), big and little, bigger and smaller, more and less, ordering and classifying. They are learning how to concentrate on the task in hand; they are sharing experiences through talk; they are imagining ('what is it like to be a duck that can dive?'; 'what would it be like to live under the sea?'; 'what would it be like to be a fish?'). They are learning about design and technology ('let's make something that floats'; 'let's join up these tubes to make the water move from one place to another'). Linguistically, they are verbalising (and verbalising is a fundamental stage of learning), crystallising and articulating their ideas, maybe to share them with another child or an adult, and moving from a restricted code of shared, non-verbalised meanings to an elaborated code of explicit vocabulary and linguistic structures. Later they may find and draw pictures of ducks, boats, divers and sea creatures. They may trace over a word to learn how to write it ('ship', 'water', 'sea', 'cup'). They may watch and discuss a multimedia presentation on sea creatures; they may keep tropical fish in an aquarium. Physically, the young child is learning fine motor control (and motor control is proximodistal[26] (from the centre out) and cephalocaudal (from the top down)).

Play is intrinsically creative. In play children may be making up their own games, activities, rules and routines. They decide the activity, they decide the levels of difficulty, they decide the rules, they enforce the rules (indeed, in many young children, more time is taken on making up and enforcing the rules than actually playing the game!). The point here, well made by Guha,[27] is that in play the locus of control is with the children; they learn democracy by practising it. They express themselves and learn to live with the consequences of that. Play is also active – socially, emotionally, physically, cognitively.

The possibilities are endless; play is a marvellous platform for learning. Behind all of these is the presence of the teacher, providing material, social, cognitive, moral, physical, emotional input, interventions and facilitation to encourage young children to maximise the learning potential of the activity in question. In the example of the playing with water, the teacher has to decide judiciously when to let the children find out for themselves and when to intervene to facilitate ('scaffold') learning through careful prompting and probing. Given this, the assertion that play is an uneconomical time-waster in early years education is simply naïve and should be dismissed.

Play has several defining features. It is, for example, frequently a spontaneous, enjoyable process rather than outcome-focused; free of explicit rules unless made up by the participants; devised and owned by children; participatory and first-hand; active and immediate.[28] It extends a child's learning, sometimes with adult intervention. Play enables young children to express, fulfil and handle their wishes and fears (for example in play therapy)[29] and to integrate and extend their understanding of the world.

Play can be structured or guided, and the environment is provided in which different kinds of play activities can take place (e.g. building, painting, constructing) with adult support for learning from the activities. This need not stifle exploratory and inventive play. There are several different types of play. In a famous delineation of learning, Bruner[30] discusses symbolic learning (through symbol systems such as language), iconic learning (through images, pictures, objects) and enactive learning (learning by doing and experiencing), and these figure significantly in types of play.

Physical play can involve, for example, running, walking, jumping, skipping, crawling, climbing, lifting, carrying, rolling, balancing, hopping, kicking, catching, digging, pulling, pushing, turning, dancing, holding and stretching. It can involve large, outdoor activities and equipment (climbing frames, digging, toy cars) and indoor activities. It encourages the development of healthy bodies, mobility and motor skills (gross to fine), agility, speed, spatial awareness, self-awareness and self-confidence.

Creative play can involve, for example, fine motor skills such as painting, drawing, 'pretend' writing, sewing, cutting, threading, model-making, gluing and sticking, constructing, building and printing. It can encourage learning about shape, size, texture, colour and patterning. This can encourage divergent thinking and enable children to experience a sense of achievement and exploration.

Symbolic play (pretending) can involve role play, for example dressing up, the home corner, playing with dolls and toys, office play, a hospital or doctor's area, a post office. It can enable children to explore adult roles and their own feelings, use language, enable socialisation and collaborative learning, develop imagination through making up situations, and learn to care for others. This can extend to playing with dolls such as those which may appear on the television (e.g. cartoon characters, children's stories, heroes and heroines). In this there is an important role for the teacher to discourage aggression (many television characters are extremely violent) and to avoid or break down stereotypes (e.g. the cute female doll, the commando male doll).

Construction play involves, for example, both commercial products (e.g. Lego, Sticklebricks) and non-commercial products to build, for example, bridges, houses, towers, railway stations, cars and farms. It can encourage language development, fine and gross motor control, spatial awareness, mathematics (e.g. size, shape, counting, ordering), science and technology (e.g. properties of materials, capacity).

Game play usually involves commercially produced equipment (e.g. board games, large mat games, counting and ordering games). It can encourage mathematical thinking (e.g. shape, order, counting and number), rule following (the rules of the game) and how to make up and apply rules, social learning (e.g. taking turns), and learning how to cope with winning and losing.

Messy play[31] involves, for example, sand, water, Play-doh, paint, finger paints, liquids, sticky substances, and maybe harmless powders (e.g. flour). These are frequently activities that children are not allowed to do at home or for which they may find themselves in trouble. They enable children to explore texture, touch and smell. Emotionally, they may offer children soothing sensations. Cognitively, they enable children to understand important properties, for example, conservation, fluidity and liquidity, shape and texture, capacity and size.

In structuring and guiding play, the teacher has a crucial role providing, for example:[32]

● a safe, secure and stimulating environment to accelerate enjoyable and fulfilling learning

- a range and balance of resources and equipment for all different kinds of play
- intervention, scaffolding and challenge to promote linguistic, cognitive, social, emotional, physical and moral development
- development of communication
- careful questioning, summarising, prompting, probing, suggesting, modelling, direct teaching, encouraging the children to learn from each other
- support and extension of spontaneous play
- a positive role model
- opportunities for children to explore their surroundings and represent their learning experiences to make sense of the world
- opportunities to develop concepts, ideas, skills and problem-solving competencies
- support for children in taking risks, socially, emotionally and cognitively
- the establishment of rules and routines
- interventions to support creativity and imagination
- information and opportunities for assessment, monitoring and feedback
- supervision (e.g. to ensure equality of access to all equipment) and conflict resolution (e.g. turn-taking)
- careful observation and assessment of the children's activities, development and progress, and its subsequent links to planning for further learning
- communication and work with parents.

In some cases it is likely that children will not know how to play; they will need to be shown. Reticent children, who would naturally self-select out of taking part, should be encouraged to participate.

SOCIALISATION

Education plays a significant role in the early socialisation of the child and is witness to her/his transformation from socialisation in the home to socialisation in the wider world. Underpinning this is the development of several key features:

- developing positive self-esteem
- security in relationships
- the development of trust in others and reliability
- behaving and interacting in a socially acceptable way
- controlling emotional outbursts
- developing independence
- learning roles and breaking stereotypes
- co-operation and relating to others
- developing social skills.

One of the EYFS principles is positive relationships. This is broken down into four areas: respecting each other; parents and partners; supporting learning; key person. The idea of a key person, sometimes called a key worker, is an important one. When a child joins an early years setting it can be a daunting experience. For that reason good practice enables children to form a close relationship with one person who they can turn to whenever they are in need of reassurance and help. Positive relationships, one of the principles, includes the idea of respecting each other. This is seen as developing children's ability to understand feelings and to form friendships.

UNDERSTANDING THE CLASSROOM

A typical early years classroom will be divided into several key areas, including some or all of the following:

- a writing area
- a drawing area
- a painting area and area for drying paintings
- a model-making and collage area with a range of small materials for cutting and sticking
- a wet area
- a wet sand area
- a dry sand area
- a science area (e.g. for growing plants, for fish)
- small-block building and construction activities (e.g. Lego)
- table-based activities (jigsaws, puzzles, language and mathematics equipment and games, shape activities)
- Play-doh, plasticine and clay areas
- role play (e.g. 'dressing up', home corner)
- computer and ICT area
- an office/police station/post office
- book corner
- a music area
- small equipment area (e.g. small cars on a mat, farm animals)
- woodwork/workshop area (with close supervision!)
- café
- shop (e.g. grocery, hairdresser)
- petrol station
- a carpeted area that can be used when the whole class meets together for sharing, circle time, story, singing, reading (e.g. with very large books), talking and watching (e.g. multimedia presentations).

A Reception class may have some different areas, for example an 'office', a shop, a nominated area for a particular feature (e.g. a visit that the children made, a speaker who came to see them, a class topic, a project display area). Some teachers may have designated or dedicated curriculum areas in the classroom, e.g. a science area, a language area, a mathematics area; others may prefer a more fluid arrangement, with some tables and spaces being used ad hoc. Student teachers will need to find out about this.

In the wet areas and 'messy' areas there must be suitable clothes protection for children. The classroom layout must be such that children can be supervised and seen. The nursery/Reception class might also have a secure separate indoor or outdoor area for larger equipment, e.g. 'solid' equipment such as slides, swings, climbing apparatus, sit-in cars/tractors/trains/trailers/tricycles, and 'soft play' equipment, which often comprises sponge-filled blocks of different shapes and sizes on which children can bounce, climb, run, roll, jump etc.

Equipment may be accessible, but not all on show, and an important early reading activity for children is connected with the careful labelling of trays of equipment. Frequently, low-level storage racks, at young children's height, are set out in the classroom in the appropriate area.

The class teacher will already have planned the layout of the classroom, and the number of tables and seats required – it may be the case that each child does not have his or her own permanent seat. Many areas will have no seats or tables (e.g. for construction activities, for some games and toys, for water and sand).

Safety is an important feature. With small equipment (e.g. scissors, very small apparatus like beads that a child may put into her/his mouth, woodwork tools) children must be taught how to access, use, return and store the equipment. With large equipment (e.g. slides, climbing apparatus) children must be taught how to use it safely and must be supervised very closely. A key factor in the running of the classroom is that the children must be taught, even trained, how to access, use and return all equipment safely. These are classroom rules that can be negotiated with the children but about which teachers must be very vigilant.

It is, perhaps, unwise to put out all the equipment at once, as a surfeit of equipment can lead to none of it being used to its maximum effect. Hence it is judicious for teachers to keep some equipment in store and bring it out when the other activities have begun to pall a little. This might be on a bi-weekly, weekly, fortnightly or monthly basis, or longer, as is deemed appropriate.

ORGANISING THE DAY

Let us imagine a typical day in an early years classroom. As the children come into the class the first matter may be to deposit anything that they have brought into the classroom and then to join the other children in the carpeted area, sitting down and waiting for the day to begin. The day may begin with the teacher talking to the whole class or, if there are several adults, with adults immediately taking some children to particular activities.

This means that the adults must have planned in advance which activities are going to be available for which children at which times, so that there is no risk of too many children from different groups being at the same activity. Many classes are divided into colour groups, so that, for example, the red group can choose from activities a, b, c and d for the first 45 minutes of the day, whilst the blue group can choose from activities e, f, g and h in the same time, and so on. The groups can rotate during the day, as set out in Box 56.

Depending on the numbers of children, some classes will timetable all or half of the class to have the large equipment at the same time. In each of the groups children will be engaged in planning with the adult. Similarly, depending on the age of the children, some of them may not be present in the morning or the afternoon, some of them may need to have a short sleep in the afternoon, and times may vary depending on whether they have lunch in the school or out of school, and whether they eat in the classroom. The schedule indicates that children will all have some reading and writing activities each day. Clearly this schedule is very formulaic and risks being mechanistic. Some activities may need longer than others; some may finish very quickly, and it is important for children not to become bored. Some children have extremely limited concentration spans (some only seconds!) and their interests may be ephemeral, so blocking off time as in the example may simply not work for some children. Some young children are able to sustain intense and prolonged concentration.[33] Indeed, some teachers will baulk at the degree of prescription in the schedule, preferring a more open style of planning to reflect each individual child's interests, concentration, tasks in hand, and the need for more collective, whole-class activities. These are matters which the student teacher must find out during preliminary visits.

If the children only come for half a day then the schedule will be completely different, for example, large apparatus may be used by everyone in the morning and the afternoon (maybe the last part of the morning, and again (for different children) in the afternoon).

Some teachers will be very experienced in their planning, and it is useful to learn from them. They will know, for example, whether it is wise to follow up a PE lesson with something quiet, individual, small-group or whole-class, whether it is a good idea to have large equipment at the

Box 56: A possible plan of an early years day

	9.00	9.20	10.00	10.45	11.30	12.00	12.45	1.00	1.45	2.30	3.00
Writing Drawing Painting Model-making/ Collage (Table-based)	Greeting, sharing, planning	Red	Yellow	Green	Sharing and review	Lunch	Greeting, sharing, planning	Yellow	Music, PE or whole-class activity	Story sharing	Preparing for home
Writing Drawing Water Wet sand Dry sand Small-block building/ construction (Table-based)		Blue	Red	Yellow					Red		
Writing Drawing Play-doh Role play/ home corner IT Book corner		Green	Blue	Red					Blue		
Writing Drawing Small equipment Woodwork Large equipment		Yellow	Green	Blue					Green		

beginning of the day, and whether it is advisable to have all the children doing a quiet but individual activity at the same time and in the same curriculum area (e.g. a language, reading or mathematics activity – may be more suited for later foundation years rather than earlier foundation years).

The key here is to ensure that a range of different types of activity is available for each group and individual so that realistic choices can be made. The teacher or adult may wish to make it clear to the children that they must undertake a particular activity, e.g. some writing, some language work, some construction play, but leave it to the child to plan how and when to do this.

The teacher may have a very different pattern to the day, for example it may be set out in a time sequence:

9.00	Children arrive
9.10	Registration and sharing activity
9.20	Language activities for all the children
9.40	Mathematics activities for all the children
10.10	Play time
10.25	Physical education
11.00	Several activities (e.g. by group or free choice)
11.50	Sharing
12.00	Lunch
13.00	Registration and sharing
13.15	Group activities (e.g. by group of free choice)
14.00	Music/television programme
14.30	Sharing/story
15.00	Home time

The attraction of this schedule is that the children are brought together to mark the start and end of each session (morning and afternoon) and that the day is punctuated by whole-class sessions as well as individual learning and choosing activities. The QCA[34] provides examples of specific activity planning and planning from the short term to the long term for the foundation years.

(See www.routledge.com/textbooks/9780415485586, Chapter 4 The Foundation Stage, Activity planning – an example.)

IMPLICATIONS FOR STUDENT TEACHERS

In preparing for teaching, student teachers on teaching practice and pre-practice visits will find it useful to address the following questions:

● How are parents involved?
● What key workers and adults are there in the class?
● Which children have designated special educational needs under the Code of Practice?
● Which children need to be drawn into greater socialisation?
● Which children have particular physical/emotional/behaviour needs, even though they are not formally 'statemented'?
● How are National Curriculum areas addressed (e.g. through subjects/integrated learning)?
● How are the six areas of learning for the foundation years planned and addressed?
● How are children's development and progress monitored and assessed?
● How is learning made active, experiential, and first-hand?
● Does the class follow a particular approach (e.g. High/Scope)?
● What planning documents are required? How is the planning done?
● When do the adults meet to share planning and review?
● How is the classroom laid out?
● How do children access and return equipment?
● How is the day organised, structured and sequenced?
● When are there quiet times?
● How structured and unstructured is the play?
● How is children's access to scarce resources planned and implemented (e.g. wet area, painting area, sand area, construction activities, home corner)?
● In what areas do children have freedom of choice and decision-making?

- How is the time organised (e.g. blocks/free choice of time by children)?
- When and for what activities do children come together as a whole class?
- How does the morning/afternoon session begin/end?
- What are the arrangements for toileting/washing/eating?
- What supervisory and safety arrangements are there for activities?
- Which activities require very close supervision?
- How are children's interests brought into their learning?
- How is indoor play organised?
- How is outdoor play organised?
- How are groups organised in the classroom? With which adults?
- How flexible and permanent are the groups?
- What assessment, recording and documentation is required?

PRIMARY TEACHING

It would be invidious to commence any outline of primary teaching and learning without an indication of some significant principles that underpin much of primary education. Drawing on a range of texts on ideological, epistemological, psychological and sociological analyses of primary education, there are several key principles that constitute primary practice:[35]

- a view of childhood as a state in itself as well as a preparation for adulthood
- the use of discovery methods and practical activity
- learning by doing – practical activity
- problem-solving approaches to teaching and learning
- the value of play and active learning
- learning in various modes – enactive, iconic, symbolic
- integration and unity of experiences; the integrated curriculum
- the value of teaching processes and skills as well as products and bodies of knowledge
- the value of content and process as complementary facets of curricular knowledge
- a view of educational activities and processes as being intrinsically worthwhile as well as having instrumental and utility value
- the value of an enriching social, emotional and physical environment
- the need to develop autonomy in children
- the provision of a curriculum which demonstrates and allows for breadth, balance, relevance, continuity and progression, differentiation and consistency
- the emphasis given to individual needs, abilities, interests, learning styles and rates as well as a received curriculum
- the fostering and satisfaction of curiosity
- the value of peer group support
- the value of self-expression
- the need for intrinsic as well as extrinsic motivation
- the use of the environment to promote learning
- the importance of the quality and intensity of a child's experience
- the uniqueness of each child
- a human-centred view of the world
- the view of the teacher as a catalyst for all forms of development
- an extended view of the 'basics' to comprehend all curriculum areas, not just the three Rs
- the need to develop literacy and numeracy through cross-curricular approaches.

We ought to say straight away that this view is not uncontentious. In two important books on primary education theory Alexander[36] argued for a much more sober examination of integrated curricula, the principle of one teacher to one class for all subjects and the notion of child-centred education. Indeed in a later work[37] he argued that debates about primary education ought to be stripped of their ideological affiliations and persuasions in order to look more closely at what primary children are actually doing and learning in classrooms and how this can be rendered more efficient and effective.[38] We proscribe the type of education debate that crudely polarises primary education, e.g. as traditional versus progressive education or as child-centred versus subject-centred curricula, as this misrepresents the complexity of teaching in primary classrooms.

In 2008 and 2009, primary education was the subject of several important reviews. The government Select Committee for Children, Families and Schools (2009) instigated a review; Ed Balls, the then Secretary of State for Education, commissioned Sir Jim Rose (2009) to review the Primary curriculum (see Chapter 3) and the Cambridge Primary Review[39] was an independent review headed by Robin Alexander (2009), based at the Faculty of Education at the University of Cambridge and is available from Routledge.

The Cambridge Primary Review had the following remit:

1   With respect to public provision in England, the Primary Review will seek to identify the purposes which the primary phase of education should serve, the values which it should espouse, the curriculum and learning environment which it should provide, and the conditions which are necessary in order to ensure both that these are of the highest and most consistent quality possible, and that they address the needs of children and society over the coming decades.

2   The Review will pay close regard to national and international evidence from research, inspection and other sources on the character and adequacy of current provision in respect of the above, on the prospects for recent initiatives, and on other available options. It will seek the advice of expert advisers and witnesses, and it will invite submissions and take soundings from a wide range of interested agencies and individuals, both statutory and non-statutory.

3   The Review will publish both interim findings and a final report. The latter will combine evidence, analysis and conclusions together with recommendations for both national policy and the work of schools and other relevant agencies.

The Review was structured to address three perspectives: Children and Childhood; Culture, Society and the Global Context; and Education. These perspectives were covered through ten themes:

Core themes: purposes, content, process and quality in primary education:

Theme 1 – Purposes and Values
Theme 2 – Learning and Teaching
Theme 3 – Curriculum and Assessment
Theme 4 – Quality and Standards
Theme 5 – Diversity and Inclusion
Theme 6 – Settings and Professionals

Contingent themes: contexts and conditions for primary education:

Theme 7 – Parenting, Caring and Educating

Theme 8 – Beyond the School
Theme 9 – Structures and Phases
Theme 10 – Funding and Governance

One of the most important features of the Primary Review was the 29 research surveys that the Review commissioned. These covered the themes as follows:

PURPOSES AND VALUES

1   *Aims as policy in English primary education.* Research survey 1/1 (John White)
2   *Aims and values in primary education: England and other countries.* Research survey 1/2 (Maha Shuayb and Sharon O'Donnell)
3   *Aims for primary education: the changing national context.* Research survey 1/3 (Stephen Machin and Sandra McNally)
4   *Aims for primary education: changing global contexts.* Research survey 1/4 (Rita Chawla-Duggan, John Lowe and Hugh Lauder)

LEARNING AND TEACHING

5   *Children's cognitive development and learning.* Research survey 2/1a (Usha Goswami and Peter Bryant)
6   *Children's social development, peer interaction and classroom learning.* Research survey 2/1b (Christine Howe and Neil Mercer)
7   *Teaching in primary schools.* Research survey 2/2 (Robin Alexander and Maurice Galton)
8   *Learning and teaching in primary schools: evidence from TLRP.* Research survey 2/4 (Mary James and Andrew Pollard)

CURRICULUM AND ASSESSMENT

9   *Curriculum and assessment policy: England and other countries.* Research survey 3/1 (Kathy Hall and Kamil Øzerk)
10 *The trajectory and impact of national reform: curriculum and assessment in English primary schools.* Research survey 3/2 (Dominic Wyse, Elaine McCreery and Harry Torrance)
11 *Primary curriculum futures.* Research survey 3/3 (James Conroy and Ian Menter)
12 *The quality of learning: assessment alternatives for primary education.* Research survey 3/4 (Wynne Harlen)

QUALITY AND STANDARDS

13 *Standards and quality in English primary schools over time: the national evidence.* Research survey 4/1 (Peter Tymms and Christine Merrell)
14 *Standards in English primary education: the international evidence.* Research survey 4/2 (Chris Whetton, Graham Ruddock and Liz Twist)
15 *Quality assurance in English primary education.* Research survey 4/3 (Peter Cunningham and Philip Raymont)

DIVERSITY AND INCLUSION

16 *Children in primary education: demography, culture, diversity and inclusion.* Research survey 5/1 (Mel Ainscow, Alan Dyson, Frances Gallannaugh and Jean Conteh)

SETTINGS AND PROFESSIONALS

PARENTING, CARING AND EDUCATING

BEYOND THE SCHOOL

STRUCTURES AND PHASES

FUNDING AND GOVERNANCE

Each survey represents an extensive and significant contribution to its field and to the Cambridge Primary Review so it is not possible to do justice to them all here (the review is available from Routledge). However, one example enables us to give an idea of the kind of coverage. John White addressed the idea of educational aims and their representation as policy.[40] White shows that a national set of aims for primary and secondary schools was proposed for the first time by the Conservative government in 1981. These proposals made a decisive break with the past in that they emphasised intellectual qualities above personal ones but the rationale for such a shift or for the aims was not made clear.

White claims that the determination of national educational aims is a matter for society as a whole and, for that reason, teachers should not have a 'special voice'; in fact, he even goes so far as to say that 'they have no more authoritative a voice than postmen or doctors in deciding the larger directions'.[41] However, it seems to us that if we accept White's suggestion that aims are not the province of teachers, once national aims exist, professional discretion in the form of 'details' that White applauds is reduced to a rather limited technical agenda because they must fit with the national aims. White doesn't seem to deal with the possibility that the very establishment of aims by government is likely to lead to and be part of other aspects of political control, including of the 'details'. Perhaps too much political control, including of aims, is one of the reasons for the incoherence of the National Curriculum which White is scathing about:

> In 1988 the government got its responsibilities relative to those of the professionals woefully back to front. Its first duty was to chart the direction of travel in the shape of substantive general aims; its second to work out in very broad terms what curricular vehicles were best suited to attain them. Neither of these things did it do. What it did do was what it had no moral authority to do. It imposed a curriculum framework which was literally almost aimless; and included in this innumerable detailed prescriptions which fell not within its own province but in that of the professionals.[42]

White claims that the new National Curriculum implemented in Key Stages 3 and 4 in 2008 was unique because for the first time the aims were made statutory, but this is not clear on examination of the statutes. The statutory basis for the National Curriculum is shown in the Education Act 1996:

> The National Curriculum shall comprise the core and other foundation subjects and specify in relation to each of them:
>
> (a) the knowledge, skills and understanding which pupils of different abilities and maturities are expected to have by the end of each Key Stage (referred to in this Part as 'attainment targets'),
> (b) the matters, skills and processes which are required to be taught to pupils of different abilities and maturities during each Key Stage (referred to in this Part as 'programmes of study'), and
> (c) the arrangements for assessing pupils in respect of each Key Stage for the purpose of ascertaining what they have achieved in relation to the attainment targets for that stage (referred to in this Part as 'assessment arrangements').

The subjects of the curriculum and the establishment of Key Stages are part of the Act, but the most recent aims of the National Curriculum that White refers to do not appear to be statutory. Aims (a) and (b) below, from the Education Act 2002, remain the same as the ones that were first introduced in the Education Act 1988, with the addition of a statement about funded nursery education.

78 General requirements in relation to curriculum
(1) The curriculum for a maintained school or maintained nursery school satisfies the requirements of this section if it is a balanced and broadly based curriculum which:
    (a) promotes the spiritual, moral, cultural, mental and physical development of pupils at the school and of society, and
    (b) prepares pupils at the school for the opportunities, responsibilities and experiences of later life.
(2) The curriculum for any funded nursery education provided otherwise than at a maintained school or maintained nursery school satisfies the requirements of this section if it is a balanced and broadly based curriculum which:
    (a) promotes the spiritual, moral, cultural, mental and physical development of the pupils for whom the funded nursery education is provided and of society, and
    (b) prepares those pupils for the opportunities, responsibilities and experiences of later life.

CHILDREN'S LEARNING IN SCHOOL

There is a need to look again at the value of topic work, extended group work, the principle of one teacher to one class, different curriculum activities taking place simultaneously in classrooms, in order to judge dispassionately the effectiveness and efficiency of children's learning in school. There is a value to subject teaching, whole-class teaching, undertaking activities in fewer curriculum areas simultaneously, more direct instruction by teachers (e.g. rather than the extended use of worksheets and resource-based learning), and a reduction of the number of teaching and learning strategies that are used in a single session. Indeed, though topic approaches can be defended if they demonstrate progression and continuity, a National Curriculum conceived in subject-specific terms flies in the face of topic-based and integrated approaches[43] and the National Curriculum means that a substantial amount of separate subject teaching will be necessary in order to cover all the programmes of study of the National Curriculum.[44] Lee and Croll[45] report that streaming and subject teaching are back on the primary agenda, particularly for Key Stage 2 children. In a survey that they carried out in two local authorities they found that over a third of the head teachers involved claimed to see value in streaming and just under a third saw value in subject specialist teaching, particularly in schools of over 300 children.

The children

An important concept to be borne in mind at all levels of teaching and learning is that of motivation, and its relevance to the primary classroom in particular needs to be kept well to the fore during teaching practice periods. First there is the matter of inner need.[46] In addition to basic needs for food, drink, warmth and shelter, etc., there are emotional and psychological needs such as love, self-esteem, the desire for recognition and responsibility, etc. All these are underpinned by the fundamental desire to learn.

There is also the stimulus to interest that comes from first-hand experience. Being involved with activities and tasks is itself highly motivating, and such involvement can be enhanced by making use of the senses – sight, sound, touch and smell in particular. Third, motivation can be generated by creating a stimulating environment. One of the many positive characteristics of British primary schools has been the imaginative and attractive environments created by class teachers. Decoration, lighting, room arrangement, noticeboards and displays have all figured prominently in this connection. Fourth, there is the importance of problem-solving as a means of stimulating children's interests. Fifth, there is competition. Where this is used sensibly it can be an effective incentive to work and to achieve. The important point here is to stress the learning aspect. Self-competition is particularly favoured in this context as the more undesirable features of competition between children are absent. Sixth and final, self-improvement is related to self-competition; helping a child to identify a set of short-term targets to reach may well stimulate learning.

It is important, also, to recognise the significance of the social world in shaping and supporting the young child's learning,[47] and of real-world, authentic tasks and learning for the developing child.

Such motivational factors as these can be all the more effective when you know your children. In order to do this it is important to:

● *Study the children's records and profiles for factual information:* Examine the evidence for general ability, high ability and low ability and especially for marked differences between ability and attainment. Look for information on any physical disabilities like poor eyesight, hearing problems, or difficulties with co-ordination. Make a note of children with learning difficulties and of home factors which may affect a child's behaviour and/or performance.

- *Talk to the class teacher(s) whose class(es) you will be teaching:* Again, ask for and make a note of factual information on work done. Find out what teaching methods have been used and how effective they are. Information on particular children should be requested, e.g. very high ability, low ability, problem children, children not realising their potential, those who have special skills, etc. In this respect, children with learning difficulties should be identified. A teacher's advice on how to deal with problem cases should always be sought and heeded.
- *Make the fullest use of your preliminary visits:* You should get the feel of a class or group and note how they respond as a group, e.g. to questions, instructions. If possible, talk to some of the children and find out what they have been doing. Examine their work. In particular, look for anything unusual, e.g. the child whose work is poor but who has good ideas, children with unusual ideas or viewpoints.

Such detailed scrutiny will enable you to identify groups of children, for example: the most able; the main body of the class; and those with low ability or learning problems. By keeping a file on each child when you start teaching, your detailed record of work and progress will assist you in lesson planning as well as with your theoretical studies at college.

The teachers

We look here at two aspects of the teacher in the primary school: his or her role and functions, and the knowledge and skills required. Some of the features of the role and function of the teacher in the primary classroom can be itemised thus:

- *manager:* she is there to manage the total learning environment, which involves the children as individuals and as a group, the learning programme, the environment and resources
- *observer:* her ultimate effectiveness depends on her ability to scrutinise the children closely, their actions, reactions and interactions
- *diagnostician:* as an integral part of observing this involves identifying the strengths and weaknesses of each child and devising programmes accordingly
- *educator:* this involves deciding on aims and objectives, the nature and content of the curriculum and the learning programme
- *organiser:* this entails organising the learning programme once its nature has been specified
- *decision maker:* choosing appropriate learning materials, deciding on topics and projects, and individual programmes
- *presenter:* this involves the teacher as expositor, narrator, questioner, explainer and instigator of discussions
- *communicator:* implied in the role of presenter, it also involves talking to other members of staff
- *facilitator:* an important aspect of the teacher's work, acting as a mediator between the child or class and the problem in hand
- *motivator:* another important feature of the role, entails arousing and sustaining interest
- *counsellor:* in this role the teacher advises on a whole range of problems and issues – educational, personal, social and emotional
- *evaluator:* a crucially professional aspect of the teacher's job, this involves evaluating, assessing and recording children's ability, achievement and progress.

It must seem fairly straightforward drawing up a list of this nature, but the teacher's role and function are not without their difficulties. In Box 57 we list a number of dilemmas identified by Pollard

Box 57: Common dilemmas faced by teachers

Treating each child as a 'whole person'.	Treating each child primarily as a 'pupil'.
Organising the children on an individual basis.	Organising the children as a class.
Giving children a degree of control over their use of time, their activities and their work standards.	Tightening control over children's use of time, their activities and their work standards.
Seeking to motivate the children through intrinsic involvement and enjoyment of activities.	Offering reasons and rewards so that children are extrinsically motivated to tackle tasks.
Developing and negotiating the curriculum from an appreciation of children's interests.	Providing a curriculum which children are deemed to need and which 'society' expects them to receive.
Attempting to integrate various elements of the curriculum.	Dealing systematically with each discrete area of the curriculum.
Aiming for quality in schoolwork.	Aiming for quantity in schoolwork.
Focusing on basic skills or on cognitive development.	Focusing on expressive or creative areas of the curriculum.
Trying to build up co-operative and social skills.	Developing self-reliance and self-confidence in individuals.
Inducting the children into a common culture.	Accepting the variety of cultures in a multi-ethnic society.
Allocating teacher time, attention and resources equally among all the children.	Paying attention to the special needs of particular children.
Maintaining consistent rules and understandings about behaviour and schoolwork.	Being flexible and responsive to particular situations.
Presenting oneself formally to the children.	Relaxing with the children or having a laugh with them.
Working with 'professional' application and care for the children.	Working with consideration of one's personal needs.

and Tann[48] with which teachers are often presented. They are not easily resolved and often it is a matter of trying to minimise the tension generated by them.

To perform effectively the kinds of roles just listed, the teacher needs to possess an impressive body of knowledge and a considerable range of skills. Dean[49] and Pollard and Tann[50] have identified the more important of these as:

● *Self-knowledge:* This entails an awareness of your strengths and weaknesses. This is a particularly valuable kind of knowledge to possess when working in the primary school where teachers are expected to teach many things.
● *Open-mindedness:* This is used by Pollard and Tann in the sense of 'being willing to reflect upon ourselves and to challenge our assumptions, prejudices and ideologies as well as those of others'.
● *A personal philosophy:* This can take quite a practical form. As Dean says, 'What you need are thought-out aims and objectives which you can use for assessing your work and for decid-

ing on approach and materials.' Those who have a clear idea of their destination are more likely to arrive there.

- *Child development:* A good grounding in the theories of child development is essential. These will include theories on intellectual, physical, emotional and social development, as well as on individual differences.
- *How children learn:* The key concepts and topics here are motivation, theories of learning, the use of rewards and punishments, and the relation between language and experience.
- *Group behaviour:* As teaching is concerned with handling groups, some awareness of group dynamics is helpful. Dean poses the following questions in this regard: What am I doing to teach children how to work together? Have I got the balance between competition and co-operating about right? Do any of my children cheat in order to win? Is this because there is too much competition? Would rather more competition stimulate some of the most able in the class?
- *Subject knowledge:* Although a teacher needs to be on top of her material, this can sometimes be difficult for the primary teacher who is expected to know a great deal. Indeed Ofsted[51] found that a teacher's subject knowledge was very strongly associated with high standards of students' achievements. There may be some areas where her expertise is slim and this can sometimes be made worse when an individual child undertakes a topic or project in an unfamiliar area. In such circumstances, where a teacher may feel vulnerable, Dean recommends (1) identifying areas in which she feels secure and working with them; (2) using other people's expertise – colleagues, parents, perhaps outsiders like the local police officer; and (3) making use of school broadcasting.

The issue of teachers' subject knowledge is topical in the current primary debate and is coupled with the issues of curriculum leadership and teachers' roles in the school. In the section of their report that is perhaps aptly titled 'The Problem of Curricular Expertise' Alexander *et al.*[52] argue that 'subject knowledge is a critical factor at every point in the teaching process: in planning, assessing and diagnosing, task setting, questioning, explaining and giving feedback. The key question to be answered is whether the class teacher system makes impossible demands on the subject knowledge of the generalist primary teacher'. Bennett *et al.*[53] and Pollard *et al.*[54] reported that the introduction of the National Curriculum had exacerbated teacher stress and that, in part, this was caused by teachers' insufficient subject knowledge. Morrison[55] has argued that subject teaching and curriculum leadership on a subject-specific basis might be very useful because curriculum leaders possess:

- academic knowledge
- professional and pedagogic knowledge (experience of how to teach the subject effectively, based on knowledge of how children learn in the subject, how to diagnose children's needs and to plan subsequent curricula and learning pathways for them, how to assess children's performance, how to plan for progression and continuity in the subject)
- awareness of the latest developments and resources in the subject
- enthusiasm for the subject.

This view was echoed by Alexander *et al.*[56] when they advocated four broad teaching roles for primary teachers:

1 *the generalist* who teaches most or all of the curriculum, probably specialising in age-range rather than subject, and does not profess specialist subject knowledge for consultancy
2 *the generalist/consultant* who combines a generalist role in part with cross-school co-ordination, advice and support in one or more subjects

3   *the semi-specialist* who teaches his/her subject, but who also has a generalist and/or consultancy role

4   *the specialist* who teaches his/her subject full-time.

In a follow-up report to Alexander *et al.*,[57] Ofsted found that in over 80 per cent of schools the teachers were generalists, with semi-specialist teaching being undertaken in 15 per cent of schools and the only specialist teaching being undertaken by bought-in part-time teachers. The student teacher will need to find out how curriculum leadership is exercised in the school so that she can approach the most appropriate teacher(s) in the school with regard to her own planning and implementation of schemes and activities.

The curriculum

We have seen how the teacher is responsible for 'mediating the curriculum'. In the course of initial visits to the school and during teaching practice itself, the student teacher will need to find out as much as she can about the way the curriculum is organised in the school as a whole and how her particular class fits into the school scheme. The following points may assist the student teacher in this respect:

- Find out the school's approach to the curriculum. Is the emphasis on direct teaching, for example, or on discovery learning? Or is there a balance between them?
- What teaching styles are used in the school and do all the teachers adopt the same approach?
- Do the teachers work together at any point in the week?
- How are the teaching groups organised?
- What is done for children with special educational needs and for those with physical disabilities?
- Do specialist teachers visit the school?
- What is the school's relationship with the parents? Are they encouraged to visit the school?
- What are the approaches to individual subjects?

A framework for analysing curriculum tasks is provided by perceiving them in terms of knowledge, concepts, skills and attitudes. Pollard and Tann[58] define these terms as follows:

- *knowledge:* the selection of that which is worth knowing and of interest
- *concepts:* the generalisations and ideas which enable pupils to classify, organise and predict – to understand patterns, relationships and meanings, e.g. continuity/change, cause/consequence, interdependence/adaptation, sequence/duration, nature/purpose, authenticity, power, energy…
- *skills:* the capacity or competence to perform a task, e.g. person/social (turn taking, sharing), physical/practical (fine/gross motor skills), intellectual (observing, identifying, sorting/classifying, hypothesising, reasoning, testing, imagining and evaluating), communication (oracy, literacy, numeracy, graphicacy), etc.
- *attitudes:* the overt expression of values and personal qualities, e.g. curiosity, perseverance, initiative, open-mindedness, trust, honesty, responsibility, respect, confidence, etc.

It has been suggested[59] that early learning focuses more on skills than on content, for example social skills, communication skills, task-related behaviours.

CLASSROOM ORGANISATION

The way one organises one's classroom exerts a powerful influence on both teaching and learning. Furthermore, the organisation must be seen to relate to the school's/teacher's philosophy, curricular aims, teaching and learning methods and interpersonal relationships. Four features of classroom organisation are especially relevant to the student teacher on teaching practice. They are: the organisation of the children for group work; the physical environment; the use of space; and resources.

Organising children for group work

Hargreaves and Hargreaves[60] indicate the significance of group work as an aid to effective learning and cognitive development. Taking their lead from Piaget, cognitive development, they aver, is more likely to be promoted when children work with their peers rather than, for example, older children or adults or, indeed, on their own. They argue that peer group learning is more effective than child–adult learning as, in peer groups, children are more likely to challenge and question each other than with adults, and that such challenges (cognitive conflict) promote learning. Indeed, peer group work can enable students to provide each other with effective 'scaffolding' for learning. By contrast, Vygotsky argues that child–adult relationships are very profitable, as the child enters a pre-structured world and learns from more knowledgeable people. He avers that higher-order learning requires group and social interaction; higher mental functions are internalised social relationships. Structured peer group work has been shown to be associated with higher levels of achievement.[61] Structured group work brings cognitive, affective and social benefits.[62] It teaches students to be co-operative and to help each other.

Kutnick and Manson[63] indicate that different kinds of group are suitable for different purposes. For example, individual work may be best for drill and practice work, paired work for cognitive problem-solving tasks, groups of 4–6 students for application and extension tasks, and whole-class work for transmission teaching and control.

It is of great importance that the student teacher be aware of the sort of situation he wants in a lesson, or at a particular point in it. This will be chiefly determined by his lesson objectives and other factors which contribute to defining the overall situation. These include:

- high–low teacher dominance
- large–small number of pupils
- high–low academic level of class
- active–passive pupil participation
- individual–co-operative effort
- contentious–non-contentious material
- strong–weak needs
- task and learning-oriented–examination-oriented, and
- directing–helping (counselling).

In writing of the whole-class approach, Pollard and Tann say:

> Such opportunities may give the teacher a chance to demonstrate discussion techniques, encourage collaborative learning and stimulate children's thinking by exploring ideas, asking more questions, sharing common problems and encouraging children to join in trying to solve them. However, if classwork is used too extensively, it may pose a severe strain on both the teacher and the listener, for it is very difficult to match the instruction appropriately to each child's different needs without sufficient individual consultation.

Alexander *et al.*[64] argue that whole-class teaching can 'provide the order, control, purpose and concentration which many critics believe are lacking in modern primary classrooms'. This echoes the research by Galton *et al.*[65] in the 1980s that showed that whole-class teaching encouraged 'solitary workers' (students working largely on their own although they interact with the teacher and their peers) and 'concentration'; this type of learning style produced the highest degree of time on task in their study (77.1 per cent). Alexander *et al.* go on to suggest that 'whole-class teaching is associated with higher-order questioning, explanations and statements, and these, in turn, correlate with higher levels of pupil performance. Teachers with a substantial commitment to whole-class teaching appear, moreover, to be particularly effective in teaching the basic subjects.'[66] Further, this style of teaching accords with their view that 'there are many circumstances in which it is more appropriate to tell than to ask, clearly an advocacy of a more didactic and instructional style of teaching'. This lies uneasily with the notion of differentiation that the same authors advocate and creates potential problems for teachers of children in the early years, where group work has been seen (and shown) to be a positive and valuable teaching strategy.

Group work, too, needs to be planned carefully. Even the most 'child-centred' classroom needs planning; indeed it is a truism to say that the more diverse, complex and 'devolved' onto children is the learning process, the more planned, structured and carefully organised it has to be by the teacher or else behaviour problems and inefficient learning might result. This echoes the important early study of primary schools by Sharp and Green[67] and the argument from Bernstein[68] that there are 'visible' and 'invisible' pedagogies in schools, neither of which neglect the need for planning. The freer the classroom apparently seems to be, the more carefully it has to be planned and structured.

The several claimed attractions of group work are summarised by Morrison and Ridley,[69] Box 58.

Bennett and Dunne[70] regard group work as an acceptable and manageable compromise between whole-class work and wholly individualised work; the former is seen as unacceptable because it is undifferentiated, the latter is seen as unworkable because there are insufficient

---

Box 58: Advantages of group work

- Helps children to work co-operatively.
- Enables students to learn from one another.
- Encourages the involvement of all children.
- Removes the stigma of failure from children.
- Enables the teacher to circulate more easily round the class.
- Enables children to work at their own pace.
- Enables children to respect others' strengths and weaknesses.
- Affords children access to scarce equipment.
- Facilitates collaborative work.
- Facilitates the integrated day (see below).
- Encourages joint decision making.
- Affords children the opportunity to exercise leadership.
- Stimulates the development of autonomy, resourcefulness and self-esteem.
- Focuses on processes as well as products.
- Promotes high-order thinking.
- Is particularly effective for problem-solving activities.
- Promotes mutual integration of children from all ethnic groups.
- Encourages children to engage the problem of disagreement.
- Improves discussion and classroom talk.

resources of time, materials and teaching staff to render this practicable. Indeed Alexander *et al.*[71] argue for the need to strike a balance between whole-class and completely individualised work; they argue that children need experience of class, group and individual work. Pollard *et al.*[72] found that this balance was being struck in about 50 per cent of the classrooms investigated.

Group work is a pedagogical strategy and not simply a seating arrangement. In a much publicised piece of research Galton *et al.*[73] found that though primary children sat in groups in fact they worked on their own; there was little collaborative work undertaken for a single, whole-group outcome. Though children sat in groups for up to 60 per cent of the time, they only worked in groups for some 5 per cent of their tasks.[74] One implication of this is that the student teacher must plan tasks, activities and routines that foster and promote interactive learning.[75] This is a significant feature if discipline and good behaviour are to be promoted in classes. Accepting that grouping is a pedagogical device requires the student teacher to be very clear on the purposes of grouping children and ensure that the children themselves understand those purposes.

There are limits to the advantages of group work. For example, putting children into groups could replace 'task-enhancing' talk with lower level 'task-related' talk.[76] Dunne and Bennett[77] found that students of all abilities improved their skills of discussion, suggesting, concluding, testing, inferring and reflecting when working in mixed-ability groups, and that they improved in terms of both co-operation and independence. Bennett and Dunne[78] found that if group work was directed towards a genuinely collaborative activity then task-related activity was very high. Muijs and Reynolds[79] report that group work risks stifling independent thinking, can produce 'group think', which may be entirely incorrect but hard to change, and can foster dependency on one or more dominant members of the group. Indeed, poorer or lazy students can 'get away' with not making a full contribution or effort.

Time will need to be spent on ensuring that children understand the 'rules of the game' in group work (e.g. about talking, moving, allotting tasks) or even on making it clear to children that co-operation is permitted. Indeed it could be that teaching time is lost to transition time in group work.[80] Kutnick and Manson[81] suggest that if tasks are ambiguous or unclear for the group then they may be ineffective.

Cohen[82] argues that students need to know what is involved in co-operation, e.g. listening, explaining, supporting, summarising, sharing ideas. Indeed Hall[83] demonstrates that children need to become aware of the purposes behind different approaches to learning, particularly when they are being asked to learn through small group discussion. Without this awareness, he argues, they do not value the various approaches to learning. This is echoed by Harwood,[84] who demonstrated that the presence of the teacher correlated with improved effectiveness of learning in group working where the teacher stimulated the students, elaborated on their ideas, and controlled group dynamics, e.g. avoiding fragmentation of groups, dominance of one student, and scapegoating.

Dunne and Bennett[85] suggest that students need to be told explicitly that they must ask each other in the group before coming to the teacher. They also suggest that teachers will have to consider carefully the type of task that groups undertake in order to anticipate the types of demands that will be made on teachers.

There is a significant body of evidence to suggest that students need to be 'trained' in group work skills, for example in sharing, participation, communication and listening skills.[86] Dunne and Bennett[87] argue that these include: knowledge of acceptable behaviour; listening; questioning; clarifying and challenging skills; posing problems and deciding what to do. Echoing Dunne and Bennett, Harwood[88] argues that teachers need to spend time in the early stages of group work on developing communication skills: listening, asking, explaining, supporting, checking for consensus, providing evidence. Indeed Muijs and Reynolds[89] suggest that it might be useful to appoint students to take certain roles in the group, for example: summariser, researcher, checker, runner, observer/troubleshooter and recorder. Cohen[90] argues that students need to review how successfully they themselves, as a group, are working co-operatively. McAllister[91] extends this point by suggesting that students benefit from analysing their own work and giving feedback to each other in groups. Cohen argues that teachers too need to give feedback to students on how successfully they are working together. McAllister is unequivocal in suggesting that discussion and detailed planning are critical for successful group work, and that these should be stressed very early in implementing group work. Galvin et al.[92] report that, though children work well in groups when the teacher works with them, the level of activity drops to around 50 per cent when the group is working without the teacher.

Further, Mortimore et al.[93] found that, whilst group work might be effective if all the groups were working in one or two curriculum areas only (e.g. everyone doing mathematics that is differentiated by task), where three or more curriculum areas were taking place simultaneously then children's learning was inefficient. This view was echoed unequivocally by Alexander et al.[94] Too many curriculum areas occurring simultaneously provided a level of complexity in organisation and implementation that detracted from efficient learning and efficient use of the teacher – procedural and managerial talk replaced instructional and pedagogical talk. Indeed Bennett and Dunne[95] suggest that teachers would have to ensure that they made abstract demands as well as action-oriented demands in group work, particularly in the areas of science, technology and mathematics. Pollard et al.[96] report that teachers who implemented group work involved themselves heavily with low-attaining children twice as much as they did with high attainers.

Actually organising the groups can be difficult – what principles or organisation does one go by? Guidance here can be found in Pollard and Tann[97] and Pollard et al.[98] who show how the criteria devised by Kerry and Sands[99] can help to overcome some of the obstacles. The criteria in question are:

- *Age groups:* These can be useful for some activities, though because of the spread of ability, achievement and interests etc., they can sometimes be counter-productive when it comes to teaching some subjects.
- *Attainment groups:* These are useful for well-defined tasks that befit the ability of the children. However, Pollard and Tann consider that they can be divisive if used permanently.
- *Interest groups:* Grouping children according to interest is always useful and has definite social advantages when there are differences of one sort of another between the children, e.g. race or social class.
- *Friendship groups:* One of the commonest forms of grouping, these go down well with the children and are a valuable means of social education. However, the teacher must bear in mind the needs of those children who do not mix well.
- *Convenience groups:* These are used for organisational rather than primarily educational purposes.
- *Mixed attainment groups.*
- *Gender groups* (single sex or both sexes).

Muijs and Reynolds[100] suggest that it is important to have co-operative groups that are of heterogeneous, but not too heterogeneous, ability. Groups which each comprised (a) high- and medium-ability and (b) medium- and low-ability students gave and received more explanations than groups which included high, medium and low abilities within each group. When only high-ability groups were formed, interaction and co-operation were limited (perhaps because the students did not feel it necessary to help each other), and when only low-ability groups were formed, the students were unable to help each other, regardless of whether they wished to or not.

Pollard *et al.*[101] found that in 1990 and 1992 80 per cent of teachers grouped children by attainment levels, particularly in mathematics and other curricular areas where differentiation by task was required (e.g. English). Mixed attainment groups and friendship groups were employed for some of the time, particularly when differentiation by outcome was operating. They reported a decrease in mixed-age groupings – even in rural schools, and a very low incidence of gender-based groups. The under-representation of gender-based groups is probably welcome, as Bennett and Dunne[102] found that if a girl was put into a group that comprised mostly boys then the amount of participation by girls was reduced and the amount of higher level talk diminished. Significantly Pollard *et al.*[103] noted the increase in the amount of grouping by attainment that had occurred since the inception of the National Curriculum.

Successful grouping occurs when 'fitness for purpose' is demonstrated. Bennett and Dunne[104] report that group work proceeds optimally when groups comprise no more than four children and where groups are involved in a whole-class activity that includes reporting-back sessions. They define different types of co-operative group work:

- where children work together on an element of a 'joint' outcome – the 'jigsaw' model
- where children work together on a whole task for a whole – joint – outcome
- where children work alone for their own individual outcomes but share resources.

The latter, of course, is a very limited view of group work. Kagan[105] suggests that having groups of odd numbers is dangerous – a group of three quickly becomes a dyad with an odd one out; a group of five again risks having an odd one out. Further, Dunne and Bennett[106] found that groups of five and six tended to splinter into smaller subgroups.

Where individual children are chosen to lead groups, as with older children, your expectations have to be explained and the requisite skills developed, for example:[107]

- *Getting ideas from the group:* These then need to be organised and appropriate follow-up action planned.
- *Allocating tasks:* Once ideas have been shaped, tasks can be allocated. It is important to clarify who should do what.
- *Pacing the work:* Monitoring progress involves helping tardy ones to catch up and redirecting early finishers.
- *Providing encouragement and support:* Leaders need to be made aware of this important part of their task.
- *Fitting it all together:* This involves seeing how the parts fit together and deciding on final presentation.

In approaching group work a series of questions need to be considered by the student teacher:

- On what basis will the children be grouped?
- How permanent is the group?
- Who will or will not work efficiently with whom if placed in the same group?
- How long will different groups have to complete the same/different tasks (i.e. what will the student teacher plan for those who finish quickly/slowly)?
- Will there be a group leader?
- Exactly what will each member of the group be required to do – are there enough tasks for each member of the group to be usefully engaged? How will each child know exactly what is expected of her/him?

●   How will the student teacher use herself and intervene most efficiently, providing instructional and cognitive talk as well as procedural and managerial talk?

●   How will group sessions begin (i.e. will some children be waiting whilst the student teacher sets others working; which children can be relied upon to wait patiently)?

●   How will sessions be rounded off (rather than simply stop for want of time)?

●   How will reporting back to the whole class be undertaken?

●   What will be done with children who do not wish to work together or who do not wish to work in any group?

●   What will be done if a child disagrees with a group decision and becomes unco-operative and uninterested?

McAllister[108] argues that in the early stages of group work students benefit from being able to work with friends of their own choice. Morrison and Ridley[109] suggest a six-stage sequence in introducing and developing group work for classes new to the idea:

●   Stage 1: Have only one or two groups working apart from the class at any one time while the remainder of the class is involved in class or individually based work.

●   Stage 2: Each group replicates the same activity.

●   Stage 3: Each group works on the same activity or focus in a variety of ways.

●   Stage 4: Each group works on a variety of aspects of a topic or focus, one aspect per group.

●   Stage 5: Each group works on a variety of aspects of a topic or focus, covering many key aspects; children do the planning.

●   Stage 6: Each group works on aspects of a variety of topics or foci.

If one stage turns out to be problematic then it is easy to revert to the previous stage, i.e. to return to a stage which had been successful. In developing group work there are a number of variables that can be progressively introduced, for example:

●   time (progressively increase the amount of time for group activities)

●   number of different activities taking place (from everybody doing the same in groups to each group maybe doing something different)

●   number of groups (from maybe only one group working apart from the whole class to complete group work)

●   number of curricular areas bring addressed (with the caveat not to have more than three or four at any one time).

If adding a variable, or increasing a variable (e.g. time) causes problems, then the advantage of staging group work over time is that it can be easily 'pulled back' to a previous stage if necessary, i.e. to reinforce a stage that was effective and successful.

Whether group work is a resounding success or a demoralising failure is often a function of planning with management issues in mind. The student teacher will have to:

●   avoid being too ambitious either for herself or for the children

●   only attempt to have more than one curriculum area simultaneously if she and the children can cope with it

●   enable children to practise being in a group (i.e. not expecting wonderful results from novice groups)

●   give clear instructions

- avoid overloading children with instructions all at once, rather stage the instructions throughout the session
- be vigilant and attend to the whole class rather than being completely absorbed in one group
- talk to the class as a whole (e.g. about how well the work is going, how well they are managing to work in the group) as well as talking to groups, i.e. avoid atomising the classroom interactions
- be prepared to stop everyone during the session to calm them down, make a teaching/ procedural/managerial/behaviour point.

When it works well group work can work very well and be very satisfying for student teachers and children.[110] In planning the classroom organisation, then, we argue that the student teacher will need to be guided by the notion of 'fitness for purpose'. For example, Wheldall *et al.*[111] argue that if one wishes students to work co-operatively then a group seating arrangement is most appropriate, whilst independent work benefits from relative isolation. They argue convincingly that it amounts to cruelty to have students seated in groups and yet expect them to work independently. Further, Hastings and Schwieso[112] suggest that having students seated in rows keeps them on task effectively in individualised work by minimising the opportunities for students to have eye contact with each other and maximising the opportunities for the teacher to have eye contact with the whole class. Group seating arrangements, on the other hand, are suitable for discussions and collaborative activities.

The physical environment

Our brief comments here can be read in conjunction with the relevant section of 'The classroom environment and situational factors' later. The fundamental aim with the classroom environment is to organise it in such a way as to back up whatever your educational purposes are.[113] Relevant considerations here might be: the values of the school (e.g. social inclusion); the requirements of the National Curriculum; how children learn and develop; how and where resources are to be kept and used; the teaching and learning strategies to be used; the views of students and teachers on the classroom and what is important/desired. Kershner[114] suggests that the environment should address such issues as: fostering personal identity; promoting involvement and self-esteem through having individuals contributing to the environment (e.g. through displays); encouraging the development of competencies; promoting ease of movement and reducing disturbance; promoting a sense of trust and security; allowing for both privacy and social interaction; providing opportunities for social, physical, motor and affective as well as cognitive growth (a feature which reinforces issues of multiple intelligences).

We advise you to begin by drawing a plan of your classroom, preferably to scale. When you have got a more or less complete picture, you can scrutinise it in the light of your own intentions. The criteria you use could include aesthetic ones:

- Do the design, layout, decoration and lighting contribute to a pleasing effect?
- Is the room pleasurable to be in?
- Is the room functional?
- Does it do what you will want it to do?
- Can practical work be undertaken efficiently?
- Is there sufficient storage?
- Can different activities take place simultaneously?
- Are there enough materials and tools?
- What are the presentational aspects like?

- Are the noticeboards and display tables adequate to your needs?
- Do they achieve what they are supposed to achieve?
- No room is perfect, so what are the possibilities for further improvements?
- Can greater use be made of the windows, or the ceiling perhaps?
- Are there enough plants in the room?

A particular aspect of the classroom is the extent to which space is used effectively, and it is to this we turn.

The use of space

Kerry and Tollitt[115] describe space as essentially a learning resource and state that for the infant teacher managing space is a vital skill. Much of that management, they explain, is about five principles:

1 providing opportunities for a variety of child-centred but teacher-directed activities (story time)
2 reinforcing children's more formal work through real experience or play (e.g. through display, or in the classroom shop)
3 setting up opportunities for tactile or imaginative play as an aid in itself (sand, water, building blocks)
4 making available the essential resources that pupils need in order to learn, and
5 creating an environment conducive to spontaneous learning.

It can be a useful exercise for the student teacher to work out how much space is required for the various activities she will be organising. This will be particularly relevant to group work. It is important to see what the differences are in this connection with respect to language skills, mathematics, science, environmental studies, art and craft, the expressive arts, play and religious education.

Space can be marked off by the appropriate use of cupboards, screens, shelves or tables. The fundamental divisions are into clean/messy activities and quiet/noisy ones. Indeed there may need to be timetabling for noisy activities, so that quieter activities are not disrupted. In Box 59 Kerry and Tollitt suggest ideas to start you thinking about 'exploiting space'.

Resources

Our last feature of classroom organisation is resources. The availability and use of resources in the primary classroom are of the greatest possible importance in the part they play in children's learning. Pollard and Tann[116] have suggested four criteria that might be borne in mind when organising and arranging resources. They are:

1 *Appropriateness:* What resources are suitable as an integral part of the learning activities?
2 *Availability:* What is available within the classroom, the school, and the wider environment?
3 *Storage:* How are the resources stored? What is under teacher control and what is freely available to the children? What safety factors need to be remembered?
4 *Maintenance:* What kind of maintenance is required and who is responsible for it?

Box 59: Exploiting space

Floor area	Layout of tables, chairs etc. will have an effect upon kinds of activities you can employ – think of spaces for individual work, group activity, story time and so on.
Wall space	Can this be exploited for display – of children's work, of stimulus materials, of resource materials around a topic of current concern?
Noticeboards	Fixing devices can be more varied here (staple guns, pins). Possible use for more long-term items, e.g. 'word ladders' of basic vocabulary, packs of stimulus cards giving tasks for pupils with 'free' moments.
Black/whiteboards	Up-dated display of day, date, season, clock-face, 'word a day' reinforcement.
Storage area	Think out problems of access, cleanliness, layout. If unsightly, how can area be disguised? E.g. doorway 'dressed' as time machine, or attractively curtained.
Horizontal surfaces	Useful for equipment (magnifying glass, Lego etc.), specimens, 3D artefacts made by children, 3D displays by teacher, plants.
Ceiling beams	In older schools it may be practical to use these as hangers for 'word trees', mobiles etc.
Bays	Can these be pressed into service as a reading corner, a group-work area, a wet area, a project base?
Windows and views	Artwork can often be displayed effectively when back-lit by window light. Window may look out on to field, with potential for watching wildlife, or onto school yard with bird-feeder.
Wet areas	As well as supporting artwork, cookery etc. these areas give potential for scientific experiments, volume and quantity work, keeping an aquarium etc.
Adjacent corridor	Can be decorated to harmonise with any theme developed in the classroom, e.g. some may lend themselves to open access bookshelves and browsing areas.
Electric points	Enable a range of audio-visual aids to be used in teaching and learning. Pupils can operate tape-recorders or simple slide viewers, so increasing potential for individual or group work, or helping non-readers.

SOME ORGANISATIONAL CONCEPTS IN PRIMARY EDUCATION

We have already introduced the notion of subject and subject specialist teaching in the primary school. There is no doubt that its influence is being felt, particularly with a subject-framed National Curriculum.[117]

Our intention here is to trace an alternative context of primary education whose history is little shorter than the elementary tradition,[118] viz. the notion of child-centred education, for example in the work of Rousseau[119] and Dewey,[120] and enshrined in the famous phrases from the Hadow Report that argued that the curriculum should be thought of in terms of activity and experience rather than knowledge to be learned and facts to be stored.[121] Child-centredness has many hues[122] – from a child-chosen curriculum to the delineation of an active, experiential and concrete form of learning.

Whilst the notion of child-centred or progressive education has become almost a term of abuse or an accusation against teachers for failing to bring students to the required standards, we argue that a cooler, less fundamentalist, less pejorative and less dismissive reading of child-centred education is tenable. This respects the individuality of the child (in differentiated activities), demonstrates the value of first-hand, experiential learning (implicit in constructivist psychology) that 'begins where the child is', and argues for some form of negotiation with children rather than a steamroller approach with heavy prescription. This will enable teachers to replace the ideological trappings of a romantic ideology for which progressive education has unfortunately been saddled with some enduring and important teaching principles that make for good practice regardless of one's ideological commitments.

A watershed in primary education that emphasised child-centred principles and methods was set out in the Plowden Report.[123] This report proved to be a powerful influence in advocating open schools and open education, concepts which when translated into school practice were to result in a marked shift from the more traditional view of children as learners. The open or progressive view of education was characterised by three broad concepts – freedom, activity and discovery – and a concern with process as opposed to content. It was also noted for its desire to broaden concepts such as education, learning and responsibility and it is such concepts and ideas that were to persist and exert an important influence on the organisation of primary school practice. The emphasis on discovery learning or 'learning to learn', for example, and the highlighting of the needs of the individual child are instances of open education's more lasting influence; likewise, the stress on the value of group work. The Plowden Report's authors saw groups as a natural social unit for primary children, which were part of the process of socialisation. 'Openness' in terms of attitudes and sharing, and in terms of relationships between teacher and pupil, pupil and pupil, and teacher and teacher also became an increasing feature of the primary world.

The notion of 'open education' was reflected not only in the pedagogical styles adopted but in the physical layout of the school building as a whole and of age-related teaching areas in particular.[124] We are referring here to the notion of an open-plan or semi-open-plan school, wherein there is joint use of space and materials, concomitant with team teaching and very flexible groupings of children. In a fully open-plan school, space is divided up by low furniture, creating bays for study; in a semi-open-plan school teaching spaces are defined by walls with openings in to other areas (often shared library, art and technology areas), and flexible open-plan schools have screens and partitions that can be moved to open or close off areas at will.[125]

There are several claimed attractions of open-plan arrangements. These are summarised in Box 60.

On the other hand, as with integrated teaching (discussed below), open-plan teaching is not universally popular and not always without its difficulties. These are summarised in Box 61.

Box 60: Advantages of open-plan arrangements

Open-plan arrangements can:

- develop children's autonomy and responsibility (e.g. for working without too close supervision)
- maximise space through shared areas
- move away from whole-class instruction to differentiated activities
- support team planning, team teaching and team assessing
- facilitate social learning and peer group learning
- reduce resource duplication
- encourage co-operative work (by children and teachers)
- support flexible group size and membership
- avoid feelings of insecurity and isolation that student teachers (and experienced teachers) may feel in more traditional 'cellular' classrooms
- facilitate consistent and supportive handling of difficult children by more than one teacher
- facilitate the sharing of ideas by students and teachers.

Box 61: Disadvantages of open-plan arrangements

Open-plan arrangements can:

- incur much transition time
- let children 'slip through the net' of being monitored
- fail with uncommitted teachers
- lead to wasteful use of resources
- cause much noise and distraction
- fail to make the most of materials and resources
- lead to over-reliance on worksheets
- cause discipline problems
- cause problems of cover if staff are absent
- cause congestion as children circulate round areas
- provide inadequate display space
- make personality clashes amongst teachers very visible
- require much time for team planning
- cause problems of supervision.

Open-plan teaching makes heavy demands on teachers and planning, echoing the issue raised by Mortimore[126] and Alexander *et al.*[127] that having too many groups doing too many different activities in too many curriculum areas is inefficient.

Two key concepts at the heart of educational practice in open and progressive classrooms are the integrated day and the integrated curriculum, both of which play an important part in primary education today.

The integrated day has been described[128] as an organisational concept, implying that 'timetables or other formalised ways of changing from one activity to another are abandoned. Instead, the flow of children's learning activities is unbroken and changes informally and often individually, with a large element of the children's own choice governing the matters.' In consequence, a variety of contrasting activities are likely to be in progress simultaneously in the room or area. 'Some children may be reading or writing, others weighing or measuring, some painting, experimenting or modelling, while yet others may be in a group being instructed or questioned by the teacher, or out of the room altogether.'[129]

Dearden considers that at least three things may be said in favour of having an integrated day. First, it allows for more individualised learning in content and pace and this makes for more interest and involvement: 'When curricula and methods are more precisely tailored success is more likely.'[130] Second, because the amount of time a teacher can devote to a particular child is limited, children learn how to learn on their own in those areas of work where this is possible:

> At the primary stage, this principally means acquiring various information-getting skills such as are involved in using reference books, using libraries and writing to relevant people. It also involves acquiring habits of initiative and persistence, so that available opportunities to find out for oneself are not shied away from ...[131]

Third, more individualised learning and developing skills of learning for oneself are closely related to the development of personal autonomy and self-direction.

Advocates of open or progressive education objected to the sharp division among subjects in traditional classrooms, arguing that learning cannot always be neatly wrapped up in separate packages. Many activities involve knowledge of, and skill in, a variety of subjects. Open educators therefore recommend an integrated curriculum in which subject boundaries are less distinct. Thus the work of a class could be organised around broad unified themes which encompass a number of subject areas. Skills are studied as they are needed by the activity and are practised in the course of significant tasks. In this connection, Dearden[132] writes:

> Integration logically presupposes differentiation, the differentiated elements being subordinated to some unitary whole. In what might be called 'loose' integration, the subordination of elements is no more than their selection according to relevance to a topic, theme or centre of interest. Thus geography, history, science, music and art may be selectively drawn upon for the contribution they can make to some such theme as canals, the sea, railways, flight, India or whatever. If the theme is the sea, then there may be maps of oceans, the history of voyages of discovery, experiments on floating in salt and fresh water, the painting of scenes beneath the sea, the playing of 'Fingal's Cave', the singing of sea shanties. Treasure Island may be read and the economic uses of the sea may be studied. No doubt the justification for such a 'loose' integration of subjects would be that it naturally follows the course of an interest without any arbitrary interruptions or divisions. And a good deal of such general knowledge is acquired in areas where it is difficult to argue that this rather than that must be known, or that this rather than that must be covered. The strongest argument for loose integration is thus motivational.

Thus the main argument in favour of an integrated curriculum is that pupils are actively involved in the learning experience. The teacher is the 'facilitator' who helps to create the conditions for learning, but it is the child who does the learning. Pollard and Tann[133] remind us of two other arguments in favour of the integrated curriculum. First, new subjects have been added to the curriculum which are inter-disciplinary and conceptually linked. An example here is environmental studies. The very nature of the subject integrated a number of disciplines. Second, where subject boundaries are reduced, it is possible to reduce the influence of subject content. As the authors explain, 'Having lessened the emphasis on particular subject knowledge, a higher priority can be given to general processes, skills and attitudes.'

Inevitably, in most integrated days there has to be a certain amount of formal timetabling. This usually occurs where the use of common or shared resources, such as in music or television programmes, is involved. Similarly, even though an integrated curriculum may be in operation, subject teaching may be important, for example:[134] 'Physical education for practical reasons, mathematics for reasons of sequence, and language skills because of their arbitrary social conventions all have to be differentiated out, at least for some of the time.'

From the child's perspective, integration in learning is natural during the early years of life. At this stage in her mental development, the child does not see what she learns as classifiable into distinct subject areas or isolated skills. She reads, records, calculates in pursuit of her current interests, and not until the age of 9 or so does she begin to classify what she learns into subject compartments. Integration stems from the child and from the natural ways in which she learns. It is the child who integrates, not the teacher.

Morrison and Ridley[135] identify five stages that the student teacher can follow in introducing the integrated day:[136]

- Stage 1: Grouping the children and training them in the access, use and return of materials; establishing discipline and control.
- Stage 2: Using one hour or one block of time to do two specific tasks, the student teacher setting the tasks and the children choosing the order and timing.

- Stage 3: The student teacher extending the periods of integration and number of tasks, perhaps doing this one group at a time.
- Stage 4: Reducing the amount of direction by the student teacher, with the children knowing what tasks to do without being told by the teacher; lengthening the period of integration; the student teacher drawing up daily plans for the children.
- Stage 5: Days of integration moving to a week of integration, perhaps one group at a time; extended use of assignment cards.

As with group work, outlined earlier, variables of time, curriculum areas, number of activities and so on are controlled. As steps to integration gather momentum so do the possible management problems. The integrated day can lead to the situation where an exhausted teacher is working much harder than the children, where noise levels rise, where lazy children 'slip through the net' (unless scrupulous records are kept and updated on an almost daily basis), where children can move around the room being distracted and distracting others, where assignment cards suffer from the 'death by worksheet' syndrome, where some children cannot handle the freedom accorded to them, and where the degree of planning required is greater than the return on the time and effort expended.

We earlier touched upon possibilities for grouping children within a class, sometimes referred to as intra-class grouping. We now consider grouping children within the school, or intra-school grouping. This can be achieved in terms of age or ability. We begin with age. There are three options here: same-age grouping (sometimes called horizontal or chronological grouping), vertical grouping (or mixed-age grouping) and transitional grouping.

Same-age grouping (or horizontal or chronological) refers to classes in which children are of the same age range. This may vary from three months to possibly one year depending on the size of the school. There are a number of advantages and disadvantages of horizontal grouping. The advantages are as follows:

- The narrow age range may enable teachers to feel more secure and the narrower range of ability may appear to make their task simpler.
- Children and teachers are both able to make a completely new beginning with each new school year.
- Classes grouped in this manner show greater social cohesion and interaction because they are at similar levels of intellectual, social and emotional development and have similar interests.

Some of the disadvantages are as follows:

- As the class is new at the start of each year, there is no continuity with the previous year.
- There is the possibility that children in the younger parallel classes may underachieve because they are known to be younger and appear less able.
- A teacher who sees his class as a fairly homogeneous group may be in danger of not noticing the exceptions.
- Teachers who tend to specialise in one age group for a number of years will automatically restrict the range of their experience.

Vertical grouping may be defined as a method of organising children in such a manner that each class contains children from each age group in the school. At the present time, vertical grouping is found chiefly in infant schools and rural schools with several ages in a single class (due to the low number of children in the school). In such classes each child will then 'run his/her own race' in a stable community guided by one teacher.

Vertical or mixed-age grouping implies a flexible organisation which provides a wide basis for a child's emotional, social and intellectual development. The distinctive strength of this arrangement lies in its fluidity, for individual, group and class work are all possible. Indeed, it is the individual needs and interests of the children, and not their ages, which lie at the basis of group formation and re-formation.

In addition to the flexible organisational structure noted above, vertical grouping possesses a number of additional advantages (some of which it shares with horizontally grouped children being taught on an individual or group basis) that may be listed thus:

● A more natural and relaxed atmosphere can result from this same flexibility.

● The organisation minimises problems arising from a child's entering the infant school for the first time – moving into a stable and secure community, the new entrant is able to adjust more quickly and successfully.

● The organisational flexibility relates more effectively to the children's motivation, to the content of learning, and to the integration of the curriculum than is the case with more traditional approaches.

● Children are better able to learn from each other as well as from the teacher.

● The structure allows more effectively for variations in personal growth and development than is the case with more rigid organisational structures, fixed age groups and set instructional procedures.

● The organisation increases the likelihood of children interacting with the environment.

● A wider range of social experience is possible, together with resultant benefits such as a greater sense of belongingness, support and security.

● Should problems arise, a child can be moved to another class without much difficulty.

● Older children develop a sense of responsibility towards the younger ones.

● The teacher is in a better position to deal with the children individually.

● Communication between teachers benefits, as each teacher is confronted with similar problems of the various age groups.

● Teachers using vertical grouping tend to speak favourably of it.

Critics of vertical grouping, however, raise the following objections:

● The duties of the teacher become excessively onerous.

● Personality clashes between a teacher and child may make it undesirable for a child to spend two or three years in the same class.

● Older children may help younger ones too much, thus hampering their own progress.

● Children on the point of entering the junior school may be given preferential treatment.

● The noise created by the younger children may disturb the older ones (partial vertical grouping can solve this problem).

● The structure presents difficulties for activities such as stories and poems, religious education, and those areas such as music and movement and physical education where skill depends on maturation.

● Groups whose teachers are uncommitted or weak will be disadvantaged by a vertically grouped structure.

● There may be hostility from parents (though this often arises from misunderstandings).

There are four basic educational principles underlying the practice of vertical grouping. These may be briefly summarised as follows:[137]

1   Being a stable and secure community, the school embodying the principles of vertical grouping provides the continuity and coherence necessary in a child's educational life.
2   A vertically grouped situation caters for a wide age range in its own right, provides for individual motivation, tempo and maturation, and thus facilitates maximal individual growth.
3   A vertically grouped structure provides for the acceptance of the child as an agent of his own learning.
4   Such an organisation provides for the fullest development of the balanced personality. It meets the need for a holistic view of child development which will foster attitudes, qualities and abilities that will enable a child to live a happy, well-adjusted life in a complex and changing social environment.

Although the one essential characteristic of vertical grouping is the age grouping, some teachers identify two further characteristics:

1   *The integrated or unstructured day:* This they perceive as crucial to the successful working of vertical grouping. In so far as it is possible, a school is thus stripped of all artificial divisions.
2   *A structured environment:* An unstructured day is only made possible by having a highly organised classroom, and success in vertical grouping rests to a large extent on a highly structured environment. Space and opportunity to spread out are essential; and every classroom should have a good range of basic equipment.

Transitional grouping is a combination of same-age and vertical grouping. Some see it as a compromise between the two. Arrangements for transitional grouping in infant, junior and first schools are extremely flexible. One such arrangement in an infant school would be to have the 5- and 6-year-olds vertically grouped in parallel classes and single-age classes for the 7-year-olds. There are advantages and disadvantages of transitional grouping.[138] Advantages include:

● With transitional grouping, children have the experience of changing to a single-age class within the security of the same school.
● Transitional grouping allows children more variety of adult contact.
● Separating children at 7 appears to eliminate the need to cater for physical education, story and music at a separate level for certain ages as within the vertically grouped class.
● It helps with the problem of younger children trying to follow too closely the lead of the older children, and losing experience of activities such as fantasy play or the investigation of the properties of materials.
● Older children also benefit in that they can expect more opportunity to use materials creatively and more teacher's help with the practice of basic skills.
● Some teachers are happier with older children. and others are more suited to younger ones.
● The system appears to be particularly advantageous in a socially deprived school.

Three disadvantages identified may be listed thus:

1   Where an individual child has not emotionally or intellectually reached the level of his companions, this is obviously more noticeable on transfer to a 7-year-old class or a vertically grouped 7- to 8-year-old class.
2   As with vertically grouped situations, there may well be misunderstandings by the parents which need sympathetic explanation by the school.

3   Where children have made friends with older or younger children in their vertically grouped class and are now separated, there may be distress on the part of the children which needs to be understood by the school.

Intra-school grouping according to ability offer two possibilities: the same or similar ability groups and mixed-ability groups. Schools organised on same-ability principles make use of setting. Where setting is seen as undesirable (for philosophical as well as practical reasons), the answer lies in mixed-ability grouping. Kerry and Tollitt[139] remind us that at infant level, mixed-ability grouping is rarely made the issue it has become in comprehensive schools. They have identified some of the reasons why teachers in infant schools prefer mixed-ability groups:

● Grading children by ability is socially divisive.
● Infant school is too early to make satisfactory judgements about children's academic potential.
● Children labelled as failures tend to fail.
● Streaming does not correspond to the way children will live in the community.
● Children of differing abilities can learn to help or be helped by classmates.

We continue by examining some of the principal teaching and learning styles to be found in primary classrooms. We concentrate on those methods that developed with the emergence of open and progressive classrooms.

TEACHING AND LEARNING STYLES IN PRIMARY CLASSROOMS

One of the most striking features of contemporary primary classrooms is the range and variety of teaching and learning styles operating in them. A teaching style is made up of a cluster of elements:

● the type of discipline
● the relationships and interactions between teachers and children
● teacher behaviour
● the organisation of the class
● the nature and extent of teacher talk
● the degree of student choice
● the nature and use of resources
● the nature of assessment
● the organisation of the curriculum
● the style of learning
● the atmosphere in the classroom.

A formal style will interpret these very differently from an informal style. For example, a formal style might be characterised by strict, overt discipline, a high degree of social distance between teachers and students, a 'chalk-and-talk' type of lesson with little interaction between one student and another, individual work with no talking, an emphasis on book work, the teacher acting as an expert, the curriculum organised in subjects and students being assessed by standardised tests. An informal style might be characterised by a freer discipline, less social distance between students and teachers, experiential and active learning using a variety of resources, children learning in groups, and assessment being diagnostic.

Our review of teaching and learning styles includes individualisation, individual attention, discovery learning, play and talk, and topics and projects. Group teaching we have already touched upon and there is enough guidance on direct, formal teaching in other parts of the book to meet the reader's need.

Individualisation

Individualisation of instruction is based on recognition of the fact that not all children can be expected to learn at the same rate. The approach is used in both traditional and open classrooms though its relationship to the content of learning is different in each case. In the traditional classroom, individualisation is achieved by varying the pace or duration of learning and by varying the mode of teaching. A consequence of this is the need for frequent evaluation and testing to check the children's progress. In open or progressive classrooms, where individualisation is a key concept, children collaborate in formulating their own curricular goals, albeit within the framework of the National Curriculum. Individualisation is sometimes misinterpreted as meaning that each child works on his own in a physical sense. But this is not the case. It simply means that his individual needs are taken into account. More often than not, these can be most effectively met by grouping – a topic we have already considered.

The key to effective individualised learning lies in the provision of adequate resources and materials, carefully structured and suitable for a child's abilities. Individualisation is but one aspect of the learning process that can benefit enormously from the technological revolution and its application to the classroom.

Individual attention

Individualisation involves encounters with the teacher, and her contribution to the teaching–learning process in the primary classroom can be considered in terms of individual attention. The burden of informal encounters between the teacher and child can be very onerous, sometimes totalling as many as a thousand interpersonal contacts a day, with two groups of children frequently receiving the most attention: the active hard workers and the active miscreants. The average child may miss out in this respect, not through any rational policy on the part of the teacher, but because the ongoing classroom pressures limit pupil contact to the two categories identified above. For the neglected child who is also diffident and therefore unlikely to talk even to those other children in his group, the classroom becomes bereft of language, either written or spoken.

However, in dividing the pupils into three sub-groups – high achievers, medium achievers and low achievers – there may be little difference in the distribution of teacher–pupil interaction between the three groups of pupils, nor any discrimination either in favour of or against any particular group of pupils according to their achievement level.

Discovery and experiential learning

Discovery and experiential learning are concepts arising from the strategies of topic and project work in progressive environments and are of central importance to the work of the primary classroom.

By means of discovery learning we may reasonably expect children to learn something new; and to do so through some initiative of their own.[140] There are three points to be borne in mind in any discussion on learning by discovery. First, what is involved primarily is the learning of facts, concepts and principles rather than skills, techniques or sensitivities; and the subjects most relevant to discovery learning are mathematics, science and environmental studies. Second, discovery learning may be contrasted with the sort of learning usually associated with the traditional class-room, i.e. learning by instruction or demonstration. And third, learning by discovery does not just happen; it comes about as a result of a particular teaching method or strategy. Numerous strategies can be distinguished in this connection; perhaps the commonest one to be found is that of guided discovery. By means of this, a teacher supports a child's self-chosen activity with questions, commentary and suggestions.

Another useful typology is that of open-ended discovery learning and planned or structural discovery. In the case of the former, the situation in which the child is put or which he chooses is such that the teacher does not know the outcome. A topic on some aspect of environmental studies would be an example here. Planned or structured discovery occurs when a teacher wants a specific aspect of learning to take place, perhaps with respect to the development or acquisition of scientific or mathematical concepts.

Topic and project work

Tann[141] defines topic work as 'an approach to learning which draws upon children's concerns and which actively involves them in the planning, executing, presenting and evaluating of a negotiated learning experience. In this form of topic work 'control' is a shared responsibility.' The use of topics, projects, themes and centres of interest has long been an important feature of primary class-rooms, especially in those where child-centred teaching prevails (not necessarily the simplistic ideologically puritan version outlined earlier but the approach that stresses first-hand, experiential learning through a negotiated order, a view that is not necessarily at odds with the National Curriculum). The reasons for our support of some form of topic work are numerous – their value in integration and discovery learning, for example, along with the social benefits that accrue from group work. Of course, the use of such approaches is not confined to the primary classroom as an examination of secondary, further and higher education will disclose. Indeed, projects play a significant role in the coursework of the GCSE. The terms topic work and project work lack precise definitions, but they do possess similarities.[142] They are practical in nature and attempt to break away from the conventional methods of teaching, placing more emphasis on the child than on the subject; they endeavour to allow the child to construct his or her own methods of approach to knowledge; they give him or her the opportunity to 'learn how to learn'; they break down barriers between school subjects; and they both utilise a child's own interests.

Topic work may be defined as individual and/or group investigations, recordings and presentations which children undertake when pursuing a topic. An individual topic is carried out by one child; a group topic is undertaken by a group of from four to six children; and a class topic by the whole class. An independent group is a self-sufficient unit contributing to one independent section of the topic; and a linked group collaborates with one or more other groups.

Generally speaking, topics should be chosen by the children on the basis of their own interests and commensurate with the requirements of the National Curriculum. They may initially require some suggestions and the teacher can help here with a compiled list of possibilities which can serve as a basis for negotiation.

The methods of undertaking a topic vary considerably with its nature and the maturity and experience of the children. The following five-stage plan, however, may serve as an organisational basis for student teachers embarking on a topic perhaps for the first time:

1   the teacher's preparation of the subject (see also Box 62)
2   introduction of the subject(s) to the class
3   the organisation of the subject(s) with the class

Box 62: Preparing for topic work

Before the topic begins, teachers should:

1   Prepare content and teaching methods
- Make flow diagrams or outlines of anticipated directions of study.
- Divide the content into the curriculum areas to be covered.
- Decide on specific teaching activities or modes for subdivision of the content.
- Refer to the school's outline scheme of work.
- Read around the subject at their own level.
- Make a list of the skills to be taught.
- Make notes on classroom management procedures (e.g. assign pupils to working groups).
- Decide on the time scale of the topic.
- Amend flow charts or plans in consultation with pupils.
- Plan lead lessons.

2   Prepare resources and materials
- Make a search of school and public libraries.
- Collect suitable audio-visual software.
- Arrange visits and speakers.
- Contact museums and other outside organisations.
- Prepare worksheets or assignment cards.
- Encourage pupils, colleagues or parents to collect materials.
- Consult TV and radio programme schedules.
- Write letters to supplying agencies.
- Visit the local Teachers' Centre.
- View in advance any area to be visited later by the class.

3   Prepare the classroom itself
- Make a display of related charts, reference books etc.
- Prepare a display area.
- Prepare resource collections.
- Decide on the layout of furniture.
- Check that any software or apparatus required is readily available.
- Provide suitable folders or storage for pupils' work.
- Organise outside or ancillary help.
- Explore the potential of school-based facilities (such as rain gauges).

4   the children's research into the subject matter
5   the end-product.

The teacher's functions throughout the sequence of stages are numerous. If the subject centres on a place or building, part of her own preparation may be a visit on her own. The form her introduction takes will depend on the nature of the subject, but it should be done in such a way as to arouse strong initial motivation. She may even adopt an imaginative approach, like telling a story or having the children act out some aspect of the theme. Once the topic is under way, the teacher is then available as a consultant and resources person. She should be careful not to direct too closely or obviously the actual course of the investigation for, as far as possible, the children themselves should determine how they wish to pursue their research and presentation. From time to time the teacher will need to restimulate interest and perhaps suggest new or alternative avenues of approach and exploration to the children as they work on their topics. She must constantly be on the alert for waning interest.

The importance of having a well-defined end-product agreed at the organisational stage cannot be over-emphasised. No matter how well motivated children are initially, they can easily lose interest as the topic gets under way. If or when this happens, the defined end-product will assist in refocusing attention and sustaining interest. What form the end-product takes will depend on a number of factors. Common forms of display and presentation include an exhibition, presentation in booklets and folders, displays and murals, recordings, mimes and plays, a talk by one or more members of the group, movies, video-recordings, models, collages, a magazine or newspaper, a festival, spoken poetry and prose, or any combination of these.[143]

In summary, the reader is reminded that the chief points to bear in mind are:

- his or her own thorough preparation, and especially the preliminary reading, research and exploration he or she needs to undertake
- the organisation of the topic with the class (availability of resources and definition of end-product are important here)
- making sure that the children enjoy the work, and
- establishing and maintaining a reasonably high level of motivation and anticipating the points where it can be expected to flag.

For a more detailed checklist for the preparation of topic work, we refer you to Box 62, the items having been devised by Kerry and Tollitt[144] with infants in mind.

It is difficult to establish a clear-cut distinction between topic work and project work. Like the topic, a project can be the work of an individual or a group. Projects, however, do tend to be more substantial than topics, thus requiring longer to accomplish. It is possible, for example, to spend a whole term on a project.

Much of what has been said on topic work will apply to projects. Social studies, environmental studies and science lend themselves particularly well to class projects. Box 63 lists some of the advantages of enquiry-based projects in primary school science.[145]

An important factor needing to be confronted in project work is that of structure. In Bonnett's[146] view, the challenge of project work for children lies in the extent to which it enables them to explore themselves in relation to the real world through the thoughtful acknowledgement and pursuit of their concerns. This challenge, Bonnett argues, 'cannot be met by attempts to 'order up' projects in advance and standardise their achievements. The structure we should be seeking is one which takes its cue from the children's own relationship with the world, their ways of revealing it to themselves.'

From his study of project work in schools, Bonnett has identified five sources of structure. These may be enshrined in the following principles:

1   *The teacher-centred principle:* This will derive largely from the teacher's own personal associations which in turn result from the teacher's own experiences and world view. As Bonnett says, 'As such it may well be highly subjective and greatly influenced by his or her own enthusiasm and areas of perceived expertise.'

2   *The knowledge-centred principle:* Where this structuring principle is paramount, the project becomes a vehicle for conveying pre-specified information, concepts, and ideas, selected, as the author says, 'on the basis that either they are of value in their own right, and/or learning

Box 63: Advantages of enquiry-based projects

- They provide a context which may help children to understand the processes of science by actually doing them.
- They may encourage children to work together, to share ideas, to challenge one another and to develop a critical awareness.
- They may change the role of the teacher from being a presenter of knowledge to that of being a resource agent and guide.
- They may encourage a degree of independence from the teacher and so begin the process of independent learning and judgement.
- They may encourage children to see science as a tentative discipline and not as an infallible one.

them forms part of the initiation of the pupil into the wider modes of knowledge and understanding from which they are derived.'

3   *The skills-centred principle:* Where this principle is operative the project is seen as a vehicle for transmitting certain skills which might be grouped under such headings as physical/manipulative, cognitive, social etc. As Bonnett explains, 'these would be pre-specified relatively independently of a particular knowledge content'.

4   *The problem-centred principle:* Here the structure is determined by the enquiry itself, and content and direction develop according to where that enquiry leads, and, as Bonnett adds, wherever it leads.

5   *The child-centred principle:* The structuring principle here is the child's own consciousness – his or her felt needs and concerns and the opportunities provided for choice and responsibility which the genuine exploration of these needs requires.

The criticisms sometimes levelled at projects – that they lack positive educational direction, that they result in mindless copying and futile experiment, and that they at best keep noisy children quiet and at worst lead to boredom and frustration – can be avoided where the practical suggestions offered above are put into practice.

11 Secondary Teaching

INTRODUCTION

Secondary classroom practices are the consequence of a range of local, institutional and individual variables, for example: the school ethos; the abilities of the pupils and the organisational arrangements to accommodate these (e.g. grouping, setting, banding, mixed-ability grouping); gender relationships; group dynamics; and characteristics of individual pupils and teachers. The pedagogical practices within secondary schools are, themselves, premised on conceptions of aims, theories of teaching and learning, interaction of variables, the learning environment, the task demands, personalities and social relationships; the focus on desired outcomes of learning; assessment and feedback.[1]

Stemler *et al.*[2] summarise research on the complexity of secondary school teaching and learning, indicating that individual differences in both the teacher and pupils are important in affecting learning outcomes, including, for example: prior knowledge, age and developmental factors, abilities, conceptions of learning, learning styles, cognitive styles, approaches to learning, effort, motivation, self-esteem, well-being, gender, ethnicity, culture and socio-economic status. Similarly, teachers' behaviours, their views of teaching and learning, and their expectations of pupils, also impact on pupil learning. Learning is also influenced by 'learning capacity',[3] which includes developing learning dispositions through broadening, deepening and strengthening the time spent learning. To address these briefly, the topics we have chosen to examine here divide into five groupings – the requisites of a secondary school student teacher; first meeting(s) with one's classes; lesson phases and presentation skills; homework; and the debate about setting, grouping and mixed-ability teaching.

It is not intended that these topics should be read exclusively by intending secondary teachers, as there is a great deal in them of relevance to primary teachers and, indeed, to anyone else concerned with professional development.

SOME REQUISITES OF A SECONDARY SCHOOL STUDENT TEACHER

The secondary school teacher is caught up in a web of different (and sometimes conflicting) demands. The whole field of certification, assessment and examinations has been the focus of considerable debate in the last decade, covering, for example:

- the moves to credentialise, award qualifications for, vocational education particularly through the introduction of diplomas in an attempt to raise the status of this area of pupils' development

- the moves to harmonise and align GCSE requirements with the National Curriculum 'big picture' changes at Key Stage 3
- the moves to diversify the post-16 curriculum through the introduction of Diplomas, Advanced Subsidiary (AS) and International Baccalaureate (IB) qualifications
- the debate about the amount, and the role of, 'controlled assessment (coursework) in public examinations
- the accreditation of 'work based' experiences and activities for public examinations
- the amount of testing taking place at Key Stages 3 and 4 leading to a 'teaching to the test' mentality approach in many schools.

Over the last decade many moves have been made to establish stronger links between the school, community and local industry. Pupils have, typically, in the past, undertaken short periods of work placement (e.g. a one-week or two-week block during Key Stage 4; one day per week for a term at age 16). The introduction of diplomas for 14–19-year-olds radically reconceives this by drawing upon the principles that suggest that learners benefit from a range of different learning contexts. This now means teachers are involved in co-ordinating interactions with a variety of key providers through developing collaborative and vocational partnerships with local colleges and industries.

Therefore, to regard the secondary school teacher as solely a teacher of one or two subjects is to seriously misconceive the diversity of the requirements placed upon the teacher. Dowson[4] differentiates between the roles of a teacher as a subject specialist and the wider role of the teacher. With regard to the teacher-as-subject-specialist she argues that the teacher must be able to:

- communicate the special relevance and rewards of the subject
- support and stretch all pupils in learning the knowledge, skills and processes of the subject in question
- achieve the best possible examination results
- contribute to the running of the department
- sustain subject expertise and enthusiasm.

In the same volume Leask[5] proposes that subject teachers require subject knowledge, professional judgement and professional knowledge. She argues that it is not enough for the teacher simply to possess academic knowledge; that has to be translated into effective learning by the pupils. This echoes Morrison[6] where he writes that subject specialists should possess both subject knowledge and pedagogical knowledge. Indeed he goes further than this to suggest that a subject specialist should possess several areas of expertise:

- academic subject knowledge
- pedagogical knowledge
- effective interpersonal behaviour
- enthusiasm and motivating skills
- understanding of social relations in schools and classrooms
- skills for developing curricula and schemes of work
- organisational skills
- understanding of how pupils learn
- awareness of current trends in the content and teaching of the subject
- management skills – leadership, communication and monitoring
- skills in assessment, evaluation and record keeping.

The effective teacher, as we discuss in the next chapter, requires skills in the fields of organisation, presentation, analysis, synthesis, assessment, management and evaluation.[7] Further, the ability to develop neutral and emotionally secure environments for learning relate positively to pupil achievement, whilst negative environments relate negatively to achievement.[8] Much of the debate about effective teaching is now taking place under the umbrella term of 'Personalised Learning'.[9] Although some would suggest the term 'personalisation' is a good idea searching for a definition, the common understanding is that personalisation offers all children the opportunity to reach or exceed national expectations and to fulfil their early promise. This is to be achieved through the setting of ambitious and individual objectives with challenging personal targets. Personalisation seeks to maintain rapid intervention, if required, and to keep pupils on a personalised learning trajectory accompanied by rigorous assessment to check and maintain pupil progress.

To achieve this, effective secondary school teachers should be business-like; effective in interpersonal relationships (being neither too focused in relationships nor uncaring about relationships); task-oriented and academically focused; careful with respect to the quantity and pace of the lesson; effective in explaining, instructing and questioning; effective in setting and building on homework; and clear in their communication of expectations and expected learning outcomes. Such teachers are adept at motivating pupils, communicating objectives, providing guidance, promoting the transfer of learning, providing opportunities for pupils to demonstrate their learning, and giving constructive and focused feedback to improve learning.[10]

They employ a range of teaching and learning strategies, including discussion; activity-based and experiential learning; exposition and explanation; questioning, peer group teaching; ICT-based learning; games and simulations; whole-class interactive teaching; individual and co-operative group work. With the move to flexible learning and the use of virtual learning environments (VLE), secondary school teachers also have to develop their skills as facilitators, not just instructors or didacts.[11]

By contrast, ineffective secondary school teachers are often over-concerned with relationships, over-emphasise the affective side of classrooms, are unable to engage with change, and lack access to discourse relating to effective teaching.[12]

In addition to possessing subject specialist abilities Leask argues that the secondary school teacher should be able to:

● integrate cross-curricular dimensions, skills and themes into her teaching
● become involved in the pastoral aspect of school life, and
● foster links between the school, the local community and industry.[13]

The National Curriculum emphasises cross-curricular teaching through its 'cross-curriculum dimensions'. These include:

● identity and cultural diversity
● healthy lifestyles
● community participation
● enterprise
● global dimension and sustainable development
● technology and the media
● creativity and critical thinking.

It is claimed that in order to achieve the aims of the curriculum, young people need to understand themselves and the world in which they live. The dimensions are supposed to provide important unifying areas of learning that will give 'relevance and authenticity' to their education. The ideas of a unified curriculum, relevance and authenticity are certainly important ones. However, it seems that, as has been the case historically, the dimensions are subservient to the curriculum subjects, rather than the driving force for organising the curriculum. The dimensions are also not statutory, unlike the National Curriculum subjects. However, they can be used as a robust basis for defending particular approaches to teaching. For example, if we take one of the dimensions, creativity and critical thinking, this could be prioritised. The National Curriculum offers guidance on this dimension including when planning for teaching:

- Build creativity objectives into your planning (you could integrate these with subject-specific objectives).
- Look for opportunities to promote creativity in your existing schemes of work and lesson plans. Could you adapt any activities so that they offer more potential for creativity?
- Devise activities that are personally and culturally authentic. Try to build on pupils' interests and experiences (both in and out of school).
- Plan for a range of teaching and learning styles so that as many pupils as possible have the opportunity to show their creativity. Role play can increase pupils' imaginative engagement and give them freedom to explore ideas. Hands-on experimentation, problem-solving, discussion and collaborative work all provide excellent opportunities for creative thinking and behaviour.
- Never lose sight of the importance of knowledge and skills. Pupils are only able to engage creatively and purposefully with the challenges they encounter if they have a solid base of knowledge and skills.

Student teachers, to become full participants in school life, will need to adopt a more synoptic, a wider view of their tasks, roles and interpersonal behaviour with staff and pupils alike. Most secondary school teachers will also be involved in teaching a programme of Personal, Social and Health Education; most will be involved in a tutorial role in the school; most will have pastoral responsibility for a named group of pupils; whilst all will have a responsibility to work with a range of other adults and agencies whilst contributing to the *Every Child Matters (ECM)* agenda.

As a 'novice teacher' on school experience, then, the student teacher will have to absorb very rapidly and become part of the several aspects of teaching that are embraced both in subject teaching and the many other aspects of school life, e.g. curricular, extra-curricular, cross-curricular, pastoral, *ECM*, disciplinary, interpersonal, managerial. Indeed Leask[14] argues that the school will have several expectations of the student teacher qua trainee professional and guest in the school, covering several areas.

Organisation and teaching approach

You will be expected to:

- be well organised
- professional and punctual, arriving at a time that allows preparation in order to arrange the classroom, check the availability of books and equipment, test out equipment new to you, talk to supporting staff and colleagues about the work and the children's progress, and clarify any safety issues
- plan and prepare thoroughly. Be conscientious in finding out what lesson content and subject knowledge are appropriate to the class you're teaching. In many cases you will be teaching mate-

rial which is new to you or which needs to be delivered in a different manner to which you were taught. Staff will expect you to ask if you're not sure but to work conscientiously to improve your subject knowledge. They will not be impressed if you are ill-prepared and have not sufficiently developed your understanding of the subject matter of the lessons you are teaching

- keep good records: have your file of schemes of work and lesson plans, pupil attendance and homework records up to date. Your evaluations of your lessons are best completed on the same day as the lesson
- know your subject
- try out different methods of teaching. Teaching practice is your opportunity to try out different approaches without having to live with the results of failure, but you have a duty to the pupils and teacher not to leave chaos behind you.

Professionalism

You will be expected to:

- act in a professional manner, e.g. with courtesy and tact; and to respect confidentiality of information
- be open to new learning
- seek advice and act on advice
- be flexible
- dress appropriately (different schools have different dress codes)
- become familiar with and work within school procedures and policies. These include record keeping, rewards and sanctions, uniform, relationships between teachers and pupils
- accept a leadership role. You may find imposing your will on pupils uncomfortable but unless you establish your right to direct the work of the class you will not be able to teach effectively
- recognise and understand the roles and relationships of staff responsible for your development
- keep up to date with your subject
- take active steps to ensure that your pupils learn
- discuss pupil progress with parents.
- act in accordance with the General Teaching Council's (GTC) code of conduct, which sets minimum standards for the regulation of the profession.

Social skills

You will be expected to:

- develop good relationships with pupils and staff
- maintain a sense of humour
- work well in teams
- be able to communicate with children as well as adults
- learn to defuse difficult situations.

The role of the secondary student teacher, then, is diffuse. We advise the student teacher to find out as much as possible during their preliminary school visits and initial contact with the school, covering, for example: the school's expectations of her; the curricular and pedagogic aspects of the teaching; the learners that she will be teaching; the staff with whom she will be working; the administrative and managerial matters in which she will be involved; the resources that she will need access to.

FIRST MEETING(S) WITH ONE'S CLASSES

We move on to try to establish a few points that will assist student teachers when meeting a class for the first time. We have deliberately pluralised the word meeting(s) in parenthesis to stress the fact that although the very first meeting between teacher and class is important, the points implemented on that occasion need to be followed up and consistently reinforced in ensuing lessons with all classes. Writing of the qualified teacher in this respect, Wragg and Wood[15] say: 'The success or failure of a whole year may rest on the impression created, the ethos, rules and relationships established during the first two or three weeks in September.'

In meeting the need for more research in this aspect of teacher–pupil encounter, they observed 313 lessons given by experienced teachers and student teachers at the beginning of the school year (in the case of the teachers) and on teaching practice. Their subsequent analysis revealed a substantial combined effort by the experienced teachers in September to establish a working climate for the whole of the academic year, and the problems the student teachers had on arriving later when, as the authors put it, 'the territory had been staked out, rules and relationships had been developed and procedures established'.

As regards the experienced teachers, they had a clear idea of how they would conduct themselves before the school year began. Their intentions, expressed in interviews given to the researchers prior to the study, were more or less fulfilled when they were observed at the beginning of the school year. The majority sought to establish a firm presence; they made up their minds about the pupils from their own experience rather than from study of the pupils' records; initial dominance and harshness was leavened by humour; and they used non-verbal means (eye movement, gesture etc.) to reinforce what they were trying to achieve. They set out to establish rules from the very first contact and, to some of these, there was a noticeable moral character.

In contrast to the experienced teachers, and as one would perhaps expect, the student teachers were less certain about their rules and what they hoped to do with their pupils. They tended to be anxious about interpersonal relationships. The research also disclosed that both the student teachers and the experienced teachers were able more often than not to establish a high level of pupil involvement with little misbehaviour in the initial lessons. The experienced teachers were considered to be more businesslike, confident, warm and friendly than the student teachers; they made more of a point of learning the pupils' names; and, in the case of the male teachers, humour was employed from quite early in the year.

From this research and related studies we have set out below a number of factors which readers might reflect on with respect to their own first and early encounters with their classes.

Information prior to meeting a class

There is a certain amount of basic information you need to know before taking a class, e.g. which pupils may have special needs, for example are there any having physical difficulties such as deafness, partial sightedness; approximately what is the range of ability; and are there any striking individual needs? Beyond these points it can sometimes be counter-productive to have too much information and too many preconceived ideas. One needs to maintain a certain amount of spontaneity and freshness as well as giving pupils an opportunity to develop a positive relationship based upon their unique relationship with their new teacher rather than their past performance and possible misdemeanours.

Thinking in advance

This entails giving due thought before a lesson to such matters as content, timing, presentations, transitions, starters and plenaries, and rules and procedures. It involves forethought on a range of issues, including, for example:[16]

- what to do if equipment is not in the classroom when it should have been set out by someone else, or if it does not work or breaks during the session
- what strategies to use if pupils work more slowly or more quickly (and finish working) than you anticipated, and what to do if your timing is misjudged
- handling misbehaviour
- what to do if pupils do not bring the required equipment or books
- defusing challenging situations (pupil to pupil, pupil to teacher, teacher to pupil), for example by moving on the lesson to increase the pace of the lesson and refocus the pupils; scanning the class; using humour to keep pupils on task; using non-verbal behaviour
- retrieving a poor lesson or having a fallback plan
- lack of personal confidence
- controlling one's own emotions (e.g. anger, uncertainty)
- how to be in charge without being preoccupied with discipline (e.g. by being businesslike and task-focused).

Introductions and appearance

Who you are and how you look are matters of great importance to a new class. In another study by Wragg and Young[17] which investigated pupils' appraisals of teachers it was found that the vast majority expected their new teacher to introduce himself or herself with his or her name together with some limited personal details about interests and hobbies as well as sharing your expectations. It can be useful in this connection to write your name on the whiteboard during the first meeting. Your general appearance will also be a matter of curiosity and it is important that you create a favourable impression in this respect. As regards clothes, for example, either smart formal or smart casual clothes are desirable.

The first lesson, its content and introduction

Particular care needs to be given to the preparation and planning of the very first lesson you will take. It is especially important to find out what prior learning has occurred with the class before your arrival so that you can extend the learning and not find yourself repeating what the usual class teacher has already done with the group. Such a state of affairs can be undermining, unless it is a planned revision lesson. The introduction to the lesson should be thought out with great care and imagination so that you can achieve maximum effectiveness. Motivation and interest are key concepts here. See also below for the suggestions given on set induction.

Ethos, image and manner

You will establish an ethos within a short space of time, so it is desirable that you create one that is favourable and to your advantage. Personality and projection are important here. Set out initially to be calm, firm but fair in a positive way, achieve a degree of control, and avoid being perceived as soft or naive. Your manner needs to be comfortable without being too informal or relaxed, yet at the same time you need to send out the message that 'you're in charge'. Other qualities you need to display are patience, self-control, fairness and respect for pupils. Project a confident image. Mentally, you should be able to visualise yourself as the leader of the learning in the classroom.

Stereotypes

Related to this last point about image is the need to avoid development of stereotypical patterns of behaviour during early meetings. Allowing verbal and physical mannerisms to become part of your classroom behaviour should also be avoided. For example, prefacing all one's statements with 'er', or frequently punctuating your statements with 'OK' are examples of the kind of things that pupils can notch on to. Avoiding such pitfalls requires a degree of self-awareness and self-monitoring that can only come with experience.

Rules and procedures

We deal with the matter of rules in a later chapter and it will be helpful to read what we say there in conjunction with this brief review of them in relation to first meetings. Following Hargreaves' advice,[18] it is desirable that the teacher establishes a minimum number of rules during his or her very first encounter with a class. As we say later, these may cover such areas as entering the room, movement about the room, modes of address, when to talk and when not to talk, work and homework, and the distribution of materials and equipment. Try to express them as clearly as possible and then ensure that they are adhered to.

Relationships

A teacher can begin to establish positive relationships with a class both collectively and individually from the very first meeting, in spite of the prohibitive nature of those rules that have to be established on this occasion. Pupils expect teachers to be firm, friendly and fair.[19] Wragg and Wood[20] describe a variety of ways in which teachers and student teachers achieved effective relationships. Briefly, they were:

- the judicious use of praise and encouragement
- giving attention to individual pupils
- being prepared to apologise when a mistake is made
- making positive offers to help individual pupils and working alongside them
- learning and using the children's names as soon as you can – it doesn't matter if you make a mistake, at least you're seen to be trying; and finally
- the leaven of humour.

As Lawrence[21] identifies, children respond well to a teacher who can share a joke with them, and especially to a teacher who can see the funny side, even when the laugh is on him or her. It means an absence of pomposity. It is also important for student teachers to think in advance of how they will respond to a potentially sensitive situation, for example, if they can't answer a pupil's question, if a pupil swears or bullies another in the classroom, or if a pupil asks a personal question or makes a personal comment.[22]

LESSON PHASES AND PRESENTATION SKILLS

Many lessons at the secondary level can be divided into five phases:[23]

1 *The entry phase* (including greeting and seating, amount of pupil talk permitted, and distributing resources and equipment). Dean[24] recommends that, at the early stage of the lesson, the teacher should not be occupied with addressing individuals, but should be focusing on managing the class as a whole group. This is usually best delivered through engaging the group through a whole-class 'starter activity'.
2 *The settling down or preparation phase* (gaining attention, with effective use of verbal and non-verbal communication; developing focus and concentration on the required task to be addressed). This requires much eye contact, the setting of a relaxed yet focused atmosphere, waiting for silence, and avoiding undue antagonism.[25] If some pupils take a long time to settle it is important not to let them dominate the classroom or interrupt the learning of the many.
3 *The lesson itself* (introduction and exposition by the teacher during which time the pupils must listen; development and pupil activity with appropriate rules for behaviour and task focus; closure in which the lesson is rounded off). This part of the lesson also requires attention not only to content but to behaviour and relationships. This requires the adapting of the lesson to the learners' needs and capabilities using a variety of pedagogical strategies to engage all learners through a series of learning episodes.
4 *The clearing up phase* (with appropriate procedures for returning equipment; rules for talking or silence; allowing enough time to tidy up and collect books and equipment; setting homework if not set at the start and answering any questions from the pupils). This phase also entails a plenary, used both as valuable feedback to the learners on their progress and for valuable feedback for the teacher on progress achieved, to aid planning for the next lesson.
5 *The exit phase* (with the teacher deciding how and when the pupils will exit).

Many lessons also involve the teacher expounding, narrating, lecturing, demonstrating, constructing, making connections, questioning, challenging, explaining and discussing. As Perrott[26] has said, 'Regardless of the level of the pupils, the necessity of exposing pupils to new facts, concepts and principles; of explaining difficult ideas; of clarifying issues or of exploring relationships more often than not places the teacher in a position where he has to do a great deal of presenting.' She goes on to identify five skills that a teacher needs to develop in order to become a successful presenter. These are:

1 set induction
2 closure
3 stimulus variation
4 clarity of explanation, and
5 use of examples.

Let us look at each in turn.

Set induction

A 'set' has been defined as 'a temporary, but often recurrent, condition of a person that (a) orients him toward certain environmental stimuli or events rather than towards others, selectively sensitising him for apprehending them; and (b) facilitates certain activities or responses rather than others.' 'Induction' simply means 'introduction'. So we are talking about saying or doing (or both) specific things prior to a learning situation that will direct the learner's attention to the task in hand. Perrott[27] says that prior learning will have an influence on the outcomes of the task and that some sets are more successful than others in achieving planned outcomes. She identifies four functions of set induction, thus:

1   Focusing a learner's attention on what is to be learned by gaining their interest.
2   As a means of transition from the familiar to the new, from the known to the unknown, from material already covered to new material about to be introduced. At the beginning of a lesson, a transition set is often resorted to using a question-and-answer session on material covered in the last lesson, thus leading on to the new learning in the current lesson. In addition, as Perrott says, a transition set may use examples from pupils' general knowledge to move to new material by use of example or analogy.
3   A set induction may be used to provide a framework or structure for a lesson. Perrott quotes research evidence which indicates that teachers can influence pupils' learning best when they are told in advance, or at the outset, what the teacher expects of them. This kind of set may perhaps be more general and will provide the class with a framework or schema for the lesson. A moment's thought will enable you to realise that there is a close logical connection between a set induction in this sense and the lesson objective, tying us into the objectives model that underpins much of this book.
4   The fourth function of set induction is to give meaning to a new concept or principle. This frequently involves the use of concrete and specific examples and analogies to assist pupils in understanding abstract ideas and concepts.

Perrott summarises the discussion of set induction in Box 64.

Closure

If set induction organises a learner's perception in a particular way at the outset of a learning session, closure, as Perrott explains, complements set induction by drawing attention to the end of a learning sequence or the end of an entire lesson by focusing attention on what has been learned. Indeed, this is its main function – to help the learners remember the main points for a future occasion. Perrott warns that closure needs to be carefully planned so that it is given due allocation of time. As she says, to be overtaken by the bell is a most ineffective end to a lesson. She identifies four occasions for using closure during the course of a lesson:

Box 64: The use of set induction

In addition to its use at the beginning of a lesson, set induction may also be used during the course of a lesson. Examples of the activities in which it is appropriate are:

- to begin a new unit of work
- to initiate a discussion
- to introduce an assignment
- to prepare for a field excursion
- to prepare for a practical session in the laboratory
- to prepare for viewing a film or TV programme
- to introduce a guest speaker.

---

1   to end a discussion by calling on a pupil to summarise the main points covered
2   to end a laboratory exercise by summarising the stages and findings of the experiment
3   as a follow-up to a DVD, TV programme or guest speaker, and
4   to follow up a piece of homework by using praise and encouragement, e.g. 'You tackled a
     difficult task very creditably, well done!' As Perrott says, this would be an example of social
     closure in contrast to cognitive closure.

Stimulus variation

The need for this skill – varying the stimulus – arises because sustained uniformity of presentation can lead to boredom and mental inactivity. Again, it is based on research evidence which indicates that changes in perceived environment attract attention and stimulate thought. Perrott identifies the chief means of varying the stimulus thus:

● *Teacher movements:* Deliberate and timed shifts about the room can help to revive and/or sustain interest. However, avoid nervous, fussy and irritating movements, like obsessively pacing up and down the same part of the room.
● *Focusing behaviours:* Communication can be aided by the use of verbal focusing (giving emphasis to particular words, statements or directions) and gestural focusing (using eye movements, facial expressions and movement of head, arms and body). As Perrott says, gestures are important as means of communication between teacher and pupil, being used to gain attention and express emotions. Verbal-gestural focusing, which is a combination of the two, can also be useful.
● *Changes in speech patterns:* This involves changing the quality, expressiveness, tone and rate of speech, all of which can increase animation. Planned silences and pauses can also be effective.
● *Changing interaction:* The need here is to ring the changes on the main types of interaction – teacher and class, teacher and pupil, and pupil and pupil.
● *Shifting sensory channels:* Information is processed by means of the five senses, and research suggests that pupils' ability to take in information can be increased by appealing to sight and sound alternately. Thus a teacher will follow up a verbal explanation with an accompanying diagram.

Clarity of explanation

Perrott again points out that research findings indicate that clarity of presentation is something that can exert considerable influence on effective teaching. She goes on to select a number of factors important in contributing to effectiveness in explanation. They are:

● *Continuity:* Maintaining a strong connecting 'narrative' thread through a lesson is a matter of great importance. This should be perfectly clear and diversions from it should be kept to a minimum.
● *Simplicity:* Try to use simple, intelligible, and grammatical sentences. As Perrott says, 'A common cause of failure is the inclusion of too much information in one sentence. Keep sentences short, and if relationships are complex consider communicating them by visual means.' As regards vocabulary, use simple words well within the class's own vocabulary. If specialist, subject-specific language is used, make sure the terms employed are carefully defined and understood.
● *Explicitness:* Perrott explains that one reason for ineffectiveness in presenting new material to

a class is the assumption that the children understand more than is in fact the case. Where explanations are concerned, one must be as explicit as possible (see the discussion of language in Chapter 13).

Use of examples

The use of examples is a fundamental aspect of teaching and it is hardly necessary to stress their importance, particularly in the presentation of new material. Perrott offers the following guidelines for the effective use of examples:

- Start with simple examples and work towards more complex ones.
- Start with examples relevant to pupils' experience and level of knowledge.
- Relate examples to the principles, idea or generalisation being taught.
- Check to see whether you have accomplished your objectives by asking the pupils to give you examples which illustrate the point you were trying to make.

HOMEWORK

There are several different kinds of homework that can be set, for example:[28]

- practice tasks, to build on what was learned in school
- preparation tasks for what will be attended to subsequently in school
- extension activities to work undertaken in class
- private study for individual work, e.g. personal projects, exploratory inquiry.

Muijs and Reynolds[29] indicate that homework can be used to:

- increase pupil achievement
- reinforce and strengthen topics taught in class
- complete unfinished work
- develop independent study skills
- develop self-discipline
- develop time-management skills
- involve parents in helping their children's learning
- allow preparation for future lessons and topics
- develop pupils' research skills
- review and practise topics taught in school
- extend the school day.

Black[30] reports that homework was most effective when it reinforced the major curriculum ideas as well as being comprised of simple practice tasks. It has been found[31] that homework can lead to improvements in several areas: cognitively and academically, it can improve retention, understanding and higher-order thinking, improve study habits, and promote positive attitudes to learning; affectively it can develop pupil autonomy and independence, self-direction and responsibility. On the other hand, too much homework can be counter-productive, leading to boredom, saturation, negative attitude to learning. Indeed, whilst many studies have found improvements associated with homework, there are also studies which have found the opposite.[32]

Homework should not be seen or used as a punishment, but as an opportunity for further learning. It should be integral to the work at school, and should be accompanied by rich feedback (see the comments on formative assessment in Chapter 16); it should be marked and returned rapidly, together with the provision of opportunities for pupils to act on the feedback. Indeed it has been found that giving rich instructional feedback on homework is more positive than simply assigning a grade or mark, as the former leads to intrinsic motivation whilst the latter leads to fear of failure or low marks. Reynolds and Muijs[33] also suggest that the teacher can learn as much from the homework as can the pupils. They reported the perhaps common-sense matter that homework which was marked and checked contributed more to pupil achievement than homework that went unmarked or unchecked. It is better to set less homework and mark it formatively rather than set more homework without marking it.[34] Muijs and Reynolds[35] suggest that homework should not be used as a way of testing pupils, and that they should all be able to complete it successfully; this suggests the need to individualise and differentiate homework. Homework should also ideally be set at the start of the lesson and then referred to throughout the lesson rather than simply being given at the end of the lesson when it might be perceived as a low priority.

Homework, they argue, is a powerful means for relating school knowledge to everyday life. Schools should have homework policies, and student teachers should find out:

● what the homework policy is
● the frequency of setting homework
● the consequences that the school applies for pupils who do not complete homework (e.g. keeping them in at break times to complete homework, negative marks, letters home in the case of persistent failure to do homework, withdrawal of privileges). Though appearing perhaps negative, allowing non-completion of homework with no negative consequences leads to pupils not taking homework seriously and to an escalation of non-completion
● how long each homework should take
● how to introduce and follow up homework in the class
● how much time to set by to address homework issues in the class
● what kind of homework is usually set
● the purpose of the homework
● how quickly it is expected that the homework is marked and returned
● what resources the pupils may or may not take home from school.

SETTING, GROUPING AND MIXED-ABILITY TEACHING

Secondary schools adopt several practices for grouping pupils, for example: banding, setting for individual subjects, and mixed-ability grouping. Though banding and streaming are declining very considerably in schools, setting appears to be on the increase.[36] Many pupils are still grouped by measured ability (e.g. non-verbal and verbal reasoning) rather than by, for example, effort (as in some South-east Asian countries), areas of study, teachers and teaching.[37]

Setting has been presumed to be the norm for grouping secondary pupils in recent government papers, not least because it is held to be most suitable for the most able learners and because it would enable teachers to match the work more effectively to pupils who were within a limited, more homogeneous range of abilities than in mixed-ability groupings, thereby facilitating whole-class interactive teaching.[38] On the other hand there have been several concerns voiced against setting, for example:[39]

● Pupils in middle-ability groups were insufficiently challenged.
● Lower-ability groups tended to have a predominance of boys and pupils with English as a second language.

- No clear link has been found between setting in ability groups and pupil attainment.[40]
- Statistically insignificant gains were found for pupils in higher ability sets, whilst statistically significant losses were found for pupils in lower sets.[41]
- Pupils in the higher sets suffer greater stress and hence their performance declines.[42]
- Incorrect allocation of pupil to groups can seriously disadvantage them, not least because the chances of mobility from one set to another are at best heavily constrained and at worst very remote.[43]
- Pupils are not always allocated on the basis of ability, but on other factors (e.g. ethnicity, social class, gender, season of birth).[44] Higher ability pupils flourish in mixed-ability groups.[45]
- The attainment of pupils in lower groups tends to deteriorate, whilst the attainment of those in upper groups tends to improve.[46]
- Ability grouping per se is no guarantee of raising standards.[47]
- Placement in lower sets negatively affects pupils' self-concept, self-esteem and motivation.[48]
- Teachers' expectations for lower sets become deflated.
- Pupils in lower ability sets become more disaffected with schooling.
- 'There is little, if any, research that supports the notion that setting enhances achievement for pupils.'[49]
- 'Setting confers small academic benefits on some high-attaining pupils, at the expense of large disadvantages for low attainers.'[50]
- Pupils' motivation is damaged for pupils in all sets.[51]

In an important study Slavin[52] found that there were no significant differences in achievement between secondary school pupils who were taught in homogeneous and heterogeneous groups. The results were the same for all subjects except for social studies, in which heterogeneous (mixed-ability) groupings seemed to produce better achievement for all pupils. Slavin argued that his findings contrast with those of other research studies that compare pupils' achievements in different tracks (streams or bands). These studies, he avers, show that a tracking system operates to the advantage of bright learners and to the disadvantage of lower ability pupils; they show that tracking has positive effects for high achievers and negative effects for low achievers.

Slavin's overall finding about ability grouping was also found in the most recent large scale study in England, Ireson et al.'s study of 6000 pupils in 45 secondary schools. This indicated that 'setting (regrouping) had little overall impact on GCSE attainment in English, mathematics or science, when prior attainment was statistically controlled'[53] (p. 454). It is suggested that factors other than ability grouping effect attainment, such as the curriculum, teachers' attitudes, pedagogy, pupil motivation and the misplacement of pupils in sets. The set in which pupils are placed (or misplaced) is one such factor that mediates the impact of ability grouping as a whole. In basic terms, the higher the set the pupil is placed in the higher their attainment will be; this is as much as one grade at GCSE in mathematics. Pupils with medium levels of attainment are most strongly affected. For example, Ireson et al. found that 'In mathematics, pupils at level 5 in Year 9 gained as much as one and a half GCSE grades from being in a top set as compared to a low set. Similarly, in English the greatest dividend was for pupils at levels 5 and 6 and in science for pupils at levels 4 and 5.' One of the reasons that pupils with medium levels of attainment are most strongly affected is that they are often placed in a range of different sets. In Ireson's study, 'they were found in as many as six different sets in schools with rigorous setting across the year group and were quite frequently found in high, middle and low sets in the same school'. It is important that teaching reflects the fact that sets are unlikely to be homogeneous and guards against low expectations on the basis of ability group.

Ireson et al. argued that, with regard to whether mixed-ability teaching or ability grouping is most effective, research internationally has not reached a definitive answer. However, on balance, it appears that educational systems across the world that feature greatest use of selective entry and/or ability grouping tend to produce the widest variation in pupil attainment. Pupils in high groups tend to benefit, while those in low groups fall behind. In view of the fact that there is no advantage for ability grouping per se, it is vital that the processes of teaching and learning that are within the system of setting are given high priority.

Streaming or banding learners is also problematic, for many of the same reasons as setting. Ireson, et al.[54] report a major study of 45 secondary comprehensive schools, indicating that setting is at its most prolific and rigorous for mathematics and at its least prolific for English. Less setting was associated with more parallel groupings.

Though many secondary schools may set pupils, the nature and amount of setting vary considerably. Student teachers on teaching practice are advised to find out about the setting arrangements and ability groupings in the school, including, for example:

- on what basis the learners are set (e.g. by tests, examinations, Key Stage tests, commercially produced tests, coursework, teacher opinion, judgements of performance or judgements of potential, evidence or feeling, behaviour and attitude, gender, social factors (e.g. friendships)), and what are the main and subsidiary factors that are taken into consideration when allocating pupils to sets, how these are justified, and on what evidence
- how and when pupils can move from one set to another if they are perhaps incorrectly placed
- who takes the decision on setting and moving pupils (and, for example, the role of parents in this, e.g. parents who request a move of set for their child)
- the number of sets
- the size of sets for different groups of pupils (e.g. smaller for the less able).[55]

Mixed-ability grouping

Mixed-ability teaching seems to be in retreat in secondary schools, perhaps as a result of the National Curriculum, with which it seems to be incompatible,[56] to be replaced with setting and whole-class teaching.[57] Mixed-ability grouping is seen to be particularly problematic in 'linear' subjects such as mathematics and foreign languages, and less problematic (and hence more widespread) in subjects like English. Whole-class teaching of pupils with alleged similar abilities disguises massive differences of ability within an allegedly 'homogeneous' group.

The case for mixed-ability grouping is advanced by the evidence that a streaming system can easily reproduce a social system, wherein, very crudely speaking, 'bright' streams contain pupils from the middle and upper classes and 'poor' streams contain pupils from the working classes. Streams and bands correlate highly with social situation.[58] Indeed one of the cornerstones of comprehensive schooling is that not only is a social mix desirable within a school, but a social mix is desirable within each class. Pupils should learn how to work with peers drawn from different social situations; indeed the school has a major function in breaking down patterns of differential status, power and class.

Given the significance of teacher expectations on pupils' performance and of the dangers of the self-fulfilling prophecy depressing pupil attainment, particularly related to cultural and ethnic stereotyping,[59] and of the high significance that grouping of pupils has on their subsequent achievement[60] and performance,[61] moves that facilitate reduction of the negative aspects of the self-fulfilling prophecy and that raise teachers' expectations (a central feature of school effectiveness) can be encouraged through mixed-ability teaching. Indeed, pupils' preferences have been shown in one study to be overwhelmingly in favour of mixed-ability teaching with 83 per cent of the pupils interviewed wanting either to return to mixed-ability teaching or to change set.[62] This dissatisfaction was not restricted to those in the lower sets.

That said, having mixed-ability teaching groups does not find universal support in schools – particularly in secondary education. The success of mixed-ability teaching is heavily dependent on the commitment to it by teachers. Ball[63] makes the perhaps sad comment that, in the school that he studied, mixed-ability teaching failed because there was little evidence of teachers moving away from a formal, didactic style of teaching. Indeed Reid *et al.*[64] comment that success of mixed-ability teaching is contingent upon the school system finding a way of coping with very many factors.

Hence, whilst this form of organisation may be desirable for a wealth of reasons (ideological, educational, academic, sociological etc.), there is clearly a need not only for teacher commitment to make this form of teaching work but also a need to solve demanding practical problems. The student teacher will need to ask her mentor about these practical issues, the nature of setting arrangements in the school, the composition of the class or set and particular problems within these. Many attempts to overcome the practical hurdles in mixed-ability teaching are addressed by encouraging collaborative group work in classes.

Arguably, it is at the extremes of the ability range where children have most need of individual attention. For student teachers, it is absolutely vital that they should plan for the range of abilities in preparing their teaching programmes. Kerry and Sands[65] identify some common problems which experienced teachers face when dealing with a range of abilities in mixed-ability classes. They concern:

- *Dead time:* This is the time between a pupil finishing one activity and starting another. Some pupils complete work quickly because tasks are often too easy for them. Other pupils can often manage only a sentence or two, and then they feel they have exhausted the topic.
- *Boredom:* This may result from spending too much time waiting for the teacher to correct work, approve progress to the next step or take remedial action.
- *Lack of motivation:* Children who are often unoccupied and bored can easily lose interest.
- *Disruption:* The creative mind continually seeks new diversions. The less able may simply be looking for something more relevant to do! The bored pupil is always a potential trouble-maker.
- *Provision of special work:* The previous four problems imply that the teacher must of necessity provide special work for pupils at both ends of the ability spectrum.
- *Increased preparation time by the teacher:* Implicitly, providing special work means spending more time in preparing lessons.
- *Linguistic and cognitive levels of worksheets and texts:* One perennial problem of mixed-ability classes is that teachers tend to 'teach to the middle'. Part of the 'special provision' for exceptional pupils is to cater for pupils who need to be stretched intellectually and to cope with others for whom the language of text or instructions may not be clear.
- *Emotional and pastoral problems:* Finally, both sets of pupils may (but not necessarily) have problems of a social nature, e.g. concerning peer-group relations. Bright pupils are sometimes rejected as 'teacher's pet', and slower learners are labelled 'thick'. The teacher needs to bear relationship problems in mind when organising classroom work and activities.

The student teacher is advised to find out how the pupils are organised in the school, together with the reasons for this, and what the implications are for his or her teaching. If the school practises mixed-ability grouping then there are several practical skills that student teachers will need to develop. We indicate these in Box 65.[66]

(See www.routledge.com/textbooks/9780415485586, Chapter 12 Secondary teaching, Advantages of mixed-ability groups and Disadvantages of mixed-ability groups.)

Box 65: Skills needed for mixed-ability group work

1 Decide beforehand how your group will be made up: self-selected, or selected by you, and if so on what criteria?
2 Decide if your groups will be static or regrouped for different activities.
3 Have the lesson carefully prepared and everything ready beforehand.
4 Ensure that each group has appropriate subject material and activities.
5 Go round from group to group quickly. Make sure you are still visible by, and still watching, other groups.
6 Do not forget to look behind you as you go round.
7 Be prepared for early finishers and have things ready for them to do.
8 Watch for signs that pupils are unoccupied – unnecessary movement and too much chat, incipient rowdiness.
9 Have a good way of ending the lesson.

12 Language in Classrooms

INTRODUCTION

Language occupies a crucial position in the classroom when we consider research evidence in relation to children and learning. Classroom dialogue has been shown to contribute to children's intellectual development and their educational attainment (Mercer and Littleton)[1] In addition, research has shown that both interaction with adults and collaboration with peers can provide opportunities for children's learning and for their cognitive development.

Barnes[2] established that language is a major means of learning and that pupils' uses of language for learning are strongly influenced by the teacher's language which prescribes them their roles as learners. This assumption thereby involves a shift of emphasis from the more traditional view of language as a means of teaching to language as a means of learning. In operational terms, therefore, this means that we learn not only by listening passively to the teacher, but by verbalising, by talking, by discussing and arguing. More recent research by Mercer and Hodgkinson[3] builds on the work of Barnes to establish the centrality of dialogue in the learning process. By studying teacher–pupil interaction, one can begin to see how classroom language might offer different possibilities for pupil learning. Should pupils merely be passive listeners? Or should they be allowed to verbalise at some point? Or should active dialogue with the student teacher be encouraged? Just three ways of pupils' participation in learning, but all under the control of the student teacher's own speech behaviour.

Like Barnes' earlier study, Mishler's work[4] takes extracts of classroom dialogue and subjects them to perceptive analysis. Unlike Barnes, however, he is more concerned with showing how different cognitive strategies as well as different values and norms are carried in the language used, chiefly in the structure of teachers' statements and in the types of exchange developed between them and the children. Mishler's main purpose is to show how teachers' cognitive strategies are conveyed in the warp and weft of classroom dialogue. To this end, he is concerned with how attention is focused, with how teachers orient themselves and their pupils to the problem under discussion; the procedures for information search and evaluation; and the structure of alternatives, that is, the number of types of alternative answers to a question and their relationship to each other. There is a very frequent pattern of questioning that takes the form of Initiation – Response – Follow-up, for example:

Initiation: How many bones are there in the human body?
Response: Two hundred and six.
Follow-up: Excellent.

This model typifies many classrooms where it is the teacher who is the initiator and who controls the talk.[5] In another study, Stubbs himself described one way in which teachers in relatively traditional lessons control classroom exchanges.[6] A characteristic of much classroom talk is the extent of the teacher's conversational control over the topic, over the relevance or correctness of what pupils say, and over when and how much pupils may speak. In traditional lessons, pupils have few conversational rights. What Stubbs shows is that a teacher is constantly monitoring the communication system in the classroom by such utterances as 'You see, we're really getting onto the topic now', or 'OK, now listen all of you', or 'Now, we don't want any silly remarks.' The teacher is thus able to check whether pupils are all on the same 'wavelength' and whether at least some of them follow what is being said. Commenting on unequal language rights between teachers and pupils in classrooms, he writes:

> Use of…language is also highly asymmetrical: one would not expect a pupil to say to a teacher: That's an interesting point. Such speech acts, in which the teacher monitors and controls the classroom dialogue are, at one level, the very stuff of teaching. They are basic to the activity of teaching, since they are the acts whereby a teacher controls the flow of information in the classroom and defines the relevance of what is said.

Wells,[7] comparing the child's experience of language at home and at school, found that:

● the number of child utterances to an adult was 122 at home and 45 at school
● the proportion for the child initiating a conversation was 63.6 per cent at home and 23.0 per cent at school
● the proportion for the child asking a question was 12.7 per cent at home and 4.0 per cent at school.

The differences are interesting: not only do children speak more at home, but their talk is more complete, more child-initiated and more extended. At school their talk is more fragmented, more teacher-initiated and more limited in its scope.

We consider the question of classroom talk in eight main areas: characteristics of talk in classrooms, direct instruction and whole-class interactive teaching, exposition, explanation, questioning, discussion, responding, and summarising. Recent research evidence to support the value of collaborative learning is also explored. Finally, the specific needs of EAL learners are considered. First, a brief history of our current understanding of why language skills need to be taught and developed throughout a child's educational career in order to maximise learning potential.

SPEAKING AND LISTENING IN EDUCATIONAL POLICY AND PRACTICE

Prior to the 1960s the idea that talk should be an important part of the English curriculum would have been greeted with some scepticism.[8] In the 1960s, educational researchers became increasingly interested in the idea that learning could be enhanced by careful consideration of the role of talk. Andrew Wilkinson's work resulted in the coining of a new word, 'oracy', as a measure of how important he thought talk was, a fact confirmed by the Oxford English Dictionary which lists Wilkinson's text historically as the first entry:

> **1965** A. WILKINSON *Spoken Eng*. 14 The term we suggest for general ability in the oral skills is *oracy*; one who has those skills is *orate*, one without them *inorate*.

The work of Wilkinson and other educationists resulted in *speaking and listening* becoming part of the National Curriculum programmes of study for the subject English.

Although the speaking and listening requirements of the National Curriculum remained statutory from 1997 onwards, the implementation of the National Literacy Strategy (NLS) meant that, in practice, speaking and listening were neglected due to a powerful focus on reading in particular, and writing to a lesser extent. It was not only the fact that speaking and listening programmes of study were not addressed by the NLS Framework for Teaching (FFT) but that the teaching methods that were strongly advocated by the NLS also resulted in weaker oral work, shown by a series of strong research studies such as that of English *et al.*[9], which found that there was a conflict between the achievement of short-term lesson objectives that are a feature of the FFT and the fostering of extended pupil contributions. In 2006 an attempt was made to address the absence of speaking and listening by including strands of objectives for speaking and listening in the new PNS framework for literacy.

At Key Stages 1 and 2 the National Curriculum conceptualises work in Speaking and Listening, Reading and Writing as part of the subject 'English'. Children's use of language is now deemed sophisticated enough to incorporate relevant and appropriate knowledge to extend their metalanguage for English. There are four main areas of speaking and listening to be addressed: children should learn how to speak fluently and confidently, listen carefully and with due respect for others; become effective members of a collaborative group; and participate in a range of drama activities. There is a further emphasis on the importance of using spoken Standard English and some thought is given to language variation. However, the emphasis of language variation seems to be the functional linguistic emphasis of language in different contexts more than learning centred on topics such as accent and dialect, language and identity, language and culture, etc.

In 2003, the Qualifications and Curriculum Authority (QCA) published a resource called *Speaking, Listening, Learning: Working with Children in Key Stages 1 and 2*. The pack was designed to support the teaching of speaking and listening in primary schools and consisted of a set of materials reflecting National Curriculum requirements in English. It included a teacher's handbook, which provided an overview, firstly emphasising the fact that children need to be taught speaking and listening skills, and acknowledging that those skills develop over time and as children mature. It put forward an argument as to why speaking and listening are so important, linking them with children's personal and social development. The handbook described the value of talk in helping children to organise their thoughts and ideas. It was pointed out that speaking and listening should not be seen as part of the subject English alone but as extending to all curriculum areas, acknowledging that different types of talk are appropriate in different subject areas. The interdependency of speaking and listening, reading and, writing was discussed and, finally, approaches to assessment.

A dedicated Speaking and Listening website can be found as part of the Secondary Framework site, which includes activities and video clips showing effective approaches to teaching speaking and listening in the English classroom from Years 7 to 11. The website states: 'Teaching Speaking and Listening is designed to help you improve your teaching of speaking and listening so that your pupils develop into confident and skilful speakers and listeners'.

SPEAKING AND LISTENING IN THE EARLY YEARS

The Early Years Foundation Stage framework puts the development and use of communication and language at the heart of young children's learning. It targets the importance of supporting children to become skilful communicators from an early age, arguing that learning to speak and listen begins from birth, emerging out of non-verbal language. It further creates overt links between speaking and listening and reading and writing, based on the idea that effective speaking and listening skills 'build the foundations for reading and writing' (p.42). Language in the EYFS comes under two main titles: 'Language for Communication' and 'Language for Thinking'. The ability to communicate verbally is seen as a crucial element to a child's overall progress.

By examining the stages of language acquisition (see Peccei for example)[10] and beginning to understand the theories of how and why this process takes place, it becomes clear that pre-school experience is an important factor in the child's language development. The significance of the way that adults interact with the child at this time should not be underestimated. It has been acknowledged that adults provide a number of important conditions for the child, for example providing access to an environment where talk has high status; providing access to competent users of language; providing opportunities to engage in talk; and providing responses that acknowledge the child as a competent language user (Wray *et al.*, 1989: 39).[11]

In addition, adults model (often in an unplanned way) the conventions of language. Adults provide feedback on the effectiveness of a child's ability to communicate through the way they respond to them. They scaffold the child's language learning, enabling them to test their current hypotheses about how language works. The ability of the adult to take into account the limited abilities of the child and adjust their language accordingly so that the child can make sense of them is intuitive for most parents.

The degree to which a rich language environment assists language development has been well documented. Two examples of relevant studies here are those of Tizard and Hughes[12] and Wells.[13] Both document the influence of language experiences from birth on a child's ability to use language and communicate effectively. Wells' study, for example, found a correlation between the amount of conversation experienced with parents and other members of their family circle and children's rates of progress in language learning.

Even though most of the language acquisition process is complete as children enter school, there is much that the teacher can do in the early years to consolidate and develop these skills. Littleton *et al.* (2005)[14] in their work with 6- and 7-year-old children, suggest that *exploratory talk* is particularly desirable and something that teachers should encourage:

> Exploratory talk demonstrates the active joint engagement of the children with one another's ideas. Whilst initiations may be challenged and counter-challenged, appropriate justifications are articulated and alternative hypotheses offered…Progress thus emerges from the joint acceptance of suggestions. (p. 173)

Children's language acquisition is likely to be stronger if they are encouraged to become active participants in conversation, if they are encouraged to be questioning (despite how frustrating this can be for some adults to deal with), to hypothesise, imagine, wonder, project and dream out loud, to hear stories and to tell stories to others, experiencing a range of telling techniques that illustrate the potential power of the spoken word. The social and cultural aspects of language development are equally important at this time as children learn, through talk, to place themselves within a specific social context, and in this way the development of language and identity are closely linked.

The quality of social experience and interaction will vary greatly between children, which is why during the early years, teachers need to be aware that some children will arrive at school appearing to be confident, articulate users of the English language, whereas others seem less comfortable language users (see Wyse and Bradford, 2008). However, teachers should beware of *deficit models* and remember that it is too easy to label a child's spoken language as 'poor', or even to say that they have 'no language', without sufficient thought about the home context and previous language experience. As an example, Bearne offers a transcription of a discussion including Sonnyboy, a 6-year-old boy from a Traveller community, demonstrating his ability to 'translate' language for other children:

Emily:	I loves them little things.
Sonnyboy:	Yeah...I loves the little things – that tiny wee spade...And this little bucket...
Teacher:	Do you think it would be a good idea to ask Cathy to get some? [Cathy runs a playgroup for the Traveller children on their site.]
Emily:	What for?
Teacher:	So that you'd have some at home.
Sonnyboy:	And who'd pay for them? Would Cathy pay?
Teacher:	No, it would be part of the kit.
Emily:	I don't know what you mean. Kit – who's Kit? Me Da's called Kit – would me Da have to pay?
Sonnyboy:	Not your Da – it's not that sort of kit, Emily. It's the sort a box with things in that you play with...like toys and things for the little ones.[15]

Bearne goes on to point out:

> Language diversity is...deeply involved with social and cultural judgements about what is valuable or worthy...Judgements are often made about intelligence, social status, trustworthiness and potential for future employment on the basis of how people speak – not the content of what they say, but their pronunciation, choice of vocabulary and tone of voice. Such attitudes can have an impact on later learning.[16]

It is important, then, that teachers understand about language diversity and the ways in which judgements are made about speakers in the classroom. From this perspective it is equally important that teachers recognise their own histories and status as language users, and resist the temptation to impose their own social criteria on the child's ongoing language development.

CHARACTERISTICS OF TALK IN CLASSROOMS

In reviewing the main characteristics of classroom talk, particularly that of older children, Edwards and Furlong[17] consider that not only is there so much of it, but that so much of what is said is both public and highly centralised. What they mean by being 'highly centralised' is that for much of the time in classrooms, there is a single verbal encounter in that whatever is being said demands the attention of all.

In pursuing the theme of centralised communication further, Edwards and Furlong explain that, although it plays a very important part in classroom interaction, its role should not be overstated, for considerable amounts of incidental and unofficial talk take place amid official exchanges. The authors further point out that, notwithstanding the occasions when children talk privately to other members of the class, when they offer comments and pose questions when requested to do so, or when they talk 'unofficially', their main communicative role, as far as traditional classrooms are concerned, is to listen. This means that the communicative rights of teacher and pupils are very unequal. In effect, the authors point out, teachers usually tell pupils when to talk, what to talk about, when to stop talking and, perhaps through informal assessment and immediate feedback, how well they talked.

The normal conversation between two equals stands in marked contrast to classroom exchanges because of this very inequality. In the former, no one has overriding claim to speak first, or more than others, or to decide unilaterally on the subject. The difference between an everyday conversation and a classroom exchange is dramatically realised when each kind is recorded and transcribed. In the case of everyday exchanges, statements are often incomplete, they clash with the statements of others and they are interrupted. There are also frequent false starts, hesitations and repetitions.[18]

By contrast, exchanges recorded in traditional classrooms are much more orderly and systematic. Indeed, Edwards and Furlong observe that they often look like a play script. As they comment, 'Most utterances are complete, and most speakers seem to know their lines and to recognise their turn to speak. Despite the large number, the talk appears more orderly.' Thus it is that, whereas in everyday informal conversations there is always the possibility that several speakers will perversely talk against one another or that one individual will eventually appropriate a disproportionate amount of the talking time, in classroom interaction contributors to a discussion must be carefully controlled. The authors point out that this is much more easily achieved if communication rights are not equally shared: 'if one participant can speak whenever he chooses to do so, can normally nominate the next speaker, and can resolve any cases of confusion'.

The authors go on to explain that in so far as pupils are ready to be taught, they are likely to acknowledge that an able teacher has the right to talk first, last and most; to control the content of a lesson; and to organise that content by allocating speaking turns to the pupils. The teacher's right to decide who speaks, when, for how long and to whom, is mirrored in the small number of interactional possibilities in a typical lesson. Edwards and Furlong refer to such arrangements of speakers and listeners as participant-structures which they define as communicative networks linking those who are in contact with one another already, or can be if they choose. Enlarging on the nature of them, Edwards and Furlong say:[19]

> What even the simplest list brings out is the limited variety of interactional patterns characteristic of lessons, and how firmly most of them are centred on the teacher. There is usually a formalised allocation of speaking and listening roles. Teachers expect both a 'proper' silence and 'proper' willingness to talk, and they manage the interaction so as to produce orderly and relevant pupil participation.

The authors go on to consider how this orderliness is achieved. In the well-ordered classroom, they explain, the teacher's turns at speaking are taken as and when she chooses, these being determined by the kinds of pupil she addresses and also the subject matter being taught. The difficulty that most teachers have is in limiting themselves to much less than two-thirds of the time available for talking. Because much of the time appropriated by teachers is taken up by giving information and instructions, censuring pupils and evaluating them, Edwards and Furlong consider that most of their talking can be described as telling.

In seeing teacher talk in this context as dominant performance, Edwards and Furlong suggest that the teacher's message is made all the more effective because of her 'front of stage' location. The traditional classroom settings serve as a means of reinforcing the centrally controlled interaction.[20] As they say:

> The conventional groupings of desks or tables channel communication to and from the teacher, who is the obvious focus of attention. He can direct his talk to any part of the room, while the natural flow of pupil-talk is either to him or to other pupils through him. It is a setting which makes it difficult for the teacher to avoid talking at pupils, or to break up the interaction into more localised encounters. In classrooms which are physically more open, no single focus of attention may be visible at all. Symbolically and practically, there is a switch of emphasis from the teacher to the learner.

But the teacher cannot monopolise the talk totally. There has to be a certain amount of pupil participation; and this presents the teacher with significant managerial problems because of the numbers of children involved. Once a teacher stops talking, Edwards and Furlong ask, how are turns taken? How is the rule of one speaker at a time maintained? Who is to answer a particular question?

Normally, it is the teacher's on-the-spot decisions that solve them: 'Turns are allocated, they are not seized, and pupils have to learn to bid appropriately for the right to speak.'[21]

We have seen how most participant-structures focus on the teacher who either does the talking or who nominates other to do it, and the significance of this for controlling the class. Watson[22] outlines three categories of teacher talk that embrace not simply introductory talk but teacher talk at the different points in a lesson. The three categories are:

1   finding out about pupils' understanding and knowledge (45 per cent of all teacher talk)
2   extending pupils' thinking (25 per cent of all teacher talk)
3   providing general feedback, e.g. on effort, task difficulty, the need to listen and pay attention, giving rewards (16 per cent of all teacher talk).

One can see the dominance of the three categories (nearly 90 per cent of all teacher talk) and the fact that these, in turn, reflect the teacher's domination of classroom talk. This finding echoes that of Carlsen[23] who argued that teachers' questioning may reflect and reproduce status differences in classrooms.

On a practical level one should note that most pupils will only be able to be involved in talk for a limited period of time (from seconds to half-hours), both as 'active listeners' and participants in talk. Talk is an oral and aural medium; many pupils cannot sustain oral and aural concentration for very long without a visual focus – be it on pictures, the chalkboard, a video, a computer screen, a piece of work, etc. One can learn from the televisual medium that concentration is highest when pupils have both an aural and visual focus. Without a visual focus a free-floating discussion can easily drift off into irrelevance and its concomitant indiscipline in classrooms.

There is the further issue of types of talk. Typically a teacher will engage in instructional talk (e.g. cognitive curricular content), procedural talk (e.g. pedagogical talk – how pupils are to work on the content) and managerial talk (e.g. how order and acceptable behaviour are promoted and sustained in a lesson). The student teacher will have to consider the emphasis that is placed on each type. Too little or too much cognitive talk and the lesson can become undemanding and boring or overwhelming respectively. Too little procedural talk and the pupil will not know how to work on an activity. Too much procedural talk and the pupils' autonomy and metacognitive development are eroded. Too little managerial talk and the lesson risks disruption. Too much managerial talk risks boredom, demotivating pupils who, in fact, might be trying hard to be successful and positive with the teacher. The Office for Standards in Education[24] found that poor pupil achievement was often accompanied by an overreliance on procedural and managerial talk (i.e. servicing and supervisory talk respectively) and an under-reliance on direct teaching.

DIRECT INSTRUCTION AND WHOLE-CLASS INTERACTIVE TEACHING

There has been a move towards increasing and enhancing direct instruction in classrooms through whole-class interactive teaching,[25] partly as a consequence of the press from the National Curriculum to cover a certain amount of content, but also because it has been shown to increase pupil achievement. The National Numeracy Strategy and the National Literacy Strategy were heavily premised on direct instruction.The benefits of whole-class interactive teaching as part of the National Literacy and Numeracy strategies were not realised, however, because in part, the 'interactive' was equated with 'whole class', which, arguably, was a stronger focus for politicians. Recent large-scale work comparing different countries has found that talk in English primary schools still appears to be marginalised in curriculum and pedagogical terms.[26] The National Strategies have further emphasised interactive whole-class teaching and focused on developing effective direct teaching approaches. However, a 2006 Ofsted report stated that:[27]

> At its best, this leads to good whole class discussion where teachers ask challenging questions, match them to pupils' ability and encourage detailed and reflective answers. In too many classes, however, discussion is dominated by the teacher, and pupils' responses are short and limited. No time is provided for reflection. Myhill and Fisher argue that the 'recitation script of "initiation, response and feedback" is still prevalent' and that the 'requirement for pre-determined outcomes and a fast pace seem to militate against reflection and exploration of ideas'. Ofsted's evidence supports this.

In order to be effective proponents of direct instruction, student teachers need to understand the complexities of this approach. To clarify therefore, direct instruction does not mean simply one-way lecturing or traditional teaching; it is more sophisticated than this. Rather, it is interactive (between pupils and teacher, and, less frequently and under the close control of the teacher, between pupils and pupils), and it involves several elements:[28]

- clear, sequenced, structured presentations
- effective pacing and timing
- effective demonstrations and modelling of a particular skill or procedure
- effective interactive structured questioning and discussion
- pupil demonstration
- paired discussion work
- interaction and individual/group practice
- effective summarising
- effective consolidation.

Whole-class interactive teaching, using direct instruction, with heavy emphasis placed on exposition and frequent questioning to ensure that all the pupils have understood, has been reported to have several successes. For example, in the UK, the celebrated ORACLE study found considerable gains in mathematics and language (excluding reading) with teachers categorised as 'class enquirers'.[29] The study of junior schools by Mortimore *et al.*[30] found that effective teaching was associated with structured sessions, higher-order and frequent questioning, and whole-class teaching. Similarly Muijs and Reynolds[31] found that mathematics teachers who spent more time in whole-class, rather than individual teaching, were more effective. A major impetus to whole-class interactive teaching came from the comparative study by Reynolds and Farrell,[32] which found that those countries, many of them East Asian and South-east Asian, which used whole-class interactive teaching, achieved significantly higher results on international tests than did other countries.

Whole-class interactive teaching not only concerns questioning, as this is what teachers do when they adopt a whole range of teaching strategies, but also the kinds of questions that they ask, to check understanding, to ask for examples, to pursue an issue in greater depth with a particular pupil or group, to ask for application of the knowledge, to check understanding of a process, as well as the product or the single right answer.

Underlying whole-class interactive teaching is the fact that it enables the teacher to have more communication and communicative contact with the pupils, itself a critical factor in effective learning.[33] This is perhaps unsurprising, when we consider that whole-class teaching enables teachers to be very vigilant and to detect immediately off-task behaviour, lack of understanding and lack of concentration, and to intervene directly.

One element of whole-class interactive teaching is frequently a demonstration. Here it is important not to provide a demonstration too early in the main teaching phase, and to consider whether the student teacher demonstration should be followed by a pupil demonstration. If the latter is to take place then the pupils should be told in advance that this will be the case, maybe commencing with a more confident pupil, and ensuring that the whole class is following either the student teacher's or the pupil's demonstration. As the pupil is demonstrating, or immediately afterwards, it is important for constructive comments and feedback to be given and received, i.e. to further the linguistic and cognitive processes in the interaction.

It can be seen that much of direct instruction and whole-class interactive teaching comprise elements of communication such as exposition, explanation, questioning, responding and summarising, and we turn to these now.

EXPOSITION

Several authors[34] argue that exposition can serve several functions:

- introducing lessons
- relaying information that pupils do not know
- introducing and using technical language in a controlled way
- relating to and building upon existing knowledge or understanding (e.g. refreshing pupils' memories of previous work)
- reinforcement and alternative representation
- clarifying a sequence of cognitive or practical steps appropriate to learners
- consolidation
- defining the nature of an activity
- informing, describing and explaining the session
- setting appropriate expectations.

These purposes can serve as criteria for judging the effectiveness of expositions, wherein student teachers clarify the purposes – objectives – of the expositions and then evaluate how successfully these purposes have been achieved, echoing the significance of the objectives model that runs throughout this book. The art of exposition is multifaceted, embracing not only the content but also the effectiveness of 'delivery' of the exposition. For example Pollard and Tann[35] set out a useful checklist of questions for evaluating the 'delivery' of the exposition (Box 66).

The exposition stage of classroom talk is a critical factor in judging the effectiveness of a lesson. If it is too long pupils 'switch off' and bad behaviour can occur. If it is too short pupils may fail to grasp both the significance of what is being said and what is required of them, again resulting in bad behaviour. As was mentioned earlier, talk is an important medium of control and the promoter of good discipline. Many pupils can only concentrate for one or two minutes (particularly young children); the best listeners can only sustain 'active concentration' for a short time – maybe 20 minutes at the very most.

In classroom talk the use of examples can root the topic in the experiences of pupils and provide an important aid to exposition, explanation, questioning, discussion, responding and summarising. The use of examples is a fundamental aspect of teaching and it is hardly necessary to stress their importance, particularly in the presentation of new material. Perrott[36] offers the following guidelines for the effective use of examples:

- Start with simple examples and work towards more complex ones.
- Start with examples relevant to pupils' experience and level of knowledge.
- Relate examples to the principles, idea or generalisation being taught.

Box 66: Questions to evaluate the 'delivery' of an exposition

- Is eye contact sustained, to hold attention and give interim feedback?
- Is an interesting, lively tone of voice used?
- Is the pace varied for emphasis and interest?
- Is the exposition varied by encouraging orderly participation?
- Are pauses used to structure each part of the exposition?
- Are appropriate examples, objects or pictures used to illustrate the main points?
- Are appropriate judgements made regarding the level of cognitive demand, size of conceptual steps, and length of the concentration span required?
- Is a written or illustrated record of key points provided as a guide, if listeners need memory aids?
- Has the student teacher planned what is going to be said?
- Has the student teacher planned the outline structure of the exposition (e.g. by means of 'advance organisers' – signposts to key points that will be met)?
- Has the student teacher selected the key points – identified and made explicit the relevance of each and their relationship to each other?
- Has the student teacher sequenced the key points appropriately?
- Has the student teacher used simple, short sentences, explained specialist vocabulary, provided concrete examples and asked pupils to generate their own?
- Has the student teacher signalled when a new point is made, summarised the key points of the exposition, and sought feedback to check understanding?

Further, Brown and Wragg[37] argue that it is often useful to convert the topics of an exposition into a series of questions (see below: questions and questioning).

In using exposition, it is often important to take pupils through one or more worked examples, without interruption, to signal the different stages carefully as they are working through a particular issue, and to explain their thinking and reasoning behind the different stages of the issue. Exposition will probably necessitate the use of specialised vocabulary, which will need to be explained and understood. Exposition, like its partner explanation, is not simply talking; it is accompanied by presentations, written guidance on layout and processes, questioning and feedback, and a clear understanding of the role of learners in the exposition – to listen, follow, understand, question and apply.

EXPLANATION

Perrott points out that research findings indicate that clarity of presentation is something that can exert considerable influence on effective teaching. Wragg[38] adds that clarity involves a clear structure, clear language, clear voice and fluency. Perrott[39] goes on to select a number of factors important in contributing to effectiveness in explanation. They are:

- *Continuity:* Maintaining a strong connecting thread through a lesson is a matter of great importance.
- *Simplicity:* Try to use simple, intelligible, and grammatical sentences. Keep sentences short, and if relationships are complex consider communicating them by visual means. As regards vocabulary, use simple words well within the class's own vocabulary. If specialist, subject-specific language is used, make sure the terms employed are carefully defined and understood.

● *Explicitness:* One reason for ineffectiveness in presenting new material to a class is the assumption that the children understand more than is in fact the case. Where explanations are concerned, one must be as explicit as possible. The explanation must be well structured and logical.

The skills involved in explaining and giving explanations have received rather patchy attention from researchers over the years, yet their importance for the teacher in the classroom cannot be overestimated. Indeed, much of his time is devoted to explaining in one way or another. Brown and Armstrong[40] have pointed out that at its lowest level the process of explaining involves presenting sets of facts or simple instructions; and that higher levels of explaining go beyond facts to consider relationships between facts and also to consider reasons, motives and causes. Wragg[41] adds to this the view that when concepts (medium and higher-order levels of explanation) are being explained the student teacher should make sure that the label or name of the concept is introduced, its attributes should be identified (with examples provided), including necessary and possible attributes. He suggests that explanations can be used to enable pupils to understand concepts, cause and effect, procedures, purposes and objectives, relationships, processes and consequences.

For Perrott[42] a clear explanation depends upon (a) identifying the elements to be related, e.g. objects, events, processes, generalisations, and (b) identifying the relationships between them, e.g. causal, justifying, interpreting, mechanical. As she says, 'This identification of the components and the relationship between them is something which the teacher has to do first for himself. The teacher's failure to do this is a primary cause of confused presentation.'

She also stresses the need to make an explanation explicit, i.e. clearly and openly stated. The danger here is in giving information about the thing in question and leaving the explanation implicit in the information supplied. It would appear from research that a student teacher's ability to make her explanations explicit has a wholly beneficial effect on pupils' attainment levels. Perrott explains that the majority of sentences which make explicit a relation between two ideas or processes use words or phrases like:

because	as a result of
why	therefore
so that	in order to
by	through

In an empirical study of explaining and explanations, Brown and Armstrong[43] adopted the following working definition; explaining is an attempt to provide understanding of a problem to others. There are three factors for the researchers to bear in mind – the explainer, the problem, and the explainees. Thus, 'The explainer has to present or elicit a set of linked statements, each of which is understood by the explainees and which together lead to a solution of the problem for that particular set of explainees.'

At the outset of their study, they used a simple typology which consisted of:

The interpretive:	which clarifies, exemplifies or interprets the meaning of terms (What is ... ?)
The descriptive:	which describes a process or structure (How is ... ? How does ... ?)
The 'reason giving':	which offers reasons or causes, the occurrence of a phenomenon (Why is ... ?)

This typology provided a basis for the analysis of explanations and for activities concerned with the preparation, design and structuring of explanations.

In the study, 27 PGCE biology pupils were required to teach two out of ten specified topics to groups of twelve 11- to 12-year-olds in two ten-minute lessons. Briefly summarising the results, the interpretive lessons revealed the importance of selection of appropriate content. Simple lessons with only one or two new concepts scored more highly than lessons in which the pupils were introduced to a large number of ideas, even though the new ideas were linked together. The lessons involving descriptive explanations disclosed the importance of careful planning and logical structuring as a framework for effective explanations. Finally, the reason-giving lessons underlined the importance of answering the central questions. The better lessons stated the problem and principles relatively early in the lessons and proceeded to elicit and give examples.

(See www.routledge.com/textbooks/9780415485586, Chapter 13 Language in classrooms, Topics for explanatory lessons.)

It is important to ensure clarity in explanations, comprising, for example: a clear structure to the explanation, clear and appropriate language, clear voice and fluency. The delivery of the explanation is also important, taking into account, for example: the pitch, volume, speed and tone of the voice; the use of non-verbal communication; the establishing and maintenance of eye contact; ensuring that the pupils are paying attention and can see and hear the student teacher (e.g. ensuring that the seating arrangements are appropriate and that the student teacher is in the most suitable part of the room whether the pupils are sitting in rows, in a horseshoe, a circle, or in groups of tables).

Wragg[44] identified several criteria that student teachers can use to evaluate their explanations. These are summarised in Box 67.

One can see that many features of effective exposition apply to explanations, indeed notions of clarity, purpose, sequencing, non-verbal support, pupil involvement, exemplification, timing and pacing are factors that apply to the aspects of classroom talk in this whole section. Kyriacou[45] suggests that the effectiveness of an explanation is enhanced by attention to: clarity (and pitched at the appropriate level for the pupils); structure (logic, coherence and split up into meaningful units); length (neither too long nor too short, and interspersed with teachers' and pupils' questions); attention (with the use of non-verbal communication); language (explaining new terms and avoiding over-complex language); exemplars (relating to pupils' own experiences); understanding (with the student teacher checking understanding through questioning).

Box 67: Criteria for evaluating explanations

- Clear introduction
- New terms clarified
- Apt word choice
- Clear sentence structure
- Vagueness avoided
- Adequate concrete examples
- Within pupils' experience
- Voice used to emphasise
- Emphasis by gesture
- Appropriate pauses
- Direct verbal cueing

- Repetition used
- Many ideas paraphrased
- Sound use of media, materials
- Pattern of explanation clear
- Parts linked to each other
- Progressive summary
- Pace or level altered
- Opportunity for pupils' questions
- Grasp of main ideas checked
- Pupil commitment sought

QUESTIONS AND QUESTIONING

Questioning is a critical skill, in the sense that, done successfully, it is amongst the most powerful tools for teaching and learning. If done less successfully, it can damage learning. Successful interactive teaching, as was argued above, depends in part on the effectiveness of the teacher's questioning and feedback; indeed an important question that student teachers can ask themselves is 'How is my questioning going to improve the pupils' learning?' It is not only the question but what is done with the response that is important: pupils and student teachers can both learn something from a pupil's response. A student teacher can know if the work is too easy or too difficult for example, if her explanations have been successful, if there are groups or individuals who need additional help, and if she needs to revise and re-present her material.

Questioning can take place throughout a lesson, and it enables a student teacher to check the pupils' understanding; to challenge pupils to think about and apply their learning; to share their ideas; and to experience success in providing the correct responses. Questioning should improve learning, not simply be a device for a pupil to display her knowledge.[46] This implies that the student teacher has to consider carefully the kind of question that is being asked. Indeed it is not only the student teacher who should be able to ask the question but also the pupil. As we showed at the start of this chapter, children ask far fewer questions in school than they do at home; exactly the place where they should be learning they are enquiring less. The paradox is striking.

It is often said that teachers are amongst a small group of adults who ask pupils questions to which they already know the answer. Anecdotally, a child did not answer a teacher who asked him what 8 + 4 'made', because, as he said, 'the teacher already knew, and I already knew, so I don't know why she asked the question'. This story from a 6-year-old makes the telling comment that teachers not only need to be sure of the purposes of the question but that they need to ensure that the pupils know what the purposes of the question are. A question can have many purposes; for example, the Leverhulme Primary Project[47] suggested 12 possible reasons why questions could be asked (Box 68).[48]

(See www.routledge.com/textbooks/9780415485586, Chapter 13 Language in classrooms, Teachers' reasons for asking questions.)

Box 68: Purposes in asking questions

- To arouse interest and curiosity concerning a topic.
- To focus attention on a particular issue or concept.
- To develop an active approach to learning.
- To stimulate pupils to ask questions of themselves and others.
- To structure a task in such a way that learning will be maximised.
- To diagnose specific difficulties inhibiting pupil learning.
- To communicate to the group that involvement in the lesson is expected, and that overt participation by all members of the group is valued.
- To provide an opportunity for pupils to assimilate and reflect upon information.
- To involve pupils in using an inferred cognitive operation on the assumption that this will assist in developing thinking skills.
- To develop reflection and comment by pupils on the responses of other members of the group, both pupils and teachers.
- To afford an opportunity for pupils to learn vicariously through discussion.
- To express a genuine interest in the ideas and feelings of the pupil.

One can see in these reasons that the teachers were using questions not only for cognitive/intellectual reasons (concerning the subject matter of the lesson) but for emotional social reasons (to cater for different personalities) and for managerial reasons (to minimise unwanted behaviour and to keep pupils on task).

Mercer and Littleton[49] further argue that questions can:

◉ encourage children to make explicit their thoughts, reasons and knowledge and share them with the class
◉ model useful ways of using language that children can appropriate for use themselves in peer group discussions and other settings, for example asking 'why' questions to elicit reasons
◉ provide opportunities for children to make longer contributions in which they express their current state of understanding, articulate ideas and reveal problems they are encountering.

So far we have discussed the student teacher's possible purposes in asking questions. Thompson and Feasey[50] argue that, in the context of science teaching, pupils themselves should be asking questions. Here teachers should encourage pupils to:

◉ generate a range of scientific questions
◉ ask pertinent questions
◉ recognise which questions can be answered
◉ appreciate that different kinds of questions can be answered in different ways
◉ appreciate that not every question has one correct answer
◉ develop a range of strategies to deal with different questions
◉ question each other and themselves in a critical manner
◉ support answers to questions using data from investigations or other sources
◉ question the validity of their own and other data.

Though this list was given in the context of science teaching, it is easy to appreciate that it can be applied in many other curriculum areas. Importantly Thompson and Feasey suggest several strategies to improve pupils' abilities to pose and answer questions through teachers' interventions. Interventions, they argue, should:

◉ be only occasional
◉ encourage observations
◉ encourage thinking
◉ reflect on what has happened and what might happen next
◉ help pupils to recognise causal links between events
◉ feed into future planning.

Teachers, therefore, should:

◉ use many different types of question
◉ ask fewer direct questions
◉ use questions to link what children know to intended learning outcomes
◉ talk less and listen more
◉ use focused questions for diagnostic purposes
◉ realise that questions have limitations
◉ encourage more questions from children

- use silence as thinking time
- support oral questioning with the same written question.

One function of questioning is to elicit information. Thus, it may probe the extent of children's prior learning before a new subject or area of learning is introduced; or it may help to revise earlier learning; or consolidate recent teaching and learning. More than this, however, questions should have teaching value; that is, in asking the question a teacher is helping the pupil to focus and clarify, and thus have thoughts and perceptions that he would not have had otherwise. Indeed the Office for Standards in Education[51] found that questioning (closely followed by exposition) was the single most important factor in pupils' achievements of high standards, where questions were used to assess pupils' knowledge and challenge their thinking.

Framing the question

Questions need to be formulated to match pupils' learning needs. It is possible to differentiate questions for different abilities and individual pupils.

The value to the student teacher of preparing questions beforehand as part of, or to accompany, a lesson plan cannot be over-emphasised. There are at least three reasons for this need. First, this provides an opportunity to think about appropriate language. Questions should be precisely and unambiguously worded so that they elicit the answer or response that the student teacher intends. The likelihood of misunderstandings and wrong answers is greater with unprepared, impromptu questions. Second, where a connected series of questions is required, it is difficult to organise them sequentially and logically on the spur of the moment. And third, a student teacher is better prepared to deal with the unexpected if she possesses a body of well-thought-out questions.

A related issue is the desirability of preparing some questions with particular pupils in mind. An apt question, for example, worded especially for a timid pupil or a pupil with learning difficulties, can help develop his/her confidence and sense of achievement.

Questions can focus on processes (to ask about procedures and 'working out' or explaining what one has done) and on products: the outcomes or answers to a particular problem. Process questions are essential to develop pupils' problem-solving skills.[52] It is also particularly useful when framing questions to distinguish two broad kinds of question – questions which test knowledge and questions which create knowledge. The former are referred to as lower-order cognitive questions and the latter as higher-order cognitive questions (you may find it easier initially to think of them as 'fact' questions and 'thought' questions respectively to distinguish the two categories, as these are terms of approximate equivalence).

Lower-order cognitive questions embrace chiefly recall, comprehension and application; higher-order questions, by contrast, involve analysis, synthesis and evaluation. Lower-order questions tend to be closed questions (when a known response is sought); higher-order questions tend to be open questions (when the type of response is known but the actual response is not, pupils being free to respond in their own way). With regard to the latter, it is important that pupils know what type of response is being sought so that their responses are relevant and apposite. Brown[53] elucidates the categories of lower to higher-order questioning thus.

Lower-order cognitive questions

Recall: Does the pupil recall what she has seen or read?
Comprehension: Does the pupil understand what she recalls?
Application: Can the pupil apply the rules and techniques to solve problems that have single correct answers?

Higher-order cognitive questions

Analysis: Can the pupil identify motives and causes, make inferences and give examples to support her statements?

Synthesis: Can the pupil make predictions, solve problems or produce interesting juxtapositions of ideas and images?

Evaluation: Can the pupil judge the quality of ideas, or problem solutions, or works of art? Can she give rationally based opinions on issues or controversies?

Studies conducted in the United States indicate that many teachers' questions fall into the recall category and that higher-order cognitive questions are rarely used.[54] Although recall questions are especially useful in testing learning and focusing attention, questioning sessions made up exclusively of them may become boring and place undue emphasis on rote-learning. Ideally, lower-order cognitive questions should be coupled with carefully selected higher-order cognitive ones so that children are led to consider the implications of the facts of the circumstances that give rise to them. It must be remembered, however, that the latter do require the skill of being able to judge the extent to which children are able to respond appropriately to the more difficult and complex examples; and such judgement must be based on knowledge of the pupils' intellectual capabilities. Once a student teacher has this knowledge, she should try to get a judicious balance of both types organised in carefully planned sequences. Some questions need to be handled carefully, or, in certain circumstances, avoided altogether. These may be briefly identified as follows.

- Questions inviting a yes or no answer should not be used excessively, for a pupil has as much chance of being right as of being wrong if he guesses. Yes and no answers follow from binary questions of the recall type, and where such answers are unavoidable, another question, such as how? or why? should follow in order to provide explanatory or supportive evidence for the yes or no. Occasionally, a yes or no answer can be of disciplinary assistance when attentions are wandering: 'Do you understand, John?'

- Questions having several equally good answers should be avoided if the teacher has only one answer in mind ('What should a driver have with him?' A map? His licence? A torch? A toolkit? A first aid box?). Formulations of this nature invite guessing. Questions having several equally good answers are permissible, however, when a teacher is building up a composite answer, e.g. when introducing a topic or project.

- Composite questions – those involving a number of interrogatives – present difficulties even with brighter children and should be avoided.

- Unless you have a well-established behaviour management strategy such as 'Hands up before speaking', avoid asking questions beginning 'Who can tell me . . . ?' or 'Does anyone know...?' as these may lead to various members of the class shouting out answers.

- Questions testing powers of expression should be treated with care. Similarly, those seeking definitions of words or concepts, especially abstract ones, should be handled carefully.

- General questions that are vague and aimless should not be used ('What do you know about the French Revolution?'). Precision and clarity should be sought from the outset.

- Guessing questions are sometimes useful for stimulating a child's imagination and actively involving him in discussion. If used too often, however, they encourage thoughtless responses.

- Leading questions (those framed in such a way as to suggest or imply the desired answer – 'Wordsworth was the author of the first sonnet we read, wasn't he?) and rhetorical questions (those to which the pupil is not expected to reply – 'Do you want me to send you outside?') should be avoided because the former tend to reinforce a pupil's dependence on the student

Box 69: Possible purposes of questioning in relation to the suggested class lesson plan

Stage	Questioning
Introduction	to establish human contact
	to assist in establishing set induction devices
	to discover what the class knows to revise previous work
	to pose problems which lead
	to the subject of the lesson
Presentation	to maintain interest and alertness
	to encourage reasoning and logical thinking
	to discover if pupils understand what is going on
Application	to focus and clarify to lead the children
	to make observations and draw inferences for themselves
	to clear up difficulties, misunderstandings and assist individual pupils
Conclusion	to revise the main points of the lesson
	to test the results of the lesson, and the extent of the pupils' understanding and assimilation
	to suggest further problems and related issues

teacher and undermine independent thought, whereas the latter may provoke unwanted or facetious replies. Questions should be asked only if the student teacher wants a real answer.

● Elliptical questions – those worded so that a child supplies a missing word or missing words – are of value when used to encourage pupils with learning or behaviour difficulties. Provided they are not used too often, they can give variety to a questioning session.

Box 69 indicates how questions may be related to a typical class.

Asking the question and receiving the answer

Questions should be asked in simple, conversational language and in a friendly and challenging manner, ensuring that the pupil knows what kind of answer is expected (i.e. there is a need to give cues to the pupils). Indeed it is important for the student teacher to make it clear whether the question is to the whole class, a group, or an individual. A useful procedure is as follows: put the question to the class, pause briefly, then name the child you wish to answer. A sequence of this kind encourages everyone to listen and prepare an answer in anticipation of being asked. Respondents should be named at random rather than in a predetermined and systematic way, thus avoiding selective listening. As suggested earlier, it is to the teacher's advantage at this point to have prepared questions with particular children in mind. The more difficult questions for brighter pupils and easier ones for pupils experiencing learning difficulties help to sustain different motivational levels and maintain the flow of the lesson. It is especially important in this respect to try to draw out the more shy members of the class. The student teacher should also counter the tendency to overlook pupils sitting at the back or sides of the classroom when distributing questions. Similarly, student teachers should resist the temptation to ignore those pupils who happen to be sitting near a supervising tutor or mentor.

Once a question has been put to a pupil, it should be left with her long enough for an answer to emerge. An appropriate waiting time might be 3–5 seconds for a low-order or factual, closed question and up to 15 seconds for an open-ended or higher-order question.[55] Waiting longer than this might lead to other pupils becoming restless or impatient, though clearly some pupils will require longer than others. Lack of preparation on the part of the student teacher, or impatience, may lead her to follow it immediately with other questions, or to modify the original, qualify it, reword it or explain it, or even to answer it herself! Such addenda merely confuse pupils or, in the latter case of the student teacher answering the question herself, lead to the feeling in pupils that, if they wait long enough, they will not have to do anything – the answer will be provided! Indeed, British research indicates that student teachers and beginning teachers often ask more questions than they receive answers.[56] Their failure to obtain answers is often due to lack of pauses and no variation in the delivery of questions.

The efficacy of the student teacher sometimes accepting two or three answers before responding should also be noted. A varied pattern of this nature thus encourages volunteering, contributes to group co-operation, and achieves a more realistic social situation which can be further enhanced by allowing other members of the class to respond to a child's answer ('John, was Peter's answer correct?').

The techniques of prompting and probing are often useful in class questioning sessions, either to an individual, group or the whole class, to pursue an issue in greater depth. Prompting involves giving hints to help a child. In addition to eliciting appropriate answers, prompts backed up with teacher encouragement help hesitant children reply more confidently. On receiving an answer, it is sometimes necessary to press a child for additional information and this may be especially the case after a factual question. Probing in this context may take the form of further information, directing the child to think more deeply about his answer, inviting a critical interpretation, focusing his response on a related issue or encouraging him to express himself more clearly. (Two illustrations of prompting and probing are given in Box 70.)[57] As Brown[58] observes, probing questions with older children tap the highest levels of their thinking.

Sometimes a correct answer needs to be repeated to make sure all have heard it. It is inadvisable to accept unsolicited answers that have been called out as such habits can lead to problems of control. Wrong answers can be of value in clearing up misunderstandings, obscurities and difficulties providing they are treated tactfully and without disrupting the lesson to any great extent (to respond to a wrong answer, for instance, with 'That's nonsense' or 'What rubbish!' is to ensure that the flow of answers from the class will quickly dry up!). Clearly, a sense of humour is an invaluable asset at this stage in a questioning session.

It is very important for pupils to receive information on the correctness or otherwise of their answers (see below: *responding*). This is especially the case for low achievers. Feedback from the teacher is the easiest way to maintain interest and is most effective when given after an individual response. In most instances, the feedback does not need to be long; a word or two will suffice to let a pupil know that she's on the right lines: 'That's right, Joanne'. Praise and censure should be used with discrimination. Praise is quickly devalued if given too readily; and undue censure can be discouraging. Excessive criticism directed at weaker pupils can do nothing but harm.

One final point remains to be briefly considered: the pupils' questions to the teacher. As Davies and Shepherd[59] note, nothing shows more clearly that a student teacher and class are on friendly terms than evidence of pupils sensibly questioning her about difficult points. Desirable as this kind of relationship is, however, it can pose problems for less experienced teachers. They must, for instance, avoid having too many interruptions and being side-tracked from the main theme of their lesson. One way of dealing with difficulties of this kind is to ensure that they have anticipated the class's questions with the ones they put to them. Another way is to invite questions from the class

Box 70: Prompting and probing

Prompting

Teacher: Would you say that nationalism in Africa is now greater or less than it was 20 years ago?
Pupil: Greater.
Teacher: Yes. Why is that?
Pupil: Because there are more nations now.
Teacher: Yes. Mmm. There's more to it than that. Can anyone else give some reasons?
Class: (Silence)
Teacher: Well, basically it's because . . .

This is an example of what frequently happens in the first discussion lessons given by a teacher. The discussion drags and degenerates into an unprepared lecture. This can be avoided by prompting any weak answers given. In the example, the teacher could have said 'Yes. That's right. There are more nations now and there are more nations because African people wanted to be independent of the Europeans. What has happened in the past 20 years which has helped them to become independent?'

Probing

Teacher: Jessica, you went to Paris this year. What did you think of it?
Jessica: Mmm. It was nice.
Teacher: What was nice about it? (Pause)
Jessica: Well, I liked walking down the avenue which had trees. I liked watching the boats on the river. I liked listening to Frenchmen. The Metro was exciting and, oh, I liked the French bread and butter.

The simple probe 'What was nice about it?' evoked from this 7-year-old girl a series of impressions which revealed her interest in sights, sounds and food.

at appropriate points in the lesson (towards the end of the presentation stage, for example). Some questions may not be directly relevant to the lesson in hand, in which case the student teacher should inform the class that they will be dealt with in future lessons. If you do not know the answer to a question, don't be afraid to admit it, but say you will find out the answers as soon as you can.

For occasions when an awkward pupil proposes a series of difficult or even silly questions, Davies and Shepherd recommend that if the questions have no direct relationship with the topic under consideration, student teachers are fully justified in making that explanation to the pupils in such a way that they do not prohibit further questions.

Student teachers anxious to acquire command of this most vital skill of questioning a class should make every effort to build short questioning sessions of from five to ten minutes into their lessons. They can then get some idea of their progress by constructing a simple self-evaluation schedule based on the suggestions outlined earlier and checking their performance, say, once a week as part of their routine lesson criticisms. In evaluating student teachers' abilities to conduct effective questioning Brown and Wragg[60] set out some errors that student teachers typically make (Box 71).

As a corollary to this they set out some key factors for effective questioning:

- *structuring* (providing signposts for the sequence of questions and the topic, indicating the types of answers expected, using 'advance organisers' to clarify what the children will be doing)

Box 71: Common errors in questioning

- Asking too many questions at once.
- Asking a question and answering yourself.
- Asking questions only of the brightest or most likeable pupils.
- Asking a difficult question too early.
- Asking irrelevant questions.
- Always asking the same types of questions.
- Asking questions in a threatening way.
- Not indicating a change in the type of question.
- Not using probing questions.
- Not giving pupils time to think.
- Not correcting wrong answers.
- Ignoring answers.
- Failing to see the implications of answers.
- Failing to build on answers.

- *pitching and putting clearly* (considering: how broad/narrow to make the question, the order of the question – low to high, the vocabulary to be used, the degree of openness or closure of the question, the level of difficulty of the question for the individual to whom it is being put, i.e. the cognitive level of the question and the pupil)
- *directing and distributing* (going around the whole class, not only accepting the answers of volunteers)
- *pausing and pacing* (allowing thinking time, particularly for more complex questions)
- *prompting and probing* (considering what to say in a prompt or a probe, rephrasing, reviewing)
- *listening and responding* (deciding the most appropriate form of response. See below: Responding)
- *sequencing* (introducing, opening out, converging, extending, lifting).

It is also important to tell the pupils how you expect them to answer, for example in a complete sentence, in a few words, in a longer explanation, using technical vocabulary, personal experience or whatever, so that they know what kind of an answer they should provide. These key factors reflect the fact that questioning is both an art and a skill that can be specifically rehearsed for classroom success.

DISCUSSION

It is in the many discussion situations in the classroom that talk as an agent of learning operates most effectively. This means that the problem for the student teacher is how to develop and improve pupils' skills in this respect, and indeed her own. In the main, discussions take place either between the student teacher and class or among small groups with or without the student teacher. There is an important issue of the physical layout of the classroom to be considered here, so that pupils have the opportunity to hear each other and feel able to contribute in a supportive environment (often facing each other rather than all facing forwards to the teacher). Tables and chairs may have to be arranged in groups.

Dean[61] advises student teachers to think out clearly what it is they hope to get from their discussions and to consider their functions. Indeed it must be made clear to pupils what is expected to come out of the discussions. The more clearly the purpose and the intended outcomes are communicated, the greater the likelihood is of a focused and purposeful discussion.

If the pupils are discussing in small groups without the teacher, then the teacher should communicate to them in advance what they will be required to do in the plenary session following the discussion, e.g. to suggest five points in favour of such-and-such and five points against such-and-such, or to identify six main issues to be addressed in building such-and-such. It is sometimes helpful here if the groups are given specific discussion points, specific tasks to come out of the discussion, specific questions to address and so on, i.e. to ensure that the discussion is focused and time-bound, and that the pupils know how much time they have to complete the discussion and how long they are advised to spend on each item. This may mean that the group has to produce a written summary of points which the teacher will collect, and appoint a spokesperson to report back in the plenary session.

If the discussion is teacher-focused then the teacher should indicate the purpose, focus and intended outcome of the discussion. This involves identifying important questions and having the pupils' language skills and general experience in mind at the same time. The issue here is that group and teacher-led discussions need very careful planning, structuring and follow-up, or else they become airings of ignorance.

It is important that the student teacher knows where she wants the discussion to go and communicates this to the pupils. In this way the student teacher and the pupils themselves know what is relevant and what is not. All too often the student teacher accepts as relevant to the discussion anything that the pupils say. This can quickly degenerate into pupils calling out anything, which makes light of the discussion and leads to discipline problems. It can render discussions inconsequential, literally pointless. Student teachers should be clear on the objectives of the discussion – where they want the discussion to go, what they want from the discussion (e.g. the intended pedagogic and knowledge outcomes), and how they will use the discussion to feed into the remainder of the lesson – and they should communicate these intentions clearly to the pupils so that the pupils see the relevance of the discussions. Even with the student teacher adopting the role of the 'neutral chairperson'[62] (e.g. in discussions of values and morals) there still needs to be a direction for, and outcome of, a discussion.

The important points that need to be remembered, in Dean's[63] view, are: how you receive the pupils' contributions; scanning the class to spot would-be contributors and those not involved; being able to interpret body language so as to know when children have had enough; and finally being able to summarise and structure ideas with a view to taking the discussion further. Discussion involves speaking, listening and taking turns. The student teacher will have to consider how participation, turn taking and listening skills can be taught and learnt by pupils.[64] Indeed Turner sets out some key points for managing a discussion (Box 72).

Pollard and Tann[65] have posed further questions which readers can reflect on, perhaps in the light of their own teaching practice experiences:

● What are the range of roles participants might play?
● What do the participants learn, including those that do not participate?
● How do different kinds of tasks, group size and composition affect group processes?
● How can we use discussion to develop and monitor the participants' discussion skills?

Box 72: Handling discussion

Rules and procedures

- Choice of subject and length of discussion (young pupils without experience may not sustain lengthy discussion).
- Physical setting: room size; arrangement of furniture so that most pupils have eye contact.
- Protocols for discourse; taking turns; length of contribution; abusive language.
- Procedures for violation of protocols, e.g. racist or sexist behaviour.
- How to protect the sensitivity of individuals; pupils may reveal unexpected personal information in the course of a discussion.
- Stance of the chairperson.

Provision of evidence

- Know the age, ability and mix of abilities of the pupils.
- Know what information is needed.
- Know sources of information.
- Decide at what point the information is introduced (before, during).

Neutral chairperson*

- Authority of the opinions of the chair should not influence the outcome.
- The opinions of the pupils are to be exposed, not those of the teachers.
- The chairperson can be free to influence the quality of the understanding, the rigour of debate and appropriate exploration of the issues.
- Pupils will understand the teacher's stance if it is made clear at the start.

Possible outcomes*

- Learn by sharing and understanding the opinion of others.
- Be exposed to the nature and role of evidence.
- Realise that objective evidence is often an inadequate basis for decision making.
- Come to know that decisions often rely on subjective value judgements.
- Realise that many decisions are compromises.

* This is in the context of discussing values and morals.

RESPONDING

In expositions, explanations, questioning and discussions, an important skill to be developed is that of responding appropriately to pupils. It is easy to miss important clues to children's understanding when you are too concerned to lead children towards a predetermined answer, for example. In addition, it is important to give children time to respond and, wherever possible, build your answers and further questions on their contributions.

Brown and Wragg[66] indicate several types of response that can be made to pupils' answers and comments. Student teachers can:

- *ignore* the response, moving on to another pupil, topic or question
- *acknowledge* the response, building it into the subsequent discussion

- *repeat* the response verbatim to reinforce the point or to bring it to the attention of those that might not have heard it
- *repeat part* of the response, to emphasise a particular element of it
- *paraphrase* the response for clarity and emphasis, and so that it can be built into the ongoing and subsequent discussion
- *praise* the response (either directly or by implication in extending and building on it for the subsequent part of the discussion)
- *correct* the response (a feature that student teachers are often reluctant to do, thereby sanctioning error and irrelevance)
- *prompt* the pupils for further information or clarification
- *probe* the pupils to develop relevant points.

These features indicate the type of response that is possible. There are also some procedural matters that echo points made so far, for example: allowing thinking time (particularly for complex responses); affording pupils the opportunity to correct, clarify and crystallise their responses, once uttered, i.e. not 'jumping onto' a response before a pupil has had time to finish it; building a pupil's contribution into the student teacher's own plans for the sequence of the discussion; using a pupil's contribution to introduce another question to be put to another pupil. There are also pedagogic matters in responding to pupils' contributions, for example giving feedback to pupils on the quality, accuracy, range, relevance, amount and significance of their contribution. Pupils need to know both the positive and the negative aspects of their contributions; to ignore the negative aspects (based, presumably, on the notion of extinction in the behaviourist view of learning) might be to leave a pupil unsure whether everything that she has said is relevant, accurate and so on. Pointing out the negative aspects need not be done negatively but in the spirit of constructive criticism and in a supportive manner.

SUMMARISING

That there are cognitive and affective aspects of summarising is reflected in the view of Proctor[67] *et al.* that effective summarising can 'reassure, consolidate [and] support' pupils. Cognitively, the student teacher needs to be able to draw together the key points of a discussion, set of questions, explanation, series of instructions and a whole lesson so that pupils can differentiate between the highly relevant/important/central points and the less relevant/trivial/marginal/peripheral points. In many cases there should be a match between the contents of a summary and the intended learning outcomes and objectives of a lesson.

Summarising in talk can be undertaken through a combination of questions, statements and restatements (by the student teacher or the pupils themselves), confirmation and highlighting of the most important features of the matters to be summarised. Summaries will link the several sections of a series of questions, discussions or stages of a lesson. They may also establish and clarify links between the current and previous or future lessons, making for and communicating to pupils the nature of the continuity, progression and relevance of the work. Summarising is a convergent exercise intended to make it clear to pupils what are the significant features of the work; it is a reductionist exercise that highlights key matters. Bruner[68] argues that the clarification and highlighting of key matters, concepts, issues etc. facilitates memorising and recall.

DIALOGIC TEACHING AND COLLABORATIVE LEARNING

In dialogic teaching pupils are encouraged, through teacher questioning, to give extended and reflective answers as opposed to brief responses. Research further suggests that dialogic teaching has the potential for similar outcomes in relation to pupil–pupil interactions; more specifically in the context of collaborative learning in group work. At the same time there is significant research to suggest that in primary classrooms, even though children mostly sit in small groups, peer inter-action in learning is rare. It is important to realise that just because several children are grouped at a table together does not mean that they are collaborating. Often the activities they are engaged in simply do not encourage or require them to work together (see for example Galton *et al.* and Baines *et al.*).[69]

Collaborative learning in group work occurs when knowledge and understanding is developed through pupils talking and working together relatively autonomously (Blatchford *et al.*, 2003; Mercer and Littleton, 2007).[70] Mercer and Littleton[71] define children as being engaged in collabora-tive learning 'when they are engaged in a co-ordinated, continuing attempt to solve a problem or in some way construct common knowledge'. The role of talk and knowledge and understanding of speaking and listening skills is therefore crucial to this process. The National Curriculum requires group discussion and interaction at Key Stages 1 and 2. Under this heading, skills that must be taught so that pupils are able to join as members of a group at Key Stage 1 and to talk effectively as members of a group at Key Stage 2 are listed. At Key Stage 3, pupils should be able to make 'different kinds of relevant contributions in groups, respond appropriately to others, propose ideas and ask questions'. They should take different roles in 'organising, planning and sustaining talk in groups'. Group work is not mentioned specifically at Key Stage 4.

It is clear, then, that group-work skills have to be taught and developed so that pupils are able to communicate effectively through listening, explaining and sharing. Many of the questioning techniques described in this chapter can be used to support the process of dialogic teaching and collaborative learning. Mercer and Littleton suggest the following to support successful collabora-tive group work activity in the classroom:

● Teachers must take an active role in guiding pupils' use of language and modelling ways it can be used for thinking collectively. Children should be encouraged to give reasons to support their views, become engaged in extended discussions of topics and encouraged to see that responding need not simply mean providing the 'right' answer.

● Establishing an appropriate set of ground rules for talk in class. For group activity to be effec-tive, children need to be taught to relate in positive ways. An atmosphere of trust and mutual respect needs to be cultivated.

● Designing appropriate curriculum-related group activities for eliciting debate and joint reasoning.

CONCLUSION

The use of language in classrooms requires the student teacher to evaluate his/her own strategies in terms of the effectiveness of: direct instruction with whole-class interactive teaching, exposition and explanation, questioning, discussion, responding, summarising and setting up tasks and activities to encourage collaborative learning. Language and the bilingual learner have also been briefly described. We have discussed the nature of effective practice in these areas and the criteria for eval-uation and self-evaluation of the student teacher's abilities here.

Most of the debates about oracy and the recent considerations of talk in teaching and learning have more to do with teaching style than a careful consideration of programmes of study. Some of these teaching styles have been explored in this chapter. If national curricula are present, as they are in England, then it is appropriate that they should specify the content of the curriculum. This can apply to communication/speaking and listening just as it can apply to reading and writing and other subjects in the curriculum. However, there is a need for clear thinking about what this content should be. If teachers' practice more routinely encouraged exploratory talk and dialogic teaching, then it may be appropriate to reduce the overall content of the programmes of study for speaking and listening. This would require renewed thinking about what the content should be and might lead to more of a focus on some of the kinds of language exploration quite rightly advocated by the Language in the National Curriculum (LINC) project of the 1980s.

13 Inclusion, Equal Opportunities and Diversity

INTRODUCTION

Since the Sex Discrimination Act 1975, the Race Relations Act 1976 and the Warnock Report on special educational needs in 1978 the issue of equal opportunities has taken an increasingly central role in the educational and curricular debate. There has been a move towards increasing inclusion in schools, whereby social exclusion for whatever reason is minimised. Inclusion concerns being educated in an ordinary school, having access to the same curriculum, and being accepted by all, regardless of gender, ethnicity, or special needs.[1] It involves being physically in the same place as other students and 'social acceptance and belonging'. Norwich argues that inclusion has come to replace integration, the latter being seen simply as physical placement in the mainstream school but having to assimilate the 'unchanged mainstream system',[2] the former implying that the mainstream system has to change to accommodate the learner's needs, restructuring itself in order to accomplish this.

A series of reports from the 1970s onwards[3] makes it very plain that all students have a right to an 'entitlement' curriculum regardless of sex, race, ethnicity, class, age, ability, special educational needs, sexuality, physical impairment, religion, cultural and linguistic background, or other background aspects in which forms of discrimination might occur.

Equality of access and opportunity for all students to learn and to make progress should feature highly on a school's planning and should touch the school's aims, objectives, curriculum and organisation, grouping of students, role models in its teachers, support for learning, and students' achievements. The school has a duty to offer high-quality education to all, to promote, foster and fulfil the potential of every student, and to prepare students for adult life after school. Indeed the Runnymede Trust in 1993[4] argued that these three concerns touch the issues of quality, identity (individual and cultural), and society respectively in addressing equality assurance in education.

The Special Educational Needs Code of Practice[5] describes the requirements for schools for supporting children with special educational needs. The National Curriculum site includes detailed guidance on inclusion.[6] The statutory requirements and non-statutory guidance are built on three principles:

Schools must:

- set suitable learning challenges
- respond to pupils' diverse learning needs
- overcome potential barriers to learning and assessment for individuals and groups of pupils.

These principles are explained in some detail on the National Curriculum website. In addition to detailed explanation, the National Curriculum provides 'inclusion case studies', which show how schools have tackled issues to do with inclusion. For example, there are case studies about:

- a culturally inclusive school
- inclusion and success for all
- personalisation and relevance
- confidence through leadership skills
- cutting exclusions through personalisation
- sharing plans for access
- supporting looked after children
- writing for real audiences
- challenging stereotypes.

The case study of writing for real audiences is part of the curriculum-in-action part of the site. It shows how pupils with severe, profound and multiple learning difficulties benefited from taking part in a city-wide reading project.

The language of equal opportunities and inclusion is also to be linked with discourses of diversity. The Runnymede Trust[7] suggests that the term 'equal opportunities' has come to be associated with the legislative framework covering gender, race and disability, whereas 'diversity' is seen to be adding another dimension to equal opportunities in terms of covering all types of difference, not simply those addressed in legislation, and in terms of its focus on individuals and organisational culture. Indeed the call to diversity has been taken up by the Qualifications and Curriculum Authority in a series of publications on inclusion and in curriculum proposals to address diversity.

The Runnymede Trust comments on the positive value of using the language of equal opportunities, as its anti-discrimination focus can move organisational climates to a more optimistic tenor in terms of 'opportunities'.[8] On the other hand the notion of what constitutes 'equal' is cloudy, e.g. treating people the same, positive discrimination, focusing on specific groups. Rather, the Trust suggests that 'diversity' catches an all-inclusive field, celebrating the value of differences and a 'higher value of harmony' and valuing people. Diversity, it is suggested,[9] concerns maximising the potential of all and including everybody, creating a culture that values all kinds of difference, e.g. age, culture, personality, ethnicity, race, behaviour, gender, abilities, disabilities, appearance, sexuality etc. The Trust suggests a synthesis, that the terms 'equal opportunities' and 'diversity' are complementary, that they can co-exist comfortably, indeed that they should. Equality and diversity are partners. It suggests that equal opportunities is an important step on the way towards, indeed a necessary condition for, valuing diversity.[10]

What is being argued here is that the issue of equal opportunities, inclusion and diversity engage very many important areas of teaching and learning, including: teachers' expectations; students' self-esteem; labelling theory and stereotyping; the formal and hidden curriculum;[11] management; resources (including time, space, materials, teachers, support staff); power and empowerment; interactions between all parties in schools; discipline; pedagogy; assessment; and a concern for high standards in all students. Newman and Triggs[12] argue that inequality comes about through stereotyping, abuse, bias, omission (i.e. non-representation in the curriculum), discriminatory behaviour, and expectations. Clearly these impact on the full gamut of experiences that students have at school and which the student teacher will need to address. Equal opportunities, inclusion and diversity then, concern:

- treating students as individuals of equal worth – regardless of gender, race, background, special needs

- addressing equality of access, uptake and outcome
- countering, challenging and eliminating stereotypes, discrimination, bias and misperceptions
- promoting a clearer understanding of equal rights and freedoms
- pre-empting discrimination
- celebrating the notion of difference and promoting positive images of a diverse populace
- identifying how to break down discriminatory practices
- developing citizenship in a non-discriminatory society.

We believe that the case for equal opportunities, inclusion and diversity needs no justification, as it is premised on the notions of justice, democracy, freedom and empowerment, i.e. the case is built on the foundations of a just society. The practical implications of these, however, do need some examination in order to ensure that they are addressed in their many forms. We discuss these in two ways. First, we look at some meanings of equal opportunities, inclusion and diversity. Second, we examine some implications of these meanings for practice, relating our discussions to gender, ethnicity and special educational needs and how these might be addressed in a student teacher's teaching practice.

In addressing equal opportunities it is inadequate simply to ensure that formal equality of opportunity is provided, i.e. that every child is entitled to a broad and balanced curriculum. Rather, teachers and schools should be concerned with equality of uptake.[13] This builds on the 'cultural capital' thesis from Bourdieu.[14] He argues that, though formal equality of opportunity to a curriculum might be offered to all students, there will be a differential uptake because students come from a variety of backgrounds. School knowledge and culture are such that some students find in school an alien culture – and hence are not able to make the most of the education that schools offer – whilst other students find that the school culture accords with their own cultural background (e.g. in terms of acceptance of authority, valuing an academic education, adopting a particular linguistic register) so that they are able to access the curriculum more easily. Equality of opportunity, in this instance, does little to break down equality of access and uptake, indeed it makes for the reproduction of inequality in the wider society (e.g. in terms of employment, power, money, class).

Moreover, equal opportunities should concern not only access and uptake; they should also address equality of outcome, i.e. the promotion of freedoms, social justice, choice in lifestyles, life chances, the moves towards an egalitarian society. In this respect we are arguing that equal opportunities has a clear political agenda that promotes empowerment in individuals, groups, cultures and society at large, that reduces illegitimate differentials of power, and that breaks down illegitimate discriminatory practices in society.

One of the key aspects of empowerment of children is the legal status of their rights; however, children's rights is an area that traditionally has not been popular in education. The legal position of children's rights in the twentieth century received a considerable boost by the important United Nations (UN) Convention on the Rights of the Child (CRC). An important precursor to the CRC was the work of Eglantyne Jebb, founder of Save the Children, who said, 'I believe we should claim certain rights for children and labour for their universal recognition'. These words stand as an important testament to her pioneering work. In 1923 she summarised some of the essential rights of children in five points. These five points became the Declaration of the Rights of the Child and were agreed by the General Assembly of the International Save the Children Union in 1923. One year later the declaration was adopted by the League of Nations and the five points subsequently became known as the Declaration of Geneva.

Following the Second World War, the United Nations concentrated on the production of the Universal Declaration of Human Rights, which was adopted in 1948. In the declaration, the rights of the child were only implicitly included and it was felt to be insufficient to safeguard their specific rights. Much work was done to persuade the UN that a separate document was needed. On 20 November 1959 the UN General Assembly adopted the Declaration of the Rights of the Child. This comprised ten articles and incorporated the guiding principle of 'working in the best interests of the child'.

To further strengthen children's statutory rights it was necessary to work on a treaty. The government of Poland submitted a draft convention on the rights of the child to the UN commission on human rights in 1978 hoping to see it adopted during the International Year of the Child. The response to their proposal was not enthusiastic and there began a decade of debate about the nature of children's rights. The involvement of non-governmental organisations in this process was significant and their impact was one of the forces that helped the drafting of the Convention on the Rights of the Child.

The convention was submitted to the General Assembly of the UN in 1989. It was adopted, without modifications on 20 November 1989, exactly 30 years after the 1959 Declaration. It achieved a record first-day response with 61 countries signing up on 26 January 1990. On 2 September 1990 the Convention on the Rights of the Child entered into force as international law.

The Convention is a comprehensive instrument that addresses children's rights in a wide range of situations including emergency and non-emergency contexts. In order to give an indication of the style of the Convention it is useful to comment on some of the articles.

Article 3

1 *In all actions concerning children, whether undertaken by public or private social welfare institutions, courts of law, administrative authorities or legislative bodies, the best interests of the child shall be a primary consideration.*

This article is important because it means that statutory bodies, including education settings such as schools, have an obligation to consider the best interests of the child. This has been replicated in the UK Children Act 1989 where, for example, the ascertainable wishes and feelings of the child have to be taken into account in cases related to the care and upbringing of the child. However, it is also important to consider the means that are used to determine the child's best interests and the extent to which children have true involvement in that process.

Article 12

1 *State parties shall assure to the child who is capable of forming his or her own views the right to express those views freely in all matters affecting the child, the views of the child being given due weight in accordance with the age and maturity of the child.*

Here the significant wording is 'all matters affecting the child'. At an institutional level there have been some instances of good practice, but, too often, even if the views are sought, there is little obligation to ensure that those views are acted upon. There are also difficulties in the potential assumption that the older the child is, the better they are able to express their views. Some people who interact daily with children have found that they are constantly forced to challenge their own age-related expectations in terms of the capabilities that children have to understand issues and express their opinions.

Article 19

1 *State parties shall take all appropriate legislative, administrative, social and educational measures to protect the child from all forms of physical or mental violence, injury*

or abuse, neglect or negligent treatment, maltreatment or exploitation, including sexual abuse, while in the care of parent(s), legal guardian(s) or any other person who has the care of the child.

In the UK, physical punishment of children by parents remains a legal act. This is often justified on the grounds of reasonable force and, ironically, in the best interests of the child, the most common example being the one where a child has run into the road and the parent smacks the child to make sure they never do it again. This remains a substantial denial of children's rights in the UK.

The second part of the Convention (articles 42 to 45) deals with the technicalities of implementation. Included within these articles are the requirements that state parties make sure that the convention is widely known about – including by children – and that they report on the progress that they have made two years after initial adoption and every five years after that.

In 2001, Wyse[15] published the first research carried out to investigate the implementation of the CRC in English schools. The research revealed a depressing picture. First and foremost, ten years after the ratification of the CRC by the UK, only one teacher out of all the pupils and school staff that had been spoken to in the course of the research had heard of the CRC. According to UNICEF this picture has changed little in the intervening years.[16]

All countries that are signatories to the UNCRC have to produce reports periodically demonstrating the extent to which they are succeeding in implementing the convention. The UK's second report was heavily condemned by the international monitoring committee in 2002:

> The report itself was very disappointing... confusing, complicated and chaotic in its presentation. It was to be hoped that the new Children and Young People's Unit would follow the guidelines more carefully in drafting the next report. The report contained much information on various Green Papers, White Papers and studies, but did not present their results. It gave no account of how compliance with the provisions of the Convention was assessed, or any information on jurisprudence related to the rights of the child.[17]

The committee's response to the third report included recognition of some positive developments. For example, the committee welcomed the development of the Children's Plan, which explicitly mentions the CRC, and also welcomed the reorganisation that led to the establishment of the Department for Children, Schools and Families. However, some of the problems with the 2002 report appeared to be the same. The most basic of these problems is that too many citizens, including children, are not aware of the CRC:

> 20. The Committee welcomes the State party's recent efforts to train professionals on the principles and provisions of international human rights instruments, including the Convention, as well as its support to the UNICEF 'Rights respecting schools' project and the collaboration with NGOs in the development and implementation of awareness-raising activities. Nonetheless, the Committee is concerned that there is no systematic awareness-raising about the Convention and that the level of knowledge about it among children, parents or professional working with children is low. Furthermore, the Committee regrets that the Convention is not part of the curriculum in schools.[18]

A starting point, then, for trainee teachers is for them to familiarise themselves with the CRC (available from http://www.unicef.org.uk/) and to find out what schools are doing to help pupils become aware of their rights including those in the CRC. Arguably, one of the most important articles in the convention is the one that requires that pupils be consulted on all matters that affect them. Even modest attempts as part of teaching to consult pupils, for examples about the activities that they are doing or their involvement in the assessment process, are an important first step in respecting their rights.

A topic that should be related to children's rights is that of *pupil voice*. In a recent report of research, Robinson and Fielding[19] found that pupils' voices were not being heard as they might because of a lack of clarity in the purposes of primary education, which had moved to an emphasis on accountability through the testing system. Robinson and Fielding acknowledge that research on pupil voice has tended to be small-scale, making it difficult to generalise to the pupil population as a whole. They also claim that there is a limited amount of research on pupil voice (see Ruddock and McIntyre for a comprehensive overview).[20] However, it may be that when thinking about pupil voice, research on children's rights should also be taken account of, as children's voices are often at the heart of research of this kind.

What we are arguing, then, is the case that every student, regardless of differences (and we are all different) should be guaranteed equality of access, uptake and outcome, and that education should further those practices that break down discrimination, i.e. that every student is of equal worth as an individual and as a citizen in society. Education, therefore, is charged with the responsibility to fulfil individual potential and to prepare students for membership of an egalitarian society. We continue our discussions with some general questions that student teachers may find useful to address in approaching equal opportunities. These concern the formal and hidden curricula of schools.

We indicated above that teachers' expectations of students exerted a considerable influence on students' learning (discussed in more detail later). Echoing the notion of the self-fulfilling prophecy,[21] the literature on school effectiveness[22] argues that teachers' expectations of students exert a powerful effect on their achievements. Crudely speaking, if teachers have low expectations of a student then the student's performance tends to drop; if teachers have high expectations of students and challenge and 'stretch' them, then their performance rises. In looking at equal opportunities, then, student teachers ought to be asking themselves about their expectations of students and whether these expectations might be affected by gender, race, class, abilities, behaviour, linguistic abilities etc. For example, do all students have their fair share of the student teacher's time and high-quality attention; do all students have equal access to resources; does the student teacher make it clear that she values all of the students equally; does the student teacher hold appropriate expectations regardless of the race, class, sex, special needs etc. of each student (i.e. to what extent is the student teacher aware of her own stereotyping)?

One can see that this simple introduction reinforces our earlier point that addressing equal opportunities, inclusion and diversity takes place in every aspect of a student's experience in school – the formal and the hidden curriculum. The field is vast and we cannot hope to do full justice to it in the space available here. However, we want to raise some issues that impinge on the student teacher in her planning, implementation and evaluation of teaching practice. By concerning ourselves with three areas of equal opportunities, inclusion and diversity – sex, ethnicity and special educational needs – we hope to use these as vehicles for exposing a range of issues in equal opportunities that go beyond simply these three cognate areas. In doing so we shall be attempting to address several issues as they are experienced by teachers and students in schools. There is clearly a difficulty in separating out these three areas as, in practice, for example, sex interacts with and is influenced by race, special needs with race, sex with special needs. Indeed all three areas are inter-penetrated with and mediated by the central issue of differentials of power – structurally, interpersonally and personally. One central purpose should be the empowerment of students (and student teachers) to fulfil their own potentials within a just society.

GENDER

Student teachers will encounter a variety of situations where sexist behaviour occurs and where they need to plan to challenge this. Discrimination is to be countered wherever it is met. The Sex

Discrimination Act 1975 identifies two kinds of discrimination: (a) treating someone unfairly because of their sex; (b) indirect discrimination, which involves setting unjustifiable conditions that appear to apply to everyone but which, in fact, discriminate against one sex.

We identify above three levels at which this might occur – structurally, interpersonally and personally. We deal with each of these in turn.

The structural level

At a structural level the student teacher will need to plan how to ensure equality of access, uptake and outcome of the curriculum; how the curriculum content and resources not only avoid sex stereotyping but actively promote sexual emancipation; how the curriculum breaks down sex stereotyping in students. Some of this will have been undertaken before the student teacher arrives in school (e.g. the subject options that students choose, the vocational options that students follow, the work experience placement that students undertake). In practical terms this might require the student teacher to consider the possible sex bias in the curriculum content (maybe addressing this per se with the students, for example, the under-representation of women in history ('invisible women')[23] and the ascription of women to domesticity in certain historical periods or in certain geographical areas of the world or in certain faiths in religious education).

The student teacher will also need to consider, for example, whether equal numbers of women and men are portrayed in resource materials, what they are doing, where they are, what they say, how much control they have over their own lives. Clearly the student teacher needs to review materials before they are used in order to spot any sexist language, so that this issue can be tackled in the classroom. This could be taken further, where the student teacher deliberately selects resources that 'counter-teach', i.e. that raise students' awareness of sexist matters and challenge sexism, for example:

● using books, workcards and media that are written by women
● using books, workcards and media that portray women in powerful and strong roles
● using books, workcards and media that portray men in gentler roles
● using books, workcards and media that present women and men in non-traditional roles
● using books, workcards and media that raise gender issues.[24]

Delamont[25] and Spender[26] suggest that in several respects schools are more sexist than the 'real' world, segregating the sexes too rigidly (e.g. in cloakrooms, in play areas, on registers, for sports, in uniforms, on records, when lining up), steering boys and girls to different areas (thereby pre-empting future career choices),[27] offering outdated role models, failing to challenge students' own sex-role stereotypes, enforcing exaggeratedly different clothes, demeanours and language.

To counter structural gender stereotyping the student teacher may decide that it is worth attempting a topic on sex stereotyping itself,[28] and the structural causes of sexual inequality in society. The student teacher will have to consider carefully whether this is appropriate, as the handling of such sensitive issues by a relative outsider (the student who arrives at a few weeks' notice and only stays for a few weeks) may require a measure of mutual understanding, mutual confidence, mutual ease, mutual trust and mutual respect that the situation cannot guarantee.

There is continuing evidence that girls are outperforming boys in school attainment. The Department for Education and Skills[29] provided data that showed a consistent pattern across calendar years from 1999–2002 and across Key Stages 1–4 to indicate that girls were outperforming boys. For example, for 2001 students in Year 5, girls consistently outperformed boys in spelling, reading and writing (in terms of the percentage achieving levels 4 and 5 on the National Curriculum). For 2002, the results were as follows:

- At Key Stage 1 girls outperform boys in English, science and mathematics by 7 percentage points, 2 percentage points and 3 percentage points, respectively.
- At Key Stage 3 girls outperform boys in English and mathematics by 13 percentage points and 4 percentage points, respectively.
- At Key Stage 4, girls achieve 11 per cent more than boys in terms of 5+ GCSEs graded A*–C.

The Department for Children, Schools and Families now includes a gender and achievement website.[30] Government also produces an enormous amount of statistical data. One place to access some of this is at the Research and Statistics Gateway.[31] As far as the provisional data on gender in 2008 was concerned the key findings were:

Key Stage 1

At Level 2 or above:

- In all subjects a higher proportion of girls than boys reached or exceeded the expected level.
- Compared to the equivalent final 2007 figures, the overall percentages achieving Level 2 or above remained the same in all subjects.

At Level 2B or above:

- As for Level 2 or above, in all subjects a higher proportion of girls than boys achieved Level 2B or above.
- Compared to the equivalent final 2007 figures, the overall percentage achieving Level 2B or above remained the same in reading and mathematics but in writing there was a fall of 1 percentage point.

At Level 3 or above:

- A higher proportion of girls than boys achieved Level 3 or above in Speaking and Listening, Reading, and Writing, whilst a higher proportion of boys than girls achieved Level 3 or above in mathematics and science.
- Compared to the equivalent final 2007 figures, the overall percentages achieving Level 3 or above dropped by 1 percentage point in all subjects.

Key Stage 2

Key Stage 2 tests by subject are as follows:

- English 81% (85% for girls, 76% for boys)
- Reading 86% (89% for girls, 83% for boys)
- Writing 67% (74% for girls, 60% for boys)
- Mathematics 78% (78% for girls, 79% for boys)
- Science 88% (89% for girls, 87% for boys).

The percentages of pupils achieving Level 5 in the 2008 Key Stage 2 tests by subject are as follows:

- English 29% (36% for girls, 23% for boys)
- Reading 48% (54% for girls, 43% for boys)

◉ Writing 20% (25% for girls, 15% for boys)
◉ Mathematics 31% (28% for girls, 35% for boys)
◉ Science 44% (45% for girls, 43% for boys).

Key Stage 3

Key Stage 3 tests by subject are as follows:

◉ English 73% (80% for girls, 66% for boys)
◉ Reading 69% (76% for girls, 62% for boys)
◉ Writing 77% (83% for girls, 70% for boys)
◉ Mathematics 77% (77% for girls, 76% for boys)
◉ Science 71% (71% for girls, 72% for boys).

The percentages of pupils achieving Level 6 or above in the 2008 Key Stage 3 tests by subject are as follows:

◉ English 33% (41% for girls, 26% for boys)
◉ Reading 33% (41% for girls, 26% for boys)
◉ Writing 36% (44% for girls, 30% for boys)
◉ Mathematics 57% (56% for girls, 58% for boys)
◉ Science 41% (40% for girls, 42% for boys).

Girls are also shown to have greater concentration than boys even at the start of schooling.[32]

Further, there may be structural forces at work in school exclusions, where, year on year, boys are permanently excluded in proportions up to five times more than girls, and boys are more likely to be excluded from a younger age than girls.[33] Ways of working which will secure the uptake of education by boys have to be addressed.

It seems as though there may be structural factors, in addition to possibly personal factors, that may lead to the situation described here. Cultural factors have their part to play, and there is concern about 'laddishness' that causes boys to adopt a stance against learning and academic achievement. The DfES issued a 'toolkit' of ways to raise boys' achievement (Box 73).[34]

The interpersonal level

At an interpersonal level the student teacher will need to examine how teaching and learning styles, groupings and interactions can be planned that will address and break down discrimination, prejudice, harassment, verbal and physical abuse, and abuse of power. This level addresses pedagogical and organisational issues. In practical terms this might require the student teacher initially to look at the seating arrangements in the classroom (where students sit and with whom), access to resources, and access to the teacher. Serbin[35] argues that boys receive more attention even if they are not close to the teacher, whereas girls have to stay close to the teacher in order to receive attention. Stanworth[36] demonstrates that boys are likely to receive twice as much attention as girls if the teacher is a woman and ten times as much attention if the teacher is a man – reinforcing the notion of 'invisible women' mentioned above.

In terms of classroom processes the student teacher will need to consider her linguistic strategies, e.g. to whom she asks questions, the frequency with which males and females are asked questions,[37] what kinds of questions are put to males and females – for example whether males are

Box 73: A toolkit to raise boys' achievement

- Develop policies that will address the negative aspects of boy culture including bullying, name calling and sexual harassment.
- Involve pupils in policy development and review.
- Begin lessons with a clear statement of learning outcomes.
- Analyse resources for gender bias.
- Investigate preferred learning styles.
- Deliver work in time-limited, bite size chunks.
- Provide challenge, competition and short-term goals.
- Give regular positive feedback and rewards.
- Allow time for reflection and review.
- Use peer support for learning.
- Develop a whole-school seating policy.
- Regard an anti-swot culture as a major threat to equal opportunities.
- Challenge stereotypes.
- Consult pupils on a wide range of issues: curricular, extra-curricular and pastoral.
- Establish a school council.
- Provide academic mentoring in a range of ways and at various stages of school life.
- Provide counselling on the same basis, including peer counselling.
- Give pupils pastoral support roles.
- Explore teachers' understanding of issues related to boys' underachievement.
- Draw up a parents' skill register.
- Map out individual pupil assessment statistics against previous data.
- Negotiate targets with pupils individually.
- Tie targets to strategies.

Deal explicitly with gender issues in PSHE, including peer pressure and sexual harassment as well as developing personal skills such as co-operation and negotiation.

asked cognitively higher-order questions and females asked cognitively lower-order questions, whether males are asked open questions and females asked closed questions (see the discussion earlier about language in classrooms) – and how the responses are handled.[38] Moreover, the student teacher will need to ensure that she is asking equally challenging questions, offering equally challenging activities, and engaging in equally demanding instruction with males and females, i.e. differentiation by input, process and outcome (discussed in Part II). It will also mean giving equal discussion rights and opportunities to males and females (see the discussion earlier on language in classrooms).

In terms of teaching and learning strategies Arnot[39] reports that in secondary schools girls tend to be more attentive and more motivated to learn. They outperform boys on tasks that require sustained concentration and which are open-ended and process-based, which are related to realistic matters and which require that they think for themselves. However, girls are less comfortable with summative examinations preferring coursework assessment, though Arnot also suggests that the selection of syllabuses may be a factor here.

On the other hand boys take to memorisation, abstractions and facts more than girls, and are more willing to opt for quick and correct answers than for deep understanding. Further, boys outperform girls on multiple-choice questions. The point here is that offering a gender-blind curriculum may not be acceptable, as it neither suits boys nor girls entirely.

Gender is mediated by ethnicity. Arnot, for example, indicates that some Asian boys will outperform some equivalent groups of Asian girls, and white boys and girls outperform African Caribbean boys and girls. Indeed she argues that 'gender never works in isolation; it both affects and is affected by ethnic patterns of performance'.[40] She also presents evidence that gender is mediated by social-class, e.g. working-class boys and girls do less well than other groups.

The student teacher will also need to consider how she will respond to sexist incidents in the classroom, for example name-calling, physical abuse, males dominating certain activities or resources (e.g. computers, constructional[41] and building apparatus in primary schools) and females dominating other activities or resources (e.g. the home corner in the infant school).[42] Domination is not simply in terms of time spent but also in terms of the quality of teaching, learning and activity that occurs.

Moreover the student teacher will need to consider the balance of activities, for example whether males have more boisterous activities than females, whether males engage in more group activities than females (or vice versa), whether females engage in more individual activities than males (or vice versa), whether females have more sedentary and quieter activities than males.[43] In connection with this the student teacher will need to look carefully at how she plans what she will be doing, with whom she will be working (also when and for how long), what sanctions and rewards she uses and whether these are unacceptably differentiated by sex. This might extend further into the student teacher reviewing the seating and grouping arrangements, the nature of and 'responsibilities' for 'jobs' undertaken by males and females,[44] the motivational strategies that she uses for males and females, and the size and constitution of the groups in the classroom. McFarlane and Sinclair[45] provide a useful checklist that student teachers can use to sensitise themselves to gender issues in the classroom (Box 74).

The personal level

At a personal level the student teacher will need to examine how she can promote in students their self-advocacy, appropriate assertiveness and empowerment – setting their own realistic goals; raising their own expectations of themselves; taking control of their own lives; raising their own

---

Box 74: Gender in practice: a checklist

- How much time do we spend responding to disruptive behaviour by boys and girls?
- How do we evaluate the time we spend with boys and girls in the classroom?
- Do we expect girls to be quieter and better behaved?
- Do we expect boys to be more imaginative, creative and resourceful?
- Do we expect girls to be more sensible and responsible?
- Do we expect boys to be stronger and more aggressive?
- Do we expect girls to be better at language work and boys to be better at maths and science?
- Do we find ourselves commenting more on girls' physical appearance?
- Do we ever refer to children by gender groupings, e.g. 'girls line up here'?
- Are we conscious of the language we use and do we actively try and avoid sexist terms or references?
- Are all classroom jobs done by both boys and girls?
- Are boys and girls ever grouped separately for different activities? If so, what questions should we ask to review the practice?
- What behaviour do we reward and punish in boys and girls?
- How do we encourage other patterns of behaviour, for instance helping girls to participate or boys to listen?

self-esteem; knowing how to behave appropriately in a group; what is and what is not acceptable to peers; how to respond to inappropriate behaviour; how to handle sexist incidents, comments and behaviour (not necessarily on their own but with the support of others); gaining insights into how they can prepare themselves to be active and authentic citizens. This rather high-sounding agenda implies that the student teacher should attempt to develop in students a self-awareness of their own life situations through an analysis of their own backgrounds and the socio-cultural, economic and perhaps political causes of their situations. This is perhaps a high-flown way of saying that the student teacher should attempt to enable all students to reach their full potential.

The notion of furthering student empowerment – teaching students to value themselves – implies, perhaps, a negotiated approach to teaching and learning, where students take a degree of responsibility for their own learning, echoing Rogers' view that 'I know I cannot teach anyone anything. I can only provide an environment in which he [sic] can learn'.[46] This is a view that is reinforced by Brandes and Ginnis[47] in their view that learning has to be 'owned' by the student and that such ownership is a combination of possession and responsibility. Clearly some students (and indeed some student teachers) may feel uncomfortable with this notion, particularly in the context of a prescribed National Curriculum. It may be the case that a step-by-step approach to such a degree of ownership is required, particularly if this has not been the custom and practice in the class(es) that the student teacher inherits. Many students will not relish the idea of ownership as it means a degree of commitment that they may not wish to give.

The student teacher will need to consider carefully how she assesses each student; what is assessed (e.g. personality characteristics?); how a student's progress is recorded (particularly in words as words can convey hidden, stereotyped messages about teachers' expectations); how feedback is given to students; what is entered onto a Record of Achievement (e.g. whether females are 'steered' to enter different achievements from boys). What we are arguing in this section is that the framework of the curriculum, the pedagogical strategies associated with it, and assessment contained within it should be empowering and enabling rather than constraining; a ladder rather than a cage.

ETHNICITY

Immigration to Britain in the last half of the twentieth century brought about fundamental changes in our society. As the Economic and Social Research Council (ESRC) website shows,[48] at the 2001 Census, 92.1 per cent of the UK population described themselves as white (though not necessarily British). The remaining 7 per cent (4.6 million) belonged to non-white ethnic minority groups. The 2001 Census figure represented a 53 per cent growth in the minority ethnic population between 1991 and 2001 (i.e. from 3.0 million in 1991, to 4.6 million).We are now an ethnically mixed and a culturally varied nation.

The government's research and statistics gateway provides data on test and exam outcomes for ethnic minorities. The key findings in 2007–08 were:

Ethnicity
Minority ethnic groups with higher achievement than the national average include Chinese, pupils of Mixed White and Asian heritage and Indian pupils who consistently achieve above the national average across Key Stage 1, Key Stage 2 and Key Stage 4.

- For example, at Key Stage 1 mathematics, 95 per cent of Chinese pupils and 93 per cent of Mixed White and Asian heritage pupils achieved the expected level or above, compared to 90 per cent nationally. Broadly similar differences to the national figure are observed in reading and writing, with a less marked difference in science.

Minority ethnic groups with lower achievement than the national average Gypsy/Romany and Traveller of Irish Heritage pupils perform considerably below the national average across Key Stages 1, 2 and 4. However, it should be noted that very small numbers of pupils were recorded in these two categories.

- For example, at Key Stage 2, around a third of both Traveller of Irish Heritage and Gypsy/Roma pupils achieved the expected level or above in KS2 English compared to at least three quarters of all pupils on average.

All the minority ethnic groups within the Black category and pupils of Mixed White and Black Caribbean heritage are consistently below the national average across Key Stages 1, 2 and 4.

- For example, in Key Stage 2 maths, 66 per cent of pupils in the Black category achieved the expected level or above compared to 77 per cent of all pupils nationally (Table 6).

The results for these groups have generally improved across each Key Stage, resulting in most cases in a narrowing of the attainment gap in many subjects.

- For example, the gap between each of these groups and the average for all pupils has narrowed for those achieving 5+ A*–C grades at GCSE or equivalent.

Bangladeshi and Pakistani pupils perform below the national average across all Key Stages.

- For example, at Key Stage 1 Reading, 77 per cent of Pakistani pupils and 79 per cent of Bangladeshi pupils achieved the expected level compared to 84 per cent of all pupils nationally.

Bangladeshi pupils' relative attainment is closer to the national average at GCSE and equivalent, with 58.4 per cent achieving 5+ A*–C at GCSE or equivalent compared to 59.3 per cent of all pupils nationally. When looking at 5+ A*–C at GCSE or equivalent including English and mathematics, there is a gap of 4 percentage points between Bangladeshi pupils and all pupils.

Pakistani pupils' relative attainment of 5+ A*–C grades at GCSE and equivalent is 6 percentage points below the national figure, 53.0 per cent compared with 59.3 per cent, increasing to a difference of 9 percentage points from the national average when English and mathematics are included.[49]

Schools must accommodate the needs of students from many different backgrounds.[50] Whether or not schools are prepared to make sufficient changes and modifications in their organisational policies and practices to meet the needs and aspirations of all their members is a matter of current concern, for, as one study shows, many teachers appear to hold what can be described as an assimilationist viewpoint with respect to many students from minority backgrounds and their needs. (Indeed it could be argued that many schools cling to the view that there is a white majority when, for example, globally speaking there is a white minority rather than a white majority.)

The term assimilationist refers to a point of view that dominated official and educational policy in the early days of immigration in the 1960s. This sought to help immigrants accommodate to the host society by giving them a working knowledge of the English language and of the indigenous culture, and was based on the belief that once English language proficiency had been acquired, all other problems would diminish.

It is our firm belief that an assimilationist viewpoint is both condescending and dismissive of other cultures and lifestyles. All over the world minority groups now actively assert their determination to maintain cultural continuity and to preserve their religious, linguistic and cultural differences. Increasingly, therefore, the host society turned its attention to the concept of cultural pluralism. What exactly does this term imply? Simply that second and third generation (43 per cent and 95 per cent of black/Asian people respectively born in Britain)[51] British-born Sikhs, Hindus and Muslims, while sharing many of the same interests and aspirations of white students, are at the same time determined to retain their involvement in the richness of their own minority cultures. Cultural pluralism, then, implies a system that accepts and celebrates the fact that people's lifestyles and customs are different and operates so as to allow equality of opportunity for all to play a full part in society. The partner of cultural pluralism is cultural diversity.

The concept of cultural pluralism represents a decisive departure from assimilationist and integrationist viewpoints with their common focus on the perceived problems of ethnic minority pupils and their proposed remedies by way of compensating for those students' disabilities. Nevertheless, cultural pluralism has come in for strong and sustained criticism. One major objection to the cultural pluralist perspective is its almost exclusive emphasis on culture, a vague, ill-defined concept that is open to many interpretations.

Preoccupation with culture, it is said, tends to obscure or to avoid the more fundamental issues to do with race, power and prejudice, i.e. it fails to address the dynamics of culture. In other words, it fails to address questions[52] in connection with:

- the economic position of black people in relation to white people
- differences in access to resources and in power to affect events
- discrimination in employment, housing and education
- relations with the police.

A second criticism of the cultural pluralist position is that it fails to confront what is regarded as the cardinal influence on the life situations of ethnic minority groups in Britain, that is, racism. In this respect, racism is not simply prejudiced attitudes held by unenlightened white people; more fundamentally, it refers to the structural aspects of racism as manifested both in the education system and in society at large.

The cultural pluralist response is at best regarded as tokenist, at worst as little better than a form of subtle racism. Rather, an anti-racist stance exposes inequalities and discrimination in society, for example in employment, in housing, in education, in careers, in 'life chances' and in income, and argues that positive discrimination is required to redress the structural inequalities and discrimination in society. The focus is also on countering discrimination and institutional racism at a structural level. In educational terms this argues for the need to raise equality, inequality, discrimination and racism per se as issues for students to study in school, directly teaching about these matters, fostering anti-racist attitudes and teaching about anti-discrimination. Negative discrimination can take many forms,[53] for example:

- illegitimately regarding others as inferior
- treating people, on racial grounds (e.g. race, colour, nationality, ethnic origin), less favourably than others
- restricting opportunities to certain sections of the community or society
- exclusive or near-exclusive focus on a particular ethnic group (i.e. avoiding the practice of

inclusiveness that values everybody's ethnic and cultural background)
● adopting an ethnocentric (often a European or nationalistic) view of society and culture
● uncritically accepting the views of one culture or group alone
● holding prejudiced views of others
● acting prejudicially.

The Race Relations Acts of 1976 and the Race Relations Act (Amendment) of 2000 make it unlawful to discriminate against anyone on grounds of race, colour, nationality (including citizenship), or ethnic or national origins. Direct discrimination occurs when someone is treated less favourably than others on grounds of race. Similarly racial abuse and harassment constitute unlawful direct discrimination. Indirect discrimination occurs when a condition or requirement is applied equally to people of all racial groups but fewer people from a particular group are able to comply with it.

The debate on multicultural education has shifted considerably during the last few years and is now beginning to reflect greater concern for the role that education can play in countering the pernicious effects of racism both within schools and in society at large. All teachers have a vital role to play in the responsible task of preparing all students for life in multiracial Britain.

The Qualifications and Curriculum Authority[54] made it clear that 'stereotypes, prejudice and discrimination are often as implicit as they are explicit'. If an open and understanding society is to be promoted, diversity must be valued and racism must be challenged, and that means raising awareness of these issues in students' and teachers' minds and behaviour. Guidance was provided by the QCA in their Respect for All website, material which was integrated in the National Curriculum in 2010. The guidance included the following areas:

● background to Respect for All
● Respect for All ethos
● the National Curriculum inclusion statement
● meeting the statutory requirements
● Ofsted guidance
● school and teacher perspectives (2001)
● subject case studies
● resources
● Respect for All audit tool kit
● how to get involved.

Indeed, the Qualifications and Curriculum Authority specifically identified, for each National Curriculum subject, how lesson planning, class management and learning activities can be addressed in order to integrate mutual understanding and positive action straightforwardly into programmes of learning. Such examples include:

● for design and technology, work on fruit and vegetables, at Key Stage 1
● for design and technology, masks and batik work, at Key Stage 2
● for English, resolving conflicts (drama work), at Key Stage 2
● for English, Anne Frank's diary, at Key Stage 3
● for history, 'who are the British?', at Key Stage 3
● for ICT, 'who are immigrants?', at Key Stage 3
● for physical education, challenging stereotypes in football, at Key Stages 2 to 4
● for religious education, white swans and black swans, at Key Stage 3.

For example, in ICT, students are taught to find, select and manipulate information that is appropriate for their work; to use the internet to access information that reflects diverse opinions and cultural representations; to challenge stereotypes and narrow-minded perspectives; to be discriminating in their use of information, questioning the plausibility and value of the information that they retrieve, identifying bias and prejudice in information; and to be sensitive to the interests, needs and cultural diversity of all.[55]

Respect for all requires all students, regardless of their cultural heritage, to value cultural diversity and to challenge racism. The Qualifications and Curriculum Authority[56] commented that, whilst schools had been adopting multicultural or anti-racist policies, current practice deals with the strengths and weaknesses of both approaches in an approach termed 'critical multiculturalism'. This term regards multiculturalism and anti-racism not in opposition to each other, but as connected. It recognises that there are different kinds and forms of racism in society (e.g. institutional racism, cultural racism), and that both multiculturalism and anti-racism can be used to tackle these problems where they occur.

Critical multiculturalism identifies the limitations of each approach (multiculturalism and anti-racism) where they apply to education. For example, it criticises multicultural education for reducing the representation of black and minority ethnic cultures to stereotyped customs, traditions and artefacts that are associated with their country of origin (e.g. steel bands in the Caribbean, and samosas in Indian culture). These, it argues, are reductionist for students living in the present-day UK.

Further, it was argued that multicultural and anti-racist education were either only for non white students or students from ethnic minorities. Not only does this fail to address the issue that multiculturalism and anti-racism apply everywhere and to everyone, but it overlooks white immigrants and the white cultural diversity that has existed in Britain for centuries (e.g. with Irish, European, Welsh, Scottish). It argues that 'ethnic problems' are not confined to non-white groups or to immigrants but they exist everywhere in the UK (e.g. in the streets of Northern Ireland, the working-class areas of Manchester, the varied communities in the East End of London, and so on); it is not only a matter of skin colour. For some time it had been held that multiculturalism and anti-racist education were only applicable in schools with a largely non-white population; now they are seen to apply to all schools – indeed they are a very pressing concern in all-white schools.[57] Russell Jones' research carried out with two teacher training institutions linked with some schools with all white pupils developed 'a typology of disappearance', which illustrated the ways in which tutors, teachers, and/or students revealed questionable ideas.[58] The quotes are things that participants in the research said but the commentary that follows them is our own:

- 'We do not have a problem here because we have no black children here.'
  Assumes that black children are a 'problem'. Suggests that it is not necessary to think about equal opportunities if you have an all white class.
- 'The child is not black because I refuse to see colour as an issue. All people are exactly the same in my eyes and I treat them as such.'
  Do we all eat the same foods; have the same religion; wear the same kinds of clothes; speak the same languages when at home and in the community? The colour-blind approach. White British teachers like this treat all children the same on the basis of their own, sometimes limited, experience. If you are a black person then colour really is an issue that white teachers need to understand and be sensitive to.
- 'I know he is being abused by the other children but this is not because he is black. It is because he is a right little swine'.
  Unprofessional language to use about a child. Would this teacher really know if it was racist abuse?

- 'Recognising ethnic identity in the classroom is pandering to the politically correct, and teaching black children should just be a matter of common sense.'
  The use of the term 'political correctness' (mainly by the media) is a cynical ploy to demean the importance of equal opportunities strategies.
- 'He is not really black but he does have coloured skin.'
  Fails to understand that 'black' is a political categorisation not a literal description of colour. Terms such as British Asian; British African, etc. are more accurate.

The National Curriculum had enacted a colour-blind policy in the face of a multicultural society, a policy which was called into question following the murder of the black teenager Stephen Lawrence.[59] The recommendations of the Stephen Lawrence inquiry pressed the government to install a National Curriculum that was aimed at valuing cultural diversity, preventing racism, and challenging stereotypes.

A response to this was a series of reforms to the curriculum by the Qualifications and Curriculum Authority in which respect for all, cultural diversity and challenging racism are high on the agenda, and the straitjacket of eurocentrism is released.[60] Indeed the curriculum must equip students with the skills to pre-empt and challenge racism.[61] The issue here is that students' curricula must move beyond simply understanding stereotypes, racism, bullying, discrimination, harassment and multiculturalism to exercising rights, responsibilities and roles in a multicultural society, including challenging and pre-empting racism, discrimination, stereotyping and harassment.[62]

A curriculum for cultural diversity

Jeffcoate[63] defines a suitable curriculum as one in which choice of content reflects the cultural diversity of British society and the world and draws significantly on the experiences of British ethnic minorities and cultures overseas. He justifies such a curriculum for the following reasons. First, there is what Jeffcoate calls a 'pathological' justification for developing a curriculum arising out of the pernicious and pervasive racism in British society. Schools, Jeffcoate believes, have a clear duty to make a concerted response to the evil of racism by promoting racial and ethnic self-respect and interracial understanding. Second, such a curriculum can be justified on the notion of minority group rights. That is to say, ethnic minorities are entitled to expect that their cultures will be positively and prominently represented in the school curriculum. Third, if it is a fundamental task of the school to present an accurate picture of society to its pupils then it follows that other races and cultures are important elements in that picture. Fourth, a cultural diversity curriculum involves pupils in more interesting, stimulating and challenging experiences than one which is not.

Having set out a justification for a suitable curriculum, how does one go about selecting learning experiences that might be incorporated within it? As with the issue of gender in the previous section, we argue that decisions for teaching can be made at three levels – the structural, the interpersonal and the personal.

The structural level

We suggest that at the structural level the student teacher will need to plan (i) how equality of access, uptake and outcome of the curriculum will be ensured; (ii) how the curriculum content and resources will not only avoid racial and ethnic stereotyping but actively promote emancipation of all groups and cultures in a culturally diverse society; (iii) how the curriculum will break down racial and ethnic stereotyping in students. For example, we need to question why African Caribbean,

Bangladeshi and Pakistani boys underperform in schools, asking whether the curriculum that is prescribed is one with which they cannot identify and engage.

One approach is to construct a learning programme around regular themes drawing on a variety of cultures for source materials with which all pupils can identify.[64] That said, there is still the need for some kind of overt, systematic study since themes of themselves cannot provide pupils with an appreciative understanding of the logic and integrity of a way of life different from their own. The humanities curriculum should divide its attention evenly between local and international studies, these serving to complement one another in the process whereby children make sense of their world. One can add to this the suggestion that positive role models from members of all ethnic groups should be incorporated into the curriculum, taking examples of the achievements of all ethnic and racial groups, i.e. 'counter-teaching'.

Having decided to incorporate minority cultures into their curricula, schools should avoid defining these cultures solely in terms of patterns of life and experience in countries and continents of origin. It may be far more pertinent for children to look at these minority cultures as they are currently evolving and taking shape here in Britain.[65] The curriculum involves a change in perspective as well as a change in content, an end, in effect, to ethnocentrism and eurocentrism which views other cultures in a disparaging, or at best condescending way.

In respect of the latter point McFarlane[66] exposes the bias in many non-fiction and textbooks about other countries and cultures. The writers argue, for example, that famine is seen as unavoidable; that reliance of the third world on the first world replaces self-help and the questioning of the legitimacy of the developed countries' exploitation of developing countries, i.e. where a climate and culture of dependency is legitimated. The writers go on to suggest that many text books regard the local culture as somehow 'deficient', 'defective', possibly corrupt and not measuring up to the standards of the west. These books communicate hidden messages about an inevitability of power and wealth differentials that go unquestioned, i.e. where an ethnocentric (and eurocentric) set of criteria is used to judge other cultures and societies.

Curriculum content, therefore, needs to ensure that not only does it draw on a diversity of cultures but that it fairly represents these cultures in their own terms, i.e. adopting an anthropological view. An anthropological view defines culture non-judgmentally. For example, Tylor[67] saw culture as 'that complex whole which includes knowledge, belief, art, morals, law, custom, and any other capabilities and habits acquired by [a person] as a member of society'; Linton[68] defined culture as 'the sum total of the knowledge, attitudes and habitual behaviour patterns shared and communicated by the members of a particular society'.

Clearly the approach concentrates on how respect for self and for others should be the cornerstone of a non-prejudiced society (but only from the point of view of the dominant community, notes Gundura).[69] Gundura has criticised such an approach for its essentially neutral stance. He points to a lack of stress on socio-political aspects of multicultural education and cites a typology for the multicultural curriculum which includes, inter alia, a socio-political perspective which asserts that what passes for knowledge is no more than the dominant ideology of a particular society. There is a need for a multicultural curriculum which challenges the value consensus in British society and thereby leaves open the possibility of a diverse society consisting of relatively separate but equal groups with equal rights and, importantly, equal powers and representation. Such an approach might focus upon the history and the literature of this country, using historical experiences and literary responses as a key to understanding the effects of colonialism upon our society. One can further suggest that a multicultural curriculum should teach about race relations and should explore the reasons for migration, government legislation and other controversial issues.

Saunders[70] suggests ways of helping students explore the cultural diversity existing in classrooms, including similarity and difference, individual differences, identity, derivation of names, culturally important categories, and who is ideal.

The former National Curriculum Council[71] argued for the need to study the origins and effects of racial prejudice in Britain and other societies. In fact this echoed the view of the Swann Report which argued that there was a need for all students to understand how racism can operate so that they can influence and be part of positive changes in society in order to reflect more fully the values of a pluralist society. This implies very strongly that multicultural and anti-racist education is not simply the task of teachers in schools that draw on ethnically diverse communities (or, for example, that draw largely on only Asian or African Caribbean or Arabic communities), but it is a task for all-white schools. Britain is a multicultural and multi-ethnic society; we regard it as a dereliction of duty if students in all-white areas are denied access to knowledge of and preparation for member-ship and practices of these diverse communities. This has implications for the images and texts that are used with all children. Materials should reflect the multi-cultural and multi-ethnic diversity of the UK and the rest of the world.[72]

Hence we suggest that the student teacher may decide to attempt a topic on racism itself and the structural, interpersonal and personal causes of this. However, just as we advocated some caution in handling issues of sex stereotyping, the student teacher will have to consider carefully whether planning a topic per se on racism is entirely appropriate, as the handling of this sensitive issue by a newcomer (and the comparatively short time that the student stays in the school) may make it difficult for the establishment of a degree of mutual trust, respect, understanding and confidence that are often the critical factors in making for the success of handling sensitive issues.

Lest we think that structural racism is not still with us, it appears that there may be structural forces at work in school exclusions, where, year on year, black Caribbean students were perma-nently excluded in proportions up to four times more than white students in 1999/2000 and up to three times more than white students in 2000/ 01, and 93 per cent of permanently excluded Asian students were boys, whilst only 7 per cent of permanently excluded Asian students were girls. Of course, it may reflect the true incidence of challenging behaviour, though the statistics are unset-tling. What are schools, society and culture doing to create such disparities?[73]

The interpersonal level

The interpersonal level concerns pedagogy. The student teacher will need to be able to draw on the experiences of students from a variety of backgrounds, to have high expectations of all students, developing high standards of achievement in all students. In particular – and this is not exclusive to teaching for ethnic diversity – the student teacher will need to consider how she can promote moti-vation, self-esteem, confidence and tolerance in students (see below: the personal level) and how mutual trust and respect can be built up in relationships between students and student teachers. Further, the Runnymede Trust[74] raises the concern that teachers themselves will need further devel-opment in pedagogies that have been identified as being successful with black and minority ethnic students.

The development of interpersonal trust, tolerance and respect has implications for the use of workshop approaches, group work and peer group learning. The student teacher will need to consider, for example, the ethnic and cultural constitution of each group as well as the ethnic and cultural content of the knowledge on which the students are working. The use of discussion-based activities can explore different aspects of the communities and cultures from which students are drawn and, in so doing, can foster tolerance, mutual respect and co-operation amongst students from diverse backgrounds.

Further, the attention to pedagogy will require the student teacher to consider the languages, dialect, accent, oral and written traditions of the students in exploring the communities from which they are drawn. This might be approached through oral and written media, discussions and drama. The Runnymede Trust[75] suggests that some practical activities can be designed so that students' learning does not depend solely on their abilities in English. The use of English can be furthered through the use of support teachers and adults who are able to work in community languages as well as English. Indeed multilingual children should have the opportunity to learn concepts in their first language as well as learning them in their second or third language. Small group learning of English can be an effective strategy also.

In England, 686,000 pupils are recorded as having a mother tongue other than English. More than 200 languages are spoken in the homes of children attending school. All bilingual or English as an Additional Language (EAL) learners are currently expected to follow the statutory National Curriculum in age-appropriate classes and teachers are expected to see EAL development as part of the overall learning needs of individual pupils. There are two relevant definitions of bilingualism here:

1   Infant or early bilingual acquisition involves the child learning two languages virtually simultaneously from the outset.

2   Child bilingual acquisition involves the successive acquisition of two languages, perhaps as a result of the family moving to another country or the child starting school where he/she is taught in a different language from the one used at home.[76]

A large-scale study of emergent bilingual pupils in America clearly showed the importance of supporting all pupils' languages:

> Non-English speaking student success in learning to read in English does not rest exclusively on primary language input and development, nor is it solely the result of rapid acquisition of English. Both apparently contribute to students' subsequent English reading achievement … early literacy experiences support subsequent literacy development, regardless of language; time spent on literacy activity in the native language – whether it takes place at home or at school – is not time lost with respect to English reading acquisition[77]

The potential of linguistic diversity in the multilingual classroom can easily be overlooked by those who insist on the exclusive use of English in their language work. Multilingual children are experts in handling language and in many ways could be more proficient than the teacher. As such, these children have considerable language skills on which the teacher can build, and they are likely to have much to offer others, particularly with regards to the subject of language study. Having said this, even if the child may be skilled in language use, he or she will still need particular support and guidance to develop greater proficiency in the use of English at school.

The language development of multilingual children often highlights a considerable gulf between the rate of oral language acquisition and the equivalent in reading and writing. In a study carried out with 2,300 11-year-olds in London, Strand (2005) found that 'EAL pupils at the early stages (1–3) of developing fluency had significantly lower KS2 test scores in all subjects than their monolingual peers. However, EAL pupils who were fully fluent in English achieved significantly higher scores in all KS2 tests than their monolingual peers' (p. 275). Consequently, the beginning teacher needs to be aware of the need to apply greater sensitivity to these children; on the one hand the child should be encouraged to use spoken English at every possible opportunity; on the other, the teacher needs to employ teaching strategies that ensure that the same child does not begin to lose confidence in their language use because they perceive themselves as failed readers and writers.

Haslam, Wilkin and Kellet[78] suggest the following strategies to support multilingual children:

- Give extra support to children who are new to the school.
- Find out about the children in your class/school: Pronunciation of names; place of birth; place of parents' birth; language background – spoken and written; religion if any.
- Show interest in learning about the different cultures including learning simple phrases from the language.
- Be sensitive to differences in cultural attitudes. For example Muslims do not eat pork and see the pig as distasteful.
- Use dual language resources: books; signs; displays, etc.
- Examine all resources for cultural bias and discrimination. Use resources which represent the different cultures: e.g. dolls and puppets in the early years.
- Don't confuse the child's development of the English language with their intelligence.
- Community languages and English need to develop together. Do not insist that children only use English at school. Bilingual children have greater levels of knowledge about language because they can compare their different languages.
- Children who are new to English have a 'quiet' phase where they listen more than talk.
- Understanding is usually far ahead of ability to talk in a new language.
- Encourage the use of community languages during lessons. Use collaborative activities which encourage speaking and listening.
- Group children who speak the same language together.
- Plan for hands-on activities which use visual resources such as photos and objects. Introduce activities orally as opposed to using worksheet.
- Occasionally use activities which specifically focus on multicultural issues. E.g. look at different scripts and number systems; use stories from different cultures, etc.
- Involve all children in understanding more about the different cultures represented by the class.
- Remember the importance of whole language experiences.
- Involve ethnic minority parents and the community in the life of the classroom/school. Create your own dual language books with help from parents.
- Take action over racist incidents – take advice from a knowledgeable and sensitive colleague. Do not ignore the issue.
- Treat all children as individuals; remember the inadequacy of stereotypes.

The issue of pedagogy also requires attention to the learning environment that teachers and students create. For example, it means that classroom displays (a) reflect cultural diversity, (b) break down stereotyping, and (c) promote positive role models in relation to cultural identity and ethnicity. At a practical level it will mean that several community languages and scripts might be represented in the displayed materials.

The National Curriculum places emphasis on the links between schools and the community. In planning for these aspects of the National Curriculum a prime opportunity is afforded for the student teacher to involve a diversity of community representatives, both by taking students out into the community and bringing people from the community into the school. The opportunity for members of the community to discuss with students several aspects of their community is one which is too good to neglect. This is not confined to schools that draw on a diverse catchment area; it applies also to all-white schools; indeed it could be argued that it is more important that all-white schools should become involved in finding out about other communities. Some all-white schools,[79] for example, run exchanges with schools whose students are drawn from culturally and ethnically diverse backgrounds.

As with sexist comments and incidents, discussed in the previous section, the student teacher will need to consider how she will respond to racist, discriminatory and prejudiced comments and incidents within and outside the classroom (e.g. verbal and physical abuse and bullying, name-calling, antagonistic remarks). As all schools should have a policy on equal opportunities it may be useful for the student teacher to examine these policies and to take other steps in order to find out what the strategies are that the school employs to deal with racist language, assumptions, behaviour and incidents.

The personal level

At a personal level the student teacher will need to plan how to ensure that all students, regardless of ethnicity, develop self-confidence, self-esteem and tolerance. Indeed the Runnymede Trust[80] suggests that all students should become confident and self-affirming rather than insecure and ashamed of their culture; they should develop an openness to change and a willingness to listen to and learn from others. The student teacher has a significant role to play in this during teaching practice as she will be the planner and provider of opportunities for students to experience success, to have a sense of personal achievement and to value their own communities and traditions. The student teacher, as the provider of opportunities, experiences and feedback on achievement, shares the important responsibility with other teachers in the school of ensuring that each student fulfils her or his own potentials and ambitions, and develops as a responsible member of a democratic society.

Hence the student teacher will need to plan opportunities for students to develop autonomy and personal worth; to resist being stereotyped and stereotyping others; to believe in their own capabilities; to learn how to handle racist comments, incidents and behaviour (not necessarily by themselves but with the support of others); to gain insights into how to work towards countering racism in its several forms; to be able to stand up for themselves; and to appreciate the value of community and cultural solidarity.

Because the issues of ethnicity and multicultural education are contentious, the student teacher will find it essential to discuss her planning and experiences with the class teacher or mentor in the school. This not only ensures that the student teacher is operating within the parameters of the school but that she has addressed the sensitivities involved in dealing with these delicate issues.

SPECIAL EDUCATIONAL NEEDS

Introduction

We regard as self-evident and incontestable the view that students with special educational needs should receive as broad and balanced an entitlement curriculum as any other students, and the same degree of choice and consultation about options as any other students (rather than, for instance, a stripped down narrow diet of 'basics', programmed reading, repetitive teaching styles and simple job training).[81] The National Curriculum should be taught to as many students as possible in ways appropriate to their abilities. Moreover, the Office for Standards in Education in a series of publications in 1995[82] made explicit its view that schools should ensure that:

- provision for special educational needs permeates the school's organisation and curricular structures and the practice in the school
- all staff work closely with the special educational needs co-ordinator
- parents know who is their main point of contact (normally the special educational needs co-ordinator) and who is the school's 'responsible person'

- resources, including staffing, are managed effectively and efficiently to support special educational needs policies and pupils' identified needs
- all staff are sufficiently aware of procedures for identifying, assessing and providing for pupils with special educational needs
- pupils' progress is monitored, especially in relation to annual reviews and individual education plans
- assessment, recording and reporting satisfy statutory requirements
- the use of specialist support from outside agencies is well managed within the school.

The Special Educational Needs and Disability Act 2001[83] makes it clear that it is unlawful for the body responsible for a school to discriminate against a disabled person:

(a) in the arrangements it makes for determining admission to the school as a pupil
(b) in the terms on which it offers to admit him to the school as a pupil; or
(c) by refusing or deliberately omitting to accept an application for his admission to the school as a pupil.

It is unlawful for the body responsible for a school to discriminate against a disabled pupil in the education or associated services provided for, or offered to, pupils at the school by that body...It is unlawful for the body responsible for a school to discriminate against a disabled pupil by excluding him from the school, whether permanently or temporarily.

For the purposes of the Act, a responsible body discriminates against a disabled person if:

(a) for a reason which relates to his disability, it treats him less favourably than it treats or would treat others to whom that reason does not or would not apply, and
(b) it cannot show that the treatment in question is justified.

Unjustified discrimination is outlawed. Yet, despite this, the levels of exclusions for pupils with a statement of special educational needs is extremely high, see Chapter 1. It seems that structural and unconscious discrimination may still be occurring.

A student teaching on teacher practice must take responsibility for finding out:

- how students with special educational needs are identified and assessed
- how provision for students' special educational needs is addressed and managed
- who is the special educational needs co-ordinator and 'responsible person'
- what resources are available to support students with special educational needs (e.g. materials, teaching and ancillary staff, specialist support)
- which students have a statement of special educational needs
- what the students' needs and difficulties are
- how recording and reporting is addressed for students with special educational needs
- how progress is planned and monitored for students with special educational needs.

Proper provision is not cheap; indeed the Audit Commission[84] found that up to 15 per cent of the education budget could be accounted for in special needs provision.

The Department for Education and Skills[85] defines special educational needs thus:

A child is defined as having special educational needs if he or she has a learning difficulty which needs special teaching. A learning difficulty means that the child has significantly greater difficulty in learning than most children of the same age. Or, it means that a child has a disability which needs different educational facilities from those that schools generally provide for children of the same age in the area.

The children who need special educational provision are not only those with obvious learning difficulties, such as those who are physically disabled, deaf or blind. They include those whose learning difficulties are less apparent, such as slow learners and emotionally vulnerable children. It is estimated that up to 20 per cent of school children may need special educational help at some stage in their school careers.

The revised Special Educational Needs Code of Practice defines special educational needs thus:[86]

Children have special educational needs if they have a learning difficulty which calls for special educational provision to be made for them. Children have a learning difficulty if they:

(a) have a significantly greater difficulty in learning than the majority of children of the same age; or

(b) have a disability which prevents or hinders them from making use of educational facilities of a kind generally provided for children of the same age in schools within the area of the local education authority; or

(c) are under the age of compulsory school age and fall within the definition at (a) or (b) above or would do so if special educational provision was not made for them.

Children must not be regarded as having a learning difficulty solely because the language or form of language of their home is different from the language in which they will be taught.

Croll and Moses[87] report that learning difficulties, as perceived by teachers, were seen as 'all-round difficulties', and comprised general learning difficulties, such as dyslexia, and specific learning difficulties such as reading, spelling, writing, mathematics, speech and language, and under-achievement. They also describe physical health, visual and hearing difficulties. Their study is important in that it shows that the categories of special educational need are mediated by gender and ethnicity.

The Children Act of 1989 indicates that 'a child is disabled if he is blind, deaf or dumb or suffers from a mental disorder of any kind or is substantially and permanently handicapped by illness, injury or congenital deformity or such other disability as may be prescribed',[88] and the Disability Discrimination Act of 1995 indicates that 'a person has a disability for the purposes of the Act if he has a physical or mental impairment which has a substantial and long-term adverse effect on his ability to carry out normal day-to-day activities'.[89]

Fundamental to the Code of Practice[90] are five principles:

1   Children with special educational needs should have their needs met.
2   The special educational needs of children will normally be met in mainstream schools or settings.
3   The views of the child should be sought and taken into account.
4   Parents have a vital role to play in supporting their child's education.
5   Children with special educational needs should be offered full access to a broad, balanced and relevant curriculum, including an appropriate curriculum for the Foundation Stage and the National Curriculum.

Supporting the view that equal opportunities should be provided for all students has certain corollaries for students with special educational needs. For example, equality of access to a wide curriculum will be a challenging task for many students and teachers.[91]

One of the most startling statistics to emerge from the Warnock Committee's celebrated and watershed report is that at some time during their school career one in five children will require some form of special educational provision. Clearly, the Warnock Committee has widened the definition of special education to include students needing relatively mild educational support, and it follows that special provision for this proportion of the school population means provision in ordinary schools as well as special schools. Research[92] surveyed by the Committee revealed that childhood disabilities giving rise to special educational needs are found in a much larger proportion of the school population than has commonly been assumed. One of the conclusions of the report, therefore, is that the tendency to equate special education with special schooling is inappropriate, given the large number of children with special educational needs in ordinary schools. Indeed the notion of special educational needs itself should avoid a 'deficiency' or 'pathology' view that confines itself to students with learning difficulties and consider, for example, the special needs and backgrounds of students:

◉ who are able and gifted
◉ with linguistic diversity
◉ with ethnic and cultural diversity
◉ with specific learning needs
◉ with short-term emotional and behavioural difficulties.[93]

We shall also consider later the gifted and talented. It is probable that many very capable students deliberately underachieve in order not to stand out as being too different from their peers. The Code of Practice 2001 regards any student as having a special educational need if any special educational provision is necessary. This includes students with special educational needs in relation to:

◉ academic attainment
◉ learning difficulties
◉ specific learning difficulties (e.g. dyslexia)
◉ emotional and behavioural difficulties
◉ physical disabilities
◉ sensory impairment (e.g. hearing or visual difficulties)
◉ speech and language difficulties
◉ medical conditions.

One must be cautious, of course, in labelling students as this can lead to the problem of teachers having low expectations of students that we mentioned earlier. It could be argued, for instance, that category labels should be replaced by an engagement with the quality of the educational experience that students have, as this recognises the complexity of the issue and the need to act positively.

What does all of this mean for the student teacher? Simply this. A student teacher in a mixed-ability class of 30 in an ordinary school should be aware that as many as six students might require some form of special provision at some time, and about four or five students will need special provision at any given time. Such students, the Warnock Report refers to as children with learning difficulties, a term it recommends should be employed to embrace students with emotional and behavioural difficulties and those receiving educational support from specialist teachers.

While special schools will continue to be providers of special education for students with severe or complex physical, sensory or intellectual difficulties, those with behavioural or emotional disorders that are so extreme that they disrupt ordinary school classes, and those with less severe difficulties who even with special help do not perform well in ordinary schools, it follows that the task of recognising early signs of possible special educational need and, where appropriate, coping with them in ordinary classrooms, will increasingly be the responsibility of teachers in ordinary schools. Indeed, the Code of Practice[94] is unequivocal in stating that 'for the vast majority of children their mainstream setting will meet all their special educational needs...A very small minority of children will have SEN of a severity or complexity that requires the LEA to determine and arrange the special educational provision their learning difficulties call for.'

Is this really feasible, readers may well ask? The answer suggested by the findings of a three-year study[95] is a resounding yes. To a far greater extent than is currently practised, the authors conclude, special educational needs can be met in ordinary schools, providing, or course, that there are the requisite commitment and resources. Hegarty, Pocklington and Lucas[96] undertook a detailed examination of 17 integration programmes in 14 LEAs, the programmes themselves varying enormously in terms of the types of special needs that were catered for and in respect of the ages and the numbers of students involved. The range and the scope of the investigation covered: developmentally delayed, communication disordered, visually impaired, hearing impaired, physically impaired and special educational needs, with needs being met by links between special schools and mainstream schools, special centres, and individual programmes for integration.

What the study clearly revealed was that integrating students with special needs into mainstream schools requires new ways of working on the part of the various professionals involved. There is, the researchers report, a need to collaborate with colleagues, share information, view students' problems in a comprehensive light, disseminate skills and generally move toward interdisciplinary and collaborative, collegial working. This is very difficult to achieve in light of such obstacles as territoriality and traditions of isolated professionalism among teachers.

In the primary sector Croll and Moses[97] found that 69.4 per cent of teachers thought that special schools were needed for students with emotional and behavioural difficulties, 58.2 per cent thought that special schools were needed for students with severe learning difficulties, 20.4 per cent thought that special schools were needed for students with physical difficulties, and 2.4 per cent thought that special schools were needed for students with sensory difficulties. Indeed this study reported that 98.3 per cent of teachers thought that there was a continuing role for special schools, with 33.3 per cent of them thinking that more, rather than fewer, students should attend special schools. The same study reported[98] that 52.2 per cent of teachers thought home and family were the main cause of students' emotional and behavioural difficulties, more than ten times the number voting for any other category except for the residual category of 'don't know' from a list of nine provided categories.

That said, the UK government is clear in its statutory guidance on inclusive schooling[99] that mainstream education is the aim for students with special educational needs.

The curriculum and education programmes

Moves towards inclusion, and moves against negative labelling and stigmatisation, have placed integration and inclusion as central issues in schools. At one pole of the debate are those who argue that a child's special needs are best catered for in special, non-mainstream schools or units,[100] as the special facilities, smaller classes and removal from an environment in which they may already have failed might be beneficial for them. They maintain that children's self-esteem is more likely to be promoted in such environments than in mainstream schools and that they can experience success in such environments rather than failure in mainstream education (i.e. that segregation protects them and fits their all-round needs well). Indeed it is argued[101] that mainstream schools simply do not have adequate material and human resources to be able to cope with children with special educational needs. At the other pole of the debate are those who argue that segregation leads to stigmatisation, negative labelling, a lack of academic press in such children's education, lack of higher-order think-ing and skills, and social isolation from their peers, lack of access to the stimulation of high achievers, and little direct teaching. That said, there is evidence of increased mainstreaming and reduced segregation over a 20-year period until 2000.[102]

A compromise position argues that children with special needs can, and should, be part of mainstream education, with withdrawal from classrooms for some time each day to follow lessons in special classrooms or units, or to receive specific attention in smaller classes, though such a compromise has been contested, arguing that the lack of co-ordination between the work done in such withdrawal classes and the work done in the mainstream class leads to the special needs child missing important parts of the curriculum.[103]

The evidence about whether children with special needs in mainstream classes achieved as well as their peers, or whether children with special needs achieved as well as their peers in 'pull-out' programmes (withdrawal during the day, whilst maintaining mainstream education) is somewhat equivocal.[104] That said, there is a slight indication of the positive effects of mainstream-ing in comparison to full-time or part-time placement in special units. Of course, the success of any of these programmes is frequently a function of the resources and the expertise available, be it in mainstream or withdrawal units, and of the nature and degree of disability. What is clear here is that the debate operates at more than one level, for example the levels of values (e.g. of inclusion) as well as empirically (whether integration works).

Reynolds and Muijs[105] argue that, for inclusion to be successful, several conditions have to be ensured, for example:

- The students in the class have to be prepared to accept the disabled student and must under-stand the needs of the student.
- The teacher must believe that the student can succeed in the inclusive classroom.
- The classroom and resources must be prepared and must be adequate.
- Staff must be properly prepared and capable in order to be able to work with the student.
- There must be good communication between all involved parties.

What of the curriculum in such programmes of integration? What is actually being offered to students with special needs in ordinary schools? The study revealed considerable diversity in prac-tice. Wade and Moore[106] suggest that the range of special educational provision can be conceived of as a continuum ranging from segregated special schooling to full attendance in a normal class, different forms of provision being seen as different points along the continuum. They argue that one can move from total segregation to locational, social, curricular and pedagogic integration that moves towards functional integration where all aspects of the development of students with special needs are both catered for and built into mainstream education, e.g. social, emotional, physical as well as academic and intellectual needs. Hegarty *et al.*[107] found a broad consensus among teachers, parents and the students themselves that students with special needs benefit greatly from being placed in integration programmes. There were gains in self-confidence and independence, and in the realistic acceptance of an individual's challenging condition. Friendly relationships between students with special needs and their peers did occur but they tended to be limited and often involved outgroups in the school. Negative relationships such as teasing were reported to be comparatively rare. Particularly encouraging was the teachers' thoroughgoing endorsement of the integration programme in their schools.

How does this impact on the work of the student teacher? As with the discussions of sex and ethnicity earlier, we organise our suggestions into three levels, the structural, interpersonal and personal.

The structural level

At a structural level the student teacher will need to consult with the teachers and the school mentor in order to find out which students have special educational needs (and which students are 'statemented' (i.e. have a formal – legal – statement of their needs and proposals for how these are to be met), which are in the process of being statemented,[108] and which students may have special needs though they are not statemented. Further, the student teacher will need to find out what the needs and difficulties are of the students in question and how they are being addressed (i.e. to find out about how equality of access and uptake are addressed). This latter will include where and how support staff are used (and when, e.g. twice a week on a withdrawal basis, three days a week with a support teacher working alongside the class teacher in the class with all of the other students etc.), details of special resources and equipment available, and particulars of individualised education plans (IEPs).

An individual education plan, a requirement of the Code of Practice, is a document, frequently drawn up each term for a student, indicating:

- the short-term, specific targets (perhaps cast in terms of SMART objectives: specific, measurable, achievable, realistic and with set time scales),[109] comprising no more than around four, set for, or by, the child
- teaching strategies
- resources and provision
- when the plan is to be reviewed,
- including success criteria, exit criteria and evidence
- outcomes (to be recorded when the IEP is reviewed).

Target setting is in accordance with the view that students with statements of special educational needs can have targets set under the 'P scales'.[110]

Under the Code of Practice each school must keep a special needs register, which indicates all the children who are subject to a formal statement of special educational needs, and what stage of the formal process each has reached.

The Special Educational Needs Co-ordinator (SENCO) in the school, a member of the teaching staff, is an important figure, and the student teacher should expect to meet her/him, to discuss specific students, their formal requirements, statement, and provision, and the implications of these for teaching the student in question during teaching practice. The Code of Practice states that the SENCO has responsibility for:[111]

- ensuring liaison with parents and other professionals in respect of children with special educational needs
- advising and supporting other practitioners in the setting
- ensuring that appropriate Individual Education Plans are in place
- ensuring that the relevant background information about individual children with special educational needs is collected, recorded and updated.

At the primary phase the SENCO and the class teacher should:[112]

- use information arising from the child's previous educational experience to provide starting points for the development of an appropriate curriculum for the child
- identify and focus attention on the child's skills and highlight areas for early action to support the child within the class

- use the curricular and baseline assessment processes to allow the child to show what they know, understand and can do, as well as to identify any learning difficulties
- ensure that ongoing observation and assessment provide regular feedback to teachers and parents about the child's achievements and experiences and that the outcomes of such assessment form the basis for planning the next steps of the child's learning
- involve parents in developing and implementing a joint learning approach at home and in school.

At the secondary phase the SENCO, the literacy and numeracy co-ordinators, departmental and pastoral colleagues should:[113]

- use information from the pupil's primary school to provide starting points for the development of an appropriate curriculum for the pupil
- identify and focus attention on the pupil's skills and highlight areas for early action to support the pupil within the class
- ensure that ongoing observation and assessment provide regular feedback to all teachers and parents about the pupil's achievements and experiences, and that the outcomes of such assessment form the basis for planning the next steps of the pupil's learning
- ensure that appropriate informal opportunities for the pupil to show what (s)he knows, understand and can do are maximised through the pastoral programme
- involve the pupil in planning and agreeing targets to meet his/her needs
- involve parents in developing and implementing a joint learning approach at home and in school.

Simply focusing on the student with special educational needs in a mainstream class can lead to the stigmatisation (perhaps unwittingly and not deliberately) of that student. Rather, we suggest that the notion of special educational needs is a societal rather than an individual issue. This implies that the students' peers should have their awareness raised of special educational needs and how to respond to and work with students with such needs. This has to be handled very sensitively, for indelicate handling can cause further stigmatisation rather than help to reduce it. With this caution, however, the student teacher can plan programmes and resources for the whole class or particular teaching groups that address special needs.

At the simplest level, perhaps, a review of texts, pictures and materials can be undertaken to ensure that there is appropriate representation of students with special needs and that that inclusion is presented positively. At another level the student teacher may wish to ensure that a 'special needs dimension' features in the curriculum content that is addressed (taking care to avoid the risk of stigmatisation).

The Qualifications and Curriculum Authority provides guidelines for working with pupils with learning difficulties. The aims of national curricula apply to all children, but as far as children with learning difficulties are concerned there are two key issues:

The curriculum for pupils with learning difficulties will provide for:

- the needs of all pupils that become priorities as they approach adulthood; for example, aspects of PSHE, the key skills and thinking skills
- the needs of particular groups of pupils; for example, developing communication skills for pupils who have difficulties with conventional speaking and listening.[114]

In addition, personal priority needs such as therapeutic needs and paramedical care of pupils with learning difficulties are essential aspects of their curriculum and need to be planned for. Teachers and schools are strongly encouraged to collaborate with other professionals; for example from healthcare settings, when thinking about planning. Close collaboration with parents is also encouraged. The Qualifications and Curriculum Authority provide some useful vignettes of pupils and their needs:

Sam

Sam is in Year 6. His severe difficulties in learning and his physical disabilities mean that he requires help in most areas of the curriculum from a teaching assistant who works with his teachers. In some subjects, the teaching assistant works with a group of children, including Sam. In PE, Sam needs specific support. He uses a rolator to help him to stand with the other pupils while the aims of the PE lesson, using large apparatus, are explained to the class. The teaching assistant stands away from the group and, as the pupils begin to work on the apparatus, she approaches Sam. Together they discuss where, how and what he would like to work on. They reach an agreement and the teaching assistant helps him to position himself on the edge of the apparatus. With encouragement and physical support, Sam pulls himself over the stand and on to a bench, and edges along on his front. The teaching assistant decides that he needs her to be close to him and constantly reassures him until he has completed the task. Sam and his peers then discuss different ways of approaching the task.[115]

The guidelines cover the following areas: General issues; Planning the curriculum; Recognising progress and achievement (see Box 75[116]); and Monitoring, evaluation and review of the curriculum.

Box 75: Guidance on recognising progress in children with special educational needs

Progress may be recognised when pupils with learning difficulties:
- develop ways to communicate from the use of concrete ways (body language and objects of reference) toward the abstract (pictures, symbols, print, signs, ICT and the spoken word)
- develop a range of responses to social interactions from defensiveness through resistance (for some pupils, a positive response) to tolerance; and from passive co-operation toward active participation with individuals, in groups and in wider social circumstances
- develop a range of responses to actions, events or experiences even if there is no clear progress in acquiring knowledge and skills
- demonstrate the same achievement on more than one occasion and under changing circumstances
- demonstrate an increase in knowledge and understanding about a subject
- demonstrate an ability to maintain, refine, generalise or combine skills over time and in a range of circumstances, situations and settings
- move from a dependence on secure and predictable routines toward a greater degree of autonomy shown by risk-taking and increased confidence
- demonstrate a reduced need for support, for example, *from another person, from technology, from individualised equipment*, in carrying out particular tasks
- develop a wider regular use of learning positions and learning environments, reducing the need to present activities in consistent and personalised ways
- show a reduction in the frequency or severity of behaviour that inhibits learning through more appropriate behaviour
- demonstrate an increased ability to cope, *for example, with frustration and failure, with new or challenging learning opportunities or situations*
- decide not to participate or to respond.

The interpersonal level

The interpersonal level concerns pedagogy. This, perhaps, lies at the heart of the notions of access and uptake of a curriculum that is formally available to all, regardless of special need. The debate continues about whether students with special educational needs should receive different pedagogical treatment from other students. In summarising a wealth of research in this area, Lewis and Norwich[117] suggest that there has been a move away from considering students with special educational needs as requiring specific and separate pedagogies, and towards a range of pedagogies that are common to all students. Planning for students' access to the curriculum can be a challenging and daunting task for the student teacher,[118] and clearly she must seek advice and support on this. In connection with providing access it is important to note that each National Curriculum subject document includes in its common requirements the statement that 'appropriate provision' should be made for pupils who need to use:

● means of communication other than speech, including computers, technological aids, signing, symbols or lip-reading
● non-sighted methods of reading, such as Braille, or non-visual or non-aural ways of acquiring information
● technological aids in practical and written work
● aids or adapted equipment to allow access to practical activities within and beyond school.[119]

There will be occasions where an 'emphasis on oral rather than written work will help some pupils with learning difficulties' and a range of communication methods should be used that make the best use of students' strengths.[120] There should be access to large print books and texts where necessary and also to audio cassettes and adapted word processors to facilitate learning. At another level the student teacher will need to plan for a multi-sensory approach to learning for some students. Further, if the abilities to communicate, and to be communicated with, are to be addressed then the student teacher will need to provide many opportunities for this to occur. This moves teaching away from the formal, didactic and individual styles and towards group work.

Planning to develop communicative competence has significant implications for the use of extended group work, collaborative and co-operative work, in pairs, small groups and larger groups.[121] We suggest that, though many students with special educational needs might find it difficult to develop, meet and practise the social, emotional, linguistic and communicative challenges and demands of being a member of a communicative situation, nevertheless, if that is how students need to develop then student teachers should be planning for such opportunities to occur. The isolates, the marginalised, the stigmatised, the emotionally and behaviourally disturbed students in the classroom are the very ones who need this situation most, even though they are often the very ones that operate worst in this situation, presenting disruptive and difficult behaviour. The student teacher will, of course, have to plan the size and constitution of each group very carefully in order to minimise difficulties in the students and to maximise their social, emotional, cognitive and behavioural development.

The expansion of technological aids in classrooms has a vital part to play in enabling students to learn and to communicate. The use of technology, including concept keyboards and various overlays for computers and word-processing packages, can 'facilitate and encourage sensory development, . . . increase the range of materials that can be accessed across the curriculum . . . [and] encourage pupil interaction'.[122] For example, technology can enable students with severe learning difficulties to generate visual and aural patterns using switches, allow choice and decision making through 'yes' and 'no' switches, and increase sensory control skills, attending skills and co-operative skills.[123]

At another level the student teacher will need to consider 'environmental factors', for example whether students are seated so that they can hear and see properly; whether the lighting is adequate for visually impaired students; whether acoustic conditions (and aids) are appropriate for students with hearing impairments; whether the furniture is arranged for easy movement of students with physical impairments.

Reynolds and Muijs[124] suggest that students with learning difficulties may require additional amounts of direct instruction; use of mnemonic strategies; breaking down tasks into smaller units and then combining them into a whole; providing regular and frequent prompts; increased use of drill and practice (as appropriate); very careful questioning; small group instruction of around three to five (rather than whole-class instruction); peer tutoring; and appropriate use of technology, particularly in reading, mathematics and social skills. They suggest that very careful attention needs to be given to the level of difficulty of the work, moving in very small, teacher-directed steps.

A problem for many students with special needs is a negative self-concept. Hence it is important for the student teacher to ensure that the child is provided with the opportunity to experience success in the full range of learning, and they argue that collaborative work is a useful tool here.

Reynolds and Muijs[125] and the Department for Education and Skills[126] synthesise several studies on strategies for keeping the attention of children for whom this is a problem, or who are unable to sit still (see Box 76).

Box 76: Suggestions for keeping the attention of students with attention deficit

- Increasing the number of ways of initially gaining the student's attention.
- Ensuring that the topic has relevance to the student's daily life.
- Presenting tasks in small steps, coupled with clear explanations of each step and its relevance along the way.
- Active involvement of the student in her/his learning.
- Setting short-term, achievable goals and having students themselves set such goals.
- Encouraging students to learn from their mistakes.
- Using a quick succession of tasks and activities in order to avoid boredom.
- Varying tasks so that there is not reliance on pencil and paper activities.
- Providing opportunities at the end of a task for the student to move around.
- Using a variety of teaching methods.
- Ensuring peer support, for example by enlisting a group of friends who identify and use strategies to help the student to sustain concentration.
- Keeping the students organised and aware of what has to be done, when it has to be done, what resources they need and when, how to organise their work, how to plan their tasks, how to store their work and resources, ensuring tidiness.
- The value of routines.
- The use of simple, direct and very clear instructions, ensuring that the student understands these (e.g. by having the student repeat them).
- Making activities and assignments very clear, and avoiding superfluous information (e.g. on handout material).
- Ensuring that students are given praise for achievements, even if they appear slight.
- Showing students how they can improve their organisation, and ensuring that they carry this out.
- Minimising distractions.
- Rewarding effort as well as achievement.
- Giving immediate feedback and feedforward that is connected to the task in hand.
- Avoiding much use of extrinsic motivation (e.g. rewards).
- Providing opportunities for students to experience success (e.g. in classroom tasks, such as tidying up).
- Giving frequent reminders.
- Establishing rules.

The authors also add the significant point that teachers should not think that there will be wonder cures or overnight success!

For children with Attention Deficit/Hyperactivity Disorder, the authors recommend the need to ensure consistency. They also suggest that such children should be placed in a position in the class so that they have the least opportunity to observe other children or to be distracted, provided that this does not provide them with a ready-made audience in the theatre of the classroom! Such students, the authors aver, should also have the opportunity to see positive behaviour models in other children. Further, it is suggested that dietary changes may need to be introduced[127] and that drug therapy may be useful (e.g. Ritalin and Dexadrine), though this is controversial.

Most teachers and student teachers will encounter emotionally and behaviourally disturbed and disturbing students. Though we deal with management and control in the next section, we ought to signal here the need for the student teacher to discuss with the class teacher the agreed and most appropriate ways of handling children whose problems cause them to present challenges to the smooth running of the classroom, who disrupt the learning of others and who disrupt their own learning by violent or disturbed behaviour. It is vital that the novice student teacher holds these discussions in order to avoid provoking the disturbed behaviour, to promote the emotional and behavioural well-being of the student, and to know how best to respond to behavioural challenges and emotionally charged behaviour.

Reynolds and Muijs[128] suggest that, for students with behavioural disorders, it is important to establish the cause and the trigger of the problem, what needs to be done to improve the behaviour, and how to reach that goal. They suggest that attention has to be shifted from a focus on the undesirable behaviours to the desired behaviours, though, as seasoned teachers know, this is frequently extremely difficult. It may be that the work is too difficult, too boring, or too demanding.

The Department for Education and Skills[129] in its guidance on inclusion suggests a range of strategies for ensuring that including students with learning difficulties is compatible with the efficient education of other children:

- praising the pupil's strengths and areas of success so that self-esteem is maintained and enhanced
- using flexible grouping arrangements including ones where the pupil can work with more able peers
- providing for all pupils experiences which will be of benefit to most pupils, particularly to the pupil with learning difficulties
- considering carefully the use of language in the classroom and strategies to promote the learning of need vocabulary
- setting appropriate targets so that personal progress can be tracked as well as progress towards externally determined goals
- considering carefully the pupil's learning styles and ensuring that this is reflected in the styles of teaching
- developing a partnership with the parents to support the pupil and the curriculum.

The Department for Children, Schools and Families has a website to address the improvement of behaviour in schools which has many useful strategies for dealing with pupils with challenging behaviour (http://www.dcsf.gov.uk/ibis/index.cfm). Where necessary the law gives teachers the power to restrain pupils in particular circumstances.

A member of the staff of a school may use, in relation to any pupil at the school, such force as is reasonable in the circumstances for the purpose of preventing the pupil from doing (or continuing to do) any of the following, namely:

    (a)   committing any offence

    (b)   causing personal injury to, or damage to the property of, any person (including the pupil himself), or

    (c)   engaging in any behaviour prejudicial to the maintenance of good order and discipline at the school or among any of its pupils, whether that behaviour occurs during a teaching session or otherwise.

Let us not understate the enormity of the task here. Students with emotional and behavioural difficulties are very draining on the capabilities of teachers to cope with routine stress, to start each day afresh and to be prepared to try to be positive over and over again with difficult students. It is likely that, in many cases, the student teacher will have to handle a student who presents a combination of emotional, behavioural and learning difficulties. Indeed some of the behavioural difficulties might stem from frustration caused by learning difficulties and the teacher's poor matching of work, e.g. overestimating the student's abilities. It is comparatively common to see in a single student a conjunction of learning and behavioural difficulties.

The same situation arises, of course, in connection with students with other special educational needs. For example, a hearing-impaired student may have difficulty in learning and this might produce difficult behaviour (e.g. out of frustration). Often it is necessary to understand and try to address the complexity of the interplay between learning difficulties, physical, emotional, behavioural and sensory difficulties.

This implies that planning to meet the needs of the student will have to take place on a variety of fronts – emotional, social, behavioural, cognitive – simultaneously. For the novice student teacher this is a daunting task in which she will need to seek and be given guidance and support from teachers with experience of handling difficult students as well as knowledge of particular individuals and how best to work with them.

Many schools will have both formal and informal strategies that are agreed for handling specific individuals and their presenting disruptive behaviour in the class, e.g. organisation for learning (maybe the use of group work); the use of practical activity; the cognitive demand, pacing and organisation of tasks; negotiation; confrontation avoidance; withdrawal; involvement of other staff; involvement of parents; the setting of individualised work and agreed contracts for work and behaviour; the use of sanctions, punishments and rewards etc. The student teacher needs to be apprised of these agreed strategies so that her actions are consistent with them. Further, many teachers (perhaps who are in the process of statementing a student) will require incidents and examples of emotional and behavioural disturbance to be formally recorded so that, if a case conference is held, evidence rather than subjective prejudice and preference will be available to support the discussions. The students with moderate or severe learning difficulties will tax the ingenuity and creativity of student teachers quite heavily, as the student teacher will have to devise several ways of addressing, introducing and cementing concepts and areas of knowledge. There will need to be multiple routes to the formation of single and several concepts in students.

As with sexist and racist comments and incidents discussed previously, the student teacher will need to consider how to respond to discriminatory comments and incidents within and outside the classroom (e.g. verbal and physical abuse to students, name calling, bullying, violent and aggressive language, violent and aggressive nonverbal communication, antagonistic remarks). This should be considered in relation to the strategies that the teacher adopts in handling such incidents generally and with particular individuals.

The personal level

Many students with special educational needs have fragile, damaged or low self-concepts and self-esteem. This is one of the most powerful arguments for taking students out of mainstream education and placing them in schools for students with moderate or severe learning difficulties or with emotional and behavioural difficulties, as mainstream education has often not only failed these students but has caused them to fail and to regard themselves as failures. The low expectations that some mainstream teachers may have of students can cause the most seriously depressing and damaging effects on students' self-esteem and motivation to learn. The reduction of threat in some form of special education is invaluable in rebuilding damaged self-concepts.

Many students, for whatever reason, need others to speak and act for them for their greatest benefit, i.e. to act as advocates for their welfare. Though advocacy on behalf of students with special needs is important, it is only one side of the coin; the other side is to develop in students their abilities in self-advocacy.[130] This is an important issue if students are to be able to have genuine control over their own lives and power to take decisions in their own best interests. Students should be enabled to find, develop and exercise their own autonomy, their 'voice'.[131] It is no accident, perhaps, that a low-ability student is called 'dumb'; it is indicative of their own inabilities and their teachers' inabilities to foster the development of their own 'voice'.

The development of self-advocacy resonates with the points made in discussing sex and ethnicity earlier, that students should be supported in their moves to become as autonomous and fulfilled as possible, and that this process can be facilitated in student-centred, negotiated and flexible learning. This need not be confined to older students; for example the High Scope curriculum accords considerable autonomy, supported decision making and responsible decision making in children from the nursery years upwards.[132] Further, Zimiles[133] demonstrates that students brought up on progressive education were able to engage weighty moral issues – punishment, goodness, wrongdoing – more effectively than students whose pedagogical and curricular diet was more formal. At a simple level this might mean that students face up to the consequences of their behaviour and take responsibility for making it more acceptable.

The great difficulty for many student teachers is coping with emotionally and behaviourally disturbed students who are severely disruptive in class. The student teacher wishes, perhaps, that they would cease to advocate themselves in the classroom! There is no simple solution to such behavioural problems; if there were it would have been discovered years ago. There is no simple solution because there is no simple problem. Many disturbed students' behaviour is the outcome of a complex interplay of many contributing factors, e.g. home circumstances and relationships; parental problems; parenting difficulties; relationships with peers; physical and mental illness; early childhood experiences; an inability to cope; difficulty in self-restraint or controlling emotions; and school matters (for example limited academic abilities).

This does not mean that nothing can be done for these students; in fact, just the opposite. It suggests that teachers, if no one else in the students' world, should be able to provide a stable, respectful and supportive environment for these students that affords them some opportunities to develop appropriate self-management skills. It also means that teachers will have to come to know and understand the biography and social and emotional make-up of the students. It involves the teacher understanding and communicating with the parties that are involved with the student, for example parents, welfare workers etc. Such intimate knowledge takes time to acquire; a student teacher who does not have that time needs, therefore, to try to gain that knowledge rapidly from the class teacher (respecting confidentiality where appropriate) and to use this to try to build up relationships with students.

Many students with special educational needs are the butt of verbal insults, taunts and abuse.

Indeed the notion of having a special educational need is often used as an insult in itself amongst students who are not themselves disadvantaged. Students with special educational needs are surrounded by messages, images and behaviour that indicate that having a special educational need renders them somehow a lesser person or a failure; this can reinforce their low self-esteem.

Given this situation it is hardly surprising that for some students with special educational needs the only way in which they can gain some positive recognition is by aggressive physical and verbal behaviour – that is all that is left open to them. The student teacher needs to discuss with the teacher(s) with whom she is working the strategies that are being used to boost self-esteem and to develop in students with special educational needs their abilities to handle themselves with self-control, avoidance of violence and violent confrontations, avoidance of acting abusively themselves, and preserving their dignity when they are the butt of abuse. That is a difficult lesson for many students to learn; it is a lesson that perhaps needs to be addressed per se as part of the curricular experience of students; developing responsibility for actions in students is an important matter, though clearly it is difficult and long term.

GIFTED AND TALENTED STUDENTS

Included in equal opportunities, inclusion and diversity is the group of students classed as 'gifted' or 'talented'. Recent attention has been focused on provision and appropriate teaching for gifted and talented students. We need to clarify the difference: whereas 'gifted' is used to denote learners with distinct abilities in one or more subjects in the National Curriculum other than in art and design, music and PE, 'talented' is used to describe those learners who have abilities in art and design, music, PE, or performing arts such as dance and drama.[134] The Qualifications and Curriculum Authority suggested that gifted and talented students work at the top 5–10 per cent of students in any school, regardless of the overall ability profile of the students, though other studies set the boundary at the top 3–5 per cent.[135] In such circumstances it is suggested that there may be generic characteristics of gifted and talented students, for example Box 77.[136]

Box 77: Generic characteristics of gifted and talented students

Gifted and talented students:

- think quickly and accurately
- work systematically
- generate creative working solutions
- work flexibly, processing unfamiliar information and applying knowledge, experience and insight to unfamiliar situations
- communicate their thoughts and ideas well
- [are] determined, diligent and interested in uncovering patterns
- achieve, or show potential, in a wide range of contexts
- [are] particularly creative
- show great sensitivity or empathy
- demonstrate particular physical dexterity or skill
- make sound judgements
- [are] outstanding leaders or team members
- [are] fascinated by, or passionate about, a particular subject or aspect of the curriculum
- demonstrate high levels of attainment across a range of subjects, within a particular subject.

The Qualifications and Curriculum Authority advocated caution in applying these criteria, as some gifted and talented students do not fit the criteria. Indeed it specifically suggested the need to look for giftedness and talent outside the regular curriculum.

Many gifted and talented students demonstrate their abilities in National Curriculum subjects and well above average assessment results, indeed they are entered for world class tests. They may also demonstrate extraordinary creative, leadership or practical abilities. Other gifted and talented students may deliberately conceal their potential, perhaps in order to avoid being singled out, being the subject of name-calling, or, indeed, to avoid being given additional work to do. Yet others may not demonstrate their abilities because of frustration, poor self-esteem, lack of challenge, or low teacher and parent expectations.[137] Indeed in the USA, one report indicates that up to 50 per cent of gifted and talented students may be underachieving, and up to 20 per cent of high school dropouts are from this pool of students.[138] This suggests that there are issues of identification, provision and assessment for such students, and that motivation is a critical factor in the development of the learning of gifted and talented students.

To address the matter of identification the Qualifications and Curriculum Authority suggested a range of ways in which teachers may become aware of gifted and talented students, for example:[139]

- how they approach routine work in class and activities outside the classroom (some learners behave quite differently in the two situations)
- observing them systematically in a range of learning contexts
- their responses to work and talking with them about what they like, dislike and what enables them to learn best
- inviting them to reflect on and talk about their own strengths, interests and aspirations, perhaps in the context of personal target-setting
- their initiative in tackling tasks or in adapting conditions to suit circumstances
- the progress they make and judging whether they achieve beyond the level of attainment expected for their age
- their performance in National Curriculum and other standardised tests, for example nonverbal reasoning tests and cognitive ability tests (CATs), or national tests and qualifications.

The same document also counsels against stereotyping, for example to suggest that black students will have sports talents but not in other areas, or that students from privileged backgrounds are brighter than those who are not from such backgrounds.

Providing a suitable teaching and learning environment for gifted and talented students involves establishing a context in which their abilities are identified, addressed, developed and applied. Such an environment should:[140]

- value learners' own interests and learning styles
- encourage independence and autonomy, and support learners in using their initiative
- encourage learners to be open to ideas and initiatives presented by others
- encourage connections across subjects or aspects of the learning programme
- link learning to wider applications
- encourage the use of a variety of resources, ideas, methods and tasks
- involve learners in working in a range of settings and contexts – as individuals, in pairs, in groups, as a class, cross-year, cross-institution and inter-institution
- encourage learners to reflect on the process of their own learning and to understand the factors that help them to make progress.

Box 78: Self-evaluation questions for planning and resourcing teaching of gifted and talented students

- How often do you encourage creative thinking by asking open-ended questions to which there are no right answers?
- How often are learners encouraged to consider the nature of a question and its possible answers?
- How often do you encourage learners to ask questions of themselves, each other and other adults in the classroom?
- How are learners involved in self-assessment and/or peer assessment?
- How effectively are the processes of formative assessment developed?
- How do you ensure that examples of gifted and talented work are on display or readily available, to raise the expectations of both learners and teachers?
- How effectively are you engaging learners in recognising and responding to challenge and taking initiative in their learning?
- How thoroughly have you checked learning activities to make sure that they offer challenges that match:

  - higher level descriptions than expected for the Key Stage and/or the exceptional performance criteria of the National Curriculum?
  - the higher tier requirements of GCSE specifications?
  - the specifications for advanced level qualifications, including the advanced extension award?

- How effectively are you involving teaching assistants, supply teachers or workplace supervisors in the identification of, and provision for, the gifted and talented?
- How effectively are you liaising with the school's library service or other local resource support services?
- How are you developing a resource collection, including lists of web resources for young people and staff in classrooms, departments, the staff room, library or resource centre? How are you making sure that resources are being used?

Indeed in the same document the Qualifications and Curriculum Authority suggested that there are several questions that teachers could ask themselves in planning for teaching and resourcing teaching (Box 78).[141]

Essentially what is being argued for here is for differentiated, suitably challenging teaching and learning. This may include, for example, accelerating learning and enrichment programmes;[142] although the terms overlap, the difference between these two is that acceleration implies faster movement through content (e.g. skipping a level or year group), whilst enrichment implies greater depth and breadth through content – greater variety, whilst not necessarily meaning gaining advanced placement.[143] Indeed a case could be made for withdrawal programmes for gifted and talented students.

Differentiation may also include: being clear on the constituent elements of higher-order thinking and applying these; promoting different ways of working with and exploring curriculum content; encouraging increasingly analytical and complex work; introducing more self-determined work (perhaps of an enquiry nature); moving beyond the given curriculum. Differentiation is maximised when teaching and learning are concept-based, exploratory and active, use formative assessment and encourage increasing independence of thought. Related to this is the need to consider progression in many forms, for example:[144]

- concrete to abstract
- simple to complex

- specific to general
- general to specific
- low order to high order
- unique instance to overarching principle
- overarching principle to unique instance
- familiar to unfamiliar
- unfamiliar to familiar
- present to future
- future to present
- near to distant
- distant to near
- basic to transformational
- single tasks to multifaceted or multi-dimensional tasks
- structured tasks to more open-ended tasks
- less independence to greater independence in planning, implementing and evaluating learning
- small steps to larger steps
- slow to fast
- fast to slow.

To provide for gifted and talented students in class may involve setting different or 'stepped' work, i.e. activities that become increasingly demanding. The Qualifications and Curriculum Authority suggested that negotiated target setting with students, linked to action planning, can be a useful means of developing their full potential. An emphasis is placed on higher-order, open-ended, autonomous thinking and exploratory activities, with a heavy emphasis placed on formative assessment, including peer assessment.[145]

To support the learning of the gifted and talented, first, teachers must help students to develop appropriate study skills. Inter alia, this will involve producing genuinely graded worksheets and instructing such students in methods of self-testing. Second, teachers need to encourage students to develop skills of higher-order thinking. This will involve teachers in looking critically at classroom interaction and at their own questioning skills.[146] Third, teachers must come to accept the 'normality' of students, particularly on the emotional level, even though they may seem 'old for their age'; they need to be rewarded for scholastic achievement and at the same time to retain their identities with the class group.

14 Managing Behaviour in the Classroom

INTRODUCTION

This section is concerned with managing behaviour in the classroom. It does not pretend to offer a panacea for all the manifold challenges and difficulties that are potentially present in the modern classroom, nor does it attempt to deal with the more problematic aspects of behaviour like violence and truancy. To do so would be to swing the balance of the pages that follow in the direction of juvenile delinquency and so distort the overall picture of classroom behaviour. In any case, should these and comparable incidents arise in the course of a student teacher's school experience, they should be referred to a senior member of staff as soon as is practically possible. What we do aim to do in this section is to offer the reader a framework for securing and maintaining the co-operation of students in classroom activities. To this end, it attempts to bring together a range of ideas, perspectives and concepts that will provide the student teacher with an operational base for achieving a positive, humane and constructive approach to management and control in the classroom.

Schools are required to have a behaviour policy,[1] and schools also set out clear indications of rewards, sanctions, punishments and procedures for handling misbehaviour. In the best schools these are found to be applied consistently, fairly and clearly.[2] Indeed, positive strategies are found to include:

- a clear statement of values to be adopted by staff and pupils
- a concise and clear code of behaviour
- well-defined basic routines
- a strong emphasis on praise and rewards
- clear explanation of the systems of rewards and sanctions.

Student teachers are advised to find out from the school not only its behaviour policy, but the required procedures to follow with rewards, sanctions, handling misbehaviour at all levels of disruption, which should frame the rules and expectations for your classroom.[3]

It is important for the reader to consider carefully and collectively the points raised in this chapter, particularly if she is concerned to achieve good standards of teaching; they cannot be viewed in isolation. This is to say, they tie in with a whole range of contextual factors, some of which are touched upon elsewhere in the book, such as preparation and planning, suitability of material, teaching methods, teacher–pupil relationships and so on. If, for example, the work you give to your class tends consistently to be too difficult, or if your relations with the class are permanently abrasive, then no amount of reading or rereading of this section will help you resolve the

Box 79: Key elements of good discipline

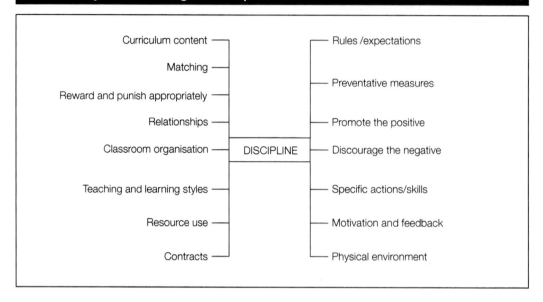

difficulties that will inevitably follow. The connections between the factors about to be discussed and the broader issues of pedagogy must be made by the reader.

The point that we wish to emphasise is that management and control is a multifaceted matter, concerning all aspects of life in schools and all aspects of a student's personality and a teacher's craft. Some key elements of good discipline and management are shown in Box 79.

This moves away from regarding 'discipline' as an extra to teaching, for example in the widespread view amongst many student teachers that discipline comes after curricular and pedagogic matters, summed up in the practice whereby a student teacher sets students some work and then the discipline comes when the student teacher spends the remainder of the lesson ensuring that students are kept 'on task' and working. Rather, the view that we espouse here is that discipline is a 'built-in' element of teaching rather than a 'bolt-on' extra – it touches every aspect of a school. This view finds support from the influential Elton Report[1] on discipline in schools, which suggested that a whole-school policy was vital for effective discipline, ensuring consistency of vision and practice in the school. Further, the Elton Report suggested that this whole-school policy should include:

● systems of incentives, sanction and support
● shared understanding and mutual support among members of a school staff
● ways of talking matters over with students
● curriculum content and teaching styles
● home/school relationships.

The attractions of the Elton Report are a realisation that a behaviour policy is not just about behaviour but that it touches every aspect of the formal and hidden curriculum of schools and their relationships with the wider community. Good behaviour and good teaching cannot be separated. A student teacher can reasonably expect to be able to look at a school's behaviour and discipline policy as a preparation for teaching practice. A school discipline policy, however, is not guaranteed to reduce misbehaviour. Hart *et al.*[5] demonstrate that there is little relationship between the school's construction and implementation of a discipline policy and the levels of students' misbehaviour or the level of teacher stress caused by misbehaviour. Rather, they aver, it is better to create a supportive atmosphere that helps teachers to cope with the misbehaviour that they have to face. The ideal situation is to provide optimally matched types of support appropriate to the demands of particular school contexts.[6]

A range of studies[7] all point in the same direction in suggesting that the promotion of good behaviour is founded on several fundamental key principles:

- the need to 'promote the positive' and to build self-esteem in students
- the centrality of motivation, interest in and enjoyment of all aspects of school life
- the promotion of empowerment, autonomy and responsibility in students
- the need for consistency
- the inclusive nature of a policy, involving and addressing all aspects of school life and curricula, all relevant parties (within and outside the school), and all aspects of the student (e.g. psychological and emotional well-being), i.e. a concern for total quality
- the need to be proactive, considering preventative measures and measures to de-escalate trouble quickly
- the need for negotiated and agreed rules, rewards and sanctions
- the need for communication, e.g. of expectations, boundaries, acceptability, responsibilities, rules, praise, feedback.

The Office for Standards in Education[8] reported that a major goal of education was to enable – and teach – students to take responsibility for their own behaviour. In this respect they provided some important guidelines:

- A minimal number of school rules governing behaviour are clearly explained and are available (often displayed) to pupils so that they understand there are good reasons for such rules to be in place and upheld by all.
- Every opportunity is taken to give pupils serious responsibility for aspects of school work and for the day-to-day running of the school, for example by running school councils, or by being permitted to work independently in the library and also to assist with the loan service at lunchtime.
- Humour is used by staff with good effect often to diffuse the build up of tensions. Sarcasm and cynicism, on the other hand, are generally loathed by pupils and are strenuously avoided by staff in the most effective schools.
- The key principle of 'fairness', which is readily understood by pupils and causes great resentment if not observed, is consistently upheld by staff.
- Rewards and praise are used effectively to acknowledge success and to reinforce positive behaviour, but not indiscriminately.
- Sanctions fit the offence with all pupils being aware of the consequences of offending behaviour.
- Genuine mistakes are not reckoned as failure so much as experiences from which to learn.

It is clear from this summary list that attention is focused on people, on intervention and on accentuating the positive. This accords with the findings of several studies[9] that punitive schools appeared to promote poor behaviour. The student teacher concerned to demonstrate effective class management and control will need to consider, amongst other things:[10]

1   how to promote positive environments
2   how to be proactive and fair
3   how to plan and implement the formal curriculum to support good discipline
4   how and when to involve other parties
5   how to make plans for management and discipline effective in practice.

With regard to 1 – how to promote positive environments – the student teacher will need to consider:[11]

Promoting the positive

● an emphasis on accentuating the positive rather than focusing on the negative
● encouraging, teaching and rewarding good behaviour and positive relationships.

Motivations, praise and enjoyment

● making school and learning interesting
● reinforcing the positive, extinguishing the negative
● providing earned and appropriate verbal and non-verbal praise
● recognising relative as well as absolute success
● publicly applauding achievement and effort (e.g. in class, assemblies).

Self-esteem and success

● promoting student autonomy, empowerment and 'voice'
● avoiding labelling
● avoiding humiliation, sarcasm, insult and ridicule
● asking for students' views/accounts and taking them seriously
● recognising non-academic achievements.

Ethos and climate

● an open, welcoming, stimulating, caring and supportive climate within the classroom envi-
    ronment (however defined).

Equal opportunities

● addressing gender, race, class, abilities, special needs: an equal opportunity to contribute and
    to learn
● intervening to reduce stereotyping and stereotyped behaviour
● responding quickly to incidents and behaviour which violate equal opportunities
● being alert to racial and sexual harassment and bullying
● being aware of statemented students and those with special needs.

Roles and relationships

● the promotion of positive role models
● being friendly and 'human'
● knowing students as individuals.

Responsibility, self-reliance and respect

- developing autonomy and responsibility in students, e.g. for their work, behaviour, learning
- being polite and respectful, expecting politeness and respect
- providing opportunities for self-discipline.

The physical environment

- a stimulating, clean and welcoming environment
- classroom display
- arrangements for moving round the classroom/teaching spaces, avoiding circulation bottle-necks
- monitoring entrance/egress of students and monitoring students outside the classroom, e.g. in corridors and play spaces
- involving students in keeping the physical environment attractive and free from graffiti, litter etc.

With regard to 2 – how to be proactive and fair – the student teacher will need to consider:[12]

Expectations and communication

- being overt, clear and precise over expectations
- communicating the criteria for acceptable behaviour
- defusing confrontations and challenging behaviour
- having high but realistic expectations in a variety of fields and communicating them
- avoiding the negative self-fulfilling prophecy
- making criticism constructive.

Being proactive and taking preventative measures

- anticipating problems and adjusting demands
- stopping unacceptable behaviour before it escalates (spotting incidents in the making)
- de-escalating unacceptable and challenging behaviour
- avoiding 'boxing students into a corner' where staff and students will lose face
- staying calm and 'taking the heat' out of situations.

Setting and communicating boundaries

- developing routines, e.g. for accessing and returning resources, giving in work, going to the toilet, moving round the classroom, starting sessions, entrance and egress, establishing attention
- maintaining eye contact
- avoiding 'bargaining', arguing with students and being pressurised by students.

Consistency, fairness and whole-school practice[13]

- adhering to the whole-school policy
- ensuring consistent application of rules, rewards, sanctions, responding to specific presenting behaviours and students
- sharing individual experiences and supporting individuals
- avoiding punishing whole groups if some individuals do not deserve it

- ensuring appropriate differentiation of application with respect to different students and situations
- ensuring fairness in administering incentives for good behaviour.

With regard to 3 – how to plan and implement the formal curriculum to support good discipline – the student teacher will need to consider:[14]

Curriculum matters

- matching, differentiation, stimulation, motivation and sustaining interest
- making demands realistic, meaningful and achievable
- marking work promptly
- communicating the purposes of the lesson and the criteria for success/achieving the purposes
- providing extension and reinforcement material
- planning curricula and activities with discipline considerations in mind
- avoiding 'slack' time (i.e. time where students can avoid being occupied) and increasing learning/teaching time.

Teaching and learning

- task orientation and a purposeful, brisk rate
- using group work for social and emotional development
- finding out about and building on students' preferred learning styles
- providing opportunities for student-centred and student-initiated/self-assessed learning
- attending to specific classroom teaching skills: beginnings, transitions, conclusions; questioning/explaining/giving instructions/listening and responding/building on students' contributions/checking understanding and working/summarising; vigilance and communicating vigilance; use of voice – volume/speed/pitch/conviction; planning and preparation; timing; accessing and returning resources; being mobile
- taking care with worksheets – avoiding 'teaching by proxy' – rather going for the human factor in teaching.

With regard to 4 – how and when to involve other parties – the student teacher will need to consider:[15]

Home, school and community

- peer group support/pressure
- two-way communication with home and school
- where relevant, involving parents early in many aspects of education and behaviour, not just as a last resort.

Non-teaching staff

- keeping all adults involved in school informed of relevant policy matters and how they impact on practice and working with students
- involving non-teaching staff in decision making
- providing support for non-teaching staff in their interactions with students.

Lunch times and breaks

● supervision by teaching and non-teaching staff
● making lunch times and playtimes interesting and constructive, e.g. with equipment, appropriate supervision, activities
● clarity on which students may/may not go into designated areas
● supervision of students who have been kept in at break times/lunch times
● rules on kinds of activities permitted and forbidden (and reasons for these).

Rules and student involvement

● involving students in devising school and classroom rules (see Wragg for different ways of establishing rules and the implications of different approaches)
● developing a limited number of agreed, explicit and memorable rules, e.g. on movement and speed, calling out, listening, going out of the classroom
● reinforcing rules frequently.

With regard to 5 – making plans for management and discipline effective in practice – the student teacher will need to consider:[16]

Rewards, sanctions and protocols

● purposes, scope and rationales of rules and their enforcement
● appropriate rewards and punishments (to fit the behaviour and the student)
● grading behaviour, rewards and sanctions to fit the incident, e.g. talking out of turn → hindering others → making unnecessary noise → work avoidance → unruly behaviour while waiting → rowdiness and verbal abuse → being cheeky → physical aggression, taking into account possible reasons for the behaviour
● avoiding over-reacting
● using a range of individual extrinsic rewards, e.g. individual and public praise, showing work to other students/adults, tokens, points, 'stickers' and badges, certificates, privileges
● using a range of group/class extrinsic rewards, e.g. points, certificates, plaques, trophies.
● rewarding/punishing the behaviour, not the student (and making this clear to the students)
● responding quickly
● avoiding 'blanket' punishments which involve non-offenders
● recording incidents and events
● arrangements for students who abscond.

Bullying

● the school's position on bullying and dealing with it (in all its forms)
● protocols for dealing with incidents of bullying, bullies and victims at the time and follow-up times; recording and reporting incidents, events and follow-up action.
● Involving parents openly and having a constructive plan to offer to all parties.

Contracts

Contracts are a strategy to be used having tried a series of other measures, and as a way to avoid the ultimate sanction of exclusion. Student teachers are unlikely to be involved in contract negotiation but we mention contracts here for information:

- contracts to promote the positive and to negotiate with students
- reporting on students on a frequent basis where appropriate
- contracts for returning to the class after a period of exclusion
- individual programmes of behaviour where appropriate.

The vast set of considerations set out above reflects the complexity of issues in establishing and maintaining effective management and discipline. No aspect of school and classroom life is untouched by management and discipline matters. The major implication of this for the student teacher is that all her planning needs to be addressed with management and discipline in mind, i.e. how to maximise learning by promoting effective discipline and diminishing discipline problems. In the following pages the several matters outlined above will be addressed in more detail.

SCHOOLS OF THOUGHT ON CLASSROOM MANAGEMENT

Wragg[17] has identified 13 commonly held views in this respect. In describing them, he warns the reader that the list is not exhaustive and that teachers should not necessarily be assigned to one category exclusively: they may change their view (and behaviour) according to the occasion. Briefly, they are as follows.

1 Authoritarian

According to this view, teachers are held to be in charge and that it is their responsibility to establish and maintain order in the school. They make the decisions and give the orders within a well-defined and fairly rigid system of roles. The justification for a teacher assuming this stance resides in his greater knowledge and experience. Opponents of this view argue that it can become repressive and that it is not appropriate to an age in which students need to learn independence if society is to become really democratic.

2 Permissive

Usually contrasted with the preceding view, the permissive school emphasises individual freedom and choice. Traditional constraints on behaviour are thus kept to a minimum. The aim is to develop pupil autonomy so that pupils can make their own decisions and be responsible for their own behaviour. The critics of permissiveness contend that it all too often degenerates into a kind of laissez-faire situation having little or no real educational significance for those participating.

3 Behaviour modification

This school holds to the views of behaviourist psychology which stresses the roles of rewards and punishments in the control of behaviour. Behaviour is controlled by the responses it receives and its consequences. Hence, if positive consequences follow desired behaviour, it is likely to be repeated, and if negative consequences follow undesired behaviour, it is less likely to be repeated; the strength of the consequence depends on the behaviour exhibited. Thus the teacher's job is to focus on rewarding desirable behaviour and discouraging undesirable behaviour by punishment or withholding suitable reinforcements. It is objected to on the grounds that the treatment is mechanistic and that this implies that the people so treated are regarded as machines and not humans – however, all classrooms utilise some form of reward and punishment and, as pointed out above, the use of extrinsic rewards is almost universally recommended in establishing positive learning environments.

4 Interpersonal relationships

The aim of this school of thought is to produce good, positive relationships between the teacher and students and among the students themselves. Emphasis on negotiation and suggestion will result in a healthy classroom climate in which learning will occur automatically. If the trick works, then problems of management will not arise. Critics of this view, however, content that good personal relationships become an end in themselves and that the real purpose of the classroom enterprise, namely the acquisition of knowledge and skills, takes second place.

5 Scientific

According to this view (which, incidentally, is one held by the present authors – though not exclusively), teaching is an activity which can be studied and analysed. It can be described as being scientific in the sense of being an objective and systematic analysis and later synthesis of the more important components of teaching and learning. It is also scientific in the sense that it draws on the findings of empirical studies as a means of establishing a body of theory on which practice can be based. Four examples are given here that draw on empirical evidence.[18] Using data from school inspections the Scottish Department of Education[19] suggested that good lesson organisation and discipline could be developed in a variety of ways, listed in Box 80.

This is paralleled by the former Department of Education and Science[20] where it gives a shorter list of recommendations for good behaviour, set out in Box 81.

One can see that there are many areas of overlap between the two studies; the extent of that congruence enables student teachers to be reasonably certain that they too can have a degree of confidence in the suggestions reported.

A third example can be given of empirical research that contains an important message for discipline. Galton *et al.*[21] showed that the impact of a student who was labelled (perhaps euphemistically!) an 'attention seeker' was greater if a whole-class teaching style were adopted in a lesson, where the attention seeker had, as it were, a theatre to attract the attention of the whole class and

---

Box 80: Promoting good discipline in school

- Classwork marked regularly and thoroughly.
- Materials and equipment readily available.
- Teachers anticipate difficulties and react positively to them.
- Teachers are seen to be 'fair' by pupils.
- Teachers show an interest in their children and work.
- Teachers arrive at class punctually.
- Pupils come into class in an orderly fashion.
- The objectives of the lesson are clear and stated in the early part.
- Lessons get off to an interesting and brisk start.
- Teachers speak clearly and are audible at all times.
- The language is simple, clear and unambiguous.
- Brief, snappy questions are used to check children's comprehension.
- Teachers avoid slowing down the pace of the lesson.
- A constant overview of the class is kept.
- Teachers are aware of what individuals are doing.
- Interventions are prompt when passions rise.

Box 81: Factors promoting good discipline

- Nurturing of genuine involvement based on understanding of the concepts which underlie those tasks and examples particular to a given lesson.
- Materials and preparation to ensure differentiation within tasks for pupils of different abilities.
- Sustained hard work on the part of the pupils as well as the teacher.
- Specific help for individual pupils without losing sight of the reactions of the whole group.
- The encouragement of pupils to contribute ideas.
- Careful attention to their contributions, with encouragement to refine their ideas in discussion.
- Flexibility in adapting a lesson plan to take account of pupils' contributions and of the mood of the group.
- Variation of the pace of a lesson to keep interest and momentum.
- Wit and humour, which help pupils to enjoy a lesson and can defuse potential problems, without recourse to sarcasm.
- Infectious enthusiasm for the subject, and for pupils and their response to it.

the teacher, than in a situation where group work was being adopted, where the attention seeker was reduced to gaining the attention of only a group, thereby diluting her/his impact – a particularly valuable point for student teachers who are faced with a disruptive attention seeker.

A fourth and longer example derives from our own experience of supervising students on teaching practice. Here we set out a series of 'tips' which, like the 'folklore' discussed later, are drawn from our observations of and recommendations for effective teaching practice. They are set out under four main headings: talk, classroom management, timing and organisation.

Talk

- Vary the voice – its pitch, tone, volume, speed.
- Avoid rhetorical questions, e.g. 'Do you know what sitting down means?' – rather give a direct order.
- Avoid general exhortations, e.g. 'Come on now' – be specific and concrete.
- Do not bargain with students, e.g. 'If you're good we will watch this programme.'
- Do not rely on students' good behaviour, e.g. 'You will be good, won't you?'
- Do not allow students to argue with you.
- Do not accept anything that students say if it is ridiculous.
- Avoid only speaking with volunteers.
- If students are supposed to have listened to an instruction and then they ask what to do, tell them off for not listening.
- Do not speak too quickly for long; it whips up an excited atmosphere in the classroom.
- Do not bombard students with instructions; stage them through the lesson.
- Do not talk over students if you are insisting on silence – it gives a mixed message that, in fact, you will tolerate noise whilst asking for silence.
- Comment on what students have done and how well they have done it.
- Speak firmly and with conviction.
- Give explicit instructions that students will understand.
- Explain how to commence work.
- Be firm without shouting or being unfriendly; maybe use humour to defuse situations.
- Do not accept students shouting out – deal with it.

- Convey a realistic sense of urgency in your voice; mean what you say.
- Avoid asking students to tell you what they were supposed to do – it is a rhetorical question.
- Avoid going to extremes too rapidly, or from extreme to extreme, e.g. flattery to crossness.

Classroom management

- Make very explicit and communicate exactly what the 'ground rules' are – what is acceptable and unacceptable.
- Monitor the whole class, even when they are working in groups, stopping regularly if necessary.
- Do not become absorbed with individuals or groups at organisationally critical times, e.g. transitions, ending a lesson.
- Be in the classroom before the students, organise their entrance and egress.
- Avoid being pinned to your desk or being the 'pied piper' with a queue of students behind you – restrict numbers moving round the classroom and in a queue at any one time. Move to the students rather than the students moving to you.
- Stop an activity if necessary, sacrificing content to control rather than vice versa.
- Insist on acceptable standards of presentation, concentration, behaviour.
- Use written work to quieten students if necessary.
- When you stop the whole class insist on complete attention.
- Anticipate trouble and 'nip it in the bud'.
- Avoid being too friendly with the class and then suddenly fierce or vice versa – be consistent.
- Be prepared to 'police' a situation at times (even if it is out of your character).
- Insist on total concentration at times, even silent working.
- Avoid saying something and then not following it through.
- Reduce students' fidgeting if they are listening.
- Veiled – unspecified – threats, e.g. 'There will be trouble if I have to come over to you again,' may be more useful than specific threats; if a specific threat is given it must be carried out if the infraction continues.
- Avoid students pressuring you into repeating something that they should have listened to earlier; it is 'their fault'.
- Repeatedly calling out students' names suffers from the law of diminishing returns.
- Avoid joking in a serious activity.
- If a student repeatedly misbehaves avoid treating each incident in isolation; deal with the cumulative effect.
- Do not accept everything that the student cares to do.
- Be vigilant, developing 'the all-seeing eye'.
- Be dynamic.
- Allow thinking time in questions; do not always provide answers to students – you may be too helpful for their own good (see earlier: questioning and responding).
- Move round the class.
- Initiate good behaviour to replace responding to unacceptable behaviour.
- Avoid letting a worksheet replace all of your teaching.
- Do not be flustered by several students suddenly requiring help.
- Shortly after students have been set to work check that they are, in fact, working.
- Do not be fooled by a quiet student or class – it may be a screen for daydreaming.
- Arrange optimum seating arrangements.
- Avoid confrontations wherever possible – though some students will not allow you to do this.

Timing

●   Allow time to commence and round off sessions.
●   Set finite time limits, e.g. 'You have ten minutes to do such-and-such', communicating these limits to the students.
●   Do not spend too long on easy or trivial points, keep a brisk pace.
●   Try to ensure that work is completed by the lunch break/end of the afternoon (for primary school student teachers).
●   Allow reasonable time for students to work – set realistic expectations.

Organisation

●   Be thoroughly prepared.
●   Be very vigilant at transition points – come out of the 'teacher-as-instructor' mode and into the 'teacher-as classroom manager' mode.
●   Anticipate problems and plan how they will be addressed.
●   Use a visual focus to support an aural focus (e.g. using 'jotters', the chalkboard, flip chart etc.).

This list of points might appear unduly antagonistic in its tone at first sight. This is not intended; rather the aim here is to signal that the student teacher needs to be proactive, clear and communicative in her work and relations with her class(es).

A key factor is vigilance in the classroom, and its associated issue of eye contact. Wragg[22] makes the point that, even though we only have a narrow field of vision in sharp focus, about two or three degrees, we have a reasonably sharp field of vision of between 30 and 40 degrees, and a less sharp field of vision of up to 180 degrees. One can draw several implications from this:

●   Teachers who only remain in one position (e.g. at their desk, near the whiteboard) may direct their attention to a limited, centrally placed group of students, to the neglect of others on the periphery.
●   Sitting near the periphery may enable students to do very little and to remain unnoticed.
●   Teachers should deliberately move their physical location and their field of vision to encompass all students, taking care not to turn their back on students.
●   Teachers should involve all learners, and take special care to involve those at the extremities of the classroom (e.g. at the back, at the sides).
●   Some students, perhaps disruptive students, deliberately occupy central positions in order to command the theatre of the classroom.
●   Some disruptive students deliberately occupy peripheral positions in order to make themselves less accessible and thereby less easy to control.

The seating arrangements are a matter for the teacher; seating is decided by the teacher in order to maximise learning, albeit hopefully, but not necessarily, with the students' assent. Choice of seating by the student, as Kyriacou[23] remarks, is a privilege, not a right. Student teachers may need to rearrange the seating arrangements for specific lessons or during the teaching practice, in order to facilitate vigilance and learning, and you should take time to consider the optimal arrangements for particular learning activities rather than assuming all effective learning is facilitated by group work.[24]

Evertson and Emmer[25] suggest a sequence of actions to be taken to de-escalate undesirable behaviour:

1   Whilst maintaining eye contact, ask the student to stop the undesirable behaviour, and maintain the eye contact until the behaviour has stopped.

2   Keep eye contact until the student settles back into the desired behaviour.

3   Keep reminding the student of what the desired behaviour is.

4   Ask the student to explain the desired behaviour.

5   Impose a penalty for breaking the rules. Repeat a procedure until it is performed correctly and acceptably. If the student deliberately does not perform the desired behaviour then impose a sanction or punishment.

6   Ensure that students have enough variety to avert boredom.

This is echoed by Arends,[26] who suggests the use of the LEAST model as a mnemonic:

Leave it alone, i.e. ignore it if it is not going to escalate or is trivial.
End the action immediately, e.g. by direct command or distraction.
Attend more fully to the students and know them and their background in depth.
Spell out directions for what should be done and what should not be done, including the implications or consequences of not carrying out the required instructions.
Track the behaviour to see if it recurs, to record evidence of the behaviour, and to follow it up if necessary.

What we are arguing here is that regarding teaching as a science enables us to identify particular teaching skills for effective management that can be developed, for example: beginnings, questioning, explaining, handling transitions, concluding, responding, being vigilant, being prepared, timing and pacing lessons, using eye contact, anticipating what might happen and how difficult situations should and should not be handled. Opponents of this perspective of teaching as a scientific activity argue that teaching is an art and cannot therefore be subjected to such an analysis. For them, teaching – and this includes class management – is intuitive and can depend upon personality.

6 Social systems

The 'social systems' view contends that the school and its inmates constitute a sub-system of a wider social system, influences from which affect the group's behaviour. These include political, social, financial, emotional emanations. The teacher thus needs to understand and be aware of these influences in order to work effectively in school, although learning is in essence an individual process. Many school problems thus need to be seen in relation to these wider contextual factors. Critics respond by arguing that teachers have little or no control over these factors and must, therefore, function within the framework of the school.

7 Folklore

If the new teacher can assimilate the received wisdom of the profession, the 'tips for teachers' and 'tricks of the trade', then he will be suitably equipped to deal with most contingencies. As Wragg[27] explains, critics consider that tips are lacking in any theoretical basis, are random and unrelated to each other, and may suit the person who proffers them but not the recipient. Box 82 contains a number of common tips identified by Wragg in his project.

Indeed in the same project Wragg outlines several differences between experienced and student teachers. These are shown in Box 83.

One can add other approaches to those from Wragg, for example:[28]

Box 82: Folklore in the classroom

As part of the Teacher Education Project, Wragg collected from student teachers tips or 'tricks of the trade' given them that they had found most useful. The 25 most common are given below in descending order of frequency. Go through the list and consider their value.

1 Start by being firm with pupils: you can relax later.
2 Get silence before you start speaking to the class.
3 Control the pupils' entry to the classroom.
4 Know and use the pupils' names.
5 Prepare lessons thoroughly and structure them firmly.
6 Arrive at the classroom before the pupils.
7 Prepare furniture and apparatus before the pupils arrive.
8 Know how to use apparatus, and be familiar with experiments before you use them in class.
9 Be mobile: walk around the class.
10 Start the lesson with a 'bang' and sustain interest and curiosity.
11 Give clear instructions.
12 Learn voice control.
13 Have additional material prepared to cope with, e.g. bright and slow pupils' needs.
14 Look at the class when speaking, and learn how to scan.
15 Make written work appropriate (e.g. to the age, ability, cultural background of pupils).
16 Develop an effective question technique.
17 Develop the art of timing your lessons to fit the available period.
18 Vary your teaching techniques.
19 Anticipate discipline problems and act quickly.
20 Be firm and consistent in giving punishments.
21 Avoid confrontation.
22 Clarify and insist on YOUR standards.
23 Show yourself as a helper or facilitator to the pupils.
24 Do not patronise pupils, treat them as responsible beings.
25 Use humour constructively.

8 Limit-setting approaches

Here the assertive teacher encourages co-operation and develops relationships with students, setting clearly defined limits on what is acceptable and what is not. Rules are made explicit so that relationships can work well, within the rule system. Positive recognition and incentives build co-operation and effective relationships, and such incentives are graded into degrees; consequences for disruption are also graded. We discuss this later in the section on Assertive Discipline.

9 Cognitive behaviourism

Cognitive approaches seek to promote students' desirable behaviour through regarding behaviour in a problem-solving approach, so that students, autonomously, can exercise self-control. This is facilitated by counselling and discussions between the students and the teacher about ways of handling situations and their behaviour in particular circumstances and environments.

Experienced teachers:

- were usually very clear about their classroom rules
- did not hesitate to describe what they thought was 'right' and 'proper'
- were conscious of the massive effort needed to establish relationships with a new class
- used their eyes a great deal to scan the class or look at individuals
- were quick to deal publicly with infraction of their rules
- were more 'formal' than usual
- were especially brisk and businesslike
- established their presence in the corridor before the class even entered the room
- introduced themselves formally.

Student teachers:

- were not so clear about classroom rules, either their own or those of other teachers in the school
- did not use terms such as 'right' and 'proper' when talking about rules
- were unaware of the massive collective effort the school and individual teachers had put into starting off the school year
- made less use of eye contact and were very conscious of themselves being looked at
- often neglected early infringements of classroom rules which then escalated into larger problems
- concentrated in their preparation on lesson content rather than rules and relationships.

10 Humanistic approaches

In this school of thought effective behaviour is encouraged by adopting a person-centred, emotional approach to their needs and learning. Such an approach is facilitated by democratic relationships in classrooms, with the teacher as a facilitator rather than simply as a director. Hence unacceptable behaviour is discussed in a problem-solving approach rather than a punitive approach, with the deployment of effective counselling and communication skills.

11 Solution-focused approaches

Solution-focused approaches strive to solve problems rather than simply to identify, understand or punish them. They identify goals (end-states) to be reached, strategies for achieving them, and identification of intermediate goals that can be reached, identification of positive exceptions to the problems, and how to reinforce and sustain the solutions and exceptions to the problems. In solution-focused approaches the teacher asks the student what life would be like if such-and-such were not a problem (i.e. if the exceptions became the norm), and then, together, identifying ways of achieving this situation.[29] In many respects solution-focused approaches resonate with the setting of SMART objectives (Specific, Measurable, Achievable, Realistic and Time-bound objectives).

12 Approaches from pioneers of discipline

Many of the approaches outlined above are related to particular seminal writers. For example[30] Glasser[31] suggested that:

- Students are rational and choose to behave in particular ways; the teacher's task is to enable beneficial choices to be made.

- Every class should have some explicit and agreed-upon rules.
- No excuses should be accepted for student misbehaviour.
- Appropriate consequences must follow particular behaviour (be it good or bad behaviour).

Kounin[32] suggested that effective behaviour is contingent on several factors:

- *Withitness:* Teachers need to be aware of what is happening in the classroom.
- *Momentum:* Lessons with a good momentum keep students on track.
- *Smoothness:* Student involvement is increased if lessons run smoothly, particularly in the presentation stages.
- *Group alerting:* There are particular strategies for gaining and sustaining student attention, and for clarifying intentions.
- *Student accountability:* Students are kept actively and attentively involved.
- *Overlapping:* Teachers attend to more than one aspect of the lesson at a time.
- *Satiation:* Teachers know when to stop – when a topic or lesson is saturating students.

Ginott[33] suggested that effective behaviour abides by several key principles:

- Ineffective teachers label and belittle students.
- Effective teachers invite co-operation and act as facilitators.
- Short reprimands and language can be effective.
- Evaluative praise (e.g. 'good boy for raising your hand to speak') can be worse than no praise at all, as it can be demeaning.
- Appreciative praise (positive feedback, and building on what students have done) is useful in responding to effort or achievement.
- It is sometimes useful to avoid using 'why' questions in relation to misbehaviour (e.g. 'Why did you hit Susan?'), as it only makes people feel guilty or elicits a shrug of the shoulders, but no solutions.
- Sarcasm is to be avoided.
- Classroom discipline has to be constantly negotiated and reinforced.

Dreikur[34] suggested several principles that underpin effective discipline:

- Discipline is best construed as self-discipline.
- Effective discipline is best practised in democratic classrooms, and rarely occurs in autocratic or over-permissive classrooms.
- Students want to feel valued, and if they do not, or if they feel isolated from the class, may resort to attention-seeking behaviour.

Finally, Charles[35] identifies a range of key principles that underpin effective synergistic discipline:

- Students are motivated by security, hope, dignity, empowerment, competence and enjoyment; effective teachers address all of these points.
- Co-operation is more effective than force.
- Students usually co-operate with teachers whom they trust.
- Teacher charisma, interest and communication are important elements of a synergistic approach.
- Confrontations should be avoided if possible, replacing them with support.

● Improving behaviour should look at causes, not just symptoms.
● Try to avoid taking misbehaviour personally; that may be incorrect.

13 Specific approaches

It is beyond the scope of this book to go into specific approaches to discipline, though we address behaviour modification and assertive discipline in a little detail towards the end of this chapter, as we regard them as important approaches. However, there is a battery of named approaches and projects to promote effective discipline. Amongst these are included:[36]

● assertive discipline
● behaviour modification
● building a better behaved school
● circle time
● positive discipline
● co-operative discipline
● discipline as self-control
● positive discipline in the classroom
● non-coercive discipline
● discipline with dignity
● inner discipline
● social discipline
● win–win discipline
● beyond discipline
● synergetic discipline.

We refer readers to Wolfgang and Charles[37] for an exposition of these. All of these approaches have received both praise and criticism.[38] For example, the work of Kounin and Jones (positive discipline) is criticised for being, at heart, a model of compliance and teacher control, and for offering simplistic recipes for a complex phenomenon. The work of Dreikur is criticised for assuming that students appreciate the links between punishments and the activities that lead to them, for being tacitly coercive (based on power), and for having adults inflict suffering on students, for promoting anger in students and for operating a counter-intuitive model of democracy as disguised autocracy and compliance. Reward-based approaches have been criticised as being simplistic, short-term and incapable of solving problems. The assertive discipline approach has been criticised for producing robotic, mechanistic students who lack compassion, principles or feelings; for using suffering to teach someone a lesson; for an essentially manipulative and competitive approach to behaviour; for teaching conformity; and for simply not working! You should, however, differentiate between approaches that seem common sense, or reflect popular beliefs, and those for which there is empirical evidence to support their effectiveness.[39]

Clearly there are many, many approaches to discipline. In this chapter we draw on these theories and approaches and attempt to glean from them key features of effective discipline in schools. Our own approach, then, is eclectic and is a synthesis of several principles and practices. Indeed teachers in schools are eclectic, using a synthesis of approaches to fit the situation in hand. This makes sense.

STUDENTS' EXPECTATIONS OF TEACHERS

Whilst there is considerable research into teachers' expectations of pupils, there is significantly less about pupils' expectations of teachers.[40] Wragg[41] notes that students are only rarely brought into the act of thinking about classroom processes. For example, most rules are decided by adults, the content of lessons is frequently chosen by the teacher, and it is assumed that students must know how to learn on their own or in groups. Wragg then refers to examples of proposals that have been put forward for involving students more in this matter of classroom processes.

Glasser,[42] for example, has suggested that students should be involved in discussion about rules and procedures during lessons. He suggests that class time should be used for the teacher to explain about classroom rules and that discussion should take place about these during which they could be adjusted, new rules could be negotiated and problems discussed.

Wragg[43] also refers to ideas put forward by Gordon. He contends that to solve a problem one must decide who 'owns it'. Is it the teacher, the students or is it shared? He recommends a six-step approach:

1 Define the problem.
2 Generate possible solutions.
3 Evaluate these solutions.
4 Decide which solutions seem best.
5 Decide how to implement the chosen solutions.
6 Assess the effectiveness of the solutions chosen.

Both Glasser's and Gordon's approaches demand greater responsibility on the part of the pupils than is normally the case.

Another view of how students see effective teachers is to be found in Gannaway's study.[44] On the basis of interviews and observation, he constructed a dynamic model by proposing that teachers are progressively typified by pupils in a given sequence. The teachers are, in effect, subjected to a systematic series of tests by students, the first of which is 'can the teacher keep order?' The next test is 'can he 'have a laugh'?' And the final test to which the teacher is subjected is 'does he understand pupils?' Gannaway suggests that providing the answer to each of these is yes, and provided the teacher can put over something of interest in the lesson, then he 'has it made'. The implications of these questions are of particular interest. The first test, for instance, 'can the teacher keep order?', implies that the students expect him to do just that, to keep order. Of equal importance is the second challenge, 'can he 'have a laugh'?' What is implied here is that in expecting the teacher to keep order, they do not expect him to be too strict, to impose a regime so harsh that the pupils will eventually rebel (we touch on this as a possible cause of misbehaviour in the next section). What is called for is a 'nice strictness' in preference to a 'nasty strictness'.[45]

The final test, 'does he understand students?', is in some ways the most interesting of the three for it implies an understanding of the class, as a class, as a group, in contrast to understanding individual students, or a group of students on an individual basis. The difference is significant for it means that understanding a group is of a different order to understanding the individual: a different standpoint is required and different knowledge and skills. For a detailed longitudinal study of what pupils expect from teachers and schooling see Ruddock, Chapplain and Wallace (1995).[46]

SOME FACTORS AFFECTING BEHAVIOUR IN CLASSROOMS

As part of his concern to understand the reasons behind students' behaviour, Fontana[47] has identified some of the differences among students which influenced how they behave. Briefly, these include the following.

Age-related differences in behaviour

The effective teacher is aware of the need to adjust the way that motives are imputed to students' behaviour as they grow older. There are also other reasons why age should be regarded as an important factor in dealing with problems of class control. Briefly, these are as follows: the nature of students' demands and expectations of the teacher change as they grow older; the nature of students' relationships with each other changes as they grow older; students grow bigger and stronger as they get older; generally students are more critical of adult behaviour the older they become; older students are often readier to blame adults for their own failures and shortcomings; and students' concentration span and their ability to do theoretical work increases as they develop intellectually.

Ability-related differences in behaviour

Differences in behaviour stemming from variations in ability which Fontana considers important may be briefly stated as follows: motivation for schoolwork will differ markedly from high ability to low ability; different ability levels in students make different demands upon the teacher in terms of personal qualities such as patience and sympathy; the criteria for success and failure differ from one ability level to the next; and the facilities and equipment available for students at different ability levels may differ markedly.

Sex-related differences in behaviour

Fontana considers that the abilities and potential that boys and girls have in common are more important from an educational point of view than any differences. Those differences that do exist are often the result of expectations. Boys are expected to be rowdy and girls more emotional, and in practice each group tends to meet such expectations.

In the primary classroom there may be clear social and academic differences. Girls are more helpful and co-operative, whereas boys show greater interest in sports and practical activities. Boys are more drawn to mathematics, while girls are attracted to reading and writing. Ideally, however, the good teacher will endeavour to minimise differences and provide the sort of learning environment that offers both boys and girls the same kind of opportunities.

The same impartiality should be evident in matters of class control. The good teacher, for example, will give praise to categories of behaviour that are the same for both boys and girls and will thus avoid the kind of situation where boys are praised for good classwork and girls for good social behaviour.

Socio-economic related differences in behaviour

Fontana argues that with the spread of comprehensive schools the differences in the socio-economic character of schools is not as great as it used to be, though it still exists. He identifies the following differences between upper socio-economic status (SES) pupils and lower socio-economic status pupils. In terms of their relevance to class control, they are: students from lower SES backgrounds tend to be lower in self-esteem, perhaps because of their underprivileged environment, than those from upper SES backgrounds; the values and standards taught in schools tend to accord more with those taught in upper SES homes than with those taught in lower SES homes; students from lower SES homes are more likely to find themselves in low-ability groups than students from upper SES homes; and upper SES students are more likely than lower SES students to practise and understand the importance of deferral of satisfaction.

Culturally related differences in behaviour

By culture, Fontana refers not only to sub-cultural variations arising from socio-economic factors, but to variables associated with a child's ethnic group. As he explains, cultural variables may overlap with socio-economic ones, but at the same time they introduce a number of factors potentially important with regard to class control. The more important of these can be summarised thus: religious and moral codes of behaviour may be more strict in certain cultural groups; religious observances and rituals may influence the school behaviours of some students; rivalry and hostility may develop between different cultural groups; students from other ethnic groups may experience language problems in the classroom; and the degree to which students from different cultural groups are taught emotional and social restraint may vary.

We shall have more to say about behavioural problems with some ethnic minority students at the end of this section.

WHAT MAKES STUDENTS MISBEHAVE?

To answer this question comprehensively would require the wisdom of Solomon and more. Fortunately, our intentions in posing it are more modest. Briefly, our suggestions are designed to identify broad types of disruptive behaviour so that the beginning teacher can know what to look for, have some idea of the cause(s), and decide what action (which may sometimes mean inaction) is called for on his part.

On a practical level Kyriacou[48] suggests that classroom misbehaviour has eight main causes:

1   boredom (including if the task is too easy or uninteresting)
2   prolonged mental effort
3   inability to do the work (e.g. frustration or if they are not sure what is required)
4   being sociable (where students' social lives and relationships 'spill over' into the lesson itself
5   low academic self-esteem (e.g. having experienced failure, lack of confidence and learned helplessness)
6   emotional difficulties (which may be out-of-school or in-school, for example bullying, which leads to attention-seeking behaviour)
7   poor attitudes (according low value to school work and school life)
8   lack of negative consequences for disruptive behaviour.

Saunders[49] has identified four main patterns of disruptive behaviour arising from social causes. These are as follows.

1 Antipathy to school

For such students, school is seen as having no place or purpose in their lives. It is an irrelevance for them and consequently they dismiss both school and teachers. The teacher's task in such circumstances is to know how to make schoolwork more relevant and meaningful. Related to this factor of antipathy is what has been termed conflicts of interest. This embraces differences in needs, values and goals between the student and the system as embodied in the teacher and usually results in a show of non-conformity by the students in question. Resolving conflicts of this kind involves negotiation. This will concern the pupil and teacher working out a mutually acceptable settlement.

2 Social dominance

Saunders regards this as an extension of the antipathetic syndrome. He writes:

> Some physically and socially mature pupils seem to have a need for frequent reinforcement in the form of attention from their peers. This is often achieved at school by challenging the authority of the teacher. If the challenge is not met it can be taken up by other pupils and the lesson ruined, and as a result the assertion of the teacher's authority becomes more difficult in future lessons.

How one counters the sort of machismo posturing that this particular problem often assumes is a perennial problem for teachers in present-day classrooms.

3 Social isolation

Some students have strong acceptance needs and a strong yearning to be wanted by their peers. However, they tend to be on the periphery of the group instead of being fully integrated into it. To achieve a sort of affiliation, therefore, they adopt the group's behaviour, though often in extreme form.

4 Inconsequential behaviour

Saunders here refers to those students who seem unable or unwilling to anticipate the consequences of their actions. Such a student, Saunders suggests, 'behaves impulsively instead of reflecting on the courses of action which are open to him and of the possible consequences of each; or he may be unable to inhibit the urge to meet a challenge'. Anticipating an action requires a degree of reflection that, judging from the frequency of this kind of problem in the classroom, many students are incapable of achieving.

To these patterns of disruptive behaviour we can add the following causes of misbehaviour set out by Gnagey.[50] One or other of them will have been experienced already by the student teacher. Thus:

5 Ignorance of the rules

Ignorance of the rules of classroom behaviour is a common cause of misbehaviour. This is particularly the case during a teacher's early contacts with a class. As we shall see in the next section, it takes time to implement a rule, for it has to be learned over a period of time by interpreting it in relation to specific concrete situations. In this respect, Gnagey distinguishes between verbal and actual rules, that is, rules that are acted upon and those that are not. As he says, 'Even if a pupil is presented with a neatly organised set of by-laws, he never really knows which statutes are operational and which are just on paper. As every seasoned teacher knows, classes have a very practical way of solving this problem. They simply proceed to try the teacher out, to see what they can get away with.'

6 Conflicting rules

Difficulties can sometimes arise for the teacher when a student is presented with two sets of conflicting rules – those of the classroom and those of his home. What is permissible in one situation is frowned upon in the other. Invariably it is the home that is the more permissive environment in this respect. Alternatively, the clash may occur between classroom norms and those of the peer group culture outside school. Where the clash is a marked one, the teacher would be best advised to seek a negotiated settlement with the student in question if lasting peace is to be achieved.

7 Displacement

As we have just seen, inappropriate behaviour may occur in the classroom because it is perfectly acceptable in another context, like the home or neighbourhood. A similar situation may occur with respect to feelings; inappropriate feelings are often displaced on the people and objects in the school. Thus, a student's hatred for his father may be transferred to his male form teacher. In an age where there is increased social dislocation through divorce, separation and one-parent families, displacement as a cause of disruptive behaviour might be more widespread than ever before.

8 Anxiety

A great deal of misbehaviour in the classroom is caused by anxious reactions to features in the educational environment – examinations, having to speak in class, being judged publicly etc. Earlier research by Gnagey[51] disclosed that disruptive students tended to be more afraid than their well-behaved classmates.

9 Leadership styles as causes of misbehaviour

Finally, Gnagey identifies a number of leadership styles on the part of teachers that can incite disciplinary problems rather than solve them. These include the despot and the nonentity. The despot, as he explains, embraces a custodial view of student control and his main concern is with keeping order. He tends to view students in negative and stereotypical terms. Student response to a lasting tyrannical style of this kind is invariably anger, which can manifest itself in a variety of ways, often indirectly as with vandalism or bullying or, in more extreme cases, arson. In a word, displacement is operating.

The nonentity, as the name suggests, is totally ineffectual. His generally over-permissive, non-interventionist approach, combined with an unwillingness to utilise such fundamental psychological principles as motivation and rewards, is likely to generate feelings of restlessness on the part of pupils and a tendency to be easily distracted.

In a study by Dierenfield[52] (quoted in Watkins and Wagner),[53] teachers in a sample of English comprehensive schools were asked to rate ten provided causes of disruptive behaviour. The proportion who rated each item as 'an important cause' was as follows:

Unsettled home environment	49.6%
Peer pressure	35.6%
Lack of interest in subject	30.7%
General disinterest in school	30.5%
Pupil psychological or emotional instability	29.4%
Inability to do classwork	21.9%
Revolt against adult authority	20.8%
Lack of self-esteem	13.7%
Dislike of teacher	12.7%
Use of drugs	4.9%

School processes can clearly be seen as a source of problems resulting in disruptive behaviour. The questionnaire also revealed that heads and deputy heads endorsed extra-school factors, i.e. home, peers and instability, as significant causes more than teachers.

When it came to the kinds of response teachers should make to such causes, the ten most frequently rated were:

1	Positive teacher personality	89.7%
2	Effective teaching methods	87.6%
3	Establishing and maintaining behaviour standards early on	86.3%
4	Firm support of teacher discipline measures by head	70.8%
5	Consistent application of behaviour standards to all pupils	69.3%
6	Support of school by parents	68.7%
7	Treating causes of behaviour problems	66.6%
8	Influence of head	56.0%
9	Pastoral care programme	40.3%
10	Strict disciplinary measures by teacher	39.9%

The teacher and school aspects feature strongly here. Measures such as exclusion, special classes, streaming and the school social worker received less support, though they were still seen as useful possibilities. Head teachers and their deputies gave above-average support to those factors involving parents and the pastoral care programme.

One way of preventing behaviour problems arising in the first place is to have adequate rules as means of controlling student behaviour. It is to a consideration of this topic that we now address ourselves.

RULES AND ROUTINES IN THE CLASSROOM

Hargreaves[54] reminds us that rules specify acceptable forms of classroom conduct and that they are either laid down by the teacher or arrived at by agreement between him and the students. Rules play an important part in helping to define the classroom situation. Although each teacher makes a somewhat different list, most rules are based on moral, personal, legal, safety and educational considerations.

Educational settings have traditionally featured too many rules, especially punitive ones,[55] and it is important that such a list be kept to a minimum for at least three reasons: (1) the number of disciplinary actions a teacher takes is kept to a minimum also; (2) rules contribute to stultifying the atmosphere of school and classroom; and (3) there is some evidence from research[56] that rules by themselves exert little influence on classroom behaviour; in other words, they need to be seen in relation to other factors in the classroom situation. The criteria for helping to achieve such a minimum list are relevance, meaningfulness and positiveness, thus:

Relevance

Making one's list relevant requires that a teacher has a clear idea of the objectives of a particular lesson or course of lessons. The list may be flexible and may vary from lesson to lesson, though not to the extent that would confuse students or give them the opportunity to justify misbehaviour.

Meaningfulness

Rules that are seen to derive logically from the nature of the task are more acceptable to students than ones that are imposed arbitrarily by the teacher and are not easily seen to relate to the task or context. What seems to be required here is a degree of negotiation between the teacher and his pupils.

Positiveness

Where possible, rules should be expressed positively since a positive statement offers a goal to work towards rather than something to avoid. Thus, 'work quietly' is preferable to 'do not talk'. A list of don'ts can have an inhibiting effect on classroom behaviour.

Hargreaves[57] suggests that the teacher should attempt to lay down her/his minimum list during the very first encounter with a class. This may cover such areas as entering the room, movement about the room, modes of address, when to talk and when not to talk, work and homework attitudes, and the distribution and use of materials and equipment. He also recommends that these should be fairly comprehensive, though not so general as to offer little guidance in specific situations; and that during subsequent meetings with the class the teacher ensures that the rules are understood, learned and conformed to, often with relation to concrete situations that arise in the class.

As well as establishing rules, the student teacher should also make explicit to the students during his early contact with them just what they can take for granted, e.g. can they use the pencil sharpener without asking permission? Clarification of this kind serves a dual purpose – it keeps formal rules to a minimum and cuts out undue fussiness.

Wragg and Wood (1984)[58] identified 11 classroom rules in secondary schools (Box 84).

Indeed Wragg[59] suggests that there will need to be rules for several areas: movement, talking (e.g. not to talk when the teacher or somebody else is talking; raising a hand to speak; no calling out), work-related matters (e.g. how to ask for help; what to do if you don't understand what to do or how to do it), presentation, safety, space, materials, social behaviour and clothing/appearance. The school may well have such rules, about which the student teacher should enquire. If these do not exist, or are selective, then it may be important for the student teacher to develop these with, and for, the students. However, many writers[60] argue that classroom rules should be limited to four or five and supported by a number of procedural routines.

Box 84: Rules in secondary school

1. There must be no talking when the teacher is talking.
2. There must be no disruptive noises.
3. There must be rules for entering, leaving and moving in classrooms.
4. There must be no interference with the work of others.
5. Work must be completed in a specified way.
6. Pupils must raise their hand to answer, not shout out.
7. Pupils must make a positive effort in their work.
8. Pupils must not challenge the authority of the teacher.
9. Respect must be shown for property and equipment.
10. There must be rules to do with safety.
11. Pupils must ask if they do not understand.

Other procedures (if not already established), though not strictly codifiable as rules, should likewise be made explicit early on, certainly during the first few contacts, e.g. do you require all the students' written work to be headed with the date? If so, make it clear to them when the first occasion for written work occurs and specify how you want it presented. A new line? On the left-hand side? Underlined? No abbreviations . . . or whatever.

In addition to rules formally laid down by the teacher or school, there are often supplementary rules of a more informal nature. Writing of such, Denscombe[61] says:

> In one sense these informal rules are much more localised than general school rules. They operate in particular classrooms, at particular times and with particular people: they are 'context specific'. So, for example, rules about the amount of noise which is permissible will depend on the kind of lesson being taught, on the teacher in charge, on the kinds of pupils, on the phase of the lesson, and on the day/week/term. Even then, these rules can be altered, suspended or renegotiated depending on the circumstances.

Indeed, as the author later points out, rules are not always imposed on students but are often the result of negotiation and renegotiation – 'the end product of a subtle bargaining procedure between teacher and students in which disagreement and resistance need to be overcome'.

In summary, good classroom management involves establishing clear rules where rules are needed, avoiding unnecessary ones, eliminating punitive ones, reviewing them periodically, and changing or dropping them when appropriate. Additionally, greater flexibility may be introduced by having recourse to more informal arrangements, frequently arrived at by negotiations and bargaining.

The partner to rules is routines. There is a certain security in routines that can promote good behaviour. So, for example, the student teacher would be well advised to assimilate the existing routines of the class(es) and, if there are none, generate some of her own and communicate these to the students, covering, for example:

- entering and leaving the classroom
- accessing, giving out, sharing and putting away materials
- having work marked
- leaving their seats and moving around the classroom
- attracting and maintaining the attention of the class
- changing activities
- catching up on incomplete work
- occupying students who complete work quickly
- going to the toilet
- using resources from other rooms
- preparing for registration/assemblies/dismissal.

We continue by identifying some of the well-tried techniques used by experienced teachers for dealing with unacceptable behaviour in the classroom.

SUGGESTIONS FOR HANDLING MINOR MISBEHAVIOUR PROBLEMS

The techniques reviewed below may be of some assistance to student teachers when dealing with minor misbehaviour problems of a passing kind such as inattention, distraction or mischievousness. When faced with infringements of this nature, the aim of the teacher should be to cut short the incipient misbehaviour before it develops and spreads, without interrupting the flow of the lesson or distracting other students unnecessarily. In many cases the secret is to pre-empt misbehaviour, rather than waiting for it to occur. Such pre-emptive strategies include:[62]

- Scan the classroom to identify difficulties, e.g. learning problems.
- Circulate round the room to identify learning problems.
- Make eye contact, particularly with a student whom you suspect of misbehaviour.
- Target your questions, including to those whom you think may be losing concentration and possibly about to misbehave, i.e. to reinvolve them.
- Use proximity: moving towards the student, not necessarily speaking, can be enough to prevent misbehaviour.
- Give academic help.
- Change activities or pace, e.g. if the students are having too many problems, becoming bored or frustrated, or if they are ready to move on.
- Notice misbehaviour, maybe through eye contact and your consequent facial expression, which can be more powerful than a verbal reprimand.
- Notice disrespect, e.g. if a student has a discourteous, poor attitude to you or to others.
- Move pupils, separating them and seating them as you require. Remember that your task as a teacher is to promote learning, so that if students' voluntary seating arrangements are not promoting learning then you have a duty to intervene. Students' seating arrangements are not an automatic right for students, but a constrained privilege.

Constant monitoring of the class

Good and Brophy[63] have emphasised the need for monitoring or scanning as an important factor in successful classroom management. By this they mean keeping the class and its individual members constantly under observation. Kounin,[64] likewise, stresses the value of this technique, noting that teachers possessing it show with-it-ness, that is, an awareness of what is happening in class. And Peters[65] says, 'The good teacher is always, as it were, 'out there' in the classroom, not wrapped up in his own involuted musings. He is aware of everything that is going on and the students sense vividly his perception of them as well as his grasp of his subject matter.' A teacher with this kind of awareness can respond immediately to a minor problem before it has time to develop into something more disruptive.

Brown[66] summarises the main signals to look for when monitoring a class in this way. Briefly, these are:

- *Posture:* Are the students turned towards or away from the object of the lesson?
- *Head orientation:* Are the students looking at or away from the object of the lesson?
- *Face:* Do the students look sleepy or awake? Do they look withdrawn or involved? Do they look interested or uninterested?
- *Activities:* Are the students working on something related to the lesson, or are they attending to something else? Where they are talking to their fellow pupils are their discussions task-oriented or not?
- *Responses:* Are the students making appropriate or inappropriate responses to your questions?

The vital need, then, is for the student teacher constantly to scan her group in an active, alert and expectant manner. Not only is she thus in a position to check or deter incipient disturbances, she also shows the class that she is in the frame of mind to know what is going on. There are some classroom situations where the student teacher is restricted in this respect – when she is writing on the whiteboard, sitting at her desk or at a piano, or when dealing with an individual student or small group. On such occasions, not only must she be extra vigilant, she must be seen to be so.

On a more positive note, lively and interested classes, as Brown notes, usually sit with their heads slightly forward, their eyes wide open and a few eagerly waiting for a chance to speak.

Ignoring minor misbehaviour

Good and Brophy[67] consider that it is not necessary for a teacher to intervene in a direct way every time he or she notices a minor control problem. Muijs and Reynolds[68] also indicate the need to avoid over-reacting when faced with misbehaviour. Research evidence[69] suggests that the combination of ignoring inappropriate behaviour and showing approval for desirable behaviour can sometimes be a more effective way of achieving better classroom behaviour. Further, the disruptive effect of the teacher's intervention, as Good and Brophy point out, can sometimes create a greater problem than the one the teacher is attempting to solve.

Having made the above recommendation, however, we need to file a caveat in the case of the student teacher experiencing his or her first teaching practice. The overlooking of a minor discipline problem by a student teacher, especially where the class knows the person teaching them is a student, could easily be misconstrued by students as either weakness or lack of awareness. They may even seize the opportunity to test the teacher out in his or her newness – 'We've got away with it once, let's go one better!' As the outcomes of a student teacher's first few encounters with the students are vital to her in defining the situation and establishing the power structure she wants, it is advisable that all early challenges to her authority be checked and that she explores the more subtle technique of 'turning a blind eye' later in her practice, when she has the measure of the group.

This is perhaps a suitable juncture for the reader to give some consideration to what is often the bane of some student teachers' lives – noise. In Box 85 we summarise some of the findings of case studies of three schools by Denscombe.[70] Review the points made in relation to yourself and your own subject specialism(s).

Box 85: Noise in the classroom

Denscombe's case studies of three schools disclosed the following broad categories of noise:

Allowable noise: This came from such lessons as PE, drama and music where it was recognised that the normal rules could not reasonably operate and where, within bounds, more noise could be tolerated without impugning the competence of the teacher in charge.

Unavoidable noise: Although the blaring of a tape-recorder or the rasping noise of classroom furniture being scraped across a floor may be a nuisance that interferes with an adjacent lesson, such noise does not immediately signify poor control.

Acceptable occasional noise: From time to time a teacher may have a lively class and a lively lesson where the presence of noise would be interpreted as a sign of action and enthusiasm rather than apathy or poor control.

Unacceptable noise: Here, pupil-initiated noise, created by pupils and/or their teacher's responses, is taken to be an indication of a lack of control in the classroom. The cacophony of talking students interspersed with the raised voice of a teacher invariably carries all the connotation of a control problem. However, noise appears to be excusable when emanating from groups that all teachers find difficult to control.

DEALING WITH REPEATED MINOR MISBEHAVIOUR

There are several techniques available to student teachers for intervening in cases of repeated minor misbehaviour when it threatens to disrupt a lesson or spread to other students in the class.[71] These should be used in preference to more dramatic procedures whenever the student teacher wishes to check, for example, persistent inattentiveness or restlessness without distracting others. The more obviously useful of these techniques include the following.

Eye contact

One of the most effective ways of checking a minor infraction is simply to look at the offender and establish eye contact with her. A cold, glassy stare has an eloquence of its own. An accompanying nod or gesture will assist in refocusing the student's attention on the task in hand.

Touch and gesture

A particularly useful technique in small group situations is the use of touch and gesture. A misbehaving student near at hand can easily be checked by touching his head or shoulder lightly (obviously taking care to avoid any behaviour that could be construed as assault), or by gesturing. The non-verbal nature of this approach ensures that others are not distracted, that is, Kounin's[72] notion of smoothness is preserved.

Physical closeness

Minor misbehaviour can also be eliminated or inhibited by moving towards the offender. This is especially useful with older students. If they know what they should be doing, the mere act of moving in their direction will assist in redirecting their attention to their work.

Inviting a response

Another effective means of summoning a student's wandering attention is to ask her a question. The utility of questioning for control purposes is often overlooked. It would seem reasonable to relate a question used for this end to the content of the lesson at the time of the incident, that is, to make it 'task-centred', not 'teacher-centred'. Thus, 'What would you have done in such a situation, John?' is preferable to 'What did I just say, John?'

Other non-verbal gestures

In addition to the ones noted above, there are other non-verbal means of expressing disapproval or checking an infraction. Common examples would include frowning, raising the eyebrows, wagging or 'clicking' a finger or shaking the head negatively.

The advantages of these and similar techniques are that they enable the teacher to eliminate minor problems without disrupting the activity or calling attention to the misdeed. Eye contact, touch and gesture, physical propinquity and other non-verbal gestures are the simplest since no verbalisation is involved.

DEALING WITH PERSISTENT DISRUPTIVE BEHAVIOUR

The techniques described so far will assist the student teacher in solving relatively minor problems of control and management. For more serious disruptions, we make the following additional suggestions.

Direct intervention

Good and Brophy[73] note that the direct intervention required for more serious misbehaviour may take two forms. First, a student teacher can command an end to the behaviour and follow this up by indicating what alternative behaviour would be appropriate. In such a situation, intervention should be short, direct and to the point. It should thus name the student, identify the misbehaviour and indicate what should be done instead. When a student knows she is misbehaving, a brief directive indicating what she should be doing should be sufficient: 'Janet, finish the exercise I gave you.'

The second direct intervention technique which Good and Brophy suggest is simply to remind the students of relevant rules and expected behaviour. As suggested earlier, clear-cut rules defining acceptable classroom behaviour should be formulated early on in the practice (or revised if you take over the class teacher's existing rules), possibly after explanation and discussion with the students if they are old enough. Where this has been done, all the student teacher has to do is to remind the class or student of them as soon as a problem manifests itself.

A third means is through the use of reprimands, and we deal with this later in this chapter.

Interview techniques

In his discussion of management techniques in the classroom, Saunders[74] outlines two forms of interview that may be used for achieving workable arrangements with those students presenting lasting behaviour problems for the teacher. The investigative interview is a useful strategy where the more serious forms of misbehaviour are present and may be used where one or more students are involved. Saunders recommends that the interview should concern only the student or students involved in the incident for, as he explains, this reduces the possibility of 'acting up' and bias resulting from group pressures. Ideally, the student or students should be given time to 'cool off'. Where more than one is involved, each should be allowed to give his version of what took place, the student teacher only interrupting to clarify questions of fact and to distinguish fact from opinion. Discrepancies in the story line should be resolved and a final account established that is acceptable to all. Saunders is of the opinion that defence mechanisms or strategies are often used by students when giving explanations in order to protect them from anxiety regarding the consequences of their behaviour. Those commonly used are denial, projection and rationalisation. Where possible these should be identified and brought out into the open. The interview will eventually lead to appropriate action which may take the form of striking a deal with the students, punishment or referral to a higher authority. Box 86 summarises the main points.

The second form of interview discussed by Saunders is the reality interview. This depends for its effectiveness on good personal relations between the student teacher and student and on the knowledge that neither will be intimidated by the other. Given these conditions, the student teacher should get the pupil to admit the misbehaviour. This achieved, the discussion should move on to an evaluation of the behaviour in question. Cause and effect links should be established. Finally, Saunders considers that the student should be encouraged to discuss a more effective course of action for the future, with the teacher impressing on her that she is responsible for her own behaviour and will subsequently be accountable for it. The main steps in this process are summarised in Box 87.

Box 86: Investigative interviews

Investigative interviews may be summarised as follows:

- Try not to become emotionally involved.
- If possible exclude anyone not involved in the incident.
- Each student should be required to give his/her own version of what happened.
- The teacher should clarify the facts and differentiate them from opinion.
- Try to recognise the use of defence mechanisms.
- If possible, explain their use to the student.
- Take further appropriate action.
- Remember your actions may serve as models for other students.

Conflict-resolving strategies and techniques

Saunders further discusses the strategies and techniques that student teachers sometimes resort to in order to resolve conflict situations. These he considers in three broad categories – avoidance strategies, diffusion strategies and confrontation strategies.

First, *avoidance strategies*. Saunders identifies strategies here which include high tolerance, feigned illness and engaging in banter. If a student teacher can build up high tolerance, she will be in a position to ignore much of the conflict in which she is involved until a breakdown point is reached. Retreating from a conflict situation under the guise of illness is another technique sometimes employed. And engaging in banter with pupils is yet another means of side-stepping conflict. As Saunders says, 'Avoidance strategies may have some survival value, but they are maladaptive in so far as the individual teacher does not receive any measure of professional satisfaction and the conflict is not resolved.'

Second, *diffusion strategies*. These include delaying action, tangential responses, evasion and appeals to generalisability. Delaying action, as it suggests, involves putting off a decision to avoid precipitating a crisis. A tangential response is one that deals with peripheral issues, thus leaving the main source of conflict unresolved. Evasion is resorted to when a student teacher is called on to justify her position and side-steps the issue. And an appeal to generalisability is resorted to when a

Box 87: Reality interviews

The principal guidelines to reality interviewing are:

- discuss in private with no hint of intimidation from either side
- start from an existing relationship, if possible
- establish the need for frankness
- evaluate the misdeed
- link cause and effect
- establish other causes of action and their consequences
- discuss the most effective action for the future.

student teacher concedes that a demand is reasonable when it is made by one person, but not if others make a similar request. Like avoidance strategies, diffusion strategies are generally unsatisfactory.

Finally, confrontation strategies. These include the use of power and negotiation strategies. A student teacher resorts to power strategies when she uses the divide-and-rule approach; when she resorts to pseudo-power by threatening sanctions she knows she cannot implement; by manipulating rewards; and by resorting to school tradition – 'This isn't the way we do it here.' Negotiation strategies are invoked when there is the possibility of a rational solution to the difficulty. Saunders identifies three approaches in this respect – compromise, affiliative appeal and pseudo-compromise.

Watkins and Wagner[75] suggest a number of principles which would serve to de-escalate a developing confrontation. These have much in common with Saunders' strategies as a comparison between the two approaches will show:

- Avoid public arenas in which people may crystallise their position in front of an audience.
- 'Is what has led to this really so important as to justify this escalation?'
- Avoid threats of any sort, especially those which could be perceived as physical.
- Look for an alternative which is presently not being explored in which both can 'win'.
- Encourage the student to say more about his/her perception of what is going on.
- Explain your own view of things clearly, and in a way which is not simplified.

With practice, Watkins and Wagner suggest that

> these principles can be applied in such a way that student teachers' common reactions about feelings of 'condoning' or 'climbing down' are not precipitated, and teachers can agree that desired behaviour from pupils is not brought about by confrontation.

Kyriacou[76] indicates six principles for handling confrontations:

1 *Stay calm.* This may help the student to calm down.
2 *Defuse the situation,* maybe by backing off temporarily and picking up the matter when everyone has cooled down. (The student teacher can do this without loss of face, simply by saying that the student is not calm enough for the matter to be dealt with at the moment, so he/she will wait until the student has calmed down.)
3 *Be aware of the heat of the moment*, and don't do something that you may later regret.
4 *Use your social skills* to avoid the student losing face, as this may pay dividends in relationships later.
5 *Design a mutual face-saver* with words and actions.
6 *Get help if necessary* (the school should have policies and procedures on this).

In summary, then, whereas the conflict-avoidance strategies may have a certain survival value to all teachers at some stage in their careers, as permanent features of one's professional behavioural repertoire they need to be regarded with suspicion because they offer neither long-term solutions nor personal satisfaction.

We next consider how a reprimand from a teacher can influence the response of the rest of the class.

THE RIPPLE EFFECT

Research by Kounin[77] revealed that a reprimand from a teacher to a student misbehaving in his class may influence the rest of the group although they are not actually party to the misdemeanour.

Kounin labelled this the ripple effect and as such it may have either positive or negative influences from the student teacher's point of view. When, for instance, a student being reprimanded is of high standing in the structure of the group, the ripple effect from an encounter with the student teacher is usually strong. If the student teacher succeeds in checking the misbehaviour, the effect on the rest of the class from the student teacher's perspective is positive in that they will tend to accept the reprimand as fair and think of the student teacher as an effective disciplinarian. In practical terms, it means that they will either improve their behaviour or be less likely to behave unsatisfactorily. If, however, the high-prestige student rebels at the student teacher's efforts to control him, this feeling may spread to his classmates, who may then consider the teacher's handling of the situation as unsatisfactory and consequently perceive him as weak and ineffectual. The practical consequences could be an escalation of the problem, with the rest of the class expressing resentment or generally creating an atmosphere not conducive to meaningful work.

Since it is therefore important to produce a positive ripple effect, that is, an improvement or inhibition of the behaviour of other pupils, certain characteristics of control need to be borne in mind. Gnagey[78] identified a number of such factors including clarity, firmness, task-centred techniques, high-prestige pupils and roughness. Each will be considered briefly.

Clarity

What Gnagey describes as a clear control technique, one embodying clarity, is one that specifies the defiant, the deviancy and the preferred alternative behaviour. Thus, 'John, stop talking and finish your essay' is preferable to 'Cut out the talking at the back there', for it is a clear command and therefore can be expected to have two beneficial effects on the rest of the class; they will be less likely to talk themselves and less likely to be disrupted in their own work than would probably be the case with a command lacking clarity.

Firmness

Firm control techniques prevent disruption more effectively than tentative ones. Gnagey recommends that they can best be implemented by moving towards the offender, issuing the command in an 'I-mean-it' tone, and following through by seeing the command is obeyed before continuing with the lesson. Kounin and Gump[79] found that students responded to rules that were actually enforced ('followed through') but ignored those lacking conviction and enforcement ('follow-through').

Task-centred techniques

A task-centred approach produces a more desirable ripple effect than one that is teacher-centred. By this is meant the need to stress the task in hand, or the effects of the deviancy on the task, rather than on the student teacher or the student teacher's relationship with the pupil. Thus, 'John, stop whispering and watch the demonstration, or else you won't understand when you have to do it yourself later' is better than 'Pay attention and listen to me.'

High-prestige students

Gnagey recommends that high-prestige students be identified and studied. He writes, 'As their responses to your influence have such a strong ripple effect on others, it will pay to find out which control techniques cause them to respond submissively with the least amount of belligerence.'

Roughness

Gnagey explains that roughness refers to the use of threatening or violent control techniques on the part of the teacher that in turn are likely to produce negative ripples – anger, resentment, feelings of injustice or displacement, as well as being illegal. Kounin *et al.*[80] found that such techniques produced a considerable amount of disruptive behaviour among students who were not originally misbehaving themselves. A further consequence was that they also held the student teacher in lower esteem because of his manner.

In summary, the beginning teacher should seek positive ripples through clarity, firmness, task-centred techniques, capitalising on high-prestige students and the avoidance of roughness. We continue by taking the important skill of giving orders and instructions a little further.

Issuing orders and instructions

Although some teachers are more effective at it than others, giving instructions to an individual, group or class is a skill that can be learned and improved with practice. Like other techniques, issuing instructions, orders and commands can be broken down into their basic components such as content, phrasing, manner of delivery and context.

The prevailing conditions play a part in the overall effectiveness of instructions; the class must be still and silent, ideally before an instruction is given. Thus, 'Stop whatever you are doing, please; no more talking, stop writing.' Then give your instruction.

The manner of delivery is also important. You have to avoid being too stern and imperious on the one hand, yet too diffident and unconvincing on the other. The one approach can induce fear (which is not desirable); the other, an ineffectualness on the teacher's part. A firm but pleasant manner is required. Marland's[81] advice in this connection is eminently practical: 'It is worth practising instructions on your own. Then listen to yourself as you give them in school and observe the response. Develop a firm warmth, or a warm firmness.'

Generally speaking, instructions tend to be more effective and to be accepted more gracefully when phrased in a positive, rather than a negative, manner. Accordingly, 'Be early for the practical lesson on Monday' in preference to 'Don't be late for Monday's lesson.' Or, 'Leave the room as tidy as you found it' rather than 'Don't leave the room in such a mess this week.'

Marland warns against framing an instruction in the form of a question. For example, the organisational and management problems encouraged by 'Anyone need paper?' will be minimised by expressing the point thus: 'Put your hands up if you're without paper.'

You should not give a second instruction until the first one has been obeyed. Take time to glance round the room and check that everyone has understood and carried out your order.

Finally, the following points may be useful to readers in their consideration of the use of commands as a technique of control:

- Task-oriented commands are often preferable to status-oriented ones. As Peters[82] observes, 'If commands are task-oriented rather than status-oriented they are a thoroughly rational device for controlling and directing situations where unambiguous directions or prohibitions are obviously necessary.'
- Generally speaking, the reason for a command should not be given, as this introduces an element of doubt or suggests that it may not or need not be obeyed. In any case, if the system of rules operating in the classroom has been explained to the group at an earlier stage, there should be no need for elaboration.
- A command should not be coupled with a statement of grievance, as this may arouse hostility

towards, or induce disrespect for, the person issuing the command. For example, avoid this sort of utterance: 'Stop moving the chairs to the back of the room. I'm tired of telling you. You do it every time you come into the room.'

● Similarly, a command couched in the language of a whine 'operates powerfully to bring about its own frustration'.[83]

● Once you have got to know your class, requests – a more polite form of command – may be all that you need to structure the situation.

● The voice issuing the command should be strong, decisive and warm.

● The student teacher's own expectations play a part, too. Students will tend to conform not so much to what she says in words but to what she actually expects. She must therefore expect more or less instant obedience to her commands as a matter of course.

● The verbal context of the message is also important. It is vital that it stands out in relief from what the teacher has said immediately preceding its issue and, especially, from what he says subsequently. A directive can easily lose much of its force by becoming indistinguishable from its context in terms of timbre, tone, dynamics, manner and speed of delivery. Timing, the judicious use of pauses and silence, social dynamics, facial expressions and a touch of drama will all assist in achieving greater salience.

● A student teacher may further enhance the effectiveness of her commands by having the class come to associate them with certain additional non-verbal features such as clapping the hands, snapping the fingers, staring, gesturing or moving to a focal point in the room.

ISSUING REPRIMANDS

It will sometimes be necessary to issue reprimands, either in private or, if deemed appropriate, in public. A reprimand is an explicit verbal comment or, indeed, a warning, and is designed to cause a behaviour to cease at very short notice, if not immediately. It cuts through the time and trouble taken to investigate, discuss, counsel and negotiate, and can be effective when used infrequently. Issuing too many reprimands suffers from the law of diminishing returns, indeed it can cause even more disruptive behaviour as students respond with increasing frustration to a 'nagging' teacher. In using reprimands student teachers should consider several important issues:[84]

● Target correctly (to the correct student).

● Be firm (in tone, expression and content).

● Express concern (e.g. that the student and others are suffering because of the misbehaviour).

● Avoid anger (i.e. avoid losing your temper, as some students will enjoy provoking you to this).

● Emphasise what is required, so that the student knows what to do.

● Maintain psychological impact, e.g. by eye contact before, during and after the reprimand.

● Avoid confrontations, even if this means following it up at the end of the lesson (and telling the student that you will follow it up with her/him at the end of the lesson).

● Criticise the behaviour, not the student, as this signals that you still care for the student (e.g. avoid insulting a student: 'George, you're behaving stupidly' can be replaced with 'George, it's time to get on with your work now', or 'George, is there a problem with your work?')

● Use private rather than public reprimands as this saves embarrassment for the student; if the student is embarrassed this could escalate the problem. A public reprimand may be necessary if you intend the message to have a 'knock-on' effect for the whole class (see the earlier discussion of the ripple effect).

● Be pre-emptive.

● State rules and rationale – the reason for the rule and the reason for the reprimand.

- Avoid making hostile remarks, e.g. sarcasm and ridicule, as this often exacerbates relationships.
- Avoid unfair comparisons, e.g. to other students or siblings.
- Be consistent in your use of reprimands and the rules/rationales that underpin them.
- Do not make empty threats, which means that you must carry out the threat if you make it. The threat must be appropriate, realistic and meaningful. Sometimes a veiled threat (e.g. 'if you don't stop interrupting then you will be in serious trouble') is as effective as an explicit threat (e.g. 'if you don't stop interrupting then I will contact your parents'), as it keeps the choice open to you, and, indeed, the punishment may be so awful as to defy being made explicit!
- Avoid reprimanding the whole class unless it is really necessary and deserved. A class discussion rather than a class threat may be more effective in reducing misbehaviour.
- Make an example, if deserved, to dissuade others ('pour encourager les autres'), a strategy that more experienced teachers sometimes use deliberately in their early meetings with a class, as it sets the rules for classroom behaviour very explicitly. Use this with caution; it may backfire as it may cause the other students to take the side of the student rather than the teacher.

Another useful guide in this context is suggested by the work of O'Leary *et al.*,[85] who studied the effects of loud and soft reprimands on the behaviour of disruptive students. Briefly, two students in each of five classes were selected for a four-month study because of their high rates of disruptive behaviour. In the first phase of the study, almost all reprimands were found to be of a loud nature and could be heard by many other students in the class. During the second phase, however, the teachers were asked to use mainly soft reprimands which were audible only to the students being reprimanded. With the institution of soft reprimands, the frequency of disruptive behaviour declined in most of the students. This sequence was repeated with the same results.

REWARDS AND PUNISHMENTS

Older books on the psychology of education make great play of the concepts of extrinsic and intrinsic rewards as aids to motivation and to a lesser extent classroom management and control. Indeed their validity and usefulness in these respects still hold good. Extrinsic rewards such as marks, grades, stars, prizes and public commendation are stock examples in this context and are there for the student teacher to exploit. Intrinsic rewards, like the warm feeling from a job well done, or satisfying one's innate curiosity, or the kick one gets from solving a problem or achieving a standard one has set oneself, belong to an individual's subjective world and are, as such, beyond the student teacher's direct control, but high-quality lessons encourage engagement and curiosity. Teachers can influence intrinsic rewards indirectly through the use of extrinsic rewards. The connection between the two is often overlooked, nor are they oppositional for the skilful manipulation of extrinsic rewards over a period of time can lead to the more desirable intrinsic kind or maintain interest when curiosity is waning.[86] Contrasting perspectives on rewards in the classroom by pupils and teachers respectively are indicated in Box 88.[87]

In general praise is more effective than punishment, for several reasons.[88] Punishment:

- does not tend to generalise across teachers, i.e. a punishment may work in stopping a student from performing an undesirable behaviour for teacher A, who administered the punishment, but not for teacher B, who did not
- is no guarantee that the desired behaviour will ensue; it may only prevent the undesired behaviour from occurring
- does not address the causes of misbehaviour, only the symptoms.

Box 88: Pupil and teacher perspectives on rewards

In a study on the relative effectiveness of various incentives and deterrents as judged by pupils and teachers, it was found that:

Pupils preferred:
- favourable home report
- to do well in a test
- to be given a prize
- to receive good marks for written work.

Whereas the staff thought the most effective rewards were:
- to be praised in the presence of others
- good marks for written work
- elected to leadership by fellow pupils
- teacher expressing quiet appreciation.

The advice, therefore, is to use it very sparingly, as a last resort and to ensure that it is linked to promoting the desired behaviour, not only to punishing the undesired behaviour.

The Office for Standards in Education found the following to be rewards that were valued by secondary school students:[89]

- privileges such as use of school equipment (IT) or rooms (music)
- mention at public meetings (assembly)
- certificates of merit
- being given more responsibility
- work displayed (particularly art and good stories)
- parents being informed
- being allowed out to the shops
- an outing at the end of term
- joining members of staff for a meal in a restaurant.

It was reported also[90] that 'the withdrawal of previously earned rewards is a practice particularly despised by pupils and can itself create a flash-point'.

Rewards

Merrett and Jones[91] classified three 'grades' of extrinsic rewards. Lower-order rewards include: praise, points, credits and tokens. Medium order rewards include: certificates, badges, being allowed privileges, comments put on reports, a letter home.[92] Higher-order rewards include prizes and very public credit. Rewards can be very motivating for students. Capel[93] indicates that students can be very motivated by achievement, enjoyment of a task, satisfaction (the feeling that one is improving) and success (e.g. in an examination). She outlines four types of reward:

1   *social rewards* (social contact and pleasant interaction with other people)
2   *token rewards* (house points, certificates)

3   *material rewards* (tangible, usable items)
4   *activity rewards* (opportunities for enjoyable activities).

Perhaps the most immediately accessible means of reward for the student teacher is the use of praise, and its value in the classroom should not be overlooked. It has been demonstrated by Madsen, Becker and Thomas[94] that showing approval for appropriate behaviour is probably the key to effective classroom management. Much of this kind of approval will take the form of verbal praise, so it is important for the teacher to understand both the constructive and damaging effects of its classroom use. Waller's[95] comments are apposite here:

> The whole matter of control by praise is puzzling and a bit paradoxical. Where it is wisely carried on, it may result in the most happy relations between students and teachers. Where it is unwisely applied it is absurdly ineffective and ultimately very damaging to the child. Praise must always be merited, and it must always be discreet, else all standards disappear. Cheap praise both offends and disappoints, and it breaks down the distinction between good and bad performances. Praise must always be measured; it must not resort to superlatives, for superlatives give the comfortable but deadening sense of a goal attained. Such praise as is used must open the way to development and not close it. Praise must always be sincere, for otherwise it is very difficult to make it sincere, and if it does not seem sincere it fails to hearten. Praise as a means of control must be adapted to particular students. It is a device to be used frequently but only on a fitting occasion rather than an unvaried policy.

Most pupils enjoy praise and you should try to direct it at the behaviour of both the individual and the class as a whole, as well as to a range of classroom behaviours – work, good behaviour, helpfulness, a quick answer. Praising, or indeed punishing, the child as opposed to their behaviour can lead to unintended negative effects. It is not always necessary to select the best work and behaviour, as one is not seeking the top performance. Nor should you invariably praise the behaviour of those who 'shine' naturally, as the idea is to get over to the child that praise is accessible to all and can be earned by them with striving. In some instances, especially where slower students are involved, it is more desirable to praise effort rather than the finished product. The rewarding of effort (as opposed to ability) is more likely to result in adaptive motivational styles in your pupils.[96]

There are two main ways of praising an individual student – either publicly or in private. Public praise in front of the rest of the class (or at morning assembly, in some circumstances) can be effective and appreciated providing it is not overdone or too effusive. The quiet private word of praise with a student is an approach which student teachers tend to overlook. In a large survey of over 1,700 8- to 11-year-olds Merrett and Man Tang[97] reported that younger children found praise more acceptable if it was given quietly. The Office for Standards in Education[98] reported that secondary school students rarely like public praise, as this causes embarrassment, but that rewards and praise, often private or within a restricted audience, were effective.

There is a whole range of non-verbal signals that can be used to indicate approval; these can be used to reinforce verbal praise or else independently. For example, a smile, an affirmative nod of the head, or a pat on the back all indicate acceptance of student behaviour. Similarly, the use and display of students' ideas, like writing comments on the board, holding up a student's work for the class to see or displaying it on a display board, can also be regarded as non-verbal expressions of approval. And merely showing interest in student behaviour and presence by establishing and maintaining eye contact is yet another rewarding (from the student's point of view) use of non-verbal signals.

Some American research findings[99] are worth mentioning in this context. Teachers use praise sparingly in standard classrooms. Further, teachers give more praise to high-achieving pupils; pupils to whom they feel more attached, or less indifferent; pupils whom they say they favour; and pupils for whom they have expectations of high future occupational status. The researches also indicate that boys receive more praise than girls and that praise varies with the social class status of the school's location. However, Bourne[100] argues that praise is not enough. She suggests that students need cognitive feedback as well as praise if their motivation (linked to successful achievements) is to be raised. She demonstrates that teachers give more feedback to high achievers so that they know how to improve, whereas teachers give only praise to low achievers, without indicating to them how they could improve their work.

Merrett and Jones[101] indicate a significant discrepancy in teachers' behaviour, wherein teachers rewarded students' academic achievements more than their achievements in terms of behaviour. In primary schools they noted that 50 per cent of teachers' comments on students' academic achievements were positive and 16 per cent were negative; only 6 per cent of teachers' comments on behaviour were positive, whilst 28 per cent were negative. In secondary schools the researchers noted that 45 per cent of teachers' comments on students' academic achievements were positive and 15 per cent were negative; only 10 per cent of teachers' comments on behaviour were positive and 30 per cent were negative. Not only does this show that more rewards were given for academic attainments rather than behaviour, but teachers were much more negative about behaviour than they were about academic matters. A curious anomaly is shown here, for, if a positive approach seems to be successful in the academic area, it is surprising that the same teachers did not use this approach for promoting good behaviour. This echoes the opening comments on class management – that it is essential to work on the positive rather than focus on the negative. In academic terms a teacher's first reaction to students making a mistake is usually to teach them; it is paradoxical that when students make a mistake in their behaviour a teacher's first reaction is to criticise or punish them.

Punishment

We consider now the subject of punishment. Discipline in a classroom is often achieved by the successful exercise of conformity to the established rules. It is when there is a serious breach of the rules, a breakdown of discipline, that the need for punishment may arise. The Elton Report[102] was careful to endorse the view that 'the punishment should fit the crime', i.e. that student teachers should avoid over-reacting and under-reacting; misbehaviour was 'graded' from the trivial to the serious in the sequence that follows:

- talking out of turn
- preventing others from working
- making unnecessary noise (not just talking but, e.g. by scraping chairs)
- leaving a seat/room without permission
- calculated idleness or avoidance of work
- general rowdiness
- verbal abuse to other students
- physical aggression to other students
- lateness or unauthorised absence
- persistence in infringement of class and school rules
- cheekiness to teachers
- physical destructiveness
- verbal abuse of teachers
- physical aggression to teachers.

The Elton Report indicated that there was a high incidence of low-level stress from low-level disruptions, a feature indicated by Wheldall and Merrett[103] and reinforced in comparative studies, e.g. one piece of research by Johnson et al.[104] in South Australia that was deliberately designed to replicate Elton's methodology and instrumentation, and a study of first and middle schools in St Helena in which, for example, the researchers reported that talking out of turn was the most commonly occurring problem[105] (43 per cent of all cases reported). Charlton and David[106] comment that the incidence of low-level behaviour infractions and irritants is responsive to relatively simple methods (outlined below).

In response to 'graded' degrees of seriousness the Elton Report indicated that several strategies were used that, themselves, were graded in order of 'seriousness', the least to the most serious in the sequence that follows:

- reasoning with a student within the classroom
- reasoning with a student outside the classroom
- setting extra work
- deliberately ignoring minor infractions
- keeping students in during and after school
- discussing with the whole class why things are going wrong
- temporarily withdrawing a student from the class
- referring a student to another teacher
- removing privileges
- sending a student to a senior figure in the school
- involving parents
- suspension from the school.

In an important study Merrett and Jones[107] classified three gradations of sanctions:

1   *low-order sanctions:* telling off (publicly and privately); detention; lines or tables; comments on reports; confiscation of property; short exclusion from the lesson
2   *middle-order sanctions:* those that involved another member of the management staff; placing a student 'on report'; sending a letter home; denying the student certain activities; meeting with parents
3   *higher-order sanctions:* exclusion; suspension; expulsion and other actions that involved an outside authority.

Johnson et al.[108] set out a list of the most to the least effective strategies for handling unacceptable behaviour in the primary school. These are shown in Box 89. The further one goes down the list the less effective is the strategy.

This list is similar to the Elton Report's suggestions for secondary school students, with the exception that detentions are seen as being more effective. The Elton Report comments that for both primary and secondary school students it is important not to ignore minor infractions that might easily escalate into major problems.

Peters[109] points out that punishment is a much more specific notion than discipline and that at least three criteria must be met if we are to call something a case of punishment. These are (1) intentional infliction of pain or unpleasantness (2) by someone in authority (3) on a person as a consequence of a breach of rules on his part. Although some actions in the school situation are loosely referred to as cases of 'punishment' without meeting all these criteria, e.g. asking a student to do a piece of work again, they do nevertheless provide us with a useful frame of reference for our brief consideration of this important subject.

Box 89: Strategies for handling unacceptable behaviour

- Discuss the problem with the student in the class.
- Have the student leave the class.
- Reason with the student outside the class.
- Remove privileges.
- Seek parental involvement.
- Have a conference with the student and the parent(s).
- Set extra work.
- Ignore minor disruptions.
- Detention.
- Refer the student to another teacher.
- Send the student to the head teacher.
- Remove the student from the school.

Although perhaps distasteful, punishment may very well have a part to play in the development and control of students. Of course, a teacher who comes to rely heavily on punishment cannot hope to succeed except in a narrow and temporary sense. Whatever he achieves will be at the cost of undue negative emotional reactions such as anxiety and frustration and a permanent impairing of relationships. Nevertheless, a teacher should not hesitate to resort to punishment when the occasion demands for, when properly used, it is a legitimate and helpful means of dealing with certain disciplinary problems.

We now consider the forms which punishment in the classroom might take, the occasions for punishment and ways of administering it.

Forms of punishment

Punishment can be used for retribution, deterrence and/or rehabilitation. Before deciding the forms of punishment you intend to use during your teaching practice, should the need for them arise, there are two points worth bearing in mind. First, you are not starting from square one: most schools will have an established system of punishment as part of their tradition and no doubt the forms it takes will be related to the rules that are operative in the school. You should thus find out what alternatives exist within the tradition so that you can use them when necessary. Do not use corporal punishment – you could be prosecuted for assault. It is illegal. Second, it is better whenever possible to anticipate and thereby avoid incidents likely to culminate in the need for punishment. As Peters[110] says, 'Under normal conditions enthusiasm for the enterprise, combined with imaginative techniques of presentation and efficient class management will avert the need for punishment. Boredom is one of the most potent causes of disorder.'

Keeping a class in after school can be an effective deterrent and a particularly useful one for the student teacher, but it must be handled within the legal requirements set out in Chapter 6: schools must give students at least 24 hours' notice of the detention, and this can weaken the connection between the offence and the punishment.

A useful form of punishment for the individual offender is that of isolation. It is important for the student teacher to remember that it is not necessary to send a student out of the room to achieve isolation. Setting him apart from the rest of the class within the classroom can be just as effective and may be achieved by having him stand in a corner, or, better still, sit at a desk away from the others. This kind of psychological banishment can be especially effective providing it does not last

Box 90: Forms of punishment

Reasonable punishment can take many forms, but some account must be taken of the forms customarily used in your school with the age range in question. Some common practices are:

- keeping a student behind for a few minutes' discussion after the rest of the class have left, so that he is last in the queue for lunch, or it causes his friends to wait for him
- formal detention with some task to do that is not directly connected with the lesson so that his antipathy for the lesson is not increased by the punishment
- detention to finish work deliberately not completed in lesson time, within the legal requirements of issuing 24 hours' notice of such a detention
- withdrawal of privileges, such as the use of a tuck shop at break, or access to a common room or class-room other than when essential
- isolation or exclusion with work, either in a corner of the classroom or in another part of the school
- if property is damaged the student may be required to repair the article, if such action is appropriate; or to do a socially useful task such as tidying the classroom or picking up paper in the playground
- as a response to unacceptable language the pupil might be required to write out the offending words several times.

too long. Offenders who have been particularly disruptive may be isolated with their work, but again the isolation should not last too long and should be appropriate to the age of the pupil.. No matter how naughty a child has been he should be given innumerable 'fresh starts'. Students have a strong corporate sense, so isolation counts as a severe punishment.

Negative utilitarian controls are frequently used by teachers. These may take the form of behaviour restrictions and limitations of privilege and may thus include missing part of a favourite lesson, a desired recreational activity, play time, or not being allowed to sit near the back of the class. You will quickly discover additional means of controlling misbehaviour along similar lines. Forms of punishment are outlined in Box 90.[111]

Punishments may include:[112]

- writing tasks such as essays on how and why to improve behaviour (though it may carry the very real risk of making writing a negative activity; we discuss this below)
- detention (the school should have a policy on this)
- loss of privileges (e.g. for social interaction, outings)
- exclusion from the classroom for defined periods of time, which is subject to the school policy and supervision requirements
- verbal interaction, e.g. a very severe reprimand from a senior member of the school
- informing significant others, for example parents, the head teacher
- symbolic punishment, e.g. a marks system which is included in the school report
- exclusion from the school, which is a matter of legal regulation.

Some kinds of punishments are better avoided and may be itemised as follows:

- School work should not be used as a punishment. A child kept in from play or games, for instance, should not be given additional school work such as writing or mathematics. These should be associated with enjoyment.

- Avoid collective punishments, such as keeping a whole class in, when only one or two individuals are culpable. Such action will provoke unnecessary resentment from the innocent members.
- Forms of mental punishment such as severe personal criticism, ridicule, sarcasm and so on are not recommended.
- Coercive sanctions, those involving a physical component such as caning, strapping, striking or shaking, should not be used; these forms of punishment are illegal.
- Only send a child to the head teacher as a last resort, or when you are confronted with a particularly serious case of misbehaviour. Such an action can be seen as weakening the teacher's authority (though in some schools it is seen very positively as the teacher simply not putting up with bad behaviour at any price). However, do not hesitate to seek advice privately from other members of staff when you need help.
- Avoid banishing a student from the classroom if possible. Where you feel isolation is warranted, try to let it be within the classroom.

Schools have policies and procedures for handling misbehaviour and sanctions, and the student teacher will need to find out what these are.

The 'when' and the 'how' of punishment

Good and Brophy,[113] in their analysis of punishment, suggest that punishment is appropriate only in dealing with repeated misbehaviour, not for single, isolated incidents, no matter how serious. It is a measure to be taken when a student persists in the same kinds of misbehaviour in spite of continued expressions of concern and disapproval from the student teacher. Resorting to punishment is not a step to be taken lightly since it signifies that neither the student teacher nor the student can handle the situation. One other point: punishment should not be administered if it is apparent that the student is trying to improve. She should be given the benefit of the doubt and, where possible, rewarded for attempts at improvement.

Punishment should be systematic and consistent in its application. So once again the efficacy of having agreed on a few basic classroom rules is brought home to us, for in providing us with an impartial frame of reference for student teacher and students alike, not only do they ensure we will achieve the consistency we seek, they also guarantee that the recipients, in recognising the logic and fairness of the punishment, will be less likely to respond emotionally.

Another factor in the punishing situation concerns the nature and extent of the talk the teacher engages in. Wright[114] explains that this can serve a number of functions, one of which helps the student 'to construe his actions in a certain way, to structure them cognitively and relate them to general rules'. In thus justifying the punishment to the student, the student teacher's explanatory talk will clarify the nature of the offence, will provide reasons for judging it wrong, will explain its effects on others and will relate it to future occasions. A consistent modus operandi of this nature will give the student the necessary criteria for making her own judgements.

A third factor concerns the temporal relationship between the offence and the punishment. Wright[115] has pointed out that punishment placing restrictions on a student will be most effective if they are related to the offence, if they follow closely after it, and if removal of the restrictions is conditional upon improvement of behaviour. Punishment being thus logically related to the offence is more easily perceived as fair. A sanction should therefore be immediate and inevitable so that the cause and effect relationship is apparent. If it is prolonged to the point where the relationship becomes tenuous, the offender may become resentful.

BEHAVIOUR MODIFICATION AND ASSERTIVE DISCIPLINE

Much behaviour is affected by its consequences. These consequences may be seen as rewarding or reinforcing if, as a result, the behaviour persists or increases, and punishing if the behaviour ceases or decreases. In some circumstances behaviour may be extinguished if there is no consequence.

Behaviour modification

The principles set out above lie at the heart of the approach to dealing with undesirable or maladaptive classroom behaviour known as behaviour modification, the techniques of which are used to change specific patterns of inappropriate behaviour, e.g. hyperactivity in the classroom, excessive movement about the room, talking too much or disobedience. This method of handling behaviour problems is preferred by those who find the use of punishment in the classroom distasteful and who seek a non-punitive, positive approach as an alternative.

The behaviour modification approach in its most basic form consists of three components:

1   specification of the undesirable behaviour to be extinguished or minimised and the preferred desirable behaviour that is to replace it
2   identification – first, of the rewards that seem to be sustaining the unwanted behaviour so that they may be avoided, and second, identification of the rewards that you believe will increase the frequency of the preferred alternative behaviour
3   the consistent and systematic application of these respective rewards and reinforcements over a period of time, together with a systematic record of changes in behaviour.

A reinforcer in this context is defined by its ability to accelerate, or increase, the rate at which a behaviour will occur, or, more simply, its effect on the learner.

There are a number of types of reinforcer that may be used in this context. The most natural and effective for teachers are social reinforcers. Student teacher attention, student teacher praise, student teacher approval and disapproval are powerful factors affecting students' behaviour, and they can be systematically varied to produce the sort of behaviour desired by the student teacher. When employing these techniques, however, the student teacher must be sure to reinforce the desirable behaviour as well as ignore the undesirable if she is to achieve her objective of creating the most favourable conditions for learning.

A particular instance of the application of behaviour modification techniques may concern some form of consistent anti-social behaviour on the part of a student in class. This kind of behaviour may often be sustained by reinforcements in the form of student teacher attention and often by the approval or perhaps disapproval of the rest of the class. If this is the case, the behaviour modification approach would recommend ignoring the attention-seeking behaviour (e.g. a student constantly moving out of his seat) and making sure that the sought-after alternative behaviour (e.g. the student remaining in his place) is rewarded or reinforced with appropriate action (attention, praise or some kind of nonverbal approval like smiling) on the part of the student teacher.

Such techniques may also be useful in the following situations providing they are employed systematically, consistently and over a period of time: failure to pay attention; day-dreaming; failure to show interest in work; not meeting work requirements; being uncommunicative and withdrawn; breaking class rules; over-reacting to stressful conditions; insensitivity to other people; anti-social behaviours; hyperactivity; attention-seeking; disobedience and disrespect.

The results of experimental studies in behaviour modification are encouraging.[116] A study by Thomas, Becker and Armstrong,[117] for example, demonstrates the possibilities of the approach. They showed that approving teacher responses served a positive reinforcing function in maintaining appropriate classroom behaviours. Disruptive behaviours increased each time approving teaching behaviour (praise, smiles, contacts etc.) was withdrawn. When the teacher's disapproving behaviours (verbal reprimands, physical restraints etc.) were tripled, there was much greater disruption, i.e. an increase in noise and movement about the room. The findings, therefore, emphasise the important role of the teacher in producing, maintaining and eliminating both desirable and disruptive classroom behaviour.

Of course, from the student teacher's point of view, teaching practice is not the most ideal context for putting the techniques of behaviour modification to the test because of its length – a few weeks at most. Nevertheless, she may be in a position to select some consistently manifested behaviour problem and attempt to remedy it along the lines suggested above. She could then at least satisfy herself that the principles are sufficiently sound to warrant further investigation at a later date.

In this regard we refer to a project by Lawrence, Steed and Young,[118] the implications of which have immediate relevance for student teachers on teaching practice in that while on the surface the approach appears to be basic common sense, it does encapsulate positive behaviour modification techniques. The project concerned a group of teachers working with a problematic class in a difficult school. The techniques the teachers used were controlled systematic rewards (praise, attention and encouragement) for appropriate behaviour, and ignoring unwanted behaviour, except when it was dangerous. 'Encouragement' with respect to this particular project included:

- praise of all kinds, for the student's work and behaviour
- attention to the student
- interest in the student
- help to the student
- increasing the student's self respect, or self-esteem.

The class in question was a third year boys' class, with 32 on the roll. All recorded IQs were low average. There were no parental occupations in social class I or II and the class was racially mixed. Six had appeared at least once before a Juvenile Court. Some of the principles emerging from the study, and which hold good for both sexes, are as follows:

- 'Encouragement' is a very powerful means of improving both a student's behaviour and the work he does.
- The more encouragement for appropriate behaviour and work she receives, the better she will behave and work.
- A teacher may think she is encouraging a student a great deal but in practice she does not, e.g. what she considers encouraging may not appear so to the student, or the encouragement may not be expressed in a way clear to the student, or it may not be enough to influence her.
- Misbehaviour can often be cancelled out if, when it is observed, the teacher ignores the student but simultaneously praises another who is behaving correctly. The teacher then returns to encourage the first student as soon as she is behaving appropriately (e.g. by saying 'That's more like it!' or 'I'm pleased to see you're behaving like an adult now').
- Another way of handling inappropriate behaviour is simply to ignore it, but to praise as soon as appropriate behaviour occurs.

Practical implications following from the project can be summarised:[119]

- Moving quickly around the class saying 'that's right' or 'good' is a way of settling the class down and getting it to work speedily.
- Small groups can be similarly encouraged.
- Encouraging a student can include having a word with him before or after a lesson.
- Students at this age like to be treated as adults.
- All work discussed in a lesson, including homework, can be used for encouragement purposes.
- 'Spell out' your praise even at the risk of overdoing it.
- Use the student's own words when praising, or make your meaning quite clear.
- Displaying a student's work is a visible sign of praise.
- A person-to-person chat at an adult level is often appreciated, e.g. especially on a topic of adult interest.

Assertive discipline

Assertive discipline[120] is premised on five key principles:

1 Clear expectations for the required behaviour are set out by the teacher.
2 Specific, concrete and verbal praise and rewards are given for the behaviour.
3 There is a graded sequence of negative consequences of undesirable behaviour.
4 The teacher is assertive in insisting on the application of the rewards and sanctions.
5 Power resides with the teacher whilst informed choice of whether to follow a path that leads to rewards or sanctions resides with the student.

The approach is sometimes termed a 'limit-setting' approach.[121] In this approach a student who is misbehaving is told to stop and told explicitly what will happen if she does not stop. The student can choose to comply with the teacher's orders, i.e. to choose to stop, or not to comply, i.e. to demonstrate the undesirable behaviour and, thereby, to incur the negative sanctions. If the unacceptable behaviour persists then stronger sanctions are imposed. There is a discipline hierarchy, with stronger sanctions applying to repeated undesirable behaviour, with suitable warnings of consequences indicated. Nicholls and Houghton[122] report that, overall, using the methods saw significant increase in teacher approval, decrease in teacher disapproval, increase in students' 'on-task' behaviour and decrease in disruptive behaviour.

On the other hand very severe questions have been put against this approach. In a hard-hitting paper Robinson and Maines[123] argue that the approach is not only under-researched but that it embodies many of the negative features of behaviourism, for example: students are passive receivers to be trained in predetermined behaviours; it demonstrates a crude instrumentalism and technicism; it replaces understanding with knee-jerk reactions; it trivialises education to the observable. Robinson and Maines argue forcefully:

- that assertive discipline confuses consequences with punishments
- that it is demeaning, humiliating and insulting to students
- that it neglects the circumstances that lead to the behaviour (resulting in a student's sense of injustice)
- that difficult students need a flexible approach with the use of encouragement rather than a rigid approach that deploys punishment
- that the public humiliation of an offender is itself 'an offence against confidentiality', and
- that it denies basic agency and freedoms because students and teachers have unequal rights to be listened to and powers to create a negotiated environment.

This litany of concerns is not empty argument. Martin[124] argues that the approach can easily fail because it needs whole staff commitment and training but that the issues and methods are so contentious that such agreement and commitment are almost impossible to secure.

Hence, though this approach is popular, the student teacher will need to consider carefully the merits and demerits of this approach. If she is in a school where it is practised, careful observation of its efficacy and its problems will repay the student teacher's time spent in evaluating its operation.

ANTICIPATING MANAGEMENT AND CONTROL PROBLEMS IN THE CLASSROOM

There are certain aspects and structural features of one's lesson that need handling with particular care and foresight because potentially they can be the cause of quite serious problems of management and control. The beginning of a lesson, for example, requires special thought because it sets the tone for the rest of the lesson. Similarly, transitions, that is occasions for a change of activity during the lesson, can also be vulnerable in their potential for disruption. As we have already considered these features of the lesson, it is sufficient for us at this point to suggest that you revise the appropriate sections.

Another important point for student teachers to bear in mind concerns their first meeting with a new class. As Wragg[125] has observed, the very first lesson with a class can go a long way towards establishing the kind of climate that will prevail for the rest of the practice or term. In the Teacher Education project, he and his colleagues observed 100 lessons given by 13 experienced teachers at the beginning of the school year, and 200 given by student teachers at the beginning of teaching practice. The differences between the two groups are listed in Box 83, and we refer readers back to this.

The importance of the first meeting with a class is also stressed by Robertson,[126] who argues that teachers who want to establish their authority should behave as if they were already in authority. Among factors highlighted by Robertson as being of crucial importance in conveying this status, especially during initial meetings, are the following.

Firmness and confidence

When a student teacher feels confident and assured, the students are consequently more responsive and this in turn reinforces his or her own confidence. If, on the other hand, the student teacher is lacking in confidence, the reverse can occur and he or she goes to pieces.

Bodily behaviour

There is an important aspect of non-verbal behaviour and two factors apply here: immediacy between a teacher and class which is achieved by a sensitive awareness of such factors as posture, positioning, bodily orientation, eye contact, gesture and touching. These, Robertson explains, focus or intensify communication between people; so too relaxation, by which Robertson means an asymmetrical positioning of the limbs, openness of arm position, a sideways lean and tilt of the head or, if seated, a more reclined position. A higher status person assumes a more relaxed posture than a lower status one.

BEHAVIOURAL PROBLEMS WITH SOME ETHNIC MINORITY STUDENTS

That there are differences in the incidence, form and extent of behavioural problems among students differentiated in terms of their ethnicity is clear. Moreover, a review of the research literature on multicultural classrooms suggests that references to 'behavioural problems with some ethnic minority students' almost invariably is concerned with students of African Caribbean origin. The research literature points to some issues that are of crucial importance to beginning (and, indeed, experienced) teachers alike. We deal with two vital areas.

Earlier in the chapter we made reference to the work of Fontana and Saunders, both of whom sought to relate socio-economic and cultural differences to the incidence of classroom misbehaviour. Saunders' concern, for example, was with antipathy to school, displayed by those students for whom school seemed irrelevant in terms of their future life chances.

Fontana's focus, inter alia, was directed towards socio-economic factors that relate to poor attitudes and to student underachievement. An appraisal[127] of Department of Social Security data, exploring the relationship between poverty and inequality and using indices such as population density, overcrowding, non-white children, levels of benefit payments and infant mortality, concluded that 'inequality in our society is clearly growing... In terms of real income, the poor have got relatively poorer and the rich have got relatively richer'. To structural factors that point to associations between, on the one hand, poor attitudes, poor behaviour and poor achievement in school and, on the other, worsening socio-economic circumstances must be added interpersonal factors that impinge directly on teacher–student relationships in schools.

Carrington's[128] case study of Hillsview Comprehensive pulls no punches in its dissection of the channelling processes initiated by teachers that directed students of African Caribbean origin away from academic pursuits and towards sporting activities, 'twentieth century gladiators for white Britain', as Carrington observes. Teachers were ingenuously open about their differential treatment of black students:

> I'm reluctant to push black kids too hard... I frequently indulge them...

> Inevitably, I'm more lenient towards blacks... I try to avoid confrontation.

Some Hillsview teachers, moreover, operated with well-documented pejorative stereotypes of African Caribbean students whose behaviour, academic abilities and parent cultures they viewed in a negative manner. There were several occasions in interview when teachers referred to the students as 'lacking in ability', 'unable to concentrate', 'indolent', 'insolent', 'aggressive' and 'disrespectful of authority'.

Green's study[129] is more disturbing still. After 3,000 observations of teacher–student interactions were recorded in each classroom, Green then invited the 70 participating teachers to complete an attitude inventory in which a 25-item prejudice scale had been 'buried'. Only after identifying 12 highly intolerant teachers did Green return to examine the interaction data. He found that highly intolerant teachers:

- gave significantly less time to accepting the feelings of children of African Caribbean origin
- gave only minimal praise to children of African Caribbean origin
- gave significantly less attention to the ideas of children of African Caribbean origin
- gave significantly more authoritative directions to children of African Caribbean origin
- gave significantly less time to children of African Caribbean origin to initiate contributions to class discussions.

The Carrington and Green studies reveal teacher behaviour that is highly injurious to the personalities, the self-esteem and the life chances of the students involved. Whereas, perhaps, the Hillsview data reflect an 'unintentional racism'[130] on the part of some members of staff, the evidence from Green's study is unequivocal in its systematic mapping of racist behaviour on the part of certain teachers. Whatever its origin, such unjust behaviour towards any student is totally unacceptable in today's classrooms. It is worthwhile, at this point, to reiterate some 'ethical absolutes' that have already appeared in our earlier discussions of equal opportunities and classroom management and control.

It is a requirement of student teachers to:

● support and stretch all students in the learning process
● remove the stigma of failure from students
● treat students as individuals of equal worth regardless of gender, race or background
● celebrate the notion of difference and promote positive images of a diverse populace
● counter stereotypes, discrimination, bias and misperceptions
● identify how to break down discriminatory practices.

CLASS MANAGEMENT ON TEACHING PRACTICE

We close this section on management and control with reference to a study by Wragg and Dooley[131] into student teachers' class management. The research was undertaken in two parts. The first part, a pilot study, involved 56 case studies of student teachers thought to be good or poor at handling classes. The subsequent main enquiry involved 204 lessons given by 34 PGCE students at six comprehensive schools, three in a city and three in other parts of the county.[132]

With regard to the pilot study, the tentative conclusions indicated that effective managers were seen as those who were well prepared, anticipated difficulties, and reacted quickly to disruption rather than allowed it to escalate. Good management was often executed with a briskness and verbal deftness. It was also noted that successful student teachers usually arrived at the classroom before the students, personally admitted them into the room, established a presence, and were seen to be in charge in an unobtrusive way. Conversely, unsuccessful managers tried to start their lessons before attention had been secured, and were unable to deal effectively with concomitant distractions like late arrivals.

With regard to the main study, analysis of the 204 lessons taught by the 34 PGCE students revealed that most acts of deviance occurring in their lessons were of a minor nature, as the authors say, 'typically the buzz of chatter punctuated by requests or commands to desist'. Few of the student teachers observed had serious discipline problems, and hardly any examples of serious disruption occurred, although many lessons became mildly chaotic and suffered from sustained mild deviance. Deviance most often occurred with 13- and 14-year-old students and then during transitions or changes of activity, particularly when movement was involved.

(See www.routledge.com/textbooks/9780415485586, Chapter 15 Managing behaviour in the classroom, Common forms of misbehaviour and Student teachers' reactions to misbehaviour.)

BULLYING

Bullying is too important an issue to leave untouched, and we make some comments on it here. Much bullying goes unreported and unnoticed by teachers; indeed more than two-thirds of secondary school students would not find it easy to tell a teacher if they were being bullied, because they fear it would not be taken seriously or because it would be seen as 'telling', or because they fear reprisals.[133] Bullying is often perpetrated in places where it will not be discovered, being frequently a surreptitious activity, therefore no action can be taken as nobody knows about it.[134] That said, successive governments have taken steps to address the issue of bullying, as it cannot be condoned in any form, be it by teachers towards students, students towards each other, or students towards teachers. Indeed a specific set of materials and websites has been set up by the government in order to tackle the problem.[135]

Being bullied can lead to lowering of self-esteem, anxiety, depression, lack of concentration, truancy and even suicide (annual figures suggest that 16 students per year commit suicide in the UK because of being bullied).[136] More girls are reported to be involved in sustained bullying than boys, who more often resort to actual violence, and more often it is group-to-one rather than one-to-one bullying that occurs.[137] Secondary school girls reported sexual bullying by boys.[138] Bullying can take place against academically motivated students, it can be racially and ethnically motivated, and can take a variety of forms. By law schools have to have an anti-bullying policy, and student teachers are advised to find out what it is, and what procedures the school has for addressing bullying if it is discovered or reported. At the least, this will probably involve completing an incident form as the precursor to further action.

Bullying is defined as:[139]

> long-standing violence, physical or psychological, conducted by an individual or group and directed against an individual who is not able to defend himself in the actual situation with a conscious desire to hurt, threaten or frighten that individual or put him under stress.

Bullying is deliberately hurtful, repeated over time and in circumstances that make it difficult for victims to defend themselves.[140] It has the following characteristics:[141]

- The behaviour is persistent and systematic (i.e. the same people behave in the same way in repeated situations).
- The behaviour induces fear in the victim.
- The behaviour is based on an imbalance of power.
- The behaviour usually takes place in a group context.

Bullying can take many forms. A study of 145 students reported in 2002 that bullying included:[142]

- direct physical aggression (40 per cent of responses)
- group versus single person (30 per cent of responses)
- taunting (making fun/teasing/swearing/asking rude or personal questions (14 per cent of responses)
- picking on someone (14 per cent of responses)
- threats of physical aggression (13 per cent of responses)
- attempt to elicit a fight (7 per cent of responses)
- allegations about self/family (7 per cent of responses)
- taking possessions (6 per cent of responses)
- older versus younger (>1 per cent of responses).

Bullying can be:[143]

- *physical:* hitting, kicking, pushing, pinching, pulling, taking or damaging belongings, using weapons
- *verbal:* name-calling, insulting, repeated teasing, sarcasm, threats, remarks and jokes, coercing into acts of stealing or bullying against others or doing things that they don't want to do, sending abusive e-mails or text messages, spreading nasty rumours

- *non-verbal:* gesturing, grimacing, sticking up one/two fingers, making fists, giving somebody bad looks
- *emotional:* excluding someone from social groups
- *spoiling bullying:* writing on school work or homework, damaging property, destroying a game
- *sexual:* lifting skirts or pulling trousers down, abusive name-calling, comments about looks and attractiveness, inappropriate touching, sexual innuendoes and propositions, possessing pornography, sexual assault
- *racist:* name-calling, racist jokes, offensive mimicry, making fun of others, inciting others to behave in a racist way, refusing to co-operate with those of another race or ethnicity, wearing provocative badges, possessing racist written materials
- *extortion bullying:* forcing someone to hand over money, sweets, mobile phones, property, valuables
- *hiding bullying:* hiding clothes, shoes, bags, valuables, books, property.

Bullies are characterised in some research as having had limited love and care as children, too much freedom, and having been exposed to power-coercive strategies of child-rearing such as physical force and violent emotional outbursts.[144] Profiles of bullies indicate that they:

- are frequently aggressive, physically strong and enjoy tormenting others
- have poor communication skills and lack empathy
- thrive on control and domination
- are attention-seeking, immature and needing to impress
- are disruptive, uncaring and manipulative
- are liars
- refuse to take responsibility and are exploitative.[145]

Victims are often characterised as having 'unusual' features, such as hair colour, weight problems, shape, speech problems (e.g. a stammer, an unusual accent), physical features such as acne, spectacles, ability in school, to suffer from low self-esteem and to be unlikely to react positively to being bullied (such that they may not report incidents). Further, racist, sexist and homophobic bullying has been reported, as have attacks because of religion, disability, gender, where students live.[146] Victims are also reported to be those children who lack close friends, who are shy, may be physically weak, do not like or use violence, are over-protected at home; they may be nuisances (e.g. who may provoke bullying), those who want to try hard at school, those who come from privileged homes, and those who are materially indulged by parents.[147]

Bullies and victims are widespread, and no respecters of age, gender, race, or socio-economic status. Bullying can start as an individual activity, but others join in and assist the bully by watching, laughing, encouraging or, indeed, doing nothing to stop it.[148] A study by the Department for Education and Employment in 1994[149] reported that 27 per cent of primary school students and 10 per cent of secondary school students had experienced being bullied. In 1997 a study of over 2,300 primary and secondary students revealed that 44.5 per cent of school children had been bullied, 4.1 per cent reporting being bullied several times per week.[150] More striking, perhaps, 26.6 per cent of primary and secondary students in the study reported bullying others. In 2003 more than half of primary school children and a quarter of secondary school children involved in a research study by Childline indicated that they had been bullied in the present school term.[151] There is some evidence that the incidence of bullying reduces in the upper end of the secondary school (as students develop coping skills and become physically stronger);[152] though physical bullying may reduce with age, indirect bullying increases.

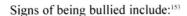

Signs of being bullied include:[153]

- becoming frightened of walking to or from school
- expressing reluctance to go to school each day
- truanting
- avoiding specific lessons or days (e.g. games, swimming)
- schoolwork starting to suffer
- coming home from school with torn clothes or damaged books
- coming home from school hungry (someone has taken dinner money)
- missing items from school bag
- bed wetting, nail biting, sleep walking or becoming withdrawn
- fear of the dark or having nightmares
- psychosomatic illnesses particularly in the morning, because s/he is scared to go to school
- stopping eating
- presenting with unexplained cuts and bruises
- beginning to bully others
- falling out with friends and family
- becoming angry or unreasonable for no particular reason
- giving improbable excuses for any of the above.

Handling incidents of bullying is problematic. Common sense might tell us that it needs simply to be punished, but common sense may not be a good guide here, as punishment may neither reduce bullying nor increase desirable non-bullying behaviour.[154] Indeed it may cause revenge attacks. Sometimes bringing the bully and the victim together in a safe environment is one treatment that can be effective, as can discussing it in classes and on a one-to-one counselling basis, or having the teacher explain what it feels like for the victim and asking for comments from others on this, followed by one-to-one counselling. Young[155] suggests that this approach had an immediate success rate of 80 per cent, with a further 14 per cent improvement to a similar level after three to five weeks. This said, clearly some sanctions must be in place, for example: removal from the group (in class); withdrawal of break and lunchtime privileges; detention; withholding participation in special events and trips; exclusion; involvement of social services and the police.[156]

The Office for Standards in Education[157] reports that engaging students in discussions of bullying can be effective in reducing it, as can having older students being vigilant throughout the school and reporting incidents. No single approach to tackling bullying will be entirely successful as the problem itself is complex; rather success in tackling it is an eclectic process. It may involve, for example, five key points:[158]

1 Never ignore suspected bullying.
2 Don't make premature assumptions.
3 Listen carefully to all accounts – several pupils saying the same does not necessarily mean they are telling the truth.
4 Adopt a problem-solving approach which moves pupils on from justifying themselves.
5 Follow up repeatedly, checking bullying has not resumed.

Additional strategies include, for example:[159]

- asking a friend or a sibling to report bullying (70 per cent of students said they would talk to a friend if they were being bullied)

- encouraging victims not to suffer in silence
- acting and reacting rapidly and consistently
- communicating disapproval unequivocally
- ensuring that the school's anti-bullying policy is operating fully
- minimising the risks to students who report bullying
- initiating consultations and discussions of bullying within schools and classrooms
- reporting bullying and action to be taken
- recognising that bullying often occurs in groups
- setting up peer support schemes
- organising anti-bullying projects
- making bullying and anti-bullying a curricular matter
- working in school on how to manage relationships with each other
- developing befriending schemes
- developing co-operative group work
- circle time (a time to discuss issues arising in the week)
- consultations with parents
- counselling for bullies and victims
- supervision practices within school
- implementing 'schoolwatch' initiatives (to patrol the school, including students, teachers, and maybe the police)
- identifying how other children can prevent and report bullying
- staff development on identifying and handling bullying
- identifying trouble spots and trouble times
- challenging bullying behaviour and language
- adopting a whole-school approach to tackling bullying
- listening services in school
- making clear what alternative desirable behaviours are
- assertiveness training for victims
- teaching children how to react (e.g. avoiding fighting back or answering provocatively, shouting 'no' very loudly, getting away quickly, telling an adult immediately)
- recognising that bullying does not end at the school gates (though schools are not directly responsible for bullying that takes place off the premises)
- involving parents of bullies and victims, and outside agencies
- training lunchtime supervisors.

For further advice we refer the reader to the work by the government's Connexions agency.[160]

The UK government has set out specific guidelines for mediation by adults and mediation by peers.[161] Mediation by adults includes the following:[162]

- Hold brief, non-confrontational, individual 'chats' with each pupil in a quiet room without interruptions – the bullying pupils first.
- Get agreement from each that the bullied pupil is unhappy and that they will help improve the situation – if they cannot suggest ways to do this, be prescriptive.
- Chat supportively with the bullied pupil – helping them to understand how to change if thought to have 'provoked' the bullying.
- Check progress a week later, then meet all involved to reach agreement on reasonable long-term behaviour – at this stage participants usually cease bullying.
- Check whether the bullying starts again or targets another pupil.

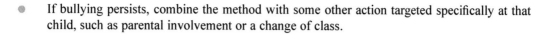

- If bullying persists, combine the method with some other action targeted specifically at that child, such as parental involvement or a change of class.

Mediation by peers includes the following.[163]

- *Define the problem:* In turn, participants describe their perspectives – without interruption, but within set time limits. The mediator clarifies the feelings of each participant and then summarises what has been said.
- *Identify key issues:* These should be listed on paper, divided into conflict and non-conflict issues.
- *Brainstorm possible options:* Both parties suggest solutions, which are written down. They consider the implications, for themselves and each other.
- *Negotiate a plan of action and agreement:* The mediator asks which solutions will most satisfy both parties. One solution is identified and a written agreement is made and signed by all participants. Both parties shake hands.
- *Follow-up:* Evaluate outcomes.

Clearly, a problem-solving approach is being adopted here. Student teachers must be alert to bullying and must take action if it is reported or discovered. Many schools have formal procedures for doing this, and the student teacher must be aware of these.

PART IV

ASSESSMENT, RECORD KEEPING AND REPORT WRITING

The rise of assessment appears to be unstoppable and, given the attention devoted to it by governments across the world, its significance in education appears unassailable. Assessment and its related aspects of recording and reporting is vast and potentially bewildering to student teachers. Part IV sets out clearly the different purposes, types and conducts of assessment. Particular emphasis is placed on formative assessment, not only because it is this which will probably engage student teachers the most on teaching practice, but also because of its potential for raising student achievement. In this respect we also include an important section on marking work. Many student teachers will be required to test their students, and new material on test construction is included in this part. Assessments and tests are never 100 per cent reliable or valid, and, indeed, the rise of testing itself may be ill-judged in educational terms. Reliability, validity and utility are significant matters, and we address them here. Assessment must be educational rather than simply following the dictates of politicians. In Part IV we strive to ensure that assessment is of educational merit. Much has been written about the recording and reporting of assessments and we update our chapter on record keeping. We provide several examples of record keeping which strives to maintain a balance between too little and too much record keeping, and to be useful and informative. Record keeping and assessment must be springboards for the improvement of learning and achievement.

15 Assessment

INTRODUCTION

As a student teacher it is inevitable that you will be involved in assessment during your teaching practice. Assessment can be a major contributor to raising standards in schools[1] in terms of teaching, learning and student achievement. Properly handled, with consistency, reliability, validity and rigour, it can have a positive effect on learning and can improve students' own understanding of how they can learn more effectively and improve. It provides information to all stakeholders – parents, teachers, learners, on learning, performance and improvement. All those involved in education are learners – students, student teachers, teachers, parents – and assessment is a powerful tool for all parties to learn in order to improve teaching, learning and achievement. Ofsted[2] argues that 'the quality of assessment has had a significant impact on attitudes to learning and on attainment in the schools by stimulating and challenging pupils to work hard and by encouraging teachers to focus on how to improve the learning of individual pupils'. Assessment is 'the process of gathering, interpreting, recording and using information about pupils' responses to educational tasks';[3] teachers have to respond to, and use, the data acquired for assessment, to make judgements, for planning, for selection, for decision making, and other matters. It comprises formal assessments, as in tests and examinations, and informal assessments, including ongoing observations, questioning, marking work and listening to students. Its scope is vast and this part addresses some of the key features of assessment.

This chapter sets out a range of issues and practices in assessment and indicates how student teachers might approach assessment on their teaching practice. It will be argued that, though assessment opportunities should be found in everyday teaching, a degree of rigour should be shown in planning, conducting, recording and reporting assessments. It is useful, first, to know the context of assessment and to find out why and how it has come to gain the centre ground in education and educational policy making. Then a series of key issues for planning assessments is outlined, including the purposes of assessment; the types of assessment; reliability and validity in assessments; methods of gathering assessment data; providing opportunities for assessment to take place; and when to assess, and the chapter part closes with some guidelines for planning assessments and marking work.

THE CONTEXT OF ASSESSMENT

The attention given to assessment is huge and world-wide. Assessment is being used on the one hand for educational improvement, increased school effectiveness and curriculum reform and, on the other, for political control of teachers, students and curricula,[4] centralised policy making,[4] narrow accountability,[5] credentialism,[6] educational selection,[7] and the determination of life chances in competitive markets.[8]

Furthermore, assessment is becoming redefined internationally as testing,[9] as can be seen in the growing emphasis on international league tables such as the Trends in International Maths and Science Study (TIMMS) and Progress in International Reading Literacy Study (PIRLS) (see http://timss.bc.edu/index.html); diagnostic and formative assessment are being overtaken by summative examinations. One can detect increasing national control of assessment, an increasing uniformity of styles and practices of assessment, an increasing importance given to assessment, an increasing amount of assessment activity, an increasing scope of assessment, and a uniformity of purposes of assessment. Harlen *et al.*[10] argue that when 'the stakes are high', e.g. when assessment is used for certification, selection, job opportunities, further and higher education, and accountability, as in the publication of 'league tables' of results of schools' examination successes, or when assessment features highly on a political agenda, then assessment takes the form of public examinations. There is also evidence that the nature of testing in England has had a number of negative consequences, in particular the distorting effect on pedagogy and the curriculum.[11]

In the United Kingdom in 2009, statutory assessment was in a period of change. The Qualifications and Curriculum Authority summarised the position:

Statutory Assessment

Assessment happens all the time, both informally and formally. Occasions during a learners' education when it takes place on a statutory basis and the results are reported are:

- At the end of the Early Years Foundation Stage by means of an observation schedule (the Early Years Foundation Stage Profile) based on progress in relation to the Early Learning Goals within the six Areas of Learning.
- At the end-of-Key Stage 1 by teachers' overall judgements. In reading, writing and mathematics these are informed by the use of nationally devised tests and tasks. In science, teachers' judgements are reported.
- At the end-of-Key Stages 2 and 3 in two forms – by judgements in English, mathematics and science based on learners' performance over time and in a range of contexts and by national tests in reading, writing, mathematics and science. The outcomes of both of these forms are reported and published. This situation will change from 2009 following the announcement of the Secretary of State to Parliament on 14 October 2008 that National Curriculum tests for pupils at the end of Year 9 (14-year-olds) will now cease to be a statutory requirement for schools. Teachers assess progress in the other subjects and report these to parents/carers.[12]

In this context procedures for moderation are vital[13] if parity across teachers, schools and regions is to be established. Informally, teachers are continuously assessing students, diagnostically, summatively and formatively, by tests or by informal means such as questioning, observation and marking of work.

An international perspective on assessment reveals that at one extreme is the burgeoning rise of the closed multiple-choice, cloze procedure style and 'tick-box' forms of assessment which focus on low-level recall of factual knowledge, where content is elevated over skills and where assessment is largely undertaken by written examination. At the other extreme is the open-ended profile of achievements which teachers and students keep and which draws on a variety of assessment evidence – written or otherwise – and which is used to record the whole gamut of achievements of a student (e.g. academic, social, extra-curricular).

The negative aspects of some examination-based forms of assessment are legion: the diminishing of education to training and drilling students to perform certain prescribed behaviours;[14] the emphasis on outcomes rather than processes; the passive nature of learning; the damage to self-esteem and learning; the elevation of trivial,[15] observable, measurable, short-term behaviours over serious, high-order, unmeasurable, creative, person-oriented, open-ended, holistic, lifelong aspects of education; the move to creating a culture of gaining and second-guessing the 'right answer'; the fragmentation and atomisation of knowledge; the creation of a nation of 'standardised minds'.[16] The move towards criterion-referenced assessments, whilst it addresses validity in requiring specific, detailed 'evidence' to inform teachers' assessments (rather than their intuitions or hunches), does not herald a move away from behaviourism; rather it provides teachers with more to measure, more to assess.

At the opposite pole of behaviourism is the open-ended profile of students' achievements which is evidenced in records of achievement (ROAs) in the United Kingdom.[17] Here assessments include the 'non-cognitive' qualities of students,[18] grades awarded in formal examination, and a whole profile of a student's achievements and awards – curricular and extra-curricular, personal, social, community-based and academic. The relaunched National Record of Achievement,[19] for example, sets out the following categories: qualifications and credits, employment history, school achievements (subject by subject), other achievements and experiences (e.g. sporting, clubs, community work, voluntary work). Whilst these have the attraction of being a personalised portfolio which motivates their owners,[20] they carry the risk of building in the prejudices and biases of teachers, of including illegitimate, value-laden and generalised statements[21] and of being insufficiently discriminating in their coverage of the significant and the trivial. Furthermore, completing this open-ended record is time-consuming.

What is being striven for is a balance between using insufficient and thereby invalid evidence formatively and so much assessment that it becomes 'interrogation without end'[22] and a means of providing material to hold teachers accountable for aspects of students' development over which they exercise little or no control.

In the United Kingdom assessment results (e.g. the results of students' test scores) are being used to serve the issue of accountability. The statutory publication of schools' results in league tables is seen as a way of ensuring that schools are accountable to the 'consumers' of education, principally parents. In this context assessment is but one of a battery of managerialist measures that have been introduced to serve accountability, e.g. teacher appraisal, the inspection and 'league tables' of school performance.

The compilation of 'value-added' indices of schools enhances accountability. Here, levels of success can be ascertained, using test scores, at every level – individual pupil, department, school, local authority, even country-wide. Schools in similar circumstances (e.g. socio-economic status, catchment area, home background, provision of free school meals, incidence of school exclusions and truancy) can be compared with each other – like with like – to see which are providing the greatest amount of added value to their students. With the rise of baseline assessment[23] the process can include the overall value-added component of specific schools – how much each school has added value to the students, compared to their starting positions, and, indeed to identify pupil progress.[24] These are important data. For example, a school in a multiply-deprived area might be achieving, overall, a lower standard than the national average, but in fact be giving vastly more added value than a school whose students are already at a higher starting point. The school in the deprived area takes students whose starting points are low and 'brings them on' enormously, whereas the school in the privileged area might have students whose starting points are high but who 'rest on their laurels' and whose rates of progress are slower.

The debate is hot: does one judge the quality of a school by an absolute standard (as in 'league tables') or in relative terms (the value-added component)? Should one be comparing like with like, which is arguably a fairer comparison than the alternative, which is to compile a rank order listing of schools, regardless of their specific circumstances and situations? The accountability issue links with the certification function of schools – a quick index of a school's success is often taken to be the number of students gaining such-and-such a number of awards at such-and-such a level. Whether this is a just or adequate basis of comparison is contested.

Assessment for certification and accountability require a degree of transparency through being related to shared, consistent, understood criteria and standards, and communicated in consistent forms so that everyone understands them in the same way. Assessment is a single device or mechanism which serves accountability, credentialism, political agendas and educational reform and improvement. Little wonder it receives so much attention.

To inform the assessment of students at the end of the Key Stages, the National Curriculum provides level descriptions, though some misalignment has been reported between these and the programmes of study. Formal assessments are, for the end-of-Key Stages, based upon a combination of teacher assessments and standard, objective assessments, though the teacher assessments have traditionally had a lower status than the Standardised Assessment Tests and Tasks.[25]

ASSESSMENT IN THE EARLY YEARS

In addition to statutory National Curriculum tests, there is also a requirement for assessment in the Early Years Foundation Stage. The EYFS curriculum is strongly influenced by the Early Learning Goals. These represent the ideal levels of attainment that children should have reached by the end of the EYFS. There is a formal requirement for early years practitioners to assess children's progress using the EYFS Profile. The purpose of this assessment is to inform Year 1 teachers about children's development and achievements. Detailed information about the profile can be found at the national strategies website in the early years section.

What characterises the best practice is careful and close documentation and assessment. This is not simply the end-of-Key Stage assessment that characterises formal National Curriculum requirements, but is much richer than this. Bertram and Pascal[26] provide a withering critique of simplistic assessment in the early years, arguing that:

- It will not yield adequate evidence to make judgements about what children know and can do and where they need to go next.
- Testing is an impoverished view of learning.
- Testing violates an essential principle of early years learning, which is that it is child-centred: testing is 'by definition' (p. 89) another person's judgement, based on a narrow set of indicators, of a child – the agenda is an outsider's, not the child's.
- Testing does not catch the art of learning and learning how to learn, which concerns motivation, socialisation and confidence.[27]

Rather, Bertram and Pascal argue persuasively for a much richer view of assessment, which includes dispositions, social competence and self-concept, and emotional well-being (p. 91). For them, effective learning concerns the child's ability to explore the world and to sustain curiosity, to enjoy learning for its own sake, to feel empowered. It entails holding a broad embrace of assessment, to include (pp. 94–101):

Dispositions

- independence
- creativity
- self-motivation
- resilience.

Social competence and self-concept

- establishing effective relationships
- empathy
- taking responsibility
- assertiveness
- awareness of self.

Emotional well-being

- emotional literacy
- empowerment
- connectedness
- positive self-esteem.

Underpinning these areas is a recognition of the significance of emotional intelligence and the close interrelatedness of feelings, socialisation and cognitive growth. At heart, as Drummond[28] suggests, assessment, must enrich children's lives and keep their interests as the highest priority.

Assessment of young children, then, must be comprehensive, covering not only academic matters but also a range of factors – social, emotional, feelings, attitudes, physical as well as intellectual development.[29] Much of the assessment 'data' are derived from informed, professional observation, and can focus on process and content of learning, social behaviour, emotional development, physical development, linguistic development, as well as the range of 'subjects' with the caveat that to arrange assessment under subject headings may be to misrepresent the nature of young children's learning, which, as this chapter has suggested, is integrated rather than subject-specific. Assessment is both formative (diagnosis which leads into formative planning) and summative (for example at the end of a Key Stage). Typically, the richer of the two kinds of assessment is formative, as it is frequently not measurement-based nor highly selective.

Sparks Linfield and Warwick[30] suggest that formative assessment of young children is time-consuming as it is often observation-based, and can involve considerable conversation with children. They suggest (p. 97) that teachers keep a notebook to jot down key observations as they occur.

Assessment can be undertaken by the adults and with the children, with facilitated self-assessment and, as in the Reggio Emilia schools, close documentation that is a document of record, a celebration of achievement, a story of a community and a planning document.

Assessment, then, focuses on:

- cognitive development
- 'academic' subjects
- physical development
- emotional and personal development

- social development
- communication, language and literacy
- knowledge and understanding of the world
- mathematical development
- creative development
- attitudes and dispositions to learning
- learning requisites, e.g. self-confidence, concentration, interest, motivations, attention, frustration tolerance (which link to personal and emotional development).

Rich assessment data are authentic, i.e. they derive from real tasks, real learning, real activities in which they have been engaged, and real behaviour. They are not a 'bolt-on' to learning, as in specific testing, but are integral to learning and are informed by, indeed in part comprised of, real events and noted observations in the day-to-day classroom. Assessment must both derive from and be a springboard into learning;[31] it must be useful. The main methods of assessment are likely to be:

- observations of children by a range of adults and in a range of situations; observations are not only ad hoc and responsive, but can be pre-ordinate (i.e. deliberately planned in terms of, for example: purpose, focus, timing, activity, curriculum area, children's interaction)
- evidence from ongoing records (e.g. notes kept by adults, samples of children's work (e.g. portfolios), records of what children have actually said)
- formal assessments (e.g. for statements of special educational need, from baseline assessment, from end-of-Key Stage 1 assessment, from annual reporting).

Assessment can be responsive, i.e. noting down issues as they occur, and it can be planned in advance, where the teacher deliberately sets up a situation in which the child can be observed. Here the teacher will need to plan:

- the purposes of the assessment
- the activity, ensuring that it serves the purposes
- the focuses/curriculum areas to be addressed (as appropriate)
- the kind of data to be collected and how they will be collected (e.g. numbers on a rating scale, teachers' notes in a notebook, sample of the child's work)
- the timing and duration of the assessment period
- the children who will be assessed (and, not least, the presence and effects of other children and adults in the classroom)
- the recording of the information
- how the activity will be introduced, developed and concluded, and what the outcome of the activity will be.

This does not mean that the assessment activity will be artificial, contrived and separate from the day-to-day 'real' activities in the classroom; rather it requires reflection on how those teaching and learning situations can be used for assessment purposes. The issue here is that the assessment is authentic, related to real-world learning and activities.

Assessment, then, should be authentic, formative, ongoing, diagnostic and summative. It can also include facilitated self-assessment by the children themselves. In many early years classrooms there is more than one adult; it is important, if only for the sake of reliability, that assessments are informed by the input from all participating adults (including parents), i.e. assessment is collaborative, for example with adults in the school, with parents, with social workers and psychologists, with the children themselves. A touchstone of assessment here is that it is evidence-based and rooted in documentation and information, rather than based on teachers' personal views.

In the UK there are several systems of assessment,[32] for example (see also Chapter 3):

- diagnostic and standardised tests produced by commercial companies
- statutory national assessments
- examinations by examination boards, typically for students at age 16 and above
- vocational and occupational examinations
- teacher assessments – either for formal requirements or as part of everyday teaching and learning.

The original proposals for national assessment[33] suggested that it should be:

1 formative (diagnostic)
2 criterion-referenced
3 moderated
4 related to progression.

However, these quickly ran into difficulties. With regard to 1, formative, diagnostic assessments – where specific information could be gathered to diagnose a student's strengths and weaknesses such that effective planning for future teaching and development could take place – were seen to place an enormous burden on teachers of extensive record keeping and time to actually undertake the diagnoses.[34] This resulted in many teachers having to set 'holding' tasks for students in the class who were not being assessed, thereby reducing the speed of their learning and risking a lowering of their standards.[35]

With regard to 2, criterion-referenced assessments – where the achievements of a student are assessed relative to predetermined specific criteria[36] – were subverted, in effect, by using the results normatively to compare students and schools (through the publication of 'league tables'). The reliability of the results could be questioned – how could students' achievement of a criterion be assured; what if they achieved the criterion on the day of the assessment and subsequently were unable to achieve it? Moreover, the intention of criterion-referencing was to provide specific and focused information; however, the data from the assessments were aggregated to give an overall score for each student on each subject – the specificity and utility were lost.[37]

With regard to 3, moderation turned out to be a very costly exercise because of the inclusion of teachers' assessments of students. Ensuring parity of standards of teachers' assessments initially required teachers to be taken out of school for training and agreement trials, though agreement trials now take place in schools.[38]

With regard to 4, progression was to be judged in terms of the National Curriculum levels, which, as was argued in Parts I and II, misrepresented the nature of students' learning and falsely assumed that each of the levels of the National Curriculum was objectively more difficult than the previous one.

Lest we be accused of adopting a solely negative stance to the assessment arrangements of students we ought to record the positive advances claimed for the increased assessment activity in schools. For example, assessments were to be based on evidence rather than intuition or hunch,[39] they would foster diagnostic teaching and increased diagnosis of students and that, in turn, would promote greater levels of match in the work set (see the discussion of differentiation in Part II).[40] Further, it was claimed that there would be a positive backwash effect, in that having to assess and report on students' achievements of all aspects of the curriculum would have consequences such that the full National Curriculum would be taught.[41] Indeed the evidence from the initial introduction of formal assessment indicated that many students positively enjoyed the increased individual attention[42] that they received from the teacher during the periods of assessment.

The contexts of assessment reveal it to be a politically and educationally highly charged activity. That level of attention suggests to us that the several elements of assessment need to be addressed and understood. This will be undertaken below and will lead into a discussion of how student teachers can plan, implement, record and report assessments and the results of assessments.

The context of assessment should also observe the significance of standards and the long-running debates on whether standards are rising or falling. In fact it is probably chimerical to try to answer this as there is little agreement on what constitutes a standard and how to hold the evidence consistent and steady when the educational, social and cultural situation is in constant flux. For example, what may constitute valid evidence of a standard in one year, culture or place may not be the same in another year, culture or place; if one holds the nature of the evidence (e.g. the test items) constant over time, culture and place whilst all around is changing, then the validity of the notion of the 'standard' is lost; if one changes the nature of the evidence (e.g. the test items) in order to take account of the changing situation, then one is not comparing like with like, so it becomes impossible to ascertain whether standards have risen or fallen; they have simply changed. However, the evidence on the impact of National Curriculum and assessment in England since 1988 suggests a number of worrying negative consequences.[43]

The situation is compounded by the further effects of the National Curriculum, in which, for example, it is specified that the 'average' child will reach Level 4 in public assessments. This has led to a shift in perception,[44] from a mean to a benchmark or minimum for all, so that, if not all or most of the students achieve Level 4, then the individual school may be deemed by the public to be problematic. The issue is particularly potent in relation to the 'standards debate', where there is difficulty in identifying what is meant by a standard, as it might be seen as comparatively arbitrary. Does a high standard of achievement, for example, mean the number of students passing at a high grade, or the criteria required to meet that grade? If it is the former then simply adjusting the quotas for the higher grades can inflate standards; if it means the latter then raising the cut-off point for each grade will raise the standard. The term is replete with ambiguity.

ASSESSING PUPILS' PROGRESS

The dangers of an inappropriate emphasis on statutory assessment and target setting were raised at the inception of the National Curriculum.[45] Since that time a growing body of evidence showing the deficits in the system (Wyse and Torrance, *op cit.*) has been accompanied by increasing dissatisfaction with the statutory testing system in society at large. As a result of this pressure, policy-makers belatedly began to take notice. In 2008, following a debacle over the external marking of statutory tests, the government, in a move that was received with incredulity, simply scrapped statutory tests for 14-year-olds. In a more considered way, trials had gone ahead for different forms of assessment. One major result of this was Assessing Pupils' Progress (APP). APP is described by the National Strategies as follows:

> APP is a process of structured periodic assessment for mathematics, reading and writing. It supports teachers by promoting a broad curriculum and by developing teachers' skills in assessing standards of attainment and the progress children have made. It involves 'stepping back' periodically to review pupils' ongoing work and relate their progress to National Curriculum levels, and provides information to help teachers plan for the next steps in children's learning.[46]

Considerable attempts are made in the documentation for APP to stress that it is not yet another bolt-on to the already over-bureaucratic nature of education in England. In fact, it is claimed 'APP is all you need'![47] The approach is 'straightforward': 1. consider evidence; 2. review the evidence; 3. make a judgement. Teachers are encouraged to accumulate evidence, perhaps in the form of portfolios (see later in this chapter for further information about portfolios), or a record of achievement, which are then reviewed periodically. Following review, the teacher makes a judgement about pupils' National Curriculum levels by comparing with the extensive and useful examples of pupils' work and teachers' assessments in 'standards files'. In spite of the attempt to simplify the assessment process through APP it still appears to require an excessive amount of documentation. APP only deals with reading, writing and mathematics, so once again we see an emphasis on a limited number of 'core' subjects at the expense of the wider curriculum. The wider curriculum is covered to a certain extent through the principles of Assessment for Learning (see http://nationalstrategies.standards.dcsf.gov.uk/node/18220).

ASSESSMENT FOR LEARNING

In 2008, government published its assessment for learning strategy, which was part of the government's commitment to personalised learning:

- *every child* knows how they are doing, and understands what they need to do to improve and how to get there. They get the support they need to be motivated, independent learners on an ambitious trajectory of improvement
- *every teacher* is equipped to make well-founded judgements about pupils' attainment, understands the concepts and principles of progression, and knows how to use their assessment judgements to forward plan, particularly for pupils who are not fulfilling their potential
- *every school* has in place structured and systematic assessment systems for making regular, useful, manageable and accurate assessments of pupils, and for tracking their progress
- *every parent and carer* knows how their child is doing, what they need to do to improve, and how they can support the child and their teachers.[48]

The National Strategy Primary has an assessment for learning site[49] and suggests that day-to-day assessment should be a natural part of effective teaching and learning:

- sharing and talking about learning objectives, learning outcomes and success criteria with children; clarifying progression
- recognising that learning is often demonstrated through oral and written language and the academic language required to show understanding has to be explicit and part of the sharing of learning objectives and success criteria
- observing and listening to gather intelligence
- questioning and whole-class dialogue to check, probe and develop understanding
- explaining and modelling to clarify progression in key concepts and skills, demonstrate thinking processes and exemplify quality
- giving oral and written feedback to support the evaluation of progress, clarify standards and help identify next steps in learning
- planning for group talk, peer assessment and self-assessment to help children develop as independent learners
- planning specific activities that give teachers an insight into the progress children are making, the standard they have achieved and the obstacles to their progress.

An important aspect of moves towards assessment for learning is the recognition that pupils should be involved in the assessment process. There are a number of personal gains that come from peer assessment and self-assessment, such as: independent learning and the ability to take responsibility for their own learning. It is recognised that these kinds of assessment do not happen automatically and like all things, pupils need support to develop appropriate ways of working:

To develop peer assessment and self-assessment, teachers will need to:

● plan peer assessment and self-assessment opportunities, for example with 'pair and share' opportunities during class questioning
● explain the intended learning outcomes behind each task and how they relate to the learning objectives, while ensuring that children are aware of the opportunities that learning presents (there may be opportunities to extend the learning for the more able children, or to relate to specific children's interests)
● provide children with clear success criteria to help them assess the quality of their work
● train children over time to assess their own work and the work of others, and develop an appropriate language
● give children opportunities in mathematics lessons to discuss and reflect on problem-solving and calculation strategies, comparing and evaluating approaches
● frequently and consistently encourage children's self-reflection on their learning
● guide children to identify their next steps.

Time needs to be built in to the lesson for structured reflection, for example using comments such as the following:

● 'Find one example you are really proud of and circle it. Tell the person next to you why you are pleased with it.'
● 'Decide with your talk partner which of the success criteria you have been most successful with and which one needs help or could be taken even further.'
● (after whole-class sharing for a minute or two) 'You have three minutes to identify two places where you think you have done this well and read them to your partner.'
● 'You have five minutes to find one place where you could improve. Write your improvement at the bottom of your work.'
● 'Look back at the problems you have solved today. Where were you successful? What approach did you take?'[50]

The renewed emphasis on formative assessment and assessment for learning was inspired by the work of Black and Wiliam,[51] who emphasised the importance of formative assessment and the close links between learning, assessment and planning. Although government seems to have embraced assessment for learning, the links that inevitably they make with national summative test standards and performance targets in many ways are in conflict with the principles of assessment for learning.

While it is good to see that assessment for learning is informed by a research base, in practice the problems with too much paper work remain. National Curriculum and assessment policy has suffered from, and continues to suffer from, a lack of a clear and logical understanding about the curriculum as a whole and the implications for teachers and pupils working with the system. This introduction serves, perhaps, to raise some cautions about assessment, its purposes and uses, the perceptions that people have of it, the power of assessment, the kind of assessment and the effects of assessment.

THE PURPOSES OF ASSESSMENT

There is a range of purposes of assessment that fairly capture the flavour and discussions of the purposes of assessment.[52] Assessments serve a series of primary functions, being used for:

- *certification*, qualifying students for their lives beyond school by awarding passes, fails, grades and marks
- *diagnosis*, identifying a student's particular strengths, weaknesses, difficulties and needs in order that an appropriate curriculum can be planned
- *improvement of learning and teaching*, providing feedback to students and teachers respectively so that action can be planned.

Assessments can serve a series of secondary functions, being used for:

- accountability of teachers and students to interested parties – to report on standards
- evaluation of the quality of teaching, learning, curricula, teachers, schools and providers of education
- motivating students and teachers,[53] though this is dependent upon the type of assessments adopted.

One can add to the secondary suggestions the control of the curriculum, for the 'backwash effect' on the curriculum is strong in 'high stakes' – external – assessment.[54] It is important to be clear on one's purposes in assessment, for, as will be argued later, the choice of method of assessment, follow-up to assessment, types of data sought, types of assessment are all governed by the notion of fitness for purpose.[55] We suggest that several of the purposes set out above are in a relation of tension to each other.[56] For example, using assessments for the purposes of selection and certification might be intensely demotivating for many students and may prevent them from improving; the award of a grade or mark has very limited formative potential, even though it would be politically attractive; internally conducted assessment has greater educational validity than externally conducted assessment. Using a diagnostic form of assessment is very different in purpose, detail, contents and implementation from assessment by an end-of-course GCSE examination. Using assessment results as performance indicators can detract from improvement and providing formative feedback to improve learning. The notion of fitness for purpose returns us to a central principle of this book, viz. the need to clarify and address the objectives of the exercise. We support the view that student teachers should be concerned with diagnostic and formative assessments that are steered to improvements in teaching and learning, as these are more educationally worthwhile and practicable over the period of a teaching practice. The purposes of assessment here are educative rather than political or managerial.

Assessment can have a backwash effect, for example to influence the contents and pedagogy of schools leading up to public examinations (e.g. at ages 7, 11, 14, 16, university entrance), and a forward effect to support learning aims.[57]

THE TYPES OF ASSESSMENT

There are several types of assessment, for example:

- norm-referenced assessment
- criterion-referenced assessment

- domain-referenced assessment
- diagnostic assessment
- formative assessment
- summative assessment
- ipsative assessment
- authentic assessment
- performance assessment.

We address these below.

(See www.routledge.com/textbooks/9780415485586, Chapter 16 Assessment, Norm-referenced assessment, Criterion-referenced assessment and Performance assessment.)

Norm-referenced assessment

A norm-referenced assessment measures a student's achievements compared to other students, for example a commercially produced intelligence test or national test of reading ability that has been standardised so that, for instance, we can understand that a score of 100 is of a notional 'average' student and that a score of 120 describes a student who is notionally above average. The concept of 'average' only makes sense when it is derived from or used for a comparison of students. A norm-referenced assessment enables the teacher to put students in a rank order of achievement.[58] That is both its greatest strength and its greatest weakness. Whilst it enables comparisons of students to be made it can risk negative labelling and the operation of the self-fulfilling prophecy.[59]

Just as a norm-referenced system guarantees a certain proportion of high grades, e.g. A and B, so, by definition, it also guarantees a proportion of low grades and failures, regardless of actual performance. The educational defensibility or desirability of this may be questionable: a 'good' student may end up failing or scoring poorly if the class or group of student with whom she/he is being compared is even better. Norm-referencing may be useful for selection, but it may not be equitable.

Criterion-referenced assessment

Criterion-referenced assessment was brought into the educational arena by Glaser[60] in 1963. Here the specific criteria for success are set out in advance and students are assessed on the extent to which they have achieved them, without any reference being made to the achievements of other students (which is norm-referencing). There are minimum competency cut-off levels, below which students are deemed not to have achieved the criteria, and above which different grades or levels can be awarded for the achievement of criteria – for example a grade A, B, C etc. for a criterion-referenced piece of coursework at GCSE level. A criterion-referenced test does not compare student with student but, rather, requires the student to fulfil a given set of criteria, a predefined and absolute standard or outcome.[61]

In a criterion-referenced assessment, unlike in a norm-referenced assessment, there are no ceilings to the numbers of students who might be awarded a particular grade. Whereas in a norm-referenced system there might be only a small percentage who are able to achieve a grade A because of the imposed quota (the 'norming' of the test), in a criterion-referenced assessment, if everyone meets the criterion for a grade A then everyone is awarded a grade A, and if everyone should fail then everyone fails.

Norm-referenced and criterion-referenced tests at first sight appear to be mutually exclusive and, indeed, in many contexts they are. However, we should not overlook the fact that implicit in criteria are norms of what we might expect a student achieving a grade A to be able to do, and how this is different from a student achieving a grade B, and so on. Further, using criterion-referenced tests still enables students' performance to be compared, e.g. comparing the grades of groups of students in a class, school, local education authority and so on.

In devising assessment, student teachers will need to be clear on whether they are going to operate a norm-referenced system of grades and marks (with quotas for each grade or mark range) or a criterion-referenced system, with everyone being able to score highly.

Domain-referenced assessment

An outgrowth of criterion-referenced testing has been the rise of domain-referenced tests.[62] Here considerable significance is accorded to the careful and detailed specification of the content or the domain which will be assessed. The domain is the particular field or area of the subject that is being tested, for example, light in science, two-part counterpoint in music, parts of speech in English language. The domain is set out very clearly and very fully, such that the full depth and breadth of the content is established. Test items are then selected from this very full field, with careful attention to sampling procedures so that representativeness of the wider field is ensured in the test items. The student's achievements on that test are computed to yield a proportion of the maximum score possible, and this, in turn, is used as an index of the proportion of the overall domain that she has grasped. So, for example, if a domain has 1,000 items and the test has 50 items, and the student scores 30 marks from the possible 50 then it is inferred that she has grasped 60 per cent ($\{30 \div 50\}$ $\times$ 100) of the domain of 1,000 items. Here inferences are being made from a limited number of items to the student's achievements in the whole domain; this requires careful and representative sampling procedures for test items.

Diagnostic assessment

Diagnostic assessment is designed to identify particular strengths, weaknesses and problems in students' learning. Though it is often reserved for specialists (e.g. educational psychologists), this is by no means always the case, as teachers are constantly diagnosing students' needs and problems. Diagnostic assessment is the foundation for formative assessment and planning, informing what a teacher should do next.

Formative assessment

Formative assessment suggests and shapes the contents and processes of future plans for teaching and learning. Formative assessment – assessment for learning – provides feedback to teachers and students on their current performances, achievements, strengths and weaknesses in such a form that it is clear what the student or the teacher can do next either to improve, enhance or extend learning and achievement. Formative assessment can be frequent and informal, thereby really assisting teachers and students in the day-to-day business of improvement. It is designed to figure highly in planning for learning.

Formative assessment should lead to rich, formative feedback to students, i.e. feedback on which they can know how to act to improve their learning and achievements, something which a mark or a grade simply does not have the power to do.

Formative feedback is feedback that relates intention to actuality – how far a student achieved his or her intentions, and what the gap was between what was desired and what was required, and the reasons for this gap, and what the gap was between ideal and actual performance. The best feedback is very specific,[63] comments on what was actually done, is clear to the student, relates to targets, goals and standards, and indicates specifically what has to be done to improve.

It can be seen that formative assessment is closely linked to principles of constructivism, which is a central theme of this book.

Summative assessment

Formative assessment contrasts with summative assessment both in timing and purpose. Summative assessment – assessment of learning – is terminal; it comes at the end of a programme and assesses, for example, students' achievements in the programme and of overall knowledge acquisition and practice. It is the stuff of the GCSE formal examination, the end of term test, the A level, the final examinations for a degree programme. A summative assessment might be to provide data on what the student has achieved at the point of time at the end of a course; it might also be more of a retrospective review of what has taken place during the course and what has been learned from it. Summative assessment is often concerned with certification, the awarding of marks and grades and public recognition of achievement.

Summative assessment carries the major risk of a negative backwash effect on the curriculum, narrowing the curriculum to that which will appear on the assessment (often the examination) and narrowing the learning to a limited range of activities. Put simply, summative assessment can become behaviourist rather than embodying the more open-ended, constructivist view of learning.

Formative and summative assessment appear to lie in tension with each other, even though there may be some degree of overlap: certification and accountability in summative assessment steer assessment towards the production of simple grades which have little formative function – they are literally largely useless for planning teaching and learning, whilst formative assessment for planning day-to-day teaching and learning requires a much fuller, detailed kind of assessment, with a different purpose and focus.

Ipsative assessment

The discussion of action planning takes us into another type of assessment to be considered here: ipsative assessment.[64] Ipsative assessment (derived from the Latin 'ipse', meaning 'herself' or 'himself') refers to a process of self-assessment in which students identify their own starting points or, in the language of action planning and school development planning, initial conditions. This is undertaken in the student's own terms (hence the appeal to the Latin root). From this analysis the student sets targets for future learning and achievements, often in conjunction with the setting of a time frame. Self-assessment works particularly well when students are very clear on the purpose and focus of learning and on the criteria for judging successful learning.

Ipsative assessment feeds directly into the process of keeping a Progress File – the contents of which are the students' own property – and is a useful parallel to, or complement to, the more academic, curriculum-oriented view of action planning. As with action planning that uses feedback from assessment formatively, ipsative assessment need not be undertaken by the student in splendid isolation; rather it can be undertaken with a teacher as facilitator and negotiator.

Authentic assessment

There has been a growing trend to render assessment more like real life, using real evidence from real situations, rather than through the use of proxy or surrogate indicators of achievement like tests. Authentic assessment relates assessment to the real world of what people actually do rather than using some easy-to-score responses to questions. What makes authentic assessment authentic is that all parties know what students can actually do in real life with the knowledge, skills and competencies that they have learnt.

What we have in authentic assessment is a major move towards increasing the validity of assessments, though the reliability is difficult to address. Even if criteria, marking schemes, grades and contents are made explicit, the problems come in applying these consistently, fairly and with equity and generalisability across different projects, students, teachers and contexts. Very many of the problems of reliability outlined in the next section present themselves squarely in authentic assessment. Moderation meetings to address reliability are time-consuming and lengthy.

Despite these problems, it remains that authentic assessment is authentic! That is not a mere tautology – it is a reminder that learning is bound to assessment; it makes learning and assessment real, meaningful and motivational.

Performance assessment

Performance assessment, as its name suggests, is that assessment which is undertaken of activities or tasks in which students can demonstrate their learning through performance in real situations. It typically uses teacher assessment, usually observation, questioning and professional judgement, rather than objective assessment and often uses some form of portfolio assessment (discussed below).

Performance assessment is already widespread in some subjects, for example communication skills, psychomotor skills (e.g. physical education and athletics, music making, drawing, science experiments, design and technology, project work, drama, social skills in group activities). It requires the learner to demonstrate knowledge, learning and understanding through a real task and application. Hence performance assessment strives to be as close to authentic assessment as possible.[65]

We commented earlier that the purposes of assessment are not only distinct but lie in tension with each – the more assessment serves one purpose the less it can serve another. This is true for some types of assessment. For example, the more we move towards summative, grade-related examinations the more we move away from formative and diagnostic assessments that required detailed – often qualitative – comments; the more we move towards standardised tests the more we move away from ipsative assessments; the more we move towards norm-referenced assessments that often yield a single score or grade the more we move away from criterion-referenced assessments that will yield specific details about a range of elements; the more we use external, objective instruments the less opportunity we have to use internal, teacher-devised instruments (often simply as a function of the time available). We suggest that student teachers should be concerned with diagnostic and formative assessments, providing useful feedback to students, i.e. feedback to improve learning, and that these can be part of ipsative assessment and action planning. Further, by involving students in ipsative assessment and by providing feedback to students upon which they can act to improve, positive interpersonal relationships are developed between students and student teachers that, themselves, support enhanced learning through engagement and motivation.

RELIABILITY AND VALIDITY IN ASSESSMENTS

As educators we need reliable data on students' achievements so that we can have confidence both in how we judge students and in what we subsequently plan for them. Black[66] reports that there has been up to a 30 per cent chance of some students being placed in the wrong level of Key Stage 3 assessments. Reliability is compromised when students of the same ability and achievements score different results on the same test, when the same student scores differently on different tests of the same matters/contents, or when the same student scores differently on the same (or very similar) test on a different occasion. Reliability means that the results are consistent and reproducible with different markers, occasions, test items, test types, marking conventions, grading procedures and contexts. Further, we need to be assured that the assessments that are made of students actually assess what they are intended to assess or else subsequent planning begins from the wrong place, i.e. to address validity.

Reliability

Reliability is an index of consistency and dependability, for example of marking practices/ conventions and of standards. An assessment would have little reliability if it yielded different results in the hands of another assessor or different results for similar students. Reliability, then, requires comparability of practices to be addressed.[67] This can be undertaken prior to assessments by agreement trials, so that a range of assessors can be clear and can agree on the specific marks and grades to be awarded for particular samples of work, examination scripts, coursework and marks scored in elements of an overall assessment, though in practice it often only becomes an issue in the post-assessment standardisation and agreement of marks and awards. Reliability, then, affects the degree of confidence that one can put on assessment data and their interpretation.

Reliability is an important issue given the significant role of teachers in formal assessments and examinations, and the need for external markers of examination scripts to be fair to all candidates, neither too harsh nor too generous in comparison with other external examiners. When external examiners commit breaches of reliability it often makes the national press; this echoes the comment made earlier that when 'the stakes are high' attention focuses on reliability in graded examinations.[68]

Not only must reliability be addressed but it must be seen to be addressed; marking must be seen to be fair. This issue was highlighted in a collection of papers from the British Educational Research Association's (BERA) Policy Task Group on Assessment, where the notion of 'transparency' was included in discussions of reliability.[69] It comes as no surprise, therefore, that the significance of reliability and transparency should lead to objective, standardised, national, externally marked tests and that this should accord with the views of a government that replaced the four criteria for assessment, specified earlier as being formative, criterion-referenced, moderated and related to progression, in favour of summative, norm-referenced, externally moderated pencil and paper tests. As was indicated earlier, assessment plays its part in a political agenda.

In an educational context most standardised tests include 'technical' details in their test manuals; these report the levels of reliability of the test. In test construction reliability is a statistical concept that refers to numerical indices of stability (the test–retest form of reliability), high correlations with results obtained in equivalent forms of a test, and high correlations between different items of a single test (internal consistency). For reasons that will become clear later when comparing validity and reliability, we shall not dwell on the formulae for calculating reliability coefficients; rather we shall remain with the concept of consistency qua concept.

Reliability in teachers' assessment at Key Stages 1, 2 and 3[70] can be improved by, amongst other things:

● joint planning between teachers in the same year or department, across years or across Key Stages
● using the programme(s) of study to agree objectives for teaching, learning and assessment developing common activities focused on agreed objectives.

It can be seen merely from the size of this (incomplete) list that reliability features highly when assessment is undertaken externally and by teachers. It enters the assessment arena at the point of agreeing marks, i.e. after the product – the examination script or the coursework for assessment, for example – has been made.

There are several threats to reliability in assessments, for example[71] with respect to examiners and markers:

- errors in marking (e.g. attributing, adding and transfer of marks)
- inter-rater reliability (different markers giving different marks for the same or similar pieces of work)
- inconsistency in the examiner/marker (e.g. being harsh in the early stages of the marking and lenient in the later stages of the marking of many scripts).

With reference to the students and teachers themselves, there are several sources of unreliability:

- Motivation and interest in the task has a considerable effect on performance. Clearly, students need to be motivated if they are going to make a serious attempt at any test that they are required to undertake, where motivation is intrinsic (doing something for its own sake) or extrinsic (doing something for an external reason, e.g. obtaining a certificate or employment or entry into higher education). The results of a test completed in a desultory fashion by resentful pupils are hardly likely to supply the student teacher with reliable information about the students' capabilities.[72] Research suggests that motivation to participate in test-taking sessions is strongest when students have been helped to see its purpose, and where the examiner maintains a warm, purposeful attitude toward them during the testing session.[73]
- The relationship (positive to negative) between the assessor and the assessee exerts an influence on the assessment. There is sufficient research evidence to show that both test takers and test givers mutually influence one another during examinations, oral assessments and the like.[74] During the test situation, students respond to such characteristics of the evaluator as the person's sex, age and personality. Although the student teacher can do little about his/her sex and age, it is important (and may indeed at times be comforting) to realise that these latent identities do exert potent influence. It could well be, for example, that the problems experienced by a female student teacher conducting a test with older secondary school boys have little if anything to do with the quality of the test material or the amount of prior preparation she has put into the testing programme.
- The conditions – physical, emotional, social – exert an influence on the assessment, particularly if they are unfamiliar. The advice generally given in connection with the location of a test or examination is that the test room should be well lit, quiet and adequately ventilated. To this we would add that, wherever possible, students should take tests in familiar settings, preferably in their own form rooms under normal school conditions. Research suggests that distractions in the form of extraneous noise, walking about the room by the examiner, and intrusions into the room all have significant impact upon the scores of the test takers, particularly when they are younger pupils.[75] An important factor in reducing students' anxiety and tension during an examination is the extent to which they are quite clear about what exactly they are required to do. Simple instructions, clearly and calmly given by the examiner, can significantly lower the general level of tension in the test room. Student teachers who intend to conduct testing sessions may find it beneficial in this respect to rehearse the instructions they wish to give to pupils before the actual testing session. Ideally, test instructions should be simple, direct and as brief as possible.

● The Hawthorne effect, wherein, in this context, simply informing a student that this is an assessment situation will be enough to disturb her performance – for the better or the worse (either case not being a fair reflection of her usual abilities).[76]

● Distractions (including superfluous information).

● A considerable and growing body of research in the general area of teacher expectancies suggests that students respond to the teacher-assessor in terms of their perceptions of what he expects of them.[77] It follows, then, that the calm, well-organised student teacher embarking purposefully upon some aspect of evaluation probably induces different attitudes (and responses) among her class of children than an anxious, ill-organised colleague.

● The time of the day, week, month will exert an influence on performance. Some students are fresher in the morning and more capable of concentration.[78]

● Students are not always clear on what they think is being asked in the question; they may know the right answer but not infer that this is what is required in the question.

● The students may vary from one question to another – a student may have performed better with a different set of questions which tested the same matters. Black[79] argues that 'two questions which seem to the expert to be asking the same thing in different ways might well be seen by the pupil as completely different questions'.

● Teachers teach to the test. This is perhaps unsurprising in high-stakes assessment, or where, as in some countries, teachers' contract renewal is contingent on students' test results, or where 'league tables' of overall performance are published.

● Teachers and students practise test-like materials. It used to be the case that pupils would practise 'intelligence' in preparation for the 11-plus examination, and there are entire lucrative businesses operating to prepare students for public tests, e.g. the GMAT and GRE tests in the USA, where entrance to university depends on test scores.

● A student may be able to perform a specific skill in a test but not be able to select or perform it in the wider context of learning.

● Cultural, ethnic and gender background affect how meaningful an assessment task or activity is to students, and meaningfulness affects their performance.

● Marking practices are not always reliable, teachers maybe being too generous, marking by effort and ability rather than performance.

● The context in which the task is presented affects performance: some students can perform the task in everyday life but not under test conditions.

With regard to the assessment items themselves, there may be problems (e.g. test bias), for example:

● The task itself may be multi-dimensional, for example testing 'reading' may require several components and constructs. Students can execute a mathematics operation in the mathematics class but they cannot perform the same operation in, for example, a physics class; students will disregard English grammar in a science class but observe it in an English class. This raises the issue of the number of contexts in which the behaviour must be demonstrated before a criterion is deemed to have been achieved.[80] The question of transferability of knowledge and skills is also raised in this connection. The context of the task affects the student's performance.

● The validity of the items may be in question (discussed below).

● The language of the assessment and the assessor exerts an influence on the assessee, for example if the assessment is carried out in the assessee's second language or in a 'middle-class' code.[81]

- The readability level of the task can exert an influence on the assessment, e.g. a difficulty in reading might distract from the purpose of an assessment which is to test the use of a mathematical algorithm.
- The size and complexity of numbers or operations in an assessment (e.g. of mathematics) – that might distract the assessee who actually understands the operations and concepts.
- The number and type of operations and stages to a task – a student might know how to perform each element, but when they are presented in combination the size of the task can be overwhelming.
- The form and presentation of questions affects the results, giving variability on students' performance.
- A single error early on in a complex sequence may confound the later stages of the sequence (within a question or across a set of questions), even though the student might have been able to perform the later stages of the sequence, thereby preventing the student from gaining credit for all she can, in fact, do.
- Questions requiring use of mechanical toys might favour boys more than girls.[82]
- Questions requiring use of dolls or kitchen work might favour girls more than boys.
- Essay questions favour boys if they concern impersonal topics and girls if they concern personal and interpersonal topics.[83]
- Boys perform better than girls on multiple choice questions and girls perform better than boys on essay-type questions (perhaps because boys are more willing than girls to guess in multiple-choice items), and girls perform better in written work than boys.[84]
- Goulding[85] indicated that continuous assessment of coursework at 16-plus enabled a truer picture of girls' achievements in mathematics to be presented than that yielded by results on a written examination. Girls may be more anxious about examinations than boys, and consequently their performance may suffer.
- Questions and assessment may be culture-bound:[86] what is comprehensible in one culture may be incomprehensible in another.
- The test may be so long, in order to ensure coverage, that boredom and loss of concentration may impair reliability.[87]

What we are saying is that specific contextual factors can exert a significant influence on learning and that this has to be recognised in conducting assessments, rendering an assessment as unthreatening and natural as possible.

With specific reference to the National Curriculum assessment tasks it has been argued that some tasks which meet the criteria for a higher level in fact might be easier than other tasks[88] for lower levels, dependent on the previous experiences of the students, i.e. as was mentioned before, there are no objective levels of difficulty. The construction of difficulty is in the mind of the individual. Further, there is a problem connected with levels of maturation and age of the students. For example, a task for a Level 5 student might be suitable for an 11-year-old but might be given to a 16-year-old; students of different ages (and not necessarily different abilities) make qualitatively different responses to the same task. This is unremarkable; student teachers who found their GCSE examinations difficult could probably pass them with ease now that they are older. Further, Hall[89] reports problems with validity in respect of the English level descriptions for assessment purposes, arguing that they do not fairly cover the domain of the component elements of the subject. Indeed Wedeen *et al.*[90] raise questions about whether a Level 3, 4, 5 means the same for a Key Stage 2 and Key Stage 3 student, and what a Level 3, 4, 5 actually means that a student can do.

Validity

Validity in assessment is defined as ensuring that the assessment in fact assesses what it purports to assess and provides a fair representation of the student's performance, achievement, potential, capabilities, knowledge skills etc. (i.e. addressing what it was intended to address). This is a problem when defining and operationalising abstract constructs like intelligence, creativity, imaginativeness, anxiety. Validity[91] refers to appropriateness, meaningfulness, usefulness, specificity, diagnostic potential, inferential utility and adequacy.

Face validity requires the assessment to assess what it was intended to assess.

Content validity requires the assessment to cover the intended contents in sufficient depth and breadth so as to be fair and adequate, and not to exceed the scope of those boundaries of content (i.e. not to cover items or contents that were not included in the programme).

Consequential validity depends on the way in which the results are used, i.e. that they should be used in the ways intended and not in other ways. Consequential validity would be violated if inferences made from the results of assessment were not sustainable or justified by the results themselves and were illegitimate. This requires the user of the results to know what the intentions of the assessment were. Of course, this is frequently violated when sensationalist headlines in the media indicate falling standards, when, in fact it was not possible to infer this legitimately from the data.

Predictive validity concerns how much the results of an assessment can be used to predict achievements in the future, e.g. how much scores at A level might be fair indicators of future degree classification. Low predictive validity (e.g. using A level scores to predict degree classification, where it is lower than 50 per cent) suggests that limited credence should be placed in such uses.

Construct validity requires the assessment to provide a fair operationalisation of the construct – often abstract – in question, e.g. intelligence, creativity, spatial awareness, problem-solving. This is usually the most difficult aspect of validity to address, not least because opinion is divided on what a fair construction of the construct actually is. For example, exactly what intelligence is, and what proxy indicators of intelligence might be, can founder at the starting line if there is disagreement on whether it is a single ability, a multiple ability (e.g. Gardner's 'multiple intelligences'), a composite, innate or capable of being developed (nature or nurture).

One statistical means of addressing construct validity is to seek inter-correlations between several items which are intended to measure the same construct (or to undertake factor analysis, itself based on inter-correlations). The principle here is that inter-correlations between items in a test, for example, that are intended to measure the same construct should be higher than inter-correlations between items that are not intended to measure the same construct or which are intended to measure different constructs. Further, different types of question that are intended to measure the same construct should have stronger inter-correlations than inter-correlations using the same types of question to assess different constructs.

So here we have a dilemma. We commented earlier on the tensions between competing purposes of assessment and competing types of assessment. We argued that one has to select which purposes and types of assessment will be used, because a single assessment could not serve all purposes and types of assessment, they being incompatible with each other. So it is with reliability and validity. The more we steer towards reliability, consistency, uniformity, standardisation and their outcomes in nominal grades, the more we move away from the rich data upon which teachers can often take action. Conversely, the more we move towards teacher- and student-defined, personalised valid data the less generalisable, standardisable, comparable and consistent are the results (though no less transparent provided that the criteria are made public). The notion of representativeness of a wide population in reliability becomes redefined as representing and capturing the specific needs, abilities and achievement of each individual student.[92] We advocate addressing the latter rather than the former set of issues. To address reliability and validity in detail could easily lead to endless assessment, and this, clearly, is not to be wished.

Moreover, Lambert[93] argues that not only are reliability and validity in a state of tension with each other but that a third factor – manageability – might reduce both reliability and validity. Manageability, reliability and validity are in tension with each other.

Assessment is an inherently inexact science.[94] Indeed it is an art rather than a science. We suggest that student teachers should be primarily concerned to address validity because this has strong individualistic, diagnostic and formative potential. This is not to suggest that reliability should be neglected; indeed student teachers will find it useful to compare their own assessments of work with those contained in the school portfolio of moderated work that are exemplars of different levels and attainment targets. We suggest that student teachers should be concerned with carefully planned and differentiated work that is well matched to students' needs. In these the intended learning outcomes for students are communicated to them and discussed with them – generating their involvement and 'ownership' – as mentioned in Part II. Diagnostic assessment feeds into diagnostic teaching. That renders validity, particularly 'consequential validity', a significant issue. Assessment takes place by identifying opportunities to undertake it in everyday teaching. Where assessment is more 'formal', i.e. less embedded in everyday teaching, care should be taken to reduce stress as much as possible and to address as far as practicable the features of reliability outlined above.

The suggestion that assessment is an inherently inexact activity suggests to us that a counsel of perfection should give way to a counsel of utility, practicability, validity, and strong formative potential. That said, it would be a useful experience if student teachers took the opportunity to conduct a standardised test or assessment.

METHODS OF GATHERING ASSESSMENT DATA

The student teacher has several ways of gathering assessment data. These can be divided into two main types: written sources of assessment data and non-written sources of assessment data. Mitchell and Koshy[95] also suggest that formative assessment by teachers can address what a student does, says and writes. Written sources include tests and written examinations (including essays); portfolios; samples of students' work; records, and self-completed, self-referenced assessments. Non-written sources include observation (visual, oral); practical activities with concrete outcomes; questioning; interviews and conferencing; presentations and exhibitions; video and audio recordings and photographs; role play and simulations. We shall deal with these in turn.

WRITTEN SOURCES OF DATA COLLECTION

Tests

The major means of gathering assessment data over the years have been tests and examinations. Published tests are commercially produced and they take various forms: diagnostic tests (e.g. the Metropolitan Diagnostic Tests);[96] aptitude tests (which predict a person's aptitude in a named area, e.g. the Comprehensive Test of Adaptive Behaviour, the McCarthy Screening Test, the Assessment for Training and Employment Test); achievement tests; norm-referenced tests (the Boehm Test of Basic Concepts); criterion-referenced tests (e.g. the GCSE examinations of coursework); reading tests (e.g. the Edinburgh Reading Test); verbal reasoning tests (e.g. the Wechsler Adult Intelligence Scale and tests published by the National Foundation for Educational Research); tests of critical thinking (e.g. the Watson-Glaser Critical Thinking Appraisal); tests of social adjustment (e.g. the

British Social Adjustment Test and the Kohn Social Competence Scale); baseline assessment tests (e.g. the Basic Achievement Skills Individual Screener). Several commercial companies hold tests that have restricted release or availability, requiring the teacher or school to register with a particular company. For example, in the United Kingdom the Psychological Corporation Ltd. not only holds the rights to a world-wide battery of tests but has different levels of clearance for different users. Having different levels of clearance attempts to ensure, for example, that students are not 'prepared' for the test by coaching on the various items.[97]

Published tests have several attractions: they are objective and standardised (as a result of piloting and refinement); they declare their levels of reliability and validity through the inclusion of statistical data; they come complete with instructions for administration and processing; they are often straightforward and quick to administer and mark, and an accompanying manual gives guidance for the interpretation of results.

On the other hand, simply because they have been standardised on a wide population and are generalisable, by definition they are not tailored to an individual institution, a local context or specific needs. Hence if published tests are to be used they must serve the desired purposes of the assessment – the notion of fitness for purpose is crucial in selecting from a battery of tests in the public domain.

A test that is devised by the teacher for a specific purpose, whilst it does not have the level of standardisation of a commercially produced test, nevertheless will be tailored to that teacher's particular needs, addressing very fully the notion of fitness for purpose. Cohen et al.[98] provide some guidelines for the construction of a test by a teacher:

●   The purposes of the test must be explicit (i.e. to provide data for a particular type of assessment).
●   The type of test must be appropriate (e.g. diagnostic, achievement, aptitude, criterion-referenced, norm-referenced).
●   The objectives of the test need to be stated in operational terms.
●   The content of the test must be suitable.
●   The construction of the test must address item analysis (e.g. ensuring that each item in the test serves one or more specified objectives), item discriminability and item difficulty (see the discussion of these topics below).

On the other hand, teacher-devised tests are prone to several problems:[99]

●   They can encourage rote learning and superficial learning, simply for the test day itself.
●   Discussions of reliability, validity and utility are not undertaken between teachers – the tests are a private creation by individual teachers.
●   Quantity can be favoured over quality.
●   There is a tendency to lead to an over-emphasis on marks and grades, to the detriment of learning and rich feedback.
●   They foster too much of a competitive mentality in learners.
●   They lead to 'learned helplessness' in students – where they are only motivated by the desire to do well rather than to learn and where they come to believe that if they fail then it is because they are not sufficiently clever and so there is nothing that can be done about it to improve, therefore they avoid risk taking and challenge.

Too much testing can be counter-productive, leading to a decline in performance, particularly if the results of the test are simply a mark or grade rather than rich feedback on how to improve. Clarke[100] summarised much research evidence to suggest that grading every piece of work is simply counter-productive.

Planning a test

In devising a test the student teacher will have to consider several stages:

1 Identify the purposes of the test

The purposes of a test are several, for example to diagnose a student's strengths, weaknesses and difficulties; to measure achievement; to measure attainment (e.g. of the National Curriculum); to measure aptitude and potential; to identify readiness for a programme ('placement testing') and is used for formative, diagnostic or summative purposes.

2 Identify the test specifications

The test specifications include:

- which programme objectives and student learning outcomes will be addressed
- which content areas will be addressed
- the relative weightings, balance and coverage of items
- the total number of items in the test
- the number of questions required to address a particular element of a programme or learning outcome
- the exact items in the test.

To ensure validity in a test it is essential to ensure that the objectives of the test are fairly addressed in the test items. Objectives should:

- be specific and be expressed with an appropriate degree of precision
- represent intended learning outcomes
- identify the actual and observable behaviour which will demonstrate achievement
- include an active verb
- be unitary (focusing on one item per objective).

One way of ensuring that the objectives are fairly addressed in test items can be done through a matrix frame that indicates the coverage of content areas, the coverage of objectives of the programme, and the relative weighting of the items on the test. Such a matrix is set out in Box 91, taking the example from a secondary school history syllabus.

Box 91 indicates the main areas of the programme to be covered in the test (content areas); then it indicates which objectives or detailed content areas will be covered (1a–3c) – these numbers refer to the identified specifications in the syllabus; then it indicates the marks/ percentages to be awarded for each area. This indicates several points:

- The least emphasis is given to the build-up to and end of the war (10 marks each in the 'total' column).
- The greatest emphasis is given to the invasion of France (35 marks in the 'total' column).
- There is fairly even coverage of the objectives specified (the figures in the 'total' row only vary from 9 to 13).

Box 91: A matrix of test items

Content areas	Objective/area of programme content			Objective/area of programme content			Objective/area of programme content			Total
Aspects of the Second World War	1a	1b	1c	2a	2b	2c	3a	3b	3c	
The build-up to the Second World War	1	2		2	1	1	1	1	1	10
The invasion of Poland	2	1	1	3	2	2	3	3	3	20
The invasion of France	3	4	5	4	4	3	4	4	4	35
The allied invasion	3	2	3	3	4	3	3	2	2	25
The end of the conflict	2	1		1	1	1	2	2		10
Total	11	10	9	13	12	10	13	12	10	100

- Greatest coverage is given to objectives 2a and 3a, and least coverage is given to objective 1c.
- Some content areas are not covered in the test items (the blanks in the matrix).

Hence we have here a test scheme that indicates relative weightings, coverage of objectives and content, and the relation between these two latter elements. Relative weightings should first be addressed assigning percentages at the foot of each column, then by assigning percentages at the end of each row, and then completing each cell of the matrix within these specifications. This ensures that appropriate sampling and coverage of the items are achieved. The example of the matrix refers to specific objectives as column headings; of course these could be replaced by factual knowledge, conceptual knowledge and principles, and skills for each of the column headings. Alternatively they could be replaced by specific aspects of an activity, for example: designing a crane, making the crane, testing the crane, evaluating the results, improving the design. Indeed these latter could become content (row) headings – see Box 92.

Here one can see that practical skills will carry fewer marks than recording skills (the column totals), and that making and evaluating carry equal marks (the row totals).

This exercise also enables some indication to be gained of the number of items to be included in the test, for instance in the example of the history test the matrix is $9 \times 6 = 54$ possible items, and in the 'crane' activity the matrix is $5 \times 4 = 20$ possible items. Of course, there could be considerable variation in this, for example more test items could be inserted if it were deemed desirable to test one cell of the matrix with more than one item (possible for cross-checking), or indeed there could be fewer items if it were possible to have a single test item that serves more than one cell of the matrix. The difficulty in matrix construction is that it can easily become a runaway activity, generating very many test items and, hence, leading to an unworkably long test – typically the greater the degree of specificity required, the greater the number of test items there will be. One skill in test construction is to be able to have a single test item that provides valid and reliable data for more than a single factor.

Having undertaken the test specifications, the researcher should have achieved clarity on (a) the exact test items that test certain aspects of achievement of objectives, programmes, contents etc.; (b) the coverage and balance of coverage of the test items; and (c) the relative weightings of the test items.

Box 92: Compiling elements of test items

Content area	Identifying key concepts and principles	Practical skills	Evaluative skills	Recording results	Total
Designing a crane	2	1	1	3	7
Making the crane	2	5	2	3	12
Testing the crane	3	3	1	4	11
Evaluating the results	3		5	4	2
Improving the design	2	2	3	1	8
Total	12	11	12	15	50

3 Select the contents of the test

Here the test is subject to item analysis. An item analysis will need to consider:[101]

- the suitability of the format of each item for the (learning) objective (appropriateness)
- the ability of each item to enable students to demonstrate their performance of the (learning) objective (relevance)
- the clarity of the task for each item.

In moving to test construction the student teacher will need to consider how each element to be tested will be operationalised: (a) what indicators and kinds of evidence of achievement of the objective will be required; (b) what indicators of high, moderate and low achievement there will be; (c) what the students will be doing when they are working on each element of the test; (d) what the outcome of the test will be (e.g. a written response, a tick in a box of multiple choice items, an essay, a diagram, a computation). Indeed the Task Group on Assessment and Testing in the UK[102] took from the work of the UK's Assessment of Performance Unit the suggestion that attention will have to be given to the presentation, operation and response modes of a test: (a) how the task will be introduced (e.g. oral, written, pictorial, computer, practical demonstration); (b) what the students will be doing when they are working on the test (e.g. mental computation, practical work, oral work, written); and (c) what the outcome will be – how they will show achievement and present the outcomes (e.g. choosing one item from a multiple choice question, writing a short response, open-ended writing, oral, practical outcome, computer output). Operationalising a test from objectives can proceed by stages:

1   Identify the objectives/outcomes/elements to be covered.
2   Break down the objectives/outcomes/elements into constituent components or elements.
3   Select the components that will feature in the test, such that, if possible, they will represent the larger field (i.e. domain referencing, if required).
4   Recast the components in terms of specific, practical, observable behaviours, activities and practices that fairly represent and cover that component.
5   Specify the kinds of data required to provide information on the achievement of the criteria.
6   Specify the success criteria (performance indicators) in practical terms, working out marks and grades to be awarded and how weightings will be addressed.

7　　Write each item of the test.

8　　Conduct a pilot to refine the language/readability and presentation of the items, to gauge item discriminability, item difficulty and distracters (discussed below), and to address validity and reliability.

Item analysis is designed to ensure that: (a) the items function as they are intended, for example, that criterion-referenced items fairly cover the fields and criteria and that norm-referenced items demonstrate item discriminability (discussed below); (b) the level of difficulty of the items is appropriate (see below: item difficulty); (c) the test is reliable (free of distracters – unnecessary information and irrelevant cues). An item analysis will consider the accuracy levels available in the answer, the item difficulty, the importance of the knowledge or skill being tested, the match of the item to the programme, and the number of items to be included.

In constructing a test the researcher will need to undertake an item analysis to clarify the item discriminability. In other words, how effective is the test item in showing up differences between a group of students? Does the item enable us to discriminate between students' abilities in a given field? An item with high discriminability will enable the researcher to see a potentially wide variety of scores on that item; an item with low discriminability will show scores on that item poorly differentiated. Clearly a high measure of discriminability is desirable.[103]

Distracters are the stuff of multiple choice items, where incorrect alternatives are offered, and students have to select the correct alternatives. Here a simple frequency count of the number of times a particular alternative is selected will provide information on the effectiveness of the distracter: if it is selected many times then it is working effectively; if it is seldom or never selected then it is not working effectively and it should be replaced.

If we wished to calculate the item difficulty of a test, we could use the following formula:

$$\frac{A}{N} \times 100$$

where A = the number of students who answered the item correctly; N = the total number of students who attempted the item.

Hence if 12 students out of a class of 20 answered the item correctly, then the formula would work out thus:

$$\frac{12}{20} \times 100 = 60\%$$

The maximum index of difficulty is 100 per cent. Items falling below 33 per cent and above 67 per cent are likely to be too difficult and too easy respectively. It would appear, then, that this item would be appropriate to use in a test. Here, again, whether the student teacher uses an item with an index of difficulty below or above the cut-off points is a matter of judgement. In a norm-referenced test the item difficulty should be around 50 per cent.

In constructing a test with item analysis, item discriminability, item difficulty and distractor effects in mind, it is important also to consider the actual requirements of the test,[104] for example:

- whether all the items in the test are equally difficult
- which items are easy, moderately hard, hard, very hard
- what kinds of task each item is addressing e.g. is it (a) a practice item – repeating known knowledge, (b) an application item – applying known knowledge, (c) a synthesis item – bringing together and integrating diverse areas of knowledge?).

4 Consider the form of the test

Much of the discussion in this chapter assumes that the test is of the pen-and-paper variety. Clearly this need not be the case, for example tests can be written, oral, practical, interactive, computer-based, dramatic, diagrammatic, pictorial, photographic, involve the use of audio and video material, presentational and role play, or simulations. This does not negate the issues discussed in this chapter, for the form of the test will still need to consider, for example, reliability and validity, difficulty, discriminability, marking and grading, item analysis, timing. Indeed several of these factors take on an added significance in non-written forms of testing; for example: (a) reliability is a major issue in judging live musical performance or the performance of a gymnastics routine – where a 'one-off' event is likely; (b) reliability and validity are significant issues in group performance or group exercises – where group dynamics may prevent a testee's true abilities from being demonstrated. Clearly the student teacher will need to consider whether the test will be undertaken individually, or in a group, and what form it will take. The test will need to consider the presentation (introduction) mode, the activity mode (what will be done in the test) and the response (outcome) mode – what product the student is expected to produce.

5 Write the test item

Many objective tests are composed of a number of items – for example, missing words, incomplete sentences or incomplete, unlabelled diagrams, true/false statements, open-ended questions where students are given guidelines for how much to write (e.g. a sentence, a paragraph, 300 words etc.), closed questions, multiple choice questions, matching pairs of statements and responses, short answer and long answer responses. They can test recall, knowledge, comprehension, application, analysis, synthesis, and evaluation, i.e. different orders of thinking. These take their rationale from the work of Bloom *et al.*[105] in 1956 on hierarchies of cognitive abilities – from low-order thinking (comprehension, application) to higher-order thinking (evaluation). Clearly the student teacher will need to know the order of the thinking being tested in the test.

Missing words and incomplete sentences
Missing word items are useful for rapid completion, and guessing is reduced because a specific response is required. On the other hand such items tend to require lower level recall and can be time-consuming to score, if the marker has to try to understand what the student has been thinking about in writing the answer.

The test will need to address the intended and unintended clues and cues that might be provided in it, for example:

- The number of blanks might indicate the number of words required.
- The number of dots might indicate the number of letters required.
- The length of blanks might indicate the length of response required.
- The space left for completion will give cues about how much to write.
- Blanks in different parts of a sentence will be assisted by the reader having read the other parts of the sentence (anaphoric and cataphoric reading cues).

There are several guidelines for constructing short-answer items to overcome some of these problems:[106]

- Make the blanks close to the end of the sentence.
- Keep the blanks the same length.

- Require a single word or short statement for the answer.
- Ensure that there can be only a single correct answer.
- Omit only the key words and avoid omitting so many key words as to make the sentence unintelligible, maybe making the blanks appear towards the end of the sentence.
- Avoid putting several blanks close to each other (in a sentence or paragraph) such that the overall meaning is obscured.
- Only make blanks of key words or concepts, rather than of trivial words.
- Avoid addressing only trivial matters.
- Ensure that students know exactly the kind and specificity of the answer required.
- Specify the units in which a numerical answer is to be given.
- Use short answers for testing knowledge recall.

Multiple choice statements

Multiple choice items can test lower-order and higher-order thinking. They are quick to complete and to mark; they are objective and are widely used in formal tests, though they may take some time to devise. In devising fixed, closed response questions there are several considerations to be borne in mind, for example:

- Make the question and requirements unambiguous and in a language appropriate for the students.
- Avoid negatives in statements.
- Avoid giving clues in the 'wrong' choices to which response is the correct one.
- Provide around four choices in order to reduce guessing, and ensure that the 'distracters' are sufficiently close to the correct response as to be worthy of consideration by the student, i.e. make the options realistic.
- Keep the choices around the same length.
- Avoid giving grammatical cues in the choices (e.g. the word 'an' in the stem requires an option that begins with a vowel; the word 'is' in the stem requires an option written in the singular).
- Ensure that one option does not contain more information than another, as this suggests to students that this is the correct option.
- Avoid the use of 'all of the above' or 'none of the above', as these tend to become the options chosen.
- Avoid value and opinion statements, as these are contestable.
- Consider the use of pictures, tables, graphics and maps, particularly for higher-order multiple choice questions (e.g. the siting of a supermarket).

It was mentioned earlier in this chapter that serious questions lie over the use of multiple choice questions. However, they are only as good as the choices offered. If they require higher-order thinking then they may be as limiting as their critics suggest (of course the problem is that they tend not to involve higher-order thinking). There are several attractions to multiple choice items, for example:[107]

- They can be completed quite rapidly, enabling many questions to be asked which, in turn, enable good coverage of each domain, thereby increasing reliability and validity.
- There is limited writing, so students' writing skills (or their lack) do not impede demonstration of knowledge.
- The opportunities for errors or biases in marking are reduced.

On the other hand they have attracted severe criticism:[108]

- They demean and reduce the complexity of knowledge, learning and education to the trivial, atomised and low level.
- They have little diagnostic or formative potential.
- Scores may be inflated through informed guessing.

In devising tests, attention has to be given to the issue of student choice; what is deemed to be unavoidably and centrally important, over which there is no option, and what might be optional is a matter for decision. Black[109] suggests that offering students choices of questions in a test does not help them to achieve higher marks, whilst it engages issues of reliability (e.g. consistency of demand across questions) and validity (e.g. to cover the required domains to be tested). Indeed some students may make unwise choices, and this might compromise reliability. The issue of choice extends further, to include whether one gives different tests to different students, for example depending on their anticipated performance, or whether one offers a single graduated test, with items becoming progressively more difficult the further one moves through the test. Black alludes to a potential gender issue here, in that girls may not choose some difficult items in mathematics as they do not want to take such risks, even though in fact they may have the ability to undertake them.

With regard to multiple choice items there are several potential problems:

- the number of choices in a single multiple choice item (and whether there is only one right answer or more than one)
- the number and realism of the distractors in a multiple choice item (e.g. there might be a number of distractors but many of them are too obvious to be chosen – there may be several redundant items)
- the sequence of items and their effects on each other
- the location of the correct response(s) in a multiple choice item.

There are several suggestions for constructing effective multiple choice test items:[110]

- Ensure that they catch significant knowledge and learning rather than low-level recall of facts.
- Frame the nature of the issue in the stem of the item, ensuring that the stem is meaningful in itself (e.g. replace the general 'Sheep: (a) are graminivorous, (b) are cloven footed, (c) usually give birth to one or two calves at a time' with 'How many lambs are normally born to a sheep at one time?').
- Ensure that the stem includes as much of the item as possible, with no irrelevancies.
- Avoid negative stems to the item.
- Keep the readability levels low.
- Ensure clarity and unambiguity.
- Ensure that all the options are plausible so that guessing of the only possible option is avoided.
- Avoid the possibility of students making the correct choice through incorrect reasoning.

True false items

True false items are useful in being quick to devise and complete, and easy to score. They offer students a 50/50 chance of being correct simply by guessing. To overcome the 'guess factor' students could be asked to indicate why a false item is false, indeed to rewrite it to make it true, where possible, with marks being awarded for the correct revision. In constructing true false items it is important to ensure that the statements are unequivocal, unambiguously true or false. This means omitting questions of value or questions in which there may be differences of opinion. Borich[111] suggests that it is important to keep the statements of approximately the same length, to avoid extremes (e.g. 'never', 'only', 'always') as these will not be chosen, and to avoid double negatives.

There are particular problems in true false questions:[112]

● ambiguity of meaning
● some items might be partly true or partly false
● items that polarise – being too easy or too hard.

To overcome these problems the authors suggest several points that can be addressed:

● Avoid generalised statements (as they are usually false).
● Avoid negatives and double negatives in statements.
● Avoid over-long and over-complex statements.
● Ensure that items are rooted in facts.
● Ensure that statements can be either only true or only false.
● Write statements in everyday language.
● Decide where it is appropriate to use 'degrees' – 'generally', 'usually', 'often' – as these are capable of interpretation.

Matching items

The use of matching items is another rapid-to-construct and easy-to-score means of testing, and is useful for measuring associations between statements and facts. It keeps the role of guessing to a minimum. Matching items comprise a descriptions list and an options list, with the options list to be matched to the appropriate descriptions list. In writing lists of matching items Borich[113] suggests that it is important to:

● keep each of the two lists of items homogeneous
● ensure that the options are plausible distractors
● ensure that the descriptions list contains longer phrases or statements than the options list
● provide clear instructions for how to indicate the matching (e.g. by joining lines, by writing a number and a letter)
● ensure that there are more options than descriptions, to address the issue of distractors
● indicate in the instructions whether the options can be used more than once.

There are also particular potential difficulties in matching items:[114]

● It might be very clear to a student which items in a list simply cannot be matched to items in the other list (e.g. by dint of content, grammar, concepts), thereby enabling the student to complete the matching by elimination rather than understanding.
● One item in one list might be able to be matched to several items in the other.
● The lists might contain unequal numbers of items, thereby introducing distractors – rendering the selection as much a multiple choice item as a matching exercise.

Difficulties in matching items can be addressed thus:

● Ensure that the items for matching are homogeneous – similar – over the whole test (to render guessing more difficult).

- Avoid constructing matching items to answers that can be worked out by elimination (e.g. by ensuring that: (a) there are different numbers of items in each column so that there are more options to be matched than there are items; (b) students can avoid being able to reduce the field of options as they increase the number of items that they have matched; (c) the same option may be used more than once).

Essay questions

A more open-ended type of written assessment is an essay. It is the freedom of response that is possible in the essay form of examination that is held to be its most important asset, enabling higher-order and sustained, in-depth and complex thinking to be demonstrated.

With regard to essay questions, there are several advantages that can be claimed. For example, an essay, as an open form of testing, enables complex learning outcomes to be measured; it enables the student to integrate, apply and synthesise knowledge, to demonstrate the ability for expression and self-expression, and to demonstrate higher-order and divergent cognitive processes. Further, it is comparatively easy to construct an essay title. On the other hand, essays have been criticised for yielding unreliable data,[115] for being prone to unreliable (inconsistent and variable) scoring, neglectful of intended learning outcomes and prone to marker bias and preference (being too intuitive, subjective, holistic, and time-consuming to mark). To overcome these difficulties the authors make the following suggestions:

- Instructions must be given as to whether the requirement is for a short or long essay.
- The essay question must be restricted to those learning outcomes that are unable to be measured more objectively.
- The essay question must ensure that it is clearly linked to desired learning outcomes; that it is clear what behaviours the students must demonstrate.
- The essay question must indicate the field and tasks very clearly (e.g. 'compare', 'justify', 'critique', 'summarise', 'classify', 'analyse', 'clarify', 'examine', 'apply', 'evaluate', 'synthesise', 'contrast', 'explain', 'illustrate').
- Time limits must be set for each essay.
- Options should be avoided, or, if options are to be given, ensure that, if students have a list of titles from which to choose, each title is equally difficult and equally capable of enabling the student to demonstrate achievement, understanding etc.
- Marking criteria should be prepared and explicit, indicating what must be included in the answers and what cognitive processes are being looked for in the essay (e.g. higher-order and lower-order thinking), together with their specification in the essay requirement (e.g. 'compare', 'speculate', 'contrast', 'evaluate', 'give reasons for'). The points to be awarded for such inclusions or ratings should be scored for the extent to which certain criteria have been met.
- Decisions should be made on how to address and score irrelevancies, inaccuracies, poor grammar and spelling.
- The scoring criteria must be agreed, e.g. for content, organisation, logic, structure, presentation, secretarial skills, reasonableness, coverage, completeness, internal consistency, originality, creativity, level of detail, persuasiveness of the argument, conclusiveness, clarity, demonstration of understanding and application, and so on.
- The marks to be awarded for each element should be agreed, including the weighting of the marks.
- The work should be marked blind, and, where appropriate, without the teacher knowing the name of the essay writer. Of course this is perhaps difficult or even undesirable for the student

teacher, who may need to know the identity of the writer. The issue here is how to avoid personal knowledge clouding an objective judgement.

Clearly these are issues of reliability. The issue here is that layout can exert a profound effect on the test. Unlike the objective test, the essay allows the candidate to organise her thoughts and to communicate them in her own style; in short, it gives her freedom to be creative and imaginative in the communication of her ideas. There are disadvantages, however, in the essay as a gatherer of information. Essays are difficult to assess reliably. With only one or two assessors a considerable degree of unreliability can creep into the assessment of essays, i.e. 'inter-rater' reliability may be limited. Black[116] suggests that a reliability coefficient of only 0.6 is likely for a single marker marking several essays, which is very low, so having essay work second marked is vital. Even with analytical marking schemes (see below) the degree of agreement between markers may be low. Since only a limited number of essay titles can be answered in one examination, only a limited part of a syllabus of work can be addressed by the candidate. The student who has the misfortune to choose the 'wrong' essay title may produce work that does not fairly represent her true abilities. Chase[117] has suggested some ways of overcoming these weaknesses in the essay form of test. First, all students might be asked to write on the same essay title(s), the principle being that individuals can only be compared to the extent that they have 'jumped the same hurdles'. Second, marking should be analytic rather than impressionistic. Analytic marking is based upon prior decisions about what exactly is being assessed in the essay – the content; the style; the grammar; the punctuation; the handwriting? (In other words, criterion-referencing should apply.) On the question of the low agreement between essay markers, Lewis[118] suggests the following ways of reducing the subjective element:

● by marking for substantive content rather than style
● by fixing a maximum penalty for mistakes in grammar, syntax and spelling
● by multiple marking followed by a further close scrutiny of those essays placed near the pass fail line.

For public examinations this problem can also be addressed by agreement trials and moderation. Again the notion of fitness for purpose must be the criterion to judge the openness of the essay and its marking frame.

6 Consider the layout of the test

This will include:[119]

● the nature, length and clarity of the instructions (e.g. what to do, how long to take, how much to do, how many items to attempt, what kind of response is required – a single word, a sentence, a paragraph, a formula, a number, a statement etc., how and where to enter the response, where to show the 'working out' of a problem, where to start new answers, e.g. in a separate booklet, whether one answer only is required to a multiple choice item, or more than one answer)
● spreading out the instructions through the test, avoiding overloading students with too much information at first, and providing instructions for each section as they come to it
● considering what marks are to be awarded for which parts of the test.

The layout of the text should be such that it supports the completion of the test and that this is done as efficiently and as effectively as possible for the student.

7 Consider the timing of the test

This refers to two areas: (a) when the test will take place (the day of the week, month, time of day); and (b) the time allowances to be given to the test and its component items. With regard to the former, in part this is a matter of reliability, for the time of day, week etc. might influence how alert, motivated, capable a student might be. With regard to the latter, the researcher will need to decide what time restrictions are being imposed and why (for example, is the pressure of a time constraint desirable – to show what a student can do under time pressure – or an unnecessary impediment, putting a time boundary around something that need not be bounded – was Van Gogh put under a time pressure to produce the painting of sunflowers?).

Though it is vital that the student knows what the overall time allowance is for the test, clearly it might be helpful to a student to indicate notional time allowances for different elements of the test; if these are aligned to the relative weightings of the test (see the discussions of weighting and scoring) they enable a student to decide where to place emphasis in the test – she may want to concentrate her time on the high scoring elements of the test.

8 Plan the scoring of the test

The awarding of scores for different items of the test is a clear indication of the relative significance of each item – the weightings of each item are addressed in their scoring. It is important to ensure that easier parts of the test attract fewer marks than more difficult parts of it, otherwise a student's results might be artificially inflated by answering many easy questions and fewer more difficult questions. Clearly, also, it is important to know in advance what constitutes a 'good answer'.[120]

The more marks that are available to indicate different levels of achievement (e.g. for the awarding of grades), the greater the reliability of the grades will be, though clearly this could make the test longer. Scoring will also need to be prepared to handle issues of poor spelling, grammar and punctuation – is it to be penalised, and how will consistency be assured here? Further, how will issues of omission be treated, e.g. if a student omits the units of measurement (miles per hour, dollars or pounds, metres or centimetres)?

Related to the scoring of the test is the issue of reporting the results. If the scoring of a test is specific then this enables variety in reporting to be addressed, for example, results may be reported item by item, section by section, or whole test by whole test. This degree of flexibility might be useful for the student teacher, as it will enable particular strengths and weaknesses in groups of students to be exposed.

Underpinning the discussion of scoring is the need to make it unequivocally clear exactly what the marking criteria are – what will and will not score points. This requires a clarification of whether there is a 'checklist' of features that must be present in a student's answer. The specification of the performance criteria is crucial, defining high-scoring, medium-scoring and low-scoring criteria. In essence, what is being required here is a rubric for the test, specifying:[121]

- the performance criteria
- what to look for in judging performance
- the range of quality of performance and how to score different levels of performance
- how to determine reliability and validity, and how these are reflected in the scoring.

Clearly criterion-referenced tests will have to declare their lowest boundary – a cut-off point – below which the student has been deemed to fail to meet the criteria. A compromise can be seen in those criterion-referenced tests which award different grades for different levels of performance of the same task, necessitating the clarification of different cut-off points in the examination. A common example of this can be seen in the GCSE examinations for secondary school pupils in the United Kingdom, where students can achieve a grade between A and F for a criterion-related examination.

9 Consider special adaptations to the test

There will be some students who will need to have special arrangements made for them for the test, for example in terms of:[122]

- the presentation format of the test (the need to read the questions slowly to a student, or in stages rather than all at the start, or to have them read aloud, or language levels adjusted, or, indeed, not to have them in written form)
- the response format (allowing dictionaries and calculators, allowing responses other than in written form, having a scribe to write the dictated answers, allowing the use of notes)
- the timing of the test (providing extra time, avoiding timed tests, providing breaks through different parts of the test, allowing an unlimited amount of time)
- the setting of the test (testing in a separate place, providing a one-to-one test situation, reducing distractions).

Ethical issues in preparing for tests

A major source of unreliability of test data derives from the extent to which students have been prepared for the test, and the ways in which this has been done. These can be located on a continuum from direct and specific preparation, through indirect and general preparation, to no preparation at all. With the growing demand for test data (e.g. for selection, for certification, for grading, for employment, for tracking, for entry to higher education, for accountability, for judging schools and teachers) there is a perhaps understandable pressure to prepare students for tests. This is the 'high-stakes' aspect of testing[123] where much hinges on the test results. At one level this can be seen in the backwash effect of examinations on curricula and syllabuses; at another level it can lead to the direct preparation of students for specific examinations. Preparation can take many forms:[124]

- ensuring coverage, amongst other programme contents and objectives, of the objectives and programme that will be tested
- restricting the coverage of the programme content and objectives to those only that will be tested
- preparing students with 'exam technique'
- practicing with past/similar papers.

Should one teach to a test; is not to do so a dereliction of duty (e.g. in criterion- and domain-referenced tests), or giving students an unfair advantage and thus reducing the reliability of the test as a true and fair measure of ability or achievement? In high-stakes assessment (e.g. for public accountability and to compare schools and teachers) there is even the issue of not entering for tests students whose performance will be low. There is a risk of a correlation between the 'stakes' and the degree of unethical practice – the greater the stakes, the greater the incidence of unethical practice. Unethical practice, observes Gipps,[125] occurs where scores are inflated but reliable inference on performance or achievement is not, and where different groups of students are prepared differentially for tests, i.e. giving some students an unfair advantage over others. To overcome such problems, she suggests, it is ethical and legitimate for teachers to teach to a broader domain than the test; teachers should not teach directly to the test, and the situation should only be that better instruction rather than test preparation is acceptable.

One can add to this list of considerations the view that:

- tests must be valid and reliable
- the administration, marking and use of the test should only be undertaken by suitably competent/qualified people (i.e. people and projects should be vetted)
- access to test materials should be controlled, for instance: test items should not be reproduced apart from selections in professional publication; the tests should only be released to suitably qualified professionals in connection with specific professionally acceptable projects.

Portfolios and samples of work

Authentic assessment may draw on portfolio assessment.[126] A portfolio is a collection of pieces of students' work, which indicate accomplishments over time and context, which may be used to represent their best achievements as they contain the samples of the best work and best represent their development. Portfolios, compiled by the student, with or without the support from, and negotiation with, the teacher, are powerful ways of involving students – a form of ipsative assessment, on which we have commented above. Portfolios are useful in that they:

- indicate best accomplishments
- help students to evaluate themselves
- indicate improvement and development over time
- comprise ongoing assessment.

The contents of a portfolio are not fixed, but they change over time and to suit different purposes and audiences, as work is selected in and selected out.[127] Clearly it is important to know the purpose of the portfolio – whether, for example, it is intended to represent the best work of the student or the typical work of the student, as this affects the selection of the contents of the portfolio. Reflecting on the choice of samples for the portfolio is important, as it encourages a student to reflect on her/his best/poorest/average/easiest/hardest piece of work and the reasons for this judgement, together with considerations of the pieces of work that demonstrate the greatest improvement and progress.

A portfolio has many purposes and uses, for example:[128]

- to act as a showcase of a student's best work, as selected by the student
- to act as a showcase of a student's best work, as selected by the teacher
- to reflect the student's interests
- to chart development, improvement and rates of progress.

Hence, in using portfolios for assessment it is important to decide:[129]

- the purpose of the portfolio (e.g. to monitor progress, to communicate what has been learnt, to inform employers, to document achievements, to grade students, to select students for employment and higher education)
- the cognitive, affective and psychomotor skills, social skills, competencies, attitudes to be addressed in the portfolio
- who will plan the portfolio (e.g. the teacher, the student, both, the parents)

●   the contents of the portfolio and the sample of work to be chosen (e.g. the best work, typical work, a range of work, a close focus on a few items).

In marking/scoring portfolios several issues should be considered:

●   Select the performance to be taught.
●   State the performance criteria: what constitutes effective learning, what are the learning outcomes, the required performance, the required activities and the required targets to be met.
●   Identify how students and teachers will be involved in the selection of the items for inclusion in the portfolio, the review of, and reflection on, the selection, and the opportunities to be provided for students to: (a) select in and out samples of work; (b) rework a particular activity or piece of work.

It is important for all parties to know the 'rules of the game' in devising and assessing portfolios, so that the criteria for inclusion and marking are transparent. There is the issue of whether it is acceptable to include poor samples of work, as students may have the right to privacy and to include only those samples of work which demonstrate their best achievements rather than the processes which led up to those achievements (should students be marked on drafts or poor work, or only on their best work?). The matter is akin to writing a curriculum vitae: we deliberately exclude our failures and weaknesses, and only include those items which present ourselves in the best light.

Portfolios are not without their difficulties, for example:[130]

●   decisions on whether to include the best work or typical work (which may not be the best work)
●   honesty (students may download materials from the internet, and pass them off as their own)
●   time (portfolios take a long time to score and mark).

Clearly these are tricky problems. At heart the portfolio is almost inevitably subjective and personal; the difficulty of reconciling this for use in a more objective style of assessment, for comparisons and comparative judgements of students, is problematic.

Throughout the years of schooling samples of work can be used to provide assessment data, be they pieces of coursework specifically undertaken for assessment purposes (for example, the coursework elements for GCSE examinations) or pieces of work undertaken as part of the everyday learning of students. As with the devising and use of tests, the use of the coursework or other written work must be appropriate to the purposes and objectives of the assessment and, like most samples, be representative of the wider range of work that a student has done. Using samples of work for assessment represents one of the most widely used means of assessment because the samples of work are ongoing and rooted in the reality of classroom life.

Ensuring that the samples of work fit the objectives and purposes of the assessment means that the criteria for setting the work in the first place must fit the assessment purposes and that the assessment or marking of the work must make explicit the criteria to be used and disclose these to the students. In the interests of good teaching and natural justice there is little justification for withholding from students the purposes of the written work and the criteria that will be used to assess the work. It is unacceptable to have students 'play a game' whose rules they have not been told. Students will be more likely to feel involved in the process of assessment if it is made clear to them what it will be and what criteria will be used (see the discussion earlier about reliability, motivation, the relations between the assessor and assessee and the assessee's 'nerves' during the assessment). This breaks with the traditional type of assessments where contents and criteria are kept secret.

Schools should have a marking policy that is consistent and consistently used through the school, and the student teacher should be able to see this. This policy might include, for example, the proportions of marks to be given for coverage of content, depth of own research, grammar, spelling, presentation, effort, achievement, together with weightings for these several elements. Guidance should be sought on what to mark for, for example:

- Was the work clear, sequenced, structured and presented?
- Was the argument clear, developmental and supported?
- Did the work keep to the point?
- Did the work address the key points comprehensively and deeply?

For marking GCSE coursework, the criteria for assessment are explicit and given by the examining body; they constitute the 'analytical' marking schemes described above. For other pieces of work and for pre-GCSE students the criteria might be those set out in the National Curriculum documentation. With reference to the National Curriculum, though it is important that the level descriptions and end-of-Key Stage statements should be used for assessment purposes, in practice some of these are too generalised to provide operational criteria; the student teacher might be better advised to refer to the programmes of study and the attainment targets in the National Curriculum for more concrete criteria – or to operationalise in more detail the level descriptors and end-of-Key Stage statements of the National Curriculum.

To be able to assess a sample of work in terms of its demonstration of the achievement of a particular aspect or subject of the National Curriculum it is important for the school and department to keep a portfolio whose samples of work have been judged by a process of internal moderation,[131] external moderation and agreement trials to demonstrate a particular level of achievement in every subject of the National Curriculum. When a teacher wishes to assess a sample of work she can refer to these samples in the school portfolio in order to match her own assessment standards with the agreed standards of work that have been decided for the samples of work contained in it. The school portfolio should include: (a) work to cover the levels of each core subject of the National Curriculum, (b) two or three examples for each level in each subject, and (c) examples of work that are at the top of each level.

A portfolio is simply a collection of samples of students' work over time, usually containing the best pieces of work in the area/field which may have been produced from previous drafts, and it will comprise different kinds of work: projects, reports, essays, assignments, reflective writing, self-assessment,[132] test materials, homework, class work. The items will vary in focus, scope, size, style, amount of teacher input and support, but may often comprise:

- a biography (of a project or piece of work, so that the reader can judge the difference between the student at the start and the end of a period of time)
- a range of works and assignments
- reflections, self-evaluation and critique: what they have learned, how they have improved, and how they have changed.

Portfolio assessment links strongly to authentic assessment, and can be used to document the kinds of activities undertaken, the best performance (a showcase of work), a record of progress over time, or, indeed, a collection of evaluated work. Though the items to be included in the portfolio may be self-selected, this may be facilitated by the teacher.

Portfolios can be used formatively and summatively, though their formative use is most frequently advocated. Because portfolios are usually selections of best practice, and because it may not always be clear how much help from parents and teachers has gone into the portfolio or how much the student has simply downloaded material from the web, their reliability, indeed their validity, may be suspect, hence they tend not to be used for high-stakes assessment. Indeed a decision has to be taken on whether to include typical or best work in the portfolio. Portfolios are very time-consuming to develop, review and mark, and this is a major problem for time-pressed teachers. Further, given that the contents of a portfolio may vary from one student to another, it becomes almost impossibly difficult to assess them fairly – consistently and comparatively – across students. Hence they tend to be used formatively rather than summatively. Portfolios are developmental and are intended to facilitate the process of communication and conferencing between teachers, learners, parents and maybe employers.

Records

Student teachers on teaching practice will be required to keep records of students' progress. The issues of record keeping will be addressed later in this part. For the present we note that the day-to-day, week-to-week and term-by-term records should provide clear evidence for student teachers' and teachers' assessments of students, in a subject-specific form as well as in terms of a student's wider development (including, for example, social and emotional factors).

Teachers are required to report on a student's progress in every National Curriculum area each year; to be able to do this entails the keeping of records throughout the year so that a student's achievement can be documented, difficulties noted and particularly strong features recorded. These records are informal though not necessarily private documents. For a formal assessment record the teacher can review the data that have been recorded that chart a student's progress, and match these to the level descriptions and attainment targets of the National Curriculum in order to document the student's level of achievement. The corollary of this is that the student teacher will be well advised to ensure that the ongoing record keeping system that she adopts is framed in terms of the National Curriculum as well as including other elements. By dating each record entry a student's rate of progress will be indicated, showing where there have been periods of rapid progress, limited progress, periods of consolidation and periods where very little seems to have happened. Student teachers would be well advised to practise writing short, punchy accounts, often in note form.[133]

Self-referenced assessments

A final type of written source of assessment data is the self-assessment undertaken by students. This was signalled in the comments earlier about ipsative assessments where it was suggested that a student could set her own targets (often in discussion with the teacher) and refer back to these at a given point in time in order to assess how successfully she has met those targets. As was mentioned earlier, these might be focused on academic knowledge and the National Curriculum subjects or they might also include other aspects of development that are not touched on in too great detail by the National Curriculum, for example developing confidence and motivation, what has been found easy or difficult (and why), what has been achieved in social behaviour, how the student has managed to stay calm in difficult settings etc.

For many students one must recognise that to give them a blank sheet of paper and ask them to complete a self-assessment in their own terms is sheer folly; they will have little or no understanding of what to do, and limited ability either to decide the focuses of the comments or to write them. In these circumstances the student teacher can offer a 'scaffolding' or framework for analysis – either provided entirely by the student teacher or arrived at through a process of discussion and negotiation with the student.

Box 93: Written sources of assessment data

Method	Strengths	Weaknesses
Tests	Targeted, specific, written, flexible, many types, marks can give credit and compensation for partial answers.	Unnatural, threatening, outcome-focused, the Hawthorne effect, simplistic, often only one 'correct' answer.
Questionnaires	Focused and specific.	Not central to the purposes of everyday teaching and learning.
Essays	Open-ended, enable individuality to be demonstrated, much formative potential.	Prone to unreliability, poor coverage of a whole course, risks of not showing a student's overall abilities, problems of comparability between different essay titles.
Portfolios and samples of work (including, for example, different kinds of writing)	Rooted in everyday teaching and learning, much formative potential, criterion-specific, public criteria, ongoing.	Need to ensure validity, much hinges on single items, problems for poor writers, neglects processes.
Records and reports	Specific, detailed, focused, much formative potential, charts rates of progress, honest, ongoing, cumulative.	Time-consuming, risk of subjectivity.
Self-referenced assessments	Authentic, focused, honest, highlight priorities, high student ownership.	Irrelevant for National Curriculum assessment, problems for poor writers, problem of institutional response only.

A summary of methods of data collection from written sources is provided in Box 93. We suggest that the use of written data for assessment purposes should select the most appropriate form(s) – to address the notion of fitness for purpose – and that caution may have to be exercised in interpreting written data, particularly from students for whom writing is difficult, demotivating or threatening. That said, many lessons which require a written outcome can also become, thereby, opportunities for assessment.

NON-WRITTEN SOURCES OF DATA COLLECTION

Non-written sources of assessment data might be particularly appropriate for students whose written abilities are limited. They enable credit to be given for work other than written work. There are several sources of non-written data, including questioning, observations, interviews and conferences, presentations, video and audio recording, and photographs.

Questions

Perhaps the most commonly used way of gathering informal assessment data is by asking the students questions, because that is what teachers do for much of their time anyway. This form of data gathering is true to everyday classroom life.[134] Effective questioning is quite a skill, as was demonstrated in Part III. Asking the 'right' questions in order to elicit required information is an art that the student teacher would do well to rehearse beforehand, rather than trying to organise her questioning on the spur of the moment. Further, the student teacher may wish to rehearse different wordings of a question so that she can have ready a different way of putting the question in order to be helpful to the respondent.

In using questions for assessment purposes, it is important to give students time to think, to respond, and to move beyond simply low-level recall questions. The student teacher will have to plan the type, sequence, level, wording, number, focus and purposes of questions if they are to yield reliable and valid data. There is also the issue of the timing of different types of question, for example at the start of a session the questions might refer back to previous teaching and then move to more speculative, open-ended questions, whereas questioning at the end of a session might be for summarising and review, using more closed questions. The focus of the questions can be derived from the purposes and focuses of the assessment that, in turn, are informed by the contents of the National Curriculum. What is required, then, is for the student teacher to operationalise the relevant contents of the National Curriculum so that appropriate, concrete, specific questions can be asked of the students. That operationalisation should not be difficult as it should have taken place at the point of planning the schemes of work and the weekly, daily and lesson plans (see Part II).

We end this section on a cautionary note. Many students may be extremely threatened if a teacher poses a battery of questions, particularly if the respondent does not know the answer. Many student teachers will have insufficient knowledge of particular students to be able to ask questions appropriately, discreetly and unthreateningly. Indeed many students might consider the posing of a range of questions by a relative outsider an invasion of their privacy. All of these constitute significant threats to reliability.

Observation

For the most part observation is a very useful tool for collecting assessment data because it need not interrupt or upset the daily life of classrooms – thereby being strong on validity and reliability. Observation can play a highly significant part in assessment. Some activities can only be assessed by observation in situ, for example in PE the student teacher will need to watch the performance of a handstand or a forward roll as it happens. Notes on the performance can be made at the same time or written up shortly afterwards. In planning observations, attention should be given to the methods and recording, focus and the role of the teacher.

With regard to methods and recording, observation can be systematic, i.e. at regular intervals of time in an activity, at certain points in or stages of the activity, or by working down the list of students to be observed. Another suggestion is that observation can be targeted at specific critical incidents (where the teacher is present when an unanticipated event occurs that yields assessment data). In truth, these two types of observation lie at two poles of a continuum in observation.

At one pole is structured observation,[135] where the observer knows in advance what she will be looking for and enters data on a previously worked out pro-forma. One such pro-forma is for event sampling. Here a tally mark is entered whenever the looked-for behaviour occurs over a given time period, for example whenever the student reads on her own, writes without assistance, addresses safety factors in the laboratory. For instance:

- The student fetches safety glasses /////
- The student checks that his shirt cuffs are tucked into an overall //
- The student keeps the Bunsen burner flame yellow when not in use ////
- The student wears gloves when handling acids ///////

In this example the event 4 occurs most frequently and event 2 least frequently. Event sampling enables the observer to note the incidence and frequency of the looked-for behaviour; that might indicate to the student teacher whether a student has learnt something and can apply it confidently and securely.

There are other forms of structured observation, viz. instantaneous sampling and interval recording. Both require data to be entered onto an observation grid of looked-for behaviours, using some form of coding symbols for speed of entry. We suggest that at this stage the student teacher would not have sufficient time available to conduct this type of observation, hence we do not dwell on it here.

In structured observation the focus of the observation can be decided by reviewing the level descriptions, the attainment targets in question or the programmes of study of the National Curriculum. It is likely that this has already been undertaken at the planning stage (see Part II); in this case the student can refer to the lesson plans where 'assessment data' and 'intended learning outcomes' were specified. These can then be operationalised into specific items to feature in the observation. We would argue against too structured an observation unless it is for in-depth assessment as it is very time-consuming, unnatural (unlike an everyday teaching situation) and potentially very threatening to students.

An unstructured observation (of critical incidents) records incidents that take place spontaneously. Here data are usually entered in the form of words and descriptions; these are reviewed later in light of the criteria used for assessment – perhaps derived from the National Curriculum level descriptions or attainment targets, lesson plans, or objectives of the scheme of work. We would argue against a completely unstructured observation as it may be time-wasting. Nevertheless a responsive observation – where a student teacher notes down an unanticipated event, reaction, outcome – may be useful for assessment purposes.

Between structured and unstructured observation comes semi-structured observation, where the teacher has a range of points about which to gather data, e.g. the students' ability to plan, undertake and evaluate a piece of design technology, but the nature of the entry about the features or behaviour looked for is open-ended, enabling a tailored response (often in words) to be written about a particular behaviour or activity in question. The observer has to know what is being looked for in the observation.[136] For example, the student teacher might be interested in assessing a student's abilities to conduct an experiment, e.g. finding out which kind of paper towel absorbs the most liquid. She might divide the assessment activity into eight areas:

1   Identifying exactly what the problem is in the experiment.
2   Identifying key variables.
3   Isolating and controlling the variables in order to conduct a fair test.
4   Operationalising the experiment.
5   Conducting the experiment.
6   Recording the results.
7   Interpreting the results.
8   Evaluating the experiment (e.g. how it could have been improved).

Each of these eight points is listed and comments are written about the student's performance in each. The comments might also include numbers (marks for the student's achievement in different aspects of the activity).

We advocate very strongly a semi-structured observation as it sets an agenda of areas and items to be observed but is sufficiently open-ended to allow an individual, 'customised' response in the form of words. That respects the student teacher's growing professional insight and judgement.

With regard to the role of the teacher in gathering observational data, attention needs to be given to whether the teacher is to be a participant or non-participant observer. We can surmise that teachers have to be aware that if they intervene too greatly in the activity this may reduce the reliability of the data that they acquire.

With regard to the focus of the observation, this should consider individual and group activities. Indeed one of our early comments indicated that the assessment activity should resemble normal classroom practice as far as possible so that the problem of the Hawthorne effect and the other threats to reliability set out earlier could be reduced. In reality this implies that collaborative group projects should feature in an assessment. Whilst this is a very positive factor it does create some problems for the assessor:

- how to minimise students copying from one another
- how to identify an individual's contribution, particularly if it did not result in a visible outcome
- the composition, size, dynamics of, and personalities in the group that might exert a significant influence on an individual's contribution, for example if there is a dominant student.

Some of these problems can be minimised if: (a) the teacher clarifies what each student will be doing in the group (perhaps after the group itself has discussed this); (b) every student has the opportunity to make a contribution; (c) it is possible to identify how each individual has enabled the task to move forward; (d) the teacher builds into the task the opportunity for individual discussions between herself and each student.

Interviews and conferencing

This 'live' form of data collection generates data that can be recorded as the interview takes place or shortly afterwards. Interviews and conferencing can take place on a one-to-one basis, with groups of students, and with the student(s), parent(s) and teacher(s) present. In the case of the latter the interview might be recorded; this is useful but very time-consuming. Interviews, like observations, vary from the structured to the unstructured. Highly structured interviews will have the contents, wording and sequence of questions worked out in advance. Semi-structured interviews will have a list of topics and questions planned but the sequence and wording will follow the flow of the interview. Questions here are open-ended as well as closed, enabling respondents/participants to address matters in their own terms and in their own words. The assessor might have a list of prompts and probes ready to use if students are unforthcoming or if they are able to be pressed into further comments respectively. Honesty, candour, depth and authenticity of response are the canons of validity in a semi-structured interview.

An unstructured interview, in parallel with an observation of an unanticipated critical incident, by definition cannot set its agenda. It is more like an everyday conversation, open-ended and uncontrived. Though this might yield assessment data it is a high risk form as it may not yield anything – just as many everyday conversations are comparatively inconsequential. We would not advocate this form of interview as it is time-consuming with the strong possibility of yielding very little assessment data.

Interviewing and conferencing have commanded significant attention, where conferences with parents, teachers and children are foundation stones. Such conferencing has been developed much more fully with all age groups and areas of school life with the rise of Records of Achievement and action planning. Both of these have conferencing at their heart, whether it be to engage in a process of review or to decide future targets, success criteria and ways of achieving the targets. In this respect the importance of interviewing and conferencing in this book's advocacy of action planning cannot be overstated. Interviews and conferencing can be motivating for students and student teachers; many students respond positively to the individual attention that they receive in a conference and this form of action planning puts student involvement and engagement in learning as a high priority. Using interviews and conferencing for teaching and learning purposes and for assessment purposes gives this form of data collection an authenticity which is derived from its rootedness in the everyday life of classrooms.

Presentations

Data can be acquired from students making short presentations to their peers or to the student teacher. A presentation might be in the form of a play, reporting what they have done in a particular lesson, leading a debate, reporting how they conducted a traffic census, introducing the work that they have done as a group, reporting on a collaborative project etc., presenting their exhibits of art or design technology work. Using an oral rather than a written medium enables students to use their own ideas in their own words. As a 'live' matter it can involve students more in their own learning and engage them in the activity in question, raising their motivation and interest. This is particularly true for students who find writing difficult or unpleasurable.

On the other hand this activity can be very threatening for inarticulate, reticent or shy students who might become a target for public embarrassment and humiliation, condemning themselves from their own mouths. Alternatively it might give centre stage to a student who loves the limelight and public acclaim and who has an ego to match. Presentations are very personality-specific; whilst that holds out the prospect of authenticity it may reduce their degree of validity.

Video and audio recordings, and photographs

These sources of assessment data capture the unfolding complexity of classrooms and are particularly suitable for acquiring data from students whose written abilities are limited. For that reason they are sources of assessment data that are frequently used with students with special educational needs. Though they can capture 'live' events they can only do so if the equipment is trained on the appropriate parties. For example, a video recorder can be selective in its focus and can cause a major disturbance if it is being taken to several locations in the classroom. Whilst these three forms can yield data that are 'strong on reality' the student teacher ought to be warned about the cost of these forms of acquiring assessment data. With regard to photography there is the cost of the film and processing; with regard to audio and video cassettes there is the cost not only in terms of equipment but in terms of time in setting up the equipment and in analysing the results – an hour's video time might take three hours of analysis, an hour's audio cassette time might take five hours of analysis. These latter two forms of acquiring assessment data are perhaps unrealistic for general and widespread use though they may be very useful indeed for in-depth, focused assessment of specific students or aspects of work.

Role play

This is an activity that might enable students who are inhibited in one context to demonstrate the looked-for abilities in another context. For example, a student who is reluctant to contribute much to a class discussion might turn out to be highly articulate in a spontaneous piece of drama. Knowing that many behaviours are context-dependent (see the discussions of reliability earlier), this is a useful way of trying to gather assessment data through additional channels. On the other hand, of course, some students may not take to role play activities; they may be overshadowed by more assertive members of a drama group and thus they may not be able to exert the freedom of decision making that might enable the student teacher to gather useful assessment data.

A summary of methods of collecting assessment data from non-written sources is presented in Box 94.

Lambert[137] also includes graphic evidence (e.g. pictures, diagrams, charts and graphs, computer printouts) and products (e.g. artefacts, models and 3D constructions). These may be particularly useful for catching assessment data from students whose written and oral skills may be undeveloped.

Box 94: Non-written sources of assessment data

Method	Strengths	Weaknesses
Questions	Focused, formative, specific, true to everyday life in school.	Threat, needs skills to put the questions, problems if students are inarticulate, perceived invasion of privacy.
Observation	Strong on reality, takes in context, high validity, reliability.	Distracting for teachers, time-consuming.
Listening	Strong on reality and authenticity, takes in context, high validity, reliability.	Time-consuming to administer and analyse, students may be inhibited. May be an intrusion on privacy.
Interviews/conferencing	Build on known relationships, can be detailed, deep and focused, enables freedom of response, links with action planning and records of achievement.	Time-consuming to administer and analyse, students may be inhibited.
Debates	Provide opportunities for students to 'shine'.	May be unfair to inarticulate, quiet or undemonstrative students; limited scope.
Presentations	Enables students to present outcomes in their own terms, useful for poor writers, captures factors that written forms miss, can be true to everyday classroom processes, motivating.	Threat, public humiliation or 'showing-off', difficult to isolate an individual's contribution, difficult to build out the influence of others, students may be inhibited.
Video/audio recording and photographs	Live, captures complexity, records the non-written, suits poor writers.	Selective, time-consuming to set up and analyse, expensive materials.
Role play and simulation	May enable a student to show different abilities.	Students may be shy, a dominant student might bias another student's 'performance'.
Models and artefacts	May enable a student to show different abilities.	May have limited motivation or interest for some students.
Web pages	Up-to-date and engaging for students.	Not achievable for all students.

As with written forms of assessment data, the selection of which non-written form of data collection to use should be covered by the criterion of fitness for purpose. Less tightly structured, non-written methods are often truer to everyday life. Unstructured methods risk being too time-wasting. As with written sources of data, we advocate semi-structured methods of data collection as these have a set agenda but are sufficiently open-ended to permit a response that is tailored to individuals. Hence in planning how to gather assessment data the student teacher needs first to be clear on the purposes of the assessment and then this will determine the level of formality of the assessment. The purposes and degree of formality will indicate whether written or graphic types of data are appropriate, how structured and closed or semi-structured and open the data collection methods are to be, and how reliability and validity will be addressed.

PROVIDING OPPORTUNITIES FOR ASSESSMENT

In addition to the obvious point that students perform differently at different times of the day and the week, a more detailed analysis reveals that opportunities have to be provided for students to demonstrate their abilities, achievements and understandings. There are plenty of occasions in classrooms when assessment data can be collected, for example: in writing times – factual, stories, poems, handwriting, spelling times; in speaking and listening times – asking and answering questions, participating in discussions; following instructions, compiling charts and spreadsheets; when students are reading all manner of literature and documents; undertaking practical activities, using equipment, solving problems, investigating, working with computers.

Moreover, not only do occasions within the field of curriculum content provide opportunities for assessment, but there is a range of pedagogical opportunities that can be used to collect assessment data, for example: working individually, in pairs, in a small group; in the home corner, in the science laboratory, in the resources centre, in the music room, in a flexible learning suite. Clearly if this is to be developed it requires teachers, departments and faculties to be prepared to share information about students other than in their own curriculum area. For example, since the publication of the Bullock Report, mentioned earlier, the point has been made that language is a cross-curricular responsibility of every teacher, yet how many secondary teachers are there who do not teach English but who have been expected to contribute to a discussion of a student's performance in English? Probably rather fewer than the Bullock Report recommended!

In devising assessments, then, opportunities not only have to be planned but seized for assessment to occur as part of the normal everyday teaching process (referring to the notion of individual – valid – assessments to be able to provide formative feedback so that improvement can take place), rendering assessment as close as possible to a 'natural' teaching situation. Put simply, not only is it desirable in principle that assessment should be integral to learning but in practice a school day, week, term or year does not have sufficient slack time to allow assessments to be extra to teaching; they are built-in not bolt-on elements of teaching. Opportunities for assessment have to be ascertained in everyday lessons. Lambert[138] suggests that a lesson plan, for example, should include references to assessment opportunities, assessment methods and evidence of attainment (see also the lesson plans set out in Part II).

DESIGNING AN ASSESSMENT TASK

So far this part has set out a range of issues in planning assessments. We turn now to seeing how these issues can be addressed in planning specific assessments. For clarity these are set out in an annotated sequential list.[139] The planning issues addressed locate assessment not only in general contexts but with specific reference to the National Curriculum.

●   Identify the target group.

Considerations: will it be one or more groups from a whole class; a whole class; students from across more than one class; one or more age groups; one or more ability groups; how will reliability be addressed if too many students are involved?

●   Decide the number of students who can be working on the activity and who can be assessed by the activity.

Considerations: will there be some students who are working on the task but who will not be assessed; what criteria will be used to decide on the numbers of students being assessed, e.g. ability, practicability, relationships, resources; how will children with special needs be part of the activity?

●   Decide the purpose of the assessment.

Considerations: will it be to grade, to diagnose, to provide feedback to students, to decide future class placement (i.e. for selection), to measure achievement, to chart rates of progress, to compare students; whose purposes and who will be the audiences of the data collected, i.e. what are the objectives of the assessment and what learning outcomes will the assessment serve (applying the objectives model adopted throughout this book)?

●   Decide the type of assessment.

Considerations: what are the most suitable types of assessment in order to serve the purposes of the assessments, e.g. criterion referenced, norm-referenced, diagnostic, formative, summative, ipsative?

●   Decide the assessment opportunities in a 'normal' teaching and learning activity.

Considerations: how can you derive assessment data from everyday activities rather than having to set a task specifically for assessment purposes; what assessment data and criteria are possible in a given lesson and its outcomes?

●   Decide what kind of task will most fittingly serve the purposes of the assessment.

Considerations: exactly what will the assessment activity be assessing; how will validity be addressed; what will the focus of the activity be?

●   Decide whether the activity is an individual or group activity and how you will assess an individual's performance in a group activity (if applicable).

Considerations: what makes the activity specifically a group activity; is the difficulty with assessing an individual's contribution to a group activity insurmountable or worth the effort; how will group interactions feature in acting on the data? Do not attempt to work with more than four groups if the students are unfamiliar with working in groups.[140]

⚫ Decide the attainment target(s) to be assessed.

Considerations: will you focus on one attainment target or more than one; what ways are there to conduct assessments in the attainment target(s)?

⚫ Decide the range of levels in which the activity will enable you to place students as a result of the assessment.

Considerations: for standard assessment tasks (SATs) the teacher has to decide the most appropriate entry level as different SATs apply to different entry levels – will you have different activities for different entry levels or different elements of an activity for different entry levels; have you looked at the criteria for achievement at the lowest and highest levels; how will you accurately be able to distinguish levels of achievement in the activity?

⚫ Decide how to render the activity as close as possible to everyday classroom practice.

Considerations: how important is it that students know that they are being assessed;[141] how will a student's awareness that she is being assessed affect her performance; is it possible to undertake the assessments without the timetable being disrupted; which children will be anxious; what can be done to allay anxieties?[142]

⚫ Decide the timing and time scale of the activity.

Considerations: examine the normal teaching timetable and activities to identify assessment opportunities in everyday teaching. How will you judge how much time is required; why might you be putting time constraints at all on a criterion-referenced assessment; what time of the day or the week is most suitable for the students; how will you make allowances for fast and slow workers?

⚫ Decide what assessment evidence you need to collect.

Considerations: will you focus on processes or outcomes, how will you decide what valid and reliable evidence is required?

⚫ Decide the most appropriate ways of gathering the assessment evidence.

Considerations: decide which parts of the assessment data can only be gathered in situ (e.g. a PE performance or musical performance) and which data can be reviewed out of school (e.g. by looking at samples of written work or notes made during an activity); decide whether, and which, written or non-written forms of data are most appropriate to address the purposes and focuses of the assessment (or whether a combination of written and non-written forms might be more suitable).

⚫ Analyse the type of task required.

Considerations: is the task an application of material already learnt, application of new material, a practice task, the synthesis of existing knowledge, the synthesis of existing and new knowledge (or a combination of these, and, if so, which parts of the task address different types of task and why are you making differential task demands); how do you know what demands the task will place on students; how precisely[143] do you know what the demands on students will be?

● Analyse the task requirements.

Considerations: look at the task requirements to see if all elements of the task are equally difficult. Why are you including elements of the task that are easier or more difficult than others; what is it that makes some elements of the task more difficult than others; are the tasks sufficiently concrete and within the experience of the students; does the number of elements in the task prevent students from demonstrating that, in fact, they might understand each element but be overwhelmed when they are put together?

● Decide options in the task.

Considerations: will some students select an easier option than others (e.g. a way of working) and what will happen if students select an easy way of working when they are capable of much more; how will the task selection process affect an individual student's recorded attainment; will the students appreciate the relevance of the task to their own lives?

● Clarify the criteria for marking (where applicable).

Considerations: how many relevant tasks does the student have to complete successfully before being credited with having reached a particular level of achievement? Consider marking conventions, criteria and weightings.

● Decide how the activity will be introduced (the presentation mode); what the students will actually be doing in the activity (the operation mode); what form the outcome will take (the response mode).

Considerations: how well matched are these modes to the students; how will you know whether, for example, a language difficulty is preventing a student from demonstrating her scientific or mathematical abilities; how will you support students whose first language is not English? Decide the method of delivery in: (a) the presentation mode (e.g. oral, written, pictorial, video, IT, practical); (b) the operation mode (e.g. mental, written, practical, oral); (c) the response mode (e.g. a multiple choice test, essay, short piece of writing, picture, oral, practical, display, presentation, role play, computer data).

● Decide how to reduce threats to reliability and validity.

Considerations: how will extraneous influences on performance be reduced; when will you address reliability issues, e.g. in devising the task (quality assurance) or in marking the outcome (quality control); attempt an assessment that is 'good enough' rather than striving for perfection – be realistic? When will you halt the activity if students are struggling; how will you take account of teacher intervention or interventions by other students; how will the situation be made less threatening; how positive are the relationships between the assessor and the assessee; how have you addressed readability; how consistent is the proposed assessment task with the usual ways of working in the class; what other contextual variables do you need to consider that might influence the reliability of the assessment and the data that it yields?

- Decide exactly which National Curriculum criteria you will be using in judging the assessment evidence.

Considerations: some level descriptions may be imprecise, in which case the attainment targets and programmes of study might be more helpful; reference to the school portfolio of agreed standards might be helpful here.

- Decide the information/records/evidence/data that will be brought to a moderation meeting.

Considerations: how will the issue of sampling be addressed, i.e. how will you decide what is a representative sample of each student's work and several students' work?

- Decide how the results will be used as part of an ongoing recording system.

Considerations: ensure that your decisions fall in line with the school policy; decide on whether and how to aggregate marks (if applicable); how often will you update your formal records?

- Decide how to report the results and to whom.

Considerations: what will be reported to students, parents, other teachers, and other interested parties; what will go into each student's portfolio?

This long list of points and considerations is perhaps daunting, yet, for the sake of reliability and validity, these are important issues that cannot be overlooked. This was a feature of the opening comments on this part that suggested that all too easily reliability and validity become the casualties of ill-prepared, over-politicised or 'high-stakes' assessments. There is no doubt that assessment in the United Kingdom is a 'high-stakes' activity, both politically and educationally, particularly since teacher assessment in the National Curriculum has assumed an almost equal footing at Key Stages 1, 2 and 3 with externally set and externally marked SATs.

That said, a much shorter list of considerations for teacher assessment was provided by the former School Examination and Assessment Council (SEAC), which built on the acronym of INFORM.[144] An updated version of the SEAC acronym can be seen below:

1 Identify the elements of the National Curriculum (attainment targets, level descriptions, programmes of study) that the lesson will address.
2 Note opportunities for the student to demonstrate attainment.
3 Focus on the performance, looking for evidence of achievement.
4 Offer the student the opportunity to discuss what was achieved.
5 Record what was identified as important and noteworthy.
6 Modify the lesson plans for the student if necessary.

What is very clear in this six-stage process is that the teacher assessment envisaged here is formative, criterion-referenced, related to progression, evidential, perhaps even related to action planning at stage 6, and, because the teacher has to relate her standard of marking to agreed criteria and standards, moderated. Hence, though formal teacher assessment and SATs might take us into simplistic summative assessments with limited formative potential, nevertheless in the day-today assessments of students a more educationally beneficial set of practices might still operate.

Drawing together the several strands of the arguments and issues raised in this part we suggest several principles that should guide the student teacher who is preparing to assess students during teaching practice:

- The purposes are to be diagnostic and formative, providing feedback and being educative.
- Teaching should be adjusted in light of assessment evidence.
- Assessment should promote, not damage, student motivation and self-esteem.
- Assessment should be constructively critical and provide rich, positive feedback and feed-forward.
- The assessments should be criterion-referenced and the criteria should be public.
- The assessments should lead to diagnostic teaching.
- Assessment should promote student self-evaluation.
- The assessments should be built on evidence rather than on intuition.
- Assessment data should be derived from everyday classroom activities.
- Assessment opportunities should be sought in everyday classroom activities.
- Semi-structured approaches to gathering data are recommended, generating words rather than numbers (measures).
- Assessments should be linked to the student teacher's and the student's action planning and target setting.
- Involve the students in the assessment process.
- Communicate the assessment criteria to students.
- Demonstrate validity and reliability in the assessments, addressing particularly 'consequential validity'.
- Demonstrate fitness for purpose in deciding the method(s) of gathering assessment data and setting assessment tasks.
- Select assessment methods that accord strongly with everyday teaching and learning processes.

MARKING WORK

Clearly it is invidious to provide detailed guidance on marking, as the notion of 'fitness for purpose' must apply. Nevertheless, we suggest some key principles of marking policies and practices here, arguing that marking should:[145]

- make clear to students its purposes and criteria, linked to the purposes of the task to be marked
- make clear the success criteria for the work (e.g. knowledge, understanding, application, presentation, effort and so on)
- provide rich, constructive, positive, criterion-referenced and high-quality feedback and 'feedforward' to students, so that they have a clear indication of what the criteria are and how to improve.

(See www.routledge.com/textbooks/9780415485586, Chapter 16 Assessment, Key principles of marking practice.)

A major study of feedback at the University of Bristol[146] – the LEARN project – provided some important insights into marking work and giving feedback. The project involved interviews with over 200 students of different ages (7–18 years) in a range of schools, and was undertaken to gather their perceptions of assessment and how assessment was being used to help them improve their learning.

The researchers found that 'students were often confused by the use of grades and found it difficult to recognise the difference between effort and attainment grades. They also found that simple praise (ticks, good or excellent) was unhelpful.' Rather, the researchers suggest, teachers should

> give narrative comments not grades or marks because narrative feedback encourages students to engage with the quality of the work while grades or marks encourage pupils to look for ways to get the best marks rather than what they need to do to improve their learning. This may result in avoidance of difficult tasks, a loss of self-esteem and increased occurrence of underachievement.

The researchers suggest that it is important to note that comments which only gave praise or criticism to students did not help them to improve; indeed it was reported that the students preferred to be given oral rather than written feedback, as this enabled them to enter into a dialogue with their teachers. Giving rich, formative feedback when marking work acts as a scaffolding for learning, not necessarily giving them the correct answers but enabling students to think for themselves.

This set of principles moves away from the simplistic awarding of a mark or grade, and towards an ongoing dialogue between teachers and learners about their learning and how to improve it. Marking work is concerned largely with improving performance. Can a mark alone indicate how to improve performance? Clearly not. Are marks and grades specific enough to improve learning? Clearly not.

If grades and marks are to be used, then their role and purpose needs to be defensible. For recording and reporting, it is important not only to have recorded the grades and marks, but also the criteria and tasks/activities, the rich feedback and the information collected and given. Without such information, the recording of a grade is entirely meaningless. It is important, then, to include comments on students' achievement of subject matter as well as to assign a grade, and it is important for the grade criteria to be transparent and communicated to the students. Clearly the awarding of a grade may cast a teacher in a dual role: as supporter as well as judge,[147] but the management of this dual role is part of a teacher's professional behaviour.

Many schools will have marking conventions (e.g. for presentational and secretarial matters) and student teachers will need to enquire about these. Further, it is important to find out: whether the school requires a mark for effort as well as for achievement; what the procedures are for learners to do 'corrections' or follow-up to the marking; the focus of the marking; the weighting to be given to different elements of marking; what the procedures are for recording and reporting marks and comments (and to whom); what kind of comments are required to be given to students.

In providing feedback to students, it is possible for 'markers' to make suggestions on what needs to be done to improve the work; to relate the achievement to the learning intentions; to provide examples of how to improve; to prompt further thinking and action; to attend to 'secretarial' matters (grammar, punctuation, spelling, presentation, handwriting); and to attend to the quality of the work and the ideas, not only its quantity of secretarial matters. Giving learners time to digest the feedback and reflect on it is important, both with marked class work and homework; if this means reducing the amount of teaching time to allow time for reading feedback and reflecting on it then so be it – it is learning time.

Some teachers have students mark their own work or mark each other's work. This may be economical in terms of teachers' time. On the other hand this can induce cheating, and, indeed, shared or paired marking has been argued to be a violation of human rights to privacy and confidentiality. If the student teacher wishes to develop paired or shared marking or shared feedback, then he/she would be well advised to find out about the existing marking and feedback practices in the school/class. If there is to be paired marking then markers – children – need to be prepared for this, to do it in a non-competitive and supportive atmosphere, with due respect to privacy, what is to be marked, and how it is to be marked. Peer assessment, properly handled, can promote self-evaluation, self-assessment and reflection in learners;[148] the criteria for such assessments must be agreed, equitable, transparent and public.

Wedeen *et al.*[149] provide some useful guidelines on giving feedback to students:

- Be realistic.
- Be specific.
- Be sensitive to the goals of the person.

Assessment moves away from simply conducting a test, to being a rich learning experience for teachers and learners alike, with formal and informal means for gathering data being utilised: observation, questioning, discussion, marking and dialogue. Informal assessment is a major contributor to formative assessment and day-to-day planning, whilst formal assessment is useful for summative and maybe diagnostic assessment, depending on how it is conducted. Informal assessment can be immediate, ongoing, direct and of great learning benefit; formal assessment takes longer, is usually delayed in providing feedback, and may have little impact on learning or improvement. Informal assessment is naturalistic, often subjective, close to reality, even covert, whilst formal assessment is predetermined, objective, often in a contrived situation and overt.[150]

So far here we have been assuming that work is produced by an individual student. What if the students have been working collaboratively? If this is the case then the teacher must specify in advance the marking criteria, for example:

- if the work is going to be a corporate effort, with each member of the group receiving the same mark, regardless of the differential effort or input into the collaborative group
- whether it is required to be able to identify each individual's exact contribution to the group product
- whether the group processes and interactions will be included in the marking
- the quality of the overall group's work (as opposed to that of individuals in the group).

A WORKED EXAMPLE OF AN ASSESSMENT ACTIVITY

Target child: The target child is a Year 2 (7-year-old) girl whom we shall call Saira. Activity/ assessment opportunity: We decide to assess her in a group situation with two other children; they will be playing a group game called 'The Snake Game'. In this game different coloured snakes have different numbers on them, some with numbers less than 10, others with numbers of 10 or greater. The number is the same for a snake of the same colour – 2 for a green snake, 3 for a yellow snake, 5 for a red snake, 10 for a brown snake, 12 for an orange snake, 15 for a white snake. The children can choose any snake if they answer a question correctly that is printed on each card of a set of cards. The cards can ask them: (a) to add single digits; (b) to add numbers greater than 10; (c) to subtract single digits from numbers between 10 and 100; (d) to subtract numbers over 10 from numbers between 11 and 100; (e) to count up the next 3 of a sequence, e.g. 2–4–6–8–10; 3–6–9–12–15; 5–10–15–20–25; (f) to count down the next 3 of a sequence, e.g. 30–25–20–15–10; 24–20–16–12–8; 30–27–24– 21–18. Each child must write down the answer to each question, though they don't need to 'show the working' if they wish. The winner is the child who is the first to reach 100.

The purpose of the assessment: the assessment is diagnostic and formative and has several purposes:

- to see how well the child can read, write and order whole numbers up to 100 and to identify areas of strength and weakness in this
- to see how secure the child's understanding is of place value up to 100, and to identify areas of strength and weakness in this
- to see how well the child can add numbers below 10, greater than 10 (whose totals do not exceed 100), both mentally and on paper, and to identify areas of strength and weakness in this
- to see how well the child can subtract numbers below 10 from totals of 100 or less, both mentally and on paper, and to identify areas of strength and weakness in this
- to see how well the child can use repeated addition and subtraction in a number pattern.

The attainment target(s) and level of the National Curriculum to be covered: mathematics, Attainment Target 2, Level 2 (though the level might turn out to be Level 1).

The timing and time scale of the activity: a 15-minute activity in the mid-morning of a Wednesday.

Presentation mode, operation mode, response mode: the teacher will show the children what to do and give them practice in the mechanics of the game; the children will play the game, writing down algorithms and 'sums' where necessary; the response will be written.

The assessment evidence to be collected: listening to the child's conversation and confidence in the activity (observation); her ability to work out 'sums' mentally (questioning); the contents of her written work (written); responses to the teacher's questions (questioning).

The (a) easy, (b) moderately difficult and (c) difficult aspects of the activity: (a) the addition (single figures) and subtraction (single figures – no decomposition); (b) addition and subtraction (double figures – no decomposition); (c) handling large numbers and subtraction with decomposition respectively.

The type of task: the application of already-learnt material.

Threats to reliability and validity: the desire to win, the effect of losing or being incorrect or having difficulty, the effects of the other two children in the group, struggling to understand the rules of the game.

Addressing threats to reliability and validity: by discussion with the child; by ensuring that the child knows exactly what to do (with a demonstration by the child and the teacher before the assessment begins); by giving the child the opportunity to practise the 'mechanics' of how to play the game (i.e. so that the rules of the game do not obstruct the processes of using algorithms).

What to do if children have difficulties: the teacher will prompt the child and indicate this in the assessment, suggesting that further work/practice is required.

The exact criteria to be used to judge the child's performance: see above – the purpose of the assessment.

The data/records to be brought to a moderation meeting: the teacher's written comments, a photocopy of the child's written work.

The record of the results: the work and the results will be held in the child's own portfolio and the teacher's record book.

Reporting the results: a summary report together with the teacher's own record for discussion with the parents.

The report of the results: Saira was eager to play the game and was able to keep the other players enthusiastic, even though they were not winning very much. Saira usually chose 'high-value' snakes (bearing numbers greater than 10). She was able to count up and down in 2s, 3s and 5s mentally but needed to write down the additions of numbers over 10 when her running total exceeded 30. Her written calculations were always correct in addition, and in subtraction where single digits were being subtracted. She sometimes used counters for this latter activity. Her subtraction of numbers over 10 from larger numbers (over 20) was correct if there was no decomposition but incorrect if decomposition was involved, e.g. $60 - 12 =$ and $53 - 15 =$. When I asked her how she 'worked out' the 'sums' in her head she was clear on place value; when I asked her 'extension' questions about adding on in patterns of 2, 3 and 5 she was clear and correct, although when she was subtracting these mentally she was clear on what to do but sometimes incorrect in actually manipulating the numbers.

Assessment analysis: Saira has a good grasp of place value to 100, mental addition to 30 and simple subtraction without decomposition. She shows understanding of, and confidence in, using the correct algorithms for these processes. She can recognise and use number patterns of 2, 3 and 5. In National Curriculum terms she is operating at Level 2 of the Mathematics Attainment Target 2.

Recommendations: Saira is ready to apply the algorithms to larger numbers in addition (up to 100) in written and mental work, and to be introduced to decomposition in subtraction – using single figures only at this stage with much practical concept reinforcement before too much written (procedural) work.

It can be seen from this fairly lengthy example that the activity bears a strong similarity to the everyday activity of a 7-year-old in school and that the assessment has been planned with reference to, or derived from, the level descriptions and programmes of study of the National Curriculum. Clearly in the day-to-day work of the teacher the level of background detail reported here would not need to be formally recorded (e.g. the details of the game, perhaps the purpose of the assessment) – the details are written here for the purpose of explication and example. They indicate, in fact, that the teacher has taken account of the several factors involved in planning the assessment; the difference between this and the normal activity of the teacher is the degree of formality involved – the teacher might be advised to go through the series of planning considerations in her mind rather than on paper.

Assessment is constantly developing. Recently the move towards 'testing when ready' rather than testing at particular ages and stages has been put onto the political agenda.[151] Computer-aided assessment is coming to the fore, not least for its ability to save teachers' time (e.g. to have electronic marking and recording),[152] to be available on demand to learners, and to test a wide range of subjects (including minority subjects) and knowledge.[153] The scene shifts constantly.

16 Record Keeping and Report Writing

INTRODUCTION

During teaching practice there is a clear obligation on the part of the student teacher to continue the day-to-day running of the classes in line with the organisation and methods employed by the regular class teachers. In certain forms of classroom and school organisation, for example where continuous assessment is practised, or where vertical grouping and related schemes operate, adequate record keeping is essential to the success of the educational programmes. Similarly, in systems practising 'individualised learning' the need for individual records is crucial. Further, with the rise of assessment and the increased attention given to the reporting of achievement there is a marked increase in the amount of record keeping that is taking place in the school.

Effective record keeping enables the student teacher to:[1]

- track the progress of individual pupils or groups of pupils
- identify patterns over time where there are many small steps in developing pupils' knowledge and skills
- confirm end-of-year and statutory end-of-key stage teacher assessment
- set individual and group targets for improvement
- discuss pupils' progress with their parents (or others with parental responsibility) and other teachers.

It is the student teacher's responsibility to participate fully in the record keeping system that is used in the school to which she/he is attached. What follows is an outline of the use of records and some suggestions for students who find themselves faced with the task of designing record systems for their own use.

Record keeping is often considered an irksome chore by many teachers. In recent years the amount of record keeping that teachers have to do has increased tremendously. In many cases the official records that schools used to keep on names, address, date of birth, previous schooling, contact telephone numbers etc. are stored on computers; these are not the present subject of discussion. Rather, our concern is with the records that the teacher keeps in connection with the ongoing work in class and the progress of students at school. In many cases there is a 'house style' of record keeping in schools, though this is usually for the more formal reporting to parents, the next school, the next teacher, the curriculum co-ordinator and the head teacher. On the other hand many teachers keep personal records on their students, often for their own personal use rather than to be shown to others. There are many considerations in record keeping that determine the records that are kept by teachers, for example:

- the purposes and uses of the record
- the use of records for reporting
- the formality of the record
- the contents and level of detail of the record
- the audience(s) of the record
- the style (format) of the record
- the timing of the record entry.

Different parties will be interested in different matters, for example a class teacher may wish to have a more detailed day-to-day record than, say, parents. A new school may seek a combination of a general record on a student's overall achievements and specific details of particular strengths and weaknesses. A head of year or age phase or a teacher concerned with the pastoral aspects of schooling may wish to have information about students who are experiencing or have experienced personal, emotional, social or behavioural difficulties and how these have been met successfully by previous teachers. The different purposes that records serve require different contents and formats. For example, it may be that parents wish to have a jargon-free and easy-to-read summary of their child's progress whereas a receiving teacher may wish to have a more detailed and diagnostic record within each National Curriculum subject. Records for a student teacher's personal use might contain notes and symbols that are unintelligible to others.

Some records might document curriculum content covered (e.g. by lists, schemes of work, web diagrams, flow charts, half-termly, weekly or daily plans that can also double up as records); others might be records of marks gained on students' written work. There might be individual students' records, group records, a whole-class record. Some records might be numerical (e.g. marks scored); others might be verbal (a teacher's comments on progress etc.); others might be samples of a student's own work; others might be photographic. Some records might be open-ended; others might be closed 'tick boxes'. As with assessment, the guiding principle for record keeping must be 'fitness for purpose'. The implication of this is that student teachers initially must be clear about the purposes of their records, so that the contents, format and detail serve the purposes clearly. Given the room for difference in record keeping there is a need for student teachers to consider purposes, contents, style and format, level of detail, uses of the information, methods of gathering and recording the information.

THE PURPOSES OF RECORD KEEPING

Throughout this book we have advocated the objectives model as one useful strategy for planning. The same holds true here; it is useful for the student teacher to be very clear on the purposes – the objectives – of the record keeping. In one study,[2] typical reasons given by teachers for keeping records were:

- to chart pupil progress and achievement
- to communicate information to other teachers
- to ensure continuity of education through the school
- to ensure continuity of education on transfer to other schools
- to guide a replacement or a supply teacher
- for diagnostic purposes – to spot problems, identify underachievement and pupils needing extra help
- to provide teachers with information on the success (or failure) of teaching methods and materials

- as a statement of 'what has happened' – to inform interested parties (parents, educational psychologists, head teacher)
- to give head teachers a general picture of achievement within the school.

A teacher may wish to augment these points by using records:

- to document effort
- to record experiences to which the students have been exposed
- to record a student's physical, emotional, social, intellectual development
- to compare students
- to chart rates of progress
- to inform subsequent curriculum planning.

Different types and contents of records are suitable for different purposes. The student teacher will need to clarify the purposes of the record before setting up a record keeping system; it is futile and time-wasting to imagine that a single record will be suitable for all purposes. This book has argued very strongly for the utility of an objectives-based approach to planning, evaluating and assessing. This has to extend to record keeping; it is only when the purposes of a record have been clarified that the student teacher can move to deciding the most appropriate contents, timing, format and nature of the entries that will be most suitable to those purposes.

THE USE OF THE RECORD FOR REPORTING PURPOSES

A distinction has to be drawn between a record and a report. Typically a report is a selection from or a summary of details contained in teachers' records. The formal requirements of reporting to parents, for instance, is that parents should receive a report at least once per year (see http://www.naa.org.uk/naa_20249.aspx). This should cover pupils' attendance, achievement and performance in each subject of the National Curriculum, including the results of statutory assessments, where relevant, and some comments on non-National Curriculum subjects, together with reports of the student's level of attainment on the ten-level scale of each National Curriculum subject at the end of each Key Stage. The report should include a commentary and explanation by the teacher of what the achievements and attainments mean.

Though such reporting can draw on teachers' detailed notes and records one can argue that this level of reporting is not specific enough for a teacher's detailed diagnostic records. Indeed reporting to parents is often of a summative nature whereas the records that teachers keep are both summative and formative.

THE FORMALITY OF THE RECORD

A record for a teacher's 'private consumption' might take the form of short notes on a particular student's progress in various areas of the National Curriculum, complemented by scores on tests and details of a student's achievement in the formal assessments of the National Curriculum (e.g. in relation to a student's level of achievement of the several attainment targets in the National Curriculum). The teacher may review and select from her private records data that are to become part of a more formal record that is for 'public consumption', e.g. for the next teacher, for a student's parents or guardians. A teacher may wish to record some particular personal details, e.g. about a student's behaviour during breaks or lunch times, that she may not wish to make public unless matters reach a critical point, though the Data Protection Act[3] makes it a requirement that students should be able to see all records that are held on them. From 2000 changes to the regulations for schools[4] made it a requirement that copies of pupil reports should form part of the pupil's educational record; that all students, regardless of their age, are entitled to have their records disclosed to them on written request unless special circumstances apply (e.g. unless they obviously do not understand what they are asking for); and that parents have a right to see their children's records. The Data Protection Act 1998 and the 2000 Regulations made it a requirement that schools should not disclose anything on a student's records which would be likely to cause serious harm to the student's physical or mental health or that of anyone else, including anything which suggests that they are, or have been either the subject of or at risk of child abuse. Guidance on the Data Protection Act is available on www.dataprotection.gov.uk.

A formal record may be more generalised than an informal record, the former being largely summative and the latter being largely formative. A formal report might include statements from the National Curriculum attainment targets or level descriptions that teachers complete with a mark against each statement. A statement of special educational needs is a legal document that specifies action to be taken to meet the special needs of a student; that requires careful consideration of the framing, terminology and detail of the record. Some formal records are anodyne or only contain positive achievements; others are very much more detailed and diagnostic.

Many trainees are encouraged to experience a parents' evening and may be involved in report writing. Many trainees will be teaching one class or more for a substantial period of time, typically up to a term for a final teaching practice. That means that they will probably have to provide teachers with specific data that they can use when completing the formal record. Further, given that student teachers eventually will become qualified themselves, it is important that they have the opportunity to look at, discuss, and provide data for the formal records that schools keep.

There is a common transfer file (CTF) that all head teachers are required to complete for students transferring to another school.[5] The common transfer file is a spreadsheet that contains a large amount of data about the pupil. The specification can be found at http://www.teachernet.gov.uk/docbank/index.cfm?id=12590

THE CONTENTS OF THE RECORD

Legalistically the contents of some records are prescribed, covering a student's coverage of and achievements in the National Curriculum. However, the National Curriculum is only one element of a student's experiences at school. There are other equally important matters that may feature in a record, for example social, emotional and moral development; a student's overall standard of behaviour; confidence; effort; motivation; interests and enthusiasms; behaviour; attendance; friends and friendship patterns. A diagnostic record will necessarily be more detailed than a summative record of achievements and progress because it is usually criterion-referenced in order that action may be taken on specific matters. The contents of a record will reflect the focus of interest, the level of detail required, the level of formality and sense of audience, and the framing of the record, for example whether it will be strictly in the terminology of the National Curriculum, whether it will comment on knowledge, concepts, skills and attitudes, subject-specific and cross-curricular matters, personal and social development, medical factors (e.g. speech, co-ordination, overall health).

Clearly not everything needs to be recorded, indeed selectivity is an important feature. Student teachers will find it useful to examine records as a way of finding out rapidly about curricula for, and assessments of students in the classes that they will be going to teach. These records might be in the form of an individual student's record (in which case permission has to be obtained to look at the record), or a record of work undertaken and curricula experienced by a whole class or particular groups.

The student teacher's own daily and weekly records concern the extent to which the students are achieving the objectives of the lessons, and what modifications need to be/have been made to the lessons in light of what has actually taken place. Hence a record may be an annotated lesson plan or notes made after the lesson, the level of detail of which is guided by the needs of the teacher for detail on individuals and groups.

The student teacher's ongoing, perhaps termly, records may comprise the schemes of work and activities which will provide assessment opportunities. The planned scheme of work is a record. Termly notes may comprise a selective note of the marking and comments written on particular pieces of work, together with a note of the extent to which the learning objectives for the term have been achieved and the kind of feedback and feed forward given to students. That said, termly records are not detailed; the close level of detail is reserved for daily and ongoing records. Teachers are able to review rates of student progress by referring to the work that students have done, the marks they obtained, the samples of work submitted, and their own ongoing notes from observations. Guidance from the National Strategies in relation to Assessing Pupils' Progress suggests:

- APP is used to periodically review your pupils' work so you will wish to gather evidence on a termly basis, or whatever fits in with your current school assessment arrangements.
- Use the work that's already in pupils' exercise books or portfolios and make use of any 'sticky notes' on which you've captured some of their spoken contributions in class. You can also take account of what you or others have seen pupils do in the course of their work. You don't need to gather weighty collections or portfolios of pupils' work.
- You won't need to look back at all of the work a pupil has done since their last APP assessment – just the pieces that you know will provide significant evidence.
- A manageable range of evidence will facilitate the process of 'scaling up' to involve all pupils in the APP approach.[6]

The student teacher may not be in the school long enough to complete an annual record, but she/he may be required to provide some information that goes towards the compilation of the annual record or towards termly reporting. The annual record is of the key aspects of the student's progress, in terms of the National Curriculum and more broadly, and in line with statutory requirements. At the end of the Key Stage this will also include the results of statutory tests and tasks, together with statutory teacher assessment.

THE AUDIENCES OF THE RECORD

Different audiences find different types of information useful. Barrs and Johnson[7] identify eight different audiences of records and indicate how the functions of records differ according to their audience(s), for example:

1 the teacher herself
2 other teachers who have contact with the student
3 receiving teachers
4 other teachers in the school
5 the head teacher
6 parents
7 local authority assessment moderators
8 wider audiences.

This is not to deny interested parties access to different information; rather it reflects different interests at work. There are many different 'stakeholders' in education who may require different types of information and who may use data for different purposes. In some respects this is akin to assessment where, at the beginning of this part, assessment was seen to serve political agendas of control and managerialist (and political) agendas of accountability of schools to their consumers. Records can be used for accountability (e.g. in the documenting and reporting of students' achievements in external tests) and for more educational purposes (e.g. planning and implementing a well-matched curriculum for students).

It is significant that Barrs and Johnson include only adults in the audiences of records, neglecting the students themselves. That reflects the bureaucratic and managerialist tenor of much record keeping. However, we commented earlier that one important purpose of assessment was to be able to give feedback to students so that they would become involved in their own learning. So it is with records; they provide information that can form the basis of, or contribute to, discussions between students and student teachers as one stage in the action planning cycle that has featured throughout this book.

The QCA identifies three main groups of people who need records of curriculum plans and about student progress, achievement and attainment:[8]

Teachers want to know:

● whether each pupil has learnt what has been taught
● who needs more help or is ready for extension work
● who is making better or worse than expected progress
● whether all pupils, including those with individual education plans (IEPs), are meeting their learning targets
● whether they need to refine any aspects of their teaching.

Head teachers, curriculum co-ordinators/heads of department and governors want to know:

● whether different groups of pupils in the school are making sufficient progress
● whether there are any major shortcomings or successes
● whether the school is on track to reach its pupil attainment targets
● how pupil attainment in the school compares with other similar schools
● which aspects of the curriculum and teaching need to be strengthened.

Parents want to know:

● whether their child is making appropriate progress
● whether their child is showing any major strengths or weaknesses
● how their child is doing in relation to the class, and to other children of the same age
● what they can do to help.

This means that different groups will need different kinds of information. Student teachers on teaching practice will need to conform to the school's practices in these respects, providing information as required.

THE STYLE AND FORMAT OF THE RECORD

There are several ways of entering data on a record that resonate with the ways of entering assessment results, for example by using numbers, words, samples of work, photographic evidence. As with the recording of assessments these ways can vary from the closed 'tick box' approach to the open-ended record that enables the student teacher to write comments about a given matter (e.g. speaking and listening skills) that are tailored to a specific student. Recording might take the form of:

1   Marks or grades recorded on coursework or non-standardised tests, ensuring that the criteria for mark ranges or grades are discrete, clear, hierarchical (i.e. progressively difficult) and defined in concrete terms, and recognising that the extremes of the lowest and highest levels might only apply to a small number of students.

2   Personal observations (from structured or semi-structured observation), for example:

> *Joanne*
>
> Mathematics: A fast worker who prefers to work alone. She can represent and access complex data on a histogram, bar chart and line graph, using appropriate scales. She is able to access data on a pie chart and can use the computer to enter data for a pie chart; she understands the notion of proportions in a pie chart and is beginning to be able to construct simple pie charts that show this understanding.

> *Shaun*
>
> English (writing): Is able to express himself well on a wide variety of matters using appropriate vocabulary and registers. He enjoys writing non-fiction accounts, where his grasp of grammatical structure and clarity of style indicate his ability to explain complex phenomena straightforwardly. Shaun is able to write imaginatively and creatively on a range of non-fiction areas though he particularly enjoys science fiction.

3   Self-recording charts that students complete as they progress through a scheme of work, for example the self-recording charts that accompany many commercially produced mathematics and language schemes of work. This form of self-recording is usually very straightforward, comprising details of the pages that have been read in a reading book, the mathematics exercises that have been completed, with maybe some very simple extensions, e.g. what was found easy/difficult/interesting, rather than a fuller type of self-assessment.

4   Results of standardised tests and assessments (e.g. of achievements of the National Curriculum) for each student, for example Box 95.

5   Ticks against statements with room for a student teacher's own comments (perhaps using the terms of the National Curriculum statements of attainment and/or level descriptions, though these may be too generalised for student teachers who are only in the school for a limited period of time, in which case they may have to use more specific terminology than used in the National Curriculum), for example Box 96 (for each child). The four statements in the box are taken from the National Curriculum for mathematics at Key Stage 4. It can be seen immediately that space (and time) can be saved if statements are not written verbatim from the National Curriculum documents but a shorthand version is used.

6   Coded entries and comments against particular statements, for example:

> *Measuring temperature using a thermometer*
>
> A tick – introduced, continue to reinforce
> A tick crossed through with another line – needs further help
> Either of the above together with a circle
> around the tick – ready to advance.

Box 95: Recording results of formal assessments

English	Level 1	Level 2	Level 3	Level 4	Level 5
	TA SAT	TA SAT	TA SAT	TA SAT	TA SAT
AT1 Speaking and listening					
AT2 Reading					
AT3 Writing					

This example identifies the starting point at which a student has been introduced to a curriculum feature. It is cumulative in practice in that each stage of recording improvement adds on to a given symbol (e.g. a tick, a line through) rather than requiring the student teacher to erase the first or second symbol in order to replace it with another. Whilst these examples show how a closed record keeping system can be used, in practice the difficulty in this type of recording is that it runs away with itself; the student teacher ends up spending as much time on the recording as the planning. Whilst this approach may be useful in providing an in-depth approach to record keeping, in practice it often becomes unworkably detailed (e.g. in a primary school it could generate 30 students $\times$ 10 subjects $\times$ 30 statements = 9,000 statements to be reviewed). The secret here is to operationalise the statements without generating a level of detail that is overwhelming; this is exactly the same problem as that mentioned earlier in connection with criterion-referenced assessment.

Box 96: Recording specific details of students' progress

Can vary the flow of electricity in a simple circuit and observe the effects	Comments
(a) Can use sampling methods, considering their reliability.	
(b) Has extended skills in handling data into constructing and interpreting histograms.	
(c) Can describe the dispersion of a set of data; can find and interpret the standard deviation of a set of data.	
(d) Understands when and how to estimate conditional probabilities.	

Box 97: A whole-class or group record

Student's name	Activity 1	Activity 2	Activity 3	Activity 4
Martin Armstrong				
Janice Asher				
Ahmet Al-Sabah				
Ruth Brown				
Soo-Lee Chang				
Joanna Davison				

This type of 'coded' response is particularly useful where the student teacher wishes to have a whole-class or group record rather than an individual student's record (see Box 97).

On this class record the student teacher can specify exactly what items 1, 2, 3 and 4 are. In each cell the student teacher can enter comments and/or a code:

| = Has had experience of
+ = Needs further reinforcement
* = Ready to move on

A second example of this approach will list the names of the students targeted and then indicate the activity that is the focus of the record, for example Box 98.

There is also a space for individual comments to be written if required.

A third example might break down an activity into significant elements, with space provided for a student teacher's comments, for example Box 99.

A fourth example of codes and comments is of a record of activities undertaken over a period of time, maybe each week, for example Box 100.

Here space is required for the student teacher to specify in more detail in the appropriate cells exactly what each student has done (unless it is possible to have included this in the column descriptor) together with relevant comments and codes to reflect effort, achievement and a diagnosis of the success of the outcome.

What we have, then, is a combination of a closed record keeping system and an open-ended system, with numbers/codes and words respectively, i.e. a double entry. Having a system that enables data about many students to be entered on a single record facilitates comparisons

Box 98: A class or group record of an activity

Student's name	Cutting sticky squares into halves and quarters	Naming the fractions formed – quarter, half, three-quarters	Finding equivalencies – quarter, half, three-quarters
Michaela Bayes			
Angela Downs			
Peter Forrest			
James Kelly			

between students to become clear. Some record keeping systems might be structured to provide room for a double entry wherein a code is used to indicate achievement and another code for effort, for example:

A = All points clearly understood
B = Reinforce a little
C = Reinforce a great deal

1 = Has made a very good effort
2 = Has made an acceptable effort
3 = Has made little or no effort

7   Multiple choice statements (where each statement must be discrete and it must be made clear whether more than one statement in a group of statements can be selected).

8   Open-ended areas for comment (where an element of, say, English is indicated, e.g. a student's response to a piece of literature) and space provided for comments to be written, or where National Curriculum statements are given, for example in mathematics:

Mathematics (understanding and using measures): Develop an understanding of the difference between discrete and continuous measures; read and interpret scales, including decimal scales, and understand the degree of accuracy that is possible, or appropriate, for a given purpose.

Alan has a sound grasp of the difference between discrete and continuous measures and has acquired this understanding through representing and interpreting different types of data using a variety of scales, including decimal scales. He is able to choose appropriate scales for different types of data and different purposes.

Box 99: Recording several aspects of an activity

Student's name	Designing a crane	Making the crane	Testing the crane	Evaluating the results	Improving the design
Sahira Anwaz					
Zoe Bond					
James Clinton					
Sean Davison					
Jane Flynn					

Another example of an open-ended record keeping system is presented in Box 101.

This type of record is useful provided that it is focused and selective (i.e. identifying priorities) and that it recognises that a particular activity may serve more than one curriculum area, for example a single activity might address language, mathematics, ICT and history. That would need to feature in the record and again, perhaps, in some subject-specific records.

A compromise between too closed and too open a record can be seen where an agenda and major foci are established but the student teacher is able to tailor comments to individuals, for example:

Speaking and listening (identifying major strengths and needs in relation to personal accounts, providing information and explanation, participation in class discussions, collaboration within a small group, awareness of register and vocabulary).

Reading (identifying major strengths and needs in relation to the range of the reading diet, fluency and reading strategies used, understanding and recall, responding to literature, study skills, enjoyment).

Writing (identifying major strengths and needs in relation to awareness of audience, conveying meaning clearly and appropriately, use of vocabulary and syntax, drafting, using different forms of writing, spelling, use of word-processing facilities).

In this example the rubric provides suggestions of areas of focus for student teachers but there is no necessity for slavish adherence to these if they are inappropriate.

Box 100: Recording activities over a period of time

Student's name	Language task	Science investigation	Art activity	History project
Yasmin Bakhtar				
Paula Bates				
John Clements				
Alan Dodds				
Susan Evans				

There is a well-documented problem in open-ended statements and comments that teachers write, viz. that the statement reflects more the biases, preferences and subjectivity of the record writer (the teacher) than the student. Law[9] draws attention to six problematical types of statement in connection with this:

Box 101: An open-ended record keeping system

Student's name	Activity/task	Knowledge, concepts, skills, attitudes	Comment on effort and achievement (what was learnt)	Action needed
Deborah Roe				
Alex Sanders				
Mary Slater				
Paula Squires				

- *Undefined statements* – that use jargon that is inappropriate for the target audience or that conceals the writer's true intentions, for example: 'has difficulty interpreting interpersonal behaviour and modifying own response when necessary' (i.e. is a major disruptive influence in the class or I don't like this student); 'can use phonic skills, particularly digraphs, in monosyllabic word attack' (i.e. can read simple single-syllable words).

- *Mixed statements* – which say more than one thing at a time. The writer is attempting a nuanced statement but a reader does not know which part of the statement to emphasise, for example: 'can take initiative but prefers guidance'; 'is absent regularly but apparently with good reason'; 'is an intelligent and amusing talker'.

- *Non-operational statements* – which, although apparently based on observed behaviours and events, use language that renders it difficult to imagine the behaviour that gave rise to the comment, for example: 'is very polite and creates a good impression' (i.e. shows off to visitors or is genuinely polite to all teachers in all lessons and all situations); 'has distinct leadership potential' (i.e. the ringleader of disruptive behaviour or is able to organise other students very positively and supportively in the series of lessons that I have taken in mathematics); 'has a very strong personality' (i.e. is awkward and a bully or reacted very well when finding the science work difficult).

- *Generalised statements* – where a statement about one facet of a student is made in such a way as to render it applicable to all facets of the student (when the teacher does not see all facets of a student), for example: 'is reluctant to try new ideas' (i.e. did not enjoy the new history topic or preferred to work on her own); 'does not like to be in the limelight' (i.e. did not want to take part in the school pantomime or was very modest about her ten grade A passes at GCSE level); 'needs constant encouragement to relate to others' (I found her very difficult in my music lessons or she was very shy in my class drama lessons).

- *Interpretive statements* – which point to underlying states and conditions rather than to specific behaviour, where the knowledge of the underlying states and conditions can only flow from an intimate knowledge of the student (that the teacher rarely has), for example: 'is capable of sustained friendships' (i.e. she always chooses to work with two other girls in my language lessons); 'has exceptional self-confidence' (i.e. did not bother to consider other approaches to solving a design and technology problem that was presented to his group); 'is very resilient' (i.e. he always undertook his mathematics corrections without complaint).

- *Value-laden statements* – where the student is judged according to the personal preferences of the teacher, for example: 'is lazy and unhelpful' (i.e. I didn't like the way that she responded to failure); 'has a friendly, helpful attitude' (i.e. I always give him the jobs to do in the classroom); 'makes constructive contributions to classroom discussions and activities' (i.e. I always ask her to speak first in a class discussion).

All of these examples show (a) how easy it can be for the writer of the record to mean something very different from the meaning read into a statement by somebody else; (b) how easy it is for the writer's personality and preferences to colour the comments that are written in a record. In one sense this is an intractable problem as long as people use words, for a writer's vocabulary can be similar to a reader's but they both bring different interpretations and connotations to the same words. A record writer, then, may find it salutary to consider whether: (a) she likes students that are like her in temperament and personality; (b) she dislikes students that are like her in temperament and personality; (c) students whom she likes have characteristics that she likes; (d) students whom she dislikes have characteristics that she dislikes. We are not suggesting that teachers deliberately misrepresent their students; rather we are arguing that biases all too easily can slip in unnoticed by the record keeper – be they positive or negative they can easily misrepresent the student.

In entering a word-based comment on a record, then, it is important for statements to be framed as objectively and evidentially as possible, so that solutions to the six problems outlined above can be met by ensuring that statements are:

- *defined:* so that everybody who reads them will understand them in the same way
- *singular:* they say one thing at a time
- *operational:* they describe what the student has been doing to give rise to the comment
- *specific:* they indicate the circumstances in which the characteristic has been demonstrated
- *guess-free:* they say that which can be correctly known about the student
- *value-neutral:* they do not voice the writer's preferences for one student over another.

This is an art that needs to be practised by student teachers looking critically at comments that are written about a student in a record. This also applies very powerfully to a Progress File where even greater opportunities exist for open-ended, subjective, prejudiced remarks to be made.

9   Comments taken from lesson, daily and weekly evaluations and plans. It is often the case that student teachers refer to particular students or groups in a class when they are writing evaluations on lessons, a day's activities or a weekly review. These evaluations can provide important data for record keeping.
10   Photographs.
11   Flow charts, web diagrams, descriptions of curricula studied (where a planning document doubles as a recording document).
12   There is also a completely open-ended type of record that begins life as a blank sheet of paper apart from a student's name, and the student teacher enters notes made about unanticipated behaviours, learning, comments by a student. This is a salutary exercise, for the student teacher can review these sheets after a few weeks and think why more notes have been made on one student than on another (e.g. is the student teacher concentrating more of her attention on one student rather than another, and if so, why?).

A standardised format enables data to be entered fairly rapidly and enables the student teacher to compare one student with another. Moreover, a standardised format may enable some useful parity to be achieved between teachers and age phases, enabling continuity to be addressed – vertically across several teachers of a specified age group and laterally across several teachers as a student moves up through a school. On the other hand tick boxes and closed forms of recording may fail to catch some important individual features about a student. In this case it may be more advisable to have a semi-structured approach to record keeping, wherein an area for comment is specified (maybe with reference to attainment targets of the National Curriculum) and space is provided for a student teacher's individual comments, carefully referenced to specific individuals and activities. There is a danger in more open forms of recording, viz. that the record may become platitudinous and generalised, saying more about the student teacher's likes and dislikes than the student's. Open-ended forms of recording must confine themselves to evidential matters, noting the context and activity that gave rise to the record entry.

There is a tension, therefore, between the need for standardisation and the need to be able to catch each student's individuality on a record. Further, there is another tension between the overall desirability of parsimony in a record – for rapidity and ease of completion – and the need for a record to be sufficiently detailed and comprehensive in order to provide useful data (i.e. data upon which action can be taken). There is a third tension between the ability of the record to enable the student teacher to enter data in her own preferred manner and the need to avoid so personalised a style or format that personal prejudices can appear.

THE TIMING OF THE RECORD ENTRY

The notion of 'fitness for purpose' that was mentioned earlier also applies to the timing of the record entries. It might be most fitting to complete a summative record each half-term whereas it might be more fitting to review detailed records on a daily or weekly basis. All data entered on a record should be dated in order that the student teacher can chart rates of progress. Timing of data entry varies according to the purpose (formative/summative) of the record, the level of detail required (the less the detail, the less frequent the record) and the focus (the more specific the focus the more frequent the entry, though the more open the entry does not necessarily imply the less frequent the entry). Moreover, we have assumed so far that the timing of the data entry will be regular – once a day, once a week, once a term etc. This need not be the case. For example, an entry in a record could be made whenever a particular event occurs – which may be once in a day or once in a week. This echoes the comments on 'event sampling' earlier, where the occurrence of the event is recorded (and dated) rather than the number of occasions on which it occurs in a given period of time. This is an important matter, for it adopts an approach termed the 'critical incident' approach,[10] in which the significance of an event can be recognised (e.g. when a child first writes her name correctly) rather than its frequency. This type of data entry enables unanticipated events, comments and behaviour to be noted.

The picture of record keeping that we have painted so far has portrayed it as being a relatively complex activity that has increased in tandem with the bureaucratisation and management of much of education. We recognise that this might be off-putting for student teachers. Nevertheless, throughout the discussion here we have provided some examples of different record keeping systems that student teachers may wish to adopt during their teaching practice. We would wish to suggest that student teachers do not confine themselves simply to recording students' achievements of the National Curriculum but that it is useful to keep notes on all aspects of a student's development, strengths, needs, interests, and social and emotional make-up.

A student teacher undertaking a short teaching practice might not be in the school or class for a sufficient length of time to be able to complete anything but the most perfunctory records. However, many student teachers are placed in a school for up to a term's duration; in light of this as a minimum requirement we suggest that a student teacher's records for a term's teaching practice should include the following:

- A record of work and activities undertaken in each curriculum area taught. This might be in the form of a web or flow diagram, a sequence of lessons, a scheme of work, an ongoing record of activities undertaken.
- A formative and diagnostic record of every student's progress in the National Curriculum areas taught, highlighting particular successes and difficulties encountered.
- A summative record of every student's achievements and efforts for every National Curriculum subject taught (for primary school student teachers this will probably be with reference to a single class of children; for secondary school student teachers this will probably be with reference to a single main subject together with personal and social education).
- A 'blank sheet' type of record for each student (though this is perhaps more practicable in primary rather than secondary school classes in the time available) that records unanticipated events, observations, comments etc. that move beyond the narrow intellectual or academic record and towards a more holistic record on a student's whole personality, personal, emotional and social development, particular strengths and needs, particular achievements and interests.

The QCA provides a useful summary chart of the purposes, uses, timing, contents, formats, audiences and storage of records (Box 102).[11]

There are several forms, timings, formats, purposes and audiences of records. Unfortunately for many teachers record keeping seems to be a bureaucratic chore. However, we suggest that this need not be the case. Records that are linked to assessment, that in turn is linked to planning, can provide important documentation for addressing progression and continuity. Above all they must be useful; a cosmetic record that has no formative or summative potential is a sheer waste of time. Students on teaching practice may find that they are requested to deposit a copy of their records with the school for the school's own record keeping purposes.

WRITING REPORTS

Student teachers may be involved either in writing reports or in contributing to the writing of reports for parents or other outside agencies. These may be end-of-year reports, end-of-term reports, or other reports as required. Indeed the student teacher may be required to submit a report on students taught during the teaching practice. The school should have its own formats for reporting, and the student teacher must find these out. Alternatively the student teacher could devise his/her own reporting systems.

There is no standardised way in which reports are written, and so each school has its own format, which may include comments, tick boxes, statements from item banks of computer-stored statements, or other elements. Item banks of statements can be found at: www.dfes.gov.uk/ cutting-burdens/goodprac/gpindex.shtml#area4. Whilst it is invidious to be prescriptive about report writing, nevertheless there are some particular points which can be raised; reports should:[12]

- be clear, concise, straightforward and jargon-free
- be written in English, though arrangements may have to be made for them to be mediated or translated into the community language or mother tongue of the recipients
- be written in the knowledge that students themselves will probably read them
- include words and numbers (e.g. in rating scales, grades, levels)
- be personal to the student in question, rather than, for example, to the whole class or to groups
- indicate cognitive and non-cognitive issues (e.g. the child's attitudes, social and emotional behaviour)
- advise recipients how they can help and support the student's development (though this is a moot point: a report is a report rather than a development document)
- indicate the student's attainments and achievements (the former referring to academic attainment, often related to the National Curriculum; the latter referring to a wider range of achievements)
- indicate progress made within, and outside, the subject areas
- include a National Curriculum level where this is a statutory requirement at the end of each Key Stage, though it does not need to do so unless there is a statutory requirement
- include teacher assessment results
- include task and test results from the National Curriculum
- indicate how the child is performing and making progress in relation to the average child of his/her age
- indicate effort as well as attainment
- indicate strengths as well as areas for improvement
- indicate targets, where relevant and appropriate, and how to achieve them (but see the comments earlier on the difference between reporting and providing information for development and improvement purposes)

Box 102: The purposes and uses of records

	Daily/weekly	Termly	Annually
Who uses the records and for what purpose?	Teacher and support staff, to plan and refine next steps.	Teacher, support staff, Special Educational Needs Co-ordinator, to adjust day-to-day teaching, track progress, set termly targets. Pupils and parents to review progress.	Next teacher, pupils and parents, senior staff to review progress and set targets. Next teacher to adjust planning.
What do the records relate to?	Short-term learning objectives identified in day-to-day lesson planning.	Significant aspects of progress identified in schemes of work and derived from the National Curriculum. Individual Education Plans.	National expectations.
Is all the information recorded?	Mainly no, because pupils' folders or exercise books and teachers' mark book will show progress. Some ephemeral evidence may be recorded.	No, except for significant assessments and some notes/comments on individuals.	Yes, for each pupil, in the annual report.
If so, what format might be used?	Day-to-day assessment in format determined by the individual teacher, for example planning notes, pupil file, mark book, comments on pupils' work in exercise books/ folders or in an evaluation box on planning sheets.	Either teacher's own records, or school pro-forma, as determined by the school. Pupils with Individual Education Plans may have their own pro-forma.	School report form. Further advice in [annual documentation on formal reporting] requirements in the Code of Practice on the Identification and Assessment of Special Educational Needs, 1994.
Should the records be retained or discarded?	Discard when information is no longer useful for planning new work.	Discard when pupils have moved on to next stage of learning. Keep most recent work and targets.	Keep and pass on information when pupil moves to next teacher.

- provide details of attendance (number of half-days attended; number of authorised absences, number of unauthorised absences, number of late arrivals).

Some reports will be accompanied by the programmes of study and level descriptions for the National Curriculum, as a reference for parents and other parties, so that readers have a clear indication of the work undertaken.

Many reports will be subject-specific and will include, for each subject:[13]

●   the effort that the student has made (maybe on a rating scale or grade)
●   the overall level of attainment/achievement in that subject, which might be on a rating scale (e.g. very poor to very good), a grade, a level
●   the levels of attainment/achievement against particular statements within each subject (maybe related to the National Curriculum statements in the programmes of study or level descriptions, for example: (a) in art and design: exploring and developing ideas; investigating and making art, craft and design; evaluating and developing work; (b) in music: joins in singing simple songs and rhymes; can listen attentively to music in a range of genres, and express responses to the music; can recognise simple rhythms and repeat them using a range of instruments and sounds)
●   a written comment on each individual subject
●   targets for the student to reach
●   achievements and areas for improvement in the foundation subjects
●   space for general comments by the child
●   space for general comments by the teacher.

The relentless focus on summative assessment and targets is clearly apparent in the example of a pupil report (Box 103).

The comments that teachers write should be specific and evidence-based, for example:

Joanne has used the word processor and drawing packages confidently and effectively in presenting her project on farms. She can use the floor turtle accurately. She is starting to be able to use the internet for searching and retrieval of information for her project work, and she has been able to send and receive e-mails from her friends.

Samson has made good progress in his mathematics this year and has tried very hard throughout the year. He is achieving above the national average for his age group. He understands numbers up to 1,000 and is good at explaining the methods that he uses for adding and subtracting and for working out problems which need more than one calculation. He is good at mental computation in adding and subtracting up to 100. He has learnt two, three, five and ten times table, and can use these in his number work. He has been using graphs and tables, sometimes with the computer, and is able to construct and interpret graphs well. His work on shape is improving, though he has some difficulties in remembering all the names and properties of squares, triangles and rectangles. He can tell the time on a clock face and digitally. Now Samson needs to improve on his shape work, to learn all his times tables up to ten, and to start some simple multiplication and division.

Sarah enjoys her science lessons, particularly when we do experiments and investigations, and she is very good at applying fair tests. She is able to classify living and non-living things on relevant properties. She has an initial understanding of electric circuits and can explain what we need to do to switch a light bulb on and off. Her attainment is at the national average for her age. Sarah now needs to be able to plan experiments and investigations for herself, whilst still keeping the tests fair.

It can be seen here that the comments are focused, include reference to achievements and attainments, progress, targets and both cognitive and non-cognitive elements, and that they are based on, and report, evidence.

Box 103: Report example

This is a brief summary of how your daughter is progressing. It is intended as a means of highlighting successes and areas for improvement.

Subject	Attitude to work	Organisation	Behaviour	Homework	Coursework up-to-date?	Estimated GCSE	GCSE Target	Teacher	
English	3	3	2	3	Y	B	A	Mr S	Good attitude, chat less
Maths	2	2	3	4	N/A	D	B	Mrs H	Missing homework
Science	3	3	3	4	N/A	C	B	Mrs B	
Art	2	2	2	2	Y	C	B	Mrs T	
Drama	3	3	3	3	N/A	C	B	Mr H	
German	3	3	3	3	Y	C	B	Miss B	More effort needed
Geography	1	1	1	2	N/A	B	B	Ms S	
PE (Core)	2	2	2	N/A	N/A	N/A	N/A	Mr O	
RS	2	2	2	2	Y	B	A	Ms B	

Attendance this term from 2nd September to 24th October: 91.9%

Brief description of attitudinal grades

1 – Outstanding/exceptional
2 – Very good
3 – Satisfactory
4 – Needs improvement
5 – Cause for concern

Attainment grades

Estimated GCSE grade:
Indicates the grade your daughter is likely to achieve at the end of the Key Stage 4, if she continues to work at her current rate.

GCSE target:
Indicates the grade your daughter should be working towards, based on her potential and past performance.

Notes and References

1 A Background to Current Developments in Education

1   Department for Children, Schools and Families (2009) *Trends in Education and Skills*. Retrieved 11 August 2008, from: http://www.dcsf.gov.uk/trends/index.cfm?fuseaction=home.showIndicator&cid= 3&iid=16

2   Chaplain, R. (2008) Stress and psychological distress among trainee secondary teachers in England. *Educational Psychology*, 28(2), 195–209.

3   Smithers, A. and Robinson, P. (2001) *Teachers Leaving*. London: National Union of Teachers and University of Liverpool: Centre for Education and Employment Research.

4   Lawton, D. (1984) *The Tightening Grip: Growth of Central Control of the School Curriculum*. Bedford Way Papers, no. 21. London: University of London Institute of Education.

5   *Ibid.*, p. 15.

6   Hargreaves, A. (1994) *Changing Teachers, Changing Times*. London: Cassell, pp. 118–20.

7   *Ibid.*, p. 14.

8   Department for Education and Employment (1998) *Reducing the Bureaucratic Burden on Teachers*. Circular 02/98. London: Her Majesty's Stationery Office.

9   Department for Children, Schools and Families (2007) *The Children's Plan: Building Brighter Futures*. Norwich: HMSO, p.3.

10   Department for Education and Employment (1997) *Excellence in Schools*. White Paper. London: Her Majesty's Stationery Office.

11   Wyse, D. and Torrance, H. (2009) The development and consequences of national curriculum assessment for primary education in England. *Educational Research*, 51(2), 213–28.

12   Department for Education and Skills (2002) *Education and Skills: Delivering Results – A Strategy to 2006*, pp. 13–15.

13   The following material is taken from Morrison, K. R. B. (2001) *The Open Society and Education in Macau*. Inaugural address for the new academic year. Macau: Inter-University Institute of Macau.

14   Popper, K. (1945, tr.1966) *The Open Society and Its Enemies*, Vols I and II. London: Routledge & Kegan Paul.

15   Popper, K. (1963) *Conjectures and Refutations*. London: Routledge & Kegan Paul.

16   Popper, K. ([1945] 1966) *op. cit.*, p. 46.

17   Popper, K. (1963) *op. cit.*

18   National Advisory Committee on Creative and Cultural Education (NACCE) (1999) *All Our Futures: Creativity, Culture and Education*. Suffolk: DfEE Publications.

19   For more information about classroom practice, research and government approach to creativity see: Wyse, D. and Dowson, P. (2008) *The Really Useful Creativity Book*. London: Routledge.

20   Wyse, D. and Goswami, U. (2008) Synthetic phonics and the teaching of reading. *British Educational Research Journal*, 34(6), 691–710.

21 Travers, C. J. and Cooper, C. L. (1993) Mental health, job satisfaction and occupational stress among UK teachers. *Work and Stress*, 7(3), 203–19; Travers, C. J. and Cooper, C. L. (1996) *Teachers under Pressure: Stress in the Teaching Profession*. London: Routledge.

22 Cf.: Cosgrove, J. (2000) *Breakdown: The Facts about Stress in Teaching*. London: RoutledgeFalmer; Kyriacou, C. (2001) Teacher stress: directions for future research. *Educational Review*, 53(1), 27–35; Moore, W. (2002) *Teachers and Stress: Pressures of Life at the Chalkface*. htttp://channel4.com/health/microsites/H/health/magazine/stress/work_teachers/html

23 PricewaterhouseCoopers (2001) *Teacher Workload Study*. Final Report, December 2001. http://www.teachernet.gov.uk/_doc/932/ACF19E2.doc

24 Department of Health, Health Development Agency (2002) *National Healthy School Standard: Staff Health and Well-being*. London: Department for Health. http://www.teacherline.org.uk/upload/TeacherSupport/documents/staffhealth.pdf

25 Troman, G. (1998) Living at a Hundred Miles an Hour: Primary Teachers' Perceptions of Work and Stress. Paper presented at the British Educational Research Association Annual Conference, Queen's University, Belfast.

26 Kyriacou, C. (2001) *op. cit.*, p. 29.

27 Gill, M. and Hearnshaw, S. (1997) *Personal Safety and Violence in Schools*. University of Leicester: The Scarman Centre for the Study of Public Order.

28 Travers, C. J. and Cooper, C. L. (1996) *op. cit.*

29 Smithers, A. and Robinson, P. (2001) *op. cit.*

30 Wilce, H. (2001) Meet the teachers who are hit and bitten and abused. *The Independent*, 12 July, p. 2.

31 Department for Education and Skills (2002) *Safe Schools*. http://www.teachernet.gov.uk/_doc/1607/safe_school_leaflet.pdf

32 Connexions (2002) *Bullying: A Reader for the Diploma for Connexions Personal Advisers*. Moorfoot, Sheffield: Connexions. http://www.connexions. gov.uk/partnerships/documents/Cnutmr11.pdf

33 Department for Education and Skills (2002) *Bullying: Don't Suffer in Silence*. London: Department for Education and Skills, pp. 10–12.

34 Connexions (2002) *op. cit.*, p. 6.

35 Department for Children, Schools and Families. (2007) *Safe to learn: Embedding anti-bullying work in schools*. Nottingham: DCSF Publishing.

36 Keddie, A. (2008) Engaging the 'maximal' intentions of the citizenship curriculum: one teacher's story. *Cambridge Journal of Education*, 38(2), 171–85.

37 Smithers, A. (2001) Comment. *The Independent*, 12 July, p. 2.

38 MacBeath, J., Gray, J., Cullen, J., Frost, D., Stewart, S. and Swaffield, S. (2007) *Schools on the Edge: Responding to Challenging Circumstances*. London: Paul Chapman Publishing.

39 Bierly, P. M. and Spender, J. C. (1995) Culture and high reliability organizations: the case of the nuclear submarine. *Journal of Management*, 21(4), 639–56; Stringfield, S. (1997) Underlying the chaos: factors explaining elementary schools and their case for high-reliability organizations, in T. Townsend (ed.) *Restructuring and Quality: Issues for Tomorrow's Schools*. London: Routledge, pp. 151–8.

40 Lieberman, A. (ed.) (1990) *Schools as Collaborative Cultures*. London: Falmer.

41 Reynolds, D. (1995) The effective school: an inaugural lecture. *Evaluation and Research in Education*, 9(2), 57–73; Stringfield, S. (1997) *op. cit.*

42 Lieberman, A. (ed.) (1990) *op. cit.*

2 Teacher Training Requirements

1 Training and Development Agency for Schools (2008) *QTS standards and ITT requirements*. Retrieved 14 August 2008 from http://www.tda.gov.uk/partners/ittstandards.aspx

2 Training and Development Agency for Schools (2008) *What are the professional standards?* Retrieved 14 August 2008 from http://www.tda.gov.uk/teachers/professionalstandards/standards.aspx

3 Maguire, M., Dillon, J. and Close, G. (2001) Reforming teachers and their work, in J. Dillon and M. Maguire (eds) *Becoming a Teacher* (2nd edition). Buckingham: Open University Press, pp. 63–73.

4   Training and Development Agency for Schools (2007) *Professional Standards for Qualified Teacher Status and Requirements for Initial Teacher Training*. London: TDA.

5   *Ibid.*, p. 16.

6   Teacher Training Agency (2002) *Qualifying to Teach: Professional Standards for Qualified Teacher Status and Requirements for Initial Teacher Training*, *op. cit.*, pp. 6–12.

7   http://www.tda.gov.uk/partners/ittstandards/guidance_08.aspx

8   Foucault, M. (1977) *Discipline and Punish: The Birth of the Prison*. London: Allen Lane, p. 138.

9   See Whitty, G. and Wilmott, E. (1991) Competence-based teacher education: approaches and issues. *Cambridge Journal of Education*, 21(3), 309–18.

10   Morrison, K. R. B. and Ridley, K. (1988) *Curriculum Planning and the Primary School*. London: Paul Chapman Publishing Ltd.

11   Training and Development Agency for Schools (2008) *QTS skills tests*. Retrieved 14 August 2008 from http://www.tda.gov.uk/skillstests.aspx

12   Teacher Training Agency (2002) *Test Coverage*. Literacy. http://www.canteach.gov.uk/support/skill-stests/literacy/index.htm

13   Teacher Training Agency (2002) *Test Coverage*. ICT http://www.canteach.gov.uk/support/skillstests/ict/index.htm

14   Tomlinson, P. (1995) *Understanding Mentoring*. Buckingham: Open University Press.

15   Mullen, C. A. and Lick, D. W. (1999) *New Directions in Mentoring: Creating a Culture of Synergy*. London: Falmer.

16   Nolder, R., Smith, S. and Melrose, J. (1994) Working together: roles and relationships, in B. Jaworski and A. Watson (eds) *Mentoring in Mathematics Teaching*. London: Falmer, pp. 41–51.

17   Tomlinson, P. (1995) *op. cit*; McPartland, M. (1995) On being a geography mentor. *Teaching Geography*, January, 35–7; Stephenson, J. (1995) Significant others – the primary student teacher's view of practice in schools. *Educational Studies*, 21(3), 323–33; Gray, C. (2001) *Mentor Development in the Education of Modern Language Teachers*. Clevedon: Multilingual Matters Ltd.

3   The Curriculum

1   Morrison, K. R. B. and Ridley, K. (1988) *Curriculum Planning and the Primary School*. London: Paul Chapman Publishing Ltd, pp. 41–5.

2   Schools Council (1983) *Primary Practice*. Working Paper 75. London: Methuen.

3   Department of Education and Science (1985) *The Curriculum from 5 to 16*. Curriculum Matters 2. London: Her Majesty's Stationery Office.

4   Jackson, P. (1968) *Life in Classrooms*. Eastbourne: Holt, Rinehart and Winston.

5   Morrison, K. R. B. (1995) Habermas and the school curriculum. Unpublished PhD thesis, University of Durham.

6   Wragg, E. C. (1997) *The Cubic Curriculum*. London: Routledge.

7   Dowson, J. (1999) The school curriculum, in S. Capel, M. Leask and T. Turner (eds) *Learning to Teach in the Secondary School* (2nd edition). London: Routledge, pp. 351–64.

8   Department for Education and Employment/Qualifications and Curriculum Authority (2000) *Curriculum Guidance for the Foundation Stage*. London: Qualifications and Curriculum Authority, unnumbered page entitled 'definition of terms'.

9   Wyse, D. (2010) Conceptions of the school curriculum, in J. Arthur, T. Grainger and D. Wray (eds), *Teaching and Learning in the Primary School* (2nd edn). London: Routledge.

10   Tyler, R. (1949) *Basic Principles of Curriculum and Instruction*. Chicago, IL: University of Chicago Press.

11   Morrison, K. R. B. and Ridley, K. (1988) *op. cit.*, pp. 38–40; Kliebard, H. M. (1995) The Tyler *rationale* revisited. *Journal of Curriculum Studies*, 27(91), 81–8; Hlebowitsh, P. S. (1995) Interpretations of the Tyler *rationale*: a reply to Kliebard. *Journal of Curriculum Studies*, 27(1), 89–94.

12   Doll, W. E. (1993) *A Post-modern Perspective on Curriculum*. New York: Teachers College Press.

13   Desforges, C. (2001) *The Challenge Ahead*. Report of the DfES Research Conference (research report CR2001). London: Department for Education and Skills.

14 Sylva, K. and Wiltshire, J. (1993) The impact of early learning on children's later development: a review prepared for the RSA inquiry 'Start Right'. *European Early Childhood Education Research Journal*, 1, 17–40.

15 Rutter, M. (2006) Is *Sure Start* an effective preventive intervention? *Child and Adolescent Mental Health*, 11(3), 135–41.

16 Department for Children, Schools and Families (2008) *Every Child Matters: Change for Children*. Retrieved 4 September 2008 from http://www.everychildmatters.gov.uk/

17 Wyse, D. and Bradford, H. (2008) 'You're supposed to tell me your name now!' speaking and listening in the early years, in D. Whitebread and P. Coltman (eds) *Teaching and Learning in the Early Years*. London: Routledge.

18 Jackson, P. W. (1968) *Life in Classrooms*. New York: Holt, Rinehart and Winston.

19 Vygotsky, L. S. (1978) *Mind in Society*. Cambridge, MA: Harvard University Press; Vygotsky, L. S. (1981) The development of higher mental functions, in J. V. Wertsch (ed.) *The Concept of Activity in Soviet Psychology*. New York: Sharpe, pp. 189–240.

20 Donaldson, M. (1993) *Human Minds*. Harmondsworth: Penguin; Dowling, M. (2000) *Young Children's Personal, Social and Emotional Development*. London: Paul Chapman Publishing.

21 LeDoux, J. (1999) *The Emotional Brain*. London: Weidenfeld & Nicolson.

22 Rogers, C. and Kutnick, P. (eds) (1990) *The Social Psychology of the Primary School*. London: Routledge.

23 Cf. Vygotsky, L. S. (1981) *op. cit.*, Bruner, J. S. (1974) *Beyond the Information Given*. London: Allen & Unwin; Tizard, B. and Hughes, M. (1984) *Young Children Learning: Talking and Thinking at Home and at School*. London: Fontana; Bruner, J. S. (1986) *Actual Minds: Possible Worlds*. Cambridge, MA: Harvard University Press.

24 Bruner's (1960) notion of a 'spiral curriculum' suggests that key concepts can be commenced early and returned to in ever more sophisticated levels throughout the learner's life.

25 Piaget, J. (1952) *The Origins of Intelligence*. New York: International Universities Press; Whitebread, D. (1996) Introduction: young children learning and early years teaching, in D. Whitebread (ed.) *Teaching and Learning in the Early Years*. London: RoutledgeFalmer, pp. 1–20.

26 Edwards, C., Gandini, L. and Foreman, G. (1998) *The Hundred Languages of Children* (2nd edition). Norwood, NJ: Ablex Publishing.

27 Forman, E. A. and Cazden, C. B. (1985) Exploring Vygotskyian perspectives in education: the cognitive value of peer interaction, in J. V. Wertsch (ed.) *Culture, Communication and Cognition*. Cambridge: Cambridge University Press, pp. 323–47.

28 Problem-solving involves choices (Dewey referred to this as a 'forked-road' situation). Dewey, J. (1933) *How We Think: A Restatement of the Relation of Reflective Thinking to the Educative Process* (2nd edition). New York: D. C. Heath and Co.; Fisher, R. (ed.) (1987) *Problem Solving in Primary Schools*. Oxford: Basil Blackwell.

29 Vygotsky, L. S. (1981) *op. cit.*; O'Hagan, M. and Smith, M. (1999) *Early Years Child Care Education Key Issues* (2nd edition). London: Harcourt Publishers Ltd.

30 Whitebread, D. (1996) *op. cit.*, pp. 6–7.

31 Donaldson, M. (1978) *Children's Minds*. London: Fontana.

32 Claxton, G. (1997) *Hare Brain, Tortoise Mind*. London: Fourth Estate.

33 Edgington, M. (2002) High levels of achievement for young children, in J. Fisher (ed.) *The Foundations of Learning*. Buckingham: Open University Press, p. 40.

34 Parliamentary Office of Science and Technology (2000) *Report on Early Years Learning*. London: Parliamentary Office of Science and Technology, p. 12.

35 *Ibid.*, p. 12.

36 Scott, W. (2002) Making meaningful connections in early learning, in J. Fisher (ed.) *The Foundations of Learning*. Buckingham: Open University Press, p. 82.

37 Pound, L. (2002) Breadth and depth in early foundations, in J. Fisher (ed.) *The Foundations of Learning*. Buckingham: Open University Press, p. 23.

38 *Ibid.*, p. 23.

39   Rogoff, B., Mistry, J., Goncu, A. and Mosier, C. (1993) Guided participation in cultural activity by toddlers and care givers. Monographs of the Society for Research. *Child Development*, 58(8), serial 236.

40   O'Hagan, M. and Smith, M. (1999) *op. cit.*, p. 15.

41   Mills, C. (1998) Britain's early years disaster. Survey of research evidence for Channel 4 television documentary *Too Much, Too Young*. Cited in T. David and A. Nurse, Inspections of under fives' education and constructions of early childhood, in T. David (ed.) (1999) *Teaching Young Children*. London: Paul Chapman Publishing, pp. 165–84.

42   Blenkin, G. and Kelly, A. V. (eds) (1994) *The National Curriculum and Early Years Learning: An Introduction*. London: Paul Chapman Publishing Ltd.

43   Wyse, D., and Goswami, U. (2008) Synthetic phonics and the teaching of reading. *British Educational Research Journal*, 34(6), 691–710.

44   Rose, J. (2008) *The Independent Review of the Primary Curriculum: Interim Report*. London: DCSF.

45   *Ibid.*, p. 16.

46   Wyse, D., McCreery, E. and Torrance, H. (2008) *The Trajectory and Impact of National Reform: Curriculum and Assessment in English Primary Schools*. (Primary Review Research Survey 3/2). Cambridge University Faculty of Education.

47   Senge, P. (1990) *The Fifth Discipline: The Art and Practice of the Learning Organization*. New York: Doubleday, p. 57.

48   Lieberman, A. (ed.) (1990) *Schools as Collaborative Cultures*. London: Falmer.

49   Smithers, A. and Robinson, P. (2001) *Teachers Leaving*. London: National Union of Teachers, and University of Liverpool: Centre for Education and Employment Research.

50   Accessed 27 February 2009 from http://curriculum.qca.org.uk/index.aspx

51   Wyse, D., McCreery, E. and Torrance, H. (2008) *The Trajectory and Impact of National Reform: Curriculum and Assessment in English Primary Schools* (Primary Review Research Survey 3/2). Cambridge: University of Cambridge Faculty of Education.

52   Department for Children, Schools and Families (2008) 14–19 education and skills. Retrieved 18 August 2008 from http://www.dcsf.gov.uk/14-19/index.cfm

53   For example, Vygotsky L. (1978) *Mind in Society: The Development of Higher Psychological Processes* (ed. M. Cole). Cambridge, MA: Harvard University Press; Hargreaves, D. H. (1982) *The Challenge for the Comprehensive School*. London: Routledge & Kegan Paul.

54   Department of Education and Science (1985) *The Curriculum from 5 to 16*, *op. cit.*

55   See Kelly, A. (1986) *Knowledge and Curriculum Planning*. London: Harper & Row; Morrison, K. R. B. and Ridley, K. (1988) *op. cit.*

56   Wyse, D. (2008) Primary education: Who's in control? *Education Review*, 21(1), 76–82.

57   Coltman, P. and Whitebread, D. (1996) 'My mum would pay anything for chocolate cake'. Organising the whole curriculum: enterprise projects in the early years, in D. Whitebread (ed.) *Teaching and Learning in the Early Years*. London: RoutledgeFalmer, pp. 55–79.

58   Blenkin, G. and Kelly, A. V. (1994) *The National Curriculum and Early Learning: An Evaluation*. London: Paul Chapman Publishing.

59   Coltman, P. and Whitebread, D. (1996) *op. cit.*, p. 56.

60   Department for Education and Employment (1998) *The National Literacy Strategy: Framework for Teaching*. London: The Stationery Office.

61   Department for Education and Employment (1999) *The National Numeracy Strategy: Framework for Teaching Mathematics*. London: The Stationery Office.

62   Wyse, D. (2003) The National Literacy Strategy: a critical review of empirical evidence. *British Educational Research Journal*, 29(6), 903–16.; Wyse, D. and Jones, R. (2008) *Teaching English, Language and Literacy* (2nd edition). London: Routledge.

63   Department for Children, Schools and Families (2008) Improving learning and teaching. Retrieved 20 August 2008 from http://www.standards.dfes.gov.uk/primaryframework/introduction/improving

64   Department for Education and Skills (DfES) (2006) *Primary Framework for Literacy and Mathematics*. London: DfES, p.6.

65   Department for Children, Schools and Families (2008) Overview of learning – Year 6 – the learner.

Retrieved 20 August 2008 from http://www.standards.dfes.gov.uk/primaryframework/introduction/overview/year6/learner

66 Department for Education and Skills (2002) *14–19: Extending Opportunities, Raising Standards.* London: The Stationery Office.

4 Information and Communications Technology

1 La Velle, L. and Nichol, J. (2000) Intelligent information and communications technology for education and training in the 21st century. *British Journal of Educational Technology*, 31(2), 99–107.

2 Becta (2008) Harnessing Technology Review 2008: The role of technology and its impact on education: full report. Available at: http://industry.becta.org.uk/display.cfm?resID=38751&page=1646&catID=1627 [Accessed November 25, 2008].

3 *Ibid.*

4 Condie, R. and Munro, B. (2006) *The Impact of ICT in Schools – A Landscape Review.* Literature review: Coventry: Becta Report: ICT Impact 2006.

5 Grabe, M. and Grabe, C. (2001) *Integrating Technology for Meaningful Learning.* Boston, MA: Houghton Mifflin Co.

6 Cox, M., Webb, M., Abbott, C. *et al.* (2003) *ICT and Pedagogy: A Review of the Research Literature.* London: DfES/Becta.

7 Castro, C. D. M. (1999) Education in the information age: promises and frustrations. *TechKnowLogia*, November/December, pp. 39–42.

8 Grabe, M. and Grabe, C. (2001) *op. cit.*

9 Condie, R. and Munro, B. (2006) *op. cit.*

10 Tondeur, J., Valcke, M. and van Braak, J. (2008) A multidimensional approach to determinants of computer use in primary education: teacher and school characteristics. *Journal of Computer Assisted Learning*, 24, 494–506.

11 Plowman, L. and Stephen, C. (2005) Children, play and computers in pre-school education. *British Journal of Educational Technology*, 36(2), 145–57.

12 Allen, J., Potter, J., Sharp, J. and Turvey, K. (2007) *Primary ICT: Knowledge, Understanding and Practice.* Exeter: Learning Matters.

13 Woollard, J. (2007) *Learning and Teaching Using ICT in Secondary Schools.* Exeter: Learning Matters.

14 Warwick, P., Wilson, E. and Winterbottom, M. (eds) (2006) *ICT and Primary Science.* Buckingham: Open University Press/McGraw-Hill.

15 Cf. Ager, R. (1998) *op. cit.*, p. 81; Lachs, V. (2000) *Making Multimedia in the Classroom.* London: RoutledgeFarmer, p. 6.; Loveless, A. and Ellis, V. (2001) *ICT, Pedagogy and the Curriculum.* London: RoutledgeFalmer, pp. 56–7.

16 Naismith, L., Lonsdale, P., Vavoula, G. and Sharples, M. (2004) *Literature Review in Mobile Technologies and Learning.* Bristol: Futurelab Report 11.

17 Kirriemuir, J. and McFarlane, A. (2004) Literature review in games and learning. Bristol: Futurelab Report 8; Kennewell, S. and Morgan, A. (2006) Factors influencing learning through play in ICT settings. *Computers and Education*, 46(3), 265–79; Williamson, B. (2006) 'Elephants can't jump: creativity, new technology and concept exploration in primary science', in P. Warwick, E. Wilson and M. Winterbottom (eds) *ICT and Primary Science.* Buckingham: Open University Press/McGraw-Hill.

18 LaJoie, S. P. (1993) Computer environments as cognitive tools for enhancing learning, in S. P. LaJoie and S. J. Derry (eds) *Computers as Cognitive Tools.* Hillsdale, NJ: Lawrence Erlbaum Associates, pp. 261–88.

19 Hennessy, S. (2006) Integrating technology into the teaching and learning of school science: a situated perspective on pedagogical issues in research. *Studies in Science Education*, 42, 1–48.

20 DFES (2003) *ICT and Attainment: A Review of the Research Literature.* London: HMSO.

21 John, P. and Sutherland, R. (2005) Affordance, opportunity and the pedagogical implications of ICT. *Educational Review*, 57(4), 405–13.

22 Higgins, S. (2001) ICT and teaching for understanding. *Evaluation and Research in Education*, 15(3), 164–71.

23   Hokanson, B. and Hooper, S. (2000) Computers as cognitive media: defining the potential of computers in education. *Computers in Human Behaviour*, 16, 537–52.

24   Smith, F., Hardman, F. and Higgins, S. (2006) The impact of interactive whiteboards on teacher–pupil interaction in the National Literacy and Numeracy Strategies. *British Educational Research Journal*, 32 (3), 443–57.

25   Nordkvelle, Y. T. and Olsen, J. K. (2005) Visions for ICT, ethics and the practice of teachers. *Education and Information Technologies*, 10, (1/2), 21–32.

26   Granger, C. A., and Morbey M. L. (2002) Factors contributing to teachers' successful implementation of IT. *Journal of Computer Assisted Learning*, 18, 480–8.

27   Wegerif, R., and Dawes, L. (2004) *Thinking and Learning with ICT*. London: Routledge.

28   Wellington, J. (2005) Has ICT come of age? Recurring debates on the role of ICT in education, 1982–2004. *Research in Science and Technological Education*, 23, 25–39.

29   Wertsch, J.V. and Tulviste, P. (1998) L.S. Vygotsky and contemporary developmental psychology, in D. Faulkner, K. Littleton and M. Woodhead (eds) *Learning Relationships in the Classroom*. London: Routledge.

30   Nordkvelle, Y. T. and Olsen, J. K. (2005) Visions for ICT, ethics and the practice of teachers, *Education and Information Technologies*, 10, (1/2), 21–32.

31   Fetherston, T. (2001) Pedagogical challenges for the world wide web. *Educational Technology Review*, 9 (1), 4.

32   Säljö, R. (1999) Learning as the use of tools: a sociocultural perspective on the human-technology link, in: K. Littleton and P. Light (eds) *Learning with Computers: Analysing Productive Interaction*. London: Routledge.

33   Salomon, G. (1993) No distribution without individuals' cognition: a dynamic interactional view, in G. Salomon (ed.) *Distributed Cognitions: Psychological and Educational Considerations*. Cambridge: Cambridge University Press, 111–38.

34   Hung, D. W. L. and Cheng, D. T. (2001) Situated cognition, Vygotskian thought and learning from the communities of practice perspective: implications for the design of web-based e-learning. *Education Media International*, 38 (1), 3–12.

35   Peterson, B. (2000) Tech talk. *LIRT News*, 22 (4), 1; Kramarski, B. and Feldman, Y. (2000) Internet in the classroom: effects on reading comprehension, motivation and metacognitive awareness. *Education Media International*, September, 37, 153.

36   Wegerif, R. and Dawes, L. (2004) *Thinking and Learning with ICT*. London: Routledge.

37   Grabe, M. and Grabe, C. (2000) *op. cit.*, pp. 149–50.

38   Vygotsky, L. S. (1981) *op. cit.*

39   Wegerif, R. (2002) Thinking skills, technology and learning. Bristol: Futurelab Report 2.

40   Wishart, J. (1990) Cognitive factors related to use involvement with computers and their effects upon learning from an educational computer game. *Computers and Education*, 15, 1–3, 145–50.

41   Loveless, A. and Ellis, V. (2001) *ICT, Pedagogy and the Curriculum*. London: RoutledgeFalmer, pp. 56–7.

42   Hawkey, R. (2004) Learning with digital technologies in museums, science centres and galleries. Bristol: Futurelab Report 9.

43   Grabe, M. and Grabe, C. (2001) *op. cit.*

44   Kramarski, B. and Feldman, Y. (2000) Internet in the classroom: effects on reading comprehension, motivation and metacognitive awareness. *Education Media International*, September, 37, 153.

45   Dawes, L. (2004) Talk and learning in classroom science. *International Journal of Science Education*, 26(6), 677–95.

46   Ross, J. and Schulz, R. (1999) Can computer-aided instruction accommodate all learners equally? *British Journal of Educational Technology*, 30(1), 5–24.

47   Higgins, S., Wall, K. and Smith, H. (2005) The visual helps me understand the complicated things: pupil views of teaching and learning with interactive whiteboards. *British Journal of Educational Technology*, 36(5), 851–67.

48   Wertsch, J.V., Tulviste, P. and Hagstrom, F. (1993) A sociocultural approach to agency, in E.A. Forman,

N. Minick and C.A. Stone (eds) *Contexts for Learning: Sociocultural Dynamics in Children's Development*. New York: Oxford University Press.

49 Underwood, J. (1998) Making groups work, in M. Montieth (ed.) *IT for Learning Enhancement*. Exeter: Intellect, pp. 29–41.

50 Bruntlett, S. (1999) Selecting, using and producing classroom-based multimedia, in M. Leask and N. Paschler (eds) *Learning to Teach Using ICT in the Secondary School*. London: Routledge, pp. 71–94.

51 Department for Education and Skills (2002) *Transforming the Way We Learn: A Vision for the Future of ICT in Schools*. London: Department for Education and Skills, p. 8.

52 Grabe, M. and Grabe, C. (2001) *op. cit.*, pp. 409–20.

53 Lachs, V. (2000) *Making Multimedia in the Classroom*. London: RoutledgeFalmer, p. 28.

54 Underwood, J. (1998) Making groups work, in M. Montieth (ed.) *IT for Learning Enhancement*. Exeter: Intellect, pp. 29–41.

55 Bialo, E. R. and Sivin-Kachala, J. (1996) *op. cit.*

56 Telem, M. (2001) Computerization of school administration: impact on the principal's role – a case study. *Computers and Education*, 37, 345–62.

57 Slenning, K. (2000) The future school manager: information and communication technology aspects. *Education Media International*, 37(4), 243–9; Telem, M. (2001) *op. cit.*, p. 354; Department for Education and Skills (2002), *op. cit.*, p. 17.

58 Kwok, L. F., Lau, C. K. and Fun, S. W. (1999) Evaluating SAMS in Hong Kong schools. *Computers and Education*, 32, 249–67.

59 Department for Education and Skills (2002) *op. cit.*, p. 17.

60 Crook, C. (1994) *Computers and the Collaborative Experience of Learning*. London: Routledge.

61 Mercer, N. and Littleton, K. (2007*) Dialogue and the Development of Children's Thinking: A Sociocultural Approach*, London: Routledge.

62 Vygotsky, L. S. (1981) *op. cit.*, p. 163.

63 Ertmer, P. A.(2005) Teacher pedagogical beliefs: the final frontier in our quest for technology integration? *Journal of Educational Administration*, 45, 33–61.

64 Tondeur, J., Valcke, M. and van Braak, J. (2008) A multidimensional approach to determinants of computer use in primary education: teacher and school characteristics. *Journal of Computer Assisted Learning*, 24, 494–506.

65 La Velle, L. and Nichol. J. (2000) *op. cit.*, p. 103; Hennessy, S. (2006) Integrating technology into the teaching and learning of school science: a situated perspective on pedagogical issues in research. *Studies in Science Education*, 42, 1–48; Hennessy, S., Deaney, R., Ruthven, K. and Winterbottom, M. (2007) Pedagogical strategies for using the interactive whiteboard to foster learner participation in school science, *Learning, Media and Technology*, 32(3), 283–301.

66 Mercer, N. (2000) *Words and Minds: How We Use Language to Think Together*. London: Routledge; Mercer, N. and Littleton, K. (2007*) Dialogue and the Development of Children's Thinking: a sociocultural approach*. London: Routledge; Mercer, N. and Wegerif, R. (1999) Is 'exploratory talk' productive talk?, in K. Littleton and P. Light (eds) *Learning with Computers: Analysing Productive Interaction*, London: Routledge; Mercer, N., Dawes, R., Wegerif, R. and Sams, C. (2004) Reasoning as a scientist: ways of helping children to use language to learn science. *British Educational Research Journal*, 30(3), 367–85.

67 Lewin, C., Scrimshaw, P., Harrison, C., Somekh, B. and McFarlane, A. (2000) *Promoting Achievement: Pupils, Teachers and Contexts*. ImpacT2 Project. London: Department for Education and Skills.

68 Esarte-Sarries, V. and Paterson, F. (2003) Scratching the surface: a typology of interactive teaching, in J. Moyles, L. Hargreaves, R. Merry, F. Paterson and V. Esarte-Sarries. *Interactive Teaching in the Primary School: Digging Deeper into Meanings*. Maidenhead: Open University Press.

69 Clariana, R. B. (1997) Considering learning styles in computer-assisted learning. *British Journal of Educational Technology*, 28(1), 66.

70 Lemke, C. and Coughlin, E. (1998) *Technology in American Schools: Seven Dimensions for Gauging Progress*. Santa Monica, CA: Milken Exchange on Education Technology. Retrieved August 1999 from http://www.mff.org/edtech/publication.taf?_function=detailandContent_uid1=158; Cooper, P. and

McIntyre, D. (1996) *Effective Teaching and Learning: Teachers' and Students' Perspectives.* Milton Keynes: Open University Press.

71   National Council for Educational Technology (1994) *Technology Works! Stimulate to Educate.* Coventry: NCET.

72   Black, P. and Harrison, C. (2001) Feedback in questioning and marking: the science teacher's role in formative assessment. *School Science Review*, 82(301), 55–61; Black, P. and Wiliam, D. (1998) Assessment and classroom learning. *Assessment in Education*, 5(1), 7–74; Smith, E. and Gorard, S. (2005) They don't give us our marks: the role of formative feedback in student progress. *Assessment in Education: Principles, Policy* and *Practice*, 12(1), 21.

73   Broadfoot, P., Daugherty, R., Gardner, J., Harlen, W., James, M. and Stobbart, G. (2002) Assessment for learning: 10 principles. Assessment Reform Goup/Nuffield.

74   Liu, Z. F. E., Lin, S. J. S. and Yuan, S. M. (2001) Design of a networked portfolio system. *British Journal of Educational Technology*, 32(4), 492–4; Department for Education and Skills (2002), *op. cit.*, p. 9.

75   Dykes, M. (2001) *op. cit.*, p. 5.

76   Collis, B., de Boer, W. and van der Veen, J. (2001) Building on learner contributions: a web-supported pedagogic strategy. *Educational Media International*, 38(4), 235.

77   Murphy, P. (2006) The impact of ICT on primary science, in P. Warwick, E. Wilson and M. Winterbottom (eds) *ICT and Primary Science*. Buckingham: Open University Press/McGraw-Hill.

78   Boklaschuk, K. and Caisse, K. (2001) *Evaluation of Educational Websites*, 1–24. http://members.fortunecity.com/vqf99

5 Legal Issues

1   Booth, I. G. (1998) *The Law and the Teacher*. University of Durham Whole School Issues PGCE Secondary Course document, 1997–8. Durham: School of Education, University of Durham, p. 20.

2   *Ibid.*, p. 20.

3   *Ibid.*, p. 20.

4   Palfreyman, D. (2001) Suffer little children: the evolution of the standard reasonably expected in the duty of care to prevent physical injury on school premises. *Education and the Law*, 13(3), 227–34. Similarly, McEwan (1999, p. 115) questions what exactly is meant by *in loco parentis*, when so many children are in his/her charge. See McEwan, V. (1999) *Education Law* (2nd edition). Welwyn Garden City: CLT Professional Publishing Ltd. Palfreyman argues for a new reading of these key terms, to put them into the context of modern professional teacher–student relationships.

5   Booth, I. G. (1998) *op. cit.*, p. 21.

6   Ford, J., Hughes, M. and Ruebain, D. (1999) *Education Law and Practice*. London: Legal Action Group Education and Service Trust.

7   Palfreyman, D. (2001) *op. cit.*, p. 230.

8   Booth, I. G. (1998) *op. cit.*, p. 21.

9   *Ibid.*, p. 22.

10   *Ibid.*, p. 23.

11   Department for Education and Employment (1988) *Section 550a of the Education Act 1996: The Use of Force to Control or Restrain Pupils*. Circular 10/98. London: Her Majesty's Stationery Office.

12   Department for Education (1994) *The Education of Children with Emotional and Behavioural Difficulties*. Circular 9/94. London: Her Majesty's Stationery Office.

13   Gilliatt, J. (1999) *Teaching and the Law*. London: Kogan Page, pp. 164–8.

14   Department for Education and Employment (1999) *Social Inclusion: Pupil Support*. Circular 10/99. London: Department for Education and Employment.

15   Department for Children, Schools and Families (2008) Permanent and fixed period exclusions from schools in England 2006/07. Retrieved 22 August 2008 from http://www.dcsf.gov.uk/rsgateway/DB/SFR/s000793/index.shtml

16   Department for Education and Skills (2002) *Statistics of Education: Permanent Exclusions from Maintained Schools in England*. London: The Stationery Office, November.

17   Department for Education and Employment (1999) *Social Inclusion: Pupil Support.* Circular 10/99. London: The Stationery Office, para. 6.4.

18   *Ibid.,* Annexe D.

19   Ford, J., Hughes, M. and Ruebain, D. (1999) *Education Law and Practice.* London: Legal Action Group Education and Service Trust Ltd., para. 8.52.

20   Department for Education and Employment (1999) *op. cit.,* para. 6.7.

21   Department for Education and Skills (2002) *op. cit.,* section 3.

22   Department for Education and Employment (1996) Education Act 1996. London: Her Majesty's Stationery Office.

23   Department for Education and Skills (2002) *op. cit.,* section 3.

24   Booth, I. G. (1998) *op. cit.,* p. 24; Berman, L., Burkhill, S., Russell, S. and Rabinowicz, J. (2001) Education negligence. *Education and the Law,* 13(1), 51–67.

25   For example, the Association for Science Education, National Association of Advisors and Inspectors in Design and Technology, the Royal Society for the Prevention of Accidents (RoSPA).

26   Booth, I. G. (1998) *op. cit.,* p. 24.

27   Department for Education and Employment (1998) *Health and Safety of Pupils on Educational Visits.* London: The Stationery Office.

28   *Ibid.,* para. 40.

29   *Ibid.,* para. 46; Royal Society for the Protection of Accidents (2001) *RoSPA Guide to Health and Safety at School.* London: Royal Society for the Protection of Accidents.

30   Department for Education and Skills (2006) *Safeguarding Children and Safer Recruitment in Education.* London: DfES.

31   Gilliatt, J. (1999) *op. cit.,* p. 110.

32   McEwan, V. (1999) *op. cit.,* p. 202.

33   University of Cambridge Centre for Applied Research in Educational Technologies, online.

34   University of Cambridge Board of Graduate Studies (2007). Accessed 19 August 2008 from http://www.caret.cam.ac.uk/copyright/

35   See Wyse, D. (2007) *The Good Writing Guide for Education Students* (2nd edition). London: Sage for full advice on accurate referencing.

36   School Teachers' Review Body (2008) Seventeenth report part 2 2008. Norwich: The Stationery Office, p. 15.

37   *Ibid.,* p. 16.

6 The Preliminary Visit

1   Hagger, H., Burn, K. and McIntyre, D. (1993) *The School Mentor Handbook.* London: Kogan Page.

2   Haysom, J. and Sutton, C. (1974) *Theory into Practice.* Maidenhead: McGraw-Hill.

3   Jackson, P. W. (1968) *Life in Classrooms.* New York: Holt, Rinehart and Winston.

4   This point is echoed in the writings of Holt, for example: Holt, J. (1969) *How Children Fail.* Harmondsworth: Penguin.

5   Cf. Turner, T. (1999) Reading classrooms, in S. Capel, M. Leask and T. Turner (eds) *Learning to Teach in the Secondary School* (2nd edition). London: Routledge, pp. 51–65.

7 Aims, Objectives and Intended Learning Outcomes

1   Department for Children, Schools and Families (2008) About the national challenge. Retrieved 23 August 2008 from http://www.dcsf.gov.uk/nationalchallenge/

2   Department for Children, Schools and Families (2008) *Autumn Performance Report 2007: Achievement against Public Service Agreement Targets.* Norwich: The Stationery Office, p. 26.

3   Blair, T. (1997) *Bringing Britain Together,* 8 December. www.cabinet-office.gov.uk/seu/index/more.html, p. 4.

4   Department for Education and Skills (2003) *About the School Curriculum.* www.nc.uk.net/about_school.html, pp. 1–2.

5   Department for Education and Employment (1999) *The National Curriculum: Handbook for Primary Teachers in England*. London: The Stationery Office, pp. 12–13.

6   White, J. (ed.) (2004) *Rethinking the School Curriculum: Values, Aims and Purposes*. London: RoutledgeFalmer.

7   Hirst, P. H. (1974) *Knowledge and the Curriculum*. London: Routledge & Kegan Paul.

8   Rowntree, D. (1974) *Educational Technology in Curriculum Development*. New York: Harper & Row.

9   Gerlach, V. S. and Ely, D. P. (1971) *Teaching and Media: A Systematic Approach*. Englewood Cliffs, NJ: Prentice-Hall.

10   Wiles, J. and Bondi, J. C. (1984) *Curriculum Development: A Guide to Practice* (2nd edition). Columbus, OH: Charles E. Merrill Publishing.

11   Note: the original painting is in the Tate Gallery, London. A colour reproduction may be found in Bullock, A. (ed.) (1971) *The Twentieth Century*, plate 80, p. 228. London: Thames and Hudson.

12   Note: photographs of the house may be found in Scully Jr., V. (1960) *Frank Lloyd Wright*. London: Mayflower. A colour photograph can be seen in Raeburn, M. (1973) *An Outline of World Architecture*. London: Octopus Books, p. 116.

13   Tyler, R. W. (1949) *Basic Principles of Curriculum and Instruction*. Chicago, IL: University of Chicago Press.

14   *Ibid.*, p. 44.

15   Shulman, L. S. and Keislar, E. R. (eds) (1966) *Learning by Discovery*. Chicago, IL: Rand McNally.

16   Saylor, J. G. and Alexander, W. M. (1974) *Planning Curriculum for Schools*. New York: Holt, Rinehart and Winston.

17   Jeffcoate, R. (1976) Curriculum planning in multiracial education. *Educational Research*, 18(3), 192–200.

18   Shipman, M. D. (1972) Contrasting views of a curriculum project. *Journal of Curriculum Studies*, 4(2), 145–53.

19   Kelly, A. V. (2004) *The Curriculum: Theory and Practice* (5th edition). London: Sage.

20   Sammons, P., Hillman, J. and Mortimore, P. (1995) *Key Characteristics of Effective Schools: A Review of School Effectiveness Research*. London: Office for Standards in Education (Ofsted) and Institute of Education, University of London.

21   Wyse, D. (2003) The National Literacy Strategy: a critical review of empirical evidence. *British Educational Research Journal*, 29(6), 903–16.

22   Brophy, J. and Good, T. (1986) Teacher behaviour and student achievement. In M. C. Wittrock (ed.) *Handbook of Research on Teaching*. New York: MacMillan.

23   Morrison, K. R. B. and Ridley, K. (1988) *Curriculum Planning and the Primary School*. London: Paul Chapman Publishing.

24   Jeffcoate, R. (1976) *op. cit.*

25   Taba, H. (1962) *Curriculum Development: Theory and Practice*. New York: Harcourt, Brace & World.

26   Peters, R. S. (1966) *Ethics and Education*. London: Routledge & Kegan Paul.

27   MacDonald-Ross, M. (1973) Behavioural objectives – a critical review. *Instructional Science*, 2, 1–51.

8 Beginning Curriculum Planning

1   Office for Standards in Education (Ofsted) (1994) *Handbook for the Inspection of Schools*. London: Ofsted. Office for Standards in Education (2003) *Inspecting Schools: The Framework for the Inspection of Schools in England from September 2003*. London: Ofsted.

2   Mortimore, P., Sammons, P. and Ecob, R. (1988) *School Matters: The Junior Years*. Shepton Mallett: Open Books; Levine, D. and Lezotte, L. (1990) *Unusually Effective Schools: A Review and Analysis of Research and Practice*. Madison, WF: NCESRD Publications; Brighouse, T. and Tomlinson, J. (1991) *Successful Schools*. Education and Training Paper No. 4. London: Institute of Public Policy Research; Alexander, R., Rose, J. and Woodhead, C. (1992) *Curriculum Organisation and Classroom Practice in Primary Schools*. London: Department of Education and Science; Reynolds, D. and Cuttance, P. (1992) *School Effectiveness: Research, Policy and Practice*. London: Cassell; Reynolds, D., Creemers, B. P. M., Stringfield, S., Teddlie, C., Schaffer, E. and Nesselrodt, P. (1994) *Advances in School Effectiveness*

Research: Policy and Practice. London: Cassell; Office for Standards in Education (1994) *Primary Matters: A Discussion of Teaching and Learning in Primary* Schools. London: Office for Standards in Education; Reynolds, D. (1995) The effective school. *Evaluation and Research in Education*, 9 (2), 57–73; Sammons, P., Hillman, J. and Mortimore, P. (1995) *Key Characteristics of Effective Schools: A Review of School Effectiveness Research*. London: Ofsted.

3   Office for Standards in Education (2002) *The Curriculum in Successful Primary Schools*. London: Ofsted, paras. 32–6.

4   *Ibid.*, para. 36.

5   For example: www.standards.dfes.gov.uk/schemes3/planning

6   Qualifications and Curriculum Authority (QCA) (2008) National Curriculum. Retrieved 18 August 2008 from http://curriculum.qca.org.uk/index.aspx

7   Department for Children, Schools and Families (2009) The National Strategies. Retrieved 1 March 2009 from http://nationalstrategies.standards.dcsf.gov.uk/

8   Department for Education and Skills (2002) *Key Stage 3 National Strategy: Designing the Key Stage 3 Curriculum*. London: The Stationery Office, p. 2.

9   Office for Standards in Education *op. cit.*, para. 49.

10   *Ibid.*, para. 46.

11   School Curriculum and Assessment Authority (1995) *Planning the Curriculum at Key Stages 1 and 2*. London: SCAA, p. 21.

12   *Ibid.*, p. 21.

13   Morrison, K. R. B. (1994) *Implementing Cross-curricular Themes*. London: David Fulton.

14   Department of Education and Science (1985) *The Curriculum from 5 to 16*. Curriculum Matters 2. London: HMSO, paras. 106–33.

15   *Ibid.*, para. 58.

16   Morrison, K. R. B. and Ridley, K. (1988) *Curriculum Planning and the Primary School*. London: Paul Chapman Publishing Ltd.

17   Department of Education and Science (1985) *op. cit.*, paras. 112–15.

18   Department of Education and Science (1981) *Curriculum 11–16: A Review of Progress*. London: HMSO, para. 2.9.6.

19   Morrison, K. R. B. and Ridley, K. (1988) *op. cit.*, pp. 130–3.

20   Department of Education and Science (1985) *op. cit.*, paras. 116–20.

21   Vygotsky, L. S. (1978) *Mind in Society: The Development of Higher Psychological Processes*. Cambridge, MA: Harvard University Press.

22   Schools Council (1981) *The Practical Curriculum*. Working Paper 70. London: Methuen.

23   Morrison, K. R. B. and Ridley, K. (1988) *op. cit.*

24   Galvin, P., Mercia, S. and Costa, P. (1990) *Building a Better Behaved School*. Harlow: Longman.

25   Vygotsky, L. S. (1978) *op. cit.*

26   Hirst, P. (1967) The logical and psychological aspects of teaching a subject, in R. S. Peters (ed.) *The Concept of Education*. London: Routledge & Kegan Paul.

27   See Morrison, K. R. B. and Ridley, K. (1988) *op. cit.*, pp. 136–7.

28   Bennett, S. N., Desforges, C., Cockburn, A. and Wilkinson, B. (1984) *The Quality of Pupil Learning Experiences*. London: Lawrence Erlbaum Associates.

29   Morrison, K. R. B. and Ridley, K. (1988) *op. cit.*, Chapter 5.

30   Withers, R. and Eke, R. (1995) Reclaiming matching from the critics of primary education. *Educational Review*, 37(1), 59–73.

31   Cf. Kyriacou, C. (1998) *Essential Teaching Skills* (2nd edition). Cheltenham: Stanley Thornes, p. 43.

32   Morrison and Ridley argue for a much more complex view of differentiation to include many variables in differentiating by process. See Morrison, K. R. B. and Ridley, K. (1988) *op. cit.*, pp. 134–6.

33   Central Advisory Council for Education (1967) *Children and their Primary Schools* (Plowden Report). London: HMSO.

34   For example Blenkin, G. and Kelly, A. V. (1981) *The Primary Curriculum*. London: Harper & Row; Walkerdine, V. (1983) It's only natural: rethinking child-centred pedagogy, in A. M. Wolpe and J. Donald

(eds) *Is There Anyone Here from Education?* London: Pluto Press; Alexander, R. (1984) *Primary Teaching.* Eastbourne: Holt, Rinehart and Winston; Morrison, K. R. B. and Ridley, K. (1988) *op. cit.*

35   Pollard, A. and Tann, S. (1993) *Reflective Teaching in the Primary School* (2nd edition). London: Cassell.

36   Alexander, R. (1984) *op. cit.*

37   Walkerdine, V. (1983) *op. cit.*

38   Entwistle, H. (1970) *Child-centred Education.* London: Methuen.

39   Eggleston, J. and Kerry, T. (1985) Integrated studies, in S. N. Bennett and C. Desforges (eds) *Recent Advances in Classroom Research.* British Journal of Educational Psychology Monographs Series No. 2. Edinburgh: Scottish Academic Press.

40   Alexander, R., Rose, J. and Woodhead, C. (1992) *op. cit,* para 64.

41   Morrison, K. R. B. (1986) Primary school subject specialists as agents of school-based curriculum change. *School Organisation,* 6(2), 175–83.

42   Senge, P. (1990) *The Fifth Discipline: The Art and Practice of the Learning Organization.* New York: Doubleday.

43   Department for Education and Employment (1996) Education Act 1996, Section 353b. London: HMSO.

44   Stenhouse, L. (1975) *An Introduction to Curriculum Research and Development.* London: Heinemann.

45   Department for Children, Schools and Families (2008) Planning principles. Retrieved 25 August 2008 from http://www.standards.dfes.gov.uk/primaryframework/foundation/ppo

46   Department for Children, Schools and Families (2008) Primary Framework for Literacy and Mathematics: Overview of Learning 3. Accessed 20 August 2008 from http://www.standards.dfes.gov.uk/primaryframework/foundation/cll/cllplanning/lm3

47   Qualifications and Curriculum Authority (2001) *op. cit.,* p. 15.

48   Qualifications and Curriculum Authority (2001) *ibid.,* p. 9.

49   Qualifications and Curriculum Authority (2002) *Designing and Timetabling the Primary Curriculum.* London: Qualifications and Curriculum Authority, p. 25.

50   *Ibid.,* p. 29.

51   Department for Children, Schools and Families (2008) Sample planning and exemplification. Retrieved 25 August 2008 from http://www.standards.dcsf.gov.uk/secondary/framework/english/fwg/pufwse/pcs

52   *Ibid.,* p. 10.

53   Bernstein, B. (1977) Class and pedagogies – visible and invisible, in B. Bernstein *Class, Codes and Control,* Vol. 3. London: Routledge & Kegan Paul.

54   Sharp, R. and Green, A. (1975) *Education and Social Control.* London: Routledge & Kegan Paul.

55   This is expounded in Morrison, K. R. B. (1993) *Planning and Accomplishing School Centred Evaluation.* Norfolk: Peter Francis Publishers.

56   Stake, R. E. (1976) The countenance of educational evaluation, cited in D. Jenkins, Six alternative models of curriculum evaluation, Unit 20, E 203, *Curriculum Design and Development.* Milton Keynes: The Open University.

57   Morrison, K. R. B. (1993) *op. cit.,* p. 41.

58   Lawton, D. (1973) *Social Change, Educational Theory and Curriculum Planning.* London: University of London Press.

59   Morrison, K. R. B. (1993) *op. cit.,* p. 2.

60   For an overview of 'connoisseurship' in educational evaluation see Eisner, E. (1985) *The Art of Educational Evaluation.* Lewes: Falmer.

61   A more structured and complete set of criteria is provided by Moyles and we advise student teachers to go into her work in detail as it is comprehensive, covering: curriculum content; relationships with students; students' progress and achievements; discipline and management; classroom administration, organisation and display; teachers' professional attitudes and personality. See Moyles, J. (1988) *Self-Evaluation: A Teacher's Guide.* Slough: National Foundation for Educational Research.

9 Learning and Teaching

1   Crowther, D. T. (ed.) The Constructivist Zone. *Electronic Journal of Science Education,* 2(2), 1–9;

Brooks, J. G. and Brooks, M. G. (1995) *The Case for Constructivist Classrooms*. Alexandria, VA: Association for Supervision and Curriculum Development. See also www.emtech.net/construc.htm.

2   Desforges, C. (2000) Integrating conceptions of learning for advancing educational practices. Paper presented at the first programme conference of the UK's ESRC Teaching and Learning Research Programme, Leicester, November. www.tlrp.org/pub/acadpub.ntml

3   Piaget, J. (1952) *The Origins of Intelligence*. New York: International Universities Press.

4   Kamii, C. (1975) Pedagogical principles derived from Piaget's theory: relevance for educational practice, in M. Golby, J. Greenwald and R. West (eds) *Curriculum Design*. London: Croom Helm and the Open University, pp. 82–93; Burton, D. and Nicholls, G. (1999) Ways pupils learn, in S. Capel, M. Leask and T. Turner (eds) *Learning to Teach in the Secondary School* (2nd edition). London: Routledge, p. 24; Shepard, L. A. (2002) The role of assessment in a learning culture, in C. Desforges (ed.) *Teaching and Learning: The Essential Readings*. Oxford: Blackwell, p. 237; Law, D. and Glover, S. (2002) *Improving Learning*. Buckingham: Open University Press, pp. 49–63.

5   Vygotsky, L. S. (1978) *Mind in Society*. Cambridge, MA: Harvard University Press; Vygotsky, L. S. (1981) The development of higher mental functions, in J. V. Wertsch (ed.) *The Concept of Activity in Soviet Psychology*. New York: Sharpe, pp. 189–240; O'Hagan, M. and Smith, M. (1999) *Early Years Child Care Education Key Issues* (2nd edition). London: Harcourt Publishers Ltd.

6   Vygotsky, L. S. (1987), p. 187.

7   Wood, D. (1998) *How Children Think and Learn* (2nd edition). London: Blackwell, p. 100.

8   Hung, D. (2001) Theories of learning and computer-mediated instructional technologies. *Education Media International*, 38(4), 281–7.

9   *Ibid.* pp. 284–5.

10 Hokanson, B. and Hooper, S. (2000) *op. cit.*, p. 548.

11 Loveless, A., DeVoogd, G. L. and Bohlin, R. M. (2001) Something old, something new ...: is pedagogy affected by ICT?, in A. Loveless and V. Ellis (eds) *ICT, Pedagogy and the Curriculum*. London: RoutledgeFalmer, pp. 63–83.

12 Sandholtz, J. H., Ringstaff, C. and Dwyer, D. C. (1997) *Teaching with Technology: Creating Student-Centered Classrooms*. New York: Teachers College Press, p. 14.

13 Doherty, P. (1998) Learner control in asynchronous learning environments. *ALN Magazine*, 2(2), 1–13.

14 Jones, B. F., Valdez, G., Nowakowski, J. and Rasmussen, C. (1995) *Plugging In: Choosing and Using Educational Technology*. Washington, DC: Council for Educational Development and Research, North Regional Educational Laboratory, p. 40.

15 Grabe, M. and Grabe, C. (2000) *Integrating the Internet for Meaningful Learning*. Boston, MA: Houghton Mifflin, pp. 46ff.

16 Fetherston, T. (2001) Pedagogical challenges for the world wide web. *Educational Technology Review*, 9(1), 8.

17 Kramarski, B. (1999) The study of graphs by computers: is easier better? *Educational Media International* 2, 203–9; Kramarski, B. and Feldman, Y. (2000) Internet in the classroom: effects on reading comprehension, motivation and metacognitive awareness. *Education Media International*, September, 37, 149–55.

18 Scardamalia, M. and Bereiter, C. (1994) Computer support for knowledge-building communities. *The Journal of Learning Sciences*, 3(3), 265–83.

19 Grabe, M. and Grabe, C. (2001) *Integrating Technology for Meaningful Learning*. Boston, MA: Houghton Mifflin Co., pp. 50–1.

20 Fetherston, T. (2001) *op. cit.*, p. 8.

21 Bloom, B., Krathwohl, D. and Masia, B. (1956) *Taxonomy of Educational Objectives. Vol. 1: Cognitive Domain*. London: Longman.

22 Glazer, C. (2000) *op. cit.*, p. 8; Grabe, M. and Grabe, C. (2001) *op. cit.*, p. 81.

23 Stoney, S. and Oliver, R. (1999) Can higher-order thinking and cognitive engagement be enhanced with multimedia? *Interactive Multimedia Electronic Journal of Computer-enhanced Learning*, 1(2). http://imej.wfu.edu/articles/1999/2/index.asp

24 Grabe, M. and Grabe, C. (2000) *op. cit.*

25   Leat, D. and Higgins, S. (2002) The role of powerful pedagogical strategies in curriculum development. *The Curriculum Journal*, 13(1), 71–86.

26   Hall, J. (2005) *Neuroscience and Education: A Review of the Contribution of Brain Science to Teaching and Learning*. Glasgow: The Scottish Council for Research in Education.

27   Howard-Jones, P. (2007) *Neuroscience and Education: Issues and Opportunities*. London: Economic and Social Research Council/Institute for Education.

28   Howard-Jones, P. (2007) *Neuroscience and Education: Issues and Opportunities*. London: TLRP, p.8.

29   Hall, J. (2005) *Neuroscience and education: A Review of the Contribution of Brain Science to Teaching and Learning*. Glasgow: The Scottish Council for Research in Education.

30   Goswami, U. (2004) Neuroscience and education. *British Journal of Educational Psychology*, 74, 1–14.

31   Hayes, J.R. (2006) New directions in writing theory, in C.A. MacArthur., S. Graham and J. Fitzgerald (eds) *Handbook of Writing Research*. New York: Guilford Press.

32   Bradford, H. and Wyse, D. (2010) 'Writing in the early years', in D. Wyse, R. Andrews and J. Hoffman (eds), *The International Handbook of English, Language and Literacy Teaching*. London: Routledge.

33   McCutchen, D. (2006) Cognitive factors in the development of children's writing, in C.A. MacArthur, S. Graham and J. Fitzgerald (eds) *Handbook of Writing Research*. New York: Guilford Press.

34   Graham, S., Harris, K.R., Mason, L., Fink-Chorzempa, B., Moran, S. and Saddler, B. (2008) How do primary grade teachers teach handwriting? *Reading and Writing*, 21, 49–69.

35   Teaching and Learning Research Programme (2008) Tlrp's evidence-informed pedagogic principles. Retrieved 27 August 2008 from http://www.tlrp.org/themes/themes/tenprinciples.html

36   Kolb, D. A. (1984) *Experiential Learning: Experience on the Source of Learning and Development*. Englewood Cliffs, NJ: Prentice Hall; Kolb, D. A. (1985) *The Learning Style Inventory* (revised edition). Boston, MA: McBer and Co. See also Heffler, B. (2001) Individual learning style and learning style inventory. *Educational Studies*, 27(3), 307–16.

37   Pachler, N. (1999) Theories of learning and ICT, in M. Leask and N. Pachler (eds) *Learning to Teach Using ICT in the Secondary School*. London: Routledge, p. 99.

38   Hall, J. (2005) *Neuroscience and Education: A Review of the Contribution of Brain Science to Teaching and Learning*. Glasgow: The Scottish Council for Research in Education.

39   Ellis, R. (ed.) *The Study of Second Language Acquisition*. Oxford: Oxford University Press, p. 506.

40   Hartley, S., Gerhardt-Powals, J., Jones, D., McCormack, C., Medley, D., Price, B. *et al.* (1996) Enhancing teaching using the internet. Report of the working group on the World Wide Web as an interactive teaching resource. Proceedings of the conference on Integrating Technology into Computer Science Education, Barcelona: Association for Computing Machinery (ACM), *SIGCSE Bulletin* 28 (SI), pp. 218–28. http://portal.acm.org/citation. cfm?doid=237466.237649

41   Lawrence, D. (1987) *Enhancing Self-esteem in the Classroom*. London: Paul Chapman Publishing Ltd.

42   Vygotsky, L. S. (1981) *op. cit.*

43   Cullen, J., Hadjivassiliou, K., Hamilton, E., Kelleher, J., Sommerlad, E. and Stern, E. (2002) Review of the current pedagogical research and practice in the fields of post-compulsory education and lifelong learning. Final report submitted to the Economic and Social Research Council by the Tavistock Institute, February 2002. London: Tavistock Institute, p. 11.

44   Kutnick, P. J. (1988) *Relationships in the Primary School Classroom*. London: Paul Chapman Publishing Ltd.

45   Adapted from Kutnick (1988) *ibid.*

46   Johnson, D. W. and Johnson, R. T. (1989) *Cooperation and Competition: Theory and Research*. Edina, MN: Interaction Book Co.

47   Schmuck, R. A. and Schmuck, P. A. (2001) *Group Processes in the Classroom* (8th edition). New York: McGraw-Hill, p. 25.

48   Slavin, R. E. (1995) *Cooperative Learning* (2nd edition). Boston, MA: Allyn & Bacon, pp. 6–12.

49   *Ibid.*, p. 12.

50   *Ibid.*, p. 45.

51   *Ibid.*, p. 60.

52   *Ibid.*, p. 60.

53   *Ibid.*, p. 70.

54   *Ibid.*, pp. 141–2.

55   Hay McBer (2000) *Research into Teacher Effectiveness: A Model of Teacher Effectiveness.* Report to the Department for Education and Skills. London: Hay McBer.

56   For additional support for the significance of teachers having high expectations of their students see Law, D. and Glover, S. (2002) *op. cit.*, pp. 49–63.

57   Barnes, B. (1987) *Learning Styles in TVEI: Evaluation Report No. 3.* Leeds University for the Manpower Services Commission.

58   Galton, M., Simon, B. and Croll, P. (1980) *Inside the Primary Classroom.* London: Routledge & Kegan Paul.

59   Flanders, N. A. (1970) *Analysing Teacher Behaviour.* Reading, MA: Addison Wesley.

60   Hamacheck, D. E. (1986) *Human Dynamics in Psychology and Education.* Boston, MA: Allyn & Bacon.

61   Combs, A. (1965) *The Professional Education of Teachers.* Boston, MA: Allyn & Bacon.

62   Marland, M. (1975) *The Craft of the Classroom.* London: Heinemann Educational.

63   Nowicki, S. and Duke, M. (2000) *Helping the Child who Doesn't Fit In.* Atlanta, GA: Peachtree.

64   Mehrabian, A. (1971) *Silent Messages.* Belmont, CA: Wadsworth.

65   Chaplain, R. (2003) *Teaching without Disruption in the Primary School.* London: RoutledgeFalmer.

66   Andersen, P. and Andersen, J. (1982) Non-verbal immediacy in instruction, in L. L. Barker (ed.) *Communication in the Classroom.* Englewood Cliffs, NJ: Prentice-Hall, pp. 98–120.

67   Neill, S. and Caswell, C. (1993) *Body Language for Competent Teachers.* London: Routledge.

68   Andersen, P. and Andersen, J. (1982) *op. cit.*

69   Wragg, E. C. (1981) *Class Management and Control: A Teaching Skills Workbook.* DES Teacher Education Project, Focus Books (series ed. T. Kerry). London: Macmillan.

70   Good, T. L. and Brophy, J. E. (1973) *Looking in Classrooms.* New York: Harper & Row.

71   For example: Good, T. L. (1970) Which pupils do teachers call on? *Elementary School Journal*, 70, 190–8; Jones, V. (1971) The influence of teacher–student introversion, achievement and similarity on teacher–student dyadic classroom interactions. Doctoral dissertation, University of Texas at Austin; Brophy, J. E. and Good, T. L. (1970) Teachers' communications of differential expectations for children's classroom performance: some behavioural data. *Journal of Educational Psychology*, 61, 365–74.

72   Lawrence, D. (1987) *op. cit.*

73   Oeser, O. (1966) *Teacher, Pupil and Task.* London: Tavistock Publications.

74   *Ibid.*, p. 54.

75   *Ibid.*, p. 55.

10   Early Years and Primary Teaching

1   Gardner, H. (1999) *The Disciplined Mind: What All Students should Understand.* New York: Simon & Schuster, pp. 86–93.

2   Cf. Morrison, G. S. (2000) *Fundamentals of Early Childhood Education* (2nd edition). Upper Saddle River, NJ: Prentice-Hall, pp. 142–5.

3   Siraj-Blatchford, I. (1999) Early childhood pedagogy: practice, principles and research, in P. Mortimore (ed.) *Understanding Pedagogy and its Impact on Learning.* London: Paul Chapman Publishing, pp. 20–45.

4   Drummond, M. J. (1996) Play, learning and the National Curriculum: some possibilities, in T. Cox (ed.) *The National Curriculum and the Early Years.* London: Falmer, pp. 129–39.

5   Moyles, J. R. (1989) *Just Playing? The Role and Status of Play in Early Childhood Education.* Milton Keynes: Open University Press; Drummond, M. J. (1996) Whatever next? Future trends in early years education, in D. Whitebread (ed.) (1996) *Teaching and Learning in the Early Years.* London: RoutledgeFalmer, pp. 33–47; Drummond, M. J. (2000) Another way of seeing: perceptions of play in a Steiner kindergarten, in L. Abbott and H. Moyett (eds) *Early Education Transformed.* London: Falmer, pp. 48–60.

6   Scott, W. (2002) Making meaningful connections in early learning, in J. Fisher (ed.) *The Foundations of Learning*. Buckingham: Open University Press, pp. 74–86.

7   Egan, K. (1991) *Primary Understanding: Education in Early Childhood*. London: Routledge.

8   Mills, C. (1998) Britain's early years disaster. Survey of research evidence for Channel 4 Television documentary *Too Much, Too Young*. Cited in Inspections of under fives' education and constructions of early childhood, in T. David (ed.) (1999) *Teaching Young Children*. London: Paul Chapman Publishing, pp. 165–84.

9   Edgington, M. (2002) High levels of achievement for young children, in J. Fisher (ed.) *The Foundations of Learning*. Buckingham: Open University Press, p. 28; Bruce, T. (1996) *Helping Young Children to Play*. London: Hodder & Stoughton.

10   Scott, W. (2002) *op. cit.*, p. 77.

11   *Ibid.*, p. 84.

12   Sylva, K. (1998) Too formal too soon? Keynote address presented at the Islington early years conference: Building on Best Practice in the early years. Cited in Changing minds: teaching young children, in T. David (ed.) *Teaching Young Children*. London: Paul Chapman Publishing.

13   Dowling, M. (2000) *Young Children's Personal, Social and Emotional Development*. London: Paul Chapman Publishing.

14   Bruner, J. S. (1986) *Actual Minds: Possible Worlds*. Cambridge, MA: Harvard University Press.

15   Office for Standards in Education (Ofsted) (1997) *Guidance on the Inspection of Nursery Education Provision in the Private, Voluntary and Independent Sectors*. London: Ofsted; Office for Standards in Education (Ofsted) (1998) *Guidance on the Inspection of Nursery Education Provision in the Private, Voluntary and Independent Sectors*. London: Ofsted; Sylva, K. (1998) *op. cit.*

16   Sylva, K. (1998) *op. cit.*, p. 76.

17   Hutt, S. J., Tyler, S., Hutt, C. and Christopherson, H. (1989) *Play, Exploration and Learning*. London: Routledge.

18   Qualifications and Curriculum Authority (2000) *Curriculum Guidance for the Foundation Stage*. London: QCA, p. 25.

19   Siraj-Blatchford, I. (1999) *op. cit.*, p. 24.

20   Cf. Aries, P. (1973) *Centuries of Childhood*. Harmondsworth: Penguin.

21   Zimiles, H. (1987) Progressive education: on the limits of evaluation and the development of empowerment. *Teachers College Record*, 89(2), 201–17.

22   Siraj-Blatchford, I. (1999) *op. cit.*, pp. 24–5; Bredekamp, S. and Copple, A. (eds) (1997) *Developmentally Appropriate Practice in Early Childhood Programs* (revised edition). Washington: National Association for the Education of Young Children; Hurst, V. and Joseph, J. (1998) *Supporting Early Learning: The Way Forward*. Buckingham: Open University Press; Morrison, G. S. (2000) *Fundamentals of Early Childhood Education* (2nd edition). Upper Saddle River, NJ: Prentice-Hall.

23   Siraj-Blatchford, I. (1999) *op. cit.*, p. 27.

24   Trudell, P. (2002) Meeting the needs of disadvantaged children, in J. Fisher (ed.) *The Foundations of Learning*. Buckingham: Open University Press, p. 71.

25   Vygotsky, L. S. (1978) *op. cit.*, p. 90.

26   Sandström, C. I. (1966) *The Psychology of Childhood and Adolescence*. Harmondsworth: Penguin, p. 66.

27   Guha, M. (1987) Play in school, in G. Blenkin and A. V. Kelly (eds) (1994) *The National Curriculum and Early Years Learning: An Introduction*. London: Paul Chapman Publishing Ltd, pp. 61–79.

28   O'Hagan, M. and Smith, M. (1999) *Early Years Child Care Education Key Issues* (2nd edition). London: Harcourt Publishers Ltd, p. 68.

29   Axline, V. M. (1964) *Dibs in Search of Self*. Harmondsworth: Penguin.

30   Bruner, J. S. (1966) *Towards a Theory of Instruction*. Cambridge, MA: Harvard University Press.

31   O'Hagan, M. and Smith, M. (1999) *op. cit.*, pp. 81–2.

32   Qualifications and Curriculum Authority (1999) *Early Learning Goals*. London: QCA, p. 12.

33   Athey, C. (1990) *Extending Thought in Young Children*. London: Paul Chapman Publishing.

34   Qualifications and Curriculum Authority (2001) *Planning for Learning in the Foundation Stage*. London: QCA, p. 13.

35   Morrison, K. R. B. and Ridley, K. (1988) *Curriculum Planning and the Primary School*. London: Paul Chapman Publishing, p. 22; Moyles, J. (1997) Just for fun? The child as active learner and meaning maker, in N. Kitson and R. Merry (eds) *Teaching in the Primary School*. London: Routledge, pp. 9–26; Gipps, C. and MacGilchrist, B. (1999) Primary school learners, in P. Mortimore (ed.) *Understanding Pedagogy and its Impact on Learning*. London: Paul Chapman Publishing, pp. 46–67.

36   Alexander, R. J. (1984) *Primary Teaching*. Eastbourne: Holt, Rinehart and Winston.

37   Alexander, R. J. (1992) *Policy and Practice in Primary Education*. London: Routledge.

38   Alexander, R. J., Rose, J. and Woodhead, C. (1992) *Curriculum Organisation and Classroom Practice in Primary Schools*. London: Routledge, para. 23.

39   Alexander, R. J., Doddington, C., Gray, J., Hargreaves, L., and Kershner, R. (eds) (2010) *The Cambridge Primary Review Research Surveys*. London: Routledge.

40   White, J. (2008) *Aims as Policy in English Primary Education* (Primary Review Research Survey 1/1). Cambridge: University of Cambridge Faculty of Education.

41   *Ibid.*, p. 7.

42   *Ibid.*, p. 7.

43   Alexander, R. J., Rose, J. and Woodhead, C. (1992) *op. cit.*, para. 66.

44   *Ibid.*, para. 71.

45   Lee, J. and Croll, P. (1995) Streaming and subject specialism at Key Stage 2: a survey in two local authorities. *Educational Studies* 21(2), 155–65.

46   Dean, J. (1983) *Organising Learning in the Primary School Classroom*. London: Croom Helm (reprinted by Routledge 1988).

47   Hargreaves, L. M. and Hargreaves, D, J. (1997) Children's development 3–7: the learning relationship in the early years, in N. Kitson and R. Merry (eds) *op. cit.*, pp. 27–47.

48   Pollard, A. and Tann, S. (1988) *Reflective Teaching in the Primary School*. London: Cassell.

49   Dean, J. (1983) *op. cit.*

50   Pollard, A. and Tann, S. (1988) *op. cit.*

51   Office for Standards in Education (1994) *Primary Matters: A Discussion of Teaching and Learning in Primary Schools*. London: Office for Standards in Education, paras. 13–19.

52   Alexander, R. J., Rose, J. and Woodhead, C. (1992) *op. cit.*, para. 77; see also Pollard, A. and Tann, S. (1993) *Reflective Teaching in the Primary School* (2nd edition). London: Cassell, p. 149.

53   Bennett, S. N., Wragg, E. C., Carr, C. G. and Carter, D. S. G. (1992) A longitudinal study of primary teachers' perceived competence in, and concerns about, National Curriculum implementation. *Research Papers in Education* 7(1), 53–78.

54   Pollard, A., Broadfoot, P., Croll, P., Osborn, M. and Abbott, D. (1994) *Changing English Primary Schools?* London: Cassell.

55   Morrison, K. R. B. (1986) Primary school subject specialists as agents of school-based curriculum change. *School Organisation* 6(2), pp. 175–83.

56   Alexander, R. J., Rose, J. and Woodhead, C. (1992) *op. cit.*, para. 146.

57   Office for Standards in Education (1993) *Curriculum Organisation and Classroom Practice in Primary School: A Follow-up Report*. London: Ofsted, para. 10.

58   Pollard, A. and Tann, S. (1988) *op. cit*; see also Department of Education and Science (1985) *The Curriculum from 5 to 16*. Curriculum Matters 2. London: HMSO.

59   Muijs, D. and Reynolds, D. (2001) *Effective Teaching: Evidence and Practice*. London: Paul Chapman Publishing, p. 136.

60   Hargreaves, L. M. and Hargreaves, D. J. (1997) *op. cit.*, pp. 42–3.

61   *Ibid.*, p. 43.

62   Muijs, D. and Reynolds, D. (2001) *op. cit.*, p. 30.

63   Kutnick, P. and Manson, I. (2000) Enabling children to learn in groups, in D. Whitebread (ed.) *The Psychology of Teaching and Learning in the Primary School*. London: RoutledgeFalmer, pp. 81 and 86.

64   Alexander, R. J., Rose, J. and Woodhead, C. (1992) *op. cit.*, para. 89.

65   For example: Galton, M., Simon, B. and Croll, P. (1980) *Inside the Primary Classroom*. London: Routledge & Kegan Paul; Galton, M. and Simon, B. (eds) (1980) *Progress and Performance in the*

Primary Classroom. London: Routledge. This view is echoed by Dunne and Bennett, see Dunne, E. and Bennett, S. N. (1991) *Talking and Learning in Groups*. Basingstoke: Macmillan.

66   Alexander, R. J., Rose, J. and Woodhead, C. (1992) *op. cit.*, para. 90.

67   Sharp, R. and Green, A. (1975) *Education and Social Control*. London: Routledge & Kegan Paul.

68   Bernstein, B. (1977) Class and pedagogies – visible and invisible, in B. Bernstein *Class, Codes and Control*, vol. 3. London: Routledge & Kegan Paul.

69   Morrison, K. R. B. and Ridley, K. (1988) *op. cit.*, pp. 85–9.

70   Bennett, S. N. and Dunne, E. (1992) *Managing Classroom Groups*. Hemel Hempstead: Simon & Schuster.

71   Alexander, R. J., Rose, J. and Woodhead, C. (1992) *op. cit.*, para. 99.

72   Pollard, A., Broadfoot, P., Croll, P., Osborn, M. and Abbott, D. (1994) *op. cit.*, p. 166.

73   Galton, M., Simon, B. and Croll, P. (1980) *op. cit.*

74   Galton, M. and Williamson, J. (1992) *Groupwork in the Primary School*. London: Routledge.

75   Pollard, A., Broadfoot, P., Croll, P., Osborn, M. and Abbott, D. (1994), *op. cit.*, p. 166.

76   Galvin, P., Mercia, S. and Costa, P. (1990) *Building a Better Behaved School*. Harlow: Longman.

77   Dunne, E. and Bennett, S. N. (1991) *op. cit.*, p. 4.

78   Bennett, S. N. and Dunne, E. (1992) *op. cit.*

79   Muijs, D. and Reynolds, D. (2001) *op. cit.*, p. 34.

80   *Ibid.*, p. 34.

81   Kutnick, P. and Manson, I. (2000) *op. cit.*, p. 81.

82   Cohen, E. (1994) Restructuring the classroom – conditions for productive small groups. *Review of Educational Research*, 64(1), 11–35.

83   Hall, K. (1995) Learning modes: an investigation of perceptions in five Kent classrooms. *Educational Research*, 3(1), 21–32.

84   Harwood, D. (1995) The pedagogy of the World Studies 8–13 Project: the influence of the presence/absence of the teacher upon primary children's collaborative group work. *British Educational Research Journal*, 21(5), 587–611.

85   Dunne, E. and Bennett, S. N. (1991) *op. cit.*, p. 31.

86   Muijs, D. and Reynolds, D. (2001) *op. cit.*, p. 32.

87   Dunne, E. and Bennett, S. N. (1991) *op. cit.*, pp. 32–3.

88   Harwood, D. (1995) *op. cit.*

89   Muijs, D. and Reynolds, D. (2001) *op. cit.*, p. 33.

90   Cohen, E. (1994) *op. cit.*

91   McAllister, W. (1995) Are pupils equipped for group work without training or instruction? *British Educational Research Journal*, 21(3), 403.

92   Galvin, P., Mercia, S. and Costa, P. (1990) *op. cit.*

93   Mortimore, P. Sammons, P. and Ecob, R. (1988) *School Matters: The Junior Years*. Salisbury: Open Books.

94   Alexander, R. J., Rose, J. and Woodhead, C. (1992) *op. cit.*, para. 97.

95   Bennett, S. N. and Dunne, E. (1992) *op. cit.*

96   Pollard, A., Broadfoot, P., Croll, P., Osborn, M. and Abbott, D. (1994) *op. cit.*, p. 161.

97   Pollard, A. and Tann, S. (1988) *op. cit.*

98   Pollard, A., Broadfoot, P., Croll, P., Osborn, M. and Abbott, D. (1994) *op. cit.*

99   Kerry, T. and Sands, M. K. (1982) *Handling Classroom Groups*. London: Macmillan.

100   Muijs, D. and Reynolds, D. (2001) *op. cit.*, pp. 33–4.

101   Pollard, A., Broadfoot, P., Croll, P., Osborn, M. and Abbott, D. (1994) *op. cit.*, p. 160.

102   Bennett, S. N. and Dunne, E. (1992) *op. cit.*, p. 27.

103   Pollard, A., Broadfoot, P., Croll, P., Osborn, M. and Abbott, D. (1994) *op. cit.*, p. 160.

104   Bennett, S. N. and Dunne, E. (1992) *op. cit.*

105   Kagan, S. (1988) *Cooperative Learning: Resources for Teachers*. University of California: Riverside Books.

106   Dunne, E. and Bennett, N. (1990) *op. cit.*, p. 27.

107   Dean, J. (1983) *op. cit.*

108 McAllister, W. (1995) *op. cit.*, p. 404.
109 Morrison, K. R. B. and Ridley, K. (1988) *op. cit.*, p. 88.
110 A useful overview of issues in this field can be found in Slavin, R. E. (1995) *Cooperative Learning* (2nd edition). Boston, MA: Allyn & Bacon.
111 Wheldall, K. *et al.* (1981) Rows versus tables: an example of behavioural ecology in two classes of eleven year old children. *Educational Psychology*, 1(2), 171–84.
112 Hastings, N. and Schwieso, J. (1995) Tasks and tables: the effects of seating arrangements on task engagement in primary classrooms. *Educational Research,* 37(3), 279–91.
113 Kershner, R. (2000) Organising the physical environment of the classroom to support children's learning, in D. Whitebread (ed.) *op. cit.*, p. 19.
114 *Ibid.*, pp. 21–2.
115 Kerry, T. and Tollitt, J. (1987) *Teaching Infants.* Oxford: Basil Blackwell.
116 Pollard, A. and Tann, S. (1988) *op. cit.*
117 Pollard, A., Broadfoot, P., Croll, P., Osborn, M. and Abbott, D. (1994) *op. cit.*, Chapter 7.
118 Blyth, W. A. L. (1965) *English Primary Education*, vol. 1. London: Routledge & Kegan Paul.
119 Rousseau, J. J. (1911) *Emile*. London: Everyman.
120 Dewey, J. (1916) *Democracy and Education*. New York: Macmillan; Dewey, J. (1938) *Experience and Education*. New York: Collier.
121 Board of Education (1931) *Report of the Consultative Committee of the Board of Education on the Primary School*. London: Board of Education, p. 93.
122 Entwistle, H. (1970) *Child-Centred Education*. London: Methuen; Morrison, K. R. B. (1985) Tensions in subject specialist teaching in primary schools. *Curriculum*, 6(2), 24–9.
123 Central Advisory Council for Education (1967) *Children and their Primary Schools* (Plowden Report). London: HMSO.
124 Morrison, K. R. B. and Ridley, K. (1988) *op. cit.*, p. 91.
125 Bennett, S. N., Andrea, J., Hegarty, P. and Wade, B. (1980) *Open Plan Schools: Teaching, Curriculum, Design*. Slough: National Foundation for Educational Research.
126 Mortimore, P., Sammons, P. and Ecob, R. (1988) *op. cit.*
127 Alexander, R. J., Rose, J. and Woodhead, C. (1992) *op. cit.*
128 Dearden, R. F. (1971) What is the integrated day?, in J. Walton (ed.) *The Integrated Day in Theory and Practice*. London: Ward Lock Educational.
129 Dearden, R. F. (1976) *Problems in Primary Education*. London: Routledge & Kegan Paul.
130 *Ibid.*
131 *Ibid.*
132 *Ibid.*
133 Pollard, A. and Tann, S. (1988) *op. cit.*
134 Dearden, R. F. (1976) *op. cit.*
135 Morrison, K. R. B. and Ridley, K. (1988) *op. cit.*, pp. 89–91.
136 Taylor, J. (1983) *Organizing and Integrating the First School Day*. London: Allen & Unwin.
137 Mycock, M. A. (1970) Vertical grouping in the primary school, in V. R. Rogers (ed.) *Teaching in the British Primary School*. London: Macmillan.
138 Allen, I., Dover, K., Gaff, M., Gray, E., Griffiths, C., Ryall, N. and Toone, E. (1975) *Working an Integrated Day*. London: Ward Lock Educational.
139 Kerry, T. and Tollitt, J. (1987) *op. cit.*
140 Dearden, R. F. (1976) *op. cit.*
141 Tann, C. S. (1988) The rationale for topic work, in C. S. Tann (ed.) *Developing Topic Work in the Primary School*. Lewes: Falmer, p. 4.
142 Rance, P. (1968) *Teaching by Topics*. London: Ward Lock Educational.
143 Kerry, T. and Eggleston, J. (1988) *Topic Work in the Primary School*. London: Routledge.
144 Kerry, T. and Tollitt, J. (1987) *op. cit.*
145 Baker, R. (1987) Developing educational relevance in primary school science. CASTME *Journal*, 7(1), 28–39.

146 Bonnett, M. (1986) Child-centredness and the problem of structure in project work. *Cambridge Journal of Education*, 16(1), 3–6.

11 Secondary Teaching

1 Simon, B. (1995) Why no pedagogy in England?, in B. Moon and A. Shelton Mayes (eds) *Teaching and Learning in the Secondary School*. London: Routledge with the Open University, pp. 10–24; Uljens, M. (1997) *School Didactics and Learning*. Hove, UK: Psychology Press Ltd; Hallam, S. and Ireson, J. (1999) Pedagogy in the secondary school, in P. Mortimore (ed.) *Understanding Pedagogy and its Impact on Learning*. London: Paul Chapman Publishing, pp. 68–97.

2 Stemler, S. E., Elliott, J. G., Grigorenko, E. L. and Sternberg, R. J. (2006) There's more to teaching than instruction: seven strategies for dealing with the practical side of teaching. *Educational Studies*, 32(1), 101–18.

3 Claxton, G. (2007) Expanding young people's capacity to learn. *British Journal of Educational Studies*, 55(2), 1–20.

4 Dowson, J. (1999) The school curriculum, in S. Capel, M. Leask and T. Turner (eds) *Learning to Teach in the Secondary School* (2nd edition). London: Routledge, pp. 351–64.

5 Leask, M. (1999) What do teachers do?, in S. Capel, M. Leask and T. Turner (eds) *op. cit.* pp. 8–17.

6 Morrison, K. R. B. (1986) Primary school subject specialists as agents of school-based curriculum change. *School Organisation*, 6(2), 175–83.

7 Hallam, S. and Ireson, J. (1999) *op. cit.*, p. 80.

8 *Ibid.*, p. 82.

9 Brophy, J. and Good, T. L. (1986) Teacher behavior and student achievement, in C. M. Wittrock (ed.) *Handbook of Research on Teaching* (3rd edition). New York: Macmillan, pp. 328–75.

10 Muijs, D. and Reynolds, D. (2005) *Effective Teaching: Evidence and Practice*. London: Sage Publications Ltd, p. 230.

11 *Ibid.*, p. 88.

12 *Ibid.*, p. 83.

13 Leask, M. (1999) What do teachers do? *op. cit.*

14 *Ibid.*, p. 20.

15 Wragg, E. C. and Wood, E. K. (1984) Teachers' first encounters with their classes, in E. C. Wragg (ed.) *Classroom Teaching Skills*. London: Croom Helm, pp. 47–78.

16 Leask, M. (1999) Taking responsibility for whole lessons, in S. Capel, M. Leask and T. Turner (eds) *Learning to Teach in the Secondary School* (2nd edition), *op. cit.*, pp. 85–8.

17 Wragg, E. C. and Wood, E. K. (1984) Pupil appraisals of teaching, in E. C. Wragg (ed.) *Classroom Teaching Skills*. London: Croom Helm, pp. 79–96.

18 Hargreaves, D. H. (1973) *Interpersonal Relations and Education*. London: Routledge & Kegan Paul.

19 Leask, M. (1999) Taking responsibility for whole lessons, *op. cit.*, p. 79.

20 Wragg, E. C. and Wood, E. K. (1984) *op. cit.*

21 Fontana, D. (1985) *Classroom Control: Understanding and Guiding Classroom Behaviour*. London: British Psychological Society and Methuen. See particularly, in this respect, pp. 138–42.

22 Leask, M. (1999) Taking responsibility for whole lessons, *op. cit.*, pp. 83–4.

23 Hargreaves, D. (1984) Rules in play, in A. Hargreaves and P. Woods (eds) *Classrooms and Staffrooms*. Milton Keynes: Open University Press, pp. 25–35; Baumann, A. S., Bloomfield, A. and Roughton, L. (1997) *Becoming a Secondary School Teacher*. London: Hodder & Stoughton, pp. 16–24; Macrae, S. and Quintrell, M. (2001) Managing effective classrooms, in J. Dillon and M. Maguire (eds) *Becoming a Teacher* (2nd edition). Buckingham: Open University Press, pp. 150–61.

24 Dean, J. (1996) *Beginning Teaching in the Secondary School*. Buckingham: Open University Press.

25 Macrae, S. and Quintrell, M. (2001) *op. cit.*, p. 153.

26 Perrott, E. (1982) *Effective Teaching: A Practical Guide to Improving your Teaching*. London: Longman.

27 *Ibid.*

28 Muijs, D. and Reynolds, D. (2005) *op. cit.*, p. 230.

29   *Ibid.*, pp. 68–9.

30   Black, P. (1997) Doing our homework on homework. *American School Board Journal*, 183(2), 48–51.

31   Cooper, H. (1989) Synthesis of research on homework. *Educational Leadership*, 47(3), pp. 58–91.

32   Farrow, S., Tymms, P. and Henderson, B. (1999) Homework and attainment in primary schools. *British Educational Research Journal*, 25(3), 323–41; Muijs, D. and Reynolds, D. (2001) *op. cit.*, p. 70.

33   Muijs, D. and Reynolds, D. (2005) *op. cit.*

34   Ornstein, A. C. (1994) Homework, studying and role taking: essential skills for students. *NASSP Bulletin*, 78(559), 58–70.

35   Muijs, D. and Reynolds, D. (2001) *op. cit.*, p. 72.

36   Ireson, J., Clark, H. and Hallam, S. (2002) Constructing ability groups in secondary school: issues in practice. *School Leadership and Management*, 22(2), 163–76.

37   Muijs, D. and Reynolds, D. (2005) *op. cit.*

38   Department for Education and Employment (1997) *Excellence in Schools*. London: The Stationery Office; Department for Education and Employment (2001) *Schools: Building on Success*. London: The Stationery Office; Department for Education and Skills (2001) *Schools Achieving Success*. London: The Stationery Office; see also Slavin, R. E. (1990) Achievement effects of ability grouping in secondary schools: a best evidence synthesis. *Review of Educational Research*, 60(3), 471–99.

39   Ireson, J., Clark, H. and Hallam, S. (2002) *op. cit.*, p. 164.

40   Slavin, R. E. (1990) *op. cit.*; Linchevski, L. and Kutscher, B. (1998) Tell me with whom you're learning and I'll tell you how much you've learned: mixed-ability versus same-ability grouping in mathematics. *Journal for Research in Mathematics Education*, 29(5), 533–53; Office for Standards in Education (2001) *Standards and Quality in – Education: The Annual Report of Her Majesty's Chief Inspector of Schools*. London: The Stationery Office.

41   Kerckhoff, A. C. (1986) Effects of ability grouping in British secondary schools. *American Sociological Review*, 51(6), 842–58; see also Boaler, J. and Wiliam, D. (2001) Setting, streaming and mixed-ability teaching, in J. Dillon and M. Maguire (eds) *op. cit.*, pp. 173–81.

42   Boaler, J. (1997) When even the winners are losers: evaluating the experience of 'top set' students. *Journal of Curriculum Studies*, 29(2), 165–82.

43   Peak, B. and Morrison, K. R. B. (1988) Investigating banding origins and destinations in a comprehensive school. *School Organisation*, 8(3), 339–49; Ireson, J., Clark, H. and Hallam, S. (2002) *op. cit.*

44   MacIntyre, H. and Ireson, J. (2002) Within-class ability grouping, group placement and self-concept. *British Educational Research Journal*, 28(2), 249–63; see also Boaler, J. (1997) *Experiencing School Mathematics: Teaching Styles, Sex and Setting*. Buckingham: Open University Press.

45   Muijs, D. and Reynolds, D. (2005) *op. cit.*, p. 145.

46   Ireson, J., Clark, H. and Hallam, S. (2002) *op. cit.*, p. 165.

47   *Ibid.*, p. 174.

48   Muijs, D. and Reynolds, D. (2001) *op. cit.*, p. 145.

49   Boaler, J. and Wiliam, D. (2001) *op. cit.*, p. 179.

50   *Ibid.*, p. 179.

51   *Ibid.*, p. 179.

52   Slavin, R. E. (1990) *op. cit.*

53   Ireson, J., Hallam, S. and Hurley, C. (2005) What are the effects of ability grouping on GCSE attainment? *British Educational Research Journal*, 31(4), 454–8.

54   *Ibid.*

55   Ireson *et al.* (*ibid.*) report that the size of the lowest sets was roughly half that of the highest sets, not least to include students with special needs in the lowest sets. They also report wide variances, with upper sets being up to four times larger than lower sets.

56   Boaler, J. and Wiliam, D. (2001) *op. cit.*, p. 174.

57   Turner, T. (1999) Differentiation, progression and pupil grouping, in S. Capel, M. Leask and T. Turner (eds) *Learning to Teach in the Secondary School* (2nd edition), *op. cit.*, pp. 134–50.

58   Bourdieu, P. (1977) Cultural reproduction and educational reproduction, in J. Karabel and A. H. Halsey (eds) *Power and Ideology in Education*. London: Oxford University Press, pp. 487–511; Woods, P. (1979) *The Divided School*. London: Routledge & Kegan Paul; Halsey, A. H., Heath, A. and Ridge, J. (1980) *Origins and Destinations*. London: Oxford University Press; Ball, S. (1981) *Beachside Comprehensive*. London: Cambridge University Press; Hargreaves, D. H. (1982) *The Challenge for the Comprehensive School*. London: Routledge & Kegan Paul.

59   Rubie-Davies, C., Hattie, J. and Hamilton, R. (2006) Expecting the best for students: teacher expectations and academic outcomes. *British Journal of Educational Psychology*, 76, 429–44.

60   Esland, G. (1971) Teaching and learning as the organization of knowledge, in M. F. D. Young (ed.) *Knowledge and Control*. Basingstoke: Collier-Macmillan, pp. 70–115; Keddie, N. (1971) Classroom knowledge, in M. F. D. Young (ed.) *Knowledge and Control*. Basingstoke: Collier-Macmillan, pp. 133–60; Hurn, C. J. (1977) *The Limits and Possibilities of Schooling*. Boston, MA: Allyn & Bacon; Woods, P. (1979) *op. cit.*; Peak, B. and Morrison, K. R. B. (1988) *op. cit.*

61   Davies, P., Telhaj, S., Hutton, D., Adnett, N. and Coe, R. (2008) Competition, cream-skimming and department performance within secondary schools. *British Educational Research Journal*. First Article, 1–17, pp. 1–16.

62   Chapman, R. (1979) Schools do make a difference. *British Educational Research Journal*, 5(1), 115–24; Smith, I. (1981) Curriculum placement in comprehensive schools. *British Educational Research Journal*, 7(2), 111–24; Reynolds, D. (1995) The effective school. *Evaluation and Research in Education*, 9(2), 57–73.

63   Ball, S. (1981) *op. cit.*

64   Reid, M., Clunies-Ross, L., Goacher, B. and Vile, C. (1981) *Mixed Ability Teaching: Problems and Possibilities*. Slough: National Foundation for Educational Research.

65   Kerry, T. and Sands, M. K. (1982) *Mixed Ability Teaching in the Early Years of the Secondary School*. London: Macmillan.

66   Adapted from Kerry and Sands, *ibid*.

12 Language in Classrooms

1   Mercer, N. and Littleton, K. (2007) *Dialogue and the Development of Thinking: A Sociocultural Approach*. New York: Routledge.

2   Barnes, D. (1971) Language and learning in the classroom. *Journal of Curriculum Studies*, 3(1), 27–38.

3   Mercer, N., and Hodgkinson, S. (2008) *Exploring Talk in School: Inspired by the Work of Douglas Barnes*. London: Sage.

4   Mishler, E. G. (1972) Implications of teaching strategies for language and cognition: observations in first-grade classrooms, in C. B. Cazden, V. P. John and D. Hymes, *Functions of Language in the Classroom*. Teachers College, Columbia University, New York: Teachers College Press, pp. 267–98.

5   Mercer, N. (1995) *The Guided Construction of Knowledge: Talk Amongst Teachers and Learners*. Clevedon: Multilingual Matters.

6   Stubbs, M. (1983) *Language, Schools and Classrooms* (2nd edition). London: Methuen.

7   Wells, G. (1986) *The Meaning Makers*. London: Routledge.

8   Wyse, D. and Bradford, H. (2008) 'You're supposed to tell me your name now!' Speaking and listening in the early years, in Whitebread, D. and Coltman, P. (eds) *Teaching and Learning in the Early Years*. London: Routledge, pp. 141–60.

9   English, E., Hargreaves, L. and Hislam, J. (2002) Pedagogical dilemmas in the national literacy strategy: primary teachers' perceptions, reflections and classroom behaviour. *Cambridge Journal of Education*, 32(1), 9–26.

10   Peccei, J.S. (ed.) *Child Language: A Resource Book for Pupils*. London: Routledge.

11   Wray, D., Bloom, W. and Hall, N. (1989) *Literacy in Action*. Barcombe: Falmer.

12   Tizard, B., and Hughes, M. (1984) *Young Children Learning*. London: Fontana.

13   Wells, G. (1986) *The Meaning Makers: Children Learning Language and Using Language to Learn*. London: Hodder & Stoughton.

14 Littleton, K., Mercer, N., Dawes, L., Wegerif, R., Rowe, D. and Sams, C. (2005) Talking and thinking together at Key Stage 1. *Early Years*, 25(2), 165–80.

15 Bearne, E. (1998) *Making Progress in English*. London: Routledge, p. 154.

16 *Ibid.*, p. 155.

17 Edwards, A. D. and Furlong, V. J. (1978) *The Language of Teaching*. London: Heinemann.

18 *Ibid.*

19 *Ibid.*

20 Stebbins, R. (1973) Physical context influences on behaviour; the case of classroom disorderliness. *Environment and Behaviour*, 5, 291–314.

21 Edwards, A. D. and Furlong, V. J. (1978) *op. cit.*

22 Watson, L. (1995) Talk and pupil thought. *Educational Psychology*, 15(1), 57–68.

23 Carlsen, W. (1991) Questioning in classrooms. *Review of Educational Research*, 61(2), 157–78.

24 Office for Standards in Education (1994) *Primary Matters: A Discussion of Teaching and Learning in Primary Schools*. London: Ofsted.

25 Reynolds, D. and Farrell, S. (1996) *Worlds Apart? A Review of International Studies of Educational Achievement Involving England*. London: HMSO.

26 Alexander, R. J. (2000) *Culture and Pedagogy: International Comparisons in Primary Education*. Oxford: Blackwell.

27 Office for Standards in Education (2006) *English 2000–05: A Review of Inspection Evidence*. London: Office for Standards in Education.

28 Muijs, D. and Reynolds, D. (2001) *Effective Teaching: Evidence and Practice*. London: Paul Chapman Publishing Ltd., Chapter 1, see also Department for Education and Employment (1999) *The Structure of the Literacy Hour*. www.standards.dfes.gov.uk/literacy/literacyhour

29 Galton, M., Simon, B. and Croll, P. (1980) *Progress and Performance in the Primary Classroom*. London: Routledge.

30 Mortimore, P., Sammons, P., Stoll, L., Lewis, D. and Ecob, R. (1988) *School Matters*. Shepton Mallett: Open Books.

31 Muijs, D. and Reynolds, D. (1999) School effectiveness and teacher effectiveness: some preliminary findings from the evaluation of the Mathematics Enhancement Programme. Paper presented at the American Educational Research Association conference, Montreal, Quebec.

32 Reynolds, D. and Farrell, S. (1996) *op. cit.*

33 Muijs, D. and Reynolds, D. (2001) *op. cit.*, p. 5.

34 For example: Wragg, E. C. (1993) *Explaining*. London: Routledge; Pollard, A. and Tann, S. (1993) *Reflective Teaching in the Primary* School (2nd edition). London: Cassell; Proctor, A., Entwistle, M., Judge, B. and McKenzie-Murdoch, S. (1995) *Learning to Teach in the Primary Classroom*. London: Routledge, pp. 78–80; Kyriacou, C. (1998) *Essential Teaching Skills* (2nd edition). Cheltenham: Stanley Thornes; Wragg, E. C. and Brown, G. A. (2001) *Explaining in the Primary School*. London: RoutledgeFalmer.

35 Pollard, A. and Tann, S. (1993) *op. cit.*

36 Perrott, E. (1982) *Effective Teaching*. London: Longman.

37 Brown, G. A. and Wragg, E. C. (1993) *Questioning*. London: Routledge, see also Wragg, E. C. and Brown, G. A. (2001) *Questioning in the Primary School*. London: RoutledgeFalmer.

38 Wragg, E. C. (1993) *op. cit.*

39 Perrott, E. (1982) *op. cit.*

40 Brown, G. A. and Armstrong, S. (1984) Explaining and explanations, in E. C. Wragg (ed.) *Classroom Teaching Skills*. London: Croom Helm, pp. 121–48.

41 Wragg, E. C. (1993) *op. cit.*; see also Wragg, E. C. and Brown, G. A. (2001) *op. cit.*

42 Perrott, E. (1982) *op. cit.*

43 Brown, G. A. and Armstrong, S. (1984) *op. cit.*

44 Wragg, E. C. (1993) *op. cit.*

45 Kyriacou, C. (1998) *op. cit.*, p. 34.

46 Urquhart, I. (2000) Communicating well with children, in D. Whitebread (ed.) *The Psychology of Teaching and Learning in the Primary School*. London: Routledge, p. 70.

47   Brown, G. A. and Wragg, E. C. (1993) *op. cit.*

48   Brown, G. A. and Edmonson, R. (1984) Asking questions, in E. C. Wragg (ed.) *Classroom Teaching Skills*. London: Croom Helm, pp. 97–120.

49   Mercer, N. and Littleton, K. (2007) *Dialogue and the Development of Thinking. A Sociocultural Approach*. New York: Routledge, p. 36.

50   Thompson, L. and Feasey, R. (1992) *Questioning in Science*. Mimeo. School of Education, University of Durham.

51   Office for Standards in Education (1994) *op. cit.*, para. 11.

52   Muijs, D. and Reynolds, D. (2001) *op. cit.*, p. 20.

53   Brown, G. A. (1975) *Microteaching*. London: Methuen.

54   Gall, M. D. (1970) The use of questioning. *Review of Educational Research*, 40, 707–21.

55   Muijs, D. and Reynolds, D. (2001) *op. cit.*, p. 23.

56   Rowe, M. B. (1986) Wait time: slowing down may be a way of speeding up. *Journal of Teacher Education*, 37 (1), 43–50.

57   Brown, G. A. (1975) *op. cit.*

58   *Ibid.*

59   Davies, W. T. and Shepherd, T. B. (1949) *Teaching: Begin Here*. London: Epworth Press.

60   Brown, G. A. and Wragg, E. C. (1993) *op. cit.*

61   Dean, J. (1983) *Organising Learning in the Primary School Classroom*. Beckenham: Croom Helm.

62   Turner, T. (1999) Moral development and values, in S. Capel, M. Leask, and T. Turner, *Learning to Teach in the Secondary School*. London: Routledge, pp. 199–211.

63   Dean, J. (1983) *op. cit.*

64   Turner, T. (1999) *op. cit.*, pp. 210–11.

65   Pollard, A. and Tann, S. (1993) *op. cit.*

66   Brown, G. A. and Wragg, E. C. (1993) *op. cit.*

67   Proctor *et al.* (1995) *op. cit.*, p. 79.

68   Bruner, J. S. (1966) *Towards a Theory of Instruction*. Cambridge, MA: Harvard University Press.

69   Galton, M., Simon, B. and Croll, P. (1980) *Inside the Primary classroom* (the ORACLE project). London: Routledge; Baines, E., Blatchford, P. and Kutnick, P. (2003) Changes in Grouping Practices over Primary and Secondary School. *International Journal of Educational Research*, 39, 9–34.

70   Blatchford, P., Kutnick, P., Baines, E. and Galton, M. (2003) Toward a Social Pedagogy of Classroom Group Work. *International Journal of Educational Research*, 39, 153–72; and Mercer, N. and Littleton, K. (2007) *Dialogue and the Development of Thinking: A Sociocultural Approach*. New York: Routledge.

71   Mercer, N. and Littleton, K. (2007) *ibid*, p.25.

13 Inclusion, Equal Opportunities and Diversity

1   Norwich, B. (2000) Inclusion in education: from concepts, values and critique to practice, in H. Daniels (ed.) *Special Education Re-formed: Beyond Rhetoric?* London: Falmer, pp. 5–30.

2   *Ibid.*, p. 8.

3   For example the Sex Discrimination Act 1975. London: HMSO; the Race Relations Act 1976. London: HMSO; Department of Education and Science (1978) *Special Educational Needs* (Warnock Report). London: HMSO; Department of Education and Science (1985) *Better Schools*. London, HMSO; Department of Education and Science (1985) *Education for All* (Swann Report). London: HMSO; Department of Education and Science (1986) *The Curriculum from 5 to 16*. London: HMSO; Department of Education and Science (1989) *From Policy to Practice*. London: HMSO; Commission for Racial Equality (1989) *Code of Practice for the Elimination of Racial Discrimination in Education*. London: Commission for Racial Equality; National Curriculum Council (NCC) (1989) *A Curriculum for All*. York: National Curriculum Council; National Curriculum Council (1989) *A Framework for the Primary Curriculum*. York: NCC; NCC (1992) *The National Curriculum and Pupils with Severe Learning Difficulties*. York: NCC; Department for Education (1992) *Choice and Diversity: A New Framework for Schools*. London: Her Majesty's Stationery Office; Office for Standards in Education

(Ofsted) (1995) *Guidance on the Inspection of Nursery and Primary Schools.* London: Ofsted, p. 77; Ofsted (1995) *Guidance on the Inspection of Secondary Schools.* London: Ofsted, p. 82; Ofsted (1995) *Guidance on the Inspection of Special Schools.* London: Ofsted, p. 80.

4   The Runnymede Trust (1993) *Equality Assurance in Schools.* London: The Runnymede Trust with Trentham Books.

5   Department for Education and Skills (2001) *Special Educational Needs Code of Practice.* London: The Stationery Office.

6   Qualifications and Curriculum Development Agency (QCDA) (2010) Equalities, diversity and inclusion. Available from: http://curriculum.qcda.gov.uk/key-stages-3-and-4/About-the-secondary-curriculum/equalities-diversity-and-inclusion/index.aspx

7   Runnymede Trust (2003) *Divided by the Same Language?* Briefing paper by S. Sanglin-Grant. London: Runnymede Trust, p. 2.

8   *Ibid.,* p. 3.

9   *Ibid.,* p. 4.

10   *Ibid.,* p. 6; see also the Cabinet Office Equality and Diversity website: www.cabinet-office.gov.uk and www.diversity-whatworks.gov.uk, and the Commission for Racial Equality: www.cre.gov.uk

11   Equal Opportunities Commission (1984) *Do You Provide Equal Educational Opportunities?* Manchester: Equal Opportunities Commission, p. 7.

12   Newman, E. and Triggs, P. (eds) (1991) *Equal Opportunities in the Primary School.* Bristol: Bristol Polytechnic, pp. 28–9.

13   Department of Education and Science (1989) *From Policy to Practice.* London: HMSO.

14   Bourdieu, P. (1976) The school as a conservative force, in R. Dale, G. Esland, M. MacDonald (eds) *Schooling and Capitalism.* London: Routledge & Kegan Paul in Association with the Open University Press, pp. 110–17.

15   Wyse, D. (2001) Felt tip pens and school councils: children's participation rights in four English schools. *Children and Society,* 15, 209–18.

16   UNICEF (2009) *United Kingdom's 3rd Quinquennial Report to the UN Committee on the Rights of the Child: Submission from UNICEF UK,* accessed 10 February 2009 from http://www.unicef.org.uk/pages.asp?page=95&nodeid=ukreport&section=

17   Committee on the Rights of the Child (2002) Summary of the 811th meeting. Considerations of reports of state's parties: Second periodic report of the United Kingdom of Great Britain and Northern Ireland (CRC/C/83ADD.3) 10–14 June 2002. Accessed 18 November 2002 from http://www.unhcr.ch/data.htm (p. 3).

18   United Nations (2008) Committee on the Rights of the Child. Forty-ninth session. Consideration of Reports submitted by States Parties under Article 44 of the Convention. Concluding observations: United Kingdom of Great Britain and Northern Ireland.

19   Robinson, C. and Fielding, M. (2007) *Children and their Primary Schools: Pupils' Voices* (Primary Review Research Survey 5/3), Cambridge: University of Cambridge Faculty of Education.

20   Ruddock, J. and McIntyre, D. (2007) *Improving Learning through Consulting Pupils.* London: Routledge.

21   Rosenthal, R. and Jacobson, L. (1968) *Pygmalion in the Classroom: Teacher Expectation and Pupils' Intellectual Ability.* New York: Holt, Rinehart and Winston; see also Hurn, C. J. (1978) *The Limits and Possibilities of Schooling.* Boston, MA: Allyn & Bacon Inc. Rosenthal's and Jacobson's findings are not uncontentious, however. Wineburg (1987) indicates that their research contained several flaws, has not been able to be replicated, and owes its high profile to its concordance with a political crest of a wave – the time was ripe for such research findings when they appeared. See Wineburg, S. S. (1987) The self-fulfilment of the self-fulfilling prophecy. *Educational Researcher* 16(9), 28–37.

22   For example, Mortimore, P., Sammons, P., Stoll, L., Lewis, D. and Ecob, R. (1988) *School Matters: The Junior Years.* Shepton Mallet: Open Books; Reynolds, D. and Cuttance, P. (1992) *School Effectiveness: Research, Policy and Practice.* London: Cassell; Sammons, P., Hillman, J. and Mortimore, P. (1995) *Key Characteristics of Effective Schools: A Review of School Effectiveness Research.* Report by the Institute of Education, University of London for the Office for Standards in

Education; Reynolds, D., Sammons, P., Stoll, L., Barber, M. and Hillman, J. (1996) School effectiveness and school improvement in the United Kingdom. *School Effectiveness and School Improvement*, 7(2), 133–58; Teddlie, C. and Reynolds, D. (eds) (2000) *The International Handbook of School Effectiveness Research*. London: RoutledgeFalmer; Reynolds, D., Hopkins, D., Potter, D. and Chapman, C. (2001) *School Improvement for Schools Facing Challenging Circumstances*. London: Department for Education and Skills.

23 Deem, R. (1978) *Women and Schooling*. London: Routledge & Kegan Paul.

24 *Ibid.*

25 Delamont, S. (1980) *Sex Roles and the School*. London: Methuen.

26 Spender, D. (1980) *Man Made Language*. London: Routledge & Kegan Paul.

27 Byrne, E. (1978) *Women and Education*. London: Tavistock.

28 McFarlane (1986) *Hidden Messages?* Birmingham: Development Education Centre.

29 Department for Education and Skills (2002) *Gender and Achievement*. www.standards.dfes.gov.uk/genderandachievement

30 Department for Children, Schools and Families (2008) Gender and achievement website. Retrieved 28 August 2008 from http://www.standards.dfes.gov.uk/genderandachievement/

31 Department for Children, Schools and Families (2008) Retrieved 28 August 2008 from http://www.dcsf.gov.uk/rsgateway/DB/SFR/s000806/index.shtml

32 Qualifications and Assessment Authority (2002) *Summary of National Sample Data*. www.qca.org.uk/ca/foundation/baseline/summary_data.asp

33 Department for Education and Skills (2002) *Statistics of Education: Permanent Exclusions from Maintained Schools in England*. Issue 09/02. London: The Stationery Office, p. 14.

34 Department for Education and Skills (2002) *Gender and Achievement: The Tool Kit*. www.standards.dfes.gov.uk/genderandachievement/goodpractice

35 Serbin, L. (1978) Teachers, peers and play preferences, in B. Spring (ed.) *Perspectives on Non-sexist Early Childhood Education*. Columbia University: Teachers College Press, pp. 243–51.

36 Stanworth, M. (1981) *Gender and Schooling: A Study of Sexual Divisions in the Classroom*. London: Women's Research and Resources Centre Publications.

37 Myers, K. (1987) *Genderwatch*. London: School Curriculum Development Committee, p. 26.

38 *Ibid.*, pp. 126–7.

39 Arnot, M. (2000) Equal opportunities and educational performance: gender, race and class, in J. Beck and M. Earl (eds) *Key Issues in Secondary Education*. London: Cassell, p. 80.

40 *Ibid.*, p. 81.

41 Equal Opportunities Commission (1984) *op. cit.*, p. 7.

42 Myers, K. (1987) *op. cit.*, p. 70.

43 *Ibid.*, p. 90.

44 *Ibid.*, p. 96.

45 McFarlane, C. and Sinclair, S. (1986) *A Sense of School*. Birmingham: Development Education Centre, p. 29.

46 Rogers, C. (1965) *Client Centred Therapy*. Boston, MA: Houghton Mifflin Co., p. 389.

47 Brandes, D. and Ginnis, P. (1986) *A Guide to Student-centred Learning*. Oxford: Basil Blackwell, p. 26.

48 ESRC (2009) Ethnic minorities in the UK. Accessed 10 February 2009 from http://www.esrcsocietytoday.ac.uk/ESRCInfoCentre/facts/UK/index39.aspx?ComponentId=12534&SourcePageId=18133

49 Department for Children, Schools and Families (2009) National Statistics First Release, accessed 10 February 2009 from http://www.dcsf.gov.uk/rsgateway/DB/SFR/s000759/index.shtml

50 Department of Education and Science (1985) *Education for All* (Swann Report). London: HMSO.

51 Gaine, C. (1991) What do we call people? in E. Newman and P. Triggs (eds) *Equal Opportunities in the Primary School*. Bristol Polytechnic.

52 Inner London Education Authority (1983) *Race, Sex and Class 3: A Policy for Equality*. London: ILEA.

53 The Race Relations Act 1976. London: HMSO; see also the Commission for Racial Equality (1989) *Code of Practice for the Elimination of Racial Discrimination in Education*. London: CRE.

54 Qualifications and Curriculum Authority (2003) *Respect for All: Valuing Diversity and Challenging Racism through the Curriculum*. London: QCA. www.qca.org.uk/ca/inclusion/respect_for_all/index.asp

55 Qualifications and Curriculum Authority (2003) *Respect for All: Information and Communication Technology (ICT) Curriculum.* London: QCA. www.qca.org.uk/ca/inclusion/respect_for_all/ict/good_practice.asp

56 Qualifications and Curriculum Authority (2003) *Respect for All: Valuing Diversity and Challenging Racism through the Curriculum.* London: QCA. www.qca.org.uk/ca/inclusion/respect_for_all/rationale.asp

57 Runnymede Trust (2000) *op. cit.*

58 Jones, R. (1999) *Teaching Racism or Tackling It.* Stoke-on-Trent: Trentham.

59 *Ibid.*

60 *Ibid.*, p. 4.

61 *Ibid.*, p. 5.

62 The Runnymede Trust provides examples of how the curriculum can be reformed to take fuller account of multiculturalism, cultural diversity and anti-racist principles, for example in PSHE, history, citizenship, English and across the whole curriculum. See, for example, Runnymede Trust (2000) *op. cit.*

63 Jeffcoate, R. (1979) A multicultural curriculum: beyond the orthodoxy. *Trends in Education* 4, 8–12; see also Gerzina, G. (1996) *Black Britain: Life Before Emancipation.* London: John Murray.

64 See also McFarlane, C. (1986) *op. cit.*

65 QCA (2003) *Respect for All: Valuing Diversity and Challenging Racism through the Curriculum.*

66 McFarlane, C. (1986) *op. cit.*

67 Tylor, E. B. (1871) *Primitive Culture.* London: Murray.

68 Linton, R. (ed.) (1940) *Acculturation.* New York: Appleton-Century-Crofts.

69 Gundura, J. (1982) Approaches to multicultural education, in Tierney, J. (ed.) *Race, Migration and Schooling.* Eastbourne: Holt, Rinehart and Winston, pp. 108–19.

70 Saunders, M. (1981) *Multicultural Teaching: A Guide for the Classroom.* Maidenhead: McGraw-Hill.

71 National Curriculum Council (1991) *Circular 11: Linguistic Diversity and the National Curriculum.* York: National Curriculum Council.

72 The book from the Runnymede Trust (1993) *Equality Assurance in Schools.* London: Trentham Books for the Runnymede Trust is an accessible source that indicates matters of direct importance to student teachers.

73 Department for Education and Skills (2002) *Statistics of Education: Permanent Exclusions from Maintained Schools in England.* Issue 09/02, *op. cit.*, p. 14.

74 Runnymede Trust (2000) *op. cit.*, p. 6.

75 The Runnymede Trust (1993) *Equality Assurance in Schools.* London: Trentham Books for the Runnymede Trust.

76 Peccei, J. S. (2006) *Child language: A resource book for students.* London: Routledge, p. 37.

77 Reese, L., Garnier, H., Gallimore, R. and Goldenberg, C. (2000) Longitudinal analysis of the antecedents of emergent spanish literacy and middle-school english reading achievement of spanish-speaking students. *American Educational research Journal.*

78 Haslam, L., Wilkin, Y. and Kellet, E. (2005) *English as an Additional Language: Meeting the Challenge in the Classroom.* London: David Fulton.

79 This counters the comments that are frequently heard in all-white schools, viz. 'we don't have a multicultural problem here!'

80 Runnymede Trust (1993) *op. cit.*, p. 13.

81 This is the view that was espoused in the 1981 Education Act and which was echoed in two important documents from the National Curriculum Council in 1989 and 1992: National Curriculum Council (NCC) (1989) *A Curriculum for All* (Curriculum Guidance 2). York: NCC; National Curriculum Council (1992) *The National Curriculum and Pupils with Severe Learning Difficulties.* York: NCC, with regard to students with special educational needs and severe learning difficulties, respectively.

82 Office for Standards in Education (Ofsted) (1995) *Guidance on the Inspection of Secondary Schools.* London: Ofsted, p. 113; Office for Standards in Education (Ofsted) (1995) *Guidance on the Inspection of Nursery and Primary Schools.* London: Ofsted, p. 107.

83 Special Educational Needs and Disability Act 2001 (Part II, paras. 11–13).

84 Long, M. (2000) *The Psychology of Education*. London: RoutledgeFalmer, p. 299.

85 Department for Education and Skills (2003) *Definition of SEN*. www.file://A:DfES,SEN2.htm

86 Department for Education and Skills (2001) *Special Educational Needs Code of Practice*. London: The Stationery Office.

87 Croll, P. and Moses, D. (2000) *Special Needs in the Primary School*. London: Cassell, p. 33.

88 Children Act 1989. Section 17(11).

89 Disability Discrimination Act 1995. Section 1.1.

90 Department for Education and Skills (2001) *Special Educational Needs Code of Practice*, *op. cit.*, para. 1.5.

91 National Curriculum Council (1992) *The National Curriculum and Pupils with Severe Learning Difficulties*. York: NCC, p. 3.

92 Pringle, M. L. K., Rutter, M. and Davie, E. (1966) *11,000 Seven Year Olds*. Harlow: Longman; Fogelman, K. (1976) *Britain's Sixteen Year Olds*. London: National Children's Bureau; Rutter, M., Tizard, J. and Whitemore, K. (1970) *Education, Health and Behaviour*. Harlow: Longman.

93 Centre for the Study of Comprehensive Schools (1994) *Managing Special Educational Needs*. School of Education, University of Leicester, Centre for the Study of Comprehensive Schools and the National Association of Head Teachers, p. 2.

94 Department for Education and Skills (2001) *Special Educational Needs Code of Practice*, *op. cit.*, para. 1.2.

95 Hegarty, S., Pocklington, K. and Lucas, D. (1981) *Educating Pupils with Special Needs in the Ordinary School*. Windsor: NFER-Nelson. For a comprehensive account of the problems of categorisation, selection, assessment and provision for children with special educational needs, see A. Cohen and L. Cohen (eds) (1986) *Special Educational Needs in the Ordinary School: A Sourcebook for Teachers*. London: Harper & Row.

96 Hegarty, S., Pocklington, K. and Lucas, D. (1981) *ibid.*

97 Croll, P. and Moses, D. (2000) *op. cit.*, p. 61.

98 *Ibid.*, p. 67.

99 Department for Education and Skills (2001) *Inclusive Schooling*. London: The Stationery Office, para. 4.

100 Long, M. (2000) *op. cit.*, p. 320; Muijs, D. and Reynolds, D. (2001) *Effective Teaching*. London: Paul Chapman Publishing, p. 114.

101 Long, M. (2000) *op. cit.*, p. 320.

102 *Ibid.*, p. 319.

103 Reynolds, D. and Muijs, D. (2001) *op. cit.*, p. 115.

104 *Ibid.*, pp. 115–17.

105 *Ibid.*, p. 117.

106 Wade, B. and Moore, M. (1992) *Patterns of Educational Integration*. Wallingford: Triangle Books Ltd.

107 Hegarty, S., Pocklington, K. and Lucas, D. (1981) *op. cit.*

108 The Department for Education and Skills (2001) *Special Educational Needs Code of Practice*, *op. cit.*, sets out a clearly defined model for assessment and statementing of students.

109 Department for Education and Skills (2001) *Supporting the Target Setting Process*. London: The Stationery Office.

110 *Ibid.*

111 Department for Education and Skills (2001) *Special Educational Needs Code of Practice*, *op. cit.*, para. 4.15.

112 *Ibid.*, para. 5.10.

113 *Ibid.*, para. 6.9.

114 Qualifications and Curriculum Authority (QCA) (2008) Determining a school curriculum for pupils with learning difficulties. Retrieved 28 August 2008 from http://www.qca.org.uk/qca_1832.aspx

115 *Ibid.*

116 *Ibid.*

117 Lewis, A. and Norwich, B. (1999) Mapping a pedagogy for learning difficulties. Report presented to the British Educational Research Association (BERA). London: BERA.

118 National Curriculum Council (1992) *The National Curriculum and Pupils with Severe Learning Difficulties*, op. cit., p. 6.

119 For example, Department for Education (1995) *Mathematics in the National Curriculum*. London: HMSO, p. 1.

120 National Curriculum Council (1989) *A Curriculum for All* (Curriculum Guidance 2), op. cit., p. 6.

121 North American research by Davidson (1990) and Slavin (1990) has shown that very considerable benefit can be derived from co-operative group work in enhancing students' performance. See Davidson, N. (1990) Co-operative learning research in mathematics. Paper given at the IACSE 5th International Convention on Co-operative Learning. Baltimore, MD; Slavin, R. (1990) *Cooperative Learning: Theory, Research and Practice*. Englewood Cliffs, NJ: Prentice-Hall.

122 National Curriculum Council (1992) *The National Curriculum and Pupils with Severe Learning Difficulties*, op. cit., p. 5.

123 *Ibid.*, pp. 48–9.

124 Reynolds, D. and Muijs, D. (2001) op. cit., pp. 117–18.

125 *Ibid.*, pp. 118–20.

126 Department for Education and Skills (2001) *Inclusive Schooling*, op. cit., p. 19.

127 Long, M. (2000) op. cit., p. 293.

128 Muijs, D. and Reynolds, D. (2001) op. cit., pp. 119–20.

129 Department for Education and Skills (2001) *Inclusive Schooling*, op. cit., p. 16.

130 Garner, P. and Sandow, S. (eds) (1995) *Advocacy, Self-advocacy and Special Needs*. London: David Fulton Publishers.

131 Fine, M. (1987) Silencing in public schools. *Language Arts*, 64(2), 157–74.

132 Hohmann, M., Bunet, B., Weikart, D. W. (1979) *Young Children in Action*. Ypsilanti, MI: High Scope Press.

133 Zimiles, H. (1987) Progressive education: on the limits of evaluation and the development of empowerment. *Teachers College Record*, 89(2), 201–17.

134 Qualifications and Curriculum Authority (2002) *Guidance on Teaching the Gifted and Talented: What Does 'Gifted' and 'Talented' Mean?* London: QCA. www.nc.uk.net/gt/general/index.htm

135 Davis, G. A. and Rimm, S. B. (1998) *Education of the Gifted and Talented* (4th edition). Boston, MA: Allyn & Bacon.

136 Qualifications and Curriculum Authority (2002) *Guidance on Teaching the Gifted and Talented: Characteristics to Look for*. London: QCA. www.nc.uk.net/gt/general/01_characteristics.htm

137 *Ibid.*; see also Davis, G. A. and Rimm, S. B. (1998) op. cit., Chapter 13.

138 Davis, G. A. and Rimm, S. B. (1998) op. cit., p. 278.

139 Qualifications and Curriculum Authority (2002) *Guidance on Teaching the Gifted and Talented: Good Practice*. London: QCA. www.nc.uk.net/gt/general/01_identifying. htm, p. 1.

140 Qualifications and Curriculum Authority (2002) *Guidance on Teaching the Gifted and Talented: Developing an Effective Learning Environment*. London: QCA. www.nc.uk.net/gt/general/05_environment.htm, p. 1.

141 *Ibid.*, p. 2.

142 Davis, G. A. and Rimm, S. B. (1998) op. cit., Chapters 5 and 6.

143 *Ibid.*, p. 105.

144 Qualifications and Curriculum Authority (2002) *Guidance on Teaching the Gifted and Talented: Levels of Challenge and Differentiation*. London: QCA. www.nc.uk.net/gt/general/05_challenge.htm; see also Morrison, K. R. B. (1988) Planning for skills progression and assessment in primary schools. *Curriculum* 9(2), 74–83.

145 Qualifications and Curriculum Authority (2002) *Guidance on Teaching the Gifted and Talented: Helpful Approaches*. London: QCA. www.nc.uk.net/gt/general/05_helpful.htm; Qualifications and Curriculum Authority (2002) *Guidance on Teaching the Gifted and Talented: Assessment*. London: QCA. www.nc.uk.net/gt/general/05_assessment.htm

146 Qualifications and Curriculum Authority (2002) *Guidance on Teaching the Gifted and Talented: Helpful Approaches*, op. cit. www.nc.uk.net/gt/general/05_helpful.htm, p. 2.

14 Managing Behaviour in the Classroom

1   Office for Standards in Education (2001) *Improving Attendance and Behaviour in Secondary Schools*. London: Ofsted.

2   *Ibid.*, p. 20.

3   Chaplain, R. (2006) Classroom management, in J. Arthur, T. Grainger and D. Wray, *Learning to Teach in the Primary School*. London: Routledge.

4   Department of Education and Science (1989) *Discipline in Schools* (Elton Report). London: HMSO.

5   Hart, P., Wearing, A. and Conn, M. (1995) Conventional wisdom is a poor predictor of the relationship between student misbehaviour and teacher stress. *British Journal of Educational Psychology*, 65 (1), pp. 27–48.

6   Chaplain, R. (2003) *Teaching without Disruption in the Primary School: A Model for Managing Pupil Behaviour*. London: RoutledgeFalmer.

7   Docking, J. (1987*) Control and Discipline in Schools*. London: Harper & Row; Department of Education and Science (1989) *Discipline in Schools* (Elton Report), *op. cit.*; McGuiness, J. (1989) *A Whole School Approach to Pastoral Care*. London: Kogan Page; Docking, J. (1990) *Managing Behaviour in the Primary School*. London: David Fulton; Galvin, P., Mercia, S. and Costa, P. (1990) *Building a Better Behaved School*, Harlow: Longman; Thompson, D. and Arora, T. (1991) Why do students bully? An evaluation of the long-term effectiveness of a whole-school policy to minimize bullying. *Pastoral Care in Education*, 9(4), 8–12; Topping, K. (1992) School-based behaviour management work with families. *Pastoral Care in Education*, 10(1), 7–17; Canter, L. and Canter, M. (1992) *Assertive Discipline*. London: Lee Canter Associates; Munn, P., Johnstone, M. and Chalmers, V. (1992) *Effective Discipline in Primary Schools and Classrooms*. London: Paul Chapman Publishing; Boulton, M. (1993) Aggressive fighting in British middle school students. *Educational Studies*, 19(1), 19–40; McGuiness, J. (1993) *Teachers, Pupils and Behaviour – A Managerial Approach*. London: Cassell; Office for Standards in Education (1993) *Achieving Good Behaviour in Schools*. London: Ofsted; Miller, A. (1995) Teachers' attributions of causality, control and responsibility and its successful management. *Educational Psychology*, 15(4), 457–71; Porter, L. (2001) *Behaviour in Schools*. Buckingham: Open University Press; Muijs, D. and Reynolds, D. (2001) *Effective Teaching*. London: Paul Chapman Publishing; Wolfgang, C. H. (2001) *Solving Discipline and Classroom Management Problems* (2nd edition). New York: John Wiley and Sons; Thompson, D., Arora, T. and Sharp, S. (2002) *Bullying: Effective Strategies for Long-term Improvement*. London: RoutledgeFalmer; Corrie, L. (2002) *Investigating Troublesome Classroom Behaviour*. London: RoutledgeFalmer; Steer, A. (2005) *Learning Behaviour: The Report of the Practitioners' Group on School Behaviour and Discipline*. London: DCSF.

8   Office for Standards in Education (1999) *Principles into Practice: Effective Education for Pupils with Emotional and Behavioural Difficulties*. London: Ofsted , para. 104.

9   For example, the Elton Report (Department of Education and Science 1989, *op. cit.*); Mortimore, P., Sammons, P., Stoll, L., Lewis, D. and Ecob, R. (1988) *School Matters: The Junior Years*. Salisbury: Open Books; Galvin, P., Mercia, S. and Costa, P. (1990) *Building a Better Behaved School*. Harlow: Longman.

10   Slee, R. (1995) *Changing Theories and Practices of Discipline*. London: Falmer Press.

11   Office for Standards in Education (1993) *op. cit.*; Department for Education (1994) *Pupil Behaviour and Discipline*. Circular 8/94. London: HMSO; Department for Education (1994) *The Education of Children with Emotional and Behavioural Difficulties*. London: HMSO; Morrison, K. R. B. (1996) Developing a whole-school behaviour policy in primary schools. *Pastoral Care in Education*, 14(1), 22–30; Office for Standards in Education (2001) *op. cit.*

12   Morrison, K. R. B. (1996) *op. cit.*

13   Chaplain, R. (2003) *op. cit.*

14   *Ibid.*

15   *Ibid.*

16   *Ibid.*

17   Wragg, E. C. (1981) *Class Management and Control: A Teaching Skills Workbook*. DES Teacher Education Project, Focus Books; Series Editor Trevor Kerry. London: Macmillan.

18   Office for Standards in Education (1993; 1999; 2001) *op. cit.*; Morrison, K. R. B. (1996) *op. cit.*

19   Scottish Department of Education (1989) *Good Discipline*. Edinburgh: Scottish Department of Education.

20   Department of Education and Science (1989) *Education Observed 5: Good Behaviour and Discipline in Schools*. London: HMSO.

21   Galton, M., Simon, B. and Croll, P. (eds) (1980) *Progress and Performance in the Primary Classroom*. London: Routledge & Kegan Paul.

22   Wragg, E. C. (2001) *Class Management in the Secondary School*. London: RoutledgeFalmer, pp. 61–2.

23   Kyriacou, C. (1998) *Essential Teaching Skills* (2nd edition). Cheltenham: Stanley Thornes, p. 87.

24   Kershner, R. and Pointon, P. (2000) Children's views of the primary classroom as an environment for working and learning. *Research in Education*, 64, 64–77.

25   Evertson, C. and Emmer, E. (1982) Effective management at the beginning of the school year in junior high classes. *Journal of Educational Psychology*, 74(4), 485–98.

26   Arends, R. I. (1998) *Learning to Teach*. Boston, MA: McGraw-Hill.

27   Wragg, E. C. (1981) *op. cit.*

28   Cf. Porter, L. (2001) *op. cit.*

29   *Ibid.*; see also Long, M. (2000) *The Psychology of Education*. London: RoutledgeFalmer, Chapter 11.

30   Charles, C. M. (2002) *Building Classroom Discipline* (7th edition). Boston, MA: Allyn & Bacon, pp. 18–19.

31   *Ibid.*, pp. 22–3.

32   *Ibid.*, p. 24.

33   *Ibid.*, pp. 26–7.

34   *Ibid.*, pp. 29–30.

35   *Ibid.*, pp. 207–8.

36   Cf. Charles, C. M. (2002) *op. cit.*; Long, M. (2000) *op. cit.*

37   Wolfgang, C. H. (2001) *op. cit.*; Charles, C. M. (2002) *op. cit.*; Porter, L. *Behaviour in Schools: Theory and Practice for Teachers*. Buckingham: Open University Press.

38   The following paragraph draws on the work of Wolfgang, C. H. (2001) *op. cit.*

39   Evans, J., Harden, A., Thomas, J. and Benefield, P. (2003) Support for pupils with emotional and behavioural difficulties (EBD) in mainstream primary classrooms: a systematic review of the effectiveness of interventions, in *Research Evidence in Education Library*. London: EPPI-Centre, Social Science Research Unit, Institute of Education, University of London.

40   Chaplain (2003) *op cit.*

41   Wragg, E. C. (1981) *op. cit.*

42   Glasser, W. (1969) *Schools without Failure*. New York: Harper & Row.

43   Wragg, E. C. (1981) *op. cit.*

44   Gannaway, H. (1976) Making sense of school, in M. Stubbs and S. Delamont (eds) *Explorations in Classroom Observation*. London: John Wiley.

45   Meighan, R. (1981) *A Sociology of Educating*. Eastbourne: Holt, Rinehart and Winston.

46   Ruddock, J., Chaplain, R. and Wallace, G. (1995) *School Improvement: What Can Pupils Tell Us?* London: David Fulton.

47   Fontana, D. (1985) *Classroom Control: Understanding and Guiding Classroom Behaviour*. London: British Psychological Society and Methuen.

48   Kyriacou, C. (1998) *op. cit.*, pp. 80–1.

49   Saunders, M. (1979) *Class Control and Behaviour Problems: A Guide for Teachers*. Maidenhead: McGraw-Hill.

50   Gnagey, W. J. (1981) *Motivating Classroom Discipline*. New York: Macmillan; London: Collier-Macmillan.

51   Gnagey, W. J. (1980) Locus of control, motives and crime prevention attitudes of classroom facilitators and inhibitors. Paper read at American Educational Research Association, Boston.

52   Dierenfield, R. B. (1982) *Classroom Disruption in English Comprehensive Schools*. Saint Paul, MN: Macalester College Education Department.

53   Watkins, C. and Wagner, P. (1987) *School Discipline: A Whole-school Approach*. Oxford: Basil Blackwell.

54   Hargreaves, D. H. (1972) *Interpersonal Relations in Education*. London: Routledge & Kegan Paul.

55   McIntyre, R. W. (1974) Guidelines for using behaviour modification in education, in R. Ulrich, T. Stachnik and J. Mabry (eds) *Control of Human Behaviour*, vol. 3. Glenview, IL: Scott, Foresman.

56   Madsen, C. H. (Jnr), Becker, W. C. and Thomas, D. R. (1968) Rules, praise and ignoring: elements of elementary classroom control. *Journal of Applied Behaviour Analysis*, 1, 139–50.

57   Hargreaves, D. H. (1972) *op. cit.*

58   Wragg, E. C. and Wood, E. K. (1984) Teachers' first encounters with their classes, in E. C. Wragg (ed.) *Classroom Teaching Skills*. London: Croom Helm, p. 67.

59   Wragg, E. C. (1984) *Classroom Teaching Skills*: London: Croom Helm, quoted in J. Davison (1999) Managing classroom behaviour, in S. Capel, M. Leask and T. Turner (eds) *Learning to Teach in the Secondary School* (2nd edition). London: Routledge, pp. 123–4.

60   For example Chaplain (2003); Canter, L. and Canter, M. (2001) *Assertive Discipline: A Take Charge Approach for Today's Educator*, Los Angeles: Lee Canter Associates.; Glasser, W. (1988) *Choice Theory in the Classroom*. New York: Quill/HarperCollins.

61   Denscombe, M. (1985) *Classroom Control: A Sociological Perspective*. London: George Allen & Unwin.

62   Kyriacou, C. (1998) *op. cit.*, pp. 86–7.

63   Good, T. L. and Brophy, J. E. (1973) *Looking in Classrooms*. New York: Harper & Row.

64   Kounin, J. S. (1970) *Discipline and Group Management in Classrooms*. New York: Holt, Rinehart and Winston.

65   Peters, R. S. (1966) *Ethics and Education*. London: George Allen & Unwin.

66   Brown, G. A. (1975) *Microteaching*. London: Methuen.

67   Good, T. L. and Brophy, J. E. (1973) *op. cit.*

68   Muijs, D. and Reynolds, D. (2001) *op. cit.*, p. 47.

69   Madsen, C. H. Jnr, Becker, W. C. and Thomas, D. R. (1968) *op. cit.*

70   Denscombe, M. (1985) *op. cit.*

71   Robertson, J. (1996) *Effective Classroom Control: Understanding Teacher–student Relationships*. London: Hodder & Stoughton.

72   Kounin, J. S. (1970) *op. cit.*

73   Good, T. L. and Brophy, J. E. (1973) *op. cit.*

74   Saunders, M. (1979) *op. cit.* Boxes 88 and 89 are adapted from Saunders (1979).

75   Watkins, C. and Wagner, P. (1987) *op. cit.*

76   Kyriacou, C. (1998) *op. cit.*, pp. 97–8.

77   Kounin, J. S. (1970) *op. cit.*

78   Gnagey, W. J. (1980) *op. cit.*

79   Kounin, J. S. and Gump, P. V. (1958) The ripple effect in discipline. *Elementary School Journal*, 35, 158–62.

80   Kounin, J. S., Gump, P. V. and Ryan, J. J. (1961) Explorations in classroom management. *Journal of Teacher Education*, 12, 235–47.

81   Marland, M. (1975) *The Craft of the Classroom*. London: Heinemann Educational.

82   Peters, R. S. (1966) *op. cit.*

83   Waller, W. (1932) *The Sociology of Teaching*. New York: John Wiley.

84   Kyriacou, C. (1998) *op. cit.*, pp. 89–91.

85   O'Leary, K. D., Kaufman, K. F., Kass, R. E. and Drabman, R. S. (1970) The effects of loud and soft reprimands on the behaviour of disruptive students. *Exceptional Students*, 37, October, 45–55.

86   Deci, E. L. and Ryan, R. M. (2000) The 'what' and 'why' of goal pursuits: human needs and the self-determination of behavior. *Psychological Inquiry*, 11, 227–68.

87   Burns, R. B. (1978) The relative effectiveness of various incentives and deterrents as judged by pupils and teachers. *Educational Studies*, 4(3), 229–43. Box 90 is an adaptation from Burns (1978).

88   Cf. Kyriacou, C. (1998) *op. cit.*, p. 93; Muijs, D. and Reynolds, D. (2001) *op. cit.*, pp. 52–3.

89   Office for Standards in Education (1999) *op. cit.*, para. 108.

90   *Ibid.*, para. 110.

91   Merrett, F. and Jones, L. (1994) Rules, sanctions and rewards in primary schools. *Educational Studies*, 20(3), 345–56.

92   Merrett, F. and Man Tang, W. (1994) The attitudes of British primary school pupils to praise, rewards, punishments and reprimands. *British Journal of Educational Psychology*, 64, 91–103.

93   Capel, S. (1999) Motivating pupils, in S. Capel, M. Leask and T. Turner, *op. cit.*, p. 113.

94   Madsen, C. H. Jnr, Becker, W. C. and Thomas, D. R. (1968) *op. cit.*

95   Waller, W. (1932) *op. cit.*

96   Chaplain, R. (2000) Helping pupils to persevere and be well motivated, in D. Whitebread (ed.) *The Psychology of Teaching and Learning in the Primary School*. London: Routledge.

97   Merrett, F. and Man Tang, W. (1994) *op. cit.*

98   Office for Standards in Education (2001) *op. cit.*, para. 77.

99   Dunkin, M. J. and Biddle, B. J. (1974) *The Study of Teaching*. New York: Holt, Rinehart & Winston.

100   Bourne, J. (1994) *Thinking through Primary Practice*. Buckingham: Open University Press.

101   Merrett, F. and Jones, L. (1994) *op. cit.*

102   Department for Education and Science (1989) *op. cit.*

103   Wheldall, K. and Merrett, F. (1988) Which classroom behaviours do primary teachers say they find most troublesome? *Educational Review*, 40(1), 14–27.

104   Johnson, B., Oswald, M. and Adey, K. (1993) Discipline in South Australian primary schools. *Educational Studies*, 19(3), 289–305.

105   Jones, K., Charlton, T. and Wilkin, J. (1995) Classroom behaviours which first and middle school teachers in St Helena find troublesome. *Educational Studies*, 21(2), 139–53.

106   Charlton, T. and David, K. (1993) *Managing Misbehaviour in Schools*. London: Routledge.

107   Merrett, F. and Jones, L. (1994) *op. cit.*

108   Johnson, B., Oswald, M. and Adey, K. (1993) *op. cit.*

109   Peters, R. S. (1966) *op. cit.*

110   *Ibid.*

111   Saunders, M. (1979) *op. cit.*

112   Kyriacou, C. (1998) *op. cit.*, pp. 93–4.

113   Good, T. L. and Brophy, J. E. (1973) *op. cit.*

114   Wright, D. (1973) The punishment of students, in B. Turner (ed.) *Discipline in Schools*. London: Ward Lock Educational.

115   *Ibid.*

116   Evans, J., Harden, A., Thomas, J. and Benefield, P. (2003) *op. cit.*

117   Thomas, D. R., Becker, W. C. and Armstrong, M. (1968) Production and elimination of disruptive classroom behaviour by systematically varying the teacher's behaviour. *Journal of Applied Behaviour Analysis*, 1, 35–45.

118   Lawrence, J., Steed, D. and Young, P. (1984) *Disruptive Students – Disruptive Schools?* London: Croom Helm.

119   See Merrett, F. (1993) *Encouragement Works Best*. London: David Fulton; and Chaplain, R. and Smith, S. (2006) *Challenging Behaviour*. London: Pearson Press, for a more detailed explanation of the application of this approach to the classroom.

120   Canter, L. and Canter, M. (1992) *Assertive Discipline*. London: Lee Canter Associates.

121   Porter, L. (2001) *op. cit.*, p. 21.

122   Nicholls, D. and Houghton, S. (1995) The effect of Canter's Assertive Discipline program on teacher and student behaviour. *British Journal of Educational Psychology*, 65(2), 197–210.

123   Robinson, G. and Maines, N. (1994) Who manages pupil behaviour? Assertive Discipline: a blunt instrument for a fine task. *Pastoral Care in Education*, 12(3), 30–5.

124   Martin, S. (1994) A preliminary evaluation of the adoption and implementation of Assertive Discipline at Robinson High School. *School Organisation*, 14(3), 321–9.

125   Wragg, E. C. (1981) *op. cit.*

126   Robertson, J. (1981) *Effective Classroom Control.* Sevenoaks: Hodder & Stoughton.

127   Reid, I. (1994) Inequality, Society and Education. Inaugural lecture, Loughborough University Department of Education, Loughborough; see also Department of Social Security (1994) *Households Below Average Income: A Statistical Analysis 1979– 1991/1992.* London: HMSO.

128   Carrington, B. (1986) Sport as a side-track: an analysis of West Indian involvement in extracurricular sport, in L. Cohen and A. Cohen (eds) *Multicultural Education: A Sourcebook for Teachers.* London: Harper & Row.

129   Green, P. A. (1982) Teachers' influence on the self-concept of ethnic minority pupils. Unpublished PhD thesis, University of Durham.

130   Rampton Committee (1981) *West Indian Children in Our Schools*, Interim Report. London: HMSO.

131   Wragg, E. C. and Dooley, P. A. (1984) Class management during teaching practice, in E. C. Wragg (ed.) *Classroom Teaching Skills.* London: Croom Helm, pp. 21–46.

132   Wragg, E. C. (1984) (ed.) *Classroom Teaching Skills.* London: Croom Helm.

133   Childline (2003) Bullying: How to Beat It. Paper presented at the conference at the Business Design Centre, Islington, London, 25 March. www.teachernet.gov.uk/teachingandlearning/resourcematerials/charities, see also Connexions (2001) *Bullying: A Reader for the Diploma for Connexions Personal Advisers.* Moorfoot, Sheffield: Connexions, p. 20.

134   Office for Standards in Education (2001) *op. cit.,* para. 89.

135   www.dfes.gov.uk/bullying/teachersindex.shtml, www.teachernet.gov.uk/management/workingwithothers/safeschools; www.teachernet.gov.uk/teachingandlearning/resourcematerials; see also Department for Education and Skills (2002) *Bullying: Don't Suffer in Silence.* London: The Stationery Office. The website of Childline is www.childline.org.uk

136   Connexions (2001) *op. cit.,* p. 16; Thompson, D., Arora, T. and Sharp, S. (2002) *Bullying: Effective Strategies for Long-term Improvement.* London: RoutledgeFalmer, p. 71.

137   Office for Standards in Education (2001) *op. cit.,* para. 89.

138   Childline (2003a) *Bullying: How to Beat It, op. cit.,* p. 2.

139   Heald, T. R. (1994) *Judgement in the Case between R. H. Walker and Derbyshire County Council.* Nottingham, County Court Records, p. 3.

140   Department for Education and Skills (2002) *Bullying: Don't Suffer in Silence, op. cit.,* p. 9.

141   Thompson, D., Arora, T. and Sharp, S. (2002) *op. cit.,* p. 58.

142   *Ibid.*

143   *Ibid.,* p. 69; Connexions (2001) *op. cit.,* p. 19; Department for Education and Skills (2002) *Bullying: Don't Suffer in Silence, op. cit.,* pp. 13–14.

144   Olweus, D. (1993) *Bullying in Schools: What We Know and What We Can Do.* Oxford: Blackwell.

145   Connexions (2001) *op. cit.,* p. 11.

146   Childline (2003b) *Bullying: Information for Teachers and Professionals Working with Young People.* London: Childline; Childline (2003c) *Bullying: Information for Primary School Pupils.* London: Childline. Childline (2003d) *Bullying: Information for Secondary School Pupils.* London: Childline.

147   Connexions (2001) *op. cit.,* p. 11; Department for Education and Skills (2002) *Bullying: Don't Suffer in Silence, op. cit.,* p. 11.

148   Department for Education and Skills (2002) *ibid.,* p. 11.

149   See Long, M. (2000) *op. cit.,* p. 286.

150   Department for Education and Skills (2002) *Bullying: Don't Suffer in Silence, op. cit.,* p. 10.

151   Childline (2003) *Bullying: How to Beat It, op. cit.,* p. 2.

152   Department for Education and Skills (2002) *Bullying: Don't Suffer in Silence, op. cit.,* p. 12.

153   Connexions (2001) *op. cit.,* pp. 12–13.

154   See Long, M. (2000) *op. cit.,* p. 289.

155   *Ibid.*

156   www.teachernet.gov.uk/management/workingwithothers/safeschools; see also Connexions (2001) *op. cit.,* p. 39.

157   Office for Standards in Education (2001) *op. cit.,* para. 90.

158   Department for Education and Skills (2002) *Bullying: Don't Suffer in Silence, op. cit.,* p. 22.

159 Connexions (2001) *op. cit.*, pp. 41–3; Department for Education and Skills (2002) *Bullying: Don't Suffer in Silence, op. cit.*; Childline (2003) *Bullying: How to Beat It, op. cit.*; www.teachernet.gov.uk/management/workingwithothers/safeschools
160 Connexions (2001) *op. cit.*
161 www.teachernet.gov.uk/management/workingwithothers/safeschools
162 Department for Education and Skills (2003) *Choosing Strategies for Reducing Bullying*. London: The Stationery Office. www.teachernet.gov.uk/management/workingwithothers/safeschools, p. 3.
163 *Ibid.*, p. 4.

15 Assessment

1 Office for Standards in Education (2003) *Good Assessment in Secondary Schools*. London: Ofsted, p. 2.
2 *Ibid.*, p. 4.
3 Lambert, D. and Lines, D. (2000) *Understanding Assessment*. London: RoutledgeFalmer, p. 4.
4 McLean, L. (1988) Possibilities and limitations in cross-national comparisons of educational achievement, in P. Broadfoot, R. Murphy and H. Torrance (eds) *Changing Educational Assessment*. London: Routledge; Harnisch, D. L. and Mabry, L. (1993) Issues in the development and evaluation of alternative assessments. *Journal of Curriculum Studies*, 25(2), 179–87.
5 Gipps, C. (1988) National assessment: a comparison of English and American trends, in P. Broadfoot *et al.*, *op. cit.*, pp. 53–64; Noah, H. J. and Eckstein, M. A. (1988) Trade-offs in examination policies: an international comparative perspective, in P. Broadfoot *et al.*, *op. cit.*, pp. 84–97.
6 Singh, J. S., Marimuthu, T. and Mukherjee, H. (1988) Learning motivation and work: a Malaysian perspective, in P. Broadfoot *et al.*, *op. cit.*, pp. 177–98.
7 Halsey, A. (1992) An international comparison of access to higher education, in D. Phillips (ed.) *Lessons of Cross-national Comparison in Education*. Wallingford: Triangle Books, pp. 11–36.
8 Okano, K. (1993) *School to Work Transition in Japan*. Clevedon: Multilingual Matters.
9 Harnisch, D. L. and Mabry, L. (1993) *op. cit.*
10 Harlen, W. (1994) Issues and approaches to quality assurance and quality control in assessment, in W. Harlen (ed.) *Enhancing Quality in Assessment*. London: Paul Chapman Publishing, pp. 2–10.
11 Harlen, W. and Deakin Crick, R. (2002) A systematic review of the impact of summative assessment and tests on students' motivation for learning (eppi-centre review, version 1.1*). *Research Evidence in Education Library*. Issue 1. Retrieved 9 January 2007, from http://eppi.ioe.ac.uk/cms/Default.aspx?tabid=108
12 Qualifications and Curriculum Authority (2009) Assessment. Accessed 13 February 2009 from http://www.qca.org.uk/qca_13581.aspx
13 Pennycuick, D. (1991) Moderation of continuous assessment systems in developing countries. *Compare*, 21(2), 145–52.
14 Nixon N. J. (1990) Assessment issues in relation to experience-based learning on placements within courses, in C. Bell and D. Harris (eds) *World Yearbook of Education and Assessment*. London: Kogan Page, p. 90.
15 Black, P. (1998) *Testing: Friend or Foe?* London: Falmer, p. 46.
16 Sacks, P. (1999) *Standardized Minds*. Cambridge, MA: Perseus Books.
17 Department of Education and Science (1984) *Records of Achievement: A Statement of Policy*. London: HMSO.
18 Law, B. (1984) *Uses and Abuses of Profiling*. London: Harper & Row.
19 Department of Education and Science (1991) *The National Record of Achievement*. London: HMSO.
20 Hargreaves, A. (1989) *Curriculum and Assessment Reform*. London: Basil Blackwell and Open University Press.
21 Law, B. (1984) *op. cit.*
22 Hargreaves, A. (1989) *op. cit.*
23 Tymms, P. B. (1999) *Baseline Assessment and Monitoring in Primary Schools*. London: David Fulton Publishers.
24 Office for Standards in Education (2003) *op. cit.*, p. 4.

25   Hall, K. (2001) Level descriptions and curriculum relatedness in English at Key Stage 1. *Educational Review*, 53(1), 47–56.

26   Bertram, T. and Pascal, C. (2002) Assessing what matters in the early years, in J. Fisher (ed.) *The Foundations of Learning*. Buckingham: Open University Press, pp. 87–101.

27   Ball, C. (1994) *Start Right: The Importance of Early Learning*. London: Royal Society of Arts, Science and Commerce.

28   Drummond, M. J. (1993) *Assessing Children's Learning*. London: David Fulton Publishers.

29   Cf. Hurst, V. and Lally, M. (1992) Assessment and the nursery curriculum, in G. Blenkin and A. V. Kelly (eds) *Assessment in Early Childhood Education*. London: Paul Chapman Publishing, p. 55; Drummond (1993) *op. cit.*, p. 10; Webber, B. (1996) *Assessment and Learning*, in T. David (ed.) *Teaching Young Children*. London: Paul Chapman Publishing, pp. 139–50.

30   Sparks Linfield, R. and Warwick, P. (1996) 'Do you know what MY name is?' Assessment in the early years: some examples from science, in D. Whitebread (ed.) *Teaching and Learning in the Early Years*. London: Routledge, pp. 81–98.

31   Webber, B. (1996) *op. cit.*, p. 143.

32   Black, P. (1998) *op. cit.*, pp. 16–17.

33   Task Group on Assessment and Testing (TGAT) (1987) *op. cit.*

34   Pollard, A., Broadfoot, P., Croll, P., Osborn, M. and Abbott, D. (1994) *Changing English Primary Schools?* London: Cassell.

35   Morrison, K. R. B. (1990) An ideological masquerade. *Forum*, 31(1), 7–8.

36   Nevo, D. (1995) *School-based Evaluation: A Dialogue for School Improvement*. Kidlington, Oxford: Pergamon.

37   Gipps, C. (1994) *Beyond Testing*. London: Falmer.

38   For example, School Curriculum and Assessment Authority (1995) *Consistency in Teacher Assessment*. London: SCAA.

39   McCallum, B., McAlister, S., Brown, M. and Gipps, C. (1993) Teacher assessment at Key Stage One. *Research Papers in Education*, 8(3), 305–27.

40   Tizard, B., Blatchford, P., Burke, J., Farquar, C. and Plewis, I. (1988) *Young Children at School in the Inner City*. London: Lawrence Erlbaum Associates; Hart, K., Johnson, D. C., Brown, M., Dickson, L. and Clarkson, R. (1989) *Children's Mathematical Frameworks: 8–13*. Windsor: NFER-Nelson.

41   Makins, V. (1995) Licence to convert a waiting room. *Times Educational Supplement*, 23 June, p. 6.

42   See, for example: Bennett, S. N., Desforges, C., Cockburn, A. and Wilkinson, B. (1984) *The Quality of Pupil Learning Experiences*. London: Lawrence Erlbaum Associates.

43   Wyse, D. and Torrance, H. (in press) The development and consequences of National Curriculum assessment for primary education in England. *Educational Research*.

44   Black, P. (1998) *op. cit*, pp. 76–7.

45   Haviland, J. (1988) *Take Care, Mr Baker!* London: Fourth Estate.

46   Department for Children, Schools and Families (2009) Assessing Pupils' Progress. Accessed 13 February 2009 from http://nationalstrategies.standards.dcsf.gov.uk/primary/assessment/assessingpupils progressapp

47   Department for Children, Schools and Families (2009) *Getting to Grips with Assessing Pupils' Progress*. Nottingham: DCSF Publications, p.2.

48   Department for Children, Schools and Families (2008) *The Assessment for Learning Strategy*. Nottingham: DCSF Publications, p. 4.

49   Department for Children, Schools and Families (2008) Assessment for learning. Retrieved 30 August 2008, from http://www.standards.dfes.gov.uk/primaryframework/assessment/dafl

50   *Ibid.*

51   Black, P. and Wiliam, D. (1998) *Inside the Black Box: Raising Standards through Classroom Assessment*. London: GL Assessment.

52   Nevo, D. (1995) *op. cit.*

53   Stiggins, J. C. and Conklin, N. F. (1992) *In Teachers' Hands: Investigating the Practice of Classroom Assessment*. New York: SUNY Press.

54 Gipps, C. (1990) *Assessment: A Teachers' Guide to the Issues*. London: Hodder & Stoughton, pp. 12–13.

55 Lambert, D. and Lines, D. (2000) *op. cit.*

56 Harlen, W. (1994) Introduction to W. Harlen (ed.) *Enhancing Quality in Assessment*. London: Paul Chapman Publishing.

57 Black, P. (1998) *op. cit.*, p. 42.

58 School Examination and Assessment Council (1990) *A Guide to Teacher Assessment Pack C: A Source Book of Teacher Assessment*. London: Heinemann for the School Examination and Assessment Council, p. 84.

59 For an introduction to the notion of the self-fulfilling prophesy see Hurn, C. (1977) *The Limits and Possibilities of Schooling*. Boston, MA: Allyn & Bacon.

60 Glaser, R. (1963) Instructional technology and the measurement of learning outcomes: some questions. *American Psychologist*, 18, pp. 519–21.

61 Cunningham, G. K. (1998) *Assessment in the Classroom*. London: Falmer.

62 Gipps, C. (1994), *op. cit.*, p. 81; Black, P. (1998) *op. cit.*, p. 64.

63 Wiggins, G. (1998) *Educative Assessment*. San Francisco, CA: Jossey-Bass, p. 46.

64 Proctor, A., Entwistle, M. Judge, B. and McKenzie-Murdoch, S. (1995) *Learning to Teach in the Primary Classroom*. London: Routledge.

65 Tombari, M. and Borich, G. (1999) *Authentic Assessment in the Classroom*. Upper Saddle River, NJ: Prentice-Hall.

66 Black, P. (1998) *op. cit.*, p. 41.

67 For example, School Curriculum and Assessment Authority (1995) *op. cit.*

68 Clear examples of this can be seen in Watts, A. (1995) Double entendre, *Times Educational Supplement*, 9 June, p. III; Hofkins, D. (1995) Cheating 'rife' in national tests. *Times Educational Supplement*, 16 June, p. 1; Maxwell, E. (1995) Anger intensifies over English tests marking. *Times Educational Supplement*, 30 June; Hofkins, D. (1995) English scripts sent back for remarking. *Times Educational Supplement*, 7 July, p. 2; Budge, D. (1995) Complaints pour in over national test results, *Times Educational Supplement*, 28 July, p. 1.

69 Harlen, W. (ed.) (1994) *Enhancing Quality in Assessment*. London: Paul Chapman Publishing.

70 For example, School Curriculum and Assessment Authority (1995) *op. cit.*

71 See Nuttall, D. (1987) The validity of assessments. *European Journal of Psychology of Education*, 11(2), 109–18; see also Black, P. (1998) *op. cit.*, pp. 38–9; Torrance, H. and Pryor, J. (1998) *Investigating Formative Assessment*. Buckingham: Open University Press, p. 17; Wedeen, P., Winter, J. and Broadfoot, P. (2002) *Assessment: What's in It for Schools?* London: RoutledgeFalmer, p. 64.

72 Gipps, C. (1990) *op. cit.*, pp. 87–94.

73 Hudson, B. (1973) *Assessment Techniques: An Introduction*. London: Methuen.

74 See, for example: Rosenthal, R. and Jacobson, L. (1968) *Pygmalion in the Classroom: Teacher Expectation and Pupils' Intellectual Ability*. New York: Holt, Rinehart & Winston; Good, T. L. and Brophy, J. E. (1974) The influence of teachers' attitudes and expectations on classroom behaviour, in R. H. Coop and K. White (eds) *Psychological Concepts in the Classroom*. New York: Harper & Row; Mortimore, P., Sammons, P., Stoll, L., Lewis, D. and Ecob, R. (1988) *School Matters: The Junior Years*. Salisbury: Open Books.

75 Lewis, D. G. (1974) *Assessment in Education*. London: University of London Press.

76 The Hawthorne Effect, wherein the act of assessment (or the research itself in the original study) can exert an effect on participants, regardless of the contents of the assessment, is discussed clearly in Hughes, J. A. (1976) *Sociological Analysis: Methods of Discovery*. Sunbury-on-Thames: Nelson, pp. 94–7.

77 Nash, R. (1976) *Teacher Expectations and Pupil Learning*. London: Routledge & Kegan Paul.

78 *Times Educational Supplement* (1995) Testing times for the timetable in Modedon Junior School. *TES*, 16 June, p. 6.

79 Black, P. (1998) *op. cit.*, p. 40.

80 Desforges, C. (1989) *Testing and Assessment*. London: Cassell.

81 Black, P. (1998) *op. cit.*, p. 50.

82 *Ibid.*, p. 50.

83   *Ibid.*, p. 50.
84   Task Group on Assessment and Testing (TGAT) (1987) *op. cit.*
85   Goulding, M. (1992) Let's hear it for the girls. *Times Educational Supplement*, 21 February, p. 38.
86   Sacks, P. (1999) *op. cit.*
87   Black, P. (1998) *op. cit.*, p. 67.
88   Mitchell, C. and Koshy, V. (1993) *Effective Teacher Assessment*. London: Hodder & Stoughton, p. 29.
89   Hall, K. (2001) *op. cit.*, p. 55.
90   Wedeen, P. *et al.* (2002) *op. cit.*, p. 22.
91   Gipps, C. (1994), *op. cit.*, Chapter 4.
92   For a fuller discussion of this see Gipps, C. (1994) *op. cit.* and Nevo, D. (1995) *op. cit.*
93   Lambert, D. (1995) Assessment and improving the quality of pupils' work, in S. Capel, M. Leask and T. Turner, *Learning to Teach in the Secondary School*. London: Routledge.
94   Sutton, R. (1993) *A Framework for Assessment* (2nd edition). Slough: NFER-Nelson, p. 48.
95   Mitchell, C. and Koshy, V. (1993), *op. cit.*, p. 38.
96   For all the texts cited here, see the publications catalogue of the Psychological Corporation. London: Psychological Corporation.
97   *Ibid.*
98   Cohen, L., Manion, L. and Morrison, K. R. B. (2000) *Research Methods in Education* (5th edition). London: RoutledgeFalmer.
99   Black, P. (1999) *op. cit.*, p. 119; Lambert, D. and Lines, D. (2000) *op. cit.*, p. 143.
100 Clarke, S. (2001) *Unlocking Formative Assessment*. London: Hodder & Stoughton, p. 55.
101 Cohen, L. *et al.* (2000) *op. cit.*
102 Task Group on Assessment and Testing (1987) *op. cit.*
103 For a discussion of item discriminability, see Cohen, L. *et al.* (2000) *op. cit.*
104 Nuttall, D. (1987) *op. cit.*; Cresswell, M. J. and Houston, J. G. (1991) Assessment of the National Curriculum – some fundamental considerations. *Educational Review*, 43(1), 63–78.
105 Bloom, B. (ed.) (1956) *Taxonomy of Educational Objectives, vol. 1: Cognitive Domain*. London: Longman.
106 Cunningham, G. K. (1998) *op. cit.*; Borich, G. (2002) *Study Guide for Educational Assessment*. Course documentation for the MSc in Education. Macau: Inter-University Institute of Macau.
107 Black, P. (1998) *op. cit.*, p. 83.
108 *Ibid.*, p. 83.
109 *Ibid.*, p. 94.
110 Cunningham, G. K. (1998) *op. cit.*; Borich, G. (2002) *op. cit.*
111 Borich, G. (2002) *op. cit.*
112 Cunningham, G. K. (1998) *op. cit.*; Borich, G. (2002) *op. cit.*
113 Borich, G. (2002) *op. cit.*
114 Cunningham, G. K. (1998) *op. cit.*; Borich, G. (2002) *op. cit.*
115 Cunningham, G. K. (1998) *op. cit.*
116 Black, P. (1998) *op. cit.*, p. 86.
117 Chase, C. I. (1974) *Measurement for Educational Evaluation*. Reading, MA: Addison-Wesley.
118 Lewis, D. G. (1974) *op. cit.*
119 Cunningham, G. K. (1998) *op. cit.*; Airasian, P. W. (2001) *op. cit.*
120 Airasian, P. W. (2001) *Classroom Assessment: Concepts and Applications* (4th edition). New York: McGraw-Hill, p. 218.
121 Wiggins, G. (1998) *op. cit.*, p. 154.
122 Airasian, P. W. (2001) *op. cit.*, pp. 222–3.
123 Harlen, W. (1994) *op. cit.*
124 Gipps, C. (1994) *op. cit.*
125 *Ibid.*
126 Haladyna, T. M. (1997) *Writing Test Items to Evaluate Higher Order Thinking*. Needham Heights, MA: Allyn & Bacon, Chapter 7; Tombari, M. and Borich, G. (1999) *op. cit.*, Chapter 9; Black, P. (1998) *op. cit.*, pp. 97–8; Airasian, P. W. (2001) *op. cit.*, p. 274; Stiggins, R. J. (2001) *op. cit.*, p. 469.

127 Stiggins, R. J. (2001) *op. cit.*, p. 467.
128 Wiggins, G. (1998) *op. cit.*, p. 190.
129 Tombari, M. and Borich, G. (1999) *op. cit.*
130 Haladyna, T. M. (1997), *op. cit.*, pp. 187–90.
131 Department for Education (1994) Circular 21/94. London: DFE.
132 Cf. Haladyna, T. M. (1997) *op. cit.*, p. 177; Wedeen, P. *et al.* (2002) *op. cit.*, p. 145.
133 Mitchell, C. and Koshy, V. (1993), *op. cit.*, p. 66.
134 Kyriacou, C. (1994) *Essential Teaching Skills*. London: Simon & Schuster, p. 37.
135 Cohen, L. *et al.* (2000) *op. cit.*
136 School Curriculum and Assessment Authority (1995) *op. cit.*
137 Lambert, D. (1995) An overview of assessment: principles and practice, in S. Capel, M. Leask and T. Turner, *op. cit.*, p. 275.
138 Lambert, D. (1995) Assessment and improving the quality of pupils' work, in S. Capel, M. Leask and T. Turner, *ibid.*, p. 296.
139 See also Morrison, K. R. B. (1990) The assessment of skills, in P. Neal and J. Palmer, *Environmental Education in the Primary School*. Oxford: Basil Blackwell, 92–7.
140 Lewis, D. G. (1974) *op. cit.*
141 Pollard, A. *et al.* (1994) indicated that 7-year-olds in 1992 showed less awareness of being assessed than 7-year-olds in 1991. See Pollard, A. *et al.*, *op. cit.*, p. 224.
142 School Examination and Assessment Council (1990) *op. cit.*, p. 16.
143 Davis, A. J. (1993) Matching and assessment. *Journal of Curriculum Studies*, 25(3), 267–79.
144 School Examination and Assessment Council (1990) *op. cit.*, p. 20.
145 Clarke, S. (2001) *op. cit.*, pp. 69–70; Lambert, D. and Lines, D. (2000) *op. cit.*, p. 137; Wedeen, P. *et al.* (2002) *op. cit.*, p. 101; Blanchard, J. (2002) *Teaching and Targets: Self-evaluation and School Improvement*. London: RoutledgeFalmer, p. 167; Ofsted (2003) *op. cit.*, p. 4.
146 Qualifications and Curriculum Authority (2001) *Feedback*. http://www.qca.org.uk/ca/5-14/afl/fb_notvery.asp
147 Airasian, P. W. (2001) *op. cit.*, p. 305.
148 Ofsted (2003) *op. cit.*, p. 29.
149 Wedeen, P. *et al.* (2002) *op. cit.*, p. 118.
150 Airasian, P. W. (2001) *op. cit.*, p. 42.
151 Ripley, M. and Walton, S. (2003) 'When ready' testing, in C. Richardson (ed.) *Whither Assessment?* London: Qualifications and Curriculum Authority, pp. 37–48.
152 Walker, A. (2003) Making technology count in formative and summative assessment, in C. Richardson (ed.) *Whither Assessment?* London: Qualifications and Curriculum Authority, pp. 67–75.
153 Collins, C., Ripley, M. and Roads, M. (2003) The opportunities for ICT in assessment, in C. Richardson (ed.) *Whither Assessment?* London: Qualifications and Curriculum Authority, pp. 49–65.

16 Record Keeping and Report Writing

1 Qualifications and Curriculum Authority (1999) *Keeping Track: Effective Ways of Recording Pupil Achievement to Help Raise Standards*. London: QCA, p. 2.
2 Clift, P., Weiner, G. and Wilson, E. (1981) *Record-keeping in Primary Schools*. Schools Council Research Studies. London: Methuen.
3 The Data Protection Act 1984. London: HMSO. See also The Data Protection Act 1998. These are interpreted for schools in Department for Education and Employment (2000) *Pupil Records and Reports*. Circular 15/2000. London: DfEE.
4 Department for Education and Employment (2000) *op. cit.* London: DfEE.
5 Teachernet (2009) Common Transfer File. Accessed 13 February 2009 from http://www.teachernet.gov.uk/management/atoz/c/commontransferfile/index.cfm?code=main
6 Department for Children, Schools and Families (2009) Assessing Pupils' Progress. Accessed 14 February 2009 from http://nationalstrategies.standards.dcsf.gov.uk/app

7   Barrs, M. and Johnson, G. (1993) *Record-keeping in the Primary School*. London: Hodder & Stoughton.

8   Qualifications and Curriculum Authority (1999) *op. cit.*, pp. 2–3.

9   Law, B. (1984) *Uses and Abuses of Profiling*. London: Harper & Row.

10   School Examination and Assessment Council (1990) *A Guide to Teacher Assessment. Pack C: A Source Book of Teacher Assessment*. London: Heinemann for the School Examination and Assessment Council, p. 38.

11   Qualifications and Curriculum Authority (1999) *op. cit.*, pp. 2–3.

12   Qualifications and Curriculum Authority (2003) *Report Writing: Working towards – Principles and Good Practice*. London: QCA, pp. 1–2. www.qca.org.uk/ca/tests/2003sample_reports.asp

13   The examples that follow were originally based closely on those provided by the Qualifications and Curriculum Authority (2003) as downloaded examples contained as hypertext links within the document from the QCA (2003) *Report Writing: Working towards – Principles and Good Practice*. London: QCA, pp. 1–2. www.qca.org.uk/ca/tests/2003sample_reports.asp. Examples of schools' work in connection with report writing can now be found at http://www.teachernet.gov.uk/casestudies/search.cfm

Bibliography

Adams, S. (1999) Dilbert. *Gazette Telegraph*, 14 October, p. 45.

Ager, R. (1998) *Information and Communications Technology in Primary Schools*. London: David Fulton Publishers.

Ager, R. (2000) *The Art of Information and Communications Technology for Teachers*. London: David Fulton Publishers.

Airasian, P. W. (2001) *Classroom Assessment: Concepts and Applications* (4th edition). New York: McGraw-Hill.

Alexander, R. J. (1984) *Primary Teaching*. Eastbourne: Holt, Rinehart & Winston.

Alexander, R. J. (1992) *Policy and Practice in Primary Education*. London: Routledge.

Alexander, R. J. (2000) *Culture and Pedagogy: International Comparisons in Primary Education*. Oxford: Blackwell.

Alexander, R. J. (ed.) (2009) *The Cambridge Primary Review Research Surveys*. London: Routledge.

Alexander, R. J., Doddington, C., Gray, J., Hargreaves, L., and Kershner, R. (eds) (2010) *The Cambridge Primary Review Research Surveys*. London: Routledge.

Alexander, R. J., Rose, J. and Woodhead, C. (1992) *Curriculum Organisation and Classroom Practice in Primary Schools*. London: Department of Education and Science.

Allen, I., Dover, K., Gaff, M., Gray, E., Griffiths, C., Ryall, N. and Toone, E. (1975) *Working an Integrated Day*. London: Ward Lock Educational.

Allen, J., Potter, J., Sharp, J. and Turvey, K. (2007) *Primary ICT: Knowledge, Understanding and Practice*. Exeter: Learning Matters.

American Psychological Association (1994) *Diagnostic and Statistical Manual of Mental Disorders* (4th edition). Washington, DC: American Psychological Association.

Amory, A., Naicker, K., Vincent, J. and Adams, C. (1999) The use of computer games as an educational tool: identification of appropriate game types and game elements. *British Journal of Educational Technology*, 30(4), 311–21.

Amundsen, C. (1993) The evolution of theory in distance education, in D. Keegan (ed.) *Theoretical Principles of Distance Education*. London: Routledge, pp. 61–79.

Andersen, P. and Andersen, J. (1982) Non-verbal immediacy in instruction, in L. L. Barker (ed.) *Communication in the Classroom*. Englewood Cliffs, NJ: Prentice-Hall, pp. 98–120.

Antifaiff, G. (2001) Integrating technology into the classroom. *Geometry Online Learning Center*, pp. 1–14. www.geometry.net/basic_i/integrating_technology_ into_the_classroom_teach_page_no_4.php

Arends, R. I. (1998) *Learning to Teach*. Boston, MA: McGraw-Hill.

Aries, P. (1973) *Centuries of Childhood*. Harmondsworth: Penguin.

Arnot, M. (2000) Equal opportunities and educational performance: gender, race and class, in J. Beck and M. Earl (eds) *Key Issues in Secondary Education*. London: Cassell, pp. 77–85.

Athey, C. (1990) *Extending Thought in Young Children*. London: Paul Chapman Publishing.

Axline, V. M. (1964) *Dibs in Search of Self*. Harmondsworth: Penguin.

Azevedo, R. and Bernard, R. (1995) Assessing the effects of feedback in computer-assisted learning. *British Journal of Educational Technology*, 26(1), 57–8.

Bailey, R. (2000) *Education in the Open Society: Karl Popper and Schooling*. Aldershot: Ashgate Publishing Ltd.

Baines, E., Blatchford, P. and Kutnick, P. (2003) Changes in grouping practices over primary and secondary school. *International Journal of Educational Research*, 39, 9–34.

Baker, R. (1987) Developing educational relevance in primary school science. *CASTME Journal*, 7(1), 28–39.

Baker, W., Hale, T. and Gifford, B. R. (1997) From theory to implementation: the mediated learning approach to computer-mediated instruction, learning and assessment. *Educom Review*, 32(5), 1–15.

Ball, C. (1994) *Start Right: The Importance of Early Learning*. London: Royal Society of Arts, Science and Commerce.

Ball, S. (1981) *Beachside Comprehensive*. London: Cambridge University Press.

Barnes, B. (1987) *Learning Styles in TVEI: Evaluation Report No. 3*. Leeds: Leeds University for the Manpower Services Commission.

Barnes, D. (1971) Language and learning in the classroom. *Journal of Curriculum Studies*, 3(1), 27–38.

Barrs, M. and Johnson, G. (1993) *Record-keeping in the Primary School*. London: Hodder & Stoughton.

Bates, A. W. (1993) *Technology, Open Learning and Distance Education*. London: Routledge.

Baumann, A. S., Bloomfield, A. and Roughton, L. (1997) *Becoming a Secondary School Teacher*. London: Hodder & Stoughton.

Bearne, E. (1998) *Making Progress in English*. London: Routledge.

Becker, H. J., Wong, Y. T. and Ravitz, J. L. (1999) *Computer Use and Pedagogy in Co-NECT Schools: A Comparative Study*. A research project of the Center for Research on Information Technology and Organizations (CRITO). University of California, Irvine http://www.crito.uci.edu/tlc/findings/co-nect/startpage.html

Becta (2008) *Harnessing Technology Review 2008: The Role of Technology and Its Impact on Education: Full report*. Coventry: Becta. Available at: http://industry.becta.org.uk/display.cfm?resID=38751&page=1646&catID=1627 [Accessed 25 November 2008].

Bennett, S. and Lockyer, L. (1999) *The Impact of Digital Technologies on Teaching and Learning in K-12 Education*. Final Report prepared for the Curriculum Corporation. Faculty of Education, University of Wollongong, 30 July. http://www.lea.co.nz/ICT/eResources/Impact_of_Digital_Technologies.pdf

Bennett, S. N., Andrea, J., Hegarty, P. and Wade, B. (1980) *Open Plan Schools: Teaching, Curriculum, Design*. Slough: National Foundation for Educational Research.

Bennett, S. N., Desforges, C., Cockburn, A. and Wilkinson, B. (1984) *The Quality of Pupil Learning Experiences*. London: Lawrence Erlbaum Associates.

Bennett, S. N. and Dunne, E. (1992) *Managing Classroom Groups*. Hemel Hempstead: Simon & Schuster.

Bennett, S. N., Wragg, E. C., Carré, C. G. and Carter, D. S. G. (1992) A longitudinal study of primary teachers' perceived competence in, and concerns about, National Curriculum implementation. *Research Papers in Education* 7(1), 53–78.

Bennett, S. W. (1995) The alternative science laboratory, in E. Boschmann (ed.) *The Electronic Classroom: A Handbook for Education in the Electronic Environment*. Medford, NJ: Learned Information, Inc., pp. 103–8

Benton Foundation (2001) *What's Working in Education*. Washington, DC. www.benton.org/Practice/Edu

Berman, L., Burkhill, S., Russell, S. and Rabinowicz, J. (2001) Education negligence. *Education and the Law*, 13(1), 51–67.

Bernstein, B. (1977) Class and pedagogies – visible and invisible, in B. Bernstein *Class, Codes and Control*, Vol. 3. London: Routledge & Kegan Paul.

Bertram, T. and Pascal, C. (2002) Assessing what matters in the early years, in J. Fisher (ed.) *The Foundations of Learning*. Buckingham: Open University Press, pp. 87–101.

Bialo, E. R. and Sivin-Kachala, J. (1996) *The Effectiveness of Technology in Schools: A Summary of Recent Research*. Washington, DC: Software Publishers Association.

Bierly, P. M. and Spender, J. C. (1995) Culture and high reliability organizations: the case of the nuclear submarine. *Journal of Management*, 21(4), 639–56.

Biggs, J. (1987) *Student Approaches to Learning and Studying*. Melbourne: Australian Council for Educational Research.

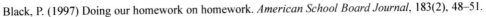

Black, P. (1997) Doing our homework on homework. *American School Board Journal*, 183(2), 48–51.

Black, P. (1998) *Testing: Friend or Foe?* London: Falmer.

Black, P. and Harrison, C. (2001) Feedback in questioning and marking: the science teacher's role in formative assessment. *School Science Review*, 82(301), 55–61.

Black, P. and Wiliam, D. (1998) Assessment and classroom learning. *Assessment in Education*, 5(1), 7–74.

Black, P. and Wiliam, D. (1998) *Inside the Black Box: Raising Standards through Classroom Assessment.* London: GL Assessment.

Blair, T. (1997) *Bringing Britain Together*, 8 December, www.cabinet-office.gov.uk/seu/index/more.html

Blakemore, S. J. and Frith, U. (2000) The implications of recent developments in neuroscience for research on teaching and learning. Report to the UK ESRC's Teaching and Learning Research Programme. www.tlrp.org/acadpub/Blakemore2000.pdf

Blanchard, J. (2002) *Teaching and Targets: Self-evaluation and School Improvement.* London: RoutledgeFalmer.

Blatchford, P., Kutnick, P., Baines, E. and Galton, M. (2003) Toward a social pedagogy of classroom group work. *International Journal of Educational Research*, 39, 153–72.

Blenkin, G. and Kelly, A. V. (1981) *The Primary Curriculum*. London: Harper & Row.

Blenkin, G. and Kelly, A. V. (eds) (1994) *The National Curriculum and Early Years Learning: An Evaluation.* London: Paul Chapman Publishing.

Bloom, B., Krathwohl, D. and Masia, B. (1956) *Taxonomy of Educational Objectives. Vol. 1: Cognitive Domain*. London: Longman.

Blyth, W. A. L. (1965) *English Primary Education*, Vol. 1. London: Routledge & Kegan Paul.

Boaler, J. (1997) *Experiencing School Mathematics: Teaching Styles, Sex and Setting*. Buckingham: Open University Press.

Boaler, J. (1997) When even the winners are losers: evaluating the experience of 'top set' students. *Journal of Curriculum Studies*, 29(2), 165–82.

Boaler, J. and Wiliam, D. (2001) Setting, streaming and mixed-ability teaching, in J. Dillon and M. Maguire (eds) *op. cit.*, pp. 173–81.

Board of Education (1931) *Report of the Consultative Committee of the Board of Education on the Primary School*. London: Board of Education.

Boklaschuk, K. and Caisse, K. (2001) *Evaluation of Educational Websites*, 1–24. http://members.fortunecity.com/vqf99

Bonnett, M. (1986) Child-centredness and the problem of structure in project work. *Cambridge Journal of Education*, 16(1), 3–6.

Booth, I. G. (1998) *The Law and the Teacher*. University of Durham Whole School Issues PGCE Secondary Course document, 1997–8. Durham: School of Education, University of Durham.

Borich, G. (2002) *Study Guide for Educational Assessment*. Course documentation for the MSc. in Education. Macau: Inter-University Institute of Macau.

Boulton, M. (1993) Aggressive fighting in British middle school students. *Educational Studies*, 19(1), 19–40.

Bourdieu, P. (1976) The school as a conservative force, in R. Dale, G. Esland, M. MacDonald (eds) *Schooling and Capitalism*. London: Routledge & Kegan Paul in Association with the Open University, pp. 110–17.

Bourdieu, P. (1977) Cultural reproduction and educational reproduction, in J. Karabel and A. H. Halsey (eds) *Power and Ideology in Education*. London: Oxford University Press, pp. 487–511.

Bourne, J. (1994) *Thinking through Primary Practice*. Buckingham: Open University Press.

Brandes, D. and Ginnis, P. (1986) *A Guide to Student-centred Learning*. Oxford: Basil Blackwell.

Bredekamp, S. and Copple, A. (eds) (1997) *Developmentally Appropriate Practice in Early Childhood Programs* (revised edition). Washington, DC: National Association for the Education of Young Children.

Brighouse, T. and Tomlinson, J. (1991) *Successful Schools*. Education and Training Paper No. 4. London: Institute of Public Policy Research.

British Educational Communications and Technology Agency (BECTA) (2002) *Information Sheet: Parents, ICT and Education*, October. www.becta.org.uk/technology/infosheets/html/parents/html

Broadfoot, P., Daugherty, R., Gardner, J., Harlen, W., James, M. and Stobbart, G. (2002) *Assessment for Learning: 10 Principles*. Assessment Reform Goup/Nuffield.

Brooks, J. G. and Brooks, M. G. (1995) *The Case for Constructivist Classrooms*. Alexandria, VA: Association for Supervision and Curriculum Development.

Brooks, J. G. and Brooks, M. G. (1999) *In Search of Understanding: The Case for Constructivist Classrooms* (second edition). Alexandria, VA: Association for Supervision and Curriculum Development.

Brophy, J. E. and Good, T. L. (1970) Teachers' communications of differential expectations for children's classroom performance: some behavioural data. *Journal of Educational Psychology*, 61, 365–74.

Brophy, J. E. and Good, T. L. (1986) Teacher behavior and student achievement, in C. M. Wittrock (ed.) *Handbook of Research on Teaching* (3rd edition). New York: Macmillan, pp. 328–75.

Brown, G. A. (1975) *Microteaching*. London: Methuen.

Brown, G. A. and Armstrong, S. (1984) Explaining and explanations, in E. C. Wragg (ed.) *Classroom Teaching Skills*. London: Croom Helm, pp. 121–48.

Brown, G. A. and Edmonson, R. (1984) Asking questions, in E. C. Wragg (ed.) *Classroom Teaching Skills*. London: Croom Helm, pp. 97–120.

Brown, G. A. and Wragg, E. C. (1993) *Questioning*. London: Routledge.

Bruce, T. (1996) *Helping Young Children to Play*. London: Hodder & Stoughton.

Bruner, J. S. (1960) *The Process of Education*. New York: Random House.

Bruner, J. S. (1966) *Towards a Theory of Instruction*. Cambridge, MA: Harvard University Press.

Bruner, J. S. (1974) *Beyond the Information Given*. London: Allen & Unwin.

Bruner, J. S. (1986) *Actual Minds: Possible Worlds*. Cambridge, MA: Harvard University Press.

Bruntlett, S. (1999) Selecting, using and producing classroom-based multimedia, in M. Leask and N. Pachler (eds) *Learning To Teach Using ICT in the Secondary School*. London: Routledge, pp. 71–94.

Budge, D. (1995) Complaints pour in over national test results, *Times Educational Supplement*, 28 July, p. 1.

Bullock, A. (ed.) (1971) *The Twentieth Century*. London: Thames and Hudson.

Burchfield, M. L. (1995) The effect of computer-assisted instruction on the science process skills of community college students. Unpublished Ed. D., Mississippi State University.

Burke, K. A., Greenbowe, T. J. and Windschitl, M. A. (1998) Developing and using conceptual computer animations for chemistry instruction. *Journal of Chemical Education*, 75(12), 1658–61.

Burns, R. B. (1978) The relative effectiveness of various incentives and deterrents as judged by pupils and teachers. *Educational Studies*, 4(3), 229–43.

Burton, D. and Nicholls, G. (1999) Ways pupils learn, in S. Capel, M. Leask and T. Turner (eds) *Learning to Teach in the Secondary Schools* (2nd edition). London: Routledge, pp. 231–59.

Byrne, E. (1978) *Women and Education*. London: Tavistock.

Canter, L. and Canter, M. (1992) *Assertive Discipline*. London: Lee Canter Associates.

Capel, S. (1999) Motivating pupils, in S. Capel, M. Leask and T. Turner (eds) *Learning to Teach in the Secondary School* (2nd edition). London: Routledge, pp. 107–19.

Capel, S., Leask, M. and Turner, T. (eds) (1995) *Learning to Teach in the Secondary School*. London: Routledge.

Capel, S., Leask, M. and Turner, T. (eds) (1999) *Learning to Teach in the Secondary School* (2nd edition). London: Routledge.

Carlsen, W. (1991) Questioning in classrooms. *Review of Educational Research*, 61(2), 157–78.

Carrington, B. (1986) Sport as a side-track: an analysis of West Indian involvement in extra-curricular sport, in L. Cohen and A. Cohen (eds) *Multicultural Education: A Sourcebook for Teachers*. London: Harper & Row.

Castro, C. D. M. (1999) Education in the information age: promises and frustrations. *TechKnowLogia*, November/December, pp. 39–42.

Central Advisory Council for Education (1967) *Children and Their Primary Schools* (Plowden Report). London: HMSO.

Centre for the Study of Comprehensive Schools (1994) *Managing Special Educational Needs*. School of Education, University of Leicester, Centre for the Study of Comprehensive Schools and the National Association of Head Teachers.

Chaplain, R. (2000) Helping pupils to persevere and be well motivated, in D. Whitebread (ed.) *The Psychology of Teaching and Learning in the Primary School*. London: Routledge.

Chaplain, R. (2003) *Teaching without Disruption in the Primary School*. London: RoutledgeFalmer.

Chaplain, R. (2006) Classroom management, in J. Arthur, T. Grainger and D. Wray, *Learning to Teach in the Primary School*. London: Routledge.

Chaplain, R. (2008) Stress and psychological distress among trainee secondary teachers in England. *Educational Psychology*, 28(2), 195–209.

Chaplain, R. and Smith, S. (2006) *Challenging Behaviour*. London: Pearson Press.

Chapman, R. (1979) Schools do make a difference. *British Educational Research Journal*, 5(1), 115–24.

Charles, C. M. (2002) *Building Classroom Discipline* (7th edition). Boston, MA: Allyn & Bacon. Charlton, T. and David, K. (1993) *Managing Misbehaviour in Schools*. London: Routledge.

Chase, C. I. (1974) *Measurement for Educational Evaluation*. Reading, MA: Addison-Wesley.

Childline (2003) Bullying: How to Beat It. Paper presented at the conference at the Business Design Centre, Islington, London, 25 March. www.teachernet.gov.uk/teachingandlearning/resourcematerials/charities

Childline (2003) *Bullying: Information for Teachers and Professionals Working with Young People*. London: Childline.

Childline (2003) *Bullying: Information for Primary School Pupils*. London: Childline.

Childline (2003) *Bullying: Information for Secondary School Pupils*. London: Childline.

Children Act 1989. London: HMSO.

Clariana, R. B. (1997) Considering learning styles in computer-assisted learning. *British Journal of Educational Technology*, 28(1), 66–8.

Clarke, S. (2001) *Unlocking Formative Assessment*. London: Hodder & Stoughton.

Claxton, G. (1997) *Hare Brain, Tortoise Mind*. London: Fourth Estate.

Claxton, G. (2007) Expanding young people's capacity to learn. *British Journal of Educational Studies*, 55(2), 1–20.

Clift, P., Weiner, G. and Wilson, E. (1981) *Record-keeping in Primary Schools*. Schools Council Research Studies. London: Methuen.

Cohen, A. and Cohen, L. (eds) (1986) *Special Educational Needs in the Ordinary School: A Sourcebook for Teachers*. London: Harper & Row.

Cohen, E. (1994) Restructuring the classroom: conditions for productive small groups. *Review of Educational Research*, 64(1), 11–35.

Cohen, J. and Stewart, I. (1995) *The Collapse of Chaos*. Harmondsworth: Penguin.

Cohen, L. and Cohen, A. (eds) (1986) *Multicultural Education: A Sourcebook for Teachers*. London: Harper & Row.

Cohen, L., Manion, L. and Morrison, K. R. B. (2000) *Research Methods in Education* (5th edition). London: RoutledgeFalmer.

Collins, C., Ripley, M. and Roads, M. (2003) The opportunities for ICT in assessment, in C. Richardson (ed.) *Whither Assessment?* London: Qualifications and Curriculum Authority, pp. 49–65.

Collis, B., de Boer, W. and van der Veen, J. (2001) Building on learner contributions: a web-supported pedagogic strategy. *Educational Media International*, 38(4), 229–40.

Coltman, P. and Whitebread, D. (1996) 'My mum would pay anything for chocolate cake'. Organising the whole curriculum: enterprise projects in the early years, in D. Whitebread (ed.) *Teaching and Learning in the Early Years*. London: RoutledgeFalmer, pp. 55–79.

Combs, A. (1965) *The Professional Education of Teachers*. Boston, MA: Allyn & Bacon.

Commission for Racial Equality (1989) *Code of Practice for the Elimination of Racial Discrimination in Education*. London: Commission for Racial Equality.

Committee on the Rights of the Child (2002) Summary of the 811th meeting. Considerations of reports of state's parties: Second periodic report of the United Kingdom of Great Britain and Northern Ireland (CRC/C/83ADD.3) 10–14 June 2002. Accessed 18 November 2002 from http://www.unhcr.ch/data.htm [p. 3].

Condie, R. and Munro, B. (2006) *The Impact of ICT in Schools – A Landscape Review*. Literature review. Coventry: Becta Report: ICT impact 2006.

Connexions (2001) *Bullying: A Reader for the Diploma for Connexions Personal Advisers*. Sheffield: Connexions. http://www.connexions.gov.uk/partnerships/documents/Cnutmr11.pdf

Cooper, H. (1989) Synthesis of research on homework. *Educational Leadership*, 47(3), 58–91.

Cooper, P. and McIntyre, D. (1996) *Effective Teaching and Learning: Teachers' and Students' Perspectives*. Milton Keynes: Open University Press.

Corrie, L. (2002) *Investigating Troublesome Classroom Behaviour*. London: RoutledgeFalmer.

Cosgrove, J. (2000) *Breakdown: The Facts about Stress in Teaching*. London: RoutledgeFalmer.

Cox, M. J. (1999) Motivating pupils, in M. Leask and N. Pachler (eds) *Learning to Teach Using ICT in the Secondary School*. London: Routledge, pp. 19–35.

Cox, M., Webb, M., Abbott, C., Blakeley, B., Beauchamp, T. and Rhodes, V. (2003) *ICT and Pedagogy: A Review of the Research Literature*. London: DfES/Becta.

Cradler, J. (1994) *Summary of Current Research and Evaluation Findings on Technology and Education*. San Francisco, CA: Far West Laboratory. WestEd http://www.wested.org/techpolicy/refind.html

Cresswell, M. J. and Houston, J. G. (1991) Assessment of the National Curriculum: some fundamental considerations. *Educational Review*, 43(1), 63–78.

Croll, P. and Moses, D. (2000) *Special Needs in the Primary School*. London: Cassell.

Crook, C. (1994) *Computers and the Collaborative Experience of Learning*. London: Routledge.

Crowther, D. T. (ed.) The constructivist zone. *Electronic Journal of Science Education*, 2(2), 1–9.

Cullen, J., Hadjivassiliou, K., Hamilton, E., Kelleher, J., Sommerlad, E. and Stern, E. (2002) Review of the current pedagogical research and practice in the fields of post-compulsory education and lifelong learning. Final report submitted to the Economic and Social Research Council by the Tavistock Institute, February 2002. London: Tavistock Institute, p. 11.

Cunningham, G. K. (1998) *Assessment in the Classroom*. London: Falmer.

Data Protection Act 1984. London: HMSO.

Data Protection Act 1998. London: The Stationery Office.

David, T. (ed.) (1999) *Teaching Young Children*. London: Paul Chapman Publishing.

Davidson, N. (1990) Co-operative learning research in mathematics. Paper given at the IACSE 5th International Convention on Co-operative Learning, Baltimore, MA.

Davies, W. T. and Shepherd, T. B. (1949) *Teaching: Begin Here*. London: Epworth Press.

Davies, P., Telhaj, S., Hutton, D., Adnett, N. and Coe, R. (2008) Competition, cream-skimming and department performance within secondary schools. *British Educational Research Journal*. First Article, 1–17, pp. 1–16.

Davis, A. J. (1993) Matching and assessment. *Journal of Curriculum Studies*, 25 (3), 267–79.

Davis, G. A. and Rimm, S. B. (1998) *Education of the Gifted and Talented* (4th edition). Boston, MA: Allyn & Bacon.

Dawes, L. (2004) Talk and learning in classroom science. *International Journal of Science Education*, 26(6), 677–95.

Dawney, M. (1977) *Interpersonal Judgements in Education*. London: Harper & Row.

Dean, J. (1983) *Organising Learning in the Primary School Classroom*. Beckenham: Croom Helm (reprinted by Routledge 1988).

Dean, J. (1996) *Beginning Teaching in the Secondary School*. Buckingham: Open University Press.

Dearden, R. F. (1971) What is the integrated day?, in J. Walton (ed.) *The Integrated Day in Theory and Practice*. London: Ward Lock Educational, pp. 84–97.

Dearden, R. F. (1976) *Problems in Primary Education*. London: Routledge & Kegan Paul.

Deci, E. L. and Ryan, R. M. (2000) The 'what' and 'why' of goal pursuits: human needs and the self-determination of behavior. *Psychological Inquiry*, 11, 227–68.

Deem, R. (1978) *Women and Schooling*. London: Routledge & Kegan Paul.

Delamont, S. (1980) *Sex Roles and the School*. London: Methuen.

Denscombe, M. (1985) *Classroom Control: A Sociological Perspective*. London: George Allen & Unwin.

Department for Children, Schools and Families (2007) *Safe to Learn: Embedding Anti-bullying Work in Schools*. Nottingham: DCSF Publishing.

Department for Children, Schools and Families (2007) *The Children's Plan: Building Brighter Futures*. Norwich: HMSO, p.3

Department for Children, Schools and Families (2008) 14–19 education and skills. Retrieved 18 August 2008 from http://www.dcsf.gov.uk/14-19/index.cfm

Department for Children, Schools and Families (2008) About the national challenge. Retrieved 23 August 2008 from http://www.dcsf.gov.uk/nationalchallenge/

Department for Children, Schools and Families (2008) *Assessment for Learning*. Retrieved 30 August 2008 from http://www.standards.dfes.gov.uk/primaryframework/assessment/dafl

Department for Children, Schools and Families (2008) *Autumn Performance Report 2007: Achievement Against Public Service Agreement Targets*. Norwich: The Stationery Office.

Department for Children, Schools and Families (2008) *Every Child Matters: Change for Children*. Retrieved 4 September 2008 from http://www.everychildmatters.gov.uk/

Department for Children, Schools and Families (2008) *Gender and achievement website*. Retrieved 28 August 2008 from http://www.standards.dfes.gov.uk/genderandachievement/

Department for Children, Schools and Families (2008) *Improving Learning and Teaching*. Retrieved 20 August 2008 from http://www.standards.dfes.gov.uk/primaryframework/introduction/improving

Department for Children, Schools and Families (2008) *Overview of Learning – Year 6 – the Learner*. Retrieved 20 August 2008 from http://www.standards.dfes.gov.uk/primaryframework/introduction/overview/year6/learner

Department for Children, Schools and Families (2008) *Permanent and Fixed Period Exclusions from Schools in England 2006/07*. Retrieved 22 August 2008 from http://www.dcsf.gov.uk/rsgateway/DB/SFR/s000793/index.shtml

Department for Children, Schools and Families (2008) *Planning Principles*. Retrieved 25 August 2008 from http://www.standards.dfes.gov.uk/primaryframework/foundation/ppo

Department for Children, Schools and Families (2008) *Primary Framework for Literacy and Mathematics: Overview of Learning 3*. Accessed 20 August 2008 from http://www.standards.dfes.gov.uk/primaryframework/foundation/cll/cllplanning/lm3]

Department for Children, Schools and Families (2008) *Sample Planning and Exemplification*. Retrieved 25 August 2008 from http://www.standards.dcsf.gov.uk/secondary/framework/english/fwg/pufwse/pcs

Department for Children, Schools and Families (2008) *National Curriculum Assessments at Key Stage 1 in England, 2008*. Retrieved 28 August 2008 from http://www.dcsf.gov.uk/rsgateway/DB/SFR/s000806/index.shtml

Department for Children, Schools and Families (2008) *The Assessment for Learning Strategy*. Nottingham: DCSF Publications, p. 4.

Department for Children, Schools and Families (2009) *Assessing Pupils' Progress*. Accessed 13 February 2009 from http://nationalstrategies.standards.dcsf.gov.uk/primary/assessment/assessingpupilsprogressapp

Department for Children, Schools and Families (2009) *Getting to Grips with Assessing Pupils' Progress*. Nottingham: DCSF Publications.

Department for Children, Schools and Families (2009) *National Statistics. First Release*. Accessed 10 February 2009 from http://www.dcsf.gov.uk/rsgateway/DB/SFR/s000759/index.shtml

Department for Children, Schools and Families (2009) *The National Strategies*. Retrieved 1 March 2009 from http://nationalstrategies.standards.dcsf.gov.uk/

Department for Children, Schools and Families (2009) *Trends in Education and Skills*. Retrieved 11 August 2008 from: http://www.dcsf.gov.uk/trends/index.cfm?fuseaction=home.showIndicator&cid=3&iid=16

Department for Education (1992) *Choice and Diversity: A New Framework for Schools*. London: Her Majesty's Stationery Office.

Department for Education (1992) *Reporting Pupils' Achievement to Parents*. Circular 5/92. London: Her Majesty's Stationery Office.

Department for Education (1993) *Protection of Children: Disclosure of Criminal Background of those with Access to Children*. Circular 9/93. London: Department for Education.

Department for Education (1994) *The Education of Children with Emotional and Behavioural Difficulties*. Circular 9/94. London: Her Majesty's Stationery Office.

Department for Education (1994) *Pupil Behaviour and Discipline*. Circular 8/94. London: Her Majesty's Stationery Office.

Department for Education (1994) *Circular 21/94*. London: Her Majesty's Stationery Office.

Department for Education (1995) *Mathematics in the National Curriculum*. London: Her Majesty's Stationery Office.

Department for Education (2000) *Learning and Skills Act 2000*. London: The Stationery Office.

Department for Education (2001) *Schools Building on Success* (green paper). London: Department for Education.

Department for Education and Employment (1988) *Section 550a of the Education Act 1996: The Use of Force to Control or Restrain Pupils*. Circular 10/98. London: Her Majesty's Stationery Office.

Department for Education and Employment (1995) *Reports on Pupils' Achievements in 1994/95*. Circular 1/95. London: Her Majesty's Stationery Office.

Department for Education and Employment (1996) *Education Act 1996*. London: Her Majesty's Stationery Office.

Department for Education and Employment (1996) *Supporting Pupils with Medical Needs: A Good Practice Guide*. London: Department for Education and Employment.

Department for Education and Employment (1997) *Education Act 1997*. London: The Stationery Office.

Department for Education and Employment (1997) *Excellence in Schools. White Paper*. London: The Stationery Office.

Department for Education and Employment (1998) *Health and Safety of Pupils on Educational Visits*. London: The Stationery Office.

Department for Education and Employment (1998) *The National Literacy Strategy: Framework for Teaching*. London: The Stationery Office.

Department for Education and Employment (1998) *Reducing the Bureaucratic Burden on Teachers*. Circular 02/98. London: The Stationery Office.

Department for Education and Employment (1998) *School Standards and Framework Act 1998*. London: The Stationery Office.

Department for Education and Employment (1998) *Supporting the Target Setting Process*. Circular 11/98. London: The Stationery Office.

Department for Education and Employment (1999) *The National Curriculum: Handbook for Primary Teachers*. London: The Stationery Office.

Department for Education and Employment (1999) *The National Numeracy Strategy: Framework for Teaching Mathematics*. London: The Stationery Office.

Department for Education and Employment (1999) *Social Inclusion: Pupil Support*. Circular 10/99. London: The Stationery Office.

Department for Education and Employment (1999) *The Structure of the Literacy Hour*. www.standards.dfes.gov.uk/literacy/literacyhour

Department for Education and Employment (2000) *Pupils Records and Reports*. Circular 15/2000. London: The Stationery Office.

Department for Education and Employment (2000) *Curriculum Guidance for the Foundation Stage*. London: The Stationery Office.

Department for Education and Employment (2000) *National Standards for Headteachers*. London: The Stationery Office.

Department for Education and Employment (2001) *Schools: Building on Success*. London: The Stationery Office.

Department for Education and Employment/Qualifications and Curriculum Authority (1999) *The National Curriculum*. London: Qualifications and Curriculum Authority.

Department of Education and Science (1978) *Special Educational Needs* (Warnock Report). London: Her Majesty's Stationery Office.

Department of Education and Science (1981) *Curriculum 11–16: A Review of Progress*. London: Her Majesty's Stationery Office.

Department of Education and Science (1981) *Education Act 1981*. London: HMSO.

Department of Education and Science (1984) *Records of Achievement: A Statement of Policy*. London: Her Majesty's Stationery Office.

Department of Education and Science (1985) *Better Schools*. London: Her Majesty's Stationery Office.

Department of Education and Science (1985) *Education for All* (Swann Report). London: Her Majesty's Stationery Office.

Department of Education and Science (1985) *The Curriculum from 5 to 16*. Curriculum Matters 2. London: Her Majesty's Stationery Office.

Department of Education and Science (1988) *Education Reform Act 1988*. London: HMSO.

Department of Education and Science (1989) *Discipline in Schools* (Elton Report). London: Her Majesty's Stationery Office.

Department of Education and Science (1989) *Education Observed 5: Good Behaviour and Discipline in Schools*. London: Her Majesty's Stationery Office.

Department of Education and Science (1989) *From Policy to Practice*. London: Her Majesty's Stationery Office.

Department of Education and Science (1989) *Report of the Records of Achievement National Steering Committee* (RANSC Report). London: Her Majesty's Stationery Office.

Department of Education and Science (1991) *The National Record of Achievement*. London: Her Majesty's Stationery Office.

Department of Education and Science Employment Department (undated) *National Record of Achievement* (accompanying paper to *The National Record of Achievement* (1991), signatories M. Howard and K. Clark).

Department for Education and Skills (2001) *Education Bill 2001*. London: The Stationery Office.

Department for Education and Skills (2001) *Inclusive Schooling*. White Paper. London: The Stationery Office.

Department for Education and Skills (2001) *Schools Achieving Success*. White Paper. London: The Stationery Office.

Department for Education and Skills (2001) *Special Educational Needs Code of Practice*. London: The Stationery Office.

Department for Education and Skills (2001) *Supporting the Target Setting Process*. London: The Stationery Office.

Department for Education and Skills (2002) *14–19: Extending Opportunities, Raising Standards*. London: The Stationery Office.

Department for Education and Skills (2002) *Autumn Performance Report 2002*, Cmnd 5689. London: The Stationery Office.

Department for Education and Skills (2002) *Bullying: Don't Suffer in Silence*. London: The Stationery Office.

Department for Education and Skills (2002) *Cutting Burdens*. London: The Stationery Office.

Department for Education and Skills (2002) *Education Act 2002*. London: The Stationery Office.

Department for Education and Skills (2002) *Education and Skills: Delivering Results: A Strategy to 2006*. London: The Stationery Office.

Department for Education and Skills (2002) *Gender and Achievement*. www.standards.dfes.gov.uk/genderandachievement

Department for Education and Skills (2002) *Gender and Achievement: The Tool Kit*. www.standards.dfes.gov.uk/genderandachievement/goodpractice

Department for Education and Skills (2002) *Guide to the National Record of Achievement*. London: The Stationery Office.

Department for Education and Skills (2002) *Key Stage 3 National Strategy: Designing the Key Stage 3 Curriculum*. London: The Stationery Office.

Department for Education and Skills (2002) *Progress File Achievement Planner, Supplement 2*. London: The Stationery Office.

Department for Education and Skills (2002) *Progress File Achievement Planner, Supplement 3*. London: The Stationery Office.

Department for Education and Skills (2002) *Safe Schools*. http://www.teachernet.gov.uk/_doc/1607/safe_school_leaflet.pdf

Department for Education and Skills (2002) *Statistics of Education: Permanent Exclusions from Maintained Schools in England*. London: The Stationery Office, November.

Department for Education and Skills (2002) *Target Setting at Key Stage 2*. London: The Stationery Office.

Department for Education and Skills (2002) *Transforming the Way We Learn: A Vision for the Future of ICT in Schools*. London: The Stationery Office.

Department for Education and Skills (2003) *About the School Curriculum.* www.nc.uk.net/about_school.html

Department for Education and Skills (2003) *Choosing Strategies for Reducing Bullying.* London: The Stationery Office. www.teachernet.gov.uk/management/workingwithothers/safeschools

Department for Education and Skills (2003) *Definition of SEN.* www.file://A:DfES,SEN2.htm

Department for Education and Skills (2003) *Excellence and Enjoyment.* London: Her Majesty's Stationery Office.

Department for Education and Skills (2003) *ICT and Attainment: A Review of the Literature.* London: HMSO.

Department for Education and Skills (2003) *Inclusion: Providing Effective Learning Opportunities for All Pupils.* www.nc.uk.net/inclusion.html

Department for Education and Skills (2003) *Planning Guidance.* www.standards.dfes.gov.uk/schemes3/planning, and also www.standards.dfes.gov.uk/schemes3/using

Department for Education and Skills (2003) *Statement of Values.* www.nc.uk.net/statement_values.html

Department for Education and Skills (2006) *Primary Framework for Literacy and Mathematics.* London: DfES.

Department for Education and Skills (2006) *Safeguarding Children and Safer Recruitment in Education.* London: DfES.

Department of Health, Health Development Agency (2002) *National Healthy School Standard: Staff Health and Well-being.* London: Department of Health. http://www.teacherline.org.uk/upload/TeacherSupport /documents/staffhealth.pdf

Department of Social Security (1994) *Households below Average Income: A Statistical Analysis 1979–1991/1992.* London: HMSO.

Desforges, C. (1989) *Testing and Assessment.* London: Cassell.

Desforges, C. (2000) Integrating conceptions of learning for advancing educational practices. Paper presented at the first programme conference of the UK's ESRC Teaching and Learning Research Programme, Leicester, November. www.tlrp.org/pub/acadpub.ntml

Desforges, C. (2001) *The Challenge Ahead.* Report of the DfES Research Conference (research Report CR2001). London: Department for Education and Skills.

Dewey, J. (1916) *Democracy and Education.* New York: Macmillan.

Dewey, J. (1933) *How We Think: A Restatement of the Relation of Reflective Thinking to the Educative Process* (2nd edition). New York: D. C. Heath and Co.

Dewey, J. (1938) *Experience and Education.* New York: Collier.

Dierenfield, R. B. (1982) *Classroom Disruption in English Comprehensive Schools.* Saint Paul, MN: Macalester College Education Department.

Disability Discrimination Act 1995. London: HMSO.

Dixon, R. (1977) *Catching Them Young: Sex, Race and Class in Children's Fiction.* London: Pluto Press.

Docking, J. (1987) *Control and Discipline in Schools.* London: Harper & Row.

Docking, J. (1990) *Managing Behaviour in the Primary School.* London: David Fulton Publishers.

Doherty, P. (1998) Learner control in asynchronous learning environments. *ALN Magazine,* 2(2), 1–13.

Doll, W. E. (1993) *A Post-modern Perspective on Curriculum.* New York: Teachers College Press.

Donaldson, M. (1978) *Children's Minds.* London: Fontana.

Donaldson, M. (1993) *Human Minds.* Harmondsworth: Penguin.

Douglas, J. (1964) *The Home and the School: A Study of Ability and Attainment in the Primary School.* London: McGibbon and Kee.

Dowling, M. (2000) *Young Children's Personal, Social and Emotional Development.* London: Paul Chapman Publishing.

Dowson, J. (1999) The school curriculum, in S. Capel, M. Leask and T. Turner (eds) *Learning to Teach in the Secondary School* (2nd edition). London, Routledge, pp. 351–64.

Drummond, M. J. (1993) *Assessing Children's Learning.* London: David Fulton Publishers.

Drummond, M. J. (1996) Play, learning and the National Curriculum: some possibilities, in T. Cox (ed.) *The National Curriculum and the Early Years.* London: Falmer, pp. 129–39.

Drummond, M. J. (1996) Whatever next? Future trends in early years education, in D. Whitebread (ed.) *Teaching and Learning in the Early Years.* London: RoutledgeFalmer, pp. 33–47.

Drummond, M. J. (2000) Another way of seeing: perceptions of play in a Steiner kindergarten, in L. Abbott and H. Moyett (eds) *Early Education Transformed*. London: Falmer, pp. 48–60.

Drury, C. J. (1995) *Implementing Change in Education: The Integration of Information Technology in Irish Post-primary Schools*. Unpublished MSc thesis, University of Leicester, 1990. http://indigo.ie/~cjdrury/thesis/chapter4.html

Dunkin, M. J. and Biddle, B. J. (1974) *The Study of Teaching*. New York: Holt, Rinehart & Winston.

Dunne, E. and Bennett, S. N. (1991) *Talking and Learning in Groups*. Basingstoke: Macmillan.

Dykes, M. (2001) *Assessment and Evaluation of Peer Interaction Using Computer-mediated Communication in Post-secondary Academic Education*. Occasional Paper: Department of Educational Communications and Technology, University of Saskatchewan.

Edgington, M. (2002) High levels of achievement for young children, in J. Fisher (ed.) *The Foundations of Learning*. Buckingham: Open University Press, pp. 25–40.

Edwards, A. D. and Furlong, V. J. (1978) *The Language of Teaching*. London: Heinemann.

Edwards, A. D. and Westgate, D. P. G. (1994) *Investigating Classroom Talk* (2nd edition). Lewes: Falmer.

Edwards, C., Gandini, L. and Foreman, G. (1998) *The Hundred Languages of Children* (2nd edition). Norwood, NJ: Ablex Publishing.

Egan, K. (1991) *Primary Understanding: Education in Early Childhood*. London: Routledge.

Eggleston, J. and Kerry, T. (1985) Integrated studies, in S. N. Bennett and C. Desforges (eds) *Recent Advances in Classroom Research*. *British Journal of Educational Psychology*. Monographs Series No. 2. Edinburgh: Scottish Academic Press.

Eisenkraft, A. (1987) The effects of computer simulated experiments and traditional laboratory experiments on subsequent transfer tasks in a high school physics course. Unpublished PhD, New York University.

Eisner, E. (1985) *The Art of Educational Evaluation*. Lewes: Falmer.

Employment Department (1991) *National Record of Achievement: A Business Guide*. Sheffield: Employment Department.

English, E., Hargreaves, L. and Hislam, J. (2002) Pedagogical dilemmas in the national literacy strategy: primary teachers' perceptions, reflections and classroom behaviour. *Cambridge Journal of Education*, 32(1), 9–26.

Entwistle, H. (1970) *Child-centred Education*. London: Methuen.

Equal Opportunities Commission (1984) *Do You Provide Equal Educational Opportunities?* Manchester: Equal Opportunities Commission.

Ertmer, P. A. (2005) Teacher pedagogical beliefs: the final frontier in our quest for technology integration? *Journal of Educational Administration*, 45, 33–61.

Esarte-Sarries, V. and Paterson, F. (2003) Scratching the surface: a typology of interactive teaching, in J. Moyles, L. Hargreaves, R. Merry, F. Paterson and V. Esarte-Sarries. *Interactive Teaching in the Primary School: Digger Deeper into Meanings*. Maidenhead: Open University Press.

ESRC (2009) *Ethnic Minorities in the UK*. Accessed 10 February 2009 from http://www.esrcsocietytoday.ac.uk/ESRCInfoCentre/facts/UK/index39.aspx?ComponentId=12534&SourcePageId=18133

Esland, G. (1971) Teaching and learning as the organization of knowledge, in M. F. D. Young (ed.) *Knowledge and Control*. Basingstoke: Collier-Macmillan, pp. 70–115.

Evans, J., Harden, A., Thomas, J. and Benefield, P. (2003) Support for pupils with emotional and behavioural difficulties (EBD) in mainstream primary classrooms: a systematic review of the effectiveness of interventions, in *Research Evidence in Education Library*. London: EPPI-Centre, Social Science Research Unit, Institute of Education, University of London.

Evertson, C. and Emmer, E. (1982) Effective management at the beginning of the school year in junior high classes. *Journal of Educational Psychology*, 74(4), 485–98.

Ewing, J. and Miller, D. (2002) A framework for evaluating computer-supported collaborative learning. *Educational Technology and Society*, 5(1), 112–18.

Farrow, S., Tymms, P. and Henderson, B. (1999) Homework and attainment in primary schools. *British Educational Research Journal*, 25(3), 323–41.

Fetherston, T. (2001) Pedagogical challenges for the world wide web. *Educational Technology Review*, 9(1), 1–11.

Fine, M. (1987) Silencing in public schools. *Language Arts*, 64(2), 157–74.

Fisher, J. (ed.) (2002) *The Foundations of Learning*. Buckingham: Open University Press.

Fisher, R. (ed.) (1987) *Problem Solving in Primary Schools*. Oxford: Basil Blackwell.

Flanders, N. A. (1970) *Analysing Teacher Behaviour*. Reading, MA: Addison-Wesley.

Flaugher, R. (1990) Item pools, in H. Wainer (ed.) *Computerized Adaptive Testing: A Primer*. Hillsdale, NJ: Lawrence Erlbaum, pp. 41–64.

Fogelman, K. (1976) *Britain's Sixteen Year Olds*. London: National Children's Bureau.

Fontana, D. (1985) *Classroom Control: Understanding and Guiding Classroom Behaviour*. London: British Psychological Society and Methuen.

Ford, J., Hughes, M. and Ruebain, D. (1999) *Education Law and Practice*. London: Legal Action Group Education and Service Trust.

Forman, E. A. and Cazden, C. B. (1985) Exploring Vygotskyian perspectives in education: the cognitive value of peer interaction, in. J. V. Wertsch (ed.) *Culture, Communication and Cognition*. Cambridge: Cambridge University Press, pp. 323–47.

Foucault, M. (1977) *Discipline and Punish: The Birth of the Prison*. London: Allen Lane.

Fulton, K. (1997) *Learning in a Digital Age: Insights into the Issues*. Santa Monica, CA: Milken Exchange on Education Technology.

Gaine, C. (1991) What do we call people?, in E. Newman and P. Triggs (eds) *Equal Opportunities in the Primary School*. Bristol: Bristol Polytechnic.

Gall, M. D. (1970) The use of questioning. *Review of Educational Research*, 40, 707–21.

Galloway, D., Rogers, C., Armstrong, D. and Leo, E. (1998) *Motivating the Difficult to Teach*. Harlow: Longman.

Galton, M. and Simon, B. (1980) *Inside the Primary Classroom*. London: Routledge & Kegan Paul.

Galton, M., Simon, B. and Croll, P. (eds) (1980) *Progress and Performance in the Primary Classroom*. London: Routledge.

Galton, M., Simon, B. and Croll, P. (1980) *Inside the Primary Classroom* (the ORACLE project). London: Routledge.

Galton, M. and Williamson, J. (1992) *Groupwork in the Primary School*. London: Routledge.

Galvin, P., Mercia, S. and Costa, P. (1990) *Building a Better Behaved School*. Harlow: Longman.

Gannaway, H. (1976) Making sense of school, in M. Stubbs and S. Delamont (eds) *Explorations in Classroom Observation*. London: John Wiley, pp. 45–81.

Gardner, H. (1999) *The Disciplined Mind: What All Students should Understand*. New York: Simon & Schuster.

Garner, P. and Sandow, S. (eds) (1995) *Advocacy, Self-advocacy and Special Needs*. London: David Fulton Publishers.

Garnett, P. J., Hackling, M. W. and Oliver, R. (1994) Visualization of chemical reactions using a multimedia instructional approach. Paper presented at the 19th Annual Conference of the Western Australia Science Education Association, Perth, AU, November.

Gerlach, V. S. and Ely, D. P. (1971) *Teaching and Media: A Systematic Approach*. Englewood Cliffs, NJ: Prentice-Hall.

Gerzina, G. (1996) *Black Britain: Life Before Emancipation*. London: John Murray.

Gill, M. and Hearnshaw, S. (1997) *Personal Safety and Violence in Schools*. University of Leicester: The Scarman Centre for the Study of Public Order.

Gilliatt, J. (1999) *Teaching and the Law*. London: Kogan Page.

Gipps, C. (1988) National assessment: a comparison of English and American trends, in P. Broadfoot, R. Murphy and H. Torrance (eds) *Changing Educational Assessment*. London: Routledge, pp. 53–64.

Gipps, C. (1990) *Assessment: A Teachers' Guide to the Issues*. London: Hodder & Stoughton.

Gipps, C. (1994) *Beyond Testing*. London: Falmer.

Gipps, C. and MacGilchrist, B. (1999) Primary school learners, in P. Mortimore (ed.) *Understanding Pedagogy and Its Impact on Learning*. London: Paul Chapman Publishing, pp. 46–67.

Glaser, R. (1963) Instructional technology and the measurement of learning outcomes: some questions. *American Psychologist*, 18, 519–21.

Glasser, W. (1969) *Schools without Failure*. New York: Harper & Row.

Glasser, W. (1988) *Choice Theory in the Classroom*. New York: Quill/HarperCollins.

Glazer, C. (2000) *The Emergence of a New Digital Divide: A Critical Look at Integrated Learning Systems*. Occasional Paper: University of Texas at Austin. EDC 385G: Literacy and Culture.

Glennan, T. K. (1995) *Fostering the Use of Educational Technology: Elements of a National Strategy*. Santa Monica, CA: The RAND Corporation. http://www. rand.org/publications/MR/MR682.html

Gnagey, W. J. (1980) Locus of control, motives and crime prevention attitudes of classroom facilitators and inhibitors. Paper read at American Educational Research Association, Boston, MA.

Gnagey, W. J. (1981) *Motivating Classroom Discipline*. New York: Macmillan; London: Collier-Macmillan.

Goleman, D. (1996) *Emotional Intelligence*. London: Bloomsbury Publishing.

Good, T. L. (1970) Which pupils do teachers call on? *Elementary School Journal*, 70, 190–8.

Good, T. L. and Brophy, J. E. (1973) *Looking in Classrooms*. New York: Harper & Row.

Good, T. L. and Brophy, J. E. (1974) The influence of teachers' attitudes and expectations on classroom behaviour, in R. H. Coop and K. White (eds) *Psychological Concepts in the Classroom*. New York: Harper & Row.

Gopnik, A., Meltzoff, A. and Kuhl, P. (eds) (1999) *How Babies Think: The Science of Childhood*. London: Weidenfeld & Nicolson.

Goswami, U. (2004) Neuroscience and education. *British Journal of Educational Psychology*, 74, 1–14.

Goulding, M. (1992) Let's hear it for the girls. *Times Educational Supplement*, 21 February, p. 38.

Grabe, M. and Grabe, C. (2000) *Integrating the Internet for Meaningful Learning*. Boston, MA: Houghton Mifflin.

Grabe, M. and Grabe, C. (2001) *Integrating Technology for Meaningful Learning*. Boston, MA: Houghton Mifflin Co.

Graham, S., Harris, K.R., Mason, L., Fink-Chorzempa, B., Moran, S. and Saddler, B. (2008) How do primary grade teachers teach handwriting? *Reading and Writing*, 21, 49–69.

Granger, C. A. and Morbey M. L. (2002) Factors contributing to teachers' successful implementation of IT. *Journal of Computer Assisted Learning*, 18, 480–8.

Gray, C. (2001) *Mentor Development in the Education of Modern Language Teachers*. Clevedon: Multilingual Matters.

Green, P. A. (1982) Teachers' influence on the self-concept of ethnic minority pupils. Unpublished PhD thesis, University of Durham.

Guha, M. (1987) Play in school, in G. Blenkin and A. V. Kelly (eds) (1994) *The National Curriculum and Early Years Learning: An Introduction*. London: Paul Chapman Publishing Ltd, pp. 61–79.

Gundura, J. (1982) Approaches to multicultural education, in Tierney, J. (ed.) *Race, Migration and Schooling*. Eastbourne: Holt, Rinehart & Winston, pp. 108–19.

Haddad, W. D. (2000) Technology for basic education: a luxury or a necessity? *TechKnowLogia*, May/June, 6–8.

Hagger, H., Burn, K. and McIntyre, D. (1993) *The School Mentor Handbook*. London: Kogan Page.

Haladyna, T. M. (1997) *Writing Test Items to Evaluate Higher Order Thinking*. Needham Heights, MA: Allyn & Bacon.

Hall, K. (1995) Learning modes: an investigation of perceptions in five Kent classrooms. *Educational Research*, 3(1), 21–32.

Hall, K. (2001) Level descriptions and curriculum relatedness in English at Key Stage 1. *Educational Review*, 53(1), 47–56.

Hall, J. (2005) *Neuroscience and Education: A Review of the Contribution of Brain Science to Teaching and Learning*. Glasgow: The Scottish Council for Research in Education.

Hallam, S. and Ireson, J. (1999) Pedagogy in the secondary school, in P. Mortimore (ed.) *Understanding Pedagogy and Its Impact on Learning*. London: Paul Chapman Publishing, pp. 68–97.

Halsey, A. (1992) An international comparison of access to higher education, in D. Phillips (ed.) *Lessons of Cross-national Comparison in Education*. Wallingford: Triangle Books, pp. 11–36.

Halsey, A. H. (1981) Education can compensate in W. Swann (ed.) *The Practice of Special Education*. Oxford: Basil Blackwell in association with the Open University Press, pp. 353–8.

Halsey, A. H., Heath, A. and Ridge, J. (1980) *Origins and Destinations*. London: Oxford University Press.

Hamacheck, D. E. (1986) *Human Dynamics in Psychology and Education*. Boston, MA: Allyn & Bacon.

Hargreaves, A. (1989) *Curriculum and Assessment Reform*. London: Basil Blackwell and Open University Press.

Hargreaves, A. (1994) *Changing Teachers, Changing Times*. London: Cassell.

Hargreaves, D. (1984) Rules in play, in A. Hargreaves and P. Woods (eds) *Classrooms and Staffrooms*. Milton Keynes: Open University Press, pp. 25–35.

Hargreaves, D. H. (1973) *Interpersonal Relations and Education*. London: Routledge & Kegan Paul.

Hargreaves, D. H. (1982) *The Challenge for the Comprehensive School*. London: Routledge & Kegan Paul.

Hargreaves, L. M. and Hargreaves, D. J. (1997) Children's development 3–7: the learning relationship in the early years, in N. Kitson and R. Merry (eds) *Teaching in the Primary School: A Learning Relationship*. London: Routledge, pp. 27–47.

Harlen, W. (1994) Introduction to W. Harlen (ed.) *Enhancing Quality in Assessment*. London: Paul Chapman Publishing.

Harlen, W. (1994) Issues and approaches to quality assurance and quality control in assessment, in W. Harlen (ed.) *Enhancing Quality in Assessment*. London: Paul Chapman Publishing, pp. 2–10.

Harlen, W. (ed.) (1994) *Enhancing Quality in Assessment*. London: Paul Chapman Publishing.

Harlen, W. and Deakin Crick, R. (2002) A systematic review of the impact of summative assessment and tests on students' motivation for learning (eppi-centre review, version 1.1*). *Research Evidence in Education Library*, 1. Retrieved 9 January 2007 from http://eppi.ioe.ac.uk/cms/Default.aspx?tabid=108

Harnisch, D. L. and Mabry, L. (1993) Issues in the development and evaluation of alternative assessments. *Journal of Curriculum Studies*, 25(2), 179–87.

Harris, D. (2001) *Information and Communication Technology in the New Zealand Educational Context*. New Zealand Ministry of Education http://www.minedu.govt.nz/web/document/document_page.cfm?id=3840a ndp=1003.1024

Hart, K., Johnson, D. C., Brown, M., Dickson, L. and Clarkson, R. (1989) *Children's Mathematical Frameworks: 8–13*. Windsor: NFER-Nelson.

Hart, P., Wearing, A. and Conn, M. (1995) Conventional wisdom is a poor predictor of the relationship between student misbehaviour and teacher stress. *British Journal of Educational Psychology*, 65(1), 27–48.

Hartley, S., Gerhardt-Powals, J., Jones, D., McCormack, C., Medley, D., Price, B. *et al.* (1996) Enhancing teaching using the internet. Report of the working group on the World Wide Web as an interactive teaching resource. Proceedings of the conference on Integrating Technology into Computer Science Education. Barcelona: Association for Computing Machinery (ACM). *SIGCSE Bulletin*, 28 (SI), 218–28. http://portal.acm.org/citation.cfm?doid =237466.237649

Harwood, D. (1995) The pedagogy of the World Studies 8–13 Project: the influence of the presence/absence of the teacher upon primary children's collaborative group work. *British Educational Research Journal*, 21(5), 587–611.

Haslam, L., Wilkin, Y. and Kellet, E. (2005) *English as an Additional Language: Meeting the Challenge in the Classroom*. London: David Fulton Publishers.

Hastings, N. and Schwieso, J. (1995) Tasks and tables: the effects of seating arrangements on task engagement in primary classrooms. *Educational Research*, 37(3), 279–91.

Haviland, J. (1988) *Take Care, Mr Baker!* London: Fourth Estate.

Hawkey, R. (2004) Learning with Digital Technologies in Museums, Science Centres and Galleries. Bristol: Futurelab Report 9.

Hawkins R. J. (2002) Ten lessons for ICT and education in the developing world. *The Global Information Technology Report 2001–2002: Readiness for the Networked World*. The World Bank Institute, World Links for Development Program. Oxford: Oxford University Press, Chapter 4.

Hay McBer (2000) *Research into Teacher Effectiveness: A Model of Teacher Effectiveness*. Report to the Department for Education and Skills. London: Hay McBer.

Hayes, J. R. (2006) New directions in writing theory in C.A. MacArthur, S. Graham and J. Fitzgerald (eds) *Handbook of Writing research*. New York: The Guilford Press.

Haysom, J. and Sutton, C. (1974) *Theory into Practice*. Maidenhead: McGraw-Hill.

Heald, T. R. (1994) *Judgement in the Case between R. H. Walker and Derbyshire County Council*. Nottingham, County Court Records.

Heffler, B. (2001) Individual learning style and learning style inventory. *Educational Studies*, 27(3), 307–16.

Hegarty, S., Pocklington, K. and Lucas, D. (1981) *Educating Pupils with Special Needs in the Ordinary School*. Windsor: NFER-Nelson.

Hennessy, S. (2006) Integrating technology into the teaching and learning of school science: a situated perspective on pedagogical issues in research. *Studies in Science Education*, 42, 1–48.

Hennessy, S., Deaney, R., Ruthven, K. and Winterbottom, M. (2007) Pedagogical strategies for using the interactive whiteboard to foster learner participation in school science. *Learning, Media and Technology*, 32(3), 283–301.

Higgins, S. (2001) ICT and teaching for understanding. *Evaluation and Research in Education*, 15(3), 164–71.

Higgins, S., Wall, K. and Smith, H. (2005) 'The visual helps me understand the complicated things': pupil views of teaching and learning with interactive whiteboards, *British Journal of Educational Technology*, 36(5), 851–67.

Hiltz, S. R. (1995) *The Virtual Classroom*. Norwood, NJ: Ablex Publishing.

Hirst, P. (1967) The logical and psychological aspects of teaching a subject, in R. S. Peters (ed.) *The Concept of Education*. London: Routledge & Kegan Paul, pp. 44–60.

Hirst, P. H. (1974) *Knowledge and the Curriculum*. London: Routledge & Kegan Paul.

Hlebowitsh, P. S. (1995) Interpretations of the Tyler *rationale*: a reply to Kliebard. *Journal of Curriculum Studies*, 27(1), 89–94.

Hofkins, D. (1995) Cheating 'rife' in national tests. *Times Educational Supplement*, 16 June, p. 1.

Hofkins, D. (1995) English scripts sent back for remarking. *Times Educational Supplement*, 7 July, p. 2.

Hohmann, M., Bunet, B. and Weikart, D. W. (1979) *Young Children in Action*. Ypsilanti, MI: High Scope Press.

Hokanson, B. and Hooper, S. (2000) Computers as cognitive media: defining the potential of computers in education. *Computers in Human Behaviour*, 16, 537–52.

Holt, J. (1969) *How Children Fail*. Harmondsworth: Penguin.

Howard-Jones, P. (2007) *Neuroscience and Education: Issues and Opportunities*. London: Economic and Social Research Council/Institute for Education.

Hudson, B. (1973) *Assessment Techniques: An Introduction*. London: Methuen.

Hughes, J. A. (1976) *Sociological Analysis: Methods of Discovery*. Sunbury-on-Thames: Nelson.

Hung, D. (2001) Theories of learning and computer-mediated instructional technologies. *Education Media International*, 38(4), 281–7.

Hung, D. W. L. and Cheng, D. T. (2001) Situated cognition, Vygotskian thought and learning from the communities of practice perspective: implications for the design of web-based e-learning. *Education Media International*, 38(1), 3–12.

Hurn, C. (1978) *The Limits and Possibilities of Schooling*. Boston, MA: Allyn & Bacon.

Hurst, V. and Joseph, J. (1998) *Supporting Early Learning: The Way Forward*. Buckingham: Open University Press.

Hurst, V. and Lally, M. (1992) Assessment and the nursery curriculum, in G. Blenkin and A. V. Kelly (eds) *Assessment in Early Childhood Education*. London: Paul Chapman Publishing, Ch. 3.

Hutt, S. J., Tyler, S., Hutt, C. and Christopherson, H. (1989) *Play, Exploration and Learning*. London: Routledge.

Inner London Education Authority (1983) *Race, Sex and Class 3: A Policy for Equality*. London: ILEA.

Ireson, J., Clark, H. and Hallam, S. (2002) Constructing ability groups in secondary school: issues in practice. *School Leadership and Management*, 22(2), 163–76.

Ireson, J., Hallam, S. and Hurley, C. (2005) What are the effects of ability grouping on GCSE attainment? *British Educational Research Journal*, 31(4), 454–8.

Jackson, P. W. (1968) *Life in Classrooms*. New York: Holt, Rinehart & Winston.

Jacobson, L. (1999) Mixed-mode simulation. *Syllabus*, 12(7), 38–42.

Jeffcoate, R. (1976) Curriculum planning in multiracial education. *Educational Research*, 18(3), 192–200.

Jeffcoate, R. (1979) A multicultural curriculum: beyond the orthodoxy. *Trends in Education*, 4, 8–12.

John, P. and Sutherland, R. (2005) Affordance, opportunity and the pedagogical implications of ICT. *Educational Review*, 57(4), 405–13.

Johnson, B., Oswald, M. and Adey, K. (1993) Discipline in South Australian primary schools. *Educational Studies*, 19(3), 289–305.

Johnson, D. W. (1978) Conflict management in the school and classroom, in D. Bar-Tal and L. Saxe (eds) *Social Psychology of Education: Theory and Research*. New York: John Wiley and Sons.

Johnson, D. W. and Johnson, R. T. (1989) *Cooperation and Competition: Theory and Research*. Edina, MN: Interaction Book Co.

Johnson, G., Hill, B. and Tunstall, P. (1992) *Primary Records of Achievement: A Teachers' Guide to Reviewing, Recording and Reporting*. London: Hodder & Stoughton.

Jonassen, D. H. (1996) *Computers in the Classroom: Mindtools for Critical Thinking*. Englewood Cliffs, NJ: Prentice-Hall.

Jonassen, D., Davidson, M., Collins, M., Campbell, J. and Haag, B. (1995) Constructivism and computer-mediated communication in distance education. *American Journal of Distance Education*, 9(2), 7–26.

Jones, B. F., Valdez, G., Nowakowski, J. and Rasmussen, C. (1995) *Plugging In: Choosing and Using Educational Technology*. Washington, DC: Council for Educational Development and Research, North Regional Educational Laboratory.

Jones, K., Charlton, T. and Wilkin, J. (1995) Classroom behaviours which first and middle school teachers in St Helena find troublesome. *Educational Studies*, 21(2), 139–53.

Jones, R. (1999) *Teaching Racism or Tackling It*. Stoke-on-Trent: Trentham.

Jones, V. (1971) The influence of teacher–student introversion, achievement and similarity on teacher– student dyadic classroom interactions. Doctoral dissertation, University of Texas at Austin.

Jukes, I. and McCain, T. (2000) *Beyond Technology to the New Literacy*. The InfoSavvy Group and Cystar. http://www.thecommittedsardine.net/handouts/btttnl.pdf

Kagan, S. (1988) *Cooperative Learning: Resources for Teachers*. University of California: Riverside Books.

Kamii, C. (1975) Pedagogical principles derived from Piaget's theory: relevance for educational practice, in M. Golby, J. Greenwald and R. West (eds) *Curriculum Design*. London: Croom Helm and the Open University, pp. 82–93.

Keddie, A. (2008) Engaging the 'maximal' intentions of the citizenship curriculum: one teacher's story. *Cambridge Journal of Education*, 38(2), 171–85.

Keddie, N. (1971) Classroom knowledge, in M. F. D. Young (ed.) *Knowledge and Control*. Basingstoke: Collier-Macmillan, pp. 133–60.

Kelly, A. (1986) *Knowledge and Curriculum Planning*. London: Harper & Row.

Kelly, A. V. (2004) *The Curriculum: Theory and Practice* (5th edn). London: Sage.

Kennewell, S. and Morgan, A. (2006) Factors influencing learning through play in ICT settings. *Computers and Education*, 46(3), 265–79.

Kerawalla, L. and Crook, C. (2002) Children's computer use at home and at school: context and continuity. *British Educational Research Journal*, 28(6), 751–71.

Kerckhoff, A. C. (1986) Effects of ability grouping in British secondary schools. *American Sociological Review*, 51(6), 842–58.

Kerry, T. and Eggleston, J. (1988) *Topic Work in the Primary School*. London: Routledge.

Kerry, T. and Sands, M. K. (1982) *Handling Classroom Groups*. London: Macmillan.

Kerry, T. and Sands, M. K. (1982) *Mixed Ability Teaching in the Early Years of the Secondary School*. London: Macmillan.

Kerry, T. and Tollitt, J. (1987) *Teaching Infants*. Oxford: Basil Blackwell.

Kershner, R. (2000) Organising the physical environment of the classroom to support children's learning, in D. Whitebread (ed.) *The Psychology of Teaching and Learning in the Primary School*. London: Routledge-Falmer, pp. 17–40.

Kershner, R. and Pointon, P. (2000) Children's views of the primary classroom as an environment for working and learning. *Research in Education*, 64, 64–77.

Kimbrough, D. (2000) Can we go the distance in chemistry? Reflections on distance learning laboratories. *Strategies for Success*, 33, 3–4.

Kimbrough, D. R., Hochgurtel, B. D. and Smith, S. S. (1997) Using internet relay chat to provide on-line tutorials in a distance learning chemistry course. Paper presented at the conference: Rocky Mountain Reforming the General Chemistry Curriculum meeting. Denver, CO: University of Colorado at Denver.

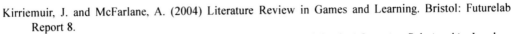

Kirriemuir, J. and McFarlane, A. (2004) Literature Review in Games and Learning. Bristol: Futurelab Report 8.

Kitson, N. and Merry, R. (eds) (1997) *Teaching in the Primary School: A Learning Relationship*. London: Routledge.

Kliebard, H. M. (1995) The Tyler *rationale* revisited. *Journal of Curriculum Studies*, 27(91), 81–8.

Kolb, D. A. (1984) *Experiential Learning: Experience on the Source of Learning and Development*. Englewood Cliffs, NJ: Prentice-Hall.

Kolb, D. A. (1985) *The Learning Style Inventory* (revised edition). Boston, MA: McBer and Co.

Kosakowski, J. (1998) *The Benefits of Information Technology*. ERIC Digest. ED420302.

Kounin, J. S. (1970) *Discipline and Group Management in Classrooms*. New York: Holt, Rinehart & Winston.

Kounin, J. S. and Gump, P. V. (1958) The ripple effect in discipline. *Elementary School Journal*, 35, 158–62.

Kounin, J. S., Gump, P. V. and Ryan, J. J. (1961) Explorations in classroom management. *Journal of Teacher Education*, 12, 235–47.

Kramarski, B. (1999) The study of graphs by computers: is easier better? *Educational Media International*, 2, 203–9.

Kramarski, B. and Feldman, Y. (2000) Internet in the classroom: effects on reading comprehension, motivation and metacognitive awareness. *Education Media International*, September, 37, 149–55.

Krysa, R. (1998) *Factors Affecting the Adoption and Use of Computer Technology in Schools*. Occasional Paper: Educational Communication and Technology, University of Saskatchewan. http://www.usask.ca/education/coursework/802papers/krysa/krysa.PDF

Kutnick, P. and Manson, I. (2000) Enabling children to learn in groups, in D. Whitebread (ed.) *The Psychology of Teaching and Learning in the Primary School*. London: RoutledgeFalmer, pp. 78–95.

Kutnick, P. J. (1988) *Relationships in the Primary School Classroom*. London: Paul Chapman Publishing.

Kwok, L. F., Lau, C. K. and Fun, S. W. (1999) Evaluating SAMS in Hong Kong schools. *Computers and Education*, 32, 249–67.

Kyriacou, C. (1994) *Essential Teaching Skills*. London: Simon & Schuster.

Kyriacou, C. (1998) *Essential Teaching Skills* (2nd edition). Cheltenham: Stanley Thornes.

Kyriacou, C. (2001) Teacher stress: directions for future research. *Educational Review*, 53(1), 27–35.

Lachs, V. (2000) *Making Multimedia in the Classroom*. London: RoutledgeFalmer.

LaJoie, S. P. (1993) Computer environments as cognitive tools for enhancing learning, in S. P. LaJoie and S. J. Derry (eds) *Computers as Cognitive Tools*. Hillsdale, NJ: Lawrence Erlbaum Associates, pp. 261–88.

Lambert, D. (1995) Assessing and recording pupils' work, in S. Capel, M. Leask and T. Turner, *Learning to Teach in the Secondary School*. London: Routledge, pp. 283–338.

Lambert, D. (1995) Assessment and improving the quality of pupils' work, in S. Capel, M. Leask and T. Turner, *Learning to Teach in the Secondary School*. London: Routledge, pp. 303–23.

Lambert, D. (1995) An overview of assessment: principles and practice, in S. Capel, M. Leask and T. Turner, *Learning to Teach in the Secondary School*. London: Routledge, pp. 284–302.

Lambert, D. and Lines, D. (2000) *Understanding Assessment*. London: RoutledgeFalmer.

La Velle, L. and Nichol, J. (2000) Intelligent information and communications technology for education and training in the 21st century. *British Journal of Educational Technology*, 31(2), 99–107.

Law, B. (1984) *Uses and Abuses of Profiling*. London: Harper & Row.

Law, D. and Glover, S. (2002) *Improving Learning*. Buckingham: Open University Press, pp. 49–63.

Lawrence, D. (1987) *Enhancing Self-esteem in the Classroom*. London: Paul Chapman Publishing Ltd.

Lawrence, J., Steed, D. and Young, P. (1984) *Disruptive Students – Disruptive Schools?* London: Croom Helm.

Lawton, D. (1973) *Social Change, Educational Theory and Curriculum Planning*. London: University of London Press.

Lawton, D. (1984) *The Tightening Grip: Growth of Central Control of the School Curriculum*. Bedford Way Papers, No. 21. London: University of London Institute of Education.

The Learning and Skills Act 2000. London: The Stationery Office.

Leask, M. (1999) Taking responsibility for whole lessons, in S. Capel, M. Leask and T. Turner (eds) *Learning to Teach in the Secondary School* (2nd edition). London: Routledge, pp. 85–8.

Leask, M. (1999) What do teachers do?, in S. Capel, M. Leask and T. Turner (eds) *Learning to Teach in the Secondary School* (2nd edition). London: Routledge, pp. 8–17.

Leask, M. and Pachler, N. (1999) *Learning to Teach Using ICT in the Secondary School*. London: Routledge.

Leat, D. and Higgins, S. (2002) The role of powerful pedagogical strategies in curriculum development. *The Curriculum Journal*, 13(1), 71–86.

LeDoux, J. (1999) *The Emotional Brain*. London: Weidenfeld & Nicolson.

Lee, J. and Croll, P. (1995) Streaming and subject specialism at Key Stage 2: a survey in two local authorities. *Educational Studies*, 21(2), 155–65.

Lemke, C. and Coughlin, E. (1998) *Technology in American Schools: Seven Dimensions for Gauging Progress*. Santa Monica, CA: Milken Exchange on Education Technology. http://www.mff.org/edtech/publication. taf?_function=detailandContent_uid1=158

Levine, D. and Lezotte, L. (1990) *Unusually Effective Schools: A Review and Analysis of Research and Practice*. Madison, WI: NCESRD Publications.

Lewin, C., Scrimshaw, P., Harrison, C., Somekh, B. and McFarlane, A. (2000) *Promoting Achievement: Pupils, Teachers and Contexts*. ImpacT2 Project. London: Department for Education and Skills.

Lewis, A. and Norwich, B. (1999) Mapping a pedagogy for learning difficulties. Report presented to the British Educational Research Association (BERA). London: BERA.

Lewis, D. G. (1974) *Assessment in Education*. London: University of London Press.

Lieberman, A. (ed.) (1990) *Schools as Collaborative Cultures*. London: Falmer.

Linchevski, L. and Kutscher, B. (1998) Tell me with whom you're learning and I'll tell you how much you've learned: mixed-ability versus same-ability grouping in mathematics. *Journal for Research in Mathematics Education*, 29(5), 533–53.

Linton, R. (ed.) (1940) *Acculturation*. New York: Appleton-Century-Crofts.

LiteracyLink PeerLit (1998) *Components of Educational Websites*, 1–2. http://littlink1.pbs.org/litteacher/ peerlit.evaluating.html

Littleton, K., Mercer, N., Dawes, L., Wegerif, R., Rowe, D. and Sams, C. (2005) Talking and thinking together at Key Stage 1. *Early Years*, 25(2), 165–80.

Liu, Z. F. E., Lin, S. J. S. and Yuan, S. M. (2001) Design of a networked portfolio system. *British Journal of Educational Technology*, 32(4), 492–4.

Long, M. (2000) *The Psychology of Education*. London: RoutledgeFalmer.

Lorson, M. V. (1991) A comparison of microcomputer-based laboratories and traditional laboratory methods in the high school chemistry laboratory. Unpublished PhD, Ohio State University, Columbus, OH.

Loveless, A. (1995) *The Role of IT: Practical Issues for Primary Teachers*. London: Cassell.

Loveless, A., Sharp, J., Potter, J. and Allen, J. (2000) *Primary ICT: Knowledge, Understanding and Practice*. Exeter: Learning Matters.

Loveless, A. and Ellis, V. (2001) *ICT, Pedagogy and the Curriculum*. London: RoutledgeFalmer.

Loveless, A., DeVoogd, G. L. and Bohlin, R. M. (2001) Something old, something new ...: is pedagogy affected by ICT?, in A. Loveless and V. Ellis (eds) *ICT, Pedagogy and the Curriculum*. London: Routledge-Falmer, pp. 63–83.

MacBeath, J., Gray, J., Cullen, J., Frost, D., Stewart, S. and Swaffield, S. (2007) *Schools on the Edge: Responding to Challenging Circumstances*. London: Paul Chapman Publishing.

MacDonald-Ross, M. (1973) Behavioural objectives – a critical review. *Instructional Science*, 2, 1–51.

MacIntyre, H. and Ireson, J. (2002) Within-class ability grouping, group placement and self-concept. *British Educational Research Journal*, 28(2), 249–63.

McAllister, W. (1995) Are pupils equipped for group work without training or instruction? *British Educational Research Journal*, 21(3), 403.

McBrien, J. L. and Brandt, R. S. (1997) *The Language of Learning: A Guide to Education Terms*. Alexandria, VA: Association for Supervision and Curriculum Development.

McCallum, B., McAlister, S., Brown, M. and Gipps, C. (1993) Teacher assessment at key stage one. *Research Papers in Education*, 8(3), 305–27.

McCarthy, B. and Lefler, S. (1983) *4MAT in Action: Creative Lesson Plans for Teaching to Learning Styles with Right/Left Mode Techniques.* Barrington: Excel Inc.

McClintock, R. (1992) *Power and Pedagogy: Transforming Education through Information Technology.* New York: Institute of Learning Technologies.

McCutchen, D. (2006) Cognitive factors in the development of children's writing, in C.A. MacArthur, S. Graham and J. Fitzgerald (eds) *Handbook of Writing Research.* New York: The Guilford Press.

McEwan, V. (1999) *Education Law* (2nd edition). Welwyn Garden City: CLT Professional Publishing Ltd.

McFarlane, C. (1986) *Hidden Messages? – Activities for Exploring Bias.* Birmingham: Development Education Centre.

McFarlane, C. and Sinclair, S. (1986) *A Sense of School.* Birmingham: Development Education Centre.

McGuiness, J. (1989) *A Whole School Approach to Pastoral Care.* London: Kogan Page.

McGuiness, J. (1993) *Teachers, Pupils and Behaviour: A Managerial Approach.* London: Cassell.

McIntyre, R. W. (1974) Guidelines for using behaviour modification in education, in R. Ulrich, T. Stachnik and J. Mabry (eds) *Control of Human Behaviour,* Vol. 3. Glenview, IL: Scott, Foresman.

McLean, L. (1988) Possibilities and limitations in cross-national comparisons of educational achievement, in P. Broadfoot, R. Murphy and H. Torrance (eds) *Changing Educational Assessment.* London: Routledge, pp. 65–83.

McPartland, M. (1995) On being a geography mentor. *Teaching Geography,* January, pp. 35–7.

Mackler, B. (1969) Grouping in the ghetto. *Education and Urban Society,* 2, 80–95.

Macrae, S. and Quintrell, M. (2001) Managing effective classrooms, in J. Dillon and M. Maguire (eds) *Becoming a Teacher* (2nd edition). Buckingham: Open University Press, pp. 150–61.

Madsen, C. H. (Jnr), Becker, W. C. and Thomas, D. R. (1968) Rules, praise and ignoring: elements of elementary classroom control. *Journal of Applied Behaviour Analysis,* 1, 139–50.

Maguire, M., Dillon, J. and Close, G. (2001) Reforming teachers and their work, in J. Dillon and M. Maguire (eds) *Becoming a Teacher* (2nd edition). Buckingham: Open University Press, pp. 63–73.

Makins, V. (1995) License to convert a waiting room. *Times Educational Supplement,* 23 June, p. 6.

Marland, M. (1975) *The Craft of the Classroom.* London: Heinemann Educational.

Martin, S. (1994) A preliminary evaluation of the adoption and implementation of assertive discipline at Robinson High School. *School Organisation,* 14(3), 321–9.

Marton, F. and Säljö, R. (1976) On qualitative differences in learning. 1 – outcome and process. *British Journal of Educational Psychology,* 46, 4–11.

Maslow, A. H. (1970) *Motivation and Personality* (2nd edition). New York: Harper & Row.

Maxwell, E. (1995) Anger intensifies over English tests marking. *Times Educational Supplement,* 30 June.

Mehrabian, A. (1971) *Silent Messages.* Belmont, CA: Wadsworth.

Meighan, R. (1981) *A Sociology of Educating.* Eastbourne: Holt, Rinehart & Winston.

Mercer, N. (1995) *The Guided Construction of Knowledge: Talk Amongst Teachers and Learners.* Clevedon: Multilingual Matters.

Mercer, N. (2000) *Words and Minds: How We Use Language to Think Together.* London: Routledge.

Mercer, N., Dawes, R., Wegerif, R. and Sams, C. (2004) Reasoning as a scientist: ways of helping children to use language to learn science, *British Educational Research Journal,* 30(3), 367–85.

Mercer, N. and Hodgkinson, S. (2008) Exploring talk in school: inspired by the work of Douglas Barnes. London: Sage.

Mercer, N. and Littleton, K. (2007) *Dialogue and the Development of Children's Thinking: A Sociocultural Approach.* London: Routledge.

Mercer, N. and Wegerif, R. (1999) Is 'exploratory talk' productive talk?, in K. Littleton and P. Light (eds) *Learning with Computers: Analysing Productive Interaction.* London: Routledge.

Merrett, F. (1993) *Encouragement Works Best.* London: David Fulton Publishers.

Merrett, F. and Jones, L. (1994) Rules, sanctions and rewards in primary schools. *Educational Studies,* 20(3), 345–56.

Merrett, F. and Man Tang, W. (1994) The attitudes of British primary school pupils to praise, rewards, punishments and reprimands. *British Journal of Educational Psychology,* 64, 91–103.

Miller, A. (1995) Teachers' attributions of causality, control and responsibility and its successful management. *Educational Psychology,* 15(4), 457–71.

Mills, C. (1998) Britain's early years disaster. Survey of research evidence for Channel 4 television documentary *Too Much, Too Young*. Cited in T. David and A. Nurse, Inspections of under fives' education and constructions of early childhood, in T. David (ed.) (1999) *Teaching Young Children*. London: Paul Chapman Publishing, pp. 165–84.

Mishler, E. G. (1972) Implications of teaching strategies for language and cognition: observations in first-grade classrooms, in C. B. Cazden, V. P. John and D. Hymes, *Functions of Language in the Classroom*. Teachers College, Columbia University, New York: Teachers College Press, pp. 267–98.

Mitchell, C. and Koshy, V. (1993) *Effective Teacher Assessment*. London: Hodder & Stoughton.

Moore, W. (2002) *Teachers and Stress: Pressures of Life at the Chalkface*. htttp://channel4.com/health/microsites/H/health/magazine/stress/work_teachers/html

Morrison, G. S. (2000) *Fundamentals of Early Childhood Education* (2nd edition). Upper Saddle River, NJ: Prentice-Hall.

Morrison, K. R. B. (1985) Tensions in subject specialist teaching in primary schools. *Curriculum*, 6(2), 24–9.

Morrison, K. R. B. (1986) Primary school subject specialists as agents of school-based curriculum change. *School Organisation*, 6(2), 175–83.

Morrison, K. R. B. (1988) Planning for skills progression and assessment in primary schools. *Curriculum* 9(2), 74–83.

Morrison, K. R. B. (1990) The assessment of skills, in P. Neal and J. Palmer, *Environmental Education in the Primary School*. Oxford: Basil Blackwell, pp. 92–7.

Morrison, K. R. B. (1990) An ideological masquerade. *Forum*, 31(1), 7–8.

Morrison, K. R. B. (1993) *Planning and Accomplishing School Centred Evaluation*. Norfolk: Peter Francis Publishers.

Morrison, K. R. B. (1994) *Implementing Cross-curricular Themes*. London: David Fulton Publishers.

Morrison, K. R. B. (1995) Habermas and the School Curriculum. Unpublished PhD thesis, University of Durham.

Morrison, K. R. B. (1996) Developing a whole-school behaviour policy in primary schools. *Pastoral Care in Education*, 14(1), 22–30.

Morrison, K. R. B. (2001) *The Open Society and Education in Macau*. Inaugural address for the new academic year. Macau: Inter-University Institute of Macau.

Morrison, K. R. B. (2002) *School Leadership and Complexity Theory*. London: RoutledgeFalmer.

Morrison, K. R. B. and Ridley, K. (1988) *Curriculum Planning and the Primary School*. London: Paul Chapman Publishing.

Mortimore, P. (1999) *Understanding Pedagogy and Its Impact on Learning*. London: Paul Chapman Publishing.

Mortimore, P., Sammons, P., Stoll, L., Lewis, D. and Ecob, R. (1988) *School Matters: The Junior Years*. Shepton Mallett: Open Books.

Moseley, D., Higgins, S., Bramald, R., Hardman, F., Miller, J., Mroz, M. *et al.* (1999) *Ways Forward with ICT: Effective Pedagogy Using Information and Communications Technology for Literacy and Numeracy in Primary Schools*. Newcastle: University of Newcastle upon Tyne and CEM Centre, University of Durham.

Moyles, J. (1988) *Self-Evaluation: A Teacher's Guide*. Slough: National Foundation for Educational Research.

Moyles, J. (1989) *Just Playing? The Role and Status of Play in Early Childhood Education*. Milton Keynes: Open University Press.

Moyles, J. (1997) Just for fun? The child as active learner and meaning maker, in N. Kitson and R. Merry (eds) *Teaching in the Primary School*. London: Routledge, pp. 9–26.

Muijs, D. and Reynolds, D. (1999) School effectiveness and teacher effectiveness: some preliminary findings from the evaluation of the Mathematics Enhancement Programme. Paper presented at the American Educational Research Association conference, Montreal, Quebec.

Muijs, D. and Reynolds, D. (2001) *Effective Teaching: Evidence and Practice*. London: Paul Chapman Publishing.

Muijs, D. and Reynolds, D. (2005) *Effective Teaching: Evidence and Practice*. London: Sage Publications Ltd.

Mullen, C. A. and Lick, D. W. (1999) *New Directions in Mentoring: Creating a Culture of Synergy*. London: Falmer.

Munby, S. (1989) *Assessing and Recording Achievement*. Oxford: Blackwell.

Munn, P., Johnstone, M. and Chalmers, V. (1992) *Effective Discipline in Primary Schools and Classrooms*. London: Paul Chapman Publishing.

Murphy, P. (2006) The impact of ICT on primary science, in P. Warwick, E. Wilson and M. Winterbottom (eds) *ICT and Primary Science*. Buckingham: Open University Press/McGraw-Hill.

Muth, R. and Guzman, N. (2000) Learning in a virtual lab: distance education and computer simulations. *Distance Education*, 15(2), 291–9.

Mycock, M. A. (1970) Vertical grouping in the primary school, in V. R. Rogers (ed.) *Teaching in the British Primary School*. London: Macmillan.

Myers, K. (1987) *Genderwatch*. London: School Curriculum Development Committee.

Naismith, L., Lonsdale, P., Vavoula, G. and Sharples, M. (2004) *Literature Review in Mobile Technologies and Learning*. Bristol: Futurelab Report 11.

Nash, R. (1976) *Teacher Expectations and Pupil Learning*. London, Routledge & Kegan Paul.

National Council for Educational Technology (1994) *Technology Works! Stimulate to Educate*. Coventry: NCET.

National Curriculum Council (1989) *A Curriculum for All*. York: National Curriculum Council.

National Curriculum Council (1989) *A Framework for the Primary Curriculum*. York: National Curriculum Council.

National Curriculum Council (1991) *Circular 11: Linguistic Diversity and the National Curriculum*. York: National Curriculum Council.

National Curriculum Council (1992) *The National Curriculum and Pupils with Severe Learning Difficulties*. York: National Curriculum Council.

Neill, S. and Caswell, C. (1993) *Body Language for Competent Teachers*. London: Routledge.

Nevo, D. (1995) *School-based Evaluation: A Dialogue for School Improvement*. Oxford: Pergamon.

Newman, E. and Triggs, P. (eds) (1991) *Equal Opportunities in the Primary School*. Bristol: Bristol Polytechnic.

Nicholls, D. and Houghton, S. (1995) The effect of Canter's assertive discipline program on teacher and student behaviour. *British Journal of Educational Psychology*, 65(2), 197–210.

Nixon, N. J. (1990) Assessment issues in relation to experience-based learning on placements within courses, in C. Bell and D. Harris (eds) *World Yearbook of Education Assessment and Evaluation*. London: Kogan Page.

Noah, H. J. and Eckstein, M. A. (1988) Trade-offs in examination policies: an international comparative perspective, in P. Broadfoot, R. Murphy and H. Torrance (eds) *Changing Educational Assessment*. London: Routledge, pp. 84–97.

Noam, E. M. (1995) Electronics and the dim future of the university. *Science*, 270, 247–9.

Nolder, R., Smith, S. and Melrose, J. (1994) Working together: roles and relationships, in B. Jaworski and A. Watson (eds) *Mentoring in Mathematics Teaching*. London: Falmer, pp. 41–51.

Nordkvelle, Y. T. and Olsen, J. K. (2005) Visions for ICT, ethics and the practice of teachers. *Education and Information Technologies*, 10(1/2), 21–32.

Norman, D. A. (1978) Notes towards a complex theory of learning, in A. M. Lesgold (ed.) *Cognitive Psychology and Instruction*. New York: Plenum, pp. 315–27.

Norwich, B. (2000) Inclusion in education: from concepts, values and critique to practice, in H. Daniels (ed.) *Special Education Re-formed: Beyond Rhetoric?* London: Falmer, pp. 5–30.

Noss, R. and Pachler, N. (1999) The challenge of new technologies: doing old things in a new way, or doing new things?, in P. Mortimore (ed.) *Understanding Pedagogy and Its Impact on Learning*. London: Paul Chapman Publishing, pp. 194–211.

Nowicki, S. and Duke, M. (2000) *Helping the Child who Doesn't Fit In*. Atlanta, GA: Peachtree.

Nuttall, D. (1987) The validity of assessments. *European Journal of Psychology of Education*, 11(2), 109–18.

Oeser, O. (1966) *Teacher, Pupil and Task*. London: Tavistock Publications.

Office for Standards in Education (1993) *Achieving Good Behaviour in Schools*. London: Ofsted.

Office for Standards in Education (1993) *Curriculum Organisation and Classroom Practice in Primary Schools: A Follow-up Report*. London: Ofsted.

Office for Standards in Education (1994) *Handbook for the Inspection of Schools*. London: Ofsted.

Office for Standards in Education (1994) *Primary Matters: A Discussion of Teaching and Learning in Primary Schools*. London: Ofsted.

Office for Standards in Education (1995) *Guidance on the Inspection of Nursery and Primary Schools*. London: Ofsted.

Office for Standards in Education (1995) *Guidance on the Inspection of Secondary Schools*. London: Ofsted.

Office for Standards in Education (1995) *Guidance on the Inspection of Special Schools*. London: Ofsted.

Office for Standards in Education (1998) *Guidance on the Inspection of Nursery Education Provision in the Private, Voluntary and Independent Sectors*. London: Ofsted.

Office for Standards in Education (1999) *Handbook for Inspecting Primary and Nursery Schools*. London: Ofsted.

Office for Standards in Education (1999) *Handbook for Inspecting Special Schools and Pupil Referral Units*. London: Ofsted.

Office for Standards in Education (1999) *Principles into Practice: Effective Education for Pupils with Emotional and Behavioural Difficulties*. London: Ofsted.

Office for Standards in Education (2001) *Improving Attendance and Behaviour in Secondary Schools*. London: Ofsted.

Office for Standards in Education (2001) *Standards and Quality in Education: The Annual Report of Her Majesty's Chief Inspector of Schools*. London: The Stationery Office.

Office for Standards in Education (2002) *The Curriculum in Successful Primary Schools*. London: Ofsted.

Office for Standards in Education (2002) *The National Literacy Strategy: The First Four Years 1998–2002*. London: Ofsted.

Office for Standards in Education (2003) *Good Assessment in Secondary Schools*. London: Ofsted.

Office for Standards in Education (2003) *Handbook for Inspecting Secondary Schools*. London: Ofsted.

Office for Standards in Education (2003) *Inspecting Schools: The Framework for Inspecting Schools in England from September 2003*. London: Ofsted.

Office for Standards in Education (2005) *Primary National Strategy: An Evaluation of its Impact in Primary Schools 2004/5*. London: Ofsted.

Office for Standards in Eduction (2006) *English 2000–05: A Review of Inspection Evidence*. London: Ofsted.

O'Hagan, M. and Smith, M. (1999) *Early Years Child Care Education Key Issues* (2nd edition). London: Harcourt Publishers Ltd.

Okano, K. (1993) *School to Work Transition in Japan*. Clevedon: Multilingual Matters.

O'Leary, K. D., Kaufman, K. F., Kass, R. E. and Drabman, R. S. (1970) The effects of loud and soft reprimands on the behaviour of disruptive students. *Exceptional Students*, 37, October, 45–55.

Olweus, D. (1993) *Bullying in Schools: What We Know and What We Can Do*. Oxford: Blackwell.

Ornstein, A. C. (1994) Homework, studying and role taking: essential skills for students. *NASSP Bulletin*, 78(559), 58–70.

Pachler, N. (1999) Theories of Learning and ICT, in M. Leask and N. Pachler (eds) *Learning to Teach Using ICT in the Secondary School*. London: Routledge, pp. 3–18.

Pachler, N. and Byrom, J. (1999) Assessment of and through ICT, in M. Leask and N. Pachler (eds) *Learning to Teach Using ICT in the Secondary School*. London: Routledge, pp. 125–46.

Palfreyman, D. (2001) Suffer little children: the evolution of the standard reasonably expected in the duty of care to prevent physical injury on school premises. *Education and the Law*, 13(3), 227–34.

Parliamentary Office of Science and Technology (2000) *Report on Early Years Learning*. London: Parliamentary Office of Science and Technology.

Peak, B. and Morrison, K. R. B. (1988) Investigating banding origins and destinations in a comprehensive school. *School Organisation*, 8(3), 339–49.

Peccei, J. S. (ed.) (1999) Child language: a resource book for pupils. London: Routledge.

Peccei, J. S. (2006) *Child language: A resource book for students*. London: Routledge, p. 37.

Pennycuick, D. (1991) Moderation of continuous assessment systems in developing countries. *Compare*, 21(2), 145–52.

Perrott, E. (1982) *Effective Teaching: A Practical Guide to Improving your Teaching*. London: Longman.

Peters, R. S. (1966) *Ethics and Education*. London: Routledge & Kegan Paul.

Peterson, B. (2000) Tech talk. *LIRT News*, 22(4), 1–3.

Piaget, J. (1952) *The Origins of Intelligence*. New York: International Universities Press.

Plowman, L. and Stephen, C. (2005) Children, play and computers in pre-school education. *British Journal of Educational Technology*, 36(2), 145–57.

Pollard, A. and Tann, S. (1988) *Reflective Teaching in the Primary School* (1st edition). London: Cassell.

Pollard, A. and Tann, S. (1993) *Reflective Teaching in the Primary School* (2nd edition). London: Cassell.

Pollard, A., Broadfoot, P., Croll, P., Osborn, M. and Abbott, D. (1994) *Changing English Primary Schools?* London: Cassell.

Popper, K. (1945, tr.1966) *The Open Society and Its Enemies*, Volumes I and II. London: Routledge & Kegan Paul.

Popper, K. (1963) *Conjectures and Refutations*. London: Routledge & Kegan Paul.

Porter, L. (2001) *Behaviour in Schools*. Buckingham: Open University Press.

Porter, L. *Behaviour in Schools: Theory and Practice for Teachers*. Buckingham: Open University Press.

Pound, L. (2002) Breadth and depth in early foundations, in J. Fisher (ed.) *The Foundations of Learning*. Buckingham: Open University Press, pp. 9–24.

PricewaterhouseCoopers (2001) *Teacher Workload Study*. Final Report, December 2001. http://www. teacher-net.gov.uk/_doc/932/ACF19E2.doc

Pringle, M. L. K., Rutter, M. and Davie, E. (1966) *11,000 Seven Year Olds*. Harlow: Longman.

Proctor, A., Entwistle, M., Judge, B. and McKenzie-Murdoch, S. (1995) *Learning to Teach in the Primary Classroom*. London: Routledge.

Prosser, M. T. and Tamir, P. (1990) Developing and improving the role of computers in student laboratories, in E. Hegarty-Hazel (ed.) *The Student Laboratory and the Science Curriculum*. London: Routledge, pp. 267–90.

Qualifications and Curriculum Authority (1999) *Developing an Assessment Strategy for NVQs and SVQs*. London: QCA.

Qualifications and Curriculum Authority (1999) *Developing National Occupational Standards for NVQs and SVQs*. London: QCA.

Qualifications and Curriculum Authority (1999) *Early Learning Goals*. London: QCA.

Qualifications and Curriculum Authority (1999) *Keeping Track: Effective Ways of Recording Pupil Achievement to Help Raise Standards*. London: QCA.

Qualifications and Curriculum Authority (2000) *Curriculum Guidance for the Foundation Stage*. London: QCA.

Qualifications and Curriculum Authority (2001) *Feedback*. http://www.qca.org.uk/ca/5–14/afl/fb_notvery.asp

Qualifications and Curriculum Authority (2001) *Planning for Learning in the Foundation Stage*. London: QCA.

Qualifications and Curriculum Authority (2001) *Planning, Teaching and Assessing the Curriculum for Pupils with Learning Difficulties: General Guidelines*. London: QCA.

Qualifications and Curriculum Authority (2002) *Designing and Timetabling the Primary Curriculum*. London: QCA.

Qualifications and Curriculum Authority (2002) *Guidance on Teaching the Gifted and Talented: Assessment*. London: Qualifications and Curriculum Authority. www.nc.uk.net/gt/general/05_assessment.htm

Qualifications and Curriculum Authority (2002) *Guidance on Teaching the Gifted and Talented: Characteristics to Look For*. London: QCA. www.nc.uk.net/gt/general/01_characteristics.htm

Qualifications and Curriculum Authority (2002) *Guidance on Teaching the Gifted and Talented: Developing an Effective Learning Environment*. London: QCA. www.nc.uk.net/gt/general/05_environment.htm

Qualifications and Curriculum Authority (2002) *Guidance on Teaching the Gifted and Talented: Good Practice*. London: QCA. www.nc.uk.net/gt/general/01_identifying.htm, p. 1.

Qualifications and Curriculum Authority (2002) *Guidance on Teaching the Gifted and Talented: Helpful Approaches*. www.nc.uk.net/gt/general/05_helpful.htm

Qualifications and Curriculum Authority (2002) *Guidance on Teaching the Gifted and Talented: Levels of Challenge and Differentiation*. London: QCA. www.nc.uk.net/gt/general/05_challenge.htm

Qualifications and Curriculum Authority (2002) *Guidance on Teaching the Gifted and Talented: What Does 'Gifted' and 'Talented' Mean?* London: QCA. www.nc.uk.net/gt/general/index.htm

Qualifications and Curriculum Authority (2002) *Including All Learners.* www.qca.org.uk/ca/inclusion/key_principles.asp

Qualifications and Curriculum Authority (2002) *Key Stage 3 National Strategy: Designing the Key Stage 3 Curriculum.* London: QCA.

Qualifications and Curriculum Agency (2002) *National Standards at Key Stage 1: English and Mathematics* http://www.qca.org.uk/ca/tests/ks1_eng_maths_2001.pdf

Qualifications and Curriculum Authority (2003) *Report Writing: Working towards – Principles and Good Practice.* London: QCA. www.qca.org.uk/ca/tests/2003sample_reports.asp

Qualifications and Curriculum Agency (2002) *Standards at Key Stage 3: English.* London: QCA. http://www.qca.org.uk/ca/tests/ks3_erg_2001.pdf

Qualifications and Curriculum Agency (2002) *Standards at Key Stage 3: Mathematics* http://www.qca.org.uk/ca/tests/ks3_maths_2001.pdf http://www.standards.dfes.gov.uk/performance/whole_ks2.pdf?version=1

Qualifications and Assessment Authority (2002) *Summary of National Sample Data.* www.qca.org.uk/ca/foundation/baseline/summary_data.asp

Qualifications and Curriculum Authority (2003) *Respect for All: Information and Communication Technology (ICT) Curriculum.* London: QCA. www.qca.org.uk/ca/inclusion/respect_for_all/ict/good_practice.asp

Qualifications and Curriculum Authority (2003) *Respect for All: Valuing Diversity and Challenging Racism through the Curriculum.* London: QCA. www.qca.org.uk/ca/inclusion/respect_for_all/index.asp

Qualifications and Curriculum Authority (2008) Determining a school curriculum for pupils with learning difficulties. Retrieved 28 August 2008 from http://www.qca.org.uk/qca_1832.aspx

Qualifications and Curriculum Authority (2008) Inclusion. Retrieved 28 August 2008 from http://curriculum.qca.org.uk/key-stages-3-and-4/organising-your-curriculum/inclusion/index.aspx

Qualifications and Curriculum Authority (2008) National curriculum. Retrieved 18 August 2008 from http://curriculum.qca.org.uk/index.aspx

Qualifications and Curriculum Authority (2009) Assessment. Accessed 13 February 2009 from http://www.qca.org.uk/qca_13581.aspx

Race Relations Act 1976. London: HMSO.

Race Relations Act (Amendment) 2000. London: The Stationery Office.

Raeburn, M. (1973) *An Outline of World Architecture.* London: Octopus Books, p. 116.

Rampton Committee (1981) *West Indian Children in Our Schools*, Interim Report. London: HMSO.

Rance, P. (1968) *Teaching by Topics.* London: Ward Lock Educational.

Reese, L., Garnier, H., Gallimore, R. and Goldenberg, C. (2000) Longitudinal analysis of the antecedents of emergent spanish literacy and middle-school english reading achievement of spanish-speaking students. *American Educational research Journal*, 37(3), 622–33.

Reid, I. (1994) Inequality, Society and Education. Inaugural lecture, Loughborough University Department of Education, Loughborough.

Reid, M., Clunies-Ross, L., Goacher, B. and Vile, C. (1981) *Mixed Ability Teaching: Problems and Possibilities.* Slough: National Foundation for Educational Research.

Reynolds, D. (1995) The effective school: an inaugural lecture. *Evaluation and Research in Education*, 9(2), 57–73.

Reynolds, D. and Cuttance, P. (1992) *School Effectiveness: Research, Policy and Practice.* London: Cassell.

Reynolds, D. and Farrell, S. (1996) *Worlds Apart? A Review of International Studies of Educational Achievement Involving England.* London: HMSO.

Reynolds, D., Creemers, B. P. M., Stringfield, S., Teddlie, C., Schaffer, E. and Nesselrodt, P. (1994) *Advances in School Effectiveness Research: Policy and Practice.* London: Cassell.

Reynolds, D., Hopkins, D., Potter, D. and Chapman, C. (2001) *School Improvement for Schools Facing Challenging Circumstances.* London: Department for Education and Skills.

Reynolds, D., Sammons, P., Stoll, L., Barber, M. and Hillman, J. (1996) School effectiveness and school improvement in the United Kingdom. *School Effectiveness and School Improvement*, 7(2), 133–58.

Rhem, J. (1995) Deep/surface approaches to learning: an introduction. *The National Teaching and Learning Forum*, 5(1), 1–5.

Ripley, M. and Walton, S. (2003) 'When ready' testing, in C. Richardson (ed.) *Whither Assessment?* London: Qualifications and Curriculum Authority, pp. 37–48.

Robertson, J. (1981) *Effective Classroom Control*. Sevenoaks: Hodder & Stoughton.

Robertson, J. (1996) *Effective Classroom Control: Understanding Teacher-student Relationships*. London: Hodder & Stoughton.

Robinson, C. and Fielding, M. (2007) *Children and Their Primary Schools: Pupils' Voices. Primary Review Research Survey*, 5/3. Cambridge: University of Cambridge Faculty of Education.

Robinson, G. and Maines, N. (1994) Who manages pupil behaviour? Assertive Discipline – a blunt instrument for a fine task. *Pastoral Care in Education*, 12(3), 30–5.

Rogers, C. (1965) *Client Centred Therapy*. Boston, MA: Houghton Mifflin Co.

Rogers, C. (1969) *Freedom to Learn*. Columbus, OH: Charles E. Merrill.

Rogers, C. and Kutnick, P. (eds) (1990) *The Social Psychology of the Primary School*. London: Routledge.

Rogoff, B., Mistry, J., Goncu, A. and Mosier, C. (1993) Guided participation in cultural activity by toddlers and care givers. Monographs of the Society for Research. *Child Development*, 58 (8), serial 236.

Roschelle, J. (1992) What should collaborative technology be? A perspective from Dewey and Situated Learning. *SIGCUE Outlook*, 21(3), 39–42.

Roschelle, J. (1992) What should collaborative technology be? A perspective from Dewey and situated learning. Paper presented at the ACM Conference on Computer Supported Collaborative Learning. http://www-scsl95.indiana.edu./cscl95/outlook/39_roschelle.html

Roschelle, J. M., Pea, R. D., Hoadley, C. M., Gordin, D. N. and Means, B. M. (2000) Changing how and what children learn in school with computer-based technologies. *Children and Computer Technology*, 10(2), Fall/Winter, 76–101. http://www.sri.com/policy/ctl/assets/images/RoschelleEtAlPackard2000.pdf

Rose, J. (2008) *The Independent Review of the Primary Curriculum: Interim Report*. London: DCSF.

Rose, J. (2009) *The Independent Review of the Primary Curriculum: Final Report*. London: DCSF.

Rosenthal, R. and Jacobson, L. (1968) *Pygmalion in the Classroom: Teacher Expectation and Pupils' Intellectual Ability*. New York: Holt, Rinehart & Winston.

Ross, J. and Schulz, R. (1999) Can computer-aided instruction accommodate all learners equally? *British Journal of Educational Technology*, 30(1), 5–24.

Rousseau, J. J. (1911) *Emile*. London: Everyman.

Rowe, M. B. (1986) Wait time: slowing down may be a way of speeding up. *Journal of Teacher Education*, 37(1), 43–50.

Rowntree, D. (1974) *Educational Technology in Curriculum Development*. New York: Harper & Row.

Royal Society for the Prevention of Accidents (2001) *RoSPA Guide to Health and Safety at School*. London: RoSPA.

Rubie-Davies, C., Hattie, J. and Hamilton, R. (2006) Expecting the best for students: teacher expectations and academic outcomes. *British Journal of Educational Psychology*, 76, 429–44.

Ruddock, J. and McIntyre, D. (2007) *Improving Learning Through Consulting Pupils*. London: Routledge.

Ruddock, J., Chaplain, R. and Wallace, G. (1995) *School Improvement: What can Pupils Tell Us?* London: David Fulton Publishers.

Runnymede Trust (1993) *Equality Assurance in Schools*. London: Trentham Books for the Runnymede Trust.

Runnymede Trust (1997) *Improving Practice*. London: Runnymede Trust in association with Nottingham Trent University.

Runnymede Trust (2000) *Curriculum 2000 – Monocultural or Multicultural?* London: Runnymede Trust.

Runnymede Trust (2003) *Divided by the Same Language?* Briefing paper by S. Sanglin-Grant. London: Runnymede Trust.

Russell, T. (2001) *Teaching and Using ICT in Secondary Schools* (2nd edition). London: David Fulton Publishers.

Rutter, M. (2006) Is sure start an effective preventive intervention? *Child and Adolescent Mental Health*, 11(3), 135–41.

Rutter, M., Maughan, B., Mortimore, P. and Ouston, J. (1979) *Fifteen Thousand Hours*. London: Open Books.

Rutter, M., Tizard, J. and Whitemore, K. (1970) *Education, Health and Behaviour*. Harlow: Longman.

Sacks, P. (1999) *Standardized Minds*. Cambridge, MA: Perseus Books.

Säljö, R. (1999) Learning as the use of tools: a sociocultural perspective on the human-technology link, in K. Littleton and P. Light (eds) *Learning with Computers: Analysing Productive Interaction*. London: Routledge.

Salomon, G. (1993) No distribution without individuals' cognition: a dynamic interactional view, in G. Salomon (ed.) *Distributed Cognitions: Psychological and Educational Considerations*. Cambridge: Cambridge University Press, 111–38.

Sammons, P., Hillman, J. and Mortimore, P. (1995) *Key Characteristics of Effective Schools: A Review of School Effectiveness Research*. Report by the Institute of Education, University of London, for the Office for Standards in Education.

Sandholtz, J. H., Ringstaff, C. and Dwyer, D. C. (1997) *Teaching with Technology: Creating Student-centered Classrooms*. New York: Teachers College Press.

Sandström, C. I. (1966) *The Psychology of Childhood and Adolescence*. Harmondsworth: Penguin.

Saunders, M. (1979) *Class Control and Behaviour Problems: A Guide for Teachers*. Maidenhead: McGraw-Hill.

Saunders, M. (1981) *Multicultural Teaching: A Guide for the Classroom*. Maidenhead: McGraw-Hill.

Saylor, J. G. and Alexander, W. M. (1974) *Planning Curriculum for Schools*. New York: Holt, Rinehart & Winston.

Schmuck, R. A. and Schmuck, P. A. (2001) *Group Processes in the Classroom* (8th edition). New York: McGraw-Hill.

School Curriculum and Assessment Authority (1995) *Consistency in Teacher Assessment*. London: SCAA.

School Curriculum and Assessment Authority (1995) *Planning the Curriculum at Key Stages 1 and 2*. London: SCAA.

School Curriculum and Assessment Authority (1996) *Nursery Education: Desirable Outcomes for Children's Learning on Entering Compulsory Education*. London: SCAA.

School Curriculum and Assessment Authority (1996) *Review of Qualifications for 16–19 Year Olds*. London: SCAA.

School Examination and Assessment Council (1990) *A Guide to Teacher Assessment. Pack C: A Source Book of Teacher Assessment*. London: Heinemann for the School Examination and Assessment Council.

School Examination and Assessment Council (1990) *Records of Achievement in the Primary School*. London: School Examination and Assessment Council.

School Teachers' Pay and Conditions Act, 1994. Crown Publications.

School Teachers' Review Body (2008) Seventeenth report, part 2 – 2008. Norwich: The Stationery Office.

Schools Council (1981) *The Practical Curriculum*. Working Paper 70. London: Methuen.

Schools Council (1983) *Primary Practice*. Working Paper 75. London: Methuen.

Scott, W. (2002) Making meaningful connections in early learning, in J. Fisher (ed.) *The Foundations of Learning*. Buckingham: Open University Press, pp. 74–86.

Scottish Department of Education (1989) *Good Discipline*. Edinburgh: Scottish Department of Education.

Scrimshaw, P. (1997) Computers and the teacher's role, in B. Somekh and N. Davis (eds) *Using Information Technology Effectively in Teaching and Learning*. London: Routledge, pp. 100–13.

Scully Jr., V. (1960) *Frank Lloyd Wright*. London: Mayflower.

Select committee: House of Commons Children Schools and Families Committee (2009) *National Curriculum. Fourth Report of Session 2008–09. Volume 1*. London: House of Commons.

Selwyn, N. (1999) Virtual concerns: restrictions of the internet as a learning environment. *British Journal of Educational Technology*, 30(1), 69–71.

Senge, P. (1990) *The Fifth Discipline: The Art and Practice of the Learning Organization*. New York: Doubleday.

Serbin, L. (1978) Teachers, peers and play preferences, in B. Spring (ed.) *Perspectives on Non-sexist Early Childhood Education*. Columbia University: Teachers College Press, pp. 243–51.

Sex Discrimination Act 1975. London: HMSO.

Sharp, J., Potter, J., Allen, J. and Loveless, A. (2000) *Primary ICT: Knowledge, Understanding and Practice*. Exeter: Learning Matters.

Sharp, R. and Green, A. (1975) *Education and Social Control*. London: Routledge & Kegan Paul.

Shepard, L. A. (2002) The role of assessment in a learning culture, in C. Desforges (ed.) *Teaching and Learning: The Essential Readings*. Oxford: Blackwell, pp. 229–53.

Shipman, M. D. (1972) Contrasting views of a curriculum project. *Journal of Curriculum Studies*, 4(2), 145–53.

Shulman, L. S. and Keislar, E. R. (eds) (1966) *Learning by Discovery*. Chicago, IL: Rand McNally.

Simon, B. (1995) Why no pedagogy in England?, in B. Moon and A. Shelton Mayes (eds) *Teaching and Learning in the Secondary School*. London: Routledge with the Open University, pp. 10–24.

Simonson, M., Smaldino, S., Albright, M. and Zvacek, S. (2000) *Teaching and Learning at a Distance: Foundations of Distance Education*. Upper Saddle River, NJ: Prentice-Hall.

Singh, J. S., Marimuthu, T. and Mukherjee, H. (1988) Learning motivation and work: a Malaysian perspective, in P. Broadfoot, R. Murphy and H. Torrance (eds) *Changing Educational Assessment*. London: Routledge, pp. 177–98.

Siraj-Blatchford, I. (1999) Early childhood pedagogy: practice, principles and research, in P. Mortimore (ed.) *Understanding Pedagogy and its Impact on Learning*. London: Paul Chapman Publishing, pp. 20–45.

Slavin, R. E. (1990) Achievement effects of ability grouping in secondary schools: a best evidence synthesis. *Review of Educational Research*, 60(3), 471–99.

Slavin, R. E. (1990) *Co-operative Learning: Theory, Research and Practice*. Englewood Cliffs, NJ: Prentice-Hall.

Slavin, R. E. (1995) *Cooperative Learning* (2nd edition). Boston, MA: Allyn & Bacon.

Slee, R. (1995) *Changing Theories and Practices of Discipline*. London: Falmer Press.

Slenning, K. (2000) The future school manager: information and communication technology aspects. *Education Media International*, 37(4), 243–9.

Sloane, A. (1997) Learning with the web: experience of using the world wide web in a learning environment. *Computers in Education*, 28(4), 207–12.

Smeets, E. and Mooij, T. (2001) Pupil-centred learning, ICT, and teacher behaviour: observations in educational practice. *British Journal of Educational Technology*, 32(4), pp. 403–17.

Smith, C. D. (1999) Using e-mail for teaching. *Computers and Education*, 33, pp. 15–25.

Smith, I. (1981) Curriculum placement in comprehensive schools. *British Educational Research Journal*, 7 (2), 111–24.

Smith, E. and Gorard, S. (2005) 'They don't give us our marks': the role of formative feedback in student progress. *Assessment in Education: Principles, Policy* and *Practice*, 12(1), 21.

Smith, F., Hardman, F. and Higgins, S. (2006) The impact of interactive whiteboards on teacher–pupil interaction in the National Literacy and Numeracy Strategies, *British Educational Research Journal*, 32(3), 443–57.

Smithers, A. (2001) Comment. *The Independent*, 12 July, p. 2.

Smithers, A. and Robinson, P. (2001) *Teachers Leaving*. London: National Union of Teachers and University of Liverpool: Centre for Education and Employment Research.

Somekh, B. (1997) Classroom investigations: exploring and evaluating how IT can support learning, in B. Somekh and N. Davis (eds) *Using Information Technology Effectively in Teaching and Learning*. London: Routledge, pp. 114–26.

Somekh, B. and Davies, R. (1991) Towards a pedagogy for information technology. *The Curriculum Journal*, 2(2), 153–70.

Somekh, B. and Davis, N. (eds) (1997) *Using Information Technology Effectively in Teaching and Learning*. London: Routledge.

Sousa, D. A. (2001) *How the Brain Learns* (2nd edition). Thousand Oaks, CA: Corwin Press Inc.

Sparks Linfield, R. and Warwick, P. (1996) 'Do you know what MY name is?' Assessment in the early years: some examples from science, in D. Whitebread (ed.) *Teaching and Learning in the Early Years*. London: Routledge, pp. 81–98.

Spears, A. and Wilson, L. (2003) *Brain-based Learning Highlights*. http://www.uwsp.edu/education/celtProject/innovations/Brain-Based%20Learning/brain-based_learning.htm, [p. 2].

Special Educational Needs and Disability Act 2001. London: The Stationery Office.

Spender, D. (1980) *Man Made Language*. London: Routledge & Kegan Paul.

Stake, R. E. (1976) The countenance of educational evaluation, cited in D. Jenkins, Six alternative models of curriculum evaluation, Unit 20, E 203, *Curriculum Design and Development*. Milton Keynes: The Open University.

Stanworth, M. (1981) *Gender and Schooling: A Study of Sexual Divisions in the Classroom*. London: Women's Research and Resources Centre Publications.

Stebbins, R. (1973) Physical context influences on behaviour: the case of classroom disorderliness. *Environment and Behaviour*, 5, 291–314.

Steer, A. (2005) *Learning Behaviour: The Report of the Practitioners' Group on School Behaviour and Discipline*. London: DCFS.

Stemler, S. E., Elliott, J. G., Grigorenko, E. L. and Sternberg, R. J. (2006) There's more to teaching than instruction: seven strategies for dealing with the practical side of teaching. *Educational Studies*, 32(1), 101–18.

Stenhouse, L. (1975) *An Introduction to Curriculum Research and Development*. London: Heinemann.

Stephenson, J. (1995) Significant others: the primary student teacher's view of practice in schools. *Educational Studies*, 21(3), 323–33.

Stiggins, J. C. and Conklin, N. F. (1992) *In Teachers' Hands: Investigating the Practice of Classroom Assessment*. New York: SUNY Press.

Stoney, S. and Oliver, R. (1999) Can higher order thinking and cognitive engagement be enhanced with multimedia? *Interactive Multimedia Electronic Journal of Computer-enhanced Learning*, 1(2). http://imej.wfu.edu/articles/1999/2/index.asp

Strand, S. (2005). English language acquisition and educational attainment at the end of primary school. *Educational Studies*, 13(3), 275–391.

Stringfield, S. (1997) Underlying the chaos: factors explaining elementary schools and their case for high-reliability organizations, in T. Townsend (ed.) *Restructuring and Quality: Issues for Tomorrow's Schools*. London: Routledge, pp. 151–8.

Stubbs, M. (1983) *Language, Schools and Classrooms* (2nd edition). London: Methuen.

Sutton, R. (1993) *A Framework for Assessment* (2nd edition). Slough: NFER-Nelson.

Sylva, K. and Wiltshire, J. (1993) The impact of early learning on children's later development: a review prepared for the RSA inquiry 'Start Right'. *European Early Childhood Education Research Journal*, 1, 17–40.

Sylva, K. (1998) Too formal too soon? Keynote address presented at the Islington early years conference: Building on Best Practice in the Early Years. Cited in T. David (1999) 'Changing minds? Teaching young children', in T. David (ed.) *Teaching Young Children*. London: Paul Chapman Publishing.

Taba, H. (1962) *Curriculum Development: Theory and Practice*. New York: Harcourt Brace & World.

Talay-Ongan, A. (1998) *Typical and Atypical Development in Early Childhood*. London: British Psychological Society.

Tann, C. S. (1988) The rationale for topic work, in C. S. Tann (ed.) *Developing Topic Work in the Primary School*. Lewes: Falmer, pp. 1–23.

Task Group on Assessment and Testing (1987) *National Curriculum Assessment and Testing: A Report*. London: HMSO.

Taylor, C. (1998) Children and student teachers learning about astronomy and ICT together. *Science Teacher Education*, 24 December, pp. 10–12.

Taylor, J. (1983) *Organizing and Integrating the First School Day*. London: Allen & Unwin.

Teaching and Learning Research Programme (2008) *TLRP's Evidence-informed Pedagogic Principles*. Retrieved 27 August 2008 from http://www.tlrp.org/themes/themes/tenprinciples.html

Teacher Training Agency (1997) *National Standards for Headteachers*. London: TTA.

Teacher Training Agency (1998) *National Standards for Qualified Teacher Status*. London: TTA.

Teacher Training Agency (1998) *National Standards for Special Educational Needs Co-ordinators*. London: TTA.

Teacher Training Agency (1998) *National Standards for Subject Leaders*. London: TTA.

Teacher Training Agency (2002) *Guidance on the Requirements for Initial Teacher Training*. London: TTA.

Teacher Training Agency (2002) *Handbook of Guidance on QTS Standards and ITT Requirements*. London: TTA.

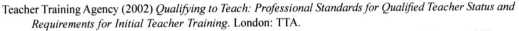

Teacher Training Agency (2002) *Qualifying to Teach: Professional Standards for Qualified Teacher Status and Requirements for Initial Teacher Training.* London: TTA.

Teacher Training Agency (2002) *Test Coverage.* Literacy. http://www.canteach.gov.uk/support/skillstests literacy/index.htm

Teacher Training Agency (2002) *Test Coverage.* Numeracy. http://www.canteach.gov.uk/support/skillstests/numeracy/testcoverage.htm

Teacher Training Agency (2002) *Test Coverage.* ICT. http://www.canteach.gov.uk/support/skillstests/ict/index.htm

Teachernet (2003) *Teaching in England: The Curriculum.* http://www.teachernet.gov.uk/teachinginengland/detail.cfm?id=9 *The Learning and Skills Act* 2000. London: The Stationery Office.

Teachernet (2009) *Common Transfer File.* Accessed 13 February 2009 from http://www.teachernet.gov.uk/management/atoz/c/commontransferfile/index.cfm?code=main

Teddlie, C. and Reynolds, D. (eds) (2000) *The International Handbook of School Effectiveness Research.* London: RoutledgeFalmer.

Telem, M. (2001) Computerization of school administration: impact on the principal's role: a case study. *Computers and Education,* 37, 345–62.

Thomas, D. R., Becker, W. C. and Armstrong, M. (1968) Production and elimination of disruptive classroom behaviour by systematically varying the teacher's behaviour. *Journal of Applied Behaviour Analysis,* 1, 35–45.

Thompson, D. and Arora, T. (1991) Why do students bully? An evaluation of the long-term effectiveness of a whole-school policy to minimize bullying. *Pastoral Care in Education,* 9(4), 8–12.

Thompson, D., Arora, T. and Sharp, S. (2002) *Bullying: Effective Strategies for Long-term Improvement.* London: RoutledgeFalmer.

Thompson, L. and Feasey, R. (1992) *Questioning in Science.* Mimeo. School of Education, University of Durham.

Thurston, J. E., Feldhusen, J. F. and Benning, J. J. (1973) A longitudinal study of delinquency and other aspects of students' behaviour. *International Journal of Criminology and Penology,* 1, November, 341–51.

Times Educational Supplement (1995) Testing times for the timetable in Modedon Junior School. *Times Educational Supplement,* 16 June, p. 6.

Tizard, B. and Hughes, M. (1984) *Young Children Learning: Talking and Thinking at Home and at School.* London: Fontana.

Tizard, B., Blatchford, P., Burke, J., Farquar, C. and Plewis, I. (1988) *Young Children at School in the Inner City.* London: Lawrence Erlbaum Associates.

Tombari, M. and Borich, G. (1999) *Authentic Assessment in the Classroom.* Upper Saddle River, NJ: Prentice-Hall.

Tomlinson, P. (1995) *Understanding Mentoring.* Buckingham: Open University Press.

Tondeur, J., Valcke, M. and van Braak, J. (2008) A multidimentional approach to determinants of computer use in primary education: teacher and school characteristics. *Journal of Computer Assisted Learning,* 24, 494–506.

Training and Development Agency for Schools (2007) *Professional Standards for Qualified Teacher Status and Requirements for Initial Teacher Training.* London: TDA.

Training and Development Agency for Schools (2008) *QTS Skills Tests.* Retrieved 14 August 2008 from http://www.tda.gov.uk/skillstests.aspx

Training and Development Agency for Schools (2008) *QTS Standards and ITT Requirements.* Retrieved 14 August 2008 from http://www.tda.gov.uk/partners/ittstandards.aspx

Training and Development Agency for Schools (2008) *What Are the Professional Standards?* Retrieved 14 August 2008 from http://www.tda.gov.uk/teachers/professionalstandards/standards.aspx

Topping, K. (1992) School-based behaviour management work with families. *Pastoral Care in Education,* 10(1), 7–17.

Torrance, H. and Pryor, J. (1998) *Investigating Formative Assessment.* Buckingham: Open University Press.

Travers, C. J. and Cooper, C. L. (1993) Mental health, job satisfaction and occupational stress among UK teachers. *Work and Stress,* 7(3), 203–19.

Travers, C. J. and Cooper, C. L. (1996) *Teachers under Pressure: Stress in the Teaching Profession*. London: Routledge.

Troman, G. (1998) Living at a hundred miles an hour: primary teachers' perceptions of work and stress. Paper presented at the British Educational Research Association annual conference, Queen's University, Belfast.

Trudell, P. (2002) Meeting the needs of disadvantaged children, in J. Fisher (ed.) *The Foundations of Learning*. Buckingham: Open University Press, pp. 57–73.

Tu, C. H. (2001) How Chinese perceive social presence: an examination of interaction in online learning environment. *Education Media International*, 38(1), 45–60.

Turner, T. (1999) Differentiation, progression and pupil grouping, in S. Capel, M. Leask and T. Turner (eds) *Learning to Teach in the Secondary School* (2nd edition). London: Routledge, pp. 134–50.

Turner, T. (1999) Moral development and values, in S. Capel, M. Leask and T. Turner (eds) *Learning to Teach in the Secondary School* (2nd edition). London, Routledge, pp. 199–211.

Turner, T. (1999) Reading classrooms, in S. Capel, M. Leask and T. Turner (eds) *Learning to Teach in the Secondary School* (2nd edition). London: Routledge, pp. 51–65.

Tweddle, S., Avis, P., Wright, J. and Waller, T. (1998) Towards evaluating websites. *British Journal of Educational Technology*, 29(3), 267–70.

Tyler, R. W. (1949) *Basic Principles of Curriculum and Instruction*. Chicago, IL: University of Chicago Press.

Tylor, E. B. (1871) *Primitive Culture*. London: Murray.

Tymms, P. B. (1999) *Baseline Assessment and Monitoring in Primary Schools*. London: David Fulton Publishers.

Uljens, M. (1997) *School Didactics and Learning*. Hove: Psychology Press Ltd. Underwood, J. (1998) Making groups work, in M. Montieth (ed.) *IT for Learning Enhancement*. Exeter: Intellect, pp. 29–41.

Underwood, J. and Brown, J. (eds) (1997) *Integrated Learning Systems: Potential into Practice*. NCET Heinemann.

UNICEF (2009) United Kingdom's 3rd Quinquennial Report to the UN Committee on the Rights of the Child: Submission from UNICEF UK, accessed 10 February 2009 from http://www.unicef.org.uk/pages.asp?page=95&nodeid=ukreport&section=

United Nations (2008) Committee on the Rights of the Child. Forty-ninth session. Consideration of Reports Submitted by States Parties Under Article 44 of the Convention. Concluding observations: United Kingdom of Great Britain and Northern Ireland. UN.

University of Bristol (1988) *Pilot Records of Achievement in Schools Evaluation: Final Report* (PRAISE Report). Bristol: University of Bristol.

University of Washington (1997) *Evaluating Educational Materials on the Web*. http://staff.washington.edu/rells/pod97/evaluate.htm

Uno, G. E. (1999) *Handbook on Teaching Undergraduate Science Courses*. Fort Worth, TX: Saunders College.

Urquhart, I. (2000) Communicating well with children, in D. Whitebread (ed.) *The Psychology of Teaching and Learning in the Primary School*. London: Routledge, pp. 57–77.

Valdez, G., McNabb, M., Foertsch, M., Anderson, M., Hawkes, M. and Raack, L. (2000) *Computer-based Technology and Learning: Evolving Uses and Expectations*. North Central Regional Educational Laboratory. http://www.ncrel.org/tplan/cbtl/toc.htm

Verduin, J. R. J. and Clark, T. A. (1991) *Distance Education: The Foundations of Effective Practice*, Vol. 1. San Francisco, CA: Jossey-Bass.

Vygotsky, L. S. (1978) *Mind in Society: The Development of Higher Psychological Processes* (ed. M. Cole). Cambridge, MA: Harvard University Press.

Vygotsky, L. S. (1981) The development of higher mental functions, in J. V. Wertsch (ed.) *The Concept of Activity in Soviet Psychology*. New York: Sharpe, pp. 189–240.

Wade, B. and Moore, M. (1992) *Patterns of Educational Integration*. Wallingford: Triangle Books Ltd.

Wainer, H. (1990) (ed.) *Computerized Adaptive Testing: A Primer*. Hillsdale, NJ: Lawrence Erlbaum.

Walker, A. (2003) Making technology count in formative and summative assessment, in C. Richardson (ed.) *Whither Assessment?* London: Qualifications and Curriculum Authority, pp. 67–75.

Walkerdine, V. (1983) It's only natural: rethinking child-centred pedagogy, in A. M. Wolpe and J. Donald (eds) *Is There Anyone Here from Education?* London: Pluto Press, pp. 79–87.

Waller, W. (1932) *The Sociology of Teaching*. New York: John Wiley.

Warwick, P., Wilson, E. and Winterbottom, M. (eds) (2006) *ICT and Primary Science*. Buckingham: Open University Press/McGraw-Hill.

Watkins, C. and Wagner, P. (1987) *School Discipline: A Whole-school Approach*. Oxford: Basil Blackwell.

Watson, L. (1995) Talk and pupil thought. *Educational Psychology*, 15(1), 57–68.

Watts, A. (1995) Double entendre, *Times Educational Supplement*, 9 June, p. iii.

Webber, B. (1996) *Assessment and Learning*, in T. David (ed.) *Teaching Young Children*. London: Paul Chapman Publishing, pp. 139–50.

Wedeen, P., Winter, J. and Broadfoot, P. (2002) *Assessment: What's In It for Schools?* London: RoutledgeFalmer.

Wegerif, R. (1998) Using computers to help coach exploratory talk across the curriculum. *Computers in Education*, 26(1–3), 51–60.

Wegerif, R. (2002) *Thinking Skills, Technology and Learning*. Bristol: Futurelab Report 2.

Wegerif, R. and Dawes, L. (2004) *Thinking and Learning with ICT: Raising Achievement in Primary Classrooms*. London: Routledge.

Wells, G. (1986) *The Meaning Makers*. London: Hodder & Stoughton.

Wellington, J. (2005) Has ICT come of age? Recurring debates on the role of ICT in education, 1982–2004. *Research in Science and Technological Education*, 23, 25–39.

Wertsch, J. V. and Tulviste, P. (1998) L.S. Vygotsky and contemporary developmental psychology, in D. Faulkner, K. Littleton and M. Woodhead (eds) *Learning Relationships in the Classroom*. London: Routledge.

Wertsch, J. V., Tulviste, P. and Hagstrom, F. (1993) A sociocultural approach to agency, in E.A. Forman, N. Minick and C.A. Stone (eds) *Contexts for Learning: Sociocultural Dynamics in Children's Development*. New York: Oxford University Press.

Westbrook, S. L. and Marek, E. A. (1991) A cross age study of student understanding of the concept of diffusion. *Journal of Research in Science Teaching*, 28(8), 649–60.

Wheldall, K. and Merrett, F. (1988) Which classroom behaviours do primary teachers say they find most troublesome? *Educational Review*, 40(1), 14–27.

Wheldall, K., Morris, M., Vaughan, P. and Ng, Y. Y. (1981) Rows versus tables: an example of behavioural ecology in two classes of eleven year old children. *Educational Psychology*, 1(2), 27–44.

White, J. (ed.) (2004) *Rethinking the School Curriculum: Values, Aims and Purposes*. London: RoutledgeFalmer.

White, J. (2008) *Aims as Policy in English Primary Education* (Primary Review Research Survey 1/1). Cambridge: University of Cambridge Faculty of Education.

Whitebread, D. (1996) Introduction: young children learning and early years teaching, in D. Whitebread (ed.) *Teaching and Learning in the Early Years*. London: RoutledgeFalmer, pp. 1–20.

Whitebread, D. (ed.) (2000) *The Psychology of Teaching and Learning in the Primary School*. London: RoutledgeFalmer.

Whitty, G. and Wilmott, E. (1991) Competence-based teacher education: approaches and issues. *Cambridge Journal of Education*, 21(3), 309–18.

Wiggins, G. (1998) *Educative Assessment*. San Francisco, CA: Jossey-Bass.

Wilce, H. (2001) Meet the teachers who are hit and bitten and abused. *The Independent*, 12 July, p. 2.

Wiles, J. and Bondi, J. C. (1984) *Curriculum Development: A Guide to Practice* (2nd edition). Columbus, OH: Charles E. Merrill Publishing.

Williams, D., Coles, L., Wilson, K., Richardson, A. and Tuson, J. (2000) Teachers and ICT: current use and future needs. *British Journal of Educational Technology*, 41(4), 307–20.

Williamson, B. (2006) Elephants can't jump: creativity, new technology and concept exploration in primary science, in P. Warwick, E. Wilson and M. Winterbottom (eds) *ICT and Primary Science*. Buckingham: Open University Press/McGraw-Hill, pp. 70–92.

Williamson, V. M. and Abraham, M. R. (1995) The effects of computer animation on the particulate mental models of college chemistry students. *Journal of Research in Science Teaching*, 32(5), 521–34.

Wineburg, S. S. (1987) The self-fulfilment of the self-fulfilling prophecy. *Educational Researcher* 16(9), 28–37.

Wishart, J. (1988) User involvement with microcomputer software. Unpublished PhD thesis, University of Surrey.

Wishart, J. (1990) Cognitive factors related to use involvement with computers and their effects upon learning from an educational computer game. *Computers and Education*, 15, 1–3, 145–50.

Wishart, J. and Blease, D. (1999) Theories underlying perceived changes in teaching and learning after installing a computer network in a secondary school. *British Journal of Educational Technology*, 30(1), 25–41.

Withers, R. and Eke, R. (1995) Reclaiming matching from the critics of primary education. *Educational Review*, 37(1), 59–73.

Wolfe, P. (2001) *Brain Matters: Translating Research into Practice*. Alexandria, VA: Association for Supervision and Curriculum Development.

Wolfgang, C. H. (2001) *Solving Discipline and Classroom Management Problems* (2nd edition). New York: John Wiley and Sons.

Wood, D. (1998) *How Children Think and Learn* (2nd edn). London: Blackwell, p. 100.

Woods, P. (1979) *The Divided School*. London: Routledge & Kegan Paul.

Woods, P. (1980) *Teacher Strategies: Explorations in the Sociology of the School*. London: Croom Helm.

Woollard, J. (2007) *Learning and Teaching Using ICT in Secondary Schools*. Exeter: Learning Matters.

Wragg, E. C. (1981) *Class Management and Control: A Teaching Skills Workbook*. DES Teacher Education Project, Focus Books (series ed. T. Kerry). London: Macmillan.

Wragg, E. C. (1984) (ed.) *Classroom Teaching Skills*. London: Croom Helm.

Wragg, E. C. (1993) *Explaining*. London: Routledge.

Wragg, E. C. (1997) *The Cubic Curriculum*. London: Routledge.

Wragg, E. C. (2001) *Class Management in the Secondary School*. London: RoutledgeFalmer.

Wragg, E. C. and Brown, G. A. (2001) *Explaining in the Primary School*. London: RoutledgeFalmer.

Wragg, E. C. and Brown, G. A. (2001) *Questioning in the Primary School*. London: RoutledgeFalmer.

Wragg, E. C. and Dooley, P. A. (1984) Class management during teaching practice, in E. C. Wragg (ed.) *Classroom Teaching Skills*. London: Croom Helm, pp. 21–46.

Wragg, E. C. and Wood, E. K. (1984) Teachers' first encounters with their classes, in E. C. Wragg (ed.) *Classroom Teaching Skills*. London: Croom Helm, pp. 47–78.

Wragg, E. C. and Wood, E. K. (1984) Pupil appraisals of teaching, in E. C. Wragg (ed.) *Classroom Teaching Skills*. London: Croom Helm, pp. 79–96.

Wray, D., Bloom, W. and Hall, N. (1989) *Literacy in Action*. Barcombe: Falmer.

Wright, D. (1973) The punishment of students, in B. Turner (ed.) *Discipline in Schools*. London: Ward Lock Educational.

Wyse, D. (2001) Felt tip pens and school councils: children's participation rights in four English schools. *Children and Society*, 15, 209–18.

Wyse, D. (2003) The national literacy strategy: a critical review of empirical evidence. *British Educational Research Journal*, 29(6), 903–16.

Wyse, D. (2007) *The Good Writing Guide for Education Students* (2nd edn). London: Sage.

Wyse, D. (2008) Primary education: Who's in control? *Education Review*, 21(1), 76–82.

Wyse, D. (2010) Conceptions of the school curriculum, in J. Arthur, T. Grainger and D. Wray (eds) *Teaching and Learning in the Primary School* (2nd edn). London: Routledge.

Wyse, D. and Bradford, H. (2008) 'You're supposed to tell me your name now!' Speaking and listening in the early years, in D. Whitebread and P. Coltman (eds) *Teaching and Learning in the Early Years*. London: Routledge, pp. 141–60.

Wyse, D. and Dowson, P. (2008) *The Really Useful Creativity Book*. London: Routledge.

Wyse, D. and Goswami, U. (2008) Synthetic phonics and the teaching of reading. *British Educational Research Journal*, 34(6), 691–710.

Wyse, D. and Jones, R. (2008) *Teaching English, Language and Literacy* (2nd edn). London: Routledge.

Wyse, D., Hilton, M., Burke, C. and Goswami, U. (eds) (2009) *A response to the independent review of the primary curriculum: Interim report* (December 2008) by Sir Jim Rose. Cambridge: PLACE Group.

Wyse, D., McCreery, E. and Torrance, H. (2008) *The Trajectory and Impact of National Reform: Curriculum and Assessment in English Primary Schools.* (Primary Review Research Survey 3/2). Cambridge University Faculty of Education.

Wyse, D. and Torrance, H. (2009) The development and consequences of national curriculum assessment for primary education in England. *Educational Research,* 51(2), 213–28.

Zhang, H. and Kortner, N. (1995) *Oral Language Development across the Curriculum, K12.* ERIC Digest. ED389029. www.ed.gov/databases/ERIC_Digests/ed38029.html

Zimiles, H. (1987) Progressive education: on the limits of evaluation and the development of empowerment. *Teachers College Record,* 89(2), 201–17.

Index